Cisco IP Communications Express:
CallManager Express with Cisco Unity Express

**Danelle Au, Baldwin Choi, Rajesh Haridas, Christina Hattingh,
Ravi Koulagi, Mike Tasker, Lillian Xia**

Cisco Press

800 East 96th Street
Indianapolis, IN 46240 USA

Cisco IP Communications Express:
CallManager Express with Cisco Unity Express

Danelle Au, Baldwin Choi, Rajesh Haridas, Christina Hattingh, Ravi Koulagi, Mike Tasker, Lillian Xia

Copyright© 2005 Cisco Systems, Inc.

Published by:
Cisco Press
800 East 96th Street
Indianapolis, IN 46240 USA

Printed in the United States of America   4 5 6 7 8 9 0

Fourth Printing January 2007

Library of Congress Cataloging-in-Publication Number: 2003114955

ISBN: 1-58705-180-X

Warning and Disclaimer

This book is designed to provide information about Cisco IP Communications Express. Every effort has been made to make this book as complete and accurate as possible, but no warranty or fitness is implied.

The information is provided on an "as is" basis. The author, Cisco Press, and Cisco Systems, Inc., shall have neither liability nor responsibility to any person or entity with respect to any loss or damages arising from the information contained in this book or from the use of the disks or programs that may accompany it.

The opinions expressed in this book belong to the author and are not necessarily those of Cisco Systems, Inc.

Trademark Acknowledgments

All terms mentioned in this book that are known to be trademarks or service marks have been appropriately capitalized. Cisco Press or Cisco Systems, Inc., cannot attest to the accuracy of this information. Use of a term in this book should not be regarded as affecting the validity of any trademark or service mark.

Corporate and Government Sales

Cisco Press offers excellent discounts on this book when ordered in quantity for bulk purchases or special sales.

For more information, please contact U.S. Corporate and Government Sales at 1-800-382-3419 or at corp-sales@pearsontechgroup.com.

For sales outside the U.S., please contact International Sales at international@pearsoned.com.

Feedback Information

At Cisco Press, our goal is to create in-depth technical books of the highest quality and value. Each book is crafted with care and precision, undergoing rigorous development that involves the unique expertise of members of the professional technical community.

Reader feedback is a natural continuation of this process. If you have any comments on how we could improve the quality of this book, or otherwise alter it to better suit your needs, you can contact us through e-mail at feedback@ciscopress.com. Please be sure to include the book's title and ISBN in your message.

We greatly appreciate your assistance.

Publisher	John Wait
Editor-in-Chief	John Kane
Cisco Representative	Anthony Wolfenden
Cisco Press Program Manager	Jeff Brady
Production Manager	Patrick Kanouse
Development Editor	Dayna Isley
Project Editor	Marc Fowler
Copy Editor	Gayle Johnson
Technical Editors	Tomoo Esaka, Sarat Khilnani, Markus Schneider
Editorial Assistant	Tammi Barnett
Book/Cover Designer	Louisa Adair
Compositor	Mark Shirar
Indexer	Tim Wright

CISCO SYSTEMS

Corporate Headquarters
Cisco Systems, Inc.
170 West Tasman Drive
San Jose, CA 95134-1706
USA
www.cisco.com
Tel: 408 526-4000
     800 553-NETS (6387)
Fax: 408 526-4100

European Headquarters
Cisco Systems International BV
Haarlerbergpark
Haarlerbergweg 13-19
1101 CH Amsterdam
The Netherlands
www-europe.cisco.com
Tel: 31 0 20 357 1000
Fax: 31 0 20 357 1100

Americas Headquarters
Cisco Systems, Inc.
170 West Tasman Drive
San Jose, CA 95134-1706
USA
www.cisco.com
Tel: 408 526-7660
Fax: 408 527-0883

Asia Pacific Headquarters
Cisco Systems, Inc.
Capital Tower
168 Robinson Road
#22-01 to #29-01
Singapore 068912
www.cisco.com
Tel: +65 6317 7777
Fax: +65 6317 7799

Cisco Systems has more than 200 offices in the following countries and regions. Addresses, phone numbers, and fax numbers are listed on the **Cisco.com Web site at www.cisco.com/go/offices.**

Argentina • Australia • Austria • Belgium • Brazil • Bulgaria • Canada • Chile • China PRC • Colombia • Costa Rica • Croatia • Czech Republic Denmark • Dubai, UAE • Finland • France • Germany • Greece • Hong Kong SAR • Hungary • India • Indonesia • Ireland • Israel • Italy Japan • Korea • Luxembourg • Malaysia • Mexico • The Netherlands • New Zealand • Norway • Peru • Philippines • Poland • Portugal Puerto Rico • Romania • Russia • Saudi Arabia • Scotland • Singapore • Slovakia • Slovenia • South Africa • Spain • Sweden Switzerland • Taiwan • Thailand • Turkey • Ukraine • United Kingdom • United States • Venezuela • Vietnam • Zimbabwe

About the Authors

Danelle Au is a product manager in the branch office IP Communications group at Cisco Systems. She was involved in the product management and marketing activities for the introduction of the Cisco CallManager Express (CME) and Survivable Remote Site Telephony (SRST) products. She was also a member of the initial team that defined and developed the Cisco Unity Express (UE) product. Her area of expertise is IP Communications, including voice security, quality of service (QoS), IP telephony interfaces, and digital signal processor (DSP) technologies. She holds an MS in electrical engineering from the University of California, Berkeley.

Baldwin Choi is a member of the technical marketing staff in the branch office IP Communications group at Cisco Systems. He has been working with Cisco sales and technical support teams on existing and new voice products, as well as in network designs and implementations. He introduced the first design guide on SRST and currently is actively involved with Cisco CME, Cisco UE, and other Cisco branch office voice solutions.

Rajesh Haridas is a member of the engineering test team of the access router and branch office IP Communications group at Cisco Systems. He has been an active member of the testing team since the inception of the Cisco CME and SRST products four years ago.

Christina Hattingh is a member of the technical staff in the branch office IP Communications group at Cisco Systems. The products in this group, including the Cisco 2600, 2800, 3600, 3700, and 3800 series platforms, were some of the first Cisco platforms to converge voice and data by offering Public Switched Telephone Network (PSTN), and private branch exchange (PBX) voice interfaces and critical QoS features on WAN interfaces. More recently, these products have integrated call control elements such as Cisco CME and Cisco UE into the router-based platform. In this role, Hattingh helps guide development projects, trains Cisco sales staff and Cisco resale partners on new router-based voice technologies, and advises customers on voice network deployment and design.

Ravi Koulagi is a technical lead in the test organization of the access router and branch office IP Communications group at Cisco Systems. He led the testing activities of the first two releases of the Cisco CME and SRST. Currently, he is leading the testing efforts of Cisco UE, which is the voice mail system for Cisco CME. In these roles, he is responsible for test strategy, development, and execution of test plans for these Cisco products.

Mike Tasker is a software architect in the branch office IP Communications group at Cisco Systems. He was the original software designer working on Cisco CME and SRST. He has extensive industry experience working with voice-related technologies, including DSPs, voice-over-packet technologies, and voice mail.

Lillian Xia is a member of the technical staff in the branch office IP Communications group at Cisco Systems. She has been actively working with product marketing, engineering, testing, and solution test teams during multiple phases of Cisco CME development and testing over the past four years. As an author of several design guides, application notes, and frequently asked questions, she has trained, helped, and guided customers and Cisco sales engineers in deploying and designing Cisco CME and SRST networks.

About the Technical Reviewers

Tomoo Esaka is a technical marketing engineer for Cisco Systems. His primary areas of expertise are Cisco Call-Manager Express and SRST. He has more than seven years of experience in the IT industry, ranging from systems administration to designing and implementing a 3000-user Cisco IP Telephony network. He holds CCNA, CCNP, CCDP, and MCSE certifications. He graduated from Carnegie Mellon University with a bachelor of science degree in 1997.

Sarat Khilnani is a product line manager at Cisco Systems and leads a team that is focused on IP Communications in the small-to-medium business and small office space. Khilnani has 18 years of direct telephony experience, having worked in software engineering, applications engineering, technical marketing, and product management of telephony products. Khilnani has a BSEE from the University of Michigan and an MBA from Santa Clara University.

Markus Schneider, CCIE No. 2863, is a diagnostic engineer for the Cisco Systems Voice Networking Team in Research Triangle Park, North Carolina. He is responsible for helping Cisco customers design, implement, and troubleshoot IP telephony solutions in their environment. He works closely with Cisco development and Technical Assistance Center (TAC) support teams to provide support for a variety of products and technologies. He has been working for Cisco as a network engineer since graduating from Georgia Tech with a BS in computer engineering in 1996.

Dedications

From Danelle Au:

To Todd and Isabelle, who make me smile, and my parents, who taught me well.

From Baldwin Choi:

To Patricia, Adrienne, and Frances for their love and support, and to my parents for their encouragement and guidance.

From Rajesh Haridas:

I would like to dedicate this book to my loving parents, Ganga Haridas and Kodathoor Haridas.

From Christina Hattingh:

To Robert Verkroost and my parents for their unfailing encouragement and support of my numerous publishing forays.

From Ravi Koulagi:

To my mother, who worked hard to give her children the best possible education.

From Lillian Xia:

To Kevin, Cindy, and my parents for their support and dedication.

Acknowledgments

Writing this book was a team effort because timing, availability, and accuracy were critical. In the fast-moving industry of voice over IP (VoIP) technology, information and products age quickly. A single author could not have produced this book in the time needed, nor does any one person know all the aspects of the system to the depth required to write all the chapters of this book. The seven authors of this book cover diverse aspects of the system in their daily work, including defining requirements, training the sales force and customers, designing and implementing the software, and testing and certifying system operation.

We would like to thank Sarat Khilnani, Tomoo Esaka, and Markus Schneider for reviewing this book and suggesting countless improvements. The larger Cisco product teams were invaluable in their support of the author team and making knowledge and equipment available toward the production of this book—in particular, Ed Leonhardt, Andy Feest, Dean Galanos, Praveen Sankaran, Vallinath Panchagnula, Subodh Shah, Narendra Hosehalli, Chandrodaya Prasad, Yuan Cai, and Haitao Zhang. Our thanks also to the Cisco management team for supporting us in this endeavor, including Michael Wood, Deependra Vaidya, Jiabin Zhao, Sarat Khilnani, and Sam Lyall. Thank you also to Tim Redpath of Metavante, who helped with questions on implementations in different industries.

Finally, a sincere thank you to John Kane, Dayna Isley, and the rest of the Cisco Press team for the editing and production of this book, and for their patience and support in dealing with seven authors.

This Book Is Safari Enabled

The Safari® Enabled icon on the cover of your favorite technology book means the book is available through Safari Bookshelf. When you buy this book, you get free access to the online edition for 45 days.

Safari Bookshelf is an electronic reference library that lets you easily search thousands of technical books, find code samples, download chapters, and access technical information whenever and wherever you need it.

To gain 45-day Safari Enabled access to this book:

- Go to http://www.ciscopress.com/safarienabled
- Complete the brief registration form
- Enter the coupon code X3JZ-36HK-3J8V-M8K3-UVYD

If you have difficulty registering on Safari Bookshelf or accessing the online edition, please e-mail customer-service@safaribooksonline.com.

## Part I

Contents at a Glance

Contents

Icons Used in This Book

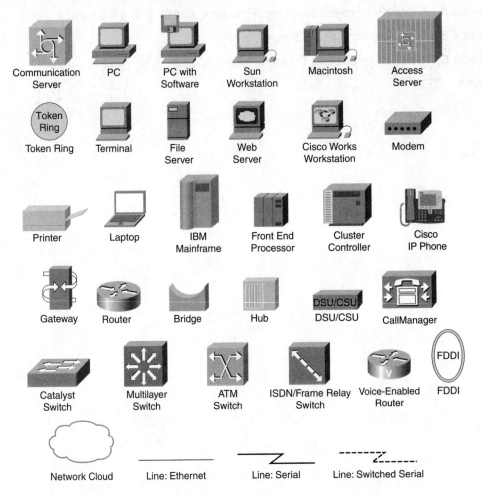

Command Syntax Conventions

The conventions used to present command syntax in this book are the same conventions used in the IOS Command Reference. The Command Reference describes these conventions as follows:

- **Bold** indicates commands and keywords that are entered literally as shown.

- *Italic* indicates arguments for which you supply actual values.

- Vertical bars (|) separate alternative, mutually exclusive elements.

- Square brackets ([ ]) indicate an optional element.

- Braces ({ }) indicate a required choice.

- Braces within brackets ([{ }]) indicate a required choice within an optional element.

Introduction

Cisco IP Communications Express: CallManager Express with Cisco Unity Express is the first comprehensive book describing Cisco converged communications solutions for the small standalone or enterprise branch office. Much has been written on solutions for larger enterprise networks, but a dearth of information exists for solutions for offices employing fewer than 100 people.

IP-based communications solutions for the small or branch office are now a reality in terms of technology, price, and product availability. Advanced features in an easy-to-use, single-box packaging now offer exciting new options for the small-business owner, or for smaller sites of a larger network. Wherever a router is deployed to provide data traffic or Internet access, that platform can also be leveraged or upgraded to provide full telephony features and data access for the office.

The small office requires a few PSTN trunks, phone handling with typical office features such as transfer and conference, an automated attendant (AA) to handle general or after-hours calls, voice mail, security features such as a firewall, and Internet access for e-mail and website applications. All this is now provided in a single Cisco router-based platform for offices of up to 240 employees.

Goals and Methods

This book tells you how to use a Cisco IPC Express system to take your business a leap forward. Perhaps you are setting up a new office or business, replacing an aging solution, wanting to move into the IP world to gain the productivity benefits of converged networks for your employees or colleagues, or starting a VoIP pilot operation as part of a larger network. Whatever the case, this book tells you how the small-office IP communications system works, how you can configure its rich set of features to meet your needs, your choices in administering the system, the features and benefits it offers, and how to isolate and correct any problems you might encounter.

For the system integrator or value-added reseller, this book arms you with the skills to offer Cisco IPC Express to your customers, to set it up quickly and efficiently, to understand its features and operation, and to save time in deploying a leading-edge VoIP system for a business owner or customer network. This book also helps you prepare for Cisco IPC Express certification.

Who Should Read This Book?

This book helps you understand the Cisco IPC Express system and its operation, regardless of whether you are the system's current or prospective owner or administrator or whether you are in the business of reselling communications systems to small-business owners.

If you own a small business and are looking for a new or upgraded communications system, this book helps you evaluate your options and prepare for your conversations with the reseller of your choice. If you already own the system, this book helps you configure, maintain, and troubleshoot it.

If you are part of the IT infrastructure of a larger enterprise, this book helps you understand how you can quickly and easily start a VoIP pilot in select offices of your organization without needing the immediate commitment or planning to do a full-scale migration to IP telephony everywhere. With Cisco IPC Express you can start small, and migrate your network at your own speed and within your budget.

If you are a reseller, Cisco IPC Express is an exciting product to add to your suite of offerings, and this book helps you prepare to sell, install, configure, and support it. If you have ideas for value-added services and applications you may offer to your customers, this book tells you how to integrate these with the system.

How This Book Is Organized

Although you can read this book cover to cover, it is designed in four main parts as different areas of interest. You can focus on the topics that are most relevant to your business, or you can progress through the chapters in sequence, learning the fundamentals before tackling more complex topics. This is particularly important if you want to become Cisco certified in reselling the system or want to be proficient in understanding its operation and features.

The following describes the parts and chapters that make up this book:

Part I, "Cisco IP Communications Express Overview," introduces Cisco IPC Express and discusses where it fits into the Cisco IP telephony portfolio. Read these chapters if you are unfamiliar with Cisco IPC Express and want to get an overview of what the system can do for you or your business, or if you are shopping for a small-office IP-based communications solution and are curious about what the industry has to offer. Also read this part of the book to see how Cisco IPC Express can benefit your business, how it fits into your network design, and to get an overview of the system architecture.

- **Chapter 1, "Introducing Cisco IPC Express,"** provides an overview of Cisco IPC Express, describes the system's components, and reviews how it fits into the overall Cisco IP telephony product portfolio. This chapter also explains the benefits and cost of ownership of Cisco IPC Express, as well as how it can be deployed in certain industries.

- **Chapter 2, "Building a Cisco IPC Express Network,"** discusses Cisco IPC Express network deployment options. It briefly covers general IP telephony network types and then covers the details of single-site and multisite network design considerations particular to Cisco IPC Express. This chapter explores networks in which every site has a Cisco IPC Express system, as well as hybrid networks that also contain sites under the control of a Cisco CallManager system.

- **Chapter 3, "Cisco IPC Express Architecture Overview,"** provides an overview of the Cisco CME and Cisco UE components of the Cisco IPC Express system. It explains the Cisco IOS software structure and foundation that Cisco CME is built on and provides background understanding for the feature operation discussion in Part II. The hardware and software architecture of Cisco UE is also explained, providing a foundation for understanding how its applications interact with Cisco CME and how the components work together to provide an integrated IP telephony system for your office.

Part II, "Feature Operation and Applications," contains detailed discussions of feature operation and configuration considerations to help you deploy Cisco IPC Express to its best advantage to solve the business problems you or your customers are facing. This part of the book is also a helpful reference if you're preparing for the Cisco CME certification exam, because it discusses in depth how the system works and interacts with surrounding applications.

- **Chapter 4, "Cisco IP Phone Options,"** provides details on the Cisco IP phones that are supported and the phone features you can use with Cisco CME.

- **Chapter 5, "Cisco CME Call Processing Features,"** discusses Cisco CME features such as PBX and key system configurations, shared-line appearances, hunt groups, ephone-dns, dial peers, overlay directory numbers (DNs), intercom, paging, call pickup, call park, transfer, forwarding, softkey customization, and billing considerations.

- **Chapter 6, "Cisco CME PSTN Connectivity Options,"** provides background information on connecting your Cisco CME system to the PSTN. It covers concepts such as analog and digital signaling on PSTN trunks, direct inward dial (DID), dialed number identification service (DNIS), and calling line ID (CLID). The characteristics of trunk type hardware and signaling are discussed to allow you to choose the PSTN connection method most appropriate for your office. Dial plans are also discussed, including dial peers and digit manipulation techniques.

- **Chapter 7, "Connecting Multiple Cisco CMEs with VoIP,"** discusses Cisco CME interactions with H.323 gatekeepers, the components and topologies of these networks, dial-plan considerations, dual-tone multifrequency (DTMF) relay, H.323 endpoint registration, H.450 supplementary services and operation, and Session Initiation Protocol (SIP) network integration and supplementary services.

- **Chapter 8, "Integrating Cisco CME with Cisco CallManager,"** covers Cisco CME interoperability with Cisco CallManager when using call modifications such as call transfer, call forwarding, and H.450.

- **Chapter 9, "Cisco IPC Express Automated Attendant Options,"** covers the AA application options available with Cisco CME. Cisco UE offers the primary AA option. The capabilities of the AA are discussed in detail, along with the scripts you use to customize the AA for your office. The AA script editor, steps, variables, and call routing options are explained, as well as the tasks required to define your own AA menu. You also learn about other AA options (not provided by Cisco UE) available with Cisco CME.

- **Chapter 10, "Cisco IPC Express Integrated Voice Mail,"** discusses the features and operation of Cisco UE as the integrated voice mail component of the Cisco IPC Express system. The types of mailboxes and the various voice mail features offered by the application are discussed from the subscriber's, caller's, and administrator's points of view. The concepts of users and names are explained, as well as how to customize these to provide the features you want in your office. Networking different sites to send voice mail messages between sites is also covered.

- **Chapter 11, "Cisco CME External Voice Mail Options,"** provides information on alternative voice mail applications that you can use with Cisco CME, including Cisco Unity and Stonevoice. Analog integration with traditional voice mail systems is also covered.

- **Chapter 12, "Additional External Applications with Cisco CME,"** explores Telephony Application Programming Interface (TAPI) and XML-based interfaces offered by Cisco CME to allow you to build and integrate your own applications with the system to enrich the productivity gains you may get from using Cisco IPC Express.

Part III, "Administration and Management," provides an in-depth discussion of the system's administration philosophy and the interfaces, access mechanisms, administration capabilities and features, tools, setup wizards, and customization. A full step-by-step configuration example is given to illustrate system setup techniques.

- **Chapter 13, "Cisco IPC Express General Administration and Initial System Setup,"** covers general administration concepts and interfaces, including the command-line interface (CLI) and the browser-based graphical access techniques. System installation and initial setup techniques and tools are covered to get you started. XML customization of the graphical user interface (GUI) interface and the Cisco CME Zero Touch Deployment option are discussed.

- **Chapter 14, "Configuring and Managing Cisco IPC Express Systems,"** provides information on how to configure the different aspects of the system. It includes prerequisite router configuration, the IP phones and extensions, the PSTN interfaces, the dial plan, hunt groups and other call processing features, AA, and voice mail. Security considerations for your Cisco IPC Express system are briefly covered.

- **Chapter 15, "Cisco IPC Express System Configuration Example,"** gives a full configuration example in which you are walked through configuring a system, from unpacking the box to full operation. The preceding chapter discusses system administration from a functional point of view, and this chapter gives the step-by-step sequence of how to set up a system.

Part IV, "Maintenance and Troubleshooting," is for the support professional installing the system or investigating trouble tickets opened against a Cisco IPC Express system. This may be your own system, or you may be supporting other businesses' systems. It contains in-depth coverage of the software components and communication between the components, typical configuration challenges and how to correct these, how to drill into a problem to isolate what part of the system may be at fault, the tools and techniques you will use for troubleshooting, and numerous tracing examples to prepare you for those inevitable situations in which things do not function the way they should.

- **Chapter 16, "Troubleshooting Basic Cisco IPC Express Features,"** provides an introduction to troubleshooting Cisco CME systems, covering basic technologies such as IP connectivity, virtual LAN (VLAN), Trivial File Transfer Protocol (TFTP), and Dynamic Host Configuration Protocol (DHCP). Phone registration and bootup scenarios are discussed in detail, as are GUI access problems when the browser is not getting the right administration login screen.

- **Chapter 17, "Troubleshooting Advanced Cisco CME Features,"** covers troubleshooting Cisco CME features, including phone lines, dial-plan patterns, transfer patterns, conference, music on hold, directory services, and class of restriction.

- **Chapter 18, "Troubleshooting Cisco CME Network Integration,"** discusses troubleshooting networks of interconnected Cisco CME systems, as well as interactions with external network components such as Cisco Unity and Gatekeeper. Network call transfers, forwards, and problems with Cisco Unity integration, such as message waiting indicator, are covered.

- **Chapter 19, "Troubleshooting Cisco UE System Features,"** covers system-level troubleshooting of Cisco UE, including logging and tracing techniques, installation problems, application startup, network connectivity, and system backup and restore.

- **Chapter 20, "Troubleshooting Cisco UE Automated Attendant,"** discusses troubleshooting Cisco UE AA topics such as calls not being answered by the AA, abnormal exits, and missing files. It provides a trace of a call flow through the AA system as well as tracing examples for every step of the call flow.

- **Chapter 21, "Troubleshooting Cisco UE Integrated Voice Mail Features,"** discusses troubleshooting Cisco UE voice mail topics such as interactions between the application and the Cisco CME software, mailbox selection problems, configuration problems, difficulties with digit manipulation and DTMF recognition, Voice Extensible Markup Language (VXML) browser problems, Lightweight Directory Access Protocol (LDAP) and database interactions, and message waiting indicator operation.

Part V, "Appendixes," supplements the topics found in the chapters.

- **Appendix A, "Cisco IPC Express Features, Releases, and Ordering Information,"** provides a concise reference list of the most common features in Cisco CME and Cisco UE. This appendix also provides ordering information for the product components.

- **Appendix B, "Sample Cisco UE AA Scripts,"** provides the full content (in text format) and a brief explanation of the AA scripts referenced in this book.

- **Appendix C, "Cisco Unity Express Database Schema,"** provides the database schema layout for Cisco UE. This helps you understand some of the troubleshooting output from Cisco UE.

What You Will Find on the Website

A simple Cisco UEs AA is used in Part IV of this book to illustrate how to isolate potential issues with AA scripting. Chapter 20 discusses the three script files that comprise this sample AA, and Appendix B shows a text representation to explain the script flow. You can download the binary script files from the website to your computer by going to http://www.ciscopress.com/title/158705180X and opening the files with the Cisco Unity Express Script Editor. (You can download the Editor application from Cisco.com.)

Cisco IP Communications Express Overview

This chapter covers the following topics:

- The benefits of Cisco IP Communications (IPC) Express to your business
- The components of the Cisco IPC Express system
- Using IP Communications in your enterprise branch or small- or medium-sized business office
- How Cisco IPC Express fits into the overall Cisco IP Telephony product portfolio

## CHAPTER 1

Introducing Cisco IPC Express

It is the summer sale season at the clothing store where you work, and the floor is swamped with shoppers. One customer inquires about an item that is unavailable. With a few keystrokes on your IP phone, you check the inventory database to see if there is a similar item in another store location. As you input the customer's account number on the phone to reserve the item, the database informs you that this person is one of your best customers. You pick up the IP phone handset and page an employee to provide special assistance to the customer. The employee intercoms you using his wireless IP phone from another section of the store and promises to head over.

When you finish assisting the customer, your IP phone message waiting indicator (MWI) light comes on. You press a button on the IP phone and scroll through your messages. You have five voice mail messages and two e-mail messages. You return an urgent message from your supplier by pressing a button on your phone before attending to the less urgent messages.

Welcome to the world of convergence, where data and voice are delivered on a single IP network through IP communications systems. The preceding example only touches on the promise of IP telephony. There are many more reasons why it can transform your business, whether you are in the retail, financial, healthcare, or any other industry. First, IP telephony delivers converged applications in a cost-effective manner to users who may not have had access to them before. Instead of providing every employee in an office with a powerful computer, an IP phone can serve as the business communications device for many employees. Second, regardless of our collective readiness, the world of convergence has arrived. Just like the Internet revolution caught some by surprise, businesses that are slow to migrate will find themselves vulnerable to competitors that provide better services and have more productive employees. Finally, from a return-on-investment perspective, IP telephony reduces the complexity of having to manage and maintain separate network infrastructures for data and voice.

This book focuses on an IP telephony system called Cisco IP Communications (IPC) Express. Cisco IPC Express is a business communications solution that offers a comprehensive set of telephony features, as well as integrated routing, security, Ethernet switching, and numerous other applications on a single platform. The primary components of the Cisco IPC Express system are

- The call processing software Cisco CallManager Express (CME)
- The IP Communications platform, ranging from the Cisco 1700 to the Cisco 3800 series Integrated Services Routers (ISRs), supporting the Cisco IOS software that provides routing, security, and numerous networking interfaces
- The IP-based applications (such as Cisco Unity Express (UE) and Cisco Unity), offering automated attendant (AA), voice mail, and various phone-based services
- The IP-based endpoints (such as IP phones and softphones)

This chapter introduces Cisco IPC Express used as an IP telephony system for small and medium businesses or an enterprise branch office. This chapter also covers the components of Cisco IPC Express and the applications that are possible over an integrated voice and data network.

The Purpose of Cisco IPC Express

In an IP telephony network, voice and data traffic converge from their separate sources onto a single IP network infrastructure. Most communications solutions available today, however, still deploy multiple platforms for different functions in the network. For instance, a private branch exchange (PBX) or key system delivers the telephony infrastructure, and a separate LAN switch delivers local data connectivity. A router manages Internet or WAN access, and a virtual private network (VPN) appliance, intrusion detection system, and firewall deliver the security infrastructure. As a result, the financial investment and management resources to deploy a multiple-platform network add up quickly.

The Cisco IPC Express system integrates data, voice, security, and routing into a single IP communications platform. No separate server or appliance is required for any of these network capabilities. You can also integrate additional features, such as content delivery, web application caching, URL filtering, LAN switching, wireless device access, network access control (NAC), and intrusion detection to protect your office from virus and worm infections into the same platform. In the Cisco IPC Express solution, all these applications are modular and can be added or turned on optionally based on what you need in your business. This means that businesses can deliver the applications that meet their initial requirements and then add other applications and functions as required when the business expands.

In addition, with data communications now a ubiquitous service in any business, adding telephony services to the existing data infrastructure is one way to protect your investment in equipment. A majority of enterprises and small or medium businesses have invested in a robust data infrastructure to communicate effectively with their vendors and customers. A business with a data infrastructure using the Cisco 2600XM, 2800, 3700, or 3800 ISRs can use these same platforms to deploy Cisco IPC Express.

Because the data infrastructure deployed by businesses today has been fine-tuned over the years to deliver reliable features, the expectation is that a telephony solution deployed on the data infrastructure will provide the same or better system reliability, flexibility, and availability. The telephony service is required to remain in operation, and users must continue to receive and make calls in the event of a network or power failure. Cisco IPC Express supports Hot Standby Router Protocol (HSRP) features and can be used with Survivable Remote Site Telephony (SRST) to deliver increased redundancy and availability for telephony features. Refer to the section "Other Cisco IP Telephony Solutions for the Enterprise Branch and Small and Medium Offices," later in this chapter for more details on SRST.

Together, all this provides a cost-effective, scalable, secure, and reliable communications solution that can be easily deployed and managed by both enterprise branch offices and small or medium businesses of one or more sites.

Benefits of Cisco IPC Express

Cisco IPC Express's unique hardware and software architecture, integrating all the telephony, routing, and application needs that may be required by a growing business, yields two categories of benefits: lower cost of ownership and productivity enhancements.

Lower Cost of Ownership

One of the most important aspects of the decision to acquire a new communications system is how it affects your budget, or cost of ownership. The cost includes direct costs, such as equipment costs, and hidden or indirect costs, such as ongoing maintenance or support fees. This section describes the benefits of Cisco IPC Express in lowering the total cost of ownership for businesses.

Reduce Equipment Costs

Cisco IPC Express allows enterprises to converge their voice and data network infrastructure from multiple vendors into a single IP-based network. By doing so, you save not only the costs of maintaining separate PBXs or key systems from a variety of vendors, but also the expense of maintaining a multiple-platform network with IP and non-IP traffic.

Some small or medium business owners require multiple devices for data and voice communications, such as phones, routers, switches, security appliances, and application servers. Such business owners not only have to incur the costs of acquiring the equipment, but also have to purchase maintenance contracts from different vendors and integrate all these devices and appliances into the network. When a communication breakdown occurs, it can be unclear which device is responsible and, therefore, which vendor to call for support. Cisco IPC Express's integrated architecture simplifies these deployment and maintenance activities and reduces equipment and support costs.

Reduce Upgrade Costs

By migrating from a PBX or key system to Cisco IPC Express, your business can eliminate the need to upgrade individual PBX and key systems, often from disparate vendors. PBX or key systems nearing the end of their product or lease life cycles must be replaced or substantially upgraded to enable the latest applications.

Reduce Wiring Costs

Cisco IPC Express lets you optimize a building's wiring. Both computers and IP phones use the same Ethernet port, thereby requiring only a single type of wiring in a building. In addition, only a single Ethernet port or jack is required for each user, because the computer can be plugged into the IP phone's data port. Traffic remains logically separated via the use of virtual LAN (VLAN) configurations. These ensure that data traffic does not interfere with voice traffic for purposes of quality of service (QoS) and security.

Reduce Network Administration Costs

Cisco IPC Express reduces network administration costs by more efficient and simplified network management, because there is only a single IP system to manage per site versus multiple devices from potentially different vendors.

In addition, because the challenges of network management are limited to maintaining a single system, a smaller system administration staff can manage a larger number of sites and provide faster response times. The same enterprise or small or medium businesses that previously may have outsourced a number of responsibilities to external network management contractors can now gain better control over their network and make configuration changes themselves. Doing so lowers maintenance costs and better utilizes IT resources. Training costs for staff are also reduced because of the converged system.

Reduce the Cost of Adds, Moves, and Changes

A growing enterprise or small- to medium-sized business that makes frequent additions to employee headcount or that wants to manage moves or transfers within an organization in a more timely manner can save money with Cisco IPC Express. The benefit of an IP endpoint, such as an IP phone, is that it moves with the employee and only has to be plugged into a working Ethernet port for it to automatically register itself to the Cisco CallManager Express (CME) call control system. No other modifications are necessary.

Quick day-to-day adjustments such as changing names and adding a new employee, extension, or mailbox can be easily accomplished via the web-based graphical user interface (GUI) by a nontechnical administrator. These tasks do not require a support call. The installation and upgrade of the system may still be performed by an external company.

Productivity Enhancements

Another consideration for businesses deciding on a communications system is how beneficial it will be to the business's overall growth or productivity and, in particular, the employees. This section describes how Cisco IPC Express improves productivity for businesses.

Improve Employee Productivity by Using IP Phones

Cisco IPC Express transforms the IP phone into a business communications device. This is crucial for the employee whose job is not desk-bound and, therefore, does not have a dedicated computer. The IP phone can collect information from various sources, such as cellular phone personal contact information and inventory or account databases, and show this information on its display screen. In addition, a built-in system directory lets employees look up other employees' names and extensions and dial these numbers with a single keystroke. Customized directories can also be accessed via XML from a single point.

XML applications used with IP phones also allow users to access the weather forecast and stock quotes, perform inventory checks, enter time-card information, reserve merchandise for customers, and more.

Improve Employee Mobility Using PC-Based Phones and Wireless Phones

PC-based IP phones, also called softphones (such as Cisco IP Communicator), eliminate or lessen the need for a desk-bound phone set. A PC can become an employee's communication device, allowing that person to set up phone calls with the click of a mouse. This is an especially powerful tool for mobile employees who need to stay in contact with the office. They have instant access to all the on-site directory and extension dialing information, as well as personal directories, and synchronization with cell phone directories. The softphone can share lines with the employees' office desk phone.

The Cisco 7920 Wireless IP Phone also introduces new productivity benefits. These phones have the same features as wired IP phones and allow employees to roam without incurring cellular phone charges. They are convenient for employees, such as store or warehouse managers or health clinic personnel, who roam about during a typical workday but who need to remain available to answer important customer calls or communicate with other employees.

Improve Communication with Advanced IP Telephony Features

Cisco IPC Express includes a number of flexible IP telephony features that can improve communication for businesses. For example, with the paging feature you can use the IP phones to call a group of users or an entire department or make overhead announcements in a store or warehouse. This transforms the IP phone into a paging terminal. Another useful IP telephony feature is the intercom function. It is used to contact a specific individual with the stroke of a key and without requiring a ring cycle, delivering instant one-to-one voice communication.

Easily Replicate Telephony Configuration

Because Cisco IPC Express offers IP telephony features on a single platform, the configuration can be easily replicated across multiple sites or branch offices. This makes deployments across multiple branch offices easy to manage and troubleshoot. In addition, it improves productivity for employees who have the same communications infrastructure and features on their IP phones, regardless of which location they work in. The easily replicated configuration also makes the customer experience consistent across multiple offices or store locations that they visit.

Simplify Network Management Using the GUI

The GUI for Cisco IPC Express is a simple, user-friendly, web-based interface that does not require technical expertise with the platform or system details. Different levels of administration are available, allowing resellers to install and debug the system and office system administrators to make day-to-day changes, such as adding phones and voice mailboxes. There also is a level for end users to access and change their individual telephony feature settings.

Although Cisco IPC Express has many benefits, it might not be the ideal communications system for certain types of businesses. The decision factors include the size of your office, the choice of centralized versus distributed call processing, the WAN environment, and the features or applications required. The section "Deciding Between Cisco IPC Express and Cisco Call Manager," later in this chapter, describes when Cisco IPC Express is the ideal choice. It also provides an overview of other Cisco IP telephony options.

Cisco IPC Express System Components

This section describes the components of a Cisco IPC Express system in detail. As previously explained, Cisco IPC Express includes the call processing software (Cisco CME), the IP Communications platform, the IP-based applications, and the IP-based endpoints.

Cisco CallManager Express

Cisco CME is a Cisco IOS-based call processing system that provides a wide range of IP telephony features for small- or medium-sized businesses and enterprise branch offices with up to 240 users. Cisco CME provides a cross section of traditional telephony features in addition to advanced converged features that are unavailable on most traditional telephony solutions. Businesses can also select between key system and PBX modes of operation or a combination of the two on a single network.

Because Cisco CME is completely IP-based call processing software, the software design has no physical connection constraints. This means that you can configure numerous phone and Public Switched Telephone Network (PSTN) trunk combinations on Cisco CME, delivering a range of applications for businesses. For example, the hunt group feature lets you program multiple phones in your business to have extensions that ring sequentially. In other words, when the first phone is busy or receives an incoming call that is not answered, the call rolls over to the second phone in the hunt group in sequential order, and so on. In a busy business environment, the hunt group feature or the shared-line/multiline appearance feature allows many options for implementing call coverage such that any group of employees can answer customer phone calls in the most efficient manner.

The initial installation of Cisco CME is accomplished easily using the Configuration Wizard. This setup tool prompts you for answers to a number of pertinent questions to set up system parameters. Voice mailboxes can also easily be added using the Cisco UE Initialization Wizard.

Cisco CME offers the option of Cisco IOS software command-line interface (CLI) or a web-based GUI for everyday administration and configuration. The CLI is the same interface used to configure routers, switches, and the IP Communications platforms and is familiar to most system administrators. For nontechnical staff, the web-based GUI is a simple GUI to add users, phones, and extensions or to make configuration changes.

Cisco CME is enabled with the purchase of a Cisco CME feature license with your Cisco IOS release for the router platform. Appendix A, "Cisco IPC Express Features, Releases, and Ordering Information," summarizes the Cisco CME features.

IP Communications Platforms

Cisco CME runs on the Cisco IPC Express platforms, including the Cisco 1700, 2600XM, 2691, and 3700 Access Router series, as well as the Cisco 2800 and 3800 ISR series. These communications platforms feature a diverse set of analog and digital PSTN trunk interfaces, analog station interfaces, and modular extension slots where you can add a variety of options such as integrated switching, hardware virtual private network (VPN) acceleration, voice mail, and intrusion detection systems. Depending on the number of users in the office, the right-sized IP communications platform can be selected to perform routing, switching, security, and other services.

Businesses already using access routers or ISRs for their data connectivity can easily deploy Cisco IPC Express on these platforms as well. Alternatively, businesses that have chosen to deploy IP telephony for new sites or offices can purchase a complete bundle package that includes the platform, software, licenses, and applications. Because the platforms provide such a wide range of features in a single chassis, it is easy to manage and configure.

The Cisco IPC Express platforms provide easy modularity. The interface cards used for value-added applications or connectivity can be reused across the portfolio of routers. In addition, if a business outgrows a Cisco IPC Express deployment and decides to move to a Cisco CallManager system, the equipment and licenses already purchased can be reused for this migration, preserving the entire investment.

The portfolio of Cisco IPC Express platforms offers a wide range of routing capacity, IP phone support, and PSTN trunk density choices to meet any small- or medium-size office. The Cisco

1700 series and Cisco 2801 platforms are the low-density services platforms, offering modular connectivity and entry-level voice services. The 2600XM series, 2691, and remaining 2800 series platforms offer extended modular connectivity. The Cisco 3700 and 3800 platforms are the high-density services platforms optimized for high performance and enhanced services. All these platforms support Cisco IOS software.

Cisco 1700 Series Platforms

The Cisco 1700 series router platforms are targeted at small businesses. Platforms that support voice include the Cisco 1751-V, 1760, and 1760-V platforms.

The Cisco 1751-V platform has a desktop form factor, whereas the 1760 and 1760-V are 19-inch rack-mounted platforms. The V extension indicates that the platforms have been fitted with the appropriate memory, IOS image, and digital signal processor (DSP) modules to support voice.

These platforms can be fitted with modular WAN interface cards (WICs) and voice interface cards (VICs) to support a variety of applications. WICs provide WAN connectivity such as broadband DSL, ISDN, leased lines, and Frame Relay, whereas VICs provide PSTN connectivity such as T1 or E1 Primary Rate Interface (PRI), Basic Rate Interface (BRI) or Foreign Exchange Office (FXO), and station-side connectivity using Foreign Exchange Station (FXS).

The Cisco 1700 series router platforms support features such as the following:

- Voice over IP (VoIP)
- High-performance routing with QoS
- Inter-VLAN routing
- VPN access with firewall options

Cisco 2600XM Series and 2691 Platforms

The Cisco 2600XM series and 2691 series routers are 19-inch rack-mounted platforms that target small and medium businesses or branch offices. Platforms in the portfolio include the Cisco 2611XM, 2621XM, 2651XM, and 2691 platforms. Like the Cisco 1700 series platforms, they support WIC and VIC slots.

In addition, the Cisco 2600XM series platforms support network module (NM) and Advanced Integration Module (AIM) slots. The NM form factor is very flexible, delivering a wide range of applications from Cisco UE voice mail and AA to high-density PSTN trunking and LAN switching. Unlike WICs, VICS, and NMs, AIMs are installed on the router's motherboard. This form factor supports security and additional voice applications, such as voice mail and digital signal processors. The Cisco 2691 platform has two AIM slots compared to the 2600XM platforms, which support only one AIM slot.

The Cisco 2600XM series and 2691 platform support a range of features:

- Multiservice voice and data integration
- VPN access with firewall and encryption options
- Analog dial access services
- Routing with bandwidth management
- Inter-VLAN routing
- Delivery of high-speed business-class DSL access
- Integration of low-density switching

Cisco 2800 Series Routers

The Cisco 2800 series routers include the 2801, 2811, 2821, and 2851 platforms. The Cisco 2800 series platforms target small and medium businesses and enterprise branch offices. They have been architected to deliver embedded voice, data, and security capability at wire-speed WAN performance for single or multiple T1 or E1 links. This means that instead of delivering services by adding optional interface cards to routers, the Cisco 2800 series routers come with core voice, data, and security features integrated on the platform chassis.

The Cisco 2811, 2821, and 2851 platforms support high-speed WICs (HWICs), VICs, NMs, and AIM slots, and the 2801 platform supports HWICs, VICs, and AIM slots. These router platforms all have motherboard slots where digital signal processor cards can be housed for onboard voice processing.

The platforms support four different NM form factor variants (network module enhanced, extended network module enhanced, double-wide network module enhanced, and extra-double-wide network module enhanced) for increased capacity and future growth potential.

The Cisco 2821 and 2851 platforms also support a high-density extension voice module (EVM) form factor that delivers up to 24 ports of analog or eight ports (16 channels) of BRI connectivity. They also feature a security hardware accelerator on the motherboard that supports the AES encryption algorithm.

Cisco 3700 Series Platforms

The Cisco 3700 series routers are high-performance platforms with extended high-density services including high-performance routing, integrated low-density switching, security, voice, IP telephony, voice mail, and content networking. These services are delivered using WICs, VICs, NMs, and AIM slots. The Cisco 3700 series includes the 3725 and 3745 platforms.

The Cisco 3725 supports two network module slots, whereas the Cisco 3745 supports four network module slots. In addition, the width of these network module slots can be adjusted to support high-density services. For example, the integrated EtherSwitch options include a

16-port NM and a 36-port, high-density service module (HDSM) version. The 36-port HDSM uses the extra capacity from the wider network module interface form factor.

Cisco 3800 Series Platforms

The Cisco 3800 series platforms, similar to the 2800 series platforms, are the latest generation of access routers and are architected for integrated services. Data, voice, and security applications are embedded into the router motherboard. This frees up modular slots to allow businesses to take advantage of new high-speed slots, such as the HWIC and network module enhanced (NME), for additional services, interfaces, and densities. VICs, NMs, and AIM slots are also supported, as are high-density extension voice module (EVM) slots. The Cisco 3800 also supports embedded VPN hardware acceleration.

The Cisco 3800 series includes the 3825 and 3845 platforms. The 3825 supports two network module slots, and the 3845 supports four network module slots.

The Cisco 2800 and 3800 series platforms significantly improve performance and integration over the corresponding Cisco 1700, 2600, and 3700 series platforms. They exhibit architectural improvements such as embedded security features, onboard DSPs, multiple new interfaces, and increased services density. For example, instead of using an NM-HDV2 network module for T1 or E1 PSTN access, you can now use a T1 or E1 voice or WAN interface card (VWIC) together with the router onboard DSP modules (PVDM2). This frees up your network module slot for other applications such as voice mail and content distribution.

Cisco IPC Express Platform Attributes

Table 1-1 summarizes the attributes of each platform.

Table 1-1 *Performance and Interface Summary for Cisco IPC Express Platforms*

Platform	WIC/VIC Slots	NM Slots	AIM Slots	EVM Slots	LAN Ports
Cisco 1751-V	2	0	0	0	1 10/100 Ethernet port
Cisco 1760, 1760-V	2	0	0	0	1 FE 10/100 Ethernet port
Cisco 2600XM	2	1	1	0	1 or 2 FE 10/100 Ethernet ports
Cisco 2691	3	1	2	0	2 FE 10/100 Ethernet ports
Cisco 2801	4	0	2	0	2 FE 10/100 Ethernet ports
Cisco 2811	4	1	2	0	2 FE 10/100 Ethernet ports
Cisco 2821	4	1	2	1	2 GE (10/100/1000) Ethernet ports
Cisco 2851	4	1	2	1	2 GE 10/100/1000 Ethernet ports
Cisco 3725	3	2	2	0	2 FE 10/100 Ethernet ports

Table 1-1   *Performance and Interface Summary for Cisco IPC Express Platforms (Continued)*

Platform	WIC/VIC Slots	NM Slots	AIM Slots	EVM Slots	LAN Ports
Cisco 3745	3	4	2	0	2 FE 10/100 Ethernet ports
Cisco 3825	4	2	2	Up to 1 EVM in NM slots	2 GE (10/100/1000) Ethernet ports
Cisco 3845	4	4	2	Up to 2 EVMs in NM slots	2 GE (10/100/1000) autosensing Ethernet ports

Cisco IPC Express Platform Capacity

Table 1-2 lists the number of phones and mailboxes supported on the Cisco IPC Express platforms (applicable to Cisco CME 3.2).

Table 1-2   *IPC Express Platform Capacity*

Platform	Maximum Number of IP Phones Supported	Maximum Number of Cisco CME DNs Supported	Cisco UE Number of Mailboxes Supported
Cisco 1751-V, 1760, 1760-V	24	120	Not supported
Cisco 2801	24	120	12, 25, or 50
Cisco 261xXM, 262xXM, 2811	36	144	12, 25, 50, or 100
Cisco 265xXM, 2821	48	144	12, 25, 50, or 100
Cisco 2691	72	288	12, 25, 50, or 100
Cisco 2851	96	288	12, 25, 50, or 100
Cisco 3725	144	500	12, 25, 50, or 100
Cisco 3745	192	500	12, 25, 50, or 100
Cisco 3825	168	500	12, 25, 50, or 100
Cisco 3845	240	720	12, 25, 50, or 100

WAN Interfaces

A variety of WAN interfaces are supported with the Cisco IPC Express platforms, delivering data connectivity via ATM, OC-3, T3/E3, channelized T1/E1, Ethernet, Frame Relay, high-speed serial, ISDN BRI, ISDN PRI, and xDSL interfaces.

IP-Based Applications

Several applications can be deployed with Cisco IPC Express to round out its business communications feature set. These include AA and voice mail applications such as Cisco UE and Cisco Unity.

Cisco Unity Express

Cisco UE is a voice mail and AA application available in a network module or advanced integration module (AIM) form factor that fits into the Cisco communications platform. The capacity of Cisco UE 2.1 is summarized in Table 1-3.

Table 1-3   *Cisco UE Capacity*

	Number of Mailboxes	**Number of Storage Hours**	**Number of Ports**
NM-CUE	12, 25, 50, or 100	100	8
AIM-CUE	12, 25, or 50	8 or 14	4 or 6

Businesses have the option of configuring Cisco UE using either CLI commands or the Cisco IPC Express web-based GUI. CLI commands are familiar to system administrators who have configured Cisco access routers in the past. CLI is also ideal for businesses that manage multiple Cisco IPC Express systems using scripting.

The web-based Cisco IPC Express GUI is integrated for both Cisco CME and Cisco UE provisioning to simplify management. Information about phones, extensions, and mailboxes is coordinated automatically between the router and the Cisco UE application module configurations.

In addition, Cisco UE features a telephony user interface (TUI) for user mailbox interaction. A simple step-by-step tutorial is provided to guide users through the first login and mailbox setup process. This tutorial lets new subscribers record a new greeting or spoken name, and set a personal identification number (PIN) to secure their mailbox.

To deploy Cisco UE, you order the hardware and purchase a feature license for the appropriate number of mailboxes. Refer to the section "Ordering Cisco Unity Express" in Appendix A for more information on Cisco UE features.

Although Cisco UE is an integrated part of the Cisco IPC Express system, Cisco CME can also be deployed with other external applications such as Cisco Unity voice or unified messaging, or non-Cisco voice messaging products.

Cisco Unity

Cisco Unity is a full-featured Windows-based voice messaging, unified messaging, and AA application. Cisco Unity features include support for up to 250,000 users and 19 languages, networking capability with Cisco UE and other traditional voice mail systems, distribution list capability, and a unified communications engine that supports both Lotus Domino and various Microsoft Exchange environments.

The unified messaging system integrates with Microsoft Outlook or Lotus Notes to deliver all messages in a single mailbox, making it easy to access and send e-mails, voice mails, and faxes from your PC with just a click of the mouse. Using Cisco Unity's text-to-speech capability, information about the messages can be played over the telephone.

Businesses with multiple sites may select a centralized Cisco Unity voice mail or messaging application over a locally deployed Cisco UE system if more sophisticated features or unified messaging are needed. However, a QoS-enabled WAN with sufficient bandwidth is required for users at remote offices to access the central location for their voice mail as well as for all call forwarding into voice mail.

IP-Based Endpoints

IP endpoints include Cisco IP phones, softphones, and Cisco IP Communicator. IP phones allow users to place telephone calls just as they do with traditional digital or analog phones. IP phones also offer additional functionality, such as XML applications, that enhance employee productivity. For example, the directory information on an executive's cellular phone can be easily transferred to the Cisco IP phone directory, making it seamless for the person to reach his or her contacts from either phone. IP phones also deliver useful information to employees, such as missed calls, received calls, call history, and directory services. IP phones are managed like any other IP device, making personnel additions, moves, and changes as easy to accomplish as plugging an IP phone into the nearest Ethernet port.

Softphones and Cisco IP Communicator are IP phone software applications running on a user's PC. They provide the same IP phone features as their hardware-based counterpart and are ideal for employees who are on the road.

Cisco IPC Express supports a wide range of IP phone endpoints and analog phone adapters. Detailed information on the endpoints supported is provided in Chapter 4, "Cisco IP Phone Options." This section provides only a brief overview and the typical combinations of endpoints that are supported in an office.

IP phones in the enterprise branch or small and medium businesses should be selected based on the telephony needs of the staff working at the office. A business office might deploy a range of different phones. For instance, it might need a Cisco 7912G for the lobby, Cisco 7960Gs for managers, a Cisco 7970G for executives, Cisco 7940Gs or 7960Gs for regular staff, and perhaps a Cisco 7920 wireless phone for anyone who is constantly on the move, such as a floor supervisor.

Cisco 7970G IP Phone

The Cisco 7970G IP Phone is ideal for executives, decision-makers, and users who do not have PCs and who use only a telephone for their business needs. Therefore, they need a sophisticated, top-of-the-line color IP phone that includes a backlit, high-resolution color touch-screen display. This phone supports an advanced XML development platform for more dynamic applications, eight telephony lines, a high-quality hands-free speakerphone, a built-in headset connection, and both Cisco prestandard Power over Ethernet (PoE) and IEEE 802.3af PoE.

Cisco 7940G/60G IP Phones

The Cisco 7940G/60G IP Phones are ideal for employees with medium-to-high telephony traffic. These phones offer a rich set of features, including a pixel display area with dynamic feature access using softkeys and an additional display area for value-added services and applications. These IP phones support a visual MWI, a services key, 24 user-selectable ringers, hands-free speakerphone capability, and a built-in headset connection. The Cisco 7940G IP Phone supports two telephone lines, whereas the Cisco 7960G Phone supports six.

Cisco 7920 Wireless IP Phone

The Cisco 7920 Wireless IP Phone is an easy-to-use IEEE 802.11b-compliant wireless IP phone that provides comprehensive voice communications in conjunction with Cisco IPC Express and Cisco wireless access points. The Cisco 7920 Wireless IP Phone increases productivity by allowing users to be reached wherever they are in a branch office.

Cisco 7905G/7912G IP Phone

The Cisco 7905G and 7912G IP Phones are entry-level business phones targeted at areas with low telephony traffic, such as lobbies and break rooms. They also can address the voice communication needs of a low-to-medium telephony user. Both phones feature a single line and fixed-feature keys, including redial, transfer, conference, and messages. They have four dynamic softkeys and a hard "hold" key. Both phones support MWI, a low-power option using the same power supply as the Cisco 7940G and 7960G, a single RJ-45 connection, and call monitor capability. They have no microphones or headset jacks.

These phones support a maximum of two calls and one directory number. The main difference between the Cisco 7905G and the 7912G is that the Cisco 7912G comes with an integrated Ethernet switch, whereas the Cisco 7905G does not.

Cisco 7935/36 IP Phone Conference Station

The Cisco 7935/36 IP Conference Station is an IP-based, hands-free conference room phone for use on desktops and in conference rooms and executive suites. IP Conference Station features include three softkeys and menu navigation keys, a pixel-based liquid crystal display (LCD) with data and time, calling party name, calling party number, digits dialed, and feature and line status.

The Cisco 7936 IP Conference Station supports additional features such as external microphone ports, an optional external microphone kit, and an audio-tuned speaker grill. The optional microphone kit includes two microphones with six-foot cords. The external microphones enable support for larger offices and conference rooms of up to 20 feet by 30 feet compared to the Cisco 7935.

Cisco 7914 IP Phone Expansion Module

The Cisco 7914 IP Phone Expansion Module is ideal for administrative assistants or receptionists who monitor and manage multiple calls. The Cisco 7914 IP Phone Expansion Module adds buttons and an LCD display to the Cisco 7960G IP Phone. A maximum of 14 buttons can be added to the existing six buttons of the Cisco 7960G IP Phone, increasing the total buttons to 20. The Cisco 7960G IP Phone can support up to two Expansion Modules, increasing the total number of buttons to 34.

You can program the buttons on each Expansion Module as a directory number (DN), line key, or speed-dial key, much like the Cisco 7960 IP Phone. When used as a DN key, a button is illuminated, allowing easy identification of the call state. For example, a steady green illuminated button means a line is in use by you, and a flashing green button means the call is on hold. A steady red button means a line is in use by someone else. Each button not programmed as a DN key may be programmed as a speed-dial button.

Cisco Analog Telephony Adaptor

The Cisco Analog Telephony Adaptor (ATA) products let you connect analog-based devices such as analog telephones, fax machines, and analog conference telephones to IP-based telephony networks. This helps you protect your investment in analog products until you are ready to migrate to IP-based devices. The Cisco ATA 188 has two voice ports, each supporting independent telephone numbers. An integrated Ethernet switch can be used to connect to a 10/100Base-T Ethernet network.

The ATA supports Skinny Client Control Protocol (SCCP) and H.323 phone loads. A fax is supported only on ATAs running an H.323 phone load.

Using Cisco IPC Express in Retail, Financial, and Healthcare Businesses

This section illustrates how Cisco IPC Express is used in the retail, financial, and healthcare industries. These case studies clarify the range and types of features available with Cisco IPC Express and how they are used in different business types. Additional industries that have found Cisco IPC Express an attractive option include education (schools), government agencies, and transportation firms.

The examples discussed in the following sections are also applicable to a wide range of small and medium businesses, such as law firms, accounting firms, and real-estate agencies. Some of the differences in small and medium business solutions are in the platforms, Cisco CME feature licenses, and phone licenses purchased because of the fewer number of users in the office. A smaller office size may also dictate the selection of analog connectivity to the PSTN rather than digital connectivity.

Retail Business

The retail sector is a highly competitive market. Retailers face intense cost and competitive pressures from the many players that exist in this space. In addition, the number of large discount stores and Internet-based companies in this market has grown, leading to price pressures that benefit customers but not retailers. Because of this, margins tend to be low. Retailers look for every opportunity to cut costs and increase per-store productivity and operations. One of the ways to decrease operational costs and increase productivity is with a streamlined IP telephony network.

Current Retail Networks

Retailers with a large number of stores and a QoS-enabled WAN are likely to deploy a centralized Cisco CallManager system for their needs. Many smaller retailers may prefer Cisco IPC Express for their call processing needs, particularly those with a limited need for store-to-store calls and infrequent communications with headquarters. WAN connections in the retail industry tend to be very low-bandwidth (56 kbps or less), lack QoS, or, in some cases, traverse the Internet via a VPN.

PSTN connectivity for retail stores depends on the size of the stores. FXO is common for smaller stores, and T1 is common for larger stores. Retailers' communication needs revolve around phones, because few businesses use PCs or laptops for the average employee in the store. Phone communication scenarios involve incoming calls from customers who are unable to stop by the store and who want to inquire about a particular item or about store hours or who want to speak to a particular person or department.

In a typical call scenario, an employee answers most incoming calls, because the human touch is important for business goals. The employee answers the calls, puts the caller on hold, uses a paging system to contact the right department or person, and then transfers the call to the proper department or employee who can help the customer.

Because a retailer's call processing system is the main source of communication with customers, the type of features supported dictates which communication system is purchased. A number of features are advantageous. These include paging, speed dial, call park and picking up a call, hookflash transfer to free up PSTN FXO trunks, multiple-line appearances, and support for wireless phones.

A store typically would use shared-line appearances on its phones, meaning that when a certain department receives a call, all the phones in that department ring. This allows any sales representative not assisting customers to pick up the call.

Voice mail systems typically are not used during regular business hours, because retailers strive to answer calls as they come in and to process the customer query immediately. Voice mail may be useful to certain store employees, such as managers and supervisors, to aid in communication with headquarters (for example, a broadcast message about new sales goals or special incentives).

Certain stores have a full-time manager who supervises the employees, walks around the store, and uses the phone frequently. In large warehouse-type stores, it can be a problem when the supervisor is paged but is located far from a wired phone, and the customer is put on hold for a long time—or worse, forgotten. Because of this, stores may equip their roaming managers with wireless phones.

When an AA exists, it is often a local AA that has menu options for personalized store hours and store direction and location information. There are few multilevel AA options, because it is desirable to have customers speak to a live person as soon as possible. Local AAs are very popular during nonbusiness hours when the AA menu either directs customers to a centralized call center or allows them to leave a voice message.

Many retailers have internal service requirements for how soon they respond to customer calls. These guidelines can include answering incoming calls by the third ring and not having customers put on hold for longer than two minutes. Retailers also like to create a hierarchical call response structure for certain departments. For example, if no sales associates are available to answer calls in the shoe department, these calls should be directed to the manager in that department. If no one is available, the calls revert to the operator.

Using Cisco IPC Express in a Retail Environment

The Cisco IPC Express solution lets retailers begin migrating new stores to an IP telephony solution. It also allows the flexibility of later deploying a centralized call processing model if the retailer decides this is a better deployment model.

A small retail store may use a Cisco 2801 IPC Express system enabled with VIC-4FXS/DID and VIC2-4FXO voice interface cards for fax and PSTN connectivity, respectively.

When customers are put on hold, a file stored on the router delivers music on hold (MOH). This file can easily be modified to include news of sale items and upcoming events during sales promotions. MOH can also connect to an external source, such as a CD player or radio.

Cisco UE AIM is added to the platform to deliver a cost-effective AA system. The AA delivers different menu options based on business hours. During regular business hours, the menu options present store hours, store directions, and the option to speak to a live operator. During nonbusiness hours, the menu options present store hours, store directions, and an option to leave a voice mail message.

A Cisco 7920 IP Phone is provided for the store manager and mobile employees within the store. It supports secure roaming across access points. It also supports up to six line appearances, similar to the Cisco 7960 IP Phone, and provides features such as hold, transfer, and conference.

A Cisco 7960G IP Phone with these same features is provided for the sales associates. A Cisco 7902G IP Phone with limited features is used in the break rooms and storerooms.

The IP phones are also equipped with a phone directory that lists important phone numbers, including nearby store sites. The directory is downloaded centrally from headquarters, easing provisioning when phone numbers change or additional stores are established.

Financial Services Business

The financial services industry in general has tended to be an early adopter of technology. Cisco IPC Express is ideal for small financial services businesses such as small banks, insurance companies, and credit unions.

Current Financial Services Network

The current financial institution network is fairly sophisticated. The WAN connectivity is typically a T1 pipe, with 64 kbps to 1.544 Mbps of bandwidth provisioned on it depending on the size of the office. The PSTN connectivity is also typically T1 for larger sites and analog FXO trunks for smaller sites. Cisco IPC Express call processing is ideal for either of these sites.

Smaller organizations, such as regional credit unions and insurance companies, typically field calls from local customers asking questions particular to the branch. Phones use the shared-line appearance feature to allow phones to ring on all desks. If representatives such as agents, cashiers, and tellers are unavailable to pick up the calls, the calls are cascaded using hunt groups to the supervisors and managers.

Similar to the retail industry, a receptionist is often preferred over an AA. An automated attendant is used outside regular business hours. Larger organizations, such as large banks, field calls from all over the country with centralized national call centers.

Certain banks have specific representatives they dedicate to their top customers. These calls receive priority, and hunt groups normally direct these calls to either a specific employee or the highest-ranking employee in a particular department.

In the banking industry, voice mail applications are often limited to bank managers, vice presidents, or other employees who find voice mail useful in their job. However, in a small insurance or mortgage company where all the employees are agents who interact with customers, all employees can be empowered with voice mailboxes.

The typical phone features used are call hold, transfer, speed dial, and shared-line appearances. Other features include intercom for assistants to communicate with managers, and paging to notify certain departments or break rooms when assistance is needed.

Using Cisco IPC Express in a Financial Services Business

A medium-sized credit union may use a Cisco IPC Express 2851 system enabled with VIC-4FXS/DID and VWIC-1MFT-1T1 voice interface cards for fax and PSTN connectivity, respectively. The T1 port provides connectivity to the WAN and PSTN, and the FXS ports are used for fax machines or analog phones.

Cisco UE AIM provides voice mail capability for the loan officer and office manager. Additional voice mailboxes can be provisioned for additional employees or when the credit union expands. Cisco UE also offers an integrated AA that can be customized for the credit union's needs.

A Cisco 7960G IP Phone is selected for the credit union tellers and office manager. The Cisco 7960G IP Phone has six line appearances and supports the myriad of features required by the credit union. A Cisco 7905G IP Phone with fewer buttons is provided for the break rooms and the lobby. A Cisco 7914 IP Phone Expansion Module is provided for the credit union receptionist, who must monitor and manage the various call states.

An integrated switch, such as the NM-16ESW-PWR, is used to connect and power the IP phones and provide connectivity to employee PCs.

Classes of service, also known as class of restriction, are defined for the Cisco 7960G IP Phones to allow only the loan officer and office manager to place long-distance calls. Lobby phones are restricted to local calls only. Account codes on the phones allow the credit union to track external calls and organize billing for specific services it provides to a customer.

IP phones are customized with XML applications that provide the latest interest rates and loan rates. When a customer calls the customer service department, a credit union representative can enter the customer's account number on the phone keypad and see details of the customer's account. This allows customer service to provide better service to higher-priority accounts.

Hunt groups are programmed to allow calls to be cascaded to the office manager when an employee is unavailable to answer them. A company-wide directory is also available on the phones to access any credit union employee with a few simple keystrokes.

Healthcare Services

Cisco IPC Express is ideal for small medical clinics or medical branch offices that are part of a larger network. These healthcare services clinics use IP telephony networks to reduce their operational costs and provide improved communication with greater staff mobility and reachability.

Current Healthcare Services Network

Healthcare services clinics and offices tend to have analog FXO lines to the PSTN and DSL access to the Internet. Small clinics typically have phones in every exam room; phones for doctors, nurses, and receptionists; and phones in common areas.

Typically, different classes of service are offered for doctors versus nurses. Popular phone features include wireless phones that allow doctors to roam around clinics. Other popular features include speed dials to connect to other extensions or departments within a medical clinic, hunt groups, and intercom.

Clinics typically interact frequently with nearby pharmacies using faxes and voice calls. Speed dials are commonly used to expedite these calls.

Phones may be available in the lobby, but long-distance calls are restricted on these phones. A required feature for the telephony system is intercom between doctors and nurses. Hunt groups are also required when receptionists are busy.

Using Cisco IPC Express in a Healthcare Services Network

A health clinic may use a Cisco IPC Express 2821 system enabled with VIC2-4FXO for PSTN access, a VIC-4FXS/DID for the fax machines, and a WIC-1ADSL interface card for DSL Internet connectivity.

The Cisco 7920 IP Phone is provided for doctors. This wireless phone allows doctors to continue being accessible while walking around the clinic. The same wireless access point that supports the Cisco 7920 IP Phone also allows doctors to access patient data and lab results using a wireless-enabled personal digital assistant (PDA) or portable computer.

The Cisco 7914 IP Phone Expansion Module is provided for the office receptionists to handle incoming calls from patients. In addition, the Cisco 7960G IP Phones are used for exam rooms and doctors' offices. The Cisco 7905G IP Phone is proposed for the nurses, the break room, and the lobby.

Different classes of service are defined for phones in the break room, lobby, and exam rooms. Long-distance calls are available only on doctors' phones.

Cisco UE's general-delivery mailboxes come in handy for the X-ray department and for the receptionists, who can use them to check for laboratory results and let patients schedule or change appointments.

Features available on the phones include speed dials to pharmacies and extensions for the receptionists, nurses, and doctors. Hunt groups are defined so that when a doctor's or nurse's phone is not answered, it is cascaded to the receptionist.

Key Cisco IPC Express Features

The features highlighted in this section were used in the different business scenarios just described. They can be modified to suit your particular business needs. A more complete list of Cisco IPC Express features can be found in Appendix A.

- **XML applications**—Customized XML applications can be written for Cisco IP phones to deliver information that would otherwise have required access to a PC. This allows retail stores to check the availability of items, healthcare clinics to check patient health history, and financial institutions to check account information or interest rates.

- **Call pickup**—Call pickup allows a business to easily answer a call that is ringing on a different phone or that someone has put on hold. The employee presses the pickup key on the IP phone and enters the number of the phone he or she wants to answer.

- **Call park**—When a call is parked, it is transferred to a "parking slot" number and put on hold until it is retrieved by another employee, who is paged with the call's park slot number.

- **Paging**—This feature is ideal for paging certain employees or for conveying important information to a group of employees. Paging groups can be designated for each group or department. When a paging number is called, each idle phone in that paging group is used in speakerphone mode, eliminating the need for an overhead paging mechanism.

- **Distinctive ringing**—IP phones have several types of ringing options so that in a busy business environment an employee can tell the phones apart. Supervisors have additional options such as monitor mode.

- **Shared-line appearance**—Shared-line appearances allow for better call coverage in a business. This feature allows several different phones to be configured with the same extension number. Ringing phones can then be answered by the closest available employee.

- **Multiple-line appearance**—This feature allows many lines to be configured on a single phone so that any of the incoming calls can be answered at that phone.

- **Speed dial**—Speed dial provides one-key dialing to a list of frequently dialed or important numbers. Up to 24 personal speed-dial numbers can be programmed on each IP phone. Speed-dial numbers can also be delivered to the phone via a central directory, making it easy to change a number and have that change reflected on the phone display of the next phone that accesses this directory.

- **Softkey customization**—This feature allows businesses to customize the phone features and remove the ones they don't want customers or certain employees to have access to. It can also prevent confusion for employees in specialized departments to have only the useful features at their phone displays.

- **Flash softkey for hookflash**—This functionality provides hookflash intervention to enable some services, such as three-way calling and call waiting. Three-way calling, for example, allows employees from two offices to speak with an employee at the head office.

- **Music on hold**—External callers who are put on hold can hear MOH audio streams supplied from an audio file or a live feed.

- **Distribution lists**—Distribution lists are lists of frequently called phone numbers and extensions to be used as broadcast recipients or voice mail recipients.

- **Wireless IP phones**—The Cisco 7920 Wireless IP Phone allows employees to roam a building but still be accessible for important calls.

- **Intercom**—This feature allows a doctor in an office or exam room to communicate with a nurse. It also lets a manager communicate with his or her administrative assistant directly without needing to dial an extension.

- **Hunt groups**—Hunt groups allow businesses to redirect calls that aren't being answered by an employee to another employee or his or her manager. Hunt groups can be sequential, or the longest idle phone can be selected for the next call.

- **Class of restriction**—Class of restriction is used to restrict certain call types, such as long-distance or international calls, from lobby phones, break room phones, and certain employee phones. It is also used to restrict calls to unwanted numbers (such as 900 numbers) for all phones.

- **Night service bell**—This feature allows organizations to cause a selected phone to ring whenever a certain number and its corresponding phones are called during a specific time period. This allows a night-shift supervisor or an employee working late to intercept calls to the operator or to a certain line.

- **Call blocking and override**—The call-blocking feature can prevent calls to a specific number during a specific time period, such as time, day, or date. This is useful to prevent calls to 900 numbers or to ensure that long-distance calls can be placed only during business hours. Call-blocking override lets you remove the call-blocking feature using a PIN.

- **Three-party conference calls**—Multiple three-party conference calls are supported based on the platform selected. Cisco CME also supports conference initiator drop-off, which allows participants in a conference to continue after the parties are introduced.

- **Called-name display**—This feature is important for businesses servicing different sets of clients, such as call centers or businesses with different departments. By identifying the number that a customer has called, the employee answering the call can respond with the appropriate greeting.

- **Do not disturb**—The do not disturb feature ensures that busy employees are not disturbed by ringing phones. They still see the details of the call and can answer it if necessary.

- **Account code**—A service-based business can enter account codes for specific customer calls. Account codes are available in the call detail records. They allow the organization to track calls as needed for billing purposes.

Other Cisco IP Telephony Solutions for the Enterprise Branch and Small and Medium Offices

The Cisco IP telephony call processing options for the enterprise branch and small or medium office include Cisco CallManager with Cisco SRST and Cisco IPC Express, which you learned about earlier in this chapter.

Cisco CallManager is made up of call processing software running on a Cisco Media Convergence Server (MCS). Cisco SRST is a backup call processing service providing local telephony features in the event of a connectivity failure between a centralized Cisco CallManager and the remote IP phone in a branch office.

This section provides an overview of the Cisco CallManager and SRST solutions. Although this is not the focus of this book, the goal is to provide enough information so that you can decide whether Cisco IPC Express or Cisco CallManager and SRST is the right technology choice for your office or customer.

Introducing Cisco CallManager and SRST

Each Cisco CallManager call processing server can support up to 7500 IP phones. Several of these servers can be clustered to support large, scalable networks of up to one million users in a system with more than 100 sites.

Although Cisco CallManager is best suited to large enterprise networks with centralized call processing, a single server can also be deployed in a medium or large office. This solution is less cost-effective than Cisco IPC Express for smaller numbers of users; however, it may still be appropriate for the office that requires any of the more sophisticated call processing features available on Cisco CallManager. Some features supported with Cisco CallManager include unified messaging, multimedia conferencing, collaborative contact centers, and interactive multimedia response systems.

Cisco SRST is used in a centralized Cisco CallManager call processing architecture. Cisco SRST is Cisco IOS-based call processing software that stays dormant in the local branch office telephony router until the WAN experiences an IP connectivity failure.

When the branch office loses connectivity to the central Cisco CallManager because of a WAN or other IP connectivity failure, SRST kicks in to provide emergency backup call processing services for the phones in the branch office. SRST delivers a long list of basic call processing features for the duration of the failure, ensuring that the phones stay up and operational.

When IP connectivity is restored in the network, the system automatically reverts call processing functions to the centralized Cisco CallManager.

A number of books describe Cisco CallManager and SRST network operation in more detail, including the following:

- *Troubleshooting Cisco IP Telephony* by Paul Giralt, Addis Hallmark, and Anne Smith. Cisco Press. 2002.

- *Cisco CallManager Fundamentals: A Cisco AVVID Solution* by John Alexander, Chris Pearce, Anne Smith, and Delon Whetten. Cisco Press. 2001.

Deciding Between Cisco IPC Express and Cisco Call Manager

You have to consider many factors when deciding between Cisco IPC Express and Cisco CallManager for the IP telephony application for your office or network. First consider the WAN environment. If the WAN has not been upgraded to deliver QoS protection for voice, or if there is limited WAN bandwidth, or if a WAN does not exist, a locally delivered call processing service is best for remote offices. In this scenario, Cisco IPC Express delivers a very cost-effective solution.

Another factor to consider is the type of operating environment required. If you require local MOH and local AA, and the business conditions are such that calls are typically placed to the PSTN rather than among different sites or offices, Cisco IPC Express may be the most appropriate solution.

You should also consider the telephony feature set required by the employees. For example, Cisco IPC Express does not support sophisticated call center applications. Therefore, if these are essential features, you would select Cisco CallManager rather than Cisco IPC Express.

For enterprise branch offices and small or medium businesses that want to explore IP telephony (either through a small pilot or by deploying it at a few sites to gain familiarity with it) and that already have a Cisco data infrastructure in place, Cisco IPC Express may be a good way to start.

Businesses that typically lack the time, financial, or technical resources to manage a sophisticated call processing system may also consider Cisco IPC Express, because it is easy to install and is a single IP communications platform to manage. The platform also is modular, allowing you to deploy the minimum level of services that you need and add options, such as security and a content engine, as your business expands. Cisco IPC Express requires no server or Windows platforms to be set up or maintained.

Understanding Migration Strategies (Cisco IPC Express to Cisco CallManager/SRST)

One of the key values of Cisco IPC Express is its flexibility and investment protection if and when larger businesses choose to migrate to a network-wide Cisco CallManager and SRST deployment.

For example, enterprise branch offices and small or medium businesses may choose to deploy a distributed Cisco IPC Express telephony solution until they build up their WAN infrastructure. When the infrastructure is voice-ready, or when the branch offices or small or medium business sites expand and seek additional functionality, they can migrate from a distributed Cisco IPC Express-based deployment to a centralized Cisco CallManager and SRST-based deployment by reusing all the equipment they acquired as part of their Cisco IPC Express rollout. Only the configuration has to change. All the IP phones, platforms, switches, feature licenses, and voice interface cards can be reused in the centralized Cisco CallManager with SRST network without any additional charge.

Summary

In this chapter, you learned about Cisco IPC Express, its cost savings and productivity benefits, the components that make up the system, and some of the features you may use in your business. You also learned how to select between Cisco IPC Express and other Cisco IP telephony options. Examples were provided of how Cisco IPC Express applies to businesses in different industries.

This chapter focused on the business or office level, the pieces of a Cisco IPC Express system, and the features benefiting end users. In the next chapter, the focus turns to the network level. You will learn about the different types of networks on which Cisco IPC Express can be deployed.

Subsequent chapters provide in-depth details on the Cisco IPC Express system architecture, deployment models, and features, and how to install, configure, and manage it for your business.

This chapter covers the following topics:

- IP Telephony network deployment models
- Cisco IP Telephony system trade-offs
- Cisco IP Communications (IPC) Express deployment models, including the standalone office, the multisite network, and the service provider managed services models

## CHAPTER 2

Building a Cisco IPC Express Network

Chapter 1, "Introducing Cisco IPC Express," provided an overview of why Cisco IP Communications (IPC) Express might be an excellent voice and data communications system for your business and how its features may apply to your needs. It also gave brief information about the router platforms, licenses, and components that comprise Cisco IPC Express. This chapter covers what your network might look like or, as it is more formally called, what *deployment models* you may consider when building a network that contains one or more sites with Cisco IPC Express.

If you own a small business that operates from a single site, your network is equally simple, so only a small portion of the information here applies to you. On the other hand, perhaps yours is a larger business with multiple sites, or you own (or work for) a firm that has an enterprise backbone network and you are considering Cisco IPC Express for some or all of the branch sites. If so, you will find the network deployment information in this chapter handy when connecting Cisco IPC Express to your existing network. Last, if you are a service provider (SP) considering Cisco IPC Express as a hosted or customer premises equipment (CPE) offering to your customers, your network has even more considerations.

IP Telephony Network Deployment Overview

Before covering Cisco IPC Express-specific deployment details, you should understand a little more about general IP telephony networks and some of the trade-offs when selecting what type of network fits your business best. This fundamental understanding is needed because Cisco IPC Express networks follow the same general architectures and trade-offs. They also represent a subset of the larger canvas of IP telephony options you may choose from for your business or branch office. Another reason to understand general IP telephony networks is because you can mix and match systems of various types in the same network. If you are already familiar with IP telephony network architectures in general, you can safely skip this introductory section, and proceed directly to the Cisco IPC Express deployment models covered in the next section.

The brain of a telephony network is the call control (or call processing) component. This component of the network generally can be located anywhere in the network in one or multiple places. It provides call features to phones such as dial tone, digit interpretation to implement a dialing plan, and setting up and tearing down voice calls (or, more technically, a *speech path* or *media stream*) from the calling user to the called user. The call control component also manages supplementary features such as call hold, transfer, conference, music on hold, call waiting tone, and the myriad voice call features you are already familiar with.

When considering where and how call processing is provided to users and phones, IP telephony networks can be classified broadly into the following types. Each of these is discussed in the subsequent sections:

- Single-site or standalone network
- Centralized network
- Distributed network
- Hybrid network

Single-Site or Standalone Network

Single-site or standalone networks are businesses or networks where all the employees are located at a single site, as shown in Figure 2-1. By definition, these types of offices or networks are predominantly small, often fewer than 30 people, and occasionally perhaps up to 100 or 150 people. Any organization larger than this most likely has multiple geographic sites.

Figure 2-1 *Single-Site Call Processing Network*

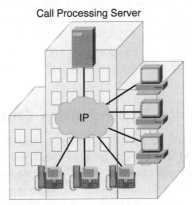

In a standalone deployment, a single instance of the call processing component is resident in the equipment at the site. In rare cases, two instances of the call processing component could be implemented in a standalone site purely for redundancy reasons. However, this is seldom required or cost-effective for such a small site. Having one or two phones directly connected to the Public Switched Telephone Network (PSTN) (or connected via a *power failover* port on the router, which you learn about in Chapter 6, "Cisco CME PSTN Connectivity Options") usually offers a backup mechanism if your business is of such a nature that redundancy is an absolute requirement.

Centralized Network

In a business with multiple geographic sites, it is very often the case that one site is larger, or more central, to a number of smaller, or remote, sites. In a centralized network topology, shown in Figure 2-2, the call processing component is located at this central or larger site, often the headquarters or main location of the business. This component provides service to all employee phones at all sites, using the network that exists between them.

Figure 2-2   *Centralized Call Processing Network*

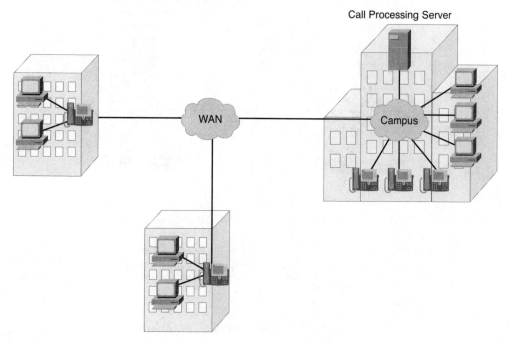

In a centralized deployment, a single instance of the call processing component is resident at one of the sites, and all the other sites connect to this component across the IP network between the sites. Calls are made via IP messaging between the remote devices (IP phones and PSTN trunks) and the central call processing component.

Centralized networks may include multiple instances of the call processing component for redundancy reasons or, in even larger networks, for sheer call capacity and load balancing. In the centralized deployment model, these call processing components are always resident (co-located) at the central site.

Distributed Network

In a network of multiple geographic sites, it is possible that each site is of roughly equal size or importance and that the site-specific network topology is duplicated at each site, as shown in Figure 2-3. In this kind of network, each site has a call processing server that provides services to the community of employees (IP phones) co-located at that site.

Figure 2-3   *Distributed Call Processing Network*

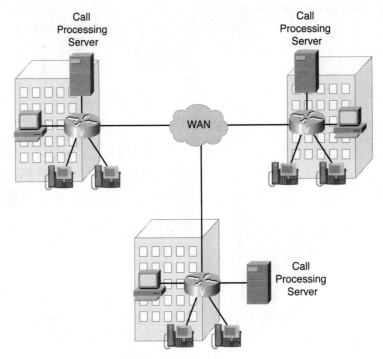

A distributed deployment, therefore, has multiple instances of the call processing component— one at each site—and each resides at its own site. Intersite calls are completed via peer-to-peer IP messaging between the two call processing components involved in the call.

This kind of network architecture has implicit redundancy, because each site has a call processing component. A network or server outage at Site A does not affect calls made at Site B. The distributed model also has implicit call capacity scalability and load balancing, because each site added to the network has its own call processing capacity. These are some of the strengths of the distributed network architecture.

Hybrid Network

The practical realities of most multisite networks often preclude a design that is either perfectly centralized or completely distributed. Instead, many networks are a hybrid of the two designs. A large network of multiple sites typically contains a number of larger locations where there are enough employees to warrant dedicated on-campus application servers (including a call processing component). A large network also sometimes has a vast number of remote sites that are much too small for this investment in equipment and management.

Reliability and availability constraints also make a purely centralized network less desirable because the single call processing component represents a single point of failure for the entire network. A small number of duplicated call processing servers distributed among a handful of key sites (each serving a larger number of remote sites) provides the best overall network availability service and coverage for large networks. A small number of servers is also cost-effective to deploy and manage.

Duplicating call processing components at multiple (but not all) sites results in most multisite networks being designed with aspects of the centralized and distributed models. This is especially true for larger networks with more than 10 to 20 sites. In this case, the attractiveness of centralized management leans toward the centralized model, while at the same time capacity and redundancy considerations necessitate a partly distributed model. This type of hybrid network includes the following characteristics from each individual call processing model:

- **Centralized**—A number of remote sites draw call processing services from another hub site across the network. The number of remote sites in large networks may be substantial—in the range of 100 to 500 sites per centralized hub.

- **Distributed**—A number of sites have call processing servers (and each of these often has a redundant configuration, or cluster). They act as hubs to the rest of the network using a centralized design. Calls between the hubs, though, represent peer-to-peer (or intercluster) calls between distributed call processing components. The number of hub sites is usually relatively small, perhaps 5 to 20, even for fairly large networks of more than 1000 sites.

Cisco IP Telephony System Trade-Offs

For the small standalone office, Cisco IPC Express is an excellent system. For larger networks of multiple sites, the decision to centralize or distribute call processing—or, more specifically, which sites should get call processing servers and which should access services from a nearby larger hub location—is key to the fundamental design of an IP telephony network. It is also one of the important factors dictating whether Cisco IPC Express is the best fit for each individual site.

Generally, two Cisco IP telephony products should be considered for the call processing component in a standalone or multisite network or a section of that network:

- **Cisco CallManager**—A separate Intel-based server (or multiple servers in a redundant configuration) available in a range of capacities from 1000 to 7500 IP phones. You can cluster these servers to form server farms with increased redundancy and availability to provide IP telephony to large campuses and to act as a hub for up to 500 remote sites. Although individual return on investment (ROI) varies, Cisco CallManager generally is not cost-effective at sites of fewer than approximately 500 phones. You can deploy Cisco CallManager in a centralized, distributed, or hybrid model.

- **Cisco IPC Express**—A Cisco IOS-integrated call processing component that is coresident in the router at the site. Cisco IPC Express is cost-effective at the low end and can provide IP telephony services at sites requiring up to 240 phones. For a multisite network, Cisco IPC Express inherently represents a distributed call processing model, because the call control is built into the router at each site.

Cisco also offers other call processing components, such as the Cisco BTS 10200 Softswitch (on Cisco.com, search for "BTS 10200") and the Cisco PGW 2200 Softswitch (on Cisco.com, search for "PGW 2200"). However, these are used primarily in SP networks for residential or large-scale voice services, such as a long-distance carrier service. They are not deployed as the call processing component in a standalone business or small or medium enterprise, which is the focus of this book. Therefore, these products are not covered here in any further detail.

Considering the Cisco CallManager and Cisco IPC Express products, the network design decision at hand is not only centralized versus distributed, but also which product is the best choice for which site. The following sections explore the key trade-offs to help you determine which design might best fit your network.

Cisco Call Manager Networks

Many large enterprises comprising hundreds or thousands of sites find a centralized Cisco CallManager network the best option. Here the term *centralized* is used in a looser sense than in the preceding sections, meaning that most phones and sites draw their call processing services from another, larger site. But inevitably, multiple Cisco CallManager servers are distributed among several of the largest, central locations, and the network is, strictly speaking, a hybrid network. The multiple servers are required for both scalability and reliability. Thus, the core of the network is a distributed model, whereas the smaller sites follow a centralized model.

In these types of networks, voice mail is often also centralized, provided by large-scale servers with thousands or tens of thousands of users per server or server farm. Many other applications, such as e-mail and business applications (for example, product ordering systems and web servers), might also be located at the same site and concentrated in the same data center(s). Therefore, they are a centralized resource to the majority of the remote sites in the network.

Providing both call processing and voice mail services in a centralized manner requires the following network and business attributes:

- Sufficient WAN bandwidth for voice calls from the remote sites to the central site where the call processing or voice mail servers are hosted

- A quality of service (QoS)-engineered WAN to all remote locations

- Network availability (uptime) commensurate with the telephone service expectations of the remote users

- A central IT management model and strong IT expertise

- A business commitment to IP telephony rollout at all or most sites

- A strongly integrated enterprise network, in terms of both technology and management practices

Although the preceding characteristics are present in most large enterprise networks, they are often not present in the majority of small and medium businesses or in smaller enterprise networks.

Cisco IPC Express Networks

At the other end of the spectrum are small standalone businesses with a single office, or small or medium businesses with a handful of sites. A Cisco CallManager server is usually oversized and not cost-effective for the former category of business. It may or may not be a reasonable choice for the latter category, partly depending on how many employees the business has.

Businesses for which a Cisco IPC Express system is a good system have some, or all, of the following attributes:

- Standalone single-site business

- Provided that a WAN is present, it often has insufficient bandwidth to carry voice calls between sites, or there are other logistical reasons for not using the WAN to carry voice traffic

- Provided that a WAN is present, QoS has not been deployed in the network and isn't yet a cost-effective proposition, or the WAN consists of Internet segments that inherently do not offer QoS guarantees

- An autonomous management model for remote locations, or a loosely integrated enterprise network, both in terms of technology and management practices

- No central IT organization or expertise

- Business voice call patterns that are predominantly among remote locations and their local PSTN-based customers, with very little call volume between locations of the enterprise

Although many businesses deploying Cisco IPC Express do not deploy intersite voice across their IP network, other businesses find this latter model a very good fit. Small or medium businesses with a smallish number of sites (for example, 10 or 20 sites) sometimes have a private, QoS-enabled WAN. Saving money on long-distance voice calls between sites may not be the driving business reason for deploying Cisco IPC Express, but it may still be a nice additional benefit.

It is possible to network different Cisco IPC Express sites across an IP infrastructure and leverage that network for voice over IP (VoIP) calls. The considerations with Cisco CallManager and Cisco IPC Express, in this case, often hinge on the following:

- The technology and features available from each product. (For example, Cisco IPC Express can do paging but Cisco CallManager can't, so if this feature is required, Cisco IPC Express is the best fit.)

- The VoIP rollout strategy may be to start with three or five networked sites (which would mean that Cisco IPC Express is a very good fit) and only much later migrate the whole network to a centralized Cisco CallManager solution.

- No clear central site or central organization that could reasonably host the call processing and, therefore, local call processing in each site is more in line with the architecture of your business. (This is often the case in the retail segment.)

- Your remote sites have considerable local autonomy (for example, a franchised business). Therefore, they prefer to run and manage their own IP phones, call processing, and voice mail services.

Hybrid Cisco Call Manager and Cisco IPC Express Networks

Like most decisions, whether to deploy *only* Cisco IPC Express or *only* Cisco CallManager in a network isn't entirely clear-cut. A hybrid network design with a centralized (again, in the looser sense of the term) Cisco CallManager servicing a number of sites and Cisco IPC Express (representing a distributed design) at a number of other sites makes sense for some networks.

Certain attributes may suggest that a hybrid approach is a good solution:

- WAN readiness
- IP telephony rollout strategy
- Varying business practices

WAN Readiness

Segments of the WAN are bandwidth- and QoS-enabled for voice traffic, but other sites are not. These sites may be connected with technology where it does not yet make economic sense to increase the bandwidth or engineer the WAN access for QoS. Or these sites may be connected such that it is not cost-effective (based on the connectivity services offered in the area) to change their WAN connectivity or bandwidth.

IP Telephony Rollout Strategy

A situation might exist where there is a desire to start an IP telephony pilot in one or more sites for a small number of users, while corporate commitment to roll out IP telephony to the entire network is a future, multiphased, multiyear strategy.

Depending on the number of users in the pilot, a Cisco CallManager may be too expensive or too large in scale for the pilot. Using Cisco IPC Express as the IP telephony entry point is an attractive option. All the phones, routers, switches, seat licenses, and other voice components can be directly reused when Cisco CallManager is later rolled out in a centralized manner to serve the users who were in the pilot.

The call processing for Cisco IPC Express is hosted inside the Cisco IOS router that is already present at the site. If it is newly purchased, it can be reused as the WAN router when the site migrates to a centralized Cisco CallManager model. This same router at that point also migrates from being the Cisco IPC Express router to becoming the Survivable Remote Site Telephony (SRST) router for the office. You can migrate from Cisco IPC Express to Cisco CallManager/SRST at your own pace, and you can make the decision independently for each site. Cisco IPC Express and Cisco CallManager sites can coexist in the network for any length of time you choose.

Varying Business Practices

A company's business may be such that some sites are tightly coupled to each other, often call each other, and are under the management of an IT organization. Other sites may be much more autonomous and loosely coupled to the rest of the enterprise based on the type of business they conduct for the enterprise. IT management for these sites may be largely left up to the sites themselves.

This situation may arise from the acquisition of a company with a different management philosophy, a larger enterprise that spins off certain parts of the business to be more autonomous, or a core parent business that franchises its agencies (which is sometimes done in the insurance industry).

Understanding Cisco IPC Express Deployment Models

This section explores Cisco IPC Express network deployments in greater detail. This assumes that one of the Cisco IPC Express models described in the preceding section—a pure Cisco IPC Express network with one or more interconnected sites, or a hybrid Cisco CallManager and Cisco IPC Express network—is a good fit for your organization.

Three general deployment models are discussed here:

- **Standalone office**—A single-site business with typically fewer than 100 employees.
- **Multisite business**—A branch or remote office interconnected to other sites in the same network.

- **Service provider (SP) managed services**—Can be either of the previous two categories. Instead of the company buying and managing the equipment for its own services, it pays a recurring charge to a local SP. This SP owns the equipment and hosts the services, typically both voice and data services.

Standalone Office

The standalone office model fits the vast number of small, single-site companies throughout the world that have fewer than 100 employees. Here are some examples:

- A dentist's office
- A small health clinic
- A professional services office for architects, lawyers, or interior decorators
- A small charity
- A florist shop with three locations in the neighborhood

These types of businesses have no IT organization, and their handful of employees are focused on conducting the company's core business. They are dentists, dental assistants, plumbers, lawyers, florists, or car mechanics, not IT professionals. Data and voice services supporting these types of businesses are either hosted by a local SP or installed and maintained on the premises by a local value-added reseller (VAR) or systems integrator (SI).

IP telephony can be as advantageous to this type of small business as it can to a large enterprise with considerable IT expertise. Voice services to small companies such as these traditionally have been provided either by centrex services or by a key system installed by a VAR or SI. Data service was provided by the local Internet service provider (ISP), which placed some type of CPE onsite and managed it from a central point.

For any site except the very smallest of perhaps only one or two employees, the CPE equipment would include a router and basic security services, such as a firewall.

The next several sections explore different aspects of the standalone office network, including the network architecture, applications, management, and security services deployed.

Network Architecture

Cisco IPC Express is an excellent choice for a single-site, standalone office. In a world before IP telephony, such an office would have had an onsite router for data services and a separate key system or centrex for voice services. Now the router can be extended to provide converged data and voice services to the office. It also can be managed in the same way as before (either by an ISP or by a VAR or SI). Furthermore, both the business and the SP can realize cost, space, and management savings.

Savings just in wiring of a new office could be enough to make Cisco IPC Express cost-effective. Because the phones and computer equipment are all Ethernet-based, only Ethernet wiring is required in the office. Furthermore, only a single Ethernet wire or jack is required to each employee location or desktop. Computer equipment can be plugged into the back of the phone, and virtual LAN (VLAN) technology can be used to provide virtual separation (and therefore security) of voice from data traffic.

Leading-edge productivity features and improved customer service IP-based applications, such as XML services, can also be deployed easily over this converged infrastructure.

Figure 2-4 shows what such a single-site office's network might look like.

Figure 2-4   *Standalone Office Network Topology*

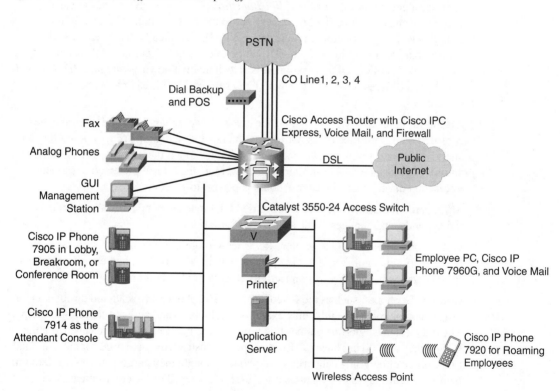

The network in Figure 2-4 has the following components:

- **Employee desktop**—Cisco 7960 IP Phones are provided for employees who work at a desk with a computer. The PC is connected via the phone's Ethernet switch. It also is connected via a single Ethernet cable to a LAN switch that provides inline power to the phones. In Figure 2-4, the LAN switch is a separate component, but it too can be integrated into the router chassis for offices requiring 50 or fewer LAN connections. The ability to connect computer equipment via the phone substantially reduces the overall number of switch ports required in the office. However, this might require that an existing LAN switch be upgraded to provide inline power for the IP phones.

- **Internet connectivity**—This is provided via a DSL or a similar type of uplink to the local ISP, which also might host the company's e-mail services. For larger offices, DSL may not have sufficient bandwidth. Internet connectivity may then be deployed via fractional T1/E1 leased-line services, or even a grouping of multiple DSL or Basic Rate Interface (BRI) lines.

- **PSTN trunks**—Small businesses often prefer familiar key system operation. In this system, individual PSTN lines are mapped to buttons on the phones labeled as Line1, Line2, Line3, and so on up to the number of lines coming in from the PSTN central office. (This arrangement is called *shared-line appearances*.) These PSTN lines are analog Foreign Exchange Office (FXO) connections to the central office (CO). Each line carries a single incoming or outgoing phone call. Caller ID is typically delivered on such connections, but direct inward dial (DID) operation is not. A variation of this offering from the PSTN offers DID operation; this is technically known as *analog DID service*. It may have a different cost than the plain FXO service. You'll read more about this in Chapter 6.

- **Attendant console**—Many small businesses with more than a handful of employees or considerable front-office customer interaction (such as a doctor's office) prefer that an attendant or receptionist answer incoming calls. Although these businesses might use an automated attendant (AA) for after-hours coverage, the typical preferred customer interaction during normal business hours is person-to-person.

- **Management station**—This is a web-based GUI management application for daily moves, adds, and changes to the system configuration.

- **Other voice services**—One or more fax machines are used by almost every type of business. A small number of analog phones may also be used around the office, such as for emergency backup PSTN connectivity if power to the building fails.

Low-end IP phones, such as the Cisco 7902 or 7905 phones, are scattered throughout the office in break rooms, health clinic exam rooms, lobbies, and perhaps conference rooms. These are often single-line phones that typically are not used to receive calls from the PSTN (they also do not have PC Ethernet ports). Instead, they are used for calls internal to the office or outgoing calls. Being IP phones, though, they participate in the intercom, paging, and display-based features often useful in a small office environment.

The Cisco 7920 wireless phone can also be a great productivity enhancer for employees whose responsibilities demand both reachability and mobility, such as a retail floor supervisor, a warehouse supervisor, a bank branch manager, or a restaurant shift manager.

Applications

For certain types of small businesses, voice mail is essential. For these businesses, such as architectural and law firms, personal contact with the customer or client is imperative to conduct business. For other types of businesses, such as restaurants or small retail outlets, an application such as voice mail may not be desired.

A small company might not use an AA application during business hours, preferring instead the personal customer interaction of a receptionist. Yet AA remains an essential application after hours to provide information such as business hours, directions to the office, and perhaps an emergency announcement informing clients that the office is closed unexpectedly because of illness or inclement weather.

Industry segment-specific XML-based applications can be tailored to each business to provide specific productivity or customer service-enhancing applications. For example, a stockbrokerage might have a stock ticker running on the phone display. A hotel might have a room status application in which the maid can update the room status from the phone in the room she just cleaned.

Management

Figure 2-4 shows a GUI management computer in the office. With the latest web-based GUI technology, a nontechnical person can make incremental modifications to the system without scheduling an appointment with the VAR or SI that installed the system. Examples of these types of changes include the following:

- Adding voice mailboxes
- Changing the spelling of employee names
- Adding or changing an extension within the office
- Adding an extension and voice mailbox for a new employee

However, system installation, initial setup and configuration, software upgrades, and turning on new services are most likely done by the SP or the SI or VAR from whom the system was purchased or leased. If any trouble is experienced, these organizations are responsible for isolating the problem and working with the system's vendor to correct system operation.

Security

Any network, especially a system connected to the Internet, requires security measures to protect the system, the applications, and the network itself from unauthorized access. At the very least, a firewall must be deployed. You probably also need a number of access control lists (ACLs) to limit access to the IP addresses and ports on the equipment connected to the Internet (router) and the systems (IP phones, application servers, or PCs) behind it. Virus protection, intrusion detection, and client network access control (NAC) are usually also necessary.

It is unlikely that the employees of the small business are directly involved in defining or setting up security measures for the office. Typically, the SP or VAR/SI that provided the system also deploys the required security filtering mechanisms during the system's initial configuration and setup.

Multisite Business or Enterprise

The multisite business or enterprise model could be a good choice for any size enterprise network. In general, Cisco IPC Express is a better fit at the low end—a network with a small number of sites and fewer than 200 employees per site. The larger the network (that is, the more sites and employees there are), the more likely it is that a centralized Cisco CallManager is the more appropriate solution.

As discussed in the earlier section "Cisco IPC Express Networks," many of these multisite networks find a centralized Cisco CallManager (for call processing) and Cisco Unity (for server-based unified messaging) the best solution for their needs. But Cisco IPC Express may still be a good choice for sites of a smaller enterprise, or certain (or all) sites of a larger enterprise, for the reason enumerated earlier.

This section considers two types of networks in the multisite enterprise model:

- **Small enterprise**—Typically a smaller number of sites (for example, fewer than ten) in the enterprise, all using interconnected Cisco IPC Express systems.

- **Hybrid enterprise**—Typically a larger number of sites overall, with only a small number of these using Cisco IPC Express. The other sites either are still using the key systems or private branch exchanges (PBXs) they have long used or are using a centralized Cisco CallManager solution.

The larger the enterprise, the more IT structure and organization it is likely to have. Therefore, these businesses tend to own their systems and equipment. They also either manage their own networks or outsource them to SPs that specialize in services for large enterprises.

IP telephony for enterprises with a large number of sites may be valuable for many reasons. These include the wiring savings outlined earlier for the standalone office, saving international calling charges, productivity-enhancing applications, and converging the network infrastructure, resulting in less equipment to manage. Another opportunity for savings is to provide a repeatable template of network equipment and topology for a large number of remote locations, all with an identical configuration. (An example is the stores of a large retailer where the bakery is always extension 5000 and the pharmacy is always 4000.)

The average branch office location for an enterprise network already has a well-used router on the premises. Adding Cisco IPC Express requires only an upgrade in software (and memory), perhaps the addition of hardware components, such as voice interface cards for the PSTN trunks, and the deployment of IP phones.

There is always an exception to every generalization, and this is also true with network deployment models. Although larger enterprise networks generally tend toward the hybrid model or the pure centralized Cisco CallManager model, several very large enterprise networks with thousands of locations deploy Cisco IPC Express at every site and interconnect the sites across their networks. This is often found in the retail industry, because this model fits its general business model.

The Small Enterprise

Typical business types that fall into the small enterprise category include

- A local credit union or small bank with a few branches in a bounded geographic area
- A local retail store with a small number of locations in a city or state
- A chain of a few health clinics belonging to a local hospital or health maintenance organization (HMO)

The next several sections look more closely at the different aspects of the small enterprise network, including the network architecture, applications, management, and security services deployed.

Network Architecture

Cisco IPC Express is an excellent choice for a small business with a limited number of sites, perhaps ten or fewer, or even up to 30 or so. The exact point where a centralized Cisco CallManager starts to make more sense depends on

- The individual business
- Its management style
- The QoS readiness of the network between the sites
- The cost basis of the intersite connectivity
- How loosely or tightly coupled the sites are to one another in the normal course of a day's business

For a business with a loosely coupled business model, individual Cisco IPC Express sites interconnected with only a minimal data network (bandwidth of less than 64 kbps and no QoS deployment) and the PSTN for voice access would suffice. An example of such a business could be a restaurant chain. This kind of network looks essentially the same as the standalone model explored in the preceding section. Because the sites have only PSTN calling between them, no VoIP binds the sites together, and the network topology of each location would look like a standalone entity (from a voice traffic perspective).

The more interesting case to consider as the multisite enterprise is when the business model dictates that VoIP connectivity between the sites for toll savings or other management reasons is advantageous.

Figure 2-5 shows a sample network topology of what such an enterprise's branch office network might look like. This representation takes a general view of the branch office.

Figure 2-5   *Multisite Distributed Cisco IPC Express Network Architecture*

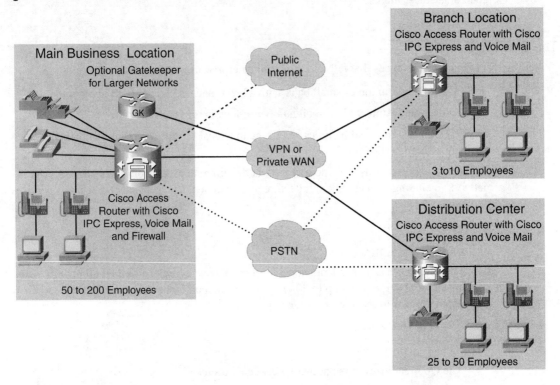

There is significant similarity between the detailed layout of the small enterprise branch office and that of the standalone single-site office discussed earlier. The new or additional considerations are as follows:

- **Employee desktop**—Depending on the business the company conducts, the percentage of employee desktops varies. A retail organization has comparatively few desk-bound employees, whereas a bank or insurance company has a higher percentage. In each case, though, there is an employee who works on the floor or at a teller location, and these stations are often not equipped with individual phones or computers. Instead, shared resources are deployed for use by these employees. Personal calls are likely made from a public payphone in the break room or from a small number of phones set aside in a shared employee space that employees can access during their breaks.

Desk-bound employees tend to have voice mail, whereas the employees on the retail floor are much less likely to find voice mail productive for their work environment and responsibilities. Sometimes voice mail is still deployed for these employees (again, accessed from a common phone or break room) for human resources or training purposes.

- **WAN connectivity** — The network between the sites is likely to be a private WAN of some type. It could also be a virtual private network (VPN) using the public Internet as the transport, but as such it is not QoS-enabled and, therefore, is not a good fit for deploying VoIP traffic.

  A VoIP-capable WAN is most likely either privately owned or provided as a single service to all the sites of the enterprise by a SP. A VPN may still be used on top of the basic network service. Each site's connectivity depends on the site's geographic location and its bandwidth needs. It could be DSL, BRI, fractional T1/E1 access, or even metro-Ethernet. Larger offices may require a full T1/E1 or may bind together multiple DSL or BRI physical access lines to provide larger bandwidth.

  The U.S. offering of integrated access, encompassing both voice and data channels sharing the same physical T1, is a very attractive offering for this type of office. The voice (PSTN) connection could be either T1 in-band signaling (T1 Channel Associated Signaling [T1 CAS]) or fractional PRI. The data connection is most likely Frame Relay.

- **PSTN connectivity** — PSTN connectivity also depends on the office's size and location. It could be low-density analog (FXO or analog DID) or BRI connections or higher-density fractional T1/E1, perhaps with (fractional) Primary Rate Interface (PRI) service.

  The business model and size of the office dictate whether the office might prefer *key system* operation (Line1, Line2, and so on appear on the buttons of each phone) or *PBX-like* operation with typically a single extension per phone and DID service from the CO. Smaller offices more often tend to use key system (shared-line) operation, because that is the traditional voice system they were likely to have had installed before migrating to IP telephony. In larger offices, it becomes impractical to have a button appearance for each incoming CO trunk. These sites tend to be better candidates for DID service. A human or AA provides receptionist services for general incoming business calls and directs clients to the correct department or employee extension.

- **Other voice services** — When a small number of sites (such as five or fewer) are interconnected, the on-net dial plan is often simple enough to be implemented directly at each site. However, this meshing of sites becomes increasingly complex to manage as the number of sites increases. For this purpose, a gatekeeper (GK) is shown at the main site in Figure 2-5. For enterprises of approximately ten or more locations, centralizing the dial plan management is well worth considering. An H.323 GK is the way to accomplish this when multiple Cisco IPC Express sites are interconnected. This way, the dial plan is administered in a single location and is not duplicated at each site, making changes to the dial plan easy to accomplish.

Applications

Voice mail and AA applications were great productivity boosters when they were introduced a decade or two ago. By now they are pervasive and essential services to most enterprises. Although a receptionist may still provide close customer interaction for general business calls and walk-in clients in the lobby, a supplementing AA or interactive voice response (IVR) system becomes increasingly indispensable as the business grows. The AA fields recurring customer queries for information such as account balances, driving directions, office hours, ordering of forms, health exam results, and other services.

Industry segment-specific XML-based applications can be tailored to each business to provide very specific productivity or customer service-enhancing applications.

Management

Figure 2-5 does not specify the equipment used to manage the network. Most likely, as with the GK shown at the main location, one site is larger or more central to the operation of the enterprise than others. All the sites are managed from this location. This may be as simple as having a single server from where the GUI of the Cisco IPC Express systems at the other individual sites is accessed, to having more sophisticated network monitoring and management tools.

Security

Security considerations for any enterprise network are imperative. Because the individual sites are most likely not directly connected to the Internet, but instead are connected to some SP offering or VPN for the enterprise, a certain amount of security is gained from the SP's equipment, firewalls, and intrusion detection systems. However, the enterprise should still employ its own mechanisms, especially if any of the sites is directly connected to the Internet or has Internet access in addition to the private WAN connection between the sites.

Figure 2-5 shows only the main location with Internet access, providing this public network entry point to all users from sites in the enterprise. This Internet connection should be fully protected by the appropriate security measures.

The Hybrid Enterprise

Hybrid enterprises include larger national and multinational banks, insurance companies, financial brokerages, and retail chains with considerable geographic coverage. Distributed call processing in a segment of the network makes sense for these enterprises primarily because of WAN connectivity attributes, franchising of stores or locations, or multiyear IP telephony roll-out schedules. These can be dauntingly large and complex in networks with up to several thousand sites or, occasionally, tens of thousands of remote sites.

In the hybrid enterprise, some of the sites, usually a smaller number, are a good fit for Cisco IPC Express for the reasons enumerated earlier. The rest of the enterprise (usually the larger number of sites) still uses either traditional time-division multiplexing (TDM) voice equipment or higher-end IP telephony solutions, such as Cisco CallManager and Cisco Unity.

The next several sections look more closely at the different aspects of the small enterprise network, including the network architecture, applications, management, and security services deployed.

Network Architecture

As shown in Figure 2-6, large enterprises have many WAN backbones designed to aggregate the traffic from an extensive number of remote sites and to provide interconnectivity between all the sites. Directly meshing a large number of sites is impractical. These networks invariably have a hierarchical, layered design. Remote sites may be connected via a plethora of different technologies, including DSL, BRI, and serial access. The aggregation network also often contains a number of technologies, such as Frame Relay, asynchronous transfer mode (ATM), and/or multiprotocol label switching (MPLS). The core network consists of high-bandwidth connections and LAN or ATM switches. A third set of technologies (such as Gigabit Ethernet, fiber transmission, and optical rings) is not directly relevant to the discussion of Cisco IPC Express.

Figure 2-6   *Multisite Enterprise WAN Backbone Network Architecture*

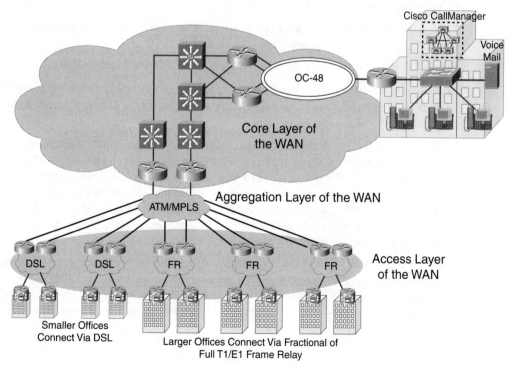

The following are three situations in which Cisco IPC Express is a good solution for a subset of the sites of a medium or large hybrid enterprise:

- The enterprise has a QoS-enabled WAN that can carry VoIP traffic, but it is not ready to deploy IP telephony everywhere. Therefore, it is starting with a pilot at a small number of sites. This is the model further discussed later in this section and shown in Figure 2-6.

- The enterprise has a QoS-enabled WAN but with sufficient bandwidth for only a small amount of VoIP traffic. The company's business model may be such that most employees speak to customers and vendors in the PSTN, and the branch manager is the only person with a frequent need to call headquarters (using intersite VoIP). This network follows the same structure as that shown in Figure 2-6, but it is likely somewhat simpler, and the branch WAN access speeds tend to be lower.

- The enterprise does not have a QoS-enabled WAN and does not want to invest in enabling it at the current time. However, it does want to start migrating toward IP telephony. In this situation, voice traffic between the sites continues to use the PSTN. The network architecture of these sites is very similar to that discussed in the "Standalone Office" section and shown earlier in Figure 2-4.

The following types of enterprises tend to find a hybrid model attractive:

- Larger banks and financial service institutions
- Large insurance companies
- National or multinational operations with a large number of individual locations and a strong central presence in one of their locations

Figure 2-7 shows what such an enterprise's branch office network might look like.

There is significant similarity between the detailed layout of this branch office and that of the smaller multisite enterprise with Cisco IPC Express at all locations. The new or additional considerations are as follows:

- **WAN connectivity**—A muscular WAN backbone exists because of the interconnection of a large number of sites. The complexity of the large WAN likely makes it cost-effective to be managed by a SP or outsourced to a management company that makes this its core business. If the business owns and manages its own WAN network (and gets only transport services from a SP), a sophisticated and dedicated IT organization resides within the enterprise. However, as with the earlier models in this discussion, IT expertise is only nominally present or completely absent in the branch office.

- **PSTN connectivity**—Only the very smallest sites in this network may prefer key system (shared-line) operation. Employees of a large enterprise are much more likely to be accustomed to PBX-like operations and to have DID services from the CO. With a VoIP-enabled WAN backbone, it is also likely that long-distance calling is consolidated into large-scale PSTN voice gateways at the central locations where the volume of traffic can provide cost-effective traffic hands-off contracts with the long-distance carrier service provider. Local PSTN calling still uses the Cisco IPC Express trunks at each local site.

Figure 2-7   *Multisite Enterprise Branch Office Network Architecture*

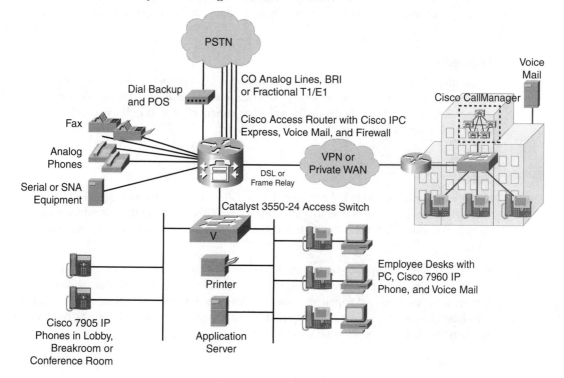

Applications

Voice mail is likely a necessity for the majority of the employees in a large enterprise. The decision to centralize or distribute voice mail services is very similar to the decision governing the provision of call processing services, but with additional considerations and caveats for specific products and feature requirements. For the hybrid enterprise, providing call processing and voice mail services under the same model often makes sense. In other words, Cisco IPC Express sites use local (distributed) voice mail, and the larger locations with central call processing also provide centralized voice mail services. However, the following converse deployment models are also valid:

- Centralized call control (Cisco CallManager) with distributed voice mail (Cisco Unity Express)

- Distributed call control (Cisco CallManager Express) with centralized voice mail (Cisco Unity)

With the larger-scale enterprise, customer contact also often takes on a more centralized character than the individual receptionist in each remote office. Customer service is likely to be provided with centralized AA and IVR systems co-located with the enterprise's data center(s) where the database information retrieved by the IVR system resides. Customers of the enterprise have toll-free access numbers to all customer service inquiries. The local branch office is relatively seldom contacted directly for routine customer service needs.

Management

As mentioned, the large enterprise has a sophisticated IT organization that manages the equipment and applications in the workplace. This is supplemented to varying degrees by outsourcing or a SP that provides additional management of aspects of the network's infrastructure and transport.

Security

Security measures are likely to be managed along with general network issues. Branch offices do not have local Internet connectivity. Sophisticated VPN servers in the central locations provide enterprise VPN connectivity to locations on the Internet, such as from employees' homes.

This type of large enterprise also has one or more data centers where the information and servers essential to the company's business are maintained and protected with sophisticated security services. Dedicated appliances such as firewalls, intrusion detection, virus detection, and client NAC services are most likely centralized services. E-mail, web servers, order entry applications, and other application servers reside in the data centers.

Service Provider Managed Multisite Network

The preceding sections made numerous references to aspects of standalone businesses or enterprise networks that are outsourced or provided by SPs. These SPs come in a wide variety of flavors. They may offer basic Internet access, web hosting, e-mail, telephony, long-distance voice services, or centrex for local services, or any combinations of these.

This section considers the SP's network used to offer these types of services. The major advantage that the SP brings to the small business is its robust network infrastructure and IT expertise. The small standalone business does not have the resources or the desire to manage the increasingly sophisticated technology necessary to operate in a competitive manner. The following two SP models alluded to throughout this chapter work for these companies:

- **Value-Added Reseller (VAR) or Systems Integrator (SI)** — The reseller provides equipment and system recommendations as well as technical expertise. The end customer buys and owns the equipment (that is, a capital expenditure model for the end-user business), and the VAR/SI installs and maintains the system. The end customer can make small changes in operation or configuration using the web-based GUI interfaces accessible to the nontechnical user, but the VAR/SI handles any major changes or upgrades.

- **Managed services**—In this model, the SP owns and manages the equipment (even if some of it is physically present at the customer premises). It also offers voice and data hosted services to the customer for a recurring monthly or annual contract charge (that is, an operational expense model for the end-user business). The SP may offer only on-net traffic services between sites belonging to the same customer. It may also offer long-distance VoIP minutes for IP-based PSTN calling between this customer and other customers or PSTN locations.

The VAR/SI model of service provision results in a network topology that is exactly the same as the standalone business and enterprise network models discussed earlier. The only difference is in who makes changes to the equipment's configuration.

The managed services model, on the other hand, results in a slightly different network architecture. The SP owns and manages a network of sites that share the same infrastructure but have to be separated into different customers' networks with appropriate security measures between them. Figure 2-8 shows the high-level architecture of this kind of network.

Figure 2-8 *SP Managed Services Network Architecture*

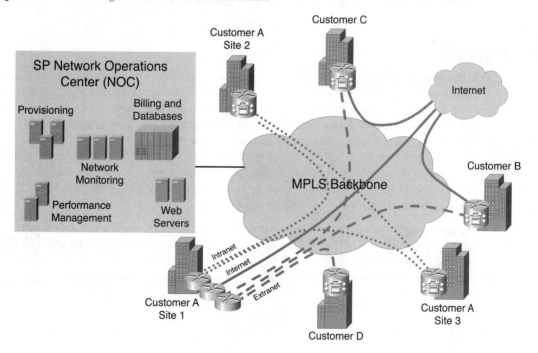

The detailed network layout within the individual branches or sites is the same as the other models discussed earlier. Differences with a managed services network lie in the following areas:

- **Management of the customer's equipment**—Although CPE equipment is present at the customer site, everything is managed centrally. The end-user business usually has no access to any management interface of the equipment.

- **Network management**—The SP has a sophisticated network operations center (NOC) where the backbone network is continuously monitored and adjusted if problems occur. Service-level agreements (SLAs), which are contractual agreements about traffic and service, are also monitored and measured on an ongoing basis.

- **Hosted services**—The SP may provide integrated applications services, such as e-mail or web services, to the end-user business. It may also provide voice services such as calling between sites and off-net PSTN hop-off (or points of presence [POPs]) services at the PSTN location nearest to the call's destination.

Cisco IPC Express is a good model for SP-managed services, because it provides an individual call processing component for each site or small business (part of the CPE). Therefore, it automatically provides separation between different customers or tenants on the network. Cisco CallManager and Cisco Unity, being centralized architectures primarily designed for a large number of users belonging to the same enterprise, may not offer the multitenant features required by many SPs to provide the demarcation between customers and provide dial plan and security barriers between one customer's traffic and the next.

Summary

In this chapter, you learned how and where to deploy Cisco IPC Express technology to its best effect for your business. You gained insight into how Cisco IPC Express fits into different types of networks and the business trade-offs for choosing Cisco IPC Express or other Cisco IP telephony options. This chapter highlighted the PSTN connectivity, WAN connectivity, applications, management, and security considerations for different types and sizes of networks. It also explored how technology and network architecture underscore your business management philosophy and decisions about network connectivity and bandwidth provisioning. Furthermore, you saw how your network might have to evolve to support IP telephony solutions such as Cisco IPC Express.

The next chapter goes into considerable detail about the features, operation, and multisite interconnection options of Cisco IPC Express, including Cisco CallManager Express (CME) and Cisco Unity Express (UE).

This chapter covers the following topics:

- Cisco IP Communications (IPC) Express system architecture
- Cisco CallManager Express (CME) architecture
- Cisco Unity Express (UE) applications architecture

## CHAPTER 3

Cisco IPC Express Architecture Overview

An IP Communications (IPC) Express system is a complete, integrated communications system for a small- or medium-sized standalone or networked office site. Fundamental to its architecture is the Cisco IOS router on which all the data and voice services offered by the system are based.

This chapter first explores the internal architecture of the Cisco IOS router on which Cisco CallManager Express (CME) is based. Then it takes a closer look at the internal architecture of the Cisco Unity Express (UE) application and its interaction with Cisco CME and the router. The packaged combination of Cisco CME and Cisco UE is called Cisco IP Communications (IPC) Express.

If you are already familiar with IP-based networks, you might approach your Cisco IPC Express system primarily as a Cisco IOS router with telephony capability. On the other hand, if you are looking at the Cisco IPC Express system as an integrated, single-box office communications system, the router technology included in the platform might be a secondary consideration for you. As covered in Chapters 1 and 2, Cisco IPC Express is supported on a range of low-end and mid-range router platforms. You can choose from among these to provide the appropriate level of connectivity and processing power for the services your office requires.

Cisco IPC Express is composed of two main components:

- The call processing engine, called Cisco CME (including communications endpoints, such as the IP phones)

- Optional applications such as automated attendant (AA), voice mail (offered by Cisco UE), and IP phone-based XML and Telephony Application Programming Interface (TAPI) applications provided by external application servers

This chapter takes an architectural overview of these components and how they interact.

Cisco IPC Express System Architecture

Figure 3-1 shows the overall software architecture of a Cisco IPC Express system. Cisco CME and its internal components are on the left, and Cisco UE and its components are on the right. The Cisco CME software (the call processing software) runs as part of Cisco IOS on the host router platform. Cisco UE runs in a Linux-based embedded environment on a hardware module that slots into the host router.

Figure 3-1 *Cisco IPC Express System Architecture*

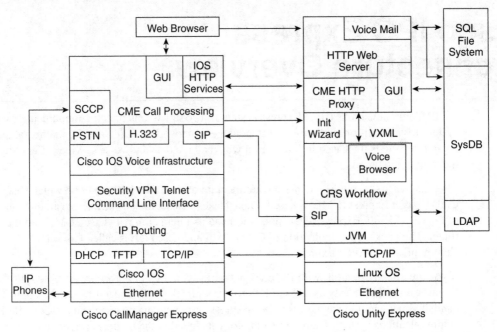

On a physical level, Cisco CME and Cisco UE communicate via an IP (Ethernet) interface across the backplane of the router chassis. As shown in Figure 3-1, there are several logical connections between the two components:

- A graphical user interface (GUI) browser interface that communicates with the router's HTTP server as well as HTTP server software on the Cisco UE module

- System management communication such as configuration lookup during the Cisco UE Initialization Wizard, and configuration synchronization with the router during the life of the system

- Call control communication using a Session Initiation Protocol (SIP) interface

- Underlying communications connectivity via TCP and Ethernet

Cisco CME Architecture

Historically, the evolution of voice support on Cisco routers first included Public Switched Telephone Network (PSTN) and Private Branch Exchange (PBX) connectivity into voice-over-packet networks, the traditional *toll bypass* voice over IP (VoIP) network architectures. This connectivity to legacy systems (the PSTN and PBXs) is often called *PSTN gateway* or *voice gateway* functionality. Support for IP phones followed next in the evolution with the development of Survivable Remote Site Telephony (SRST). When all these technologies were in place, a comprehensive standalone telephony solution such as Cisco CME was a natural next step. All the Cisco CME phone features are built on top of these two foundation elements: the router engine and the VoIP infrastructure first developed to provide PSTN and PBX gateway connectivity on a router. This is an important perspective to embrace in understanding Cisco CME and its architecture.

This inheritance has some advantages and also some disadvantages. The primary advantages include the fact that Cisco CME leverages the extensive base of Cisco IOS IP routing and voice technologies. This lets Cisco CME interoperate with a large installed base of IP network types and different voice protocols and technologies. It also means that new developments in the Cisco IOS IP and voice technology area tend to get bundled automatically with each new release of the Cisco CME software. This significantly reduces the risk of rapid marketplace obsolescence inherent in any new technology. Considering the ongoing competition in the VoIP marketplace between the International Telecommunication Union (ITU)-sponsored H.323 and Internet Engineering Task Force (IETF)-sponsored SIP technologies, this has particular importance for anyone concerned about picking the "wrong" technology. Because Cisco CME is based on Cisco IOS voice technology, it includes both H.323 and SIP support. It will continue to evolve as these technologies unfold in the industry.

The disadvantage of this integrated approach is that the Cisco CME platform was not originally designed to be a phone system. It was designed as a router with the ability to handle voice traffic. This means considerations and compromises are reflected in how Cisco CME is designed, configured, and managed and in how it operates. How you view these trade-offs may depend in part on whether you are looking for a phone system as a standalone technology purchasing decision or as part of a larger communications infrastructure and longer-term investment.

If you are approaching Cisco CME from the point of view of an integrated and converged voice and data communications infrastructure, you are more likely to see the extra complexity and capabilities that come with the Cisco IOS foundation as a good thing and as necessary to meet your business networking needs. The complexity that's inherent in Cisco IOS isn't arbitrary. It has evolved over many years of dealing with the real-world network intricacies that exist when you try to interconnect multiple pieces of equipment, and evolve your network in several phases over an extended period of time.

Cisco CME Software Architecture

The Cisco CME phone features in Cisco IOS are built on top of the Cisco IOS voice infrastructure foundation. This gives Cisco CME access to both H.323 and SIP interfaces. It also lets Cisco CME be protocol-agnostic regarding H.323 versus SIP for VoIP calls across intersite links. The protocol used to control local IP phones is the lightweight Cisco Skinny

Client Control Protocol (SCCP), often simply called "Skinny." This protocol gives Cisco CME tight control over the IP phones and lets it offer a rich set of phone features from a call control, phone user interface, and provisioning point of view.

SCCP is a Cisco-specific interface that is used only internally between the Cisco CME router and the IP phones it controls. The external interface that Cisco CME exposes to phone connections across its public IP link to other sites uses the standards-based H.323 or SIP protocols. Figure 3-2 shows the VoIP protocols used by a Cisco CME system.

Figure 3-2   *Protocols Used by a Cisco CME System*

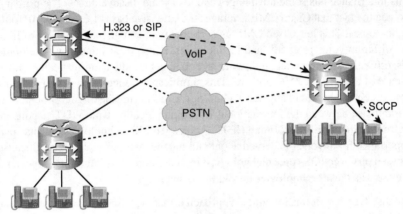

The internal use of SCCP to its attached IP phones also allows Cisco CME to bypass some of the significant challenges that often arise when Network Address Translation (NAT) is deployed with voice protocols such as H.323 and SIP. NAT is often required in VoIP networks to avoid the need for a large number of public IP addresses—one for each IP phone. Cisco CME requires only a single public IP address to handle external H.323 or SIP calls, regardless of the number of IP phones deployed in the office.

The Cisco CME SCCP-based IP phones can be deployed using private IP addresses and still have access to external H.323 and SIP networks (without requiring the use of NAT). This approach provides Cisco CME with standard interfaces for connecting it to external devices. This approach also takes advantage of a Cisco-owned and -controlled protocol with which to build enhanced internal phone features.

Building advanced phone features using agreed-upon, fully ratified, interoperable standard protocols is very difficult. In many cases, no agreed-upon standards exist for implementing some phone features, especially in a fully peer-to-peer protocol environment. Getting even basic features such as call transfer, call hold, and call forwarding to work in a truly standards-based, vendor-independent manner is still a tough business and engineering challenge. Nevertheless, as the standards evolve to specify how these advanced features might be achieved, Cisco CME will also evolve to support them. Right now, however, a SCCP-based phone is the or˹v way to accomplish advanced IP phone features.

Just as Cisco CME is built on top of the Cisco IOS voice infrastructure, the Cisco IOS voice infrastructure functions are, in turn, built on top of the underlying Cisco IOS IP infrastructure. This gives Cisco CME access to quality of service (QoS) facilities such as voice packet marking, classification, prioritization, and Resource Reservation Protocol (RSVP). The IOS IP infrastructure also includes many other useful elements, such as Dynamic Host Configuration Protocol (DHCP), Trivial File Transfer Protocol. (TFTP), virtual LAN (VLAN), HTTP, access control lists (ACLs), and an extensive choice of WAN interface types and protocols. These include Ethernet, Frame Relay, Asynchronous Transfer Mode (ATM), DSL, fiber, ISDN, high-speed serial, and several more. These concepts and terms are briefly defined in the glossary near the end of this book. The following lists the layered components, top to bottom, that underlie Cisco CME:

- **CME IP phone services**—SCCP, GUI interface
- **IOS voice services**—Telephony interfaces, H.323, SIP, RSVP, RTP Control Protocol (RTCP)
- **Cisco IOS protocols**—IP routing, TFTP, DHCP, HTTP, virtual private network (VPN), security, Telnet
- **Cisco IOS network interfaces**—Ethernet, Frame Relay, ATM, DSL, VLAN, wireless LAN

The following sections introduce the Cisco IOS voice infrastructure functions that Cisco CME relies on to provide PSTN trunking and VoIP services.

Cisco IOS Voice Infrastructure

To understand Cisco CME fully, you should have at least a basic understanding of the Cisco IOS voice infrastructure functionality used for the Cisco IOS PSTN and PBX gateways. This section gives a brief overview of the Cisco IOS voice infrastructure. For additional resources that cover this topic in greater depth, see the "Recommended Reading" section at the end of this chapter.

The Cisco IOS voice infrastructure software has three primary components:

- Telephony interfaces (Foreign Exchange Office [FXO], ear and mouth [E&M], Foreign Exchange Station [FXS], T1, E1, Primary Rate Interface [PRI], and Basic Rate Interface [BRI])
- Application layer software (session application plus the Toolkit Command Language [TCL] and Voice Extensible Markup Language [VXML] scripting languages)
- Voice-over-packet interfaces (H.323, SIP, voice over Frame Relay [VoFR], voice over ATM [VoATM])

These components communicate with each other primarily through an internal IOS call control application interface called Call Control Application (CCAPI). CCAPI itself has two main interfaces:

- The first connects to the telephony and packet interfaces. These are collectively known as service provider interfaces (SPIs).
- The second connects to the application layers.

CCAPI acts primarily as a middle software layer. It attempts to provide a protocol-independent abstraction between the upper application software layer and the lower-layer SPIs. The intent of this design is two-fold. It allows the application layer to operate on the lower-level SPIs and to largely be able to manipulate call legs (bridged segments of an end-to-end call) without regard for their fundamental type (telephony, VoIP, and so on). For example, the topmost application layer can set up a telephone call to a particular phone number mostly without needing to know if the phone number corresponds to a PSTN or VoIP endpoint. The resolution of a telephone number as being either a PSTN or VoIP destination is usually determined by database-like command-line interface (CLI) configuration entries called dial peers. Figure 3-3 shows the layered design of the Cisco IOS voice infrastructure software.

Figure 3-3 *Basic IOS Voice Gateway Software Structure*

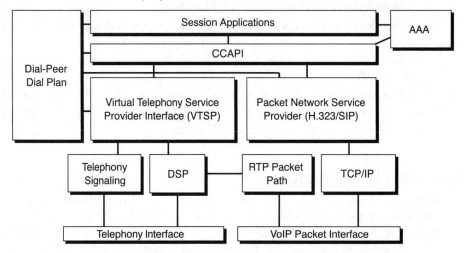

A voice call that passes through a Cisco IOS PSTN gateway is typically composed of two call legs or call segments. One call leg normally exists between the physical telephony (PSTN) interface and the application layer. The second call leg exists between the application layer and the VoIP packet interface. The application layer joins (or bridges) the two call legs to create a composite call. This example describes a call consisting of one telephony leg and one VoIP leg, which is typical for a router used as a PSTN-to-VoIP voice gateway. However, calls can also be constructed that have two telephony call legs (for example, for analog phone-to-PSTN calls or fax-to-PSTN calls). Also, calls can be constructed that have two VoIP call legs. (You'll read more about this in Chapter 7, "Connecting Multiple Cisco CMEs with VoIP.")

The following sections discuss the telephony and VoIP call leg components in greater detail.

Cisco IOS Voice Telephony Interfaces

Cisco IOS voice-enabled routers provide a wide range of modular telephony interface options offering significant choices of analog and digital PSTN connectivity. More information on the hardware and signaling variations supported appears in Chapter 6, "Cisco CME PSTN

Connectivity Options." Here the discussion centers on the Cisco software infrastructure that handles the Cisco IOS voice router telephony interfaces.

The Cisco IOS voice software architecture to a large extent mirrors the physical construction of the telephony interfaces. As shown in Figure 3-3, below the CCAPI layer on the telephony side is a telephony abstraction layer called Virtual Telephony Service Provider (VTSP). This layer provides a software abstraction layer that hides the telephony protocol specifics of the physical telephony interface. Below the VTSP layer are alternative software adapters that provide telephony-specific protocol support for the various types of telephony interfaces (such as FXO, FXS, and E&M). You will read more about this software layer shortly, when IP phone connectivity is discussed. This architecture is shown in Figure 3-4.

Figure 3-4   *Telephony Interface Internals*

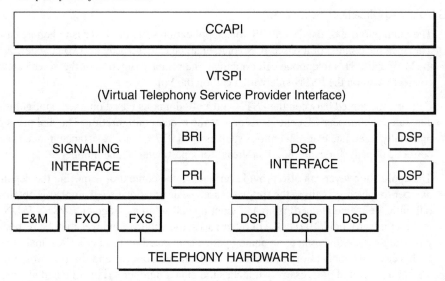

IOS Voice-Over-Packet Interfaces

The Cisco IOS voice infrastructure software includes support for a range of voice-over-packet interfaces, including the VoIP H.323 and SIP interfaces used by Cisco CME. Also included are protocols such as Media Gateway Control Protocol (MGCP) and VoATM using AAL2 (VoAAL2) encapsulation. Cisco CME does not support MGCP or VoAAL2. In addition, the Cisco IOS voice infrastructure software supports the older Layer 2 voice protocols, such as VoFR and VoATM using AAL5 encapsulation. Cisco CME provides some limited interworking with the VoFR and VoATM protocols. This interworking is primarily supported to provide a migration path for networks upgrading from VoFR/VoATM technologies to H.323/SIP VoIP. The primary interfaces of concern in the Cisco CME context—and those addressed in the rest of this book—are the H.323 and SIP VoIP interfaces.

An important point to highlight in this discussion of interfaces is that the various SPI interfaces are largely modular and independent of each other. The SIP and H.323 interfaces operate without significant awareness of the type of analog/digital telephony interface involved. This is an important point to be aware of for the discussion of the Cisco CME extensions to the Cisco IOS voice infrastructure.

In addition to the basic H.323 and SIP protocol support for making VoIP calls, the Cisco IOS VoIP SPIs provide access to voice QoS controls such as RSVP, IP precedence, or DiffServ Code Point (DSCP) marking of voice packets and low-latency queuing (LLQ) of voice media packets. Also included is support for H.323 gatekeeper (GK) (and SIP Registrar) registration of endpoint telephone numbers (for call routing purposes).

Cisco IOS Voice Application Software

The main purpose of the Cisco IOS voice application software layer is to handle call routing. This is in the context of a Cisco IOS voice-enabled router acting as a voice gateway between the VoIP and PSTN telephone call domains. The primary function of the voice gateway is to connect a call on the PSTN side with a call on the VoIP side.

Calls can be routed between the PSTN and VoIP domains based on fixed configurations contained in dial peer CLI entries as part of the router configuration. The dial peers can optionally reference external entities such as an H.323 GK for assistance in determining the correct call path (for example, IP address) for a particular phone number.

The application layer can also provide services in the context of acquiring the destination number for placing a call. In the simplest case, the destination called number is obtained *en bloc* (all digits delivered at once) from an incoming call setup message on a PSTN ISDN interface (a direct inward dial [DID] call). In other cases, the application layer may be responsible for providing simple dial tone to an analog phone connected to a router's FXS analog voice port. In this case, the application layer code collects dialed digits in one-digit-at-a-time mode from the phone user and progressively matches the dialed number string collected against the dial peer information until an unambiguous match is found. The application then routes the call based on the information in the matched dial peer (SIP, H.323, or plain old telephone service [POTS], for example).

The IOS voice application layer can provide an interactive voice response (IVR) interface to a caller. It also can operate a dialog in which the IVR plays voice prompts and collects the caller's response in the form of dual-tone multifrequency (DTMF) digits. An example of an IVR dialog would be to answer incoming calls by playing a voice prompt that presents the caller with a short list of menu choices, 1 to 9. For example, a prompt such as "Press 1 for sales; press 2 for support" can be used. The caller then presses a digit in the appropriate range, and the application layer routes the call to a preconfigured destination.

Phone dialogs for IVR can be constructed using either Tool Command Language (TCL) scripts or Voice Extensible Markup Language (VXML). TCL scripts are typically loaded into the router's internal Flash memory or can be fetched from a remote server using TFTP. VXML dialogs are typically accessed from a remote web server using HTTP. IVR dialogs can be used for both incoming PSTN calls and calls that arrive at the router over VoIP.

Cisco CME Extensions to the Cisco IOS Voice Infrastructure

Even though the Cisco CME IP phones use VoIP technology, an IP phone is first and foremost still a *telephone*. As a result, the IP phones fit within the set of Cisco IOS voice telephony interfaces, as shown in Figure 3-5.

Figure 3-5   *SCCP IP Phone Extension to Cisco IOS Voice*

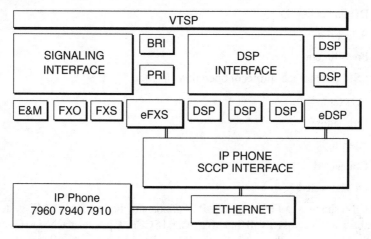

From the perspective of the higher application software layers, the basic operations performed on an IP phone are the same as that for an analog phone connected to an FXS port on a router. Both types of phones signal an off-hook event when the handset is lifted for an outgoing call, and both types of phones expect to get dial tone in response. The logic that drives analog and IP phones is very similar. This is also the reason for some of the terminology that Cisco CME uses to describe its IP phones. In Cisco CME, the SCCP-based IP phones are called *ephones* (for Ethernet phones). This conceptually helps differentiate the SCCP-based IP phones from SIP- and H.323-based VoIP phones.

This may not be the architectural approach you might have expected. After all, an SCCP phone is indeed an IP phone, and it uses VoIP technology, so you might more reasonably expect it to be handled as part of the VoIP interface software infrastructure. One of the main reasons for this is that the Cisco CME IP phones use SCCP for control. SCCP is a master/slave-type protocol (and is similar in many ways to MGCP). The H.323 and SIP protocols are peer-to-peer protocols and behave in significantly different ways. From a purely logical point of view, there isn't much difference between using SCCP to control an IP phone and using a proprietary time-division multiplexing (TDM)-based (D channel) protocol to control a digital phone handset on a legacy digital PBX. The main difference between these two is in the physical transport layer used to convey the messages between the phone and the software that controls it. Consider the following basic operations that are communicated via SCCP to an IP phone, and compare them to the operations that are used in the peer-to-peer H.323/SIP context.

Analog phone and SCCP operation examples include

- On-hook and off-hook
- Dial tone on and off
- Digit press
- Ringer on and off
- Display caller ID
- Select line
- Press function key

H.323/SIP peer-to-peer protocol operations include

- Call setup
- Proceeding
- Alerting
- Connected
- Disconnected

Figure 3-6 shows a call from an SCCP IP phone attached to Cisco CME system 1 using H.323 to establish a call across a VoIP link to a second SCCP IP phone attached to Cisco CME system 2. This figure illustrates the relative roles of SCCP, which is used for local phone control, and H.323 (or SIP), which is used to make calls between independent peer systems. This figure provides only a simplified view of the message exchange for clarity. It does not include the SCCP messages for softkey selection, call state notification, and other functions.

It's worth noting that IP phones that natively support H.323 and SIP do indeed communicate with the Cisco IOS voice software through the H.323 and SIP voice-over-packet interfaces. In this case, operations such as *dial tone* and *digit press* are handled entirely and autonomously within the H.323/SIP phone itself. In this scenario, the IP phones act as fully independent VoIP network peers. They don't need assistance from the router for basic tasks such as collecting dialed digits before an outbound call is placed. This also means that the router can't easily control the phone actions and user interface over protocols such as H.323 and SIP because of the degree of autonomy that peer-to-peer protocols provide to the phone.

NOTE   A peer-to-peer protocol provides a means to establish communication between two equivalent devices. A master/slave protocol provides the means for one device (with more intelligence or network awareness) to control another (with less intelligence).

Figure 3-6 *SCCP IP Phone Call Between Two Cisco CME Systems Using H.323*

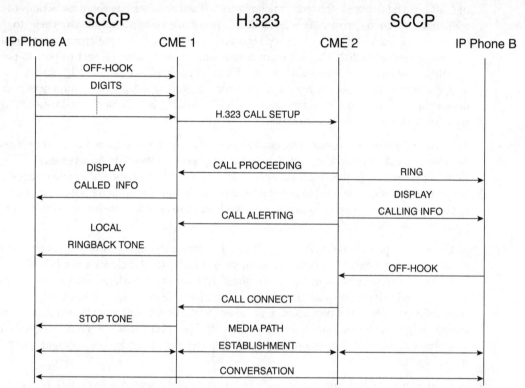

Using SCCP to *control* the Cisco CME IP phones provides some significant advantages, as explained in the following section.

Introducing SCCP

SCCP was developed by a company called Selsius, which Cisco acquired in 1998. This acquisition brought the Cisco CallManager IP PBX product to the Cisco product portfolio. Cisco CallManager primarily addresses the enterprise market for VoIP-based phone systems. SCCP was developed as a lower-cost alternative to H.323 given the larger CPU and memory demands of H.323 (because H.323 is designed as a peer-to-peer protocol and requires significant intelligence on both communicating devices). As such, H.323 doesn't directly support the operations needed to provide PBX phone features. Selsius developed SCCP to support the creation of low-cost VoIP phones using Ethernet interfaces to connect the phones to a system controller (a PC running Microsoft Windows). SCCP has remained mostly unchanged since the Selsius days, even though the IP phones themselves have gone through considerable changes from the original Selsius models. SCCP mostly predates the SIP and MGCP standards.

SCCP is designed to provide endpoint control of VoIP telephones. The key word here is *control*. In most private telephone networks, maintaining full and absolute control of the actions of telephones within the network is a key concern. Telephone system administrators need to control which features a particular phone can access, as well as which telephone numbers the phone is permitted to dial. This is a fundamentally different paradigm from true peer-to-peer operation. Normally the designation of a device as a peer implies that it largely can act *independently* of other peer devices in the network. Enforcing a degree of control over peer devices in a network from a central control point is possible, but it's harder to do, more complex, and more easily circumvented.

The easiest form of peer control that can be imposed is control of actions that cross network boundaries (such as controlling which external telephone numbers can be accessed). Controlling the actions that occur between peers in a local network is much more difficult, however. In addition, the need to assert different permissions for different peer devices also implies the need for a strong authentication mechanism to be able to positively identify which peer device is which.

SCCP does not provide just call control. It also provides a significant ability to control the IP phone user interface (softkey buttons and phone display). SCCP includes a number of provisioning functions as well. These two items are normally considered outside the scope of the H.323 and SIP peer-to-peer protocols and, therefore, are not readily subject to standardization. However, provisioning and user interface functions must be addressed when constructing a real phone system. From a call control perspective, SCCP has many things in common with the MGCP standard that is used in the telephony service provider and enterprise market spaces.

SCCP runs over TCP/IP and usually uses TCP port 2000. At startup, an SCCP IP phone runs through three main phases:

- **Registration**—The phone locates a controller (such as Cisco CME or Cisco CallManager) and identifies itself to the controller. The newer-model SCCP phones can also perform certificate-based authentication as part of the registration process.

- **Provisioning**—The controller gives the phone information about the functions of the phone's buttons (button template and softkey sets) as well as the phone numbers associated with the phone. Some provisioning steps also occur using TFTP in which the phone uses TFTP to read a phone configuration file from the controller.

- **Operation**—The phone can make and receive calls.

Within the operational state, the phone acts mostly as a dumb endpoint. It signals the following discrete user actions to the controller as they occur:

- On-hook
- Off-hook
- Numeric keypad button press
- Softkey button press
- Line button press

The phone receives the following detailed command instructions from the SCCP controller:

- Ringer on
- Ringer off
- Call progress tone on or off
- Calling and called number display
- Softkey set display selection (per line context)
- Call state notification, including on-hook, off-hook, alerting, connected, ringing, hold, transfer, and so on
- Media control (voice path), including the voice compression codec selection, such as G.711 or G.729

The SCCP phone has autonomous control over some local context items such as speakerphone and headset activation, as well as some local provisioning such as ringer volume, ringer sound, and handset and speakerphone volume settings. Most SCCP phones also autonomously maintain internal directories of recently received, missed, and placed calls.

In addition to SCCP, most of the IP phones equipped with a display also support a simplified and limited web browser function using the HTTP and XML protocols. Operation of the HTTP protocol is largely independent of SCCP. In most cases, the web browser function is used only when the phone is not being used for telephone calls. The web browser function allows the IP phone to be used as an information access point. The HTTP and XML interfaces are made available to non-Cisco third-party developers to construct information services and applications. The phone also uses the web browser interface to provide access to the Cisco CME system's internal telephone directory.

Cisco CME as a Gateway to the PSTN

As covered in the previous sections, the voice gateway functions (providing PSTN connectivity) of a voice-enabled Cisco IOS router are mostly independent of the Cisco CME IP phone functions. This has its good points and its not-so-good points.

On the positive side, the independent functions may simplify the overall network architecture. You can use and provision the Cisco IOS PSTN trunk functions independent of whatever Cisco CME functions you choose to use. This means that a single router can fulfill the roles of phone system controller and PSTN gateway, rather than needing two separate devices for these roles. Perhaps you already have a Cisco IOS voice-enabled router you are using to provide a toll-bypass link between a key system or small PBX at a remote site and a central headquarters campus phone network. If so, you can turn on Cisco CME features without disrupting existing operations. In addition, you can continue to operate and administer your toll-bypass network without much regard for the presence of Cisco CME systems in your network. Of course, you will probably have to make some dial plan configuration changes simply to accommodate the phone numbers you choose to associate with the Cisco CME system.

The downside of this separation of Cisco CME and PSTN trunk functions is that you can't easily view Cisco CME as a single, simple, self-contained system. You have to embrace the modular nature of Cisco IOS functions, and this inevitably deprives you of a truly monolithic administration and management solution. This isn't surprising when you consider the huge breadth of features built into Cisco IOS and the fact that the voice features are only a small fraction of the services that Cisco IOS offers. Your Cisco CME router is probably also your Internet gateway and access concentrator, firewall, Ethernet switch, terminal server, and DHCP server or relay agent.

Cisco CME as a Gateway to SCCP Phones

In addition to seeing your Cisco IOS router as an Internet gateway, a PSTN gateway, and potentially a toll-bypass gateway, you can also view the router's Cisco CME functions as providing a gateway to SCCP and SCCP IP phones. This is consistent with the overall role of Cisco IOS to provide protocol conversion and interworking for a broad set of voice and data protocols.

Leveraging Cisco IOS Voice Infrastructure Functionality for SCCP

Cisco CME provides Cisco IOS with an interworking function that allows the connection of SCCP IP phones to other IP-based protocols such as SIP and H.323. This construction allows for evolution within the SIP and H.323 network environments without directly affecting SCCP-based phone services. At the same time, SCCP services and SCCP-based IP phones can evolve without the delay implied in the development and standardization processes of the IETF and ITU. This "divide and conquer" approach provides the best of both worlds: standardization and third-party interworking where that is required, and flexibility and rapid product innovation where those are needed. In addition, the modular separation of the local phone system internal protocols from the "long-distance" VoIP backbone network protocols provides a degree of insurance against future changes in the Internet and WAN connectivity environments.

Although H.323 and SIP are currently the protocols of primary interest in the small office and remote branch office market space, there's no guarantee that this direction will not change at some point in the future. For example, although Cisco CME 3.2 doesn't support direct interworking between SCCP and MGCP, there's no architectural reason that this cannot be added if needed in the future. The same is true of other protocols that may possibly evolve in the voice-over-DSL, voice-over-cable, and even voice-over-wireless network markets.

It is also worth noting the close relationship between the Cisco CME and SRST Cisco IOS feature set. SRST lets a Cisco IOS voice-enabled router act as a failover call controller for Cisco CallManager in voice networks that operate the SCCP protocol from a centralized Cisco CallManager cluster to SCCP IP phones located at remote sites (across a WAN link). SRST provides an enhanced degree of fault tolerance to guard against remote-site IP phones having no dial tone upon a WAN link or an IP connectivity outage to a central site Cisco CallManager network cluster. An SRST router provides a Cisco CallManager of last resort to the SCCP IP phones at a remote office site should WAN connectivity fail.

The core software engine that provides the SCCP support for Cisco CME is the same software that underpins SRST. The Cisco IOS product features licenses for the SRST and Cisco CME that are largely interchangeable. If you buy a Cisco CME system for an autonomous office environment, you can easily evolve the network into a centralized Cisco CallManager-based system later, and you can migrate your Cisco CME licenses to the SRST environment. The PSTN trunks on the router and the IP phones can simply be reconfigured to move a remote office from being a phone system under local Cisco CME control to a centralized Cisco CallManager system with SRST redundancy.

IP Phone Address Scope and NAT/Firewall

Another advantage of using SCCP as the protocol for local IP phone control is that it avoids problems with NAT and firewalls that often arise in the H.323 and SIP contexts. If you operate H.323 or SIP as your phone endpoint protocol, this usually means that the phone's IP address must be reachable by all other endpoints that need to exchange telephone calls with it. The simplest way of doing this is to give every H.323/SIP phone in your network a public IP address. This approach creates two problems:

- A shortage of 32-bit IPv4 addresses, which makes this approach unworkable for phone systems of any real size

- A need to protect any phone with a public IP address from hackers by using a firewall

If you introduce a firewall, the firewall software must be able to understand all the H.323/SIP messages that pass through it. The firewall must read all the H.323/SIP messages so that it can decide which messages are associated with legitimate phone calls it should pass and which messages are potentially hostile actions from a hacker. This means that every time a new feature or function is added to the H.323/SIP protocol, the firewall software potentially needs to be upgraded as well.

With SCCP used as the internal protocol, there is no need to allow the H.323/SIP messages to enter the internal network behind the firewall. You have the option of terminating the H.323/SIP messages outside the firewall in a less heavily protected area of your network.

The alternative approach to providing a public IP address for every H.323/SIP phone is to use NAT. NAT allows you to insert a NAT gateway device between a group of IP phones that use private IP addresses and the public Internet. NAT takes advantage of the fact that each IP address can be accessed on a range of different TCP/UDP port numbers. There are 65,536 port numbers available for each IP address. (Actually, there is effectively a separate pool of 65,536 port numbers for each distinct IP protocol, such as TCP and UDP.) NAT allows you to use the single IP address of the NAT gateway to represent the pool of IP phones, and then multiplex the IP connection between the phone and the Internet by using a different port number on the NAT gateway for each individual phone. This approach is used extensively within IP networks to significantly reduce the number of unique IPv4 addresses needed.

The problem with NAT is similar to the problem with firewalls. The NAT software also must understand every H.323/SIP message that passes through it so that it can provide the appropriate NAT translation for every IP address that is embedded in the H.323/SIP messages. This means that every time new fields and messages are added to the H.323/SIP protocols, the NAT software has to be upgraded as well.

Of course, another solution to the IPv4 address shortage issue is to use IPv6. However, this has widespread ramifications for your entire network infrastructure, and this topic is beyond the scope of this book.

The Cisco CME SCCP gateway architecture provides a solution similar to NAT. Like NAT, it lets the SCCP IP phones use private IP addresses. Where the SCCP gateway approach wins over the NAT approach is that there's no direct need to intercept and translate messages as they pass through. In the Cisco CME SCCP gateway router case, the H.323/SIP messages are terminated on the router instead of passing through. This hides the complicated detail of the H.323/SIP protocol implementation from the SCCP IP phones. What's more, not only are the H.323/SIP control messages terminated on the Cisco CME router, but so are the H.323/SIP media streams. The Cisco CME router public WAN IP address is used as the termination point for both the H.323/SIP control and media IP packets. Termination of the media stream using the Cisco CME router's external public IP address avoids the need for NAT to contend with the complexity of voice protocols. Passing the H.323/SIP protocol through NAT requires NAT to look at all H.323/SIP control messages, and then translate all the media IP addresses they contain. NAT may still be required for other nonvoice services such as HTTP, but NAT support for HTTP is generally much less complex.

Media Path Handling and QoS

The media path for calls between local IP phones on the same Cisco CME system runs directly between the IP phones. SCCP is used to set up the connection path and provide each IP phone with the IP address and port number to use when sending voice media packets intended for the other phone. The packets are then switched as needed by your Layer 2 Ethernet switch infrastructure, or perhaps they are Layer 3 IP routed if the phones are on different LAN segments. This is mostly pure IP connectivity. Basically, no voice-aware software is involved in transferring packets from one phone to the other. If you use a VLAN for your phone network (recommended), the phones may add priority marking of the packets using the VLAN Class of Service (CoS) priority field in the VLAN Layer 2 encapsulation. (VLAN CoS is set to five by the phones themselves for media stream packets.)

For calls between IP phones and the PSTN trunk voice ports, the media stream for a call flows from the IP phone to the router and then is internally routed to the router's PSTN voice port. For the reverse media flow direction from the router voice port to the phone, the media packets are given internal priority over most other packets to ensure that they are transmitted first on the Ethernet interface connecting to the phone LAN or VLAN. This avoids packet queuing and congestion caused by any contention between the voice media flow and other data flowing through the Ethernet interface (such as HTTP and FTP data traffic).

For a voice call that runs from the SCCP IP phone to the Cisco CME router's WAN connection using H.323/SIP, the voice packets are transmitted by the phone and addressed to the Cisco CME router's IP address (typically to the default gateway IP address for the LAN segment that the phone is on). The IP media packet from the phone is terminated on the router. The IP and UDP headers are stripped from the packet, leaving just the voice payload with its Real-Time Transport Protocol (RTP) encapsulation header. This packet is then passed to the H.323/SIP software stack in the router. The H.323/SIP software applies a new IP and UDP header using the destination media address and port number negotiated by the H.323/SIP protocol with the far-end H.323/SIP endpoint device. The H.323/SIP software also usually rewrites the RTP SSRC (the Synchronization Source field defined in IETF RFC 1889, which covers RTP) source identifier field. This address translation is shown in Figure 3-7.

Figure 3-7   *Cisco CME Media Path Handling*

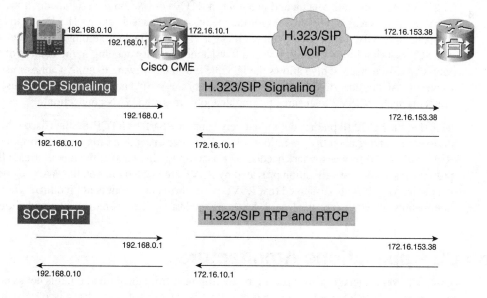

Example 3-1 presents the relevant extract of the Cisco CME router's configuration for this figure.

Example 3-1   *IP and DHCP Configuration for the Cisco CME Router*

```
Router#show running-config
ip dhcp pool cme-phones
   network 192.168.0.0 255.255.0.0
   default-router 192.168.0.1
   option 150 ip 192.168.0.1
!
interface FastEthernet0/0
 ip address 192.168.0.1 255.255.0.0
!
```

continues

Example 3-1 *IP and DHCP Configuration for the Cisco CME Router (Continued)*

```
interface Multilink1
  ip address 172.16.10.1 255.255.255.0
  max-reserved-bandwidth 100
  service-policy output qos-policy
  ppp multilink
  ppp multilink group 1
!
interface Serial0/0:0
  no ip address
  max-reserved-bandwidth 100
  encapsulation ppp
  ppp multilink group 1
```

The H.323/SIP software sets up and maintains a RTCP connection for each media flow. This disassembly and reassembly process for the media stream packets allows H.323/SIP to apply independently whatever packet treatment it needs. This may include setting the IP precedence or DSCP marking for the packet flow and low-latency priority queuing in the context of the egress WAN interface. It also allows the H.323/SIP router software to apply Call Admission Control (CAC) policies to avoid oversubscription of the WAN bandwidth, plus make use of protocols such as RSVP to ensure appropriate QoS across the WAN connection.

Note that the SCCP IP phones do not natively support RSVP or RTCP. So the Cisco CME disassembly and reassembly operations allow the router to act as a proxy device to support RSVP and RTCP services where needed. The assumption here is that the media stream flow protection and strict prioritization provided by RSVP are needed only on the WAN segment of the media path. It is also assumed that RSVP per-flow management is not required within the high-bandwidth context of the local LAN (over the last hop between the router and phone).

Cisco UE Applications Architecture

Cisco UE was designed as an applications environment from the ground up. It is not as heavily based on the Cisco IOS router architecture as the Cisco CME software. The Cisco UE hardware module is a Linux-based environment with local storage and CPU capacity that communicates with the host router via a logical IP interface. From a communications and system architecture point of view, the interface between the Cisco UE hardware and the host router looks like an Ethernet interface to both sides. This is true even though there is no physical cabling, and the communication runs across the backplane of the router chassis.

Although Linux is the operating system (OS) underlying the Cisco UE software, it is an entirely embedded system. It is invisible and inaccessible to the system's external interfaces (CLI, GUI, IP). Likewise, Cisco UE's database and Lightweight Directory Access Protocol (LDAP) directory components are purely internal to the architecture; they have no external access or interfaces.

Cisco UE can be deployed with Cisco CME or Cisco CallManager as the call control agent. Only the Cisco CME deployment architecture is within the scope of this book. Go to http://www.cisco.com/go/cue for more information on how to deploy Cisco UE in Cisco CallManager/SRST networks.

Cisco UE Hardware Architecture

The Cisco UE application is based on an Intel Pentium-based hardware module that fits into the router chassis. It is available in two form factors:

- Network module (NM-CUE)
- Advanced Integration Module (AIM-CUE)

The NM form factor contains a hard disk for persistent storage, whereas the AIM form factor uses an industrial-strength compact Flash card.

The Cisco UE hardware module (irrespective of form factor) has a back-to-back Fast Ethernet connection to the host router. The host router sees an Ethernet interface through its Peripheral Component Interconnect (PCI) backplane that is internally hard-wired to a second Ethernet interface. The second interface (called the *service-engine interface*) is controlled by the Cisco UE module, as shown in Figure 3-8.

Figure 3-8   *Router IP Interface to Cisco UE Hardware Module*

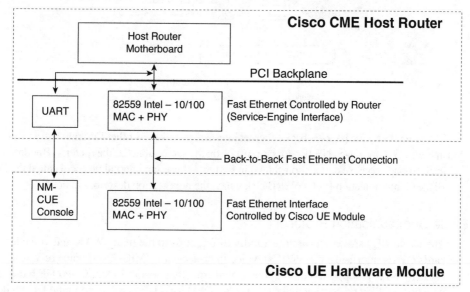

A 100-Mbps data communication channel lies between the Cisco UE module and the host router (with the exception of the Cisco 2600XM series, where it is 10 Mbps). A Universal

Asynchronous Receiver/Transmitter (UART) chip connection also is used for the console connection and management of the Cisco UE module from the router console.

IP Communication with the Host Router

IP connectivity between the Cisco UE module and host router is imperative for the functioning of Cisco UE. The Cisco UE hardware has no external ports, connectivity, or cabling. Its only interface to the network is via the back-to-back Ethernet and console interfaces to the host router. An external Ethernet port resides on the NM form factor, but this is permanently disabled and cannot be used for Cisco UE access.

Figure 3-9 shows IP and console communication between the host Cisco CME router and the Cisco UE hardware.

Figure 3-9 *Cisco UE Hardware Architecture*

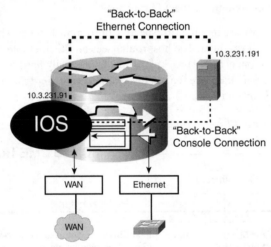

The router treats the back-to-back Ethernet interface just like any other Ethernet interface. As shown in Figure 3-9, the Cisco UE IP address must be on the same subnet as the router's IP addressing. The back-to-back console connection shown in Figure 3-9 uses an internal protocol called the Router Blade Communication Protocol (RBCP), which the next section describes in detail.

Router Blade Communication Protocol

The Cisco UE hardware is architecturally different from the many WAN and voice interface cards (WAN interface cards [WICs], voice interface cards [VICs], and voice or WAN interface cards [VWICs]) supported on the router platforms that host it, in that Cisco UE hardware contains a CPU and storage and runs its own OS. Cisco UE is a self-contained, embedded, Linux-based application software environment, whereas the router is IOS-based. In this design, a control protocol is crucial for communication between the router and Cisco UE hardware, especially before IP connectivity is configured or established.

RBCP is used to communicate basic configuration information such as IP addressing, the default gateway setting, and other parameters to the Cisco UE module until IP connectivity is established. RBCP runs directly over Ethernet, so it requires both Ethernet interfaces (the router and the Cisco UE hardware) to be up and the drivers to be operational. The Cisco UE hardware must reach a steady state in the RBCP protocol state machine to operate properly.

RBCP messages can broadly be classified into two types:

- **Request response**—A transaction-oriented communication that is made up of a request sent by one side and a response from the other side.

- **Unsolicited notifier**—An unsolicited notification sent from one side to the other. There is no acknowledgment.

Every RBCP message has the following fields:

- Source Address (SA)
- Destination Address (DA)
- Operation Code (Op)
- Sequence Number (Sq)
- Length of Message (Ln)
- Information (I)
- Flags
- Payload

Table 3-1 lists the RBCP operational codes (opcodes) and messages used between Cisco IOS and the Cisco UE hardware. These messages and codes are important when troubleshooting the system.

Table 3-1   *RBCP Opcodes*

Opcode	Message Type
0x0011	SERVICE_MODULE_PING
0x0012	SERVICE_MODULE_HEARTBEAT
0x0013	SERVICE_MODULE_REGISTER
0x0014	SERVICE_MODULE_REG_REQ
0x0051	SERVICE_MODULE_SHUTDOWN
0x0052	SERVICE_MODULE_SHUTDOWN_COMPLETE
0x0053	SERVICE_MODULE_RELOAD
0x0054	SERVICE_MODULE_IP_ADDRESS
0x0059	SERVICE_MODULE_IP_DEFAULT_GATEWAY
0x005A	SERVICE_MODULE_PLATFORM_INFO

A brief explanation of the various codes follows:

- **SERVICE_MODULE_PING** — The router sends this message to test basic connectivity.

- **SERVICE_MODULE_HEARTBEAT** — When the Cisco UE module state machine reaches a steady state, the router periodically sends this message to monitor the Cisco UE module's health.

- **SERVICE_MODULE_REGISTER** — The Cisco UE module uses this message to register itself with the router.

- **SERVICE_MODULE_REG_REQ** — After booting up, the router sends this message to the Cisco UE module, asking it to register.

- **SERVICE_MODULE_SHUTDOWN** — This message from the router instructs the Cisco UE module to shut down.

- **SERVICE_MODULE_SHUTDOWN_COMPLETE** — This message from the Cisco UE module confirms that it is shutting down.

- **SERVICE_MODULE_RELOAD** — This message is sent from the router to the Cisco UE module to initiate a reload.

- **SERVICE_MODULE_IP_ADDRESS** — This message is sent from the router to the Cisco UE module to configure the internal interface. It includes information on the IP address and subnet mask.

- **SERVICE_MODULE_IP_DEFAULT_GATEWAY** — This message is sent from the router to the Cisco UE module to set the IP default gateway address.

- **SERVICE_MODULE_PLATFORM_INFO** — This message is sent from the router to the Cisco UE module upon receiving the registration message (0x13). This message provides information such as the serial number and router type to the Cisco UE module.

For every IP address configuration action, RBCP messages are transmitted from the router to the Cisco UE module. If a response is not received within five seconds, the router retransmits the same RBCP message (with a different sequence number).

NOTE   RBCP messages can flow even when the Cisco UE module interface is in a shutdown state. This is necessary because RBCP is the only way to monitor the Cisco UE module's health.

When the router boots up, or after an Online Insertion and Removal (OIR) action has been performed on the Cisco UE hardware, the state machine enters the INIT (initialization) state. OIR is a technique by which network modules can be inserted into and removed from the host router without powering down the router. OIR is applicable only to the NM form factor, not to the AIM. It is available only on some of the higher-end router platforms, such as the Cisco 3745 and 3845 platforms.

In the INIT state, the router transmits a registration request message (0x0014) and transitions to the REGISTRATION_WAIT state (in which it waits for a registration event). The router periodically retransmits this registration request until it receives a registration response (0x0013) from the Cisco UE module. At this time, it transitions to the STEADY_STATE (the normal state when both sides are in contact with each other and no errors have occurred). The router then sends RBCP messages (0x0054 and 0x0059) to configure the IP and gateway address that were previously configured under the service engine interface. If the registration request times out, the router sends a reset to the Cisco UE module and transitions to the RECOVER_FROM_ERROR state (in which error recovery actions take place).

Cisco UE Software Architecture

Cisco UE is made up of many software components. Apart from the base hardware and OS infrastructure, Cisco UE uses the Cisco Customer Response Solutions (CRS) software for call control, media termination, AA application development, and configuration. It also uses many other components, including a directory for user information, a Structured Query Language (SQL) database to store voice mail messages and configuration, and a web server for the GUI and VXML implementations. The voice mail component is implemented using a VXML VoiceBrowser. Caller and subscriber interaction with the voice mail system is implemented with VXML scripts.

OS Infrastructure

The Cisco UE software contains various OS infrastructure components offering basic, system-wide services that are not particular to the application software running on top of them. These include elements such as interprocess communication and arbitration (sysDB), startup and shutdown logic, an HTTP server, a CLI engine, and the LDAP directory and SQL database underlying the applications. Figure 3-10 shows the infrastructure components used in Cisco UE software.

The sysDB component is the system's central data warehouse and arbiter. It runs on top of the Linux OS. SysDB coordinates all data read and write operations to the system databases. sysDB is implemented as a memory-based database. It maintains a copy of data as it is being written to permanent storage so that all software components can query it when needed without reading the disk or Flash.

The data that sysDB keeps is organized using directories, nodes, and attributes. sysDB provides consumer and provider services via an application programming interface (API) to the higher-layer software components. sysDB is implemented using shared memory to allow efficient access in real time to data that changes frequently. sysDB can be loosely compared to the Windows Registry structure, ensuring data consistency throughout the system.

Figure 3-10 *Cisco UE OS Infrastructure*

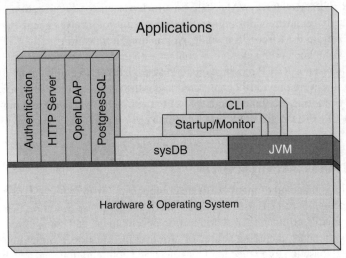

A Java Virtual Machine (JVM) is used by several system software components, including the Cisco CRS infrastructure (part of the Applications layer shown in Figure 3-10) and the HTTP web server. There is also a component that monitors the startup and synchronization of the other software components, ensuring that they are running (shown as Startup/Monitor in Figure 3-10).

The CLI server process services commands from the CLI client. Cisco UE software uses an HTTP web server to serve the VXML scripts that implement the voice mail subsystem and the GUI administration pages. Cisco UE software uses a Postgres SQL database to store voice mail messages and mailbox configuration data. Cisco UE software also contains an OpenLDAP directory server, used to store user and group information. The LDAP component uses the same schema as the Cisco CallManager. However, all the components (for example, the SQL database and the LDAP directory) are embedded and have no external interfaces to other software or hardware in the network.

Figure 3-11 shows all the different software components of the Cisco UE system and how they interact.

The subsystems in the CRS component are shown on the top left of Figure 3-11. These are explained in greater detail in the next section. The voice mail system components are shown at the top right. The voice mail components store voice mail messages directly to the SQL database, as well as mailbox configuration and greeting information using the sysDB provider. User profile and spoken-name information is stored in the LDAP directory, which is accessed via sysDB by the CRS and voice mail components.

Figure 3-11   *Cisco UE Software Components and Their Interaction*

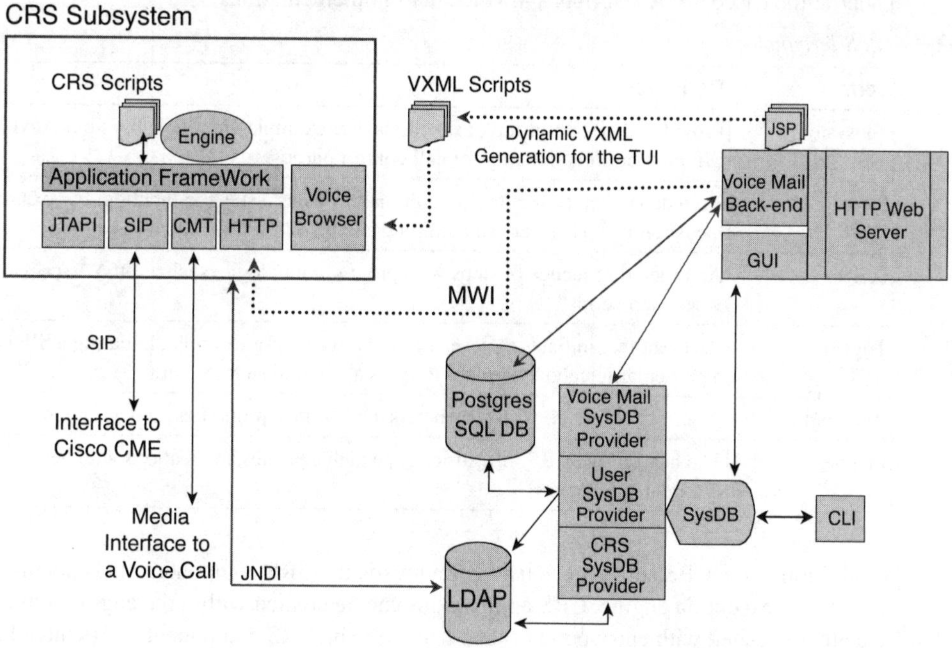

Customer Response Solutions Component

Cisco UE leverages the CRS software infrastructure used in other Cisco application software. The CRS software has many subsystems of its own. The most important components of the Cisco UE software structure include

- Application framework subsystem

- Call control subsystem, which includes SIP

- Media subsystem (Cisco Media Termination [CMT])

- Java Telephony Application Programming Interface (JTAPI) (this subsystem is not used with Cisco CME, but instead is used when Cisco UE is deployed with Cisco CallManager)

NOTE	Cisco UE connects with Cisco CallManager via a JTAPI, so this subsystem exists in the Cisco UE architecture. However, the functionality and configuration of this component of the Cisco UE system are not explored in any detail here or in the remainder of this book, because it is dormant in a Cisco CME deployment. Instead, Cisco UE uses SIP to communicate with Cisco CME, so this architecture is explored in greater detail.

Table 4-2 explains key CRS terminology. This terminology and the components it describes underlie the Cisco UE AA scripts and voice mail implementations.

Table 3-2   *CRS Terminology*

Term	Definition
Subsystem	Provides a specific group of functions. For example, the SIP subsystem provides SIP protocol functionality for call control purposes.
Steps	An independent programming unit that provides a specific function. For example, the Accept step answers an incoming call using SIP.
Script	An ordered sequence of steps with programming logic, such as an AA script or a voice mail script.
Trigger	An event that initiates the execution of a script. For example, initiating a SIP call to a particular telephone number triggers a script to start executing.
Application	A script configured with parameters, call control properties, and a trigger.
Engine	The heart of the CRS infrastructure, which executes applications with help from different subsystems.

In addition to the CRS subsystems listed previously, the CRS component also contains an application execution engine. CRS applications can be created within the engine framework and are associated with entry points called triggers. The CRS component offers three kinds of triggers:

- Call
- E-mail
- HTTP

The Cisco UE application uses only the call and HTTP triggers.

Call triggers are associated with telephone numbers. This part of the architecture constitutes the AA and voice mail pilot numbers you configure to use the Cisco UE features. When a call comes into the call control subsystem for a particular called number, the called number is mapped to a trigger that, in turn, starts the application associated with that trigger. Each application is a logical flow of steps, created using a graphical editor provided as part of the Cisco UE software.

Each step is an independent programming unit that provides a specific function. For example, the Get Digit String step collects DTMF digits pressed by the caller. Different steps play static and dynamically constructed prompts (for example, PlayPrompt and PlayGeneratedPrompt). In addition, you can use many generic programming steps such as *If, Set* (to set the value of a variable) to construct unique applications. The Cisco UE AA and its voice mail components are implemented as CRS applications. The voice mail application uses the VoiceBrowser step provided by the CRS software.

The LDAP directory is the main data store for the CRS software component. CRS stores user information (such as spoken names, dial-by-name strings, and extensions), engine and application configurations, trigger configurations, and scripts in LDAP. System and user prompts are stored in the file system.

Cisco UE Voice Mail Component

The voice mail component is composed of the Telephony User Interface (TUI) and the voice mail back-end server.

User interaction (the TUI) is implemented using the CRS VoiceBrowser step. When voice mail answers a call, the VXML browser starts executing VXML scripts by communicating with the voice mail back end. The CMT component of CRS is used to play prompts and record messages.

The voice mail back-end server is implemented in the HTTP server and interacts with TUI, GUI, and CLI commands. The voice mail back end runs Java Server Pages (JSP) inside the HTTP web server and interacts with the database to serve additional VXML scripts. Which scripts are executed depends on the current status of the user and the mailbox. Figure 3-12 illustrates the architectural operation of the voice mail component.

Figure 3-12   *Voice Mail Architecture*

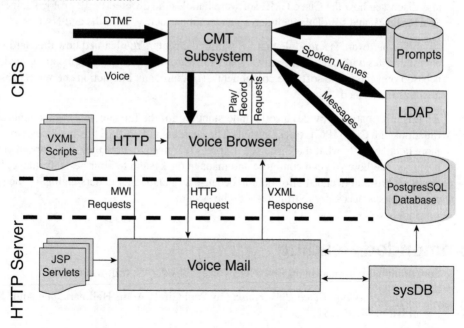

All voice messages and mailbox configurations are stored in the SQL database, and spoken names are stored in and retrieved from LDAP.

The voice mail back end turns on the message waiting indicator (MWI) using CRS's HTTP trigger mechanism. The MWI state changes from on to off (or vice versa) when a new message arrives in a mailbox or a message is deleted. A change in MWI status is affected by the voice mail back end by sending an HTTP request to the CRS HTTP server. The mailbox extension and the desired change (MWI on or MWI off) are passed in the request. The request triggers the CRS software to place an outgoing call to the Cisco CME extension controlling the MWI state (the Cisco CME MWI on or off directory number [DN]). In that turn, triggers the phone's lamp to be turned on or off via an SCCP message to the IP phone.

Summary

This chapter provided an architectural overview of the two main Cisco IPC Express components: Cisco CME, the router-based call processing engine, and Cisco UE, the AA and voice mail applications engine.

The Cisco CME architecture was discussed within the larger scope of Cisco IOS-based voice services. This chapter covered how Cisco CME features and services fit within, and reuse, fundamental Cisco IOS voice infrastructure, such as dial peers and PSTN trunk interfaces. It also discussed how the Cisco CME software handles the different VoIP protocols, including SCCP, H.323, and SIP. This included considerations such as firewalls and NAT.

Cisco UE hardware is a module that fits within the router. You learned how this hardware communicates with the router hardware and software. The Cisco UE applications environment is based on Linux. The software components, structure, and interactions between subsystems also were explained.

All this information provides a solid understanding for the fundamental components and functions of a Cisco IPC Express system. The chapters in Part II of this book describe in much more detail exactly what the Cisco IPC Express features are, how they can work in your business, and how you can configure and manage the system to your best advantage. Part III draws on this architectural information, because a fundamental understanding of the system components is necessary to troubleshoot the system.

Recommended Reading

For additional information on Cisco IOS voice, consider the following books:

- *Troubleshooting Cisco IP Telephony* by Paul Giralt, Addis Hallmark, and Anne Smith. ISBN 1587050757.

- *Voice over IP Fundamentals* by Jonathan Davidson, James Peters, and Brian Gracely. ISBN 1578701686.

- *Integrating Voice and Data Networks* by Scott Keagy. ISBN 1578701961.

PART II

Feature Operation and Applications

This chapter covers the following topics:

- Features and capabilities of the following Cisco IP Phones: 7970G, 7940G, 7960G, 7914 Expansion Module, 7910G, 7905G, 7912G, 7902G, 7935 and 7936 Conference Stations, and 7920 wireless phone
- Cisco Analog Telephony Adapter (ATA)
- Cisco IP Communicator softphone
- Firmware files for the IP phones
- Resetting and restarting the IP phones
- Erasing the IP phone configuration
- Accessing call parameters for an active call

## CHAPTER 4

Cisco IP Phone Options

Cisco CallManager Express (CME) supports a range of phones that meet various customer needs, from the simple low-end Cisco 7902G IP Phone to the advanced Cisco 7970G color touch-screen phone, the 7936 Conference Station, and the Analog Telephony Adaptor (ATA) that lets you connect analog phones to Cisco CME. This chapter discusses the various phones supported by Cisco CME to give you a better understanding of how these devices operate and which features are supported. After reviewing the main hardware features of each phone, you learn the configuration steps necessary for each phone type. This chapter also covers some phone-specific information such as firmware loads, resetting the phone, erasing the phone configuration, and accessing call parameters from the phone.

The Cisco 7940G and 7960G IP Phones

The Cisco 7940G and 7960G, shown in Figure 4-1, were the first phones available with Cisco CME. These phones support all the features currently supported with Cisco CME 3.2.

Figure 4-1   *Cisco 7940G and 7960G IP Phones*

NOTE	Although this chapter refers primarily to the current G-series phones (such as the 7960G and 7940G), Cisco CME also supports the previous generation of phones, such as the Cisco 7960 and 7940. The only difference between the G and non-G phones is in how their buttons are labeled: with English words (the non-G phones) or with language-independent icons (the G series).

Hardware

The Cisco 7960G and 7940G IP Phones look identical, except for the number of buttons on each phone. The Cisco 7940G has two line buttons, whereas the Cisco 7960G has six line buttons and can have an additional 28 lines with the addition of up to two Cisco 7914 expansion modules. The phones require 48V DC power for operation.

The Cisco 7960G and 7940G IP Phones include a 10/100 Ethernet switch port that allows a PC to be connected via the phone's Ethernet connection. The two Ethernet ports on the phone are marked as 10/100SW and 10/100PC. The 10/100SW should be connected to the Ethernet switch port, and the 10/100PC port can be connected to a UNIX workstation or PC, as shown in Figure 4-2.

Figure 4-2   *Connecting a PC to an IP Phone*

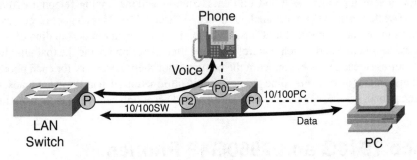

Both phone ports are capable of autonegotiation. 48V power is required for the phone to operate. This can be provided by an external power supply unit or via a LAN switch with inline power capability. The inline power LAN switch might be an external switch or an integrated Layer 2 LAN switching module resident in the network module or high-speed WAN interface card (HWIC) slot of the Cisco CME router. Only the 10/100SW port can receive inline power from a LAN switch or similar device. The phone supports 802.3/Ethernet, 802.1p/q, and Inter-Switch Link (ISL) encapsulations at Layer 2.

The line buttons of the Cisco 7960G and 7940G IP Phones can be configured as regular phone lines, speed-dial buttons, or intercom buttons. The phone also has a headset jack and button.

NOTE   In the rest of this section, "phone" refers to both 7940G and 7960G phone types.

The liquid crystal display (LCD) screen can display up to eight lines of text plus a row of softkeys. The four softkey buttons at the bottom of the LCD screen are used for programmable functions such as hold, conference, and call forward. The label and function of the softkeys change according to the phone's current state. For example, if the phone is on-hook, you find functions such as redial and new call assigned to the softkeys. Similarly, when the phone is on an active call, you see functions such as hold, conference, and transfer. The softkey presented for each state is customizable if you are using Cisco CME 3.2 or later.

The phone has a standard dial keypad (0 to 9, *, #), a speakerphone, and a microphone. The volume control buttons are located above the speakerphone, mute, and headset buttons. You can adjust the volume of the speakerphone, headset, and ringer using these buttons. Pressing the up or down arrow buttons adjusts the volume of the speakerphone, handset, or ringer, depending on the phone's state. For example, if the phone is on-hook, pressing the volume buttons adjusts the ringer volume. If the phone is off-hook via the speakerphone, pressing the volume buttons adjusts the speakerphone volume.

The phone also has a ? button with four more buttons around it. The standard functions for these buttons are as follows:

- **Messages**—Pressing the messages button autodials the voice mail number (if configured).
- **Directories**—The directories button has options to view call records; access a directory search; and view missed calls, received calls, and placed calls. You also can search for a directory number by the caller name associated with the number. This menu also has an option for local speed dial and personal speed dial. Cisco CME configuration is required for the local directories and speed-dial options on this menu to work.
- **Services**—The services button lets you access the various XML services configured on Cisco CME.
- **Settings**—Pressing the settings button gives you the following options on the phone display:
    - Contrast
    - Ring Type
    - Network Configuration
    - Model Information
    - Status

You can scroll through the options by using the blue rocker button and pressing the select button at the bottom of the LCD screen. A number assigned to each option allows you to select the option by keying in the corresponding number directly from the dial pad. This saves you time when you have to scroll down the more than 30 options available on the Network Configuration menu.

The contrast and ring type options adjust the LCD screen's contrast and select a different ring type for your phone, respectively. The remaining three options are primarily intended for use by a system administrator.

The Settings->Network Configuration menu has information such as IP address, subnet mask, and Dynamic Host Configuration Protocol (DHCP) server. Some of these parameters can be manually configured or edited from the phone itself, but in most cases, manual configuration is not needed. The next section covers how to make manual adjustments.

The Settings->Model Information menu contains phone details such as firmware version and boot load. The Settings->Status menu lets you view network status and statistics information such as packets received and packets sent. You can also access phone settings via a web browser by pointing it to the phone's IP address.

Configuring the Cisco 7940G and 7960G IP Phones

The phone's default behavior is to get its required network parameters via DHCP from a DHCP server. It is also possible to configure these parameters manually from the phone. The most common reason for performing manual editing of the phone's configuration occurs when you move a phone from one Cisco CME or Cisco CallManager system to another. Manual editing of the phone configuration is also sometimes needed to force parameter updates to stop the phone from attempting to access its old Cisco CME or Cisco CallManager servers. To configure the network parameters manually from the phone, you should first disable the DHCP service on the phone. The phone Settings menu by default is locked to prevent manual editing of parameters.

Here's the step-by-step process to disable DHCP:

Step 1   Press the **settings** button.

Step 2   Select Network Settings by pressing button **3** or by scrolling through the options using the rocker button and pressing the **select** softkey.

Step 3   When you are in Network Settings, select the **DHCP Enabled** option by scrolling down the menu using the rocker button.

Step 4   Unlock the phone by entering the key combination ****#**. If the phone is already unlocked, entering the key combination ****#** locks the phone instead. You can see the lock's current status on the second line of the LCD display toward the right side.

Step 5   Select **no** to disable the DHCP service.

Step 6   Press the **save** softkey to save the current settings.

After you disable DHCP, you can overwrite the phone's IP and Trivial File Transfer Protocol (TFTP) server addresses. The TFTP server address is the key parameter controlling the identity of the Cisco CME (or Cisco CallManager) system that the IP phone attempts to register with.

Chapter 16, "Troubleshooting Basic Cisco IPC Express Features," provides many more details about the IP phone bootup sequence and how the phone uses DHCP and TFTP.

The Cisco 7914 Expansion Module

The Cisco 7914 Expansion Module is an add-on device that attaches to the Cisco 7960G IP Phone to increase the number of line buttons. Figure 4-3 shows a Cisco 7914 Expansion Module attached to a Cisco 7960G IP Phone.

Figure 4-3   *Cisco 7960G with a 7914 Add-on Module*

Hardware

The Cisco 7914 expansion module has 14 buttons and a single-line LCD screen for each button. Each module adds 14 lines to the Cisco 7960G host phone that it is attached to. You can add a maximum of two expansion modules to a Cisco 7960G IP Phone and, thus, increase the phone's total lines to 34.

A separate 48V DC power supply is required for the Cisco 7914 module. Inline power from an Ethernet switch cannot provide power to a Cisco 7914 module. An RS-232 cable provides the communication link between the Cisco 7914 module and the Cisco 7960G IP Phone. The buttons are lit amber, red, or green, depending on the state of the line associated with the button.

Configuring the Cisco 7914 Expansion Module

You can configure the 14 lines on the Cisco 7914 module as individual lines, speed dials, intercom, or monitored lines. The Cisco 7914 module is not configured as a separate device under Cisco CME; hence, it doesn't require the network parameter configuration required for other IP phones.

The Cisco 7914 module does, however, require firmware for its operation. The firmware for the module depends on the version of Cisco CME you are using. It should be configured under the **telephony-service** configuration prompt using the **load** command. The buttons are considered a continuation of the buttons on the Cisco 7960G IP Phone to which it is attached. Hence, the first button on a Cisco 7914 is configured as the seventh button on the Cisco 7960G IP Phone, and the 14th button of the Cisco 7914 is configured as the 20th button. Example 4-1 shows a typical configuration for a Cisco 7960G IP Phone with a Cisco 7914 module attached.

Example 4-2 *Cisco 7914 Configuration*

```
Router#show running-config
telephony-service
max-dn 10
max-ephone 10
ip source address 10.0.0.1 port 2000
load 7940-60 P00303020214
load 7914 OSX001124351
create-cnf file
ephone-dn 1
  number 1001
ephone-dn 2
  number 1002
..
..
ephone-dn 7
  number 1007
ephone-dn 8
  number 1008
ephone 1
  mac-address 1111.2222.3333
  add-on 1 7914
  button 1:1 2:2 3:3 4:4 5:5 6:6 7:7 8:8
  speed dial 1 2001
  speed dial 2 2002
```

With the configuration in Example 4-1, the first and second buttons of the Cisco 7914 have the extension number 1007 and 1008, respectively. The third and fourth buttons have the speed dials 2001 and 2002, respectively.

The Cisco 7910G IP Phone

The Cisco 7910G IP Phone, shown in Figure 4-4, is a low-end phone that is part of the same family of phones as the Cisco 7960G and 7940G. The primary difference is that the Cisco 7910G phone has only a two-line display and no softkeys. The Cisco 7910G supports English only and does not support XML capabilities.

Figure 4-4   *Cisco 7910G IP Phone*

Hardware

The Cisco 7910G IP Phone comes in two flavors: the Cisco 7910G and the Cisco 7910G+SW models. The Cisco 7910G has a standard 10 Mbps Ethernet interface, and the Cisco 7910G+SW is equipped with two 10/100 Ethernet interfaces. The ports are marked as 10/100SW and 10/100PC, respectively. The functionality of the ports is similar to the Cisco 7960G IP Phone, where one port can be connected to a LAN switch and the other port can be connected to a PC.

The Cisco 7910G supports only a single line (extension) and has a two-line, text-only LCD screen. The phone does not have a microphone, although it does have a "listen-only" speakerphone. If you put a call on "listen-only" speakerphone, the far-end party can't hear you. The phone has fixed function buttons for two speed dials, redial, hold, conference, transfer, accessing voice mail, and configuring call-forward from the phone.

Configuring the Cisco 7910G IP Phone

Configuring network parameters for a Cisco 7910G is similar to doing so for a Cisco 7960G IP Phone. The phone's default behavior is to use DHCP to obtain the network parameters. You can also manually configure these parameters from the phone by unlocking the phone and disabling DHCP services first.

Pressing the Settings button takes you through a menu with various options. This menu is comparable to the Settings menu for a Cisco 7960G. Because of the limited display and softkeys available, some of the functions on this menu work differently on a Cisco 7910G IP Phone than on a Cisco 7960G.

To unlock the phone, press the key combination ****#** before pressing the settings button. You can see the lock's status in the top-right corner of the LCD screen after pressing the settings button.

The menu gives you the following options, with a number assigned to each option:

- Handset Vol
- Speaker Vol
- Ringer Vol
- Model Information
- LCD Contrast
- Network Config
- Ringer Type
- Timers

Do the following to unlock the phone and disable DHCP services:

Step 1 Press **# to unlock the phone.

Step 2 Press the **settings** button.

Step 3 Choose Network Settings by selecting option **6**.

Step 4 Scroll down until you see the disable DHCP option.

Step 5 Press the * button to get the option yes. Use the volume control button to scroll between the options yes and no. Select the option **no**.

Step 6 Press the # button to make the selection.

Step 7 Press the # button again to save the selection.

As soon as the DHCP service is disabled, you can manually configure the IP address, subnet mask, and default gateway.

The Cisco 7905G and 7912G IP Phones

The Cisco 7905G and 7912G are entry-level IP phones. Figure 4-5 shows the Cisco 7905G IP Phone. The physical appearance of these two phones is very similar, except for the additional Ethernet port available on the Cisco 7912G.

Figure 4-5 *Cisco 7905G IP Phone*

Hardware

The Cisco 7905G has a single 10-Mb Ethernet interface. The device requires 48V DC power to operate, which can be provided from an inline Cisco LAN switch or an external power supply unit. The Cisco 7905G has a pixel-based LCD screen.

NOTE	The Cisco 7905G IP Phone is the *only* model where Cisco CME supports *only* the G-series model and not the ordinary Cisco 7905 IP Phone. The Cisco 7905 is an H.323 phone, and Cisco CME supports only SCCP-based phones (such as the Cisco 7905G).

The Cisco 7912G has two 10/100 Mbps Ethernet ports and functions similar to the Cisco 7960G phone. The power supply can be provided from an inline power LAN switch or an external power supply.

Both the Cisco 7905G and 7912G phones support a single-line button and have an additional four buttons for hold, transfer, conference, and dialing voice mail. The phone is also equipped with a "listen-only" speakerphone, mute button, volume control keys, and a rocker button to scroll through the LCD screen. The function of the softkeys changes depending on the phone's state. The softkeys can be programmed for various states of the phone, such as the Cisco 7960G. The hold function button is not a part of the softkey set. A dedicated button for this function is located on the left side of the rocker button; it has a hexagon symbol resembling a stop sign. The button on the right side of the rocker button takes you to the Settings menu, similar to the phones discussed previously.

Configuring the Cisco 7905G and 7912G IP Phones

The Cisco 7905G and 7912G IP Phones obtain their IP address and other network information by default from DHCP. You can also configure these parameters from the phone after disabling DHCP. The phone is equipped with a set of menus similar to the Cisco 7960G IP Phone to view and configure some of the phone and network parameters. The key combination to unlock and reset the phone is the same as for the Cisco 7960G IP Phone.

The phone load and phone type should be configured under the telephony-services and ephone configuration modes, respectively, for a successful registration of the phone. The phone can be configured with two single-line directory numbers (DNs) or a single dual-line DN.

The Cisco 7970G IP Phone

The general look and feel of the Cisco 7970G IP Phone, shown in Figure 4-6, is similar to that of a Cisco 7960G, with added buttons, features, and a color display.

Figure 4-6 *Cisco 7970G IP Phone*

Hardware

The Cisco 7970G IP Phone has an LCD color display that is bigger than the Cisco 7960G display and has touch-screen capability. The phone has eight line buttons and five softkeys. The line buttons are light emitting diode (LED) lit with different colors indicating different phone states (for example, ringing or hold).

The phone's network capabilities are similar to that of a Cisco 7960G IP Phone. The phone also has a sleep/wake button for the LCD screen. The phone needs a 48V DC power supply to operate; it can be provided from a LAN switch capable of inline power or from an external power supply. If the phone is powered from an inline power LAN switch, the LCD screen does not operate with full brightness (this requires an external power supply). The Cisco 7970G IP Phone supports 802.3af inline power.

Configuring the Cisco 7970G IP Phone

The Cisco 7970G is supported on Cisco CME 3.2.1 and later. Configuring a Cisco 7970G is the same as with a Cisco 7960G. The phone requires certain firmware depending on the version of Cisco CME you are using. This firmware version is configured in telephony-service configuration mode.

You also can configure the phone manually from the Settings menu. You can configure the system message and softkeys for various phone states from the Cisco CME router console.

The Cisco 7902G IP Phone

The Cisco 7902G, shown in Figure 4-7, is the lowest-end IP phone in the portfolio supported by Cisco CME. The phone's physical appearance is similar to a Cisco 7905G IP Phone but without an LCD screen.

Figure 4-7   *Cisco 7902G IP Phone*

Hardware

The default configuration of network parameters for a Cisco 7902G IP Phone is via the DHCP mechanism. Because of the lack of display, manual configuration is carried out via a built-in English-only interactive voice response (IVR) menu on the phone. The Cisco 7902G has a single 10-Mb Ethernet interface and requires a 5V DC external power supply to operate.

The four fixed function buttons provide redial, transfer, conference, and voice mail functionality. You can configure up to ten speed dials for a Cisco 7902G. To place a call using speed-dial, press and hold (for about two seconds) the number on your keypad (0 to 9) assigned as a speed-dial number.

Configuring the Cisco 7902G IP Phone

The Cisco 7902G IP Phone has hold and function keys. Pressing the hold button puts an active call on hold. The same action retrieves a call if one is on hold. Pressing the function button when the phone is off-hook activates the IVR menu that allows you to manually configure the phone's various network and service parameters.

The Cisco 7935 and 7936 IP Conference Station

The Cisco 7935 and 7936 IP Conference Stations are IP-based, hands-free conference room stations. Figure 4-8 shows the Cisco 7935 IP Conference Station.

Figure 4-8 *Cisco 7935 IP Conference Station*

Hardware

The Cisco 7935 and 7936 conference stations provide a speakerphone for a large conference room. The general look and feel of the Cisco 7935 and 7936 are the same. Both have 10/100 Mbps Ethernet interfaces to connect to a LAN switch and operate from a 19V DC external power supply. The Cisco 7935 and 7936 do not support inline power.

The conference station has standard dial pad, off-hook, volume control, and mute buttons. Additional buttons are available on the phone to configure and navigate through the network and phone parameters.

The conference station does not have a handheld receiver. Hence, the phone's off-hook button should be used to make a call. The Cisco 7935 can cover a 10 ft. by 12 ft. (3 m by 3.6 m) conference room, and the Cisco 7936 can support a room as big as 20 ft. by 30 ft. (6 m by 9.1 m). The Cisco 7936 has two external microphones that can be connected to the main unit.

Configuring the Cisco 7935 and 7936 Conference Stations

Configuring a Cisco 7935 or 7936 conference station is similar to doing so with the IP phones mentioned in the previous sections. You can manually configure the phone's network parameters from the phone in a similar fashion. The Cisco 7935 and 7936 should be configured with their respective device types when configured under Cisco CME.

The menu button on the conference station provides access to network and phone-specific parameters. This menu is slightly different from the one on the phones discussed in the previous sections. You can access the network parameters by selecting the option admin setup. This menu is password-protected; it comes with a factory default password of 12345. As soon as you have access to this menu, you can change or edit the conference station's network parameters.

The Cisco 7920 Wireless IP Phone

The Cisco 7920 Wireless IP Phone, shown in Figure 4-9, is an 802.11b wireless communication device supported by Cisco CME.

Figure 4-9   *Cisco 7920 Wireless IP Phone*

Hardware

The Cisco 7920 Wireless IP Phone needs a Cisco Aironet 802.11b access point to work with Cisco CME. The phone uses a Lithium-ion battery for power; it can be charged using an external AC adaptor.

This phone has the following buttons:

- A standard dial pad button
- A left and right key that activates the softkey above it
- An answer/send key to answer a call or send the number
- Arrow keys to navigate through the phone menu
- A power/end key to turn off the phone, silence a ringing call, or end a connected call

You can configure up to six lines on the Cisco 7920 Wireless IP Phone.

Configuring the Cisco 7920 Wireless IP Phone

The Cisco 7920 Wireless IP Phone is supported by Cisco CME 3.0 and later. This phone is configured like any other wireless device. Go to http://www.cisco.com/go/wireless for more information on setting up your wireless network for voice traffic.

The Cisco CME configuration required for a Cisco 7920 Wireless IP Phone is no different from any of the other IP phones discussed in the previous sections. This phone requires certain firmware depending on the version of Cisco CME you are using. This firmware version should be configured in telephony-service configuration mode. You also can configure the phone manually from the phone's menu.

The Cisco Analog Telephony Adaptor

The Cisco Analog Telephony Adaptor (ATA) is a small gateway device that provides an interface between Skinny Client Control Protocol (SCCP), used for IP phones, and a standard analog phone. Thus, the ATA lets you register an analog phone with Cisco CME as if it were an IP phone. The Cisco ATA device comes in two models: the Cisco ATA 186 and Cisco ATA 188 (shown in Figure 4-10). The models look similar from the front, but from the rear you can see the additional Ethernet port available on the ATA 188.

Figure 4-10   *Cisco ATA 186 and ATA 188*

Hardware

Both the ATA models connect one or two analog telephones. The hardware features for the ATA 186 include the following:

- Function button
- Two RJ-11 Foreign Exchange Station (FXS) ports
- RJ-45 10Base-T Ethernet uplink port
- Network activity (ACT) LED
- Power connector

One of the major differences between the two models is that the Cisco ATA 188 has two RJ-45 10/100-Mbps Ethernet ports, whereas the Cisco ATA 186 has only a single10 Mbps Ethernet port. One of the ports on the Cisco ATA 188 is an uplink port, and the other one is a data port.

The FXS interfaces can be used to connect two standard analog telephones or fax machines. The Cisco ATA is connected to the network via an Ethernet interface and can be configured via DHCP or manually. The Cisco ATA needs a 5V DC external power supply to operate. Inline Ethernet power does not apply to the Cisco ATA devices, because they do not support phones on Ethernet ports.

NOTE   Cisco CME 3.2 does not support a fax machine using SCCP. A fax machine on a Cisco ATA device must use H.323.

Configuring the Cisco ATA

A Cisco ATA by default uses DHCP to obtain the network's parameters. You can change this behavior by manually disabling DHCP. Configuring the Cisco ATA manually is different from configuring the phones. Instead of a visual display, the Cisco ATA has an English-only IVR menu that lets you configure the parameters.

You can also view and edit the parameters via a web browser. Accessing the parameters via a browser requires the Cisco ATA to have network connectivity. Thus, a newly installed Cisco ATA can be configured either via DHCP or manually via the IVR menu.

You can access the IVR menu by connecting a phone to the first RJ-11 port on the Cisco ATA. Activate the IVR by pressing the LED lit button on the Cisco ATA when the phone connected to the RJ-11 port is in an off-hook state. As soon as the ATA receives the IP address, you can access the web configuration page (see Figure 4-11) located at http://ipaddress/dev, where ipaddress is the ATA's IP address.

Figure 4-11 *Web Configuration Page for the Cisco ATA*

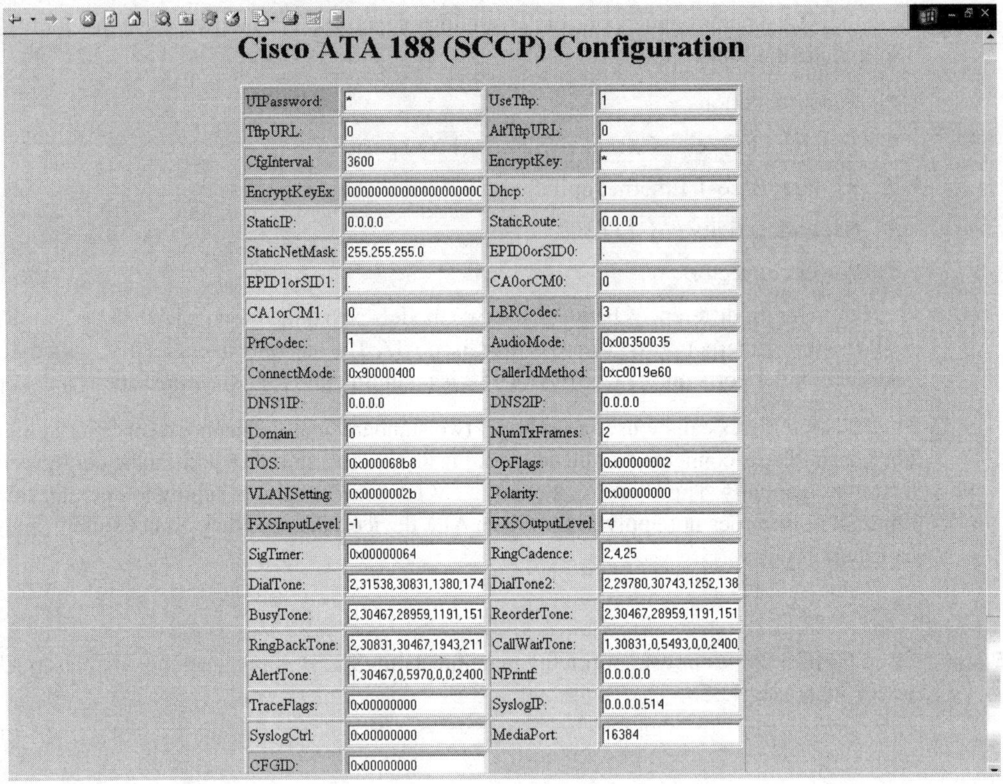

Cisco ATA 188 (SCCP) Configuration

UIPassword:	*	UseTftp:	1
TftpURL:	0	AltTftpURL:	0
CfgInterval:	3600	EncryptKey:	*
EncryptKeyEx:	00000000000000000000	Dhcp:	1
StaticIP:	0.0.0.0	StaticRoute:	0.0.0.0
StaticNetMask:	255.255.255.0	EPID0orSID0:	
EPID1orSID1:		CA0orCM0:	0
CA1orCM1:	0	LBRCodec:	3
PrfCodec:	1	AudioMode:	0x00350035
ConnectMode:	0x90000400	CallerIdMethod:	0xc0019e60
DNS1IP:	0.0.0.0	DNS2IP:	0.0.0.0
Domain:	0	NumTxFrames:	2
TOS:	0x000068b8	OpFlags:	0x00000002
VLANSetting:	0x0000002b	Polarity:	0x00000000
FXSInputLevel:	-1	FXSOutputLevel:	-4
SigTimer:	0x00000064	RingCadence:	2,4,25
DialTone:	2,31538,30831,1380,174	DialTone2:	2,29780,30743,1252,138
BusyTone:	2,30467,28959,1191,151	ReorderTone:	2,30467,28959,1191,151
RingBackTone:	2,30831,30467,1943,211	CallWaitTone:	1,30831,0,5493,0,0,2400,
AlertTone:	1,30467,0,5970,0,0,2400,	NPrintf:	0.0.0.0
TraceFlags:	0x00000000	SyslogIP:	0.0.0.0.514
SyslogCtrl:	0x00000000	MediaPort:	16384
CFGID:	0x00000000		

You should configure each FXS port on the Cisco ATA as a separate device on Cisco CME. The Media Access Control (MAC) address for the first analog port is the MAC address of the Cisco ATA itself. The MAC address of the second analog port on the Cisco ATA is created by dropping the leftmost two digits and adding 01 to the rightmost digits. For example, if the MAC address of the Cisco ATA device is 0007.0EA2.6032, the MAC address of the second port is 070E.A260.3201.

The Cisco IP Communicator Softphone

The Cisco IP Communicator is a software-based application that allows users to place and receive calls from their PCs. IP communication between your personal computer and Cisco CME should be in place for successful operation of Cisco IP Communicator. Also, the IP network connecting your PC should be designed to carry voice traffic. Figures 4-12 and 4-13 show the Cisco IP Communicator interface with the default skin and the alternate skin, respectively.

Figure 4-12   *Cisco IP Communicator Default Skin*

Figure 4-13   *Cisco IP Communicator Alternate Skin*

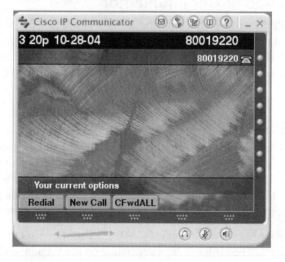

Hardware

The minimum PC hardware and software required for Cisco IP Communicator to function are as follows:

- Windows 2000 Professional with service pack 3.0 or later or Windows XP Professional with service pack 1.0 or later
- 450-MHz Pentium III or the equivalent
- 128 MB of RAM for Windows 2000, or 192 MB of RAM for Windows XP
- Screen resolution of 800×600
- A minimum of 100 MB of free disk space
- Non-ISA full-duplex sound card (integrated or PCI-based) or USB sound device
- 10/100-Mbps Ethernet network interface card
- SVGA video card

The interface of the Cisco IP Communicator is very similar to the Cisco 7970G IP Phone. In addition to the buttons available on the interface, the Cisco IP Communicator provides keyboard shortcuts for many functions. Also, you can access some of the user options such as different skin types, user options, and preferences by right-clicking.

Configuring the Cisco IP Communicator

Configuring the Cisco IP Communicator involves two steps. The first is to install the Cisco IP Communicator software on your PC, and the second is to configure Cisco IP Communicator on Cisco CME. Cisco IP Communicator is configured like any other phone mentioned in the previous sections, except that the PC's MAC address is used for the phone's MAC address.

Firmware Files for IP Phones

Each type of IP phone requires firmware to register and function properly with Cisco CME. The version of the firmware depends on the type of phone and version of Cisco CME you are using. The firmware should be placed on a TFTP server accessible to the router and should be copied to the Cisco CME router. Also, the telephony-service configuration should have the firmware specified for each type of phone connected to the Cisco CME system.

The configuration shown in Example 4-2 lists the firmware for the Cisco 7940G, 7960G, and 7905G IP Phones. These files change depending on the version of Cisco CME you're using.

Check Cisco.com for the correct version of these files for your system. The files in Example 4-2 are shown to illustrate where they are configured.

Example 4-3 *Phone Firmware*

```
Router#show running-config
telephony-service
max-dn 10
max-ephone 10
ip source address 10.0.0.1 port 2000
load 7940-60 P00303020214
load 7914 S00103020002.bin
load 7905 CP79050101SCCP030530B31.zup
```

All the phones come with factory default firmware installed. During the registration process, the phone compares its current firmware with the load configured under telephony services, as shown in Example 4-2. If the configured firmware and the current firmware match, the phone continues with the registration process. If the firmware is different from what is configured, the phone tries to download the new firmware from Cisco CME.

It is necessary to have the right version of phone firmware for the version of Cisco CME you are using to have all the features working as designed.

In certain cases, a firmware upgrade or downgrade is not a one-step process. Also, in certain cases, you cannot downgrade the phone firmware to a lower version. For example, you cannot downgrade the firmware on a Cisco 7960G IP Phone from a signed load to an unsigned load. This process is covered in much more detail in Chapter 16.

Resetting and Restarting the Phones

You may have to reset or restart the phones when you make changes to the Cisco CME configuration. When a phone is reset, it goes through the entire bootup sequence. A phone reset is very similar to power-cycling the phone (powering it on and off). When a phone is restarted, it clears its current registration with Cisco CME and registers again. Restart is faster than reset. A restart is sufficient for configuration changes such as adding another line or speed dial to the phone. A reset is required for system-level changes such as upgrading a phone load or changing the URL for a directory search.

Cisco IP phones can be reset from a Cisco CME router console, from the Cisco CME GUI, or from the phone itself. A restart can be issued from the Cisco CME console or the Cisco CME GUI. You can reset or restart individual phones from the Cisco CME router console by issuing the **reset** or **restart** command, respectively, from the ephone configuration prompt.

You can reset from the phone itself by entering the key combination **#** from the phone dial pad. The phone should be in the on-hook state when you enter the key combination.

Erasing the Phone Configuration

In rare situations, you may have to erase a phone's current configuration. One such situation is when you physically move the phone from one Cisco CME system to another.

The running configuration of a Cisco 7960G, 7940G, or 7970G IP Phone can be erased from the phone. This provision is available on the Settings->Network Configuration menu. Scrolling through this menu using the rocker button or entering the number 36 takes you to the option erase configuration. If the phone is in an unlocked state, you should see a softkey labeled yes. Pressing the yes softkey gives you another softkey labeled save. If you select the save softkey, the phone's current configuration is erased, and the phone reboots.

Accessing Call Parameters for an Active Call

The Cisco 7940G, 7960G, and 7970G IP Phones have a provision to view call parameters such as the number of packets sent and received, the codec used for the current call, and delay and jitter readings for an active call. This is helpful when you're troubleshooting issues related to voice quality.

When a call is active, press the ? button twice to show the current parameters on the LCD screen. The parameters are updated dynamically. If there are two or more active calls on the phone, the display reflects the parameters for the call that is in the connected state.

Summary

In this chapter, you learned about the different phones that can be connected to a Cisco CME system and the options and features available for each device. It also included a discussion of the hardware capabilities, the key (button) operation, and the configuration of each phone.

The next chapter covers some of the important call processing features available on a Cisco CME system and how to configure them.

This chapter covers the following topics:

- IP phones and lines
- Shared lines
- Hunt groups
- Intercoms
- Paging
- Line overlays
- Call pickup
- Softkey customization
- Call transfer and forward

## CHAPTER 5

Cisco CME Call Processing Features

This chapter describes the primary call processing features of Cisco CallManager Express (CME) and shows how you can combine them to produce an extensive set of call handling behaviors. It includes a basic discussion of the advantages of IP telephony for the small office and relates these to the more traditional time-division multiplexing (TDM) or analog-based telephone systems historically used in the small private branch exchange (PBX) and Key System marketplace.

This chapter explains the terminology and Cisco IOS commands (command-line interface [CLI]) used to configure IP phones, extension lines, shared lines, overlays, intercom, paging, call park and pickup, hunt groups, and other forms of call coverage. One of the key perspectives to understanding Cisco CME is that it is built on top of a Cisco IOS router. This means that the same modular feature approach that dominates the general Cisco IOS command-line organization is carried forward into the Cisco CME structure. The result is that individual component features are designed to be as modular and flexible as possible. It also means that it is often possible to combine features to produce some fairly complex operations. Some of these combinations are not obvious from a quick glance at the CLI. This chapter is intended to help you understand and use some of the available flexibility.

The sample configurations in this chapter are presented using the Cisco IOS CLI. Many of the configurations described can also be generated using the web browser graphical user interface (GUI). In both cases, the configurations generated are stored identically in the router's nonvolatile memory in CLI format. The CLI presentation is more compact and easier to grasp than an equivalent series of GUI screen shots. The CLI presentation also shows the integration of some Cisco CME-specific functions with the CLI commands for related but generic Cisco IOS router functions, because the generic Cisco IOS commands usually don't have a GUI equivalent. The CLI format is also convenient for many readers who may already be very familiar with the Cisco IOS CLI. The GUI is more extensively covered in Chapter 13, "Cisco IPC Express General Administration and Initial System Setup," and Chapter 14, "Configuring and Managing Cisco IPC Express Systems."

The objective of this chapter is to give you a broad understanding of the options that Cisco CME provides. It's not meant to be an exhaustive manual on how to configure a Cisco CME system to meet every possible combination of network design circumstances you might encounter. System configuration is covered in Chapter 14. For the more sophisticated configurations, consult the detailed Cisco IOS feature and Cisco CME administration documentation available online at Cisco.com.

The less-complex configurations are generally simple to build, even using the CLI. At the same time, the broad range and component-level adaptability of the Cisco IOS software platform is available if required to deal with the complexity of real-life network situations. Hopefully by reading this chapter, you will at least have a good idea of what you're looking for when you decide to tackle the extensive Cisco IOS, voice over IP (VoIP), and Cisco CME documentation that's available online.

IP Phones and IP Phone Lines

IP phones may appear to be very similar in appearance to the digital phones used with a TDM-based PBX, at least on initial inspection. IP phones do behave in very similar ways for basic call operations. When you lift the handset, you hear dial tone. When an incoming call arrives, the phone rings. Phone users expect this behavior, which makes the introduction of IP phone technology as a replacement for traditional TDM-based telephony relatively painless for the vast majority of (nontechnical) phone users. In the case of traditional TDM-based telephony, the basis of the phone user interface is rooted in the physical structure of the typical digital TDM PBX. This in turn has its roots in the analog PBX systems that preceded it.

With IP telephony, some conscious and deliberate effort has gone into replicating the traditional phone user interface, because many of the historic engineering considerations that dictated design in the TDM PBX world are no longer applicable. This is well illustrated by considering the idea of "phone extensions" or "phone lines" for IP phones. In an analog PBX or Key System, the number of twisted-pair cables connected to the phone determines how many lines the phone has access to. If you want more phone lines, you have to add more wires. This is still mostly true for digital TDM phones. An example is a Basic Rate Inerface (BRI) phone with a twisted-pair cable carrying 2B + D—that is, two bearer channels (audio) plus one data channel (signaling).

For an IP phone, there is no direct relationship between the physical wiring and the number of lines that an IP phone supports. IP phones based on 100-Mbps Ethernet connections can theoretically support hundreds of phone lines. How many lines an IP phone supports is instead determined solely by the design of the phone user interface, not the physical connectivity to the system equipment cabinet. The user interface might be a traditional looking one that has a dedicated physical button for each *line* the phone supports. Alternatively, the IP phone might simply have a touch screen. In this case, the number of square inches available on the display may determine the maximum number of lines accessible to the user. Other variations on user interface design might include the use of pull-down menus or scroll bars to select a phone line. The extreme example of this is the PC softphone. A softphone is simply an application program running on a PC where you select a phone line from the PC display with a mouse click.

The next section describes how Cisco CME deals with phones and phone lines.

Cisco CME Ephone and Ephone-dn

In the Cisco CME product, an IP phone device is called an ephone (short for Ethernet phone). The phone lines that are associated with the ephone are called ephone-dn (Ethernet phone directory number [DN]). An ephone-dn is made up of the following two subcomponents:

- Virtual voice port
- Dial peer

The virtual voice port is the nearest direct equivalent to a physical phone line in a Cisco CME system. The virtual voice port is the object that maintains the call state (on-hook or off-hook). The dial peer is the object that determines the phone number associated with the virtual voice port. A dial peer can do many additional things besides control the virtual voice port's phone number, such as apply translations to called and calling numbers. A virtual voice port can be associated with multiple dial peers and, therefore, can have multiple phone numbers associated with it.

Figure 5-1 shows that ephone-dn 7 creates, or is associated with, virtual voice port 50/0/7 and a plain old telephone service (POTS) dial peer that references virtual voice port 50/0/7. The dial peer contains the voice port's phone number. It is used for call-routing purposes for incoming calls. The virtual voice port contains the station ID that sets the caller ID properties (name and number) for the ephone-dn (used for outgoing calls).

Figure 5-1   *Ephone-dn Components: Voice Port and Dial Peer*

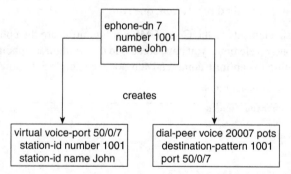

The terms dial peer and voice port are inherited from the Cisco IOS router voice infrastructure functions that have historically been used for applications such as VoIP gateways in toll-bypass networks (using protocols such as H.323, Session Initiation Protocol [SIP], and Media Gateway Control Protocol [MGCP]). In the router voice gateway context, a voice port typically refers to an interface that connects to the Public Switched Telephone Network (PSTN) (or PBX), but it also includes interfaces that directly connect to analog telephones. The behavior and usage of a virtual voice port is similar in many ways to a physical voice port used to connect to an analog telephone (specifically, a Foreign Exchange Station [FXS]). As a result of this similarity, you will see virtual voice ports called eFXS voice ports. In this terminology, the term eFXS means ephone-dn virtual FXS voice port.

You can configure a virtual voice port to have one or two subchannels. Each subchannel can accept a single voice call. This arrangement is similar to the two bearer channels present on an ISDN BRI voice port. An ephone-dn that is configured in dual-line mode creates a virtual voice port that can handle two simultaneous calls. The primary use of the dual-line option is to provide a simple way to handle features such as call waiting. The *dual-line* option also provides a way to support the second call instance required by features, such as third-party conferencing and call transfer with consultation.

When you select the dual-line option, the Cisco IP phone provides a rocker button or (blue) navigation bar that is used as a scroll key to select between two call instances presented on the IP phone display. For example, in the case of call waiting, the phone display shows you the active (connected) call and the waiting (ringing) call. You can press the hold softkey to place the active call on hold, use the navigation bar to scroll the IP phone display, and then select the answer softkey for the waiting call.

Alternatively, call waiting can be supported simply by using an IP phone that has two (or more) physical line buttons. In this case, you configure each button with a separate phone line instance (ephone-dn). Instead of configuring a single ephone-dn in dual-line mode, you configure two ephone-dns with the same phone number using the default ephone-dn single-line mode (and the **no huntstop** option, which you'll learn more about later, in the section "Cisco IOS Voice Dial Peer Hunting"). This provides a simpler and more traditional multiline user interface. You perform navigation between two simultaneous calls by simply pressing one of the line buttons to select the desired call. The previously active call is automatically placed on hold. This mode of operation is often called one *button*, one *call*.

The most basic elements of the Cisco CME configuration are the ephone and ephone-dn. You bind the ephone-dn elements you have created to the configured ephone entries using the button command within the **ephone** command submode. Example 5-1 shows a very simple example.

Example 5-1 *Simple Ephone-dn Configuration*

```
router#show running-config
ephone-dn 4 dual-line
        number 1001

ephone 7
        mac-address 000d.aa45.3f6e
        button 1:4
```

Example 5-1 shows a single IP phone (ephone 7) that is uniquely identified by its Ethernet MAC address (000d.aa45.3f6e). You can find the Ethernet MAC address on a sticker on the underside of your Cisco IP phone or from the phone's shipping carton label. In many cases, the MAC address can be autodiscovered after the phone is plugged into your Cisco CME router's LAN network. Example 5-1 also shows a dual-line ephone directory number (ephone-dn 4). This ephone-dn has telephone extension number 1001. Ephone-dn 4 is then associated or bound to the first line button of ephone 7 using the **button** command (**button 1:4**).

Example 5-2 shows a slightly expanded view of the CLI configuration in Example 5-1.

Example 5-2   *Expanded Ephone-dn Configuration*

```
router#show running-config
tftp-server flash:P00303020214.bin

ip dhcp pool cme
network 192.168.0.0 255.255.255.0
default-router 192.168.0.1
option 150 ip 192.168.0.1

interface FastEthernet0/1
   ip address 192.168.0.1 255.255.255.0
duplex auto
speed auto

telephony-service
   ip source-address 192.168.0.1
   load 7960-7940 P00303020214
   max-ephones 24
   max-dn 24
   create cnf-files

ephone-dn 4 dual-line
   number 1001

ephone 7
   mac-address 000d.aa45.3f6e
   button 1:4
```

The configuration shown in Example 5-2 is all that's needed to register your first IP phone provisioned with a single line button and to produce dial tone when you lift the handset. The only assumptions made here are that the phone is a Cisco 7960 IP Phone, that the phone firmware desired is the file P00303020214.bin, and that the firmware file is loaded into the router's Flash memory.

The **tftp-server**, **ip dhcp pool**, and **interface FastEthernet 0/1** commands shown are standard Cisco IOS CLI router commands that are outside the scope of this book, but you are most likely familiar with their basic function in the IP world. These commands are included just to provide a context for the Cisco CME-specific commands **ephone**, **ephone-dn**, and **telephony-service**.

Cisco CME also has a **telephony-service setup** command that you can use to bring up a set of phones and provide basic service. This command includes automatic creation of the Dynamic Host Configuration Protocol (DHCP) pool CLI entry if you need it.

Using a PBX Versus a Key System

The Cisco CME product addresses phone systems in the roughly 1-to-240-phone marketplace. This product spans the range from a small, independent, four-person professional services office (perhaps running on a Cisco 2801 router) to a mid-sized company to a large branch office of a multinational enterprise (running on a Cisco 3845 router). This marketplace has traditionally been addressed by a range of simple Key Systems (with perhaps two PSTN trunk lines and four extensions) to hybrid and small PBX systems (with multiple T1 Primary Rate Interface [PRI] digital PSTN interface trunks). Within this market space, the phone user interface expectations include simple one-extension per-phone configurations (usually with call waiting) to direct PSTN trunk appearance presence on all phones (any phone can answer any PSTN call).

The next sections describe typical deployments for PBX systems and Key Systems.

PBX Usage: One Phone Line and One Phone

In a typical PBX-like deployment, you expect to see digital PSTN trunk lines, with direct inward dial (DID) for direct access to individual phone extensions and one or more receptionists. The receptionist answers calls to the company's primary public phone number and transfers these calls to the individual phone users. Each phone user has his or her own private extension number (and probably also a personal voice mailbox to handle busy or unanswered calls). In this arrangement, each IP phone normally has only a single phone number associated with it. You saw a sample configuration for the one-phone-to-one-extension case in Example 5-1.

You are likely to see a few exceptions to the one-phone-to-one-extension rule, such as in the case of a company executive who has an assistant. In this case, the assistant's phone usually has two extension numbers—one shared with the executive (to allow the assistant to answer the executive's calls) and one personal extension for calls intended for the assistant. This configuration is shown in Example 5-3.

Example 5-3 *Two Extension Numbers Per Phone*

```
router#show running-config
ephone-dn 4 dual-line
   number 1001
   name Boss

ephone-dn 5 dual-line
   number 1002
   name Assistant

ephone 7
   mac-address 000d.aa45.3f6e
   button 1:4

ephone 8
   mac-address 000d.bb46.2e5a
   button 1:5 2:4
```

In Example 5-3, ephone 7 is the executive's phone, with extension 1001 on line button 1. Ephone 8 is the assistant's phone, with the assistant's personal extension 1002 on button 1 and the executive's extension 1001 shared on button 2. When a call arrives for 1001, both phones ring, and either phone can answer the call. When a call arrives for 1002, only the assistant's phone rings. When the executive is using extension 1001, the assistant's phone is unable to access the line. However, the display on the IP phone indicates that that line is in use so that the assistant knows that the executive is busy with a call.

Key System: One Phone Line and Many Phones

In the typical PBX environment described in the preceding section, an analysis of call traffic often shows that there are more internal extension-to-extension calls than external PSTN-to-extension calls. A result of this is the need for the one-person-to-one-phone-number configuration.

In a small four-person office, extension-to-extension calls may be nonexistent. It's often easier to walk over and speak to a coworker than it is to phone him or her. In this environment, calls are predominantly PSTN-to-extension. Furthermore, incoming PSTN calls are the lifeblood of the small company, because each call can potentially be from a customer.

In this environment, often there is no need for personal extension numbers. What is important in this case is that somebody always promptly answers the incoming PSTN calls. A small four-person company, however, often cannot afford to hire a dedicated telephone receptionist. Example 5-4 gives a sample configuration for this type of environment.

Example 5-4   *PSTN Lines on All Phones*

```
router#show running-config
ephone-dn 1
   number 4085550101
   no huntstop
   preference 0

ephone-dn 2
   number 4085550101
   preference 1

ephone 1
   mac-address 000d.aa45.3f6e
   button 1:1 2:2

ephone 2
   mac-address 000d.bb46.2e5a
   button 1:1 2:2

ephone 3
   mac-address 000d.cc47.1d49
   button 1:1 2:2

ephone 4
   mac-address 000d.dd48.0c38
   button 1:1 2:2
```

In Example 5-4, you see that ephone-dn 1 and ephone-dn 2 both have the same phone number. The phone number configured is the small company's (fictitious) public PSTN phone number. This is the number that is displayed on the IP phones and also the PSTN number that customers dial to reach the company. You can configure the Cisco CME router's PSTN interface to direct incoming PSTN calls to the first ephone-dn (for example, **connection plar opx** configured on an Foreign Exchange Office [FXO] port connected to the PSTN). If ephone-dn 1 is busy, calls automatically roll over to ephone-dn 2. To make this happen, you configure the ephone-dn with the same number, and then set explicit *preference* values to indicate the order for selection between the ephone-dns. The lower-preference 0 value attached to ephone-dn 1 indicates that ephone-dn 1 should be selected first. Also note that the **no huntstop** command gives the Cisco CME system permission to try to find an alternative destination for the incoming call if the first ephone-dn is busy. (You'll read more about huntstop in the section "Cisco IOS Voice Dial Peer Hunting.")

Note how easy it is to expand this basic two-by-four configuration to include more PSTN trunks and more IP phones. There is no specific limit on how many IP phones can share a single IP phone line. There is a limit on how many phone lines can be directly assigned to each IP phone. This limit is set by the number of available line buttons on the IP phone. For example, a Cisco 7960 IP Phone has six buttons, so you cannot directly assign more than six PSTN lines using the simple configuration method shown in Example 5-4. However, you can attach up to 60 lines to a 7960 IP Phone using a configuration option called **overlay-dn**. (You'll read more about this in the section "Using Overlay-dn.")

You can see from the examples that the simple binding arrangement between IP phone and IP phone lines creates a significant amount of flexibility. This allows the Cisco CME to support multiple styles of phone usage to meet different end-customer expectations. The PBX and Key System configuration styles are not mutually exclusive. You can combine configuration styles by simply adjusting the IP phone-to-IP phone line bindings as needed.

The one phone line and many phones configuration model applies much more broadly than just the four-person Key System example given here. Even within a larger company's phone system, there are cases in which the one phone line and many phones model is appropriate. One example is for a company loading dock, where you might have several hundred square feet of loading/unloading storage space in a shipping and receiving department. In this situation, you may find it desirable to place multiple phones so that they are spread out across a wide physical area. In addition, any phone can be used to place and receive calls on the same line.

Implementing Shared Lines and Hunt Groups

Although it is widely used, the term *hunt group* seems to mean different things to different people and in different contexts. It's a general term that covers the distribution of calls among a group of phones. In this chapter, the term call coverage refers to the general concept of call distribution across phones. This helps avoid confusion with the Cisco CME CLI command **ephone-hunt**. The **ephone-hunt** command is used to configure a specific kind of call coverage that involves sequential selection among a group of selected phone lines.

Many other types of call coverage are addressed with other commands, combinations of commands, and configurations. Examples include the use of shared lines, overlay-dn, call forwarding, secondary ephone-dn numbers, and combinations of these.

This section describes a number of different types of call coverage:

- Simple sequential ringing of a selected set of phone lines
- Ringing of multiple phone lines at the same time, referred to here as parallel hunting
- Call forwarding from one line to another using call forward on busy or no-answer
- Combination sequences that involve sequential ringing of multiple phone lines, referred to here as sequential parallel hunting

Notice that all these refer to ringing phone *lines*, not *phones*. Calls are sequenced through an ordered set of phone lines. Which phones ring depends on the binding of the lines to the phones. Each line can be bound to multiple phones.

The following sections discuss several types of call coverage.

Cisco IOS Voice Dial Peer Hunting

A good place to start a discussion of call coverage for Cisco CME is to look at the voice dial peer hunting mechanism that is a standard component of the Cisco IOS voice infrastructure. Dial peers have a very large number of configuration options. The most basic options are related to matching a telephone number and directing the call to a specific voice port or VoIP destination. More advanced options relate to number manipulation (using translation rules or translation profiles), application selection (including custom TCL scripts), protocol options (such as fax relay and dual-tone multifrequency [DTMF] relay), voice codec selection, and caller ID manipulation and restriction.

Some dial peer operations relate to selecting a dial peer associated with the call's originator (incoming dial peer matching) and selecting a dial peer associated with the call destination (outgoing dial peer matching). Multiple parameters can affect the selection of the incoming and outgoing dial peers, but the primary matching criteria are the called and calling party numbers.

Describing all the dial peer options in detail is outside the scope of this book; however, numerous books deal with this subject in more depth, including the following:

- *Deploying Cisco Voice over IP Solutions* by Jonathan Davidson (Cisco Press, 2001).
- *Cisco Voice over Frame Relay, ATM, and IP*, edited by Steve McQuerry, Kelly McGrew, and Stephen Foy (Cisco Press, 2001).

This section provides a simplified overview of dial peers to provide a basic understanding of some of the options that apply to call coverage—specifically, dial peer hunting. Example 5-5 shows two basic dial peers.

Example 5-5 *Two Basic Dial Peers*

```
router#show running-config
dial-peer voice 100 pots
   destination-pattern 1001
   port 1/0/0

dial-peer voice 200 voip
   destination-pattern 20..
   session target ipv4:10.0.4.2
```

The first dial peer (dial peer 100) is a POTS dial peer. This type of dial peer is used to reference a local telephony voice port connected to the router.

The second dial peer (dial peer 200) is a VoIP dial peer used to reference a remote telephony device accessed via IP, usually across a WAN data link.

Both dial peers have a **destination-pattern** parameter. This associates a telephone number or range of telephone numbers with the dial peer. In the VoIP dial peer, you can see that the destination pattern contains the wildcard character "." (to match any digit). In this example, the **destination-pattern 20..** command matches telephone numbers in the range 2000 to 2099.

Both dial peers associate a destination device with the phone number selected by the destination pattern. In the POTS dial peer case, the destination is a physical voice port on the router designated as **port 1/0/0**. Your router's exact port numbering may vary by router type and voice interface type, but the basic numbering structure is slot/card/port.

In the VoIP dial peer case, the destination is an IP address, as indicated by the session target ipv4:10.0.4.2 parameter.

In Example 5-5, you can see how a dial peer is used to associate a telephone number (or range) with a destination, either a voice port or an IP address.

The dial peer hunting function comes into play when you create two or more dial peers that match the same telephone number but reference different destination devices. You can set many parameters to adjust the order in which matching dial peers are selected. The default behavior is called *longest match*. For longest match, the dial peer that most exactly matches the telephone number is preferred. A longest match selects the destination pattern that matches the desired number using the fewest "." wildcard characters. The best kind of longest match is an exact match, where no wildcards are used and the destination pattern and telephone number match literally and exactly. This is often the case with POTS dial peers, where you assign a specific phone number to a specific port.

Example 5-6 shows a dial peer configuration that illustrates some of the matching capabilities.

Example 5-6   *Simple Dial Peers*

```
router#show running-config
dial-peer voice 101 pots
   destination-pattern 2001
   port 1/0/0

dial-peer voice 102 pots
   destination-pattern 2007
   port 1/0/1

dial-peer voice 200 voip
   destination-pattern 20..
   session target ipv4:10.0.4.2
```

In Example 5-6, two POTS dial peers associate the phone numbers 2001 and 2007 to (local) voice ports 1/0/0 and 1/0/1. All other numbers in the 2000 to 2099 range are associated with the VoIP dial peer and are resolved somewhere in the VoIP space. This configuration provides a simplified way of indicating that the numbers 2001 and 2007 are local numbers. The remaining numbers in the range 2000 to 2099—specifically, 2002 to 2006 and 2008 to 2099—are remote and can be accessed via VoIP.

As a result of the longest-match rule, a call to 2001 selects POTS dial peer voice 101 in preference to VoIP dial peer 200. This is because the destination pattern for dial peer 101 has an exact match to the called number 2001, whereas VoIP dial peer 200 uses "." wildcard digits to match 2001.

Example 5-7 shows a more complex configuration.

Example 5-7   *More Complex Dial Peers*

```
router#show running-config
dial-peer voice 101 pots
   destination-pattern 2001
   preference 1
   port 1/0/0

dial-peer voice 102 pots
   destination-pattern 2001
   preference 2
   port 1/0/1

dial-peer voice 200 voip
   destination-pattern 20..
   session target ipv4:10.0.4.2
```

In Example 5-7, you can see that the two POTS dial peers now both have the same number. Because both dial peers provide an exact match to the number 2001, the longest-match criteria cannot distinguish between them. You also see that the dial peers now have an extra parameter,

preference. The **preference** command is used to define a specific preference order for selecting the dial peers. The call to 2001 goes to the dial peer with the lowest preference value. The default preference value is 0.

In Example 5-7, when an incoming call to 2001 arrives, it first goes to POTS dial peer 101 with preference 1. Only if the port 1/0/0 associated with this dial peer is busy does the dial peer matching process hunt to the second dial peer 102 (preference 2). This provides the first basic mode of call coverage hunting: dial peer hunt on busy.

You may notice that there is a potential problem with the dial peer hunt-on-busy arrangement in this example: What if the second port is also busy? If ports 1/0/0 and 1/0/1 are both busy, the dial peer hunting mechanism takes the call to the next best available match. The next best match in this example is the VoIP dial peer 200. This dial peer matches the 2001 number, because it has a wildcard-based match range that spans the entire range 2000 to 2099. This range includes the number 2001.

In most cases, you do not want the call to hunt on busy into the VoIP dial peer, because (in this example) there is no resolution for the number 2001 in the VoIP space. If a call to 2001 gets routed to the VoIP destination, the call will fail with a cause code (returned by the remote VoIP system) indicating that the number 2001 does not exist. This condition returns a fast-busy tone (number not in service) indication to the caller. This is not the correct behavior. What is needed is to return a simple user busy tone indication to the caller.

You can solve this problem by adding the dial peer option **huntstop**, as shown in Example 5-8.

Example 5-8   *Huntstop in a Dial Peer*

```
router#show running-config
dial-peer voice 101 pots
   destination-pattern 2001
   preference 1
   port 1/0/0

dial-peer voice 102 pots
   destination-pattern 2001
   preference 2
   huntstop
   port 1/0/1


dial-peer voice 200 voip
   destination-pattern 20..
   session target ipv4:10.0.4.2
```

The **huntstop** command option tells the dial peer hunting mechanism not to try to find any further dial peer matches. Instead, the dial peer hunting stops at the dial peer containing the **huntstop** command. If no available voice port is found, it returns a busy tone to the caller.

Example 5-9 shows another variation using dial peers to manage call coverage.

Example 5-9   *Dial Peer Variation*

```
router#show running-config
dial-peer voice 101 pots
   destination-pattern 2001
   preference 1
   port 1/0/0

dial-peer voice 102 pots
   destination-pattern 2001
   preference 2
   huntstop
   port 1/0/1

dial-peer voice 102 pots
   destination-pattern 2007
   huntstop
   port 1/0/1
```

In Example 5-9, port 1/0/1 can be accessed by dialing 2001 or 2007. A call to 2001 first tries port 1/0/0. If this port is busy, it hunts to port 1/0/1. A call to 2007 goes directly to port 1/0/1.

Note that the default for the **huntstop** parameter under dial peer is for **huntstop** to be disabled. As you will see later (in the section "Cisco IOS Voice Dial Peer Hunting"), the default for **huntstop** when applied to the ephone-dn configuration is for **huntstop** to be enabled.

Ephone-dn Dial Peers and Voice Ports

The preceding section provided an overview of dial peers as used by the generic Cisco IOS voice infrastructure software. This section shows how Cisco CME uses dial peers to enable routing of calls to IP phones. The Cisco CME CLI configuration of IP phones and IP phone lines does not directly include dial peers or (virtual) voice ports. Instead, the dial peer and virtual voice port resources used by Cisco CME are hidden inside the **ephone-dn** command. This simplifies the configuration steps needed to create an IP phone line. It avoids the manual process of creating POTS dial peers to bind phone numbers to virtual voice ports.

Here is the original **ephone-dn** command from the beginning of this chapter, modified with a user name added and a specific dial peer preference included:

```
ephone-dn 4
   number 1001
   name John Smith
   preference 1
```

This **ephone-dn** command generates the configuration subelements shown in Example 5-10.

Example 5-10 *Ephone-dn Subelements*

```
router#show running-config
dial-peer voice 20004 pots
   destination-pattern 1001
   preference 1
   huntstop
   port 50/0/4

voice-port 50/0/4
   station-id number 1001
   station-id name John Smith
```

The **ephone-dn** command is more compact and saves you from entering some information twice, such as the number 1001. The **station-id** commands (under the **voice-port** command) set the caller ID properties (name and number) for the IP phone line. This establishes the calling party name and number for calls originated by the ephone-dn. Note that the dial peer destination pattern by itself is not a good way to set the caller ID information. This is because in the general case, you can have multiple POTS dial peers that reference the same voice port. Because each dial peer can specify a different destination pattern phone number for the voice port, you can see that attempting to imply the caller ID calling party number from the dial peer creates ambiguity. With multiple dial peers for the same voice port, determining which dial peer to choose to represent the calling party number is difficult. There are specific rules for incoming dial peer selection that select the calling party number from the dial peers, but these are outside the scope of this chapter. The dial peer destination pattern is used as the calling party number for calls from the voice port only if the **station-id** command is omitted from the voice port configuration. As you can see, the **ephone-dn** configuration takes care of this detail for you.

Note the presence of the **huntstop** command in the generated dial peer in Example 5-10. This is discussed in the section "Cisco IOS Voice Dial Peer Hunting."

Also note the (virtual) voice port numbering 50/0/4. The numbering convention varies by router type, but it's typically slot/card/port. The value 50 was arbitrarily chosen as the virtual "slot" number for the virtual voice ports just to avoid contention with the routers' physical network module slots. Currently, no routers (that support Cisco CME) have 50 physical slots, so there's no confusion with physical hardware slot numbers. The middle card number value is always 0. The port number, 4 in this example, matches the ephone-dn tag value (as in ephone-dn 4). The dial peer tag numbering (20004) is not significant, but it usually has some correlation to the ephone-dn tag number, which is 4 in this example.

The only place that the virtual voice port port number is significant is in the binding of the ephone-dn dial peer to the virtual voice port. In most cases, you never need to be aware of the virtual voice port port numbers in your Cisco CME system.

If you execute the IOS command **show running-config**, you see only the **ephone-dn** commands you have entered, not the dial peer and virtual voice port commands. This is because the

ephone-dn command automatically manages these subcommands for you, and there is no need for these to take up space in the router configuration. However, you can see the ephone-dn generated dial peers and virtual voice ports using the Cisco IOS commands **show dial-peer summary** and **show voice-port summary**.

The important point for you to understand here is that the dial peer and voice port configurations created by the ephone-dn do exist in the router configuration, even though they are not included in the output of **show running-config**. This point helps you understand how the Cisco CME configuration interacts with any general Cisco IOS voice infrastructure configuration that is included in your router, as well as for troubleshooting Cisco CME (covered in Part IV, "Maintenance and Troubleshooting").

Ephone-dn Secondary Number

The ephone-dn secondary number allows you to associate a second phone number with the same IP phone line. You can use this to create a simple hunt-on-busy configuration. This allows you to use the dial peer hunt-on-busy mechanism to make a call roll over from one line to another, even when the lines have different primary phone numbers. Example 5-11 shows an example.

Example 5-11 *Ephone-dn Secondary Number*

```
router#show running-config
ephone-dn 4
   number 1001 secondary 1007
   name John Smith
   preference 1 secondary 2
```

This **ephone-dn** command generates the configuration subelements shown in Example 5-12.

Example 5-12 *Ephone-dn Subelements*

```
router#show running-config
dial-peer voice 20004 pots
   destination-pattern 1001
   preference 1
   huntstop
   port 50/0/4

dial-peer voice 30004 pots
   destination-pattern 1007
   preference 2
   huntstop
   port 50/0/4

voice-port 50/0/4
   station-id number 1001
   station-id name John Smith
```

If you compare this with the earlier Example 5-7, you can begin to see how the **ephone-dn** command can leverage the IOS voice infrastructure dial peer hunting mechanism to provide simple call coverage. The configuration in this example causes incoming calls to both 1001 and 1007 to be routed to the IP phone line created by the **ephone-dn 4** command, provided that no other dial peer elements in the system preempt the call routing path with a destination pattern match that has a lower numeric preference value.

Example 5-13 shows how you can use the ephone-dn secondary number to create dial peers that provide a simple form of call coverage.

Example 5-13 *Ephone-dn Secondary Number*

```
router#show running-config
ephone-dn 4
    number 1001 secondary 1007
    name John Smith
    no huntstop
    preference 1 secondary 2

ephone-dn 5
    number 1007 secondary 1001
    name Jane Smith
    no huntstop
    preference 1 secondary 2
```

Example 5-14 shows the dial peers and voice port configurations that these commands generate.

Example 5-14 *Ephone-dn Subelements*

```
router#show running-config
dial-peer voice 20004 pots
    destination-pattern 1001
    preference 1
    no huntstop
    port 50/0/4

dial-peer voice 30004 pots
    destination-pattern 1007
    preference 2
    no huntstop
    port 50/0/4

dial-peer voice 20005 pots
    destination-pattern 1007
    preference 1
    no huntstop
    port 50/0/5

dial-peer voice 30005 pots
    destination-pattern 1001
    preference 2
    no huntstop
```

Example 5-14 *Ephone-dn Subelements (Continued)*

```
    port 50/0/4

voice-port 50/0/4
    station-id number 1001
    station-id name John Smith

voice-port 50/0/5
    station-id number 1007
    station-id name Jane Smith
```

With the configuration in Example 5-14, you can see that an incoming call to 1001 first goes to dial peer 20004 (preference 1) and tries virtual voice port 50/0/4 (for ephone-dn 4). If this port is busy, the call hunts on busy from dial peer 20004 to dial peer 30005 (preference 2) and tries virtual voice port 50/0/5 (for ephone-dn 5). In a similar manner, you can see that a call to 1007 first goes to ephone-dn 5 and then hunts to ephone-dn 4.

The dial peer hunting mechanism works only for hunt on busy. It does not provide hunting on no-answer timeout.

Note the use of the **no huntstop** command under ephone-dn. Without having this command present, the dial peer hunting stops at the first dial peer it reaches. The literal command text for **no huntstop** does not actually appear in the dial peers if you examine them using the **show dial-peer** Cisco IOS commands. This is because **no huntstop** is the default configuration for a dial peer, and default configuration items normally are not included in the IOS **show running-config** command display output. The **no huntstop** text is included in the preceding dial peer examples for clarity only. The **no huntstop** command is required under ephone-dn. This is needed to turn off the default ephone-dn configuration, which has huntstop enabled by default.

Using Call Forwarding for Call Coverage

In the examples of dial peer matching, you saw how calls can be distributed over a number of ephone-dn IP phone lines without changing the called number for the call. You can also use call forwarding to provide simple forms of call coverage. Cisco CME supports call forwarding for busy, no-answer, and unconditional (or call-forward all). When you use call forwarding to provide call coverage, the called number for the call changes. This can affect what is displayed on the IP phone receiving the forwarded call and entry into voice mail. Example 5-15 shows an example of a call forwarding configuration.

Example 5-15 *Call Forwarding*

```
router#show running-config
ephone-dn 4 dual-line
    number 1001
    name John Smith
    call-forward busy 1007
    call-forward noan 1007 timeout 20
```

continues

Example 5-15 *Call Forwarding (Continued)*

```
ephone-dn 5 dual-line
   number 1007
   name Jane Smith
   call-forward busy 1001
   call-forward noan 1001 timeout 20
```

In Example 5-15, you can see that John and Jane's phones are set to call forward on busy or no-answer (**noan**) to each other's phone. There's an issue with this configuration, because it potentially creates an infinite forwarding loop. If neither phone is answered, the call is repeatedly forwarded back and forth between the two phones until the caller hangs up.

You can limit the number of times the call forwarding loop is traversed by setting the **max-redirect** command under **telephony-services**. The **max-redirect** command has a range of 5 to 20 and a default value of five. This is a global command and limits call forwarding system-wide.

Using Shared Lines for Call Coverage

The previous examples showed you how to use the Cisco IOS voice infrastructure dial peer hunting mechanism to control the routing distribution of incoming calls across more than one line (virtual voice port). These examples assume that each different IP phone line is associated with a different IP phone. In this section, you learn how to distribute calls between multiple phones using only a single IP phone line. Example 5-16 uses a simple shared-line configuration to move a call between phones by dynamically moving the line ownership between phones instead of moving the call between lines.

Example 5-16 *Shared-Line Configuration*

```
router#show running-config
ephone-dn 1
   number 1001
   name John Smith

ephone-dn 2
   number 1002
   name Jane Smith

ephone-dn 3
   number 5001
   preference 1
   no huntstop
   name SalesLine1

ephone-dn 4
   number 5001
   preference 2
   name SalesLine2
```

Example 5-16 *Shared-Line Configuration (Continued)*

```
ephone 12
   mac-address 000d.1234.0efc
   button 1:1 2:3 3:4

ephone 15
   mac-address 000d.5678.0dcf
   button 1:2 2:3 3:4
```

Example 5-16 shows two IP phones. Ephone 12 belongs to John Smith and has John's personal phone line on button 1 (button 1:1). Ephone 15 belongs to Jane Smith and has Jane's personal phone line on button 1 (button 1:2). Note that the personal line on button 1 is the default line that's selected for outgoing calls when the phone's handset is taken off-hook (you can change this with the **auto-line** command).

Both phones have ephone-dns 3 and 4 associated with buttons 2 and 3. Ephone-dns 3 and 4 both have the same telephone number—5001. The ephone-dns are set up so that the first call to the sales line goes to ephone-dn 3. If ephone-dn 3 is busy, a second incoming call will dial peer hunt on busy to ephone-dn 4.

Both ephone-dns 3 and 4 are present on both IP phones so that calls to either ephone-dn ring both IP phones. John and Jane can see at a glance which lines are in use.

Either John or Jane's phone can answer the first incoming call to 5001 SalesLine1. The second call rolls over to 5001 SalesLine2 and also goes to both phones. The phone that is busy with the first call sees the second call as call waiting (and hears a call waiting beep, which can be disabled). The other phone rings.

Furthermore, John can place his call on hold. This makes the call fully visible to Jane because it is on a shared line, and she can pick up the call simply by pressing the corresponding line button on her phone. Note that in this case of shared line pickup on hold, the call does not change lines. Rather, the active ownership of the line moves between the phones. The call stays on the same line throughout the call.

Using Overlay-dn

The preceding section described a simple two-by-two arrangement in which two phones share two IP phone lines. This type of arrangement can be expanded to, say, four lines shared by eight phones. However, there is a limit on how far you can go with this arrangement. A Cisco 7960 IP Phone has only six line buttons, so the maximum number of lines that it can directly share is six. If you also consider that the line buttons on a Cisco 7960 IP Phone can also be configured for speed dial or other uses, such as personal extensions and intercoms, you can see that it's fairly easy to run out of buttons.

The Cisco CME overlay-dn configuration provides a way around the physical button limit for many cases.

Example 5-17 shows an alternative arrangement for John and Jane's phones that provides a simple example of an overlay-dn configuration.

Example 5-17 *Overlay-dns*

```
router#show running-config
ephone-dn 1
   number 1001
   name John Smith
ephone-dn 2
   number 1002
   name Jane Smith
ephone-dn 3
   number 5001
   preference 1
   no huntstop
   name SalesLine1
ephone-dn 4
   number 5001
   preference 2
   name SalesLine2
ephone 12
   mac-address 000d.1234.0efc
   button 1:1 2o3,4
ephone 15
   mac-address 000d.5678.0dcf
   button 1:2 2o3,4
```

The only thing that is different about this configuration relative to Example 5-16 is the **button** command **button 1:1 2o3,4**.

To configure a button for overlay use, you simply replace the colon **button:dn** separator with the letter *o*, for overlay. Following the **o** separator, you provide a list of two to ten ephone-dn tag numbers. You must have at least two ephone-dns in the overlay set to use the **o** separator.

You can see that this configuration uses only two buttons instead of the three buttons used originally. This leaves the additional buttons available for use as speed dial buttons, for example. Alternatively, you can use a lower-cost IP phone, such as the Cisco 7940 IP Phone, which has only two buttons instead of the six buttons of a Cisco 7960 IP Phone.

An overlay-dn arrangement works as a multiplexor. This works in a similar way to an old-fashioned printer-sharer device that allows multiple PCs to drive a shared printer.

When an incoming call arrives on one of the ephone-dns in the IP phone's button overlay set, the ephone-dn with the ringing call is multiplexed onto the appropriate button. At any time, only one ephone-dn in the overlay set is actively bound to the IP phone. When all ephone-dns in the overlay set are idle, the first ephone-dn in the set is the one that is actively bound to the phone. You can see this multiplexing activity using the **show ephone** command (examples of this are provided later in this book).

The ephone-dn is multiplexed into the active slot for the button when it needs to be used, as shown in Figure 5-2.

Figure 5-2   *Overlay-dn Multiplexes Multiple Lines to a Single Button*

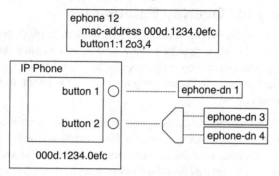

When an outgoing call is attempted on a button that is configured for an overlay, the first available idle ephone-dn in the overlay set is selected based on the left-to-right order of the ephone-dn tags used in the phone's **button** overlay command.

The one drawback of the overlay-dn configuration is that you cannot perform the shared-line pickup on hold operation described in Example 5-16. Also, overlay-dn lines do not provide call waiting indication when multiple calls are present in the overlay set. This is because with ten lines mapped to a single button, the number of waiting calls can be rather large and generate too many interruptions.

When you use the overlay-dn configuration in a shared-line configuration (as in this example), it is recommended that you have at least as many lines in the overlay set as there are phones sharing. If there are more phones than lines in the shared-line overlay, when all ephone-dns are in use, you can get situations where there is no available ephone-dn to multiplex onto a phone. There is no specific harm in this situation, except the user confusion that may result when a user presses the line button and does not get dial tone (because no line is available).

An IP phone can have as many overlay sets as it has buttons. Each overlay set on each button on each IP phone can contain a unique set of ephone-dn tags. If you apply a ten-way overlay set to each of the six buttons on a 7960 IP Phone, 60 ephone-dns can be associated to the phone.

You can use an overlay-dn to support multiple lines, even on a phone such as the Cisco 7912 IP Phone, which normally is considered a single-line phone. The key difference between a single-line phone with a six-way overlay and a six-button phone with one ephone-dn per button is in the ability to see and navigate between calls. With a six-way overlay onto a single-line phone, you can see the status of only one line at a time. You also have no direct choice over which of the six lines is being used. The overlay multiplex mechanism makes the choice for you. With a six-button phone, you can see all the calls at once, and select between them by pressing the line button for the call you want.

The section "Using Overlay to Overcome Phone Button Count Limits" has more information on using overlays.

Called Name Display for Overlay Extensions

In most cases, when you overlay multiple extensions onto a single button, the set of extensions included in the overlay set is usually closely related, so you often don't need to distinguish between the individual extensions in an overlay set. But if you assign multiple unrelated extensions to the same phone button using an overlay, the phone user needs to know which extension is being called.

Cisco CME 3.2 introduced the called-name dialed number identification service (DNIS) to address this problem. This uses the command **service dnis overlay** (set under **telephony-service**). If this command is active, an incoming call on the (hidden) second through last members of the overlay set displays the extension name that is being called on the bottom line of the Cisco IP phone display. This name is set using the **name** command in the ephone-dn extension configuration. This allows the phone user to see at a glance which extension is ringing and allows the phone user to answer the call with a greeting appropriate to the specific extension. When the first (primary) extension in the overlay set is called, no name display appears, because the identity of the first extension line is implicitly indicated by the extension number display next to the phone line button itself.

Another thing to note about overlays is that if you put an overlay call on hold, the phone displays the extension number of the specific extension from the overlay set. This is useful if you want to perform a call on-hold extension pickup using the phone's pickup softkey.

Called Name Display for Non-Overlay Extensions

If you want to see the called name in cases where you are not using an overlay, you can use the **service dnis dir-lookup** command (under **telephony-service**). This command is useful when you are taking calls from the PSTN using a digital PRI trunk configured to receive calls for a large block of numbers and where each number is associated with a separate person or company.

For example, consider a doctor's answering service, where an agent may be taking messages for a group of 30 different doctors and where each doctor has a different answering service phone number for patients. In this simple example, assume that all the phone numbers are part of a specific block of numbers, say 555-0500 to 555-0529.

It's easy to set up a single Cisco CME extension to accept these calls using the "." wildcard character as part of the extension number:

```
ephone-dn 20
  number 55505..
```

This takes care of routing the call to the right place, but it doesn't tell you which specific number is being called. To display the called name (for example, Dr. Smith for calls to 555-0500 or Dr.

Jones for calls to 555-0501), you enable the service **dnis dir-lookup** command and configure the phone number-to-name associations that you want using the **directory entry** command as follows:

```
telephony-service
   service dnis dir-lookup
   directory entry 1 5550500 name Dr. Smith
   directory entry 2 5550501 name Dr. Jones
```

You can create a list of up to 100 directory entries to be used in this way. With this configuration, an incoming call to 555-0500 rings ephone-dn 20 and displays Dr. Smith, whereas a call to 555-0501 displays Dr. Jones. This allows the agent who answers the call to greet the caller with "Dr. Smith's answering service" or "Dr. Jones's answering service," as appropriate.

The ephone-hunt Command

The **ephone-hunt** command gives you a simple way to configure a sequential call group based on a list of extension numbers. You can configure up to ten ephone-hunt groups in a Cisco CME system (as of CME 3.0). Each ephone-hunt group can contain a list of up to ten extension numbers. Note that you should make sure that the global **max-redirect** limit set for your system (under **telephony-service**) is higher than the maximum number of internal forwards needed by your hunt groups.

You can choose from three ephone-hunt modes:

- **Sequential mode**—This gives a simple ordered list of extension numbers. Each extension number in the list is tried in turn, always starting from the beginning of the list. If the end of the list is reached without finding an available number, the call is forwarded to a number configured as a final destination.

- **Peer mode**—This gives a circular list of extension numbers. The starting point in the list for a new call is set by the last number tried for the preceding call. Because the list is circular, you have to set a parameter to limit how many times a call can be sequenced from one extension to the next. This value has to be less than the global call forwarding hop count limit set for the entire Cisco CME system by the **max-redirect** command. You have to do this to avoid an infinite hunting loop. You control it by setting the maximum number of hops for the call in the **ephone-hunt** command's subcommands. As soon as the maximum number of hops has been reached, the call is forwarded to the number defined as the final destination for the hunt group.

- **Longest idle**—This also gives a circular list of extension numbers. The starting point in the list for a new call is set by the number that has been on-hook for the longest period of time. Again, because the list is circular, you have to set a parameter to limit how many times a call can be sequenced from one extension to the next. As soon as the maximum number of hops has been reached, the call is forwarded to the number defined as the final destination for the hunt group. The longest idle option was introduced in Cisco CME 3.2.

Example 5-18 provides a configuration for these modes.

Example 5-18 *ephone-hunt* Command

```
router#show running-config
ephone-hunt 1 sequential
    pilot 5001
    list 1001, 1003, 1007, 1008
    final 6001
    preference 1
    timeout 15

ephone-hunt 2 peer (or longest-idle)
    pilot 5002
    list 1002, 1003, 1008, 1009
    final 6002
    hops 3
    preference 1
    timeout 15
```

If you look at the two **ephone-hunt** commands in Example 5-18, you can see that some of the extension numbers are present in both ephone-hunt lists. This illustrates one of the advantages of ephone-hunt. In the previous examples, hunting to the IP phone ephone-dn lines is based on binding telephone numbers directly to the ephone-dns themselves. Because you can directly bind only two numbers per ephone-dn (the primary and secondary numbers), you are limited in how many simultaneous ways you can route calls to the ephone-dn.

In Example 5-13, you saw how both phones could be called using the numbers 1001 and 1007. This was done using the ephone-dn secondary number of the individual ephone-dns. You cannot add a third phone using this technique.

Example 5-17, which uses an overlay-dn, allows for greater expansion, but at the expense of consuming additional ephone-dns (at about 50 *KB* of memory per ephone-dn).

The other issue with using hunt numbers directly associated with the ephone-dns is that the call hunting path goes directly through each ephone-dn. This means that if you set any type of call forwarding on the ephone-dn (forward all, on busy, or no-answer), this forwarding affects the call hunt path too.

This is not true when you use the **ephone-hunt** command. You can set call forwarding on the individual ephone-dn without affecting the call hunt path defined by the ephone-hunt list.

When you use the **ephone-hunt** command and enter a list of numbers, here's what happens:

- The system searches for all ephone-dn entries that have primary numbers that match the ephone-hunt list.

- For each ephone-dn that matches, the ephone-dn builds an additional dial peer. This dial peer has a number that's derived from the ephone-hunt pilot number plus the relative position of the matched number in the ephone-hunt list. The dial peer also includes the virtual voice port number from the matching ephone-dn.

When you configure call forwarding under ephone-dn, the call forwarding information is inserted into the dial peers that are directly bound to the ephone-dn. The call forwarding information is not included in the dial peers created by the **ephone-hunt** command.

You also notice that the ephone-hunt command lets you set a preference value. As you might expect, this is a dial peer preference. The dial peer preference is inserted into the dial peer that is created by ephone-hunt to match the ephone-hunt pilot number.

For the **ephone-hunt** configuration examples shown, at least five dial peers are created. One dial peer is created for the pilot number. One dial peer is created for each ephone-dn that is found that matches one of the numbers in the list. If multiple ephone-dns match the individual numbers in the list, each of those ephone-dns causes the creation of an additional dial peer.

Here is a description of what you see for ephone-hunt 1 in Example 5-18:

- The pilot number creates a dial peer with destination pattern 5001. This dial peer has call forward all set to the first dial peer in the hunt list.

- The first member of the list creates a dial peer with destination pattern A5001A0001. This dial peer contains the virtual voice port number of the ephone-dn that has 1001 as its primary number. This dial peer has call-forward busy and call-forward no-answer set to the next ephone-hunt dial peer. The call-forward timeout value is set by the **timeout** subcommand under **ephone-hunt**.

- The second member of the list creates a dial peer with destination pattern A5001A0002. This dial peer contains the virtual voice port number of the ephone-dn that has 1003 as its primary number. This dial peer has call-forward busy and call-forward no-answer set to the next ephone-hunt dial peer.

- The third member of the list creates a dial peer with destination pattern A5001A0003. This dial peer contains the virtual voice port number of the ephone-dn that has 1007 as its primary number. This dial peer has call-forward busy and call-forward no-answer set to the next ephone-hunt dial peer.

- The fourth and final member of the list creates a dial peer with destination pattern A5001A0004. This dial peer contains the virtual voice port number of the ephone-dn that has 1008 as its primary number. This dial peer has call-forward busy and call-forward no-answer set to the number defined as the final destination for the ephone-hunt.

The digit A in the destination pattern is the DTMF digit A from the extended set of DTMF digits A to D. The digits A to D are routable digits within the Cisco IOS voice infrastructure software and can be used just like the digits 0 to 9 and *. The digit # is often used as a dial digit string terminator.

You can view all the dial peers created by the **ephone-hunt** command using the Cisco IOS command **show dial-peer voice summary**. Example 5-19 shows the dial peers associated with ephone-hunt 1 in Example 5-18.

Example 5-19   *Ephone-hunt 1 Dial Peers*

```
router#show dial-peer voice summary
TAG     TYPE ADMIN OPER DEST-PATTERN PREF   SESS-TARGET
20051   pots up    up   1001         0      50/0/1
20053   pots up    up   1003         0      50/0/3
20057   pots up    up   1007         0      50/0/7
20058   pots up    up   1008         0      50/0/8
20069   pots up    up   A5001A000    1      50/0/1
20070   pots up    up   5001         1      50/0/1
20071   pots up    up   A5001A001    1      50/0/3
20072   pots up    up   A5001A002    1      50/0/7
20073   pots up    up   A5001A003    1      50/0/8
```

The SESS-TARGET column shows the virtual voice port numbers that correspond to ephone-dns 1, 3, 7, and 8.

Using Ephone-dn Dual Line

The several previous call coverage examples included ephone-dns configured in the default single-line mode. This helps keep the examples relatively simple. If you use ephone-dn dual-line mode, you should consider how you want to treat call waiting calls.

When you create an ephone-dn configured as dual line, you provide the ephone-dn with a virtual voice port that has two subchannels so that it can accept two simultaneous calls. This operates in a similar manner to an ISDN BRI voice port that has two bearer channels. By default, for a dual-line ephone-dn, when the first subchannel is busy with an active call, a second call is routed onto the second channel.

This behavior is usually not wanted in a hunt group. You normally want the second call to go to the next member of the hunt group instead of being present as a waiting call on the first member.

If you configure the ephone-dn as a single line, you don't need to worry about this behavior. In this case, no second channel exists, so there is no choice but for the second call to go to the next hunt group member.

To prevent the presentation of call waiting calls in a hunt group situation, you should use the command **huntstop channel**. This command can be used independently of, and in addition to, the plain **huntstop** command. The **huntstop channel** command prevents incoming calls from hunting on busy from the first virtual voice port channel to the second channel. It does not affect hunting between dial peers. It influences channel hunting only within the voice port. The **huntstop channel** command can be used in any dual-line ephone-dn. Its use is not restricted to ephone-hunt.

The effect of the **huntstop channel** command is to prevent incoming calls from reaching the second channel of a dual-line ephone-dn. This effectively reserves the second channel for outgoing calls from the ephone-dn. This can be used to guarantee the availability of the second channel to support the second call instance required for features such as three-party conference and call transfer with consultation.

If you use ephone-dn configured as dual line within a hunt group situation, it is recommended that you also use the **huntstop channel** command, as shown in Example 5-20.

Example 5-20   huntstop channel *Command*

```
router#show running-config
ephone-dn 1 dual-line
    number 1001
    huntstop channel
ephone-dn 3 dual-line
    number 1003
    huntstop channel
ephone-dn 7 dual-line
    number 1007
    huntstop channel
ephone-dn 8 dual-line
    number 1008
    huntstop channel
ephone-hunt 1 sequential
    pilot 5001
    list 1001, 1003, 1007, 1008
    final 6001
    preference 1
    timeout 15
```

Hunting Chains

Cisco CME provides a flexible set of mechanisms to support call coverage. These mechanisms are based on creating dial peers that are linked using hunt-on-busy arrangements and call forwarding.

The **ephone-hunt** command includes the option to set a final destination to forward calls to, when all hunt group members are busy. The number you forward to is itself resolved by another dial peer somewhere in the system. There is no restriction on the nature of the dial peer this number is linked to. The dial peer selection for the final number is based on the normal Cisco IOS voice infrastructure rules, taking into consideration criteria such as longest match and dial peer preference.

You can set the final destination of one ephone-hunt group to be the pilot number of a second ephone-hunt. The only restriction to consider is that the total number of times a call is forwarded cannot exceed the maximum set by the **max-redirect** command (under **telephony-service**). This has an allowed range of 5 to 20. You must count the internal forwarding hops included in each ephone-hunt when you figure the forwarding limit.

Also note that there is no restriction on the ephone-dn configuration matched by the ephone-hunt list. The ephone-dns matched to the ephone-hunt list can be part of more complex configurations. For example, you can use shared lines and overlay-dn as matches for the ephone-hunt list. This lets you create some very complex call coverage arrangements, including arrangements that perform sequential-parallel hunting, in which different groups of phones ring in a defined linear or circular sequence.

One final point here is that setting **call-forward all** for an ephone-dn that is part of a hunt group does not break the hunt group forwarding sequence. This is because the call-forward all is applied only to the ephone-dn's main dial peer, not to the subsidiary dial peers that are generated by the **ephone-hunt** command. To temporarily remove a phone from a hunt group, you simply put the phone into Do-Not-Disturb mode (the Cisco CME 3.2 DND feature).

Immediate Diversion of Calls to Voice Mail

In earlier sections, you saw the use of the **call-forward busy** and **call-forward noan** (no answer) commands to control call forwarding of calls for busy and no-answer extensions. In many cases, the number the call is forwarded to is the pilot number for a voice mail system.

Cisco CME 3.2 and later allows the person receiving a call to cause the incoming call to be forwarded immediately without having to wait for the no-answer timer to expire. (This is applicable only on Cisco IP phones that have softkeys.) When an incoming call is presented, the phone user sees two softkeys: answer and DND (Do Not Disturb). If the user's phone has call-forward no-answer configured, pressing the DND softkey causes the incoming call to be forwarded immediately to the number configured for call-forward no-answer (typically the voice mail number).

If no call-forward no-answer is configured for the extension, pressing the DND key simply mutes the phone's ringer until the call is cancelled (by the caller hanging up). The ringer mute DND action is temporary and applies only to the current call when used in the manner described. The phone can also be placed in a permanent muted ringer state by pressing the DND softkey while the phone is in the idle state. This allows the phone user to screen incoming calls, because the phone display is still active and shows the caller ID for incoming calls. If a phone user wants to avoid all incoming calls, you can use the cfwdall (call forward all) softkey to set up unconditional forwarding of incoming calls to voice mail (or another extension). In this case, there is no indication of incoming calls on the user's phone.

Call Coverage Summary

This section has described a wide array of techniques for providing call coverage solutions. You can use the dial peer hunting mechanisms provided by the Cisco IOS voice infrastructure features. You can use call forwarding. You can use the ephone-hunt mechanism. You also have the option of using overlay-dn. You may combine several of these options to produce complex call coverage paths.

Creating an Intercom

Cisco CME supports single-button push-to-talk and push-to-respond intercom lines. You can create an intercom arrangement between any two (multiline) IP phones that support speakerphone operation. You can even operate an intercom across a VoIP connection using either SIP or H.323. Cisco CME's intercom function is built using two functions:

- Autodial at the initiating end of the intercom
- Autoanswer-with-mute at the receiving end

To create an intercom you assign a line button on each of the two phones to operate as an intercom line. Pressing the intercom line button selects the line and triggers the autodial function toward the second phone. The receiving phone receives the incoming intercom call on its intercom line. This line autoanswers the call and activates the phone in speakerphone mode and sounds a beep. It also forces the speakerphone to mute to protect the privacy of the intercom recipient. The audio path is open from the initiator to the receiver. To respond to the intercom, the recipient simply presses the mute button to unmute the audio path back to the originator.

The intercom Command

Example 5-21 shows a configuration of an intercom between two IP phones.

Example 5-21   *Intercom Lines*

```
router#show running-config
ephone-dn 1 dual-line
   number 1001
   name John Smith
ephone-dn 2 dual-line
   number 1002
   name Jane Smith
ephone-dn 3
   number 1111
   intercom 1112 label Jane
ephone-dn 4
   number 1112
   intercom 1111 label John
ephone 12
   mac-address 000d.1234.0efc
   button 1:1 2:3
ephone 15
   mac-address 000d.5678.0dcf
   button 1:2 2:4
```

Example 5-21 shows two phones. John's phone has button 1 as his primary extension line. Button 2 on John's phone is an intercom line. This line is set to autodial Jane's phone using the number 1111. The button is labeled "Jane" to show that pressing the button intercoms to Jane.

The intercom lines are configured in the default single-line mode.

Jane's phone is configured to match to John's phone. Button 1 on Jane's phone is her primary line. Button 2 is set to autodial John's phone and shows the label "John" next to the button. The default configuration for an intercom line is that it autoanswers with mute for any incoming call. Autoanswer can be disabled if desired using the **no-auto-answer** command option.

Example 5-21 shows a fully symmetric two-way intercom arrangement. John can intercom to Jane, and Jane can intercom to John.

Individual phones may have more than one intercom. The maximum number of intercoms per phone is limited only by the number of available buttons. In general, using intercoms on single-line phones such as the Cisco 7910, 7905, and 7912 is not recommended. These phones do not have a built-in (hands-free) microphone and, therefore, cannot be unmuted without lifting the phone's handset.

Many-to-One Intercom

In the previous example you saw that an intercom line autoanswers *any* incoming call. The incoming intercom does not perform any type of cross-check on the calling party to ensure that it matches the outgoing intercom destination. This arrangement lets you create a many-to-one intercom, which is useful when you have a single shared assistant working for multiple executives, as shown in Example 5-22.

Example 5-22 *Shared-Line Intercom*

```
router#show running-config
ephone-dn 1 dual-line
    number 2101
    name Executive1
ephone-dn 2 dual-line
    number 2102
    name Executive2
ephone-dn 3 dual-line
    number 2103
    name Executive3
ephone-dn 4 dual-line
    number 2201
    name Assistant
ephone-dn 5
 number 1110
    intercom 1110 label Intercom
ephone-dn 6
    number 1111
    intercom 1110 label Intercom
ephone-dn 7
    number 1112
```

Example 5-22 *Shared-Line Intercom (Continued)*

```
   intercom 1110 label Intercom
ephone-dn 8
   number 1113
   intercom 1110 label Intercom
ephone 12
   mac-address 000d.1234.0efc
   button 1:1 2:6
ephone 13
   mac-address 000d.5678.0dcf
   button 1:2 2:7
ephone 14
   mac-address 000d.4321.0ef7
   button 1:3 2:8
ephone 15
   mac-address 000d.4132.f7e4
   button 1:4 2:5
```

In Example 5-22, ephones 12 to 14 belong to the three executives 2101 to 2103. The fourth phone, ephone 15, belongs to the assistant. Each of the four phones has its primary line associated with button 1. The second buttons on the three executive phones are configured to intercom to the assistant's intercom line. This configuration provides a many-to-one intercom. Any of the executives can press the button 2 intercom on his or her phone to talk to the assistant. Of course, only one intercom conversation can exist at one time.

Note that the assistant's intercom (ephone-dn 5) is set to autodial itself. It is not possible to create a one-to-many intercom path. The assistant's phone could also be configured to autodial one of the executives.

One-Way Intercoms

In the previous many-to-one intercom example, you saw that the assistant's intercom is configured as a one-way or receive-only intercom. This is done by configuring the intercom line to autodial itself. When the assistant presses the intercom button, he or she hears busy tone.

You can use this technique to configure a one-way intercom even in a simple one-to-one intercom arrangement. A better configuration for a one-way, one-to-one intercom is to use the **noautoanswer** command option, as shown in Example 5-23.

Example 5-23 *One-to-One Intercom*

```
router#show running-config
ephone-dn 1 dual-line
   number 2101
   name Executive
ephone-dn 4 dual-line
   number 2201
   name Assistant
ephone-dn 5
```

continues

Example 5-23 *One-to-One Intercom (Continued)*

```
      number 1110
      intercom 1111 label Intercom
ephone-dn 6
      number 1111
      intercom 1110 label Intercom no-auto-answer
ephone 12
      mac-address 000d.1234.0efc
      button 1:1 2:6
ephone 15
      mac-address 000d.4132.f7e4
      button 1:4 2:5
```

With this arrangement, you still have a direct one-to-one dedicated line between the executive and the assistant. Only the assistant's phone autoanswers incoming calls presented to its intercom line. If the assistant presses the intercom line, the phone still autodials the executive's intercom line. The executive's phone simply rings as for a normal call.

Dialable and Private Intercoms

All the previous intercom examples in this chapter show intercoms configured with ordinary extension numbers. This means that you can dial into the intercom lines from any phone, not just the phones configured for intercom. You can even put the intercom numbers into the Cisco CME system directory or speed-dial lists.

You can make the intercom more restrictive by using the extended DTMF digits A–D as part of the intercom phone number. Because IP phones do not have the A–D DTMF digit keys available on their keypads, if the phone number includes A–D digits, it cannot be dialed from an ordinary phone.

Example 5-24 shows how to restrict intercom numbers so that they cannot be dialed from an ordinary telephone.

Example 5-24 *Nondialable Intercom*

```
router#show running-config
ephone-dn 1 dual-line
    number 2101
    name Executive
ephone-dn 4 dual-line
    number 2201
    name Assistant
ephone-dn 5
    number A110
    intercom A111 label Intercom
ephone-dn 6
    number A111
    intercom A110 label Intercom
ephone 12
```

Example 5-24 *Nondialable Intercom (Continued)*

```
    mac-address 000d.1234.0efc
    button 1:1 2:6
ephone 15
    mac-address 000d.4132.f7e4
    button 1:4 2:5
```

In this example, you see that the intercom numbers are set to A110 and A111 using the DTMF A digit as the first digit. This technique is also useful if you are using a dial plan that has only two- or three-digit phone numbers. Use of the extra A–D digits for intercom can free up space in the normal number range for use on regular extension numbers.

Courtesy Phone

A *courtesy phone* is a phone in a publicly accessible area. The phone is allowed to make calls only to internal numbers, such as calls from a lobby, to request assistance. The phone is not allowed to make calls directly to other extensions or to make external calls.

You can create a courtesy phone using the Cisco CME intercom feature. If you configure a multiline phone with normal extensions and intercom extensions, the phone automatically selects the first available normal extension when you lift the phone handset. The phone never auto selects the intercom line, even if all available normal extension lines are in use (for example, by shared phones).

You can configure an IP phone with only a single line where that single line is an intercom. In this case, when you lift the handset off-hook, the only possible line selection is the intercom line. This line is selected, and the phone autodials to the configured intercom destination. You can use this configuration technique to create a courtesy phone that always dials a fixed destination when the phone is taken off-hook.

Using Private Lines

Similar in some ways to the courtesy phone application for the **intercom** command, Cisco CME 3.2 introduces the FXO **trunk** command. This can be used to provide an emulation of a dedicated private PSTN line for a specific phone user. This allows Cisco CME to create the user appearance that one of the buttons on a Cisco IP phone is directly connected to a specific PSTN subscriber line (usually a dedicated FXO port connected to a specific PSTN phone number). One potential application for this is in a bank branch office where the bank manager has an internal extension number for regular calls (perhaps forwarded to the manager by a receptionist) plus a direct private line used for important clients. The private line also has voice mail service provided by the PSTN. This provides message waiting indication (MWI) by way of a stutter dial tone. To hear the MWI indication, the manager selects the private line and hears dial tone provided by the PSTN.

Example 5-25 shows how the trunk command is used to create a private line on an IP phone.

Example 5-25 *FXO* **trunk** *Command*

```
router#show running-config
voice-port 1/0/0
    connection plar-opx 1082
dial-peer voice 82 pots
    destination-pattern 82
    port 1/0/0
ephone-dn 10
    number 1010
    name manager
ephone-dn 11
    number 1082
    name private-line
    trunk 82
ephone 1
    button 1:10 2:11
```

Example 5-25 shows ephone 1 configured with two lines. Button 1 is a normal extension (number 1010) using ephone-dn 10. Button 2 is the private line using ephone-dn 11. Incoming PSTN calls on FXO port 1/0/0 are routed directly to ephone 11 (extension number 1082) by the **connection plar-opx 1082** command that is shown under **voice-port 1/0/0**.

Outgoing calls on the private line are routed to voice port 1/0/0 by the **trunk 82** command within ephone-dn 11. This causes all calls dialed on ephone-dn 11 to have the digits 82 prefixed to the dialed number. The 82 prefix causes the calls to match to the **destination-pattern 82** in dial peer 82 and, thus selects voice port 1/0/0 for the outbound call.

When the phone user dials the number, such as 555-0510, the **trunk** command prefixes the digits 82 to create the number 825550510. The leading digits 82 match the destination pattern for the voice port dial peer. The leading 82 digits are stripped off, and the remaining digits, 5550510, are forwarded to the PSTN line. Note that in some cases, you may need to adjust the time delay before the digits are passed to the PSTN line to avoid their being sent before the PSTN line is ready to accept them. You can do this using the **prefix** command (under the POTS dial peer) and using commas to insert 1-second units of delay. For example, the command **prefix ,,** inserts 2 seconds of delay.

The appearance that the phone button is directly connected to the FXO port's PSTN line is obtained by means of the one-to-one association that's created by the combination of the **connection plar-opx** binding of the FXO port to the ephone-dn, plus the **trunk** binding of the ephone-dn back to the FXO port. Because of this arrangement, whenever the FXO port is in use, it follows that the ephone-dn is also in use. Therefore, the ephone-dn's status reflects the FXO port's status.

To maintain this direct one-to-one binding, call operations that could break the one-to-one binding are disabled by the **trunk** command. This means that functions such as call transfer and call forwarding are not supported when the trunk configuration is used. However, functions such as call hold and conference are supported, including the ability to join two ephone-dn trunk lines in a three-party conference.

You can use the **trunk** command and **connection plar-opx** command independent of each other. For example, you can create other private line-like call behaviors where incoming calls are directly routed to a specific extension using the **connection plar-opx** command but outgoing calls use the common "Dial 9 for an outside line" approach.

Paging

You can set up a Cisco CME system to provide audio paging using the speakers of your IP phones to broadcast the paging audio output. This feature works in conjunction with IP phones that have a speakerphone mode. Only IP phones that are idle are used to output paging audio. IP phones can still be used to make or receive calls during paging. When the phone is used, it simply drops out of the page.

You can create paging groups or zones that output paging audio only on specific groups of IP phones. You can also combine multiple paging groups to output audio paging to multiple paging groups at the same time.

Using your IP phones to provide an audio paging system can save the additional cost of installing a separate overhead audio paging system. If you already have a conventional overhead audio paging system, you can also use this with Cisco CME. You simply need an available physical voice port on your router that can connect to the paging system. Ear and mouth (E&M) voice ports are the easiest to use because they do not usually require external adapter hardware. Because E&M ports usually come in pairs, you can also use the second E&M port as an input to connect to an external music on hold audio source.

The following sections describe how you can use the Cisco CME paging features.

Paging Groups

To configure an IP phone-based paging group, you first set up an ephone-dn entry in your system to act as the pilot number for the paging group. Like most of the special-purpose ephone-dns you create for your Cisco CME system, the paging ephone-dn is not directly bound to any of your IP phones. You don't use this ephone-dn in a **button** command.

The paging group pilot number is the number you dial from a phone to output audio to the paging group. A sample configuration is shown in Example 5-26. Note that you can dial into a paging group from any phone, including via a VoIP connection. You can also set up speed-dial buttons on your IP phones to dial into the paging number for one-button push-to-page operation.

Example 5-26 *Paging Pilot Number Configuration*

```
router#show running-config
ephone-dn 14
   number 6112
   name Sales
   paging ip 239.1.1.1 port 2000
```

The paging-dn is set up with a pilot number of 6112. When you make a call to 6112, it is answered by the paging-dn. The audio stream from your phone to the paging-dn is broadcast to all the phones in the paging group for ephone-dn 14 using IP Multicast on address 239.1.1.1 and port 2000.

As soon as you have created your paging-dn, you then create a group of IP phones to include in your paging group, as shown in Example 5-27. You do this using the **paging-dn** command within the ephone command mode. Set the **paging-dn** command in the ephone command mode to select the tag number of the ephone-dn that you configured as a paging-dn (14 in this example).

Example 5-27 *Paging on IP Phones*

```
router#show running-config
ephone 12
   mac-address 000d.1234.0efc
   button 1:1 2:6
   paging-dn 14
ephone 15
   mac-address 000d.4132.f7e4
   button 1:4 2:5
   paging-dn 14
```

With the configuration shown in Example 5-27, when you dial the number 6112 from any phone, the speakerphone on ephones 12 and 15 activates, provided that the phones are idle and the audio from the call is IP Multicast to both phones and output via the speakerphone.

There is no limit on the number of IP phones that can be included in a paging group. There is no specific limit on the number of paging-dns and corresponding paging groups you can create. Each paging group consumes one of the finite number of ephone-dns in your Cisco CME system. You can create individual paging groups for each department in your organization — for example, sales, accounts, and service.

Each IP phone can belong directly to only a single paging group. You can enter only one **paging-dn** configuration per ephone.

Combining Paging Groups

After you have created the individual paging groups, you can combine up to ten paging groups. You use the **paging group** command followed by a list of the **paging-dn** tag numbers you want to include in the group. Example 5-28 shows how two paging groups are combined.

Example 5-28   *Using the* **paging group** *Command*

```
router#show running-config
ephone-dn 14
   number 6112
   name Sales
   paging ip 239.1.1.2 port 2000
ephone-dn 16
   number 6113
   name Accounts
   paging ip 239.1.1.3 port 2000
ephone-dn 17
   number 6120
   name Sales&Acccounts
   paging ip 239.1.1.20 port 2000
   paging group 14,16
ephone 12
   mac-address 000d.1234.0efc
   button 1:1
   paging-dn 14
ephone 15
   mac-address 000d.4132.f7e4
   button 1:2
   paging-dn 14
ephone 19
   mac-address 000d.5678.13f4
   button 1:24
   paging-dn 15
ephone 21
   mac-address 000d.8765.23e5
   button 1:27
   paging-dn 15
```

In Example 5-28, you can see that **paging-dn** in **ephone-dn 14** creates the paging group for the sales department with pilot number 6112. This group contains ephones 12 and 15. Ephone-dn 16 creates the paging group for the accounts department with pilot number 6113. This group contains ephones 19 and 21.

The combined paging group is created by ephone-dn 17. It uses the pilot number 6120. This combines the paging groups of paging-dn ephone-dns 14 and 16 by listing the ephone-dn tag values after the **paging group** command.

When you call the pilot number 6120 for the combined group, all four of the IP phones are used to output the paging audio. Note that each paging-dn uses a different multicast IP address. Using different IP Multicast addresses for each paging group allows you to have simultaneous paging to different groups. In this example, it allows you to have unrelated paging to the sales and accounts department at the same time.

Multicast Routing for Paging

An IP Multicast address is any IP address in the range 224.0.0.0 to 239.255.255.255. However, you cannot use the 224.x.x.x address range, because it is typically reserved, and most Cisco IP phones do not accept IP Multicast streams in this range. For most normal use, the IP Multicast address range 239.x.x.x is recommended. This address range is locally scoped and is not routed outside your network. The details of IP Multicast routing are more formally defined in RFC 1112, *Host Extensions for IP Multicasting*.

For simple Cisco CME systems where all your IP phones are connected to the same local LAN, you do not need to configure your router(s) for multicast routing to use the Cisco CME paging mechanism. The Cisco CME software takes care of directing multicast packets to the appropriate local Ethernet interface(s) that connect to your IP phones. Because the IP phones maintain SCCP communication with CME over TCP/IP, the Cisco CME router has direct knowledge of the locations of the phones and, therefore, does not need to rely on multicast routing mechanisms to distribute IP Multicast packets. If you have a small number of IP phones that are not directly connected to the Cisco CME router local LAN, you can still include these in paging by configuring individual IP phones to use unicast paging. Add the **unicast** option to the phone's paging configuration under the **ephone** command, as shown in Example 5-29.

Example 5-29 *Unicast Paging*

```
router#show running-config
ephone 12
   mac-address 000d.1234.0efc
   button 1:1
   paging-dn 14 unicast
```

You can have up to ten unique output destinations in a paging audio IP stream, where a destination is either a router interface (Ethernet port) or a phone's unique IP (unicast) address. This means that if the multicast IP audio stream is sent out on only a single Ethernet port for the benefit of the majority of your phones, you may additionally include up to nine nonmulticast phone destinations using individual unicast paging.

For more complex local networks that involve multiple routing hops, you most likely need to configure multicast routing on the routers that are located between the Cisco CME router and your IP phones.

Implementing Overlays

The Cisco CME overlay feature provides a way to work around the physical button limits on your IP phones. Instead of a normal one-line-to-one-button mapping arrangement, you can map up to ten lines or ephone-dns to the same physical phone button. This allows you to use the same phone button to answer incoming calls on any of the up to ten ephone-dns associated with the button.

NOTE	Although you can map ten ephone-dns to the same button, you can work with and see only one ephone-dn at a time.

Earlier, you saw one usage (in Example 5-17) for overlay-dns, where it allowed access to multiple instances of ephone-dns that have the same telephone number. See Figure 5-2 earlier in this chapter.

The Purpose of an Overlay-dn

An overlay-dn associates or binds from two to ten ephone-dn IP phone lines onto a single IP phone button (even on single-line IP phones). You can use separate overlay-dn arrangements on each separate IP phone button. Each IP phone can use an independent set of ephone-dns for overlay for each of the phone's buttons.

An overlay-dn acts as a multiplexor. It dynamically selects the most appropriate ephone-dn to present on an IP phone button from within the configured overlay-dn set. When you receive incoming calls, the first ringing ephone-dn in the overlay set is presented. When you make an outgoing call, the first idle ephone-dn in the overlay set is selected.

You can configure the ephone-dns used in an overlay set as either single line or dual line. However, all the ephone-dns in the same overlay set must be of the same type (single or dual line).

Using Overlay to Overcome Phone Button Count Limits

The simplest use of overlay-dn is to overcome the limited number of physical buttons available on an IP phone. In a simple Key System case where you have four incoming PSTN trunk lines and four IP phones, you can make each line available on all phones simply by using one button per line. You can do this using a Cisco 7960 IP Phone, which has six buttons. With this arrangement, you can answer any of the four incoming lines on any of the four IP phones.

However, you cannot use this simple one-button-to-one-line mapping if you want to have ten incoming PSTN lines and ten IP phones (assuming a six-line Cisco 7960 IP Phone). There simply aren't enough line buttons to do this (unless you add a Cisco 7914 IP Phone Expansion Module to your Cisco 7960 IP Phones).

Example 5-30 shows how you can map ten incoming PSTN lines to a single button on an IP phone.

Example 5-30 *Overlay-dn Configuration*

```
router#show running-config
ephone-dn 101
   number 4085550101
   no huntstop
ephone-dn 102
   number 4085550101
   preference 1
   no huntstop
ephone-dn 103
   number 4085550101
   preference 2
   no huntstop
ephone-dn 104
   number 4085550101
   preference 3
   no huntstop
ephone-dn 105
   number 4085550101
   preference 4
   no huntstop
ephone-dn 106
   number 4085550101
   preference 5
   no huntstop
ephone-dn 107
   number 4085550101
   preference 6
   no huntstop
ephone-dn 108
   number 4085550101
   preference 7
   no huntstop
ephone-dn 109
   number 4085550101
   preference 8
   no huntstop
ephone-dn 110
   number 4085550101
   preference 9
ephone 1
   mac-address 000d.1234.ecfd
   button 1o101,102,103,104,105,106,107,108,109,110
ephone 2
   mac-address 000d.4321.a6b7
   button 1o101,102,103,104,105,106,107,108,109,110
ephone 3
   mac-address 000d.5678.b923
   button 1o101,102,103,104,105,106,107,108,109,110
```

The key to this configuration is the *o* separator used in the button command in place of the normal **:** separator character. In this configuration example, the **preference** and **huntstop** commands are used to control the order of selection of the incoming lines (in preference order from 101 to 110).

This configuration allows any incoming call to be answered on any of the IP phones. The example shows only the first three IP phones. There is no specific limit on the number of phones that can share the lines as shown. But, in general, you want to limit the number of phones so as not to exceed the number of lines. If there are more phones than lines, some phones can't access any lines if they are all in use.

Using Overlay with Intercom

You can include ephone-dns configured for intercom within an overlay set. In general, you would do this only for one-way intercoms where the phone with the overlay intercom is not expected to initiate an outgoing intercom call. This allows you to attach an incoming-only intercom to an IP phone without using up one of the phone's buttons. If the intercom is used as incoming only, there is no need to assign a phone button to select the intercom. One example of incoming-only intercom is the many-to-one intercom case discussed earlier.

Overlays and Shared Lines

In the section "Using Shared Lines for Call Coverage," you saw how a call can be put on hold on one phone by pressing the hold softkey and then picked up by pressing the resume softkey on a second phone that shares the line.

This form of shared-line direct call pickup is unavailable in the case of lines shared by a phone in an overlay set. As soon as an ephone-dn is dynamically associated to a specific phone using an overlay, the ephone-dn is no longer accessible on other phones that share the ephone-dn using overlay. It is available on phones that directly share the line using a simple nonoverlay button assignment (for example, by using the **:** separator, as in **button 1:tag**).

You can still move calls between phones in this arrangement by using the pickup softkey, provided that you carefully number the ephone-dns within the overlay set so that they can be uniquely selected. Example 5-31 uses a simplified form of the previous configuration.

Example 5-31   *Simplified Overlay-dn Configuration*

```
router#show running-config
ephone-dn 101
   label 4085550101
   number 101 secondary 4085550101
   no huntstop
ephone-dn 102
   number 102 secondary 4085550101
   preference 1
   no huntstop
```

continues

Example 5-31 *Simplified Overlay-dn Configuration (Continued)*

```
ephone-dn 103
   number 103 secondary 4085550101
   preference 2
   no huntstop
ephone-dn 104
   number 104 secondary 4085550101
   preference 3
ephone 1
   mac-address 000d.1234.ecfd
   button 1o101,102,103,104,105,106,107,108,109,110
ephone 2
   mac-address 000d.4321.a6b7
   button 1o101,102,103,104,105,106,107,108,109,110
```

In Example 5-31, you can see that the PSTN telephone number is moved to the ephone-dn's secondary number field. The primary number field is provisioned with a unique number 101, 102, 103, 104, and so on for each ephone-dn. This makes each ephone-dn in the overlay set uniquely identifiable.

The first ephone-dn in the overlay set also includes the **label 4085550101** command. The **label** command overrides the normal line display behavior to prevent the phone from displaying the ephone-dn's primary number (in this case 101) and instead displays the desired PSTN number.

With this arrangement, consider an incoming call answered on ephone 1. When ephone 1 puts the call on hold, the phone display shows the ephone-dn primary number of the specific ephone-dn in use and that now has the call on hold. The phone display shows Hold [101]. The call can then be accessed by another ephone (for example, ephone 2) by pressing the pickup softkey and entering the ephone-dn extension number displayed.

Another way to move the call from one phone to another in this arrangement is to use *call park*. (You'll read more about this shortly.)

Invoking Call Pickup

The call pickup feature allows you to retrieve calls on hold in a park slot and to move calls from one phone to another. You invoke the call pickup feature from the phone you want to move the call to. You can move calls that are in either the (incoming) ringing state or the call hold state. To invoke call pickup, simply press the pickup softkey on the IP phone, and enter the extension number of the ephone-dn that has the call you want to move.

Call pickup is also often used in conjunction with paging. In this case, you place a call on hold, either at an extension or in a park slot, and then use the paging system to request that a coworker pick up the call you just parked. The park-and-pickup combination is a popular feature used in the retail store environment.

Pickup of a Ringing Extension

You can use the pickup softkey to move a call on a ringing extension on another phone to your phone. When you invoke call pickup, the Cisco CME system triggers a call forward from the phone with the ringing extension to your phone. Because the call pickup for a ringing extension uses the call forwarding mechanism, the general restrictions and considerations that apply to forwarded calls (forward on no-answer) also apply to calls for pickup on ringing. This means that the **max-redirects** limit set under **telephony-service** may affect the call pickup feature.

Pickup of a Call on Hold

You can use the pickup softkey to move a call that is on hold at an extension on another phone and move it to your phone. When you invoke call pickup, the Cisco CME system triggers a blind call transfer from the phone with the on-hold call to phone. Because the call pickup for an on-hold call uses the call transfer mechanism, the general restrictions and considerations that apply to transferring calls also apply to calls for pickup on hold.

Pickup Groups

The group pickup feature operates in a manner similar to simple extension pickup. To use the group pickup feature, press the gpickup softkey and enter a pickup group number. You can use the group pickup feature to pick up any ringing call in a designated group of phones. You cannot use the group pickup feature to pick up calls that are on hold.

You can assign each phone in your Cisco CME system to a pickup group. You can have any number of pickup groups in your Cisco CME system.

If you create only a single pickup group in your Cisco CME system, you can pick up calls from within the single pickup group by simply pressing the gpickup softkey. If your Cisco CME system has only a single pickup group, there is no need to enter a pickup group number.

If you have more than one pickup group, you can pick up calls from within a phone's local pickup group by pressing the gpickup softkey followed by the star (*) key. This provides a shortcut instead of requiring you to enter the phone's own pickup group number.

To assign a phone to a specific pickup group, use the **pickup-group** command within the ephone configuration command mode, as shown in Example 5-32.

Example 5-32 *Pickup Group Configuration*

```
router#show running-config
ephone 1
   mac-address 000d.1234.ecfd
   button 1:10
   pickup-group 201
```

You can assign any number you want to the pickup group. In general, it's a good idea not to use pickup group numbers that are the same as extension numbers in your Cisco CME system. Also, it's a good idea for all your pickup group numbers to have the same number of digits—for example, for all pickup groups to have three-digit numbers. If you do have pickup group numbers with varying digit lengths, make sure the leading digits of your pickup group numbers are different. For example, you cannot have a pickup group numbered as 20 and also have a pickup group numbered as 201.

Call Park

The Cisco CME call park feature allows you to create park slots to use as temporary holding locations for calls. You create park slots using the **ephone-dn** command and by setting the ephone-dn to operate in park-slot mode. Calls parked in a call park slot hear your Cisco CME system's music on hold.

You park calls by pressing the park softkey on your IP phone when the phone has a call in the connected state. Note that the park softkey is displayed on your phone only if you have created at least one park slot for your Cisco CME system. Also, you may need to press the more softkey one or more times on your IP phone to display the park softkey.

When you press the park softkey, the call is transferred to a park slot that has the number that most closely matches the extension number you used to answer the call. So if you are using extension 312 and you park a call from that extension, the call is parked in a park slot with a number ending in 12 if available. For example, if you create park slots with numbers 711, 712, 713, and 714, a call parked from extension 312 uses park slot 712 if possible. If no park slot with a matching number is available, any available park slot is used. You can use the Cisco CME extension-to-park slot association to create personal park slots for individuals who frequently use the park feature. There is no limit on the number of park slots you can create in your system other than the overall limit on the number of available ephone-dns.

When you park a call, the park-slot number selected is displayed on your IP phone's display. To retrieve a parked call, simply press the pickup softkey followed by the park-slot number. To retrieve the last call parked by your phone (or notified to your phone), simply press the pickup softkey followed by the star (*) key on the phone's keypad.

You can also park calls by pressing the transfer softkey and entering a park slot number as the destination for the blind transfer. This operation, called *directed park*, allows you to park calls to a specific slot. This is useful when you want to dedicate specific park slots for particular types of calls. For example, you might choose to park a call specifically for the sales department and then page the sales department for someone to pick up the call from the sales department park slot. To accommodate multiple calls for the same department, you can create multiple park slots with the same park-slot number. Calls are picked up from the park slot in first-in, first-out order.

You can also configure your park slots to provide a call parked on hold reminder at programmed intervals. By default, the call reminder goes to the phone that originally parked the call. You can also configure your park slots to send a reminder to a specific phone number as well as to the park originator, or instead of to the park originator. Example 5-33 shows a park-slot configuration.

Example 5-33 *Park-Slot Configuration*

```
router#show running-config
ephone-dn 102
   number 711
   park-slot timeout 30 limit 20 notify 310 only
```

This example creates a single park-slot instance with number 711. It sets the reminder interval to 30 seconds and configures 20 as the maximum number of reminders. As soon as the maximum number of reminders has been sent (after 20 * 30 = 600 seconds [10 minutes]), the call in the park slot is disconnected.

The reminder notifications are sent to all IP phones with extension 310. To send reminders to both the park originator and extension 310, simply omit the **only** keyword in the **park-slot** command.

If you create multiple park slots with the same number, remember to include the **no huntstop** command to allow the Cisco CME system to search for alternative park slots if the first instance with a particular number is in use.

You can use the ephone-dn secondary number to give your park slot two different extension numbers, as shown in Example 5-34.

Example 5-34 *Park-Slot Configuration on the Secondary Ephone-dn*

```
router#show running-config
ephone-dn 102
   number 711 secondary 700
   no huntstop
   park-slot timeout 30 limit 20 notify 310 only
ephone-dn 102
   number 712 secondary 700
   no huntstop
   park-slot timeout 30 limit 20 notify 310 only
```

This configuration allows you to use the directed park feature and transfer-park the call to 700. The IP phone display shows you the park-slot (primary) number that actually received the call—in this case, 711 or 712. You can pick up the call by using the specific park-slot number (711 or 712), or you can get the first parked call from either park slot by performing a pickup using the shared secondary number, 700.

Note that after you have created your first park slot within your Cisco CME system, you need to reset or restart your IP phone(s) before the park softkey becomes visible on the phone. Because the call park mechanism uses the Cisco CME router's call transfer mechanism, you should ensure that your system is correctly configured for call transfer before attempting to use call park.

Customizing Softkeys

Cisco CME 3.2 and later allow you to customize the set of softkeys displayed to the phone user in each stage of a phone call. For example, by default in the connected call state, a Cisco 7960 IP Phone shows the following six softkeys:

- Acct (account code entry)
- Confrn (three-party conference)
- Endcall
- Flash (sends a hookflash signal to the PSTN line)
- Hold
- Trnsfer (call transfer)

Because a Cisco 7960 IP Phone has only four physical softkey buttons, the phone displays a more softkey as the rightmost button to allow the phone user to scroll to access all the keys. Because the more softkey itself uses one of the physical buttons, the user sees the feature softkeys in two sets:

- Hold
- Trnsfer
- EndCall
- More

- Confrn
- Acct
- Flash
- More

The softkey customization feature allows you to change this default behavior, and choose the set of keys you want to display. It also allows you to control the order of the keys so that you can move the more frequently used keys to the first page. For example, you may choose to remove the Acct and Flash keys from the connected state key set, leaving just the following four keys:

- Hold
- Trnsfer
- EndCall
- Confrn

Because this reduces the number of keys to just four, there is no need for a more softkey, allowing you to use all four physical phone buttons and present the softkeys as a single page.

The **ephone-template** command is used to provide this configuration, as shown in Example 5-35. The order of the command options determines the order in which the softkeys appear on the phone.

Example 5-35 **ephone-template** *Command*

```
router#show running-config
ephone-template 1
   soft-key connected hold trnsfr endcall confrn
ephone 1
   ephone-template 1
```

Cisco CME 3.2 and later allow you to create up to five different ephone templates. Each template lists the softkeys available for each of the four configurable call states:

- Idle
- Seized
- Alerting
- Connected

The ringing call state for inbound calls cannot be configured because it offers only two softkeys: Answer and DND. As soon as you have created the ephone templates, you can apply them on a per-ephone basis. This allows you to optimize the soft key sets to support several different types of phone users. It also allows removal of softkeys in cases where you need to restrict access to certain functions for some phone users.

Table 5-1 shows the full set of customizations for all customizable call states.

Table 5-1   *Softkey Support Per Call State*

Call State	Available Softkeys
Idle	Redial, CFwdAll, DND, PickUp, GPickUp, Newcall, Login
Seized	Redial, CFwdAll, PickUp, GPickUp, EndCall
Alerting	Acct, EndCall, CallBack
Connected	Acct, Confrn, Hold, Trnsfr, Endcall, Flash, Park

The Seized call state is the initial dial tone state after going off-hook to place an outbound call. The Alerting state is the name of the call state after the telephone number has been dialed and the user is waiting for the called number to answer (or hears busy tone).

Configuring Call Transfer and Forward

Configuring call transfer and forwarding for H.323 VoIP calls is a fairly complex task in most real-world H.323 VoIP networks. This is especially true if you have a mixture of H.323 VoIP systems from different vendors. Even if you have an all-Cisco H.323 VoIP network, there are still interactions to consider, unless all your VoIP systems are running relatively up-to-date Cisco IOS software. This means having at least Cisco IOS 12.3 software in all your voice-enabled routers. Ideally, you should have Cisco IOS 12.3(4)T or later software (this is the Cisco CME 3.0 base code version). There are also some special considerations if you are using a Cisco CallManager in addition to your Cisco IOS-based Cisco CME systems, which you'll learn more about in Chapter 7, "Connecting Multiple Cisco CMEs with VoIP." The good news is that with the right software and configuration, there are workable solutions for most of your VoIP call transfer and forwarding needs.

In a VoIP network, getting an optimized system working for call transfer and forwarding requires the active cooperation of all endpoints involved in a call transfer or call forward. This means your ability to perform a call transfer or forward depends on the capabilities of the calling party's VoIP system as well as your Cisco CME system configuration. A call transfer also depends on the capabilities of the final VoIP system that you are transferring the call to.

In traditional TDM-based PBX telephony, call transfer and forwarding usually operate within the limited scope of a single PBX system and, therefore, are simpler operations. For example, you are often limited to call transfers between extensions on the same PBX only.

In a VoIP-based system, you can potentially transfer or forward calls between any VoIP endpoints, regardless of their physical location. Of course, being able to do this in practice requires making sure that you have support for transfer and forwarding built into all your VoIP endpoints.

With Cisco CME, you have three basic choices for the protocol used to support call transfer and forwarding for H.323 VoIP calls:

- **Standards-based H.450**—Strongly recommended because it provides for optimal call paths and unlimited sequential transfers and forwards

- **Cisco-proprietary H.323 extension**—Mostly obsolete, but useful if you are using software older than Cisco IOS 12.2(15)T

- **Hairpin call routing**—Maximum compatibility but uses more WAN bandwidth and results in higher delay and jitter

The default H.323 call transfer protocol used by Cisco CME is the Cisco-proprietary mechanism. This mechanism supports only blind call transfer (that is, no transfer consultation). It is selected as the default simply for purposes of backward compatibility with earlier Cisco IOS versions.

The default call forwarding mechanism provides for automatic local forwarding only (that is, within the same Cisco CME system). It does not provide forwarding display update notification of the call forwarding to the calling party's IP phone. For incoming VoIP calls from another Cisco CME system that are nonlocally forwarded to a third Cisco CME system, the Cisco-proprietary H.323 protocol extensions are used.

Even if you do not require H.323 VoIP call transfers (because you do not need to make calls across an IP connection to another site), you should still select the H.450 configuration method for call transfers. This enables call transfer with consultation for local calls within your system and for PSTN calls that use PSTN voice ports that are physically on your Cisco CME router. (PSTN voice ports on a router other than the Cisco CME system appear as H.323 VoIP calls to the Cisco CME system.) It also prepares your system to use the standards-based H.450 protocol in case you want to add support for H.323 or SIP VoIP transfer and forwarding to another site at some point in the future.

Call Transfer Terminology

To fully comprehend the different call flows when talking about transfers, you should be familiar with the following terms:

- **Transferee**—The person who is being transferred. Usually this is the person who placed the original call.

- **Transferor**—The person who invokes the transfer. Usually this is the initial recipient of the incoming call.

- **Transfer-to**—The person who becomes the final recipient of the call after the transfer has been completed.

- **Consultation call**—The call between the transferor and transfer-to parties. This is usually the call that introduces the transfer where the transferor and transfer-to parties talk (consult) before the transferee is connected to the transfer-to party.

- **Transfer commit at connect**—The act of completing the (consultative) transfer after the transferor and transfer-to party have talked to each other. The transferee party does not hear the transfer-to party's phone ring. The transfer-to party's phone shows the transferor as the (initial) calling party.

- **Transfer commit at alerting**—The act of committing the (consultative) transfer during the time that the transfer-to party's phone is ringing. In this case, a consultation call is placed but is abandoned before the transfer-to party answers the phone. The transfer-to party's phone shows the transferor as the (initial) calling party. The transferee party hears the transfer-to party's phone ringing. Note that in a VoIP system, it's usually not possible to commit a transfer to a busy destination, unless you use the blind transfer approach. You can commit a transfer to a busy destination that has call forward-on-busy, provided that the forward-to destination itself is available (for example, forward on busy to voice mail). However, none of this is necessarily visible to the transferor.

- **Blind transfer**—This is also called *unsupervised transfer* and sometimes *full blind transfer*. It is the act of invoking a call transfer without first checking to see if the transfer-to party is available. In the traditional TDM PBX world, this is often considered to be the same as commit at alerting when the transferor commits the transfer without waiting to hear the transfer-to party's phone ring, usually by hanging up the phone. The transfer-to party's phone shows the transferee as the calling party.

In the VoIP world, there are two key differences between the blind and commit-at-alerting case. The first difference is in the calling party information sent in the H.323 call setup request toward the transfer-to party. In the blind case, this is the transferee, and in the commit at alerting/ connect case, it's the transferor. This can affect the billing for the call. The second difference is that a blind transfer doesn't involve doing a call replace operation, which is needed to switch the transfer-to party's call between transferor and transferee. So you might sometimes want to consider the blind form of transfer, because it eliminates the transfer capability dependency on the transfer-to endpoint VoIP system.

Call Transfer Methods for VoIP

This section describes several methods for implementing call transfer across VoIP networks:

- H.450 and SIP
- Hairpin routing
- H.450.12
- Empty Capability Set

H.450 and SIP

The ITU-T standards-based H.450.2 transfer method and the Cisco-proprietary method operate in a similar fashion. In both cases, when a call transfer occurs, a control message is sent back to the transferee party to request that the transferee initiates a follow-on call from the transferee to the final transfer-to destination. In the H.450.2 case, the follow-on call originated by the transferee can act to replace the transfer consultation call that's in progress between the transferor and the transfer-to destination party. The consultation call between transferor and transfer-to and the original transferee-transferor call are not torn down until the "replaces" operation is completed successfully. The term *replaces* is used here in the context of "Call 2 replaces call 1." If for any reason the replaces operation fails, it's usually possible for the transferor to reconnect the call to the transferee. The H.450.2 mechanism works in a manner similar to the REFER method used for SIP VoIP calls. The Cisco-proprietary transfer mechanism does not support the call replacement mechanism and, therefore, allows you to perform only blind call transfers. This proprietary method is similar to the older BYE/ALSO method that was used to perform blind transfers for SIP VoIP calls. The BYE/ALSO method has been mostly superceded by the SIP REFER method.

Both of these H.323 call transfer methods result in an optimal direct call path between the transferee and the transfer-to party after the call transfer is committed.

Hairpin Routing

The third alternative is to hairpin route the VoIP call transfer. In this case, the original transferee-to-transferor VoIP call leg is kept, and a second transferor to transfer-to VoIP call leg is created for the consultation call phase of the transfer. When the transfer is committed, the original and consultation call legs are simply bridged together at the Cisco CME router. This method has the advantage that it has no end-to-end dependency on the capabilities of the transferee or transfer-to VoIP endpoint.

It also has disadvantages. One significant disadvantage is that the final transferred call is relayed through the transferor's Cisco CME system. This means that the transferred call continues to consume resources on the transferor Cisco CME system even after the transfer is committed. It also means that the media path for voice packets for the transferred call may hairpin route through the transferor's Cisco CME system, so both the original call and the transferred call continue to consume WAN bandwidth. If the amount of WAN bandwidth is limited, this may prevent new VoIP calls from being established until the transferred call is terminated. The other significant disadvantage of hairpin routing calls is the cumulative bandwidth, delay, and jitter problems that occur if a call is transferred multiple times (chained or sequential transfers).

H.450.12

You can compromise between the H.450.2 and hairpin routing call methods by turning on the H.450.12 protocol on your Cisco CME system (this is recommended). You must be using at least Cisco CME 3.1 to use H.450.12. With H.450.12 enabled, your Cisco CME system can use the H.450.12 protocol to automatically discover the H.450.x capabilities of VoIP endpoints within your VoIP network. When H.450.12 is enabled, the Cisco CME system can automatically detect when an H.450.2 transfer is possible. When it isn't possible, the Cisco CME system can fall back to using VoIP hairpin routing. Cisco CME also can automatically detect a call from a (non-H.450-capable) Cisco CallManager.

Empty Capabilities Set

For the sake of completeness, it's worth mentioning a fourth alternative for call transfers: Empty Capabilities Set (ECS). Cisco CME does not support the instigation of transfer using ECS. But because a Cisco CME router also has the full capabilities of the Cisco IOS H.323 voice infrastructure software, it can process receipt of an ECS request coming from a far-end VoIP device. In other words, a Cisco CME system can be a transferee or transfer-to party in an ECS-based transfer. A Cisco CME system does not originate a transfer request using ECS. The problem with ECS-based transfers is that in many ways they represent a combination of the worst aspects of the end-to-end dependencies of H.450.2 together with the cumulative problems of hairpin for multiple transfers. Many ECS-based transfer implementations don't allow you to transfer a call that has already been transferred in the general case of VoIP intersystem transfers.

Cisco CME VoIP Call Transfer Options

Your Cisco CME system by default is set up to allow local transfers between IP phones only. It uses the Cisco-proprietary H.323 call transfer extensions to transfer calls that include an H.323 VoIP participant.

To configure your Cisco CME system to use H.450.2 transfers (this is recommended), set **transfer-system full-consult** under the **telephony-service** command mode. You also have to use this configuration for SIP VoIP transfers.

To configure your Cisco CME system to permit transfers to nonlocal destinations (VoIP or PSTN), set the **transfer-pattern** command under **telephony-service**. The **transfer-pattern** command also allows you to specify that specific transfer-to destinations should receive only blind transfers. You also have to use this configuration for SIP VoIP transfers. The **transfer-pattern** command allows you to restrict trunk-to-trunk transfers to prevent incoming PSTN calls from being transferred back out to the PSTN (employee toll fraud). Trunk-to-trunk transfers are disabled by default, because the default is to allow only local extension-to-extension transfers.

To allow the H.450.12 service to automatically detect the H.450.2 capabilities of endpoints in your H.323 VoIP network, use the **supplementary-services** command in voice service voip command mode.

To enable hairpin routing of VoIP calls that can't be transferred (or forwarded) using H.450, use the **allow-connections** command. Example 5-36 shows a call transfer configuration using this command.

Example 5-36 *Call Transfer Configuration*

```
router#show running-config
voice service voip
   supplementary-service h450.12
   allow-connections h323 to h323
telephony-service
   transfer-system full-consult
   transfer-pattern .T
```

The configuration shown in Example 5-36 turns on the H.450.2 (**transfer-system full-consult**) and H.450.12 services, allows VoIP-to-VoIP hairpin call routing (**allow-connections**) for calls that don't support H.450, and permits transfers to all possible destinations (**transfer-pattern**). The transfer permission is set to **.T** to provide full wildcard matching for any number of digits. (The T stands for terminating the transfer destination digit entry with a timeout.)

Example 5-37 shows a configuration for more restrictive transfer permissions.

Example 5-37 *More Restrictive Call Transfer Configuration*

```
router#show running-config
telephony-service
   transfer-system full-consult
   transfer-pattern 1...
   transfer-pattern 2... blind
```

This example permits transfers using full consultation to nonlocal extensions in the range 1000 to 1999. It also permits blind transfers to nonlocal extensions in the range 2000 to 2999.

Call Transfer Billing Considerations

You should consider what your billing requirements are for transferred calls. Most enterprise VoIP networks have no requirement for separate billing for VoIP call legs within an internal VoIP network. Most enterprise networks are concerned only with billing for external PSTN call legs.

The billing for a PSTN call leg usually goes to the party identified as the calling party on the outbound PSTN call setup. For a PSTN call using ISDN BRI/PRI, the calling party number is passed from the Cisco CME extension that originated the call. You can use the Cisco CME **dialplan-pattern** or Cisco IOS voice dial peer **translation rule** commands to convert from two-to-five-digit abbreviated extension numbers into a national number format acceptable to your PSTN service provider. If you are using simple analog FXO port connections to connect to the PSTN (simple subscriber line), you have no control over the billing party information, so you can probably skip the rest of this section. Calls on an analog subscriber line are simply billed to the number associated with the subscriber line by the PSTN service provider.

For the ISDN PRI/BRI case, this is an area where the difference between transfer commit at connect/alerting and blind transfers may be significant. It's also an area in which hairpin call routing may provide you with some advantages.

When an H.450.2-style transfer is committed at alerting/connected, the calling party number for the consultation call setup to the transfer-to party (from the transferor) is normally equal to the transferor's phone number. This is usually the bill-to number that's associated with the call. If the consultation call involves a PSTN call leg using PRI/BRI (either a direct PSTN connection on the Cisco CME router or a remote PSTN gateway call reached via an intermediate VoIP leg), it's useful to have the initial calling party number for the outbound PRI/BRI PSTN leg equal to the transferor's phone number. This assumes that you want any transferred call to be billed (or traceable) to the person who invokes the transfer. When the replaces operation is triggered to connect the transferee to the transfer-to party, the calling party information associated with the PSTN leg normally does not change. This means that even after the transferor has dropped out of the call, the call continues to be billed to the transferor, at least as far as the external PSTN call leg is concerned. This is true for PSTN access that's directly on your Cisco CME router and also when the PSTN access is on a remote VoIP-PSTN gateway accessed via a VoIP link. This is because the H.450.2 call transfer replaces operation is confined to the H.323 VoIP network. The replaces operation normally cannot extend into the PSTN connection.

Transfers that use the blind mechanism work differently. In the blind transfer case, the transferor does not originate a consultation call. The initial call received by the transfer-to party in an H.450.2 transfer case by default has the transferee's phone number as the calling party. The transferee is often a phone number belonging to some external party. You are often not permitted to bill calls to this phone number even if you want to. Your PRI/BRI PSTN connection is very likely to reject any outbound calls that attempt to claim an external number as the calling party identifier.

You can work around this issue in a couple of different ways, depending on the reason you chose to select the blind transfer method. For example, you may be using blind transfer to avoid the H.450.2 replaces operation if it is not supported by your PSTN access voice gateway. The workaround methods include the following:

- You can place a translation rule on the dial peer associated with the outgoing PRI/BRI PSTN port that overwrites the transferee calling party number with the general public phone number for your company.

- You can elect to force hairpin VoIP routing with transfer commit-at-alerting/connect as an alternative to blind transfer such that the outgoing PSTN call carries the transferor's phone number.

To use the first alternative, you must have control of the PSTN gateway. This is true if the PSTN access is local to your Cisco CME router. This may not be true if you get remote PSTN access across a WAN connection from a VoIP telephony service provider (TSP). In this case, your VoIP TSP may share the PSTN access ports across multiple end customers.

The second hairpin case is the most robust approach, because it forces a separate call leg to be generated for the outgoing PSTN call segment.

To force hairpin VoIP call routing, you can switch on H.450.12 services on your Cisco CME router and use a separate PSTN gateway router on which H.450.12 is disabled (or not supported). Alternatively, you can explicitly turn off H.450.2 service on your Cisco CME voice dial peers that route calls to the PSTN gateway router. You do this using the **no supplementary-service** h450.2 command, as shown in Example 5-38.

Example 5-38 *Turning Off H.450 on a Dial Peer*

```
router#show running-config
dial-peer voice 100 voip
   destination-pattern 9.T
   session target ipv4:10.0.1.20
   no supplementary-service h450.2
```

Because Cisco CME includes the standard Cisco IOS voice infrastructure functionality, you can also connect your Cisco CME system to a Remote Authentication Dial-In User Service (RADIUS) server to capture call records for more detailed call tracking information collected. If you don't have a RADIUS server, you can also configure your Cisco CME system to generate SYSLOG messages that include call details. You can use a simple PC as a SYSLOG server to record the call data, using one of several freeware SYSLOG programs available on the Internet.

Call Forward Methods for VoIP

This section describes different mechanisms for handling call forwarding in a VoIP network:

- H.450.3 call forwarding
- H.323 Facility Message
- VoIP hairpin call forwarding

You can configure your Cisco CME to handle VoIP call forwarding in several different ways. Select the method to use depending on how you want forwarding to operate.

H.450.3 Call Forwarding

You can use the ITU-T H.450.3 standard for call forwarding (this is recommended). It has some similarities to H.450.2 (call transfer). When a call is forwarded, an H.450.3 message is sent back to the calling party requesting that the caller reoriginate a follow-on call to the forwarded-to destination. If Cisco CME is configured to use H.450.3, it is used even if the forward-to destination is another local IP phone within the same Cisco CME system as the forwarding phone (or forwarder). Use this method if you want the calling VoIP party to always be able to see the phone number he or she is being forwarded to. Just like the H.450.2 transfer case, use of H.450.3 requires that all the VoIP endpoints in your VoIP network support H.450 services.

H.323 Facility Message

The second choice is to use the quasi-standard H.323 Facility Message mechanism for forwarding. This is the default call forwarding configuration for Cisco CME. This method is used as the default, because it provides backward compatibility with earlier (and current) Cisco IOS releases. It's also quite widely supported by third-party and non-Cisco IOS VoIP systems. When this mechanism is used, an H.323 Facility Message is sent back to the VoIP caller only for the case of forwarding to a nonlocal number. If the forward-to destination is local to the forwarding phone, the call forward operation is handled internally within the Cisco CME system. In this case, the remote calling IP phone cannot update its display to show the forwarded destination.

VoIP Hairpin Call Forwarding

Your third choice is to use VoIP call hairpin routing. This is similar to the call transfer hairpin option. A second independent VoIP call leg is created for the forwarded call leg. This leg is bridged to the original incoming VoIP call leg. As for the transfer hairpin case, the disadvantage of this approach occurs if you have to support sequential or chained forwarding. Sequential hairpin forwarding of VoIP calls results in accumulated bandwidth and jitter/delay issues.

Just like the call transfer discussion, if you have to deal with only local LAN and PSTN connections and do not have to route VoIP H.323 calls across a WAN connection, you can just configure your system for H.450.3 operation to get your system ready to interoperate with other H.450-capable endpoints should you need this in the future.

You can also compromise between the H.450.3 and hairpin configuration by using the H.450.12 service to automatically detect H.450.3-capable VoIP endpoints, and fall back to hairpin routing for calls that don't support H.450.3.

Cisco CME VoIP Call Forwarding Options

Your Cisco CME system by default is configured to support internal local forwarding. It sends only H.323 Facility Messages back to the VoIP caller for nonlocal VoIP forwarding destinations. If you have direct PSTN access on your Cisco CME system, PSTN destinations accessed via local ports are considered local for the purposes of this discussion.

To turn on H.450.3 services for VoIP calls, you use the **call-forward pattern** command under **telephony-service**. This command lets you conditionally select H.450.3 service based on matching the calling party's telephone number. This lets you invoke H.450.3 for calls only from VoIP phone numbers that you know support H.450.3. You can configure the matching pattern to use **.T** to match all possible calling party numbers. This is similar to the match-all configuration used with the **transfer-pattern** command.

To permit VoIP-to-VoIP hairpin (or tandem) call routing for forwarded calls, set the **allow-connections** command under **voice services voip**. If you've already done this to allow hairpin transfers, you don't need to do it again for call forwarding.

As with the H.450.2 transfer case, you can turn on the H.450.12 service to compromise and allow H.450.3 where possible, and fall back to hairpin forwarding otherwise. Note that H.450.12 support was introduced in Cisco CME 3.1.

Example 5-39 shows a basic configuration.

Example 5-39 *Turning On H.450 on a Dial Peer*

```
router#show running-config
voice service voip
   supplementary-service h450.12
   allow-connections h323 to h323
telephony-service
   call-forward pattern .T
```

Call Forward Billing Considerations

Similar billing issues apply to call forwarding as for call transfer. You can choose to have the calling party information for the forwarded call reflect the party being forwarded (in the H.450.3 case). You also can have the information show the calling party number of the phone that requested the forwarding (in the VoIP hairpin case). As for the call transfer case, you can use the **dialplan-pattern** command and voice dial peer **translation rule** options to control the format of the calling party on outgoing PSTN PRI/BRI calls. Again, this issue does not apply for PSTN analog subscriber line connections via FXO ports.

Transfer and Forward Proxy Function

The transfer and forward discussion so far in this chapter has related to the configuration of a single Cisco CME system to cope with various possible VoIP network scenarios, including networks that have endpoints with mixed capabilities. If you have a network of Cisco CME systems, you should consider partitioning it to provide a section that contains only H.450-capable endpoints. This allows you to gain the full set of H.450 service benefits within the group of VoIP network devices that support them. You can then link this segment of your VoIP network to the non-H.450 network using a Cisco IOS router configured to act as an H.450 Tandem Gateway.

An H.450 Tandem Gateway can act as a proxy for H.450.2 and H.450.3 services on behalf of VoIP devices that don't support H.450. Calls between the H.450 and non-H.450 devices can be routed to pass through the H.450 Tandem Gateway. H.450 messages originated by Cisco CME systems can be terminated on the H.450 Tandem Gateway, which can invoke hairpin call routing for transfers and call forwarding as needed.

An H.450 Tandem Gateway makes the most sense if your network topology is arranged in a hub-and-spoke fashion. Consider a network design that has a number of Cisco CME systems located at the end of WAN link spokes connected to a central hub network. In this type of network, it often makes sense to locate an H.450 Tandem Gateway at the central hub and to use it as a linkage point to act as a bridge into the non-H.450 segment of the VoIP network. With an H.450 Tandem Gateway, calls that enter the H.450 network segment through the Tandem Gateway can be transferred and forwarded using H.450 services within the H.450 segment of the network. Calls transferred or forwarded to destinations outside the H.450 segment are hairpin routed as needed by the H.450 Tandem Gateway. If the H.450 Tandem Gateway is located at a central hub location, hairpin routing the call at the hub is a better option than hairpin routing the call from a Cisco CME system located at the far end of one of the network spokes over a WAN link. (Figure 5-3 in the next section shows a Tandem Gateway.)

Call Transfer and Forward Interoperability with Cisco CallManager

Cisco CallManager (version 4.0 and earlier) does not support H.450 services. Cisco CME 3.1 can automatically detect H.323 calls that go to or come from Cisco CallManager. It does this using H.323 information elements included in H.323 call setup, progress, alerting, and connect messages. You can optionally turn on H.450.12 services for calls to Cisco CallManager, and use the lack of H.450.12 indications to invoke hairpin VoIP call routing by your Cisco CME systems, but this is not required.

You may have a VoIP network in which turning on H.450.12 produces ambiguous results as far as the detection of H.450.2 and H.450.3 capabilities. One example of this occurs when you have older Cisco CME 3.0 (or even Cisco ITS [Cisco CME's earlier name] 2.1) systems in your network. Although Cisco CME 3.0 systems do support H.450.2 and H.450.3, they don't support H.450.12 capabilities indications. If you turn on H.450.12 on your Cisco CME 3.1 systems and you also have some older Cisco CME 3.0 routers, the CME 3.1 systems assume that the CME

3.0 routers cannot perform H.450.2/3 services, because no H.450.12 indication is forthcoming from the Cisco CME 3.0 systems. So in a network with a mixture of Cisco CME 3.0, Cisco CME 3.1, and Cisco CallManagers, it makes sense to turn off the H.450.12 service and assume that all endpoints can perform H.450.2/3 except for the endpoints that are detected as explicitly being Cisco CallManager systems.

Also, if you have a Cisco CallManager system, it's likely to be located at a central corporate site with Cisco CME systems at branch offices. This arrangement lends itself naturally to a hub-and-spoke network design with the Cisco CallManager at the hub and the Cisco CME systems at the ends of the network spokes. This type of network design is a good candidate for an H.450 Tandem Gateway using the H.450 Tandem Gateway to front-end the Cisco CallManager and act as a proxy for H.450 services between the Cisco CallManager and the network of Cisco CME systems. The H.450 Tandem Gateway can also be configured to act as the PSTN Voice Gateway for the Cisco CallManager system (using either H.323 or MGCP), so you don't need to dedicate a separate router for the H.450 Tandem Gateway. It can also provide centralized PSTN access for the Cisco CME systems. Performance wise, calls that pass through the H.450 Tandem Gateway consume a similar amount of CPU and memory resources as a call terminated by the router as a PSTN gateway call. See Figure 5-3.

Figure 5-3   *H.450 Tandem Gateway*

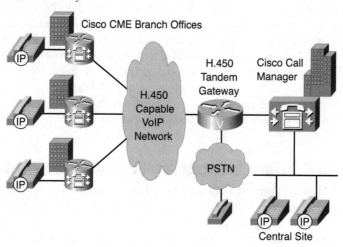

A Cisco CallManager (version 4.0 or earlier) should be configured to interface with Cisco CME systems or an H.450 Tandem Gateway using H.323 Inter-Cluster Trunk (ICT) mode and a Media Termination Point (MTP). In addition, Cisco CallManager version 3.3(3) should be configured to disable H.323 fast-start.

Call Transfer and Forwarding with Routed Signaling H.323 Gatekeepers

An H.323 gatekeeper that uses routed signaling acts as a call proxy for basic A-to-B calls. All calls that reference the gatekeeper have H.323 signaling that passes through the gatekeeper. The presence of this type of gatekeeper in your network has a significant impact on your network from the H.450 service point of view. Your routed signaling gatekeeper may or may not support H.450 services. It may be able to pass through H.450 messages transparently, or it may block some or all of them. It may even be able to act as an H.450 Tandem Gateway.

A worst-case design approach for dealing with a routed signaling gatekeeper would be to assume that H.450.2/3 services do not work through the gatekeeper. In this case you can configure your Cisco CME systems to force hairpin routing of all VoIP calls that have to transfer or forward back into the VoIP network. You can do this by turning off H.450 services under the voice service voip command, as shown in Example 5-40.

Example 5-40   *Turning Off H.450 Services*

```
router#show running-config
voice service voip
   no supplementary-service h450.2
   no supplementary-service h450.3
   allow-connections h323 to h323
telephony-service
   call-forward pattern .T
   transfer-system full-consult
   transfer-pattern .T
```

Note that by default, the H.450.12 service is disabled, so there's no need to specifically include commands to turn it off.

Summary

In this chapter, you read about some of the more popular Cisco CME phone and call processing features. You saw examples of how these features can be configured and combined to provide a rich and flexible set of functions. You also saw how to configure call transfer and forwarding functions in a variety of network scenarios.

This chapter covers the following topics:

- Cisco CallManager Express (CME) analog and digital Public Switched Telephone Network (PSTN) interface hardware, configuration, and features
- PSTN call switching and routing options
- Digit manipulation tools to translate phone numbers
- PSTN trunk failover options

## CHAPTER 6

Cisco CME PSTN Connectivity Options

In previous chapters, you learned about the Cisco IP Communications (IPC) Express platforms and architecture, Cisco IOS voice infrastructure software features, and configuring call routing features between endpoints such as IP phones and Public Switched Telephone Network (PSTN) interfaces.

This chapter focuses on the hardware options, configurations, and detailed features that Cisco IPC Express offers for connecting your business to the PSTN. This PSTN connectivity is not particular to Cisco IPC Express but is part of the generic voice-enabled feature set of the Cisco router platforms.

Router PSTN connectivity is generically referred to as *voice gateway* functionality, offering a *gateway* for voice over IP (VoIP) calls to, and from, traditional analog or digital PSTN or private branch exchange (PBX) calls. You can use a router voice gateway to connect to PSTN central office (CO) switches, private branch exchanges (PBXs), Key Systems, time-division multiplexing (TDM)-based interactive voice response (IVR) systems, traditional TDM-based voice mail systems, and any other legacy (non-IP) voice processing or telephone equipment.

This chapter explores several aspects of Cisco CME connectivity to the PSTN, including the following:

- Standards-based telephony signaling systems and protocols supported by Cisco IOS, which, in turn, determine what traditional TDM or analog systems you can connect to and what features you get when using this type of connection

- A brief overview of the Cisco voice gateway hardware choices and the voice port densities and features they provide

- Sample Cisco IOS configurations for different types of PSTN connections

- Network design and call switching considerations for connecting to the PSTN from your IP network

Traditional telephony terminology is used throughout this chapter. It has a more precise meaning here than in other chapters, because the topic of discussion is connecting a traditional telephony system, the PSTN. If you are unfamiliar with the telephony meanings of terms such as trunks, lines, caller ID, direct inward dial (DID), and dialed number information service (DNIS), refer to the glossary to review these terms.

Trunk Signaling Systems

Cisco IOS PSTN connectivity complies with the relevant standard signaling systems used by the PSTN and other telephony-switching systems. Cisco IOS routers support all the signaling variations in general use in the world today. No matter where your business is located, you should be able to connect easily to the PSTN with the analog or digital signaling options described in this section.

Analog Signaling

Low-density PSTN connectivity typically implies an analog connection. In some geographies Basic Rate Interface (BRI) is used instead, as discussed in the "Digital Signaling" section. Analog signaling is also used for connections to analog stations (such as fax machines and traditional analog phones). Table 6-1 summarizes the analog signaling variations supported by Cisco IOS voice gateways.

Table 6-1   *Analog Signaling Support by Cisco IOS*

Signaling	Description	Typical Use
FXS	Foreign Exchange Station	Used to connect to analog phone sets or fax machines. Occasionally also used to connect to a PBX or Key System if it offers only FXO interfaces.
FXO	Foreign Exchange Office	Generally used to connect to an analog PSTN line. Also used to connect to a PBX or Key System FXS interface. Can be connected to any interface where a standard analog phone is currently connected.
E&M	Ear and Mouth	Used to connect to an analog PBX.
Analog DID	Analog Direct Inward Dial	Used to connect to an analog PSTN line that has DID service on it.
CAMA	Centralized Automatic Message Accounting	Used to connect to the PSTN for emergency services (911 calls) in North America.

To connect your Cisco CME system to the PSTN for normal analog business line service, you use FXO interfaces. FXO ports, like all the other analog interfaces, carry one call per port, so each RJ-11 port on your Cisco CME router connects to one line from the PSTN and carries a single call at a time. (A second call gets busy tone if it tries to use the same port or line.)

NOTE   Note that on voice interface cards such as the NM-HDA and EVM-HD-8FXS/DID, which contain a single RJ-21 50-pin connector, the individual analog ports carried in the single cable are broken into separate RJ-11 ports by a break-out box.

The FXS and FXO voice interfaces are asymmetric, but most of the other signaling methods are symmetric. This means that if the PSTN offers an FXS interface (a normal business line), your Cisco CME router connects to that with an FXO interface. On the other hand, perhaps you have a Key System with FXO interfaces. (Maybe it used to connect to the PSTN, and now you want to connect those same ports to your Cisco CME router.) You require FXS interfaces on the router to connect to these ports.

Asymmetric also means that although you can make calls in both directions across FXS and FXO connections, services typically work in only one direction. For example, caller ID is *sent* on an FXS interface and *received* on an FXO interface, but not the other way around.

Analog trunks all support a single call per physical connection or port, so you need as many ports connected to the PSTN as you require simultaneous calls from your business to the PSTN.

FXO connections do not provide dialed digits (DNIS), introducing challenges in providing automatic call switching. You'll learn more about this in the later section "PSTN Call Switching." Analog DID is a variation of FXO that provides DNIS on what is, essentially, an FXO interface. Note, though, that these trunks are one-way and can only receive calls from the PSTN (they cannot make calls to the PSTN). If you use analog DID for incoming calls from the PSTN, you still need some FXO trunks as well to be able to make outgoing calls to the PSTN.

Digital Signaling

If you require only a small number of simultaneous calls to the PSTN, you will most likely use analog FXO connections. In geographic locations outside North America, ISDN BRI is a likely alternative option for low-density PSTN connectivity. However, if you have a larger office and require more than approximately 10 to 16 simultaneous calls to the PSTN, a digital T1 or E1 trunk might provide a more cost-effective option. Table 6-2 summarizes the digital signaling variations supported by Cisco IOS routers.

Table 6-2   *Digital Signaling Support by Cisco IOS*

Signaling	Description	Typical Use
BRI Q.931	Basic Rate Interface	An ISDN connection to the PSTN or a PBX carrying two simultaneous voice calls. It uses the Q.931 ISDN specification. Calls are controlled via a dedicated channel called the D channel. The term 2B+D is often used for BRI describing two voice channels (or bearer [B] channels) and one signaling channel (or data [D] channel).
BRI QSIG	Basic Rate Interface	Used for PBX ISDN connectivity. It uses the Q Signaling (QSIG) variation of the basic ISDN specification.
T1 CAS	T1 Channel Associated Signaling	Used widely in North America to connect to the PSTN or PBXs. Several variations of this signaling exist, including T1 FXS, T1 FXO, and T1 E&M. T1 E&M signaling supports delay dial, wink, and immediate dial.

continues

Table 6-2 *Digital Signaling Support by Cisco IOS (Continued)*

Signaling	Description	Typical Use
T1 FGD	Feature Group D	The T1 CAS variations generally cannot convey caller ID. T1 FGD can. It's used to connect to the PSTN where caller ID is required and PRI is not an option. T1 FGD is an asymmetric protocol.
T1 and E1 PRI	Primary Rate Interface	An ISDN connection to the PSTN carrying 23 (T1) or 30 (E1) simultaneous voice calls, giving rise to the terms 23B+D and 30B+D. It uses the Q.931 ISDN specification. Calls are controlled via a dedicated signaling channel (D channel).
T1 PRI NFAS	Non-Facility Associated Signaling	A variation of PRI available only on T1 that uses a single D channel to control multiple spans of T1s with only B channels (voice calls).
T1 and E1 QSIG	Primary Rate Interface	Used for PBX ISDN connectivity. It uses the QSIG variation of the basic ISDN specification.
E1 R2	The Regional System 2 (R2) CAS protocol	Used in South America and Asia for PSTN connectivity. Numerous country-specific variations of the R2 protocol exist.
J1	Japan interface	PBX connectivity in Japan. Japan also uses the T1 standard.

BRI connectivity on the Cisco IOS routers is supported only for switch (PSTN, PBX, or Key System) connectivity, not for ISDN BRI phones.

All ISDN variations listed in Table 6-2 support both DID and caller ID, which is implicitly supported in the ISDN protocol. The CAS protocols (T1 CAS and E1 R2) may or may not support caller ID. Typically T1 CAS does not, but T1 FGD is a variation that does. All digital trunk types support DNIS and DID.

Cisco IOS PSTN Telephony Interfaces

You can add numerous modular cards to your Cisco CME router to support PSTN connections of the types discussed in the preceding section. These technologies and hardware cards are not particular to Cisco CME. They can be used on any Cisco router platform that supports the card in question, independent of whether Cisco CME is enabled on the router. For example, you may choose to have two separate routers in your office—one configured for Cisco CME and the other as the PSTN voice gateway. Or you can combine both functions in the same router.

The following sections cover these hardware choices in greater detail, first looking at analog and then at digital PSTN trunks.

Analog Trunks

Voice interfaces range from two- and four-port FXO/FXS/E&M/DID cards up to 96/120-channel quad T1/E1 interfaces. The physical telephony interface for analog and BRI ports is provided by a plug-in voice interface card (VIC) and for a T1/E1 port by a voice or WAN interface card (VWIC).

Using various combinations of VICs and VWICs on a Cisco IOS router, you can build a Cisco CME system that includes a range of physical telephone interfaces. You can assemble a small analog telephony system with a few FXO ports used to connect to PSTN subscriber lines, or you can use digital telephony interfaces such as T1/E1 and ISDN BRI/PRI, or any combination of these. The specific hardware cards offering analog trunk and station (analog phone or fax machine) interfaces are discussed next.

Analog Trunk and Station Hardware

The analog interface cards listed in Table 6-3 are used to provide low-density analog PSTN interfaces. VICs are placed in a WAN interface card (WIC) slot (supported on the Cisco 1751 and 1760), in a high-speed WIC (HWIC) slot on the router (supported on the Cisco 2800 and 3800 series), or inside a network module (Cisco 2600, 2800, 3700, and 3800 series) such as the NM-HD-1V, NM-HD-2V, NM-HD-2VE, or NM-HDV2. For high-density analog PSTN interfaces, the NM-HDA (supported on the Cisco 2600, 2811, 2821, 2851, 3700, and 3800 series) or the EVM-HD-8FXS/DID card (supported on the Cisco 2821, 2851, and 3800 series) can be used.

Table 6-3   *Analog Interfaces, Signaling, and Density*

Interface Card	Signaling	Density
VIC-4FXS/DID	FXS and analog DID	Four ports
VIC2-2FXO	FXO and CAMA	Two ports
VIC-2DID	Analog DID	Two ports
VIC2-4FXO	FXO and CAMA	Four ports
VIC2-2FXS	FXS	Two ports
VIC2-2E/M	E&M	Two ports
NM-HDA-4FXS, EM-HDA-8FXS, and EM-HDA-4FXO	FXS and FXO	Four ports on the baseboard, but can be expanded up to 12 FXS ports by adding an EM-HDA-8FXS card to the network module (NM), or up to eight FXO ports by adding two EM-HDA-4FXO cards to the NM.
EVM-HD-8FXS/DID, EM-HDA-8FXS, EM-HDA-6FXO cards, and EM-HDA-3FXS/ 4FXO	FXS, FXO, CAMA, and analog DID	Eight ports on the baseboard that can be FXS or DID. You can expand the EVM-HD to up to 24 FXS ports by adding two EM-HDA-8FXS cards, or up to 12 FXO ports by adding two EM-HDA-6FXO cards, or various combinations of FXS and FXO by adding one or two EM-HDA-3FXS/ 4FXO cards. The EVM-HD supports any combination of two EM cards.

The cards that support multiple signaling systems (such as FXS or DID, and FXO or CAMA) can be software configured on a per-port basis to support one or the other. For example, the VIC2-4FXO card can be configured to support one CAMA and three FXO ports, or two CAMA and two FXO ports.

Configuring Analog Trunks and Stations

All PSTN interfaces are configured as voice ports on the router. When you insert the card into the router, the configuration automatically creates and shows the corresponding voice ports. Directing calls to a voice port is based on the dial plan and is implemented with plain old telephone service (POTS) dial peers.

A full discussion of Cisco IOS dial plan features on POTS and VoIP dial peers is beyond the scope of this book. However, note the use of the 9T directive in the **destination-pattern** command of the dial peer in Example 6-1, which shows a basic FXO port configuration.

Example 6-1   *FXO Port and Dial Peer Configuration*

```
Router#show running-config
voice-port 1/0/0

voice-port 1/0/1

dial-peer voice 100 pots
 description PSTN
 destination-pattern 9T
 port 1/0/0

dial-peer voice 100 pots
 description PSTN
 destination-pattern 9T
 port 1/0/1
```

This command is a quick way of dealing with variable-length PSTN dial plans. The T denotes a timeout. The command **destination-pattern 9T** instructs the dial peer to match any dialed digits that start with a nine, regardless of how many digits follow. When the timeout expires, the digits are forwarded from the voice port to the PSTN. There are other, more explicit ways to make your destination-pattern commands match calls to the PSTN more exactly, including **9911**, **9411**, **91T**, and **9[2-9]**.

The dial peers shown in Example 6-1 direct all calls (of a varying number of digits) that start with a nine to the two PSTN FXO trunks, ports 1/0/0 and 1/0/1. If no preference is given on the dial peers and both trunks are free, the Cisco IOS software chooses one of the two trunks at random. You can control the order in which they are chosen by adding a **preference** command to the dial peer. The **dial-peer hunt** command offers additional control over the sequence in which dial peers, and therefore voice ports, are chosen.

You can also direct calls to different destinations over different trunks if you want to. This is shown in Example 6-2, where calls to the 408 area code always use voice port 1/0/0, and calls to the 415 area code always use voice port 1/0/1. This way, if you have different local and long-distance PSTN provider connections, you can connect to each independently and direct different types of calls to the correct trunks.

Example 6-2 *Different PSTN Numbers to Different Trunks*

```
Router#show running-config
voice-port 1/0/0

voice-port 1/0/1

dial-peer voice 100 pots
 description PSTN
 destination-pattern 9408.......
 port 1/0/0

dial-peer voice 101 pots
 description PSTN
 destination-pattern 9415.......
 port 1/0/1
```

If you require CAMA connectivity to comply with North American emergency calling regulations, you can configure one or more of your FXO ports for CAMA operation. This is shown in Example 6-3, where port 2/0/3 on a VIC2-4FXO card is configured for CAMA signaling.

Example 6-3 *CAMA Configuration*

```
Router#show running-config
voice-port 2/0/0

voice-port 2/0/1
   signal ground-start

voice-port 2/0/2

voice-port 2/0/3
   signal cama KP-NPD-NXX-XXXX-ST
```

Analog Trunk Features

With analog FXO interfaces, caller ID information received for an incoming PSTN call is displayed on the IP phones. You can optionally enable the Flash softkey on your IP phones. Pressing the Flash softkey on the IP phone generates a hookflash signal on the FXO port and allows you to exercise PSTN subscriber line services, such as PSTN call waiting and three-way calling. However, Cisco IOS FXO ports do not support PSTN call waiting caller ID display.

You can also set up a direct link between a specific PSTN telephone line and an individual button on an IP phone. This is useful if you want to use PSTN-based voice mail services where a stutter dial tone on the PSTN line indicates that a message is waiting.

As mentioned earlier, in the section "Analog Signaling," FXO interfaces are asymmetric. As such, calls can be disconnected in only one direction in pure FXO operation. The historic reasons for this are beyond the scope of this book. Suffice it to say that today FXO ports are widely used as two-way trunks, and special care must be taken that calls disconnect properly in both directions and do not hang the port. You can use the following Cisco IOS commands on the voice port to facilitate proper call disconnect on FXO ports:

- **signal groundstart**
- **battery-reversal**
- **supervisory disconnect dualtone**
- **supervisory disconnect anytone**

Which of these methods you should use depends on the complementary features provided by your PSTN CO switch. It also varies based on your geographic location and the technology available in the CO you connect to.

In addition, FXO signaling does not receive dialed digits (that is, DNIS). This means that an incoming call from the PSTN to an FXO port cannot be switched automatically by your Cisco CME system to an extension, because there are no digits from the PSTN to tell Cisco CME where to switch it. You can overcome this shortcoming of FXO signaling by using auto-terminate directives on the FXO voice port to switch the call to a predetermined destination. Commands you can explore include **connection plar** and **connection plar-opx**, which you will learn more about in the later section "PSTN Call Switching."

Digital Trunks

Digital trunks can be low-density (for example, BRI with two calls per port) or high-density T1 or E1 ports with 24 or 30 calls per port, respectively. The specific hardware cards offering digital trunk interfaces are discussed next.

Digital Trunk Hardware

The digital interface cards listed in Table 6-4 are used to provide a range of low- to high-density digital PSTN interfaces.

Table 6-4 *Digital Interfaces, Signaling, and Density*

Interface Card	Signaling	Density
VIC2-2BRI-NT/TE	Q.931 or QSIG BRI	Two ports and four voice channels.
NM-HDV	T1 and E1	Up to two T1/E1 ports. Up to 48 (T1) or 60 (E1) voice channels. Used in conjunction with a VWIC-1MFT-T1/E1 or VWIC-2MFT-T1/E1.
NM-HD-2VE	Analog, BRI, T1, and E1	Up to four T1/E1 ports, or two T1/E1 and two BRI ports, or four BRI ports. Up to 24 voice channels. Used in conjunction with a VWIC-1MFT-T1/E1, VWIC-2MFT-T1/E1, or VIC2-2BRI-NT/TE.
NM-HDV2	Analog, BRI, T1, and E1	Up to four T1/E1 ports, or two T1/E1 ports and two BRI ports. Up to 120 voice channels. Has up to two onboard T1/E1 ports. For the additional ports, a VWIC-1MFT-T1/E1 or VWIC-2MFT-T1/E1 is used. For BRI, the VIC2-2BRI-NT/TE card is used inside the NM.
EVM-HD-8FXS/DID, EM-4BRI-NT/TE	Analog and BRI	Up to eight BRI ports (16 voice channels).
VWIC-1MFT-T1/E1 or VWIC-2MFT-T1/E1 in a WIC slot	T1 and E1	Up to two T1/E1 ports. Channel density depends on the router platform and where the DSPs are accessed from.

In the general case, a T1 port offers 24 voice channels, and an E1 port offers 30 channels. When using ISDN signaling, where one channel is dedicated to call control signaling (the D channel), a T1 carries 23 voice channels, and an E1 carries 30 voice channels. (An E1 always has a channel dedicated to signaling, no matter what type of protocol is used. With T1 this is not normally the case; using ISDN takes away one of the standard channels.)

You do not have to use the maximum number of channels on these ports, depending on what your PSTN service provider offers. You can configure your Cisco IOS router with any number of channels on the T1 or E1 interface, but it has to be complemented by what is configured on the PSTN CO on the other side.

Fractional T1 service is quite common in North America, where you can subscribe to PSTN T1 service with, for example, only 12 or 16 channels of service (and this service costs less than a full T1 of 24 channels). This service can be either T1 CAS or T1 PRI. Another service is to multiplex your WAN connection (Frame Relay or Point-to-Point Protocol [PPP]) on some channels of the same physical T1 used for your PSTN voice connection. For example, channels 1 to 6 could offer a 384-Kbps PPP WAN connection, and channels 10 to 20 could offer ten channels of PSTN voice service using T1 E&M signaling.

Fractional E1 service is much less common or isn't available at all. Your lower-density PSTN connectivity options in geographies that use E1 connectivity may be multiples of BRI until such time as a full E1 makes sense for your business.

Configuring Digital Trunks

Digital PSTN interfaces are configured in general just like analog interfaces—that is, as voice ports and POTS dial peers on the router to direct calls to the ports. The dial peer control and configuration are exactly the same, regardless of what type of voice port you're using.

T1/E1 ports, however, show up as controllers in your basic configuration (by just inserting the hardware into the router). Unlike an analog interface, the voice port is not created until you add more configuration details to the controller. T1/E1 ports are used for both data and voice access. Until you add specific configuration statements, the router does not know what your intention is with the T1/E1 port. You add a voice configuration to a T1/E1 port by using either the **ds0-group** or **pri-group** command. A data T1/E1 port is configured with the **channel-group** command.

You often see the terms CAS and *common channel signaling* (*CCS*) when reading about T1/E1 trunks. CAS generally means that the signaling to control the call uses the same channel (or timeslot) as the call's media path. This is common on T1 interfaces. (It is also called *robbed-bit signaling* because a few bits out of the 64-kbps channel are "stolen" from the media path to convey call control information, such as on-hook and off-hook.) CCS means that a channel is dedicated to signaling. This channel carries the call control information for all the voice calls (media paths) on that same T1/E1 interface. For example, channel 16 on an E1 is used exclusively for call control and carries the control information for all the other channels (1 to 15 and 17 to 31) on that interface.

Example 6-4 shows a T1 CAS (E&M immediate start) PSTN connection using a **ds0-group** configuration. In this example, you can see that the second port on the VWIC shows up as controller T1 2/1. This means that the hardware has been detected but no configuration has been done for this port.

Example 6-4 *T1 CAS Configuration*

```
Router#show running-config
controller T1 2/0
 framing esf
 clock source internal
 linecode b8zs
 ds0-group 0 timeslots 1-24 type e&m-immediate-start
```

Example 6-4   *T1 CAS Configuration (Continued)*

```
controller T1 2/1

voice-port 2/0:0
 signal immediate

dial-peer voice 100 pots
 description PSTN
 destination-pattern 9T
 port 2/0:0
```

In this example, all 24 channels on the T1 are configured. But you could as easily have stated **ds0-group 0 timeslots 1-10** if you agreed with your provider to get only ten channels of PSTN service on this T1 (fractional T1 service). The result of the **ds0-group** command is that voice port 2/0:0 is created. The POTS dial peer, in this example, looks the same as the one in the FXO example earlier, except that it now points to voice port 2/0:0, which is a T1 port.

If you are using ISDN PRI service to the PSTN, you use the **pri-group** command to insert a voice configuration on a T1 or E1 controller. Example 6-5 shows a sample configuration for a T1 PRI trunk.

Example 6-5   *T1 PRI Configuration*

```
Router#show running-config
isdn switch-type primary-5ess

controller T1 2/0
 framing esf
 linecode b8zs
 pri-group timeslots 1-24

interface Serial2/0:23
 no ip address
 isdn switch-type primary-5ess
 isdn incoming-voice voice

voice-port 2/0:23
 echo-cancel coverage 64

dial-peer voice 100 pots
 description PSTN
 destination-pattern 9T
 port 2/0:23
```

Geographic variants of ISDN are controlled by the **switch-type** setting. A default router setting, seen in Example 6-5 as the first line in the configuration, is specified at the Cisco IOS global level (the **isdn switch-type** command). This default can be overridden on a per-interface basis by the **switch-type** statement under the controller. In Example 6-5, both are set to **primary-5ess**, but they could be different. If they are different, the statement on the controller takes precedence.

The D channel interface (**interface Serial 2/0:23**) and voice-port (**voice-port 2/0:23**) commands are automatically created by the insertion of the **pri-group** command on the controller. The POTS dial peer again looks exactly the same as in Examples 6-1, 6-2, and 6-4. You simply have to adjust the voice port it refers to.

Digital Trunk Features

For PRI/BRI interfaces using ISDN signaling, you can optionally allow the IP phone's full DID name and number to be used as the calling party's identity for outgoing calls. This puts extension-specific information into the PSTN billing records for the call. This can be useful if you want to rely on the PSTN provider's billing information to track the internal origin point of PSTN calls made from your Cisco CME system. Alternatively, you can block IP phone extension-specific information from the outgoing ISDN call and instead substitute the general public phone number for your system.

Generally, PSTN providers do not use name information delivered to the PSTN by a subscriber system. Although the name can be included in the ISDN call setup, the PSTN typically overrides this with the information associated with the subscriber in the PSTN's own databases. You can, however, receive name display information from the PSTN on ISDN trunks, and display this on the IP phones in your business.

All digital trunks provide DID (or DNIS) information. ISDN trunks also provide caller ID delivery. Fractional CAS and PRI are supported on the Cisco IOS routers. If you configure fractional PRI, the D channel for the T1 must be on channel 24 and for E1 on channel 16. This cannot be customized. The voice channels (B channels) can be any subset of the remaining channels.

ISDN channels cannot be customized to be incoming only or outgoing only. However, through creative use of dial peers, you can limit the number of incoming or outgoing calls to and from your business. You just cannot specify the exact channel each call should use. With T1 CAS, you have more granular control, because you can specify separate ds0-groups (up to a ds0-group per channel). Each ds0-group creates a separate voice port that you can control via dial peers as to what calls may reach those channels. Example 6-6 shows a sample configuration for this.

Example 6-6 *T1 CAS Configuration with Separate Voice Ports*

```
Router#show running-config
controller T1 2/0
 framing esf
 clock source internal
 linecode b8zs
 ds0-group 0 timeslots 1-10 type e&m-immediate-start
 ds0-group 1 timeslots 15-20 type e&m-immediate-start
```

Example 6-6   *T1 CAS Configuration with Separate Voice Ports (Continued)*

```
controller T1 2/1

voice-port 2/0:0
 signal immediate

voice-port 2/0:1
 signal immediate

dial-peer voice 100 pots
 description PSTN
 destination-pattern 9408.......
 port 2/0:0

dial-peer voice 101 pots
 description PSTN
 destination-pattern 9415.......
 port 2/0:1
```

The **ds0-group 0 timeslots 1-10** command results in voice **port 2/0:0**, and the **ds0-group 1 timeslots 15-20** command creates voice **port 2/0:1**.

DSP Hardware

Digital signal processor (DSP) technology provides voice compression, echo cancellation, tone generation, and voice packetization functions for servicing voice interfaces and converting the voice for transport over packet networks. To drive a PSTN voice connection, the analog or digital voice ports must have access to a DSP for the call.

Some voice NMs include internal slots into which DSP modules can be plugged, and others have fixed DSP configurations. In some router models, such as the Cisco 1760, 2800, and 3800 series, you can plug DSP cards directly into the router's motherboard.

VWIC cards offer only physical T1/E1 port connections, and VIC cards offer only the physical analog or BRI ports. If a VIC or VWIC card is inserted into a router WIC slot (supported on the Cisco 1751, 1760, 2800, and 3800 series), the DSPs are typically provided by the onboard DSP cards. A VIC or VWIC inserted into an NM typically draws on DSPs resident on the NM itself.

One other variation is to use a VWIC in a WIC slot on the Cisco 2600 or 3700 series platforms, which do not support onboard DSPs. For this configuration, you can use a DSP AIM card such as the AIM-VOICE-30 or the AIM-ATM-VOICE-30 card. (An Advanced Integration Module [AIM] is an internal plug-in module that fits on the router's motherboard.) The AIM-based DSPs cannot drive analog or BRI VIC cards, only T1/E1 VWICs.

DSP cards for motherboard and NM-based slots come in many densities and use various DSP technologies. All are called packet voice/fax DSP module (PVDM) cards.

PSTN Trunks Integrated with or Separate from Cisco CME

In a typical deployment, the PSTN connectivity for your business is integrated into your Cisco CME router. However, you could also use a separate router platform as your PSTN gateway. You may choose to do this because you already have a router that acts as your PSTN gateway in your office or because the slot density on your Cisco CME router is insufficient for the PSTN connectivity your office requires.

For PSTN trunks integrated onto your Cisco CME router, the voice call is switched directly from the POTS interface to the IP phone and is straightforward to configure. Placing the PSTN gateway on a different platform gives you an H.323 (or SIP) call leg between the PSTN gateway and the Cisco CME call controller where the IP phones are managed. This requires POTS dial peers to direct calls to the PSTN interfaces, as shown in the previous configuration examples in this chapter. It also requires H.323 dial peers to direct calls from the PSTN gateway to IP phones, as well as from the IP phones to the PSTN gateway. From an H.323 standpoint, this configuration is similar to connecting two separate Cisco CME systems via an H.323 VoIP interface between them. This is shown in Figure 6-1.

Figure 6-1 *Integrated or Separate PSTN Gateways*

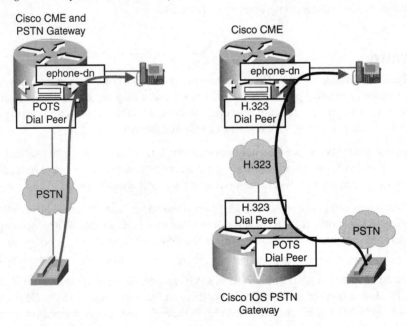

It is recommended that you deploy Cisco CME with an integrated PSTN gateway, because this results in a much simpler network design and configuration. Another consideration is that if Cisco Unity Express (UE) is used for the automated attendant (AA) or voice mail on your Cisco CME system, the H.323 VoIP leg must be converted to a SIP call leg before the call can successfully terminate on the Cisco UE application. In Cisco CME 3.2 and later, you can do this using the Cisco IOS translation shown in Example 6-7. In Cisco CME 3.1 and earlier, a workaround using loopback-dns can be used, but this is not recommended. It complicates your configuration considerably and has several caveats about particular call flows that are not supported with loopback-dns, such as T.38 fax relay. It is better to upgrade to Cisco CME 3.2.

Example 6-7 *H.323 to SIP Translation for Calls into Cisco UE*

```
Router#show running-config
voice service voip
 allow-connections h323 to sip
```

PSTN Call Switching

The preceding sections explored the various PSTN trunk types, signaling methods, and router hardware you can use to connect to the PSTN. But there are more considerations than just physical connectivity. One thing to keep in mind is that the PSTN numbers and your internal extension numbers are almost certainly not the same, at least not the same length. Digit translation must occur to map one set of numbers to another. You'll learn more about this in the later section "Digit Manipulation."

Another consideration is what PSTN numbers (and how many) your business has or needs. Do you have just one main office number, and the receptionist directs all calls to the correct employee? Do you need an AA menu to have callers switch to the person or service they want to speak to? Should you have DID numbers for all or some of your employees? Do you prefer a Key System type of operation, where a series of PSTN numbers appear as distinct line appearances on a number of phones, and any employee can pick up any call? There is interaction between your business needs, the PSTN service you get from your provider, the capabilities of the physical connection to the PSTN, and the Cisco CME configuration (IP phone button appearances) to use.

The physical connection is likely dictated in large part by cost, your office's geographic location, and the number of voice channels your office needs. You may desire DID service for your business. However, if it's not offered in your area at a cost-effective level, you have little choice but to settle for non-DID service.

The following sections explore considerations about how calls may be routed depending on whether you have DID service and, even if you do, how you can handle calls to non-DID destinations within your business.

PSTN Call Switching with DID Enabled

Many offices deploying Cisco CME have DID capability from the PSTN provider for some subset of employees. PSTN calls to DID destinations can be switched automatically to the employee's phone without any manual intervention.

There are two situations to consider, depending on how DID numbers are allocated to destinations within your business:

- All employees, the AA, and voice mail pilot numbers have DID numbers assigned. In this configuration, PSTN calls can be switched as follows:

    — The main office number (non-DID calls) terminates on the AA pilot (for AA assistance) or on an IP phone extension (for receptionist assistance).

    — Employee DID numbers terminate on the extension for that person's IP phone.

    — The number employees call from PSTN locations to check their voice mail terminates on the voice mail pilot number.

- Some employees have DID numbers assigned, and others do not. In this configuration, PSTN calls are handled as follows:

    — Calls to the main office number and for PSTN voice mail checking are handled as per the preceding scenario.

    — Calls to employees with DID numbers terminate on the extension for that person's phone.

    — Calls to employees without DID numbers terminate on the AA (or receptionist's extension). These callers then can dial through or be transferred to the extension of the person they want to reach.

PSTN Call Switching with DNIS But No DID

PSTN call switching with DNIS and no DID is not a likely configuration, but it is possible. In this configuration, your business does not have DID service and, therefore, has only a single main office number from the PSTN provider even though you have multiple trunks. Or even if you have multiple PSTN numbers, they are not associated with particular employees, but instead are just alternate main office numbers.

Although the dialed number is delivered via DNIS from the PSTN to the PSTN gateway, it is of little use to switch calls to individual destinations. In this situation, you have two configuration choices:

- Regardless of the dialed number, all PSTN calls are terminated on the AA pilot (for AA assistance) or on a specific phone extension (for receptionist assistance).

- All PSTN lines appear on multiple phones (Key System operation). Any employee at these phones can answer any of the lines, regardless of what number the caller dialed.

If all calls are directed to the AA (or a receptionist), *caller-busy* conditions must be carefully considered. For example, you need to determine what should happen if all AA ports are busy or all the receptionists are busy. If you do not want busy tone returned, more ports or receptionists may be required, or alternate destinations to switch calls to (lower-preference dial peers) or DID service may be needed for high-volume destinations in your business.

PSTN Call Switching with No DNIS (FXO Trunks)

If the office has only FXO trunks, no DNIS (or DID) capability is technically possible. This scenario is very common for a small standalone office or a small branch of a bigger network that has only a few business lines from the local CO.

Because no dialed digits (DNIS) are available on FXO trunks, these calls must be autoterminated on a predetermined destination, most often the AA or the receptionist's extension. This can be achieved with a private line automatic ringdown (PLAR) configuration on the voice port where a particular destination extension is associated with the trunk, and all calls arriving on that trunk are switched as if they had dialed the configured extension. This syntax is shown in Example 6-8, where all calls arriving on the FXO trunk on slot 1/0/0 are switched as if they had dialed extension 6800.

Example 6-8   *PLAR Syntax for FXO Trunks*

```
Router#show running-config
voice-port 1/0/0
  connection plar opx 6800
```

Most small offices have multiple FXO trunks to the PSTN because each trunk can carry only a single call. One or more PSTN numbers may be associated with these trunks or this trunk group, depending on the PSTN service the business subscribes to. Generally, there are two possibilities:

- **A single PSTN main office number**—In this configuration, all calls from the PSTN are terminated (via the PLAR feature) to the AA pilot (for AA assistance) or to a specific phone extension (for receptionist assistance).

- **Multiple PSTN numbers**—You could have one PSTN number for the main office and another for voice mail retrieval by employees. In this case, calls on main office trunks are switched as in the preceding case, and calls to voice mail are switched (via PLAR) to the voice mail pilot number. Clearly, these two types of calls must be delivered on different physical trunks or trunk groups so that each is autoterminated to the correct destination.

Sharing all FXO trunks across all PSTN calls (the first case in the preceding list) results in better trunk utilization than assigning distinct FXO trunk(s) to the main office number and other distinct FXO trunk(s) to the voice mail pilot number (the second case).

Digit Manipulation

There are various reasons to manipulate the digits dialed by the caller on a voice system. The most common reason is to allow both internal calls (from other extensions) and external calls from the PSTN (where a full E.164 phone number is delivered) to terminate directly on the user's phone without needing a receptionist to intercept and redirect the call.

NOTE	E.164 is an International Telecommunication Union (ITU) specification that describes international telephone dial plans. It specifies phone number attributes such as international dialing codes, regional (area) codes, and the minimum and maximum length of each field in the phone number. Voice systems use the E.164 specification to parse and interpret phone numbers. PSTN numbers are always fully qualified E.164 numbers, whereas extensions within your business typically aren't, because they are private numbers of local significance only.

Here are some other reasons to translate (or manipulate) digits:

- To allow IP phone users to call each other directly by extension, and also to access the PSTN
- To allow for site access codes in a multisite on-net dial plan and to strip these digits to extract the extension as soon as the destination site is reached
- To allow for variable-length external (off-net) dialing while maintaining fixed-length internal dialing
- To block calls to certain numbers
- To redirect calls to certain numbers

For example, suppose your employee, Grace, is at extension 3001, and her PSTN DID number is 444-555-3001. Without some form of digit manipulation or live intercept, a call incoming from the PSTN that dialed 444-555-3001 will not match the ephone-dn definition for Grace's phone, which contains only her extension, 3001. Therefore, a method is needed to translate the string 4445553001 to 3001.

Several Cisco IOS digit manipulation tools can translate phone numbers. The following are the most common:

- Dial peer commands
- Cisco CME **dialplan-pattern** command
- IOS translation rules

Dial Peer Commands

You can include several commands on a POTS dial peer to add, suppress, or substitute the digits forwarded to the PSTN trunk interface:

- **destination-pattern**
- **digit-strip**
- **forward-digits**
- **prefix**

- **translate-outgoing**
- **translation-profile**

Dial peer commands are handy if only small changes to the beginning or end of the dialed number are necessary, such as prefixing an area code, prefixing a CO designator (NXX) to an extension number, or forwarding only the last four digits of a longer number. The wildcard matching within the **destination-pattern** command automatically deletes the numbers explicitly matched. For example, when 5553001 is dialed and is matched by a dial peer that contains the command destination-pattern 555...., the default operation is to forward only the digits 3001.

Cisco IOS Translation Rules

For more extensive digit manipulation, such as a wholesale change of a number or substituting digits in the middle of a number, translation rules are much more powerful. Translation rules are regular expressions attached to the dial peer with the **translation-profile** command.

Like the other dial peer commands discussed in the preceding section, translation rules are a generic Cisco IOS feature that allows manipulation of called numbers, calling numbers, and number types. It can also be attached in such a way that it translates calls in only one direction, either incoming or outgoing.

Example 6-9 gives a configuration extract for a T1 PRI trunk, with translation profile **to_261x** attached for incoming calls (calls from the PSTN to the Cisco IOS PSTN gateway). Translation profile **to_261x**, in turn, references **translation rule 23**, which has ten rules specified. This CLI segment intercepts all calls incoming from the PSTN over this T1 PRI that contains a dialed number ending in the range 12610 to 12619. It does not matter what (or how many) numbers precede this range; for example, it could be 555-331-2610 or 551-2618. The numbers that match the rule (12610 to 12619) are translated pointblank to a completely unrelated number so that none of the original digits survive. To illustrate, if a call with a dialed number of 555-331-2610 arrives, it is translated to 32085, and an IP phone (or other dial peer) associated with that extension receives the call. A PSTN call with a dialed number of 551-2618 results in extension 79988 receiving the call.

Example 6-9 *Translation Rules*

```
Router#show running-config
voice translation-rule 23
 rule 1 /12611/ /37002/
 rule 2 /12612/ /37262/
 rule 3 /12613/ /37990/
 rule 4 /12614/ /57514/
 rule 5 /12615/ /30631/
 rule 6 /12616/ /50043/
 rule 7 /12617/ /28787/
 rule 8 /12618/ /79988/
 rule 9 /12619/ /68278/
 rule 10 /12610/ /32085/
```

continues

Example 6-9 *Translation Rules (Continued)*

```
voice translation-profile to_261x
 translate called 23

controller T1 2/0
 framing esf
 linecode b8zs
 pri-group timeslots 1-24

interface Serial2/0:23
 no ip address
 no logging event link-status
 isdn switch-type primary-5ess
 isdn incoming-voice voice

voice-port 2/0:23
 echo-cancel coverage 64

dial-peer voice 1261 pots
 translation-profile incoming to_261x
 incoming called-number 1261.
 direct-inward-dial
 port 2/0:23
```

The syntax for translation rules can be cryptic if you are unfamiliar with regular expressions. But it is a very powerful facility to manipulate digits, and it is not tied to Cisco CME, so you can use it on any Cisco IOS voice-enabled router.

Here are some considerations when using the Cisco IOS voice translation rules feature:

- It's a very powerful feature that can do almost any translation of digits required, but it can be obscure and, therefore, error-prone to those who are unfamiliar with it.
- Being a generic Cisco IOS feature, the feature's rules apply to all calls that traverse the router. It can be applied at a global level, dial peers, and ephone-dns (Cisco CME IP phones).
- The digits are manipulated before dial peer matching and call termination.
- Calling and/or called numbers can be manipulated on every call based on what is configured.
- The rules can be directionally applied to incoming or outgoing calls (or both).

When applying translation rules to ephone-dns, there is a side effect that if no rule is matched, an extra post-dial delay is incurred. As a workaround, create a dummy translation rule that acts as a pass-through. For example, if no rule is applied to extension-to-extension calls, and the extensions all start with five, add a rule that "translates" five to five, just to make sure that a rule is always matched, and the delay is not incurred.

Cisco CME dialplan-pattern Command

The Cisco CME **dialplan-pattern** command allows E.164 numbers to be mapped to extension numbers or, put another way, to extract the extension number from a longer DID number. The **dialplan-pattern** command does not actually translate the number (although the effect from a call routing point of view is the same). It instead creates multiple dial peers that allow different dialed numbers to terminate on the same phone.

The **dialplan-pattern** command can be used in some cases (calls to IP phones) to achieve the same call routing as can be achieved by using translation rules. Because these two features operate differently, you should think carefully about which method to use. If you use both methods, you should be clear about how these might interplay with each other to affect your call routing. The **dialplan-pattern** command is explained in more detail in Chapter 7, "Connecting Multiple Cisco CMEs with VoIP."

The CLI shown in Example 6-10 does the same mapping as the number translation discussed previously for employee Grace.

Example 6-10   *Cisco CME* **dialplan-pattern** *Command*

```
Router#show running-config
telephony-service
 load 7960-7940 P00303020214
 max-ephones 48
 max-dn 192
 ip source-address 10.1.3.1 port 2000
 system message CUE System 2691
 create cnf-files version-stamp 7960 Jul 15 2003 13:48:12
 dialplan-pattern 1 510395.... extension-length 4
 voicemail 6800
 max-conferences 8
 web admin system name cue password cue
 dn-webedit
 time-webedit
```

Some considerations about using the Cisco CME **dialplan-pattern** feature include the following:

- It's an easy-to-use, user-friendly feature.

- It's a Cisco CME feature, so it applies only to calls to and from IP phones controlled by Cisco CME. It does not apply to calls from the PSTN gateway directly to the AA or voice mail pilot numbers. Therefore, if digit manipulation is needed on these calls, one of the other two methods must be used.

- The IP phone extension must have at least one digit in common with the original called number and be in the same sequence. (If the extension is completely different from the called number, or not in sequence, Cisco IOS translation rules must be used to manipulate the digits.)

- Like Cisco IOS translation rules, the digits are manipulated before dial peer matching and call termination.

- It manipulates the **called** number on a call to an IP phone and the *calling* number of a call from an IP phone. This operation is implicit and cannot be controlled or altered.

- The E.164 number patterns generated by the **dialplan-pattern** command can be registered to an H.323 gatekeeper or SIP proxy. Digit translations done with Cisco IOS translation rules are not registered to H.323 gatekeepers or SIP proxies.

PSTN Trunk Failover

Larger offices that use a digital trunk, such as a PRI, often need a backup method to connect to the PSTN. This requirement results in the PRI being the main PSTN connection point in addition to a handful of FXO trunks (typically to back up a T1) or BRI interfaces (typically to back up an E1) used if the main interface is down.

In this configuration, the dial peers directing calls to the main interface must be duplicated to also point to the backup interface. You can force calls to use the main interface when it is available by using the **preference** command on the dial peers pointing to these trunks. The use of the **preference** command is covered in Chapter 5, "Cisco CME Call Processing Features."

Another need is to have a backup mechanism for a small office with FXO trunks if a power failure should occur. FXO hardware supports a feature called FXO Power Failover that allows a hardware (relay) connection between a *red* phone (a specially dedicated analog telephone in your office that normally is not in use) and the PSTN line, in case the router is not powered.

On Cisco voice hardware, the NM-HDA-4FXS FXO expansion card (the EM-HDA-4FXO) and the EVM-HD-8FXS/DID FXO expansion card (the EM-HDA-6FXO) each have one port per card that has this power failover capability. Other Cisco FXO hardware cards do not support this feature.

Summary

In this chapter, you learned how to connect your Cisco CME system to the PSTN. You reviewed the different signaling mechanisms and the features each provides to your business. You also learned about the Cisco IOS voice-enabled router hardware you can choose from to connect to the PSTN.

The latter part of this chapter focused on PSTN call switching and routing considerations to help you set up and optimize your office to handle PSTN calls in the manner that best fits your business model.

This chapter covers the following topics:

- General considerations when integrating Cisco CallManager Express (CME) in H.323 and Session Initiation Protocol (SIP) voice over IP (VoIP) networks
- Integrating Cisco CME into an H.323 network with or without a gatekeeper
- dual-tone multifrequency (DTMF) relay for H.323
- Call transfer and call forwarding within an H.323 network using H.450
- Integrating Cisco CME into a SIP network

## CHAPTER 7

Connecting Multiple Cisco CMEs with VoIP

This chapter describes the ways in which you can use Cisco CME as a component of a larger network using the two major voice over IP (VoIP) protocols—H.323 and SIP—to link multiple Cisco CME systems. It examines some of the considerations that apply within a networked environment that do not arise in simpler standalone configurations. This chapter focuses on the call handling implications of using Cisco CME in a network. The administration of networked systems is covered in Chapter 14, "Configuring and Managing Cisco IPC Express Systems."

Considerations When Integrating Cisco CME in H.323 and SIP VoIP Networks

H.323 is the dominant protocol deployed for VoIP networks from an installed-base perspective. Because H.323 is more mature than SIP, you can expect to see increased real-world interoperability between different vendors' H.323 products, particularly with basic call handling. However, many of the high-level VoIP networking considerations that apply to H.323 apply equally in the SIP context. Some technical and protocol-specific differences exist between H.323 and SIP VoIP networking, but for the most part, you'll find more commonality than difference, at least at the level of technical detail that this chapter addresses.

The shared aspects of the two protocols means that the overall high-level architecture and distribution of hardware and primary component roles within your VoIP network don't significantly depend on which protocol you choose to use for intersite VoIP. For networks built on either H.323 or SIP, you are dealing with peer-to-peer communication between sites. Therefore, you also need some kind of telephone number directory system to be able to resolve the IP address of the appropriate destination VoIP peer device for intersite calls.

In contrast, this similarity between H.323 and SIP does not extend to Media Gateway Control Protocol (MGCP) (and also Skinny Client Control Protocol [SCCP]), which takes a significantly different approach to telephony. Of course, it is still possible to connect Cisco CME to MGCP networks, primarily using either H.323 or SIP. Many MGCP Call Agent implementations (using MGCP internally for phone control) use H.323 or SIP to connect separate Call Agents (as intersystem peer-to-peer). Cisco CME itself does not support control of MGCP endpoints. Cisco CME uses SCCP for phone control, and SCCP shares many common traits with MGCP.

The term *VoIP* here specifically describes "long-distance" VoIP telephone calls that traverse a WAN. This interpretation excludes SCCP used to control local IP phones. Although SCCP technically does use VoIP technology, it is primarily used in the context of operating voice calls within the confines of a LAN with more or less unlimited bandwidth and many fewer concerns about security.

You can view the H.323/SIP versus SCCP contrast as the difference between interbranch office voice traffic and intrabranch office voice traffic, or alternatively as long distance (WAN) versus local VoIP (LAN). This division is useful in many ways, because it inherently supports the often-necessary difference in treatment of calls between internal and external phone users.

In some cases, you will want to treat H.323 calls as internal calls and won't want a high degree of differentiation in the treatment of LAN versus WAN calls, such as calls between separate systems on two floors of the same building. Cisco CME has features that address this, although currently you cannot treat a network of many Cisco CME systems as if they are a single logical entity with full intersite feature transparency. Both H.323 and SIP still have obstacles to overcome before this is really possible. Not least of these are issues surrounding meaningful interoperability with non-Cisco devices for services beyond basic calls.

When you extend VoIP calling into the WAN space, you might also have to consider the difference between VoIP calls that come from other Cisco CME nodes within your WAN network versus VoIP calls that are from VoIP Public Switched Telephone Network (PSTN) gateways or even from other independent external/wholesale VoIP carrier networks. You can link independent VoIP networks together and into your corporate VoIP network using IP-to-IP gateways. This arrangement may be desirable if you want to obtain international and long-distance phone service directly from a carrier-class VoIP service provider and have this linked at the VoIP level to your private enterprise VoIP network.

SIP potentially has some advantages over H.323 in terms of separating intersite VoIP calls from true external VoIP calls, because SIP uses the Internet concept of domains. It's a fair assumption that all of the intersite calls will use the same root domain name and that this fact can be used to make the required distinction. However, from a purely practical security point of view, most likely you will want any truly external VoIP traffic entering your corporate VoIP network to pass through an IP-to-IP gateway and also a firewall, regardless of whether you choose to use SIP or H.323. This means that you should have the opportunity to appropriately classify and mark the external calls at the point of entry in either type of network.

Alternatively, you can keep your VoIP network entirely separate at the IP level and simply connect into VoIP service provider carrier networks through time-division multiplexing (TDM)-based PSTN-like gateways (at some cost in terms of increased end-to-end voice path delay). For the sake of simplicity and clarity, the rest of this chapter ignores the IP-to-IP possibility and includes only the PSTN gateway scenario. For many reasons, what is on the far side of the gateway—whether PSTN or IP-to-IP—isn't hugely significant. It's the gateway's job to take care of whatever adaptation is needed to provide the interconnection path.

Integrating Cisco CME in an H.323 Network

There are two basic approaches to connecting a Cisco CME system to an H.323 network: the first uses no gatekeeper (GK), and the second does. A direct interconnection of sites with H.323 implies that each site must be knowledgeable about how to reach every other site. This works well in small networks of only a handful of nodes, but as the network grows larger, the configuration becomes increasingly cumbersome to maintain. In its simplest form, a gatekeeper is a device that provides a directory service that translates a telephone number into an IP address. Using a gatekeeper provides significant scalability by centralizing the interconnection of the individual sites so that each site needs to be aware of only the gatekeeper and not every other site in the network.

The following sections discuss different approaches to building Cisco CME networks. Rather than being alternative approaches, they represent a simpler approach for smaller networks with only a few nodes and a more scalable approach for larger multinode networks.

A Simple Two-Node Topology with H.323

In the simplest case, you can just connect two Cisco CME systems via an IP-enabled serial data link (or Ethernet), and configure VoIP dial peers on each system to symmetrically direct calls that are destined for nonlocal extension numbers to the other Cisco CME system. In other words, if the Cisco CME recognizes that the extension number being dialed isn't present in its internal list of phone numbers, it can assume that it should send the call to the other Cisco CME, as shown in Figure 7-1.

Figure 7-1   *Simple Two-Node Cisco CME H.323 Network*

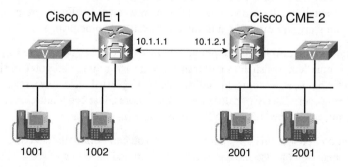

Example 7-1 shows the relevant configuration extracts of the two systems. It shows a pair of Cisco CME systems that have extensions 1000 to1099 on CME 1 (IP address 10.1.1.1) and 2000 to 2099 on CME 2 (IP address 10.1.2.1).

Example 7-1 *Dial Peers for Figure 7-1*

```
CME 1:
Router#show running-config
dial-peer voice 2000 voip
     destination-pattern 20..
     session target 10.1.2.1
     dtmf-relay h245-alphanumeric
     codec g729r8


CME 2:
Router#show running-config
dial-peer voice 1000 voip
     destination-pattern 10..
     session target 10.1.1.1
     dtmf-relay h245-alphanumeric
     codec g729r8
```

NOTE   The dtmf-relay configuration portion of the output is explained later, in the section "DTMF Relay for H.323."

You can use this simple symmetrical VoIP dial peer technique to join two Cisco CME systems even within a single site to increase the total phone count supported beyond the capacity of a single Cisco CME system. The downside of doing this is that it doesn't give you a truly monolithic system from a configuration, inter-CME feature transparency, and management point of view. This arrangement requires you to administer the two systems separately, which may be acceptable if the two systems are split between naturally different and separate sections of your company (for example, administration and manufacturing).

This arrangement also limits the phone features you can use across the two systems. You can operate simple features such as call transfer and forwarding, and you can share a single voice mail device between systems, including inter-CME distribution of message waiting indication (MWI). However, Cisco CME does not support more advanced features, such as shared line and call pickup, across the H.323 or SIP interconnection.

One final point about this arrangement is that you can optionally choose to provide a physical PSTN connection on just one Cisco CME system and have that Cisco CME system also act as a VoIP PSTN gateway for the second Cisco CME system.

Although this discussion considers H.323 and SIP "long-distance" protocols, the use of these protocols is not related to physical distance. You can use H.323/SIP to link systems 1000 feet apart the same as you would link systems 1000 miles apart. This ability is one of the key advantages of VoIP technology over traditional TDM systems. With the appropriate IP infrastructure, you can link systems and users more or less independent of the physical distance that separates them. This means that you can give a remotely located Cisco CME system a phone extension number and voice mailbox that appears to your phone users to belong to their local Cisco CME system (with the aforementioned restriction on advanced phone feature operation between systems across VoIP). The historical out-of-area-code restrictions that apply to traditional TDM-based centrex phone systems largely do not apply in the VoIP context.

The one caveat in this area is the effect on access to public emergency services. Users dialing for emergency assistance (such as police, fire, or ambulance) should be routed into the PSTN via a PSTN connection that is local to their physical location. The calling party information provided to the PSTN connection and emergency services operator for this type of call must display an appropriate phone number (and therefore an associated physical location) that is within the emergency services area of the PSTN link being used.

A Large Multinode Topology with H.323

If you want to connect more than two Cisco CME systems, you can extend the basic approach used to connect two systems and add a third, fourth, or more Cisco CME systems—up to a point. For a low number of systems, such as five or six, it's usually possible to add VoIP dial peers to your Cisco CME system that indicate the static IP address of the other system to reach. This is especially true if your dial plan is reasonably well segmented such that you can infer to which Cisco CME system the call should be sent based on the first one or two digits of the dialed extension number. For example, Cisco CME system 1 is given extension numbers 5000 to 5099, Cisco CME system 2 is given extension numbers 5100 to 5199, and so on.

Even if your dial plan isn't entirely evenly divided, you can still use this approach if you're prepared to build the necessary dial peer-based configuration. At the limit of this method, you can construct systems in which you create an individual H.323 VoIP dial peer on each Cisco CME system for each remotely located extension number. You can follow this approach as far as available memory and your patience in creating and maintaining the configuration allow. As the number of dial peers increases, the post-dial delay increases somewhat, because the Cisco CME system might need to search through a couple hundred dial peers to find the right information. In the very worst case, a network of five Cisco CME systems with 20 extensions each would need 80 VoIP dial peers created (and maintained) on each system. That's assuming that your extension number distribution is fully random across the full set of Cisco CME systems. Troubleshooting such a system in the event of misconfiguration is challenging, however.

Another drawback of the multiple dial peer configuration is that there's no good way to do call admission control (CAC) to prevent too many voice calls from trying to use the same WAN link at the same time. This may be an issue if your expected maximum call volume might be greater than the capacity of your WAN links. See the next section for more on this issue.

Alternatively, you can use the VoIP tandem call routing feature of Cisco CME 3.1 and above. This allows you to construct hub-and-spoke or hop-by-hop call routing arrangements. Hub-and-spoke call routing arrangements are historically common in small-scale voice over Frame Relay (VoFR) and voice over ATM (VoATM) networks. In these small-scale networks, you might have a single larger "hub" Cisco CME system with approximately 100 users at a primary site, with perhaps five satellite Cisco CME systems, each with 20 users linked on VoIP "spokes" to the primary. In this arrangement, only the central hub site needs VoIP dial peers to be configured to define the location of all network-wide extensions. The spoke satellite sites only need to know to send nonlocal calls to the hub site. The central hub site can then relay the call to the final spoke site destination.

This type of arrangement makes the most sense if the physical Layer 1/Layer 2 connection topology of your IP transport network mirrors the same hub-and-spoke arrangement as the dial plan. With this situation, IP packets that flow between different spoke sites inevitably get IP Layer 3 routed via the central hub site Cisco CME router. The hub-and-spoke dial plan arrangement causes the VoIP calls and voice packets to get routed by the application layer instead, with relatively minor added delay, as shown in Figure 7-2.

Figure 7-2 *Multinode Cisco CME Tandem H.323 Network*

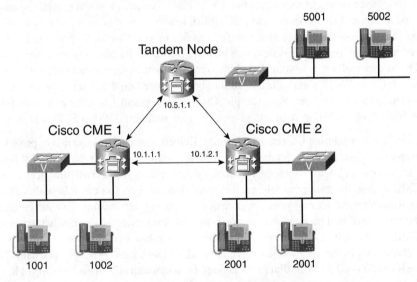

Example 7-2 shows the relevant configurations of the nodes shown in the network.

Example 7-2 *Node Configurations*

```
CME 1:
Router#show running-config
dial-peer voice 2345 voip
    destination-pattern [2345]0..
    session target ipv4:10.1.5.1
```

Example 7-2 *Node Configurations (Continued)*

```
CME 2:
Router#show running-config
dial-peer voice 1345 voip
  destination-pattern [1345]0..
session target ipv4:10.1.5.1

Tandem Node:
Router#show running-config
voice service voip
   allow-connections h323 to h323
   dial-peer voice 1000 voip
      destination-pattern 10..
      session target ipv4:10.1.1.1
   dial-peer voice 2000 voip
      destination-pattern 20..
      session target ipv4:10.1.2.1
```

Using a single dial peer at the spoke sites to direct calls to the hub site and all far-end spoke sites beyond it also allows you to more easily use CAC per dial peer call-counting mechanism (which you'll learn more about in the following section). This is shown in Figure 7-2. You can use UNIX-style regular expressions in dial peer destination patterns. For example, if you need a single dial peer that references extensions in multiple ranges, such as 10xx, 30xx, 40xx, and 50xx (not including 20xx), you can use the following command:

    destination-pattern [1345]0..

The values in square brackets ([ ]) provide a list of alternative values—in this case, 1, 3, 4, and 5. You can also use this to encompass a continuous range. For example, you can also write the preceding example as 1,3-5:

    destination-pattern [13-5]0..

However, an even better and fundamentally more scalable approach to inter-CME H.323 VoIP call routing is to use an H.323 GK (as you will see in the next section). This is the most practical approach to link tens or hundreds of Cisco CME systems.

The Role of an H.323 Gatekeeper

The primary role of an H.323 gatekeeper is to provide a conversion lookup between a telephone number and an IP address. This service essentially centralizes the dial plan (all the telephone numbers in the network and how to reach them) in a single place in the network, as opposed to each node needing the configuration information to do this. This significantly eases the management of a large network.

Gatekeepers also provide other services, depending on the type of gatekeeper used. These services are discussed in this section:

- Telephone address lookup
- Call admission control
- Billing
- Proxy

Figure 7-3 shows a sample gatekeeper network.

Figure 7-3 *Multinode Cisco CME Gatekeeper Network*

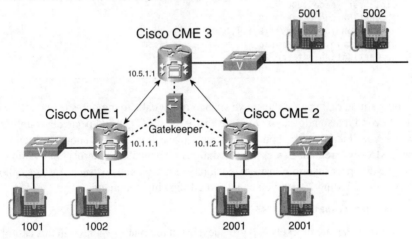

Example 7-3 shows the relevant dial peer configurations of the nodes shown in the network. Note the use of **session target ras**; it is explained in the next section.

Example 7-3 *CME Node and Gatekeeper Configurations*

```
CME 1:
Router#show running-config
dial-peer voice 2345 voip
   destination-pattern [2345]0..
   session target ras


CME 2:
Router#show running-config
dial-peer voice 1345 voip
   destination-pattern [1345]0..
   session target ras


CME 3:
Router#show running-config
dial-peer voice 1234 voip
   destination-pattern [1234]0..
   session target ras
```

Example 7-4 shows a more detailed example from an individual Cisco CME router setup to interwork with an H.323 gatekeeper connected via the Cisco CME router's Ethernet interface. Note the **gk ipaddr** that defines the gatekeeper's IP address.

Example 7-4   *Cisco CME Gatekeeper Connectivity*

```
Router#show running-config
interface FastEthernet0/0
ip address 10.1.1.1 255.255.0.0
load-interval 30
duplex auto
speed auto
no cdp enable
h323-gateway voip interface
h323-gateway voip id gk ipaddr 10.1.10.1 1719
h323-gateway voip h323-id cme1
h323-gateway voip tech-prefix 1#
h323-gateway voip bind srcaddr 10.1.1.1

dial-peer voice 1234 voip
       destination-pattern [1-4]0..
       session target ras
```

Telephone Address Lookup

The simplest type of gatekeeper provides only telephone number-to-IP address resolution. When a Cisco CME system uses a gatekeeper to help route a call, it sends a message to the gatekeeper to request the IP address that corresponds to a certain specific phone number. As soon as Cisco CME gets the correct IP address, it can send an H.323 call setup message for the desired phone number to the IP address of the remote Cisco CME system (provided by the gatekeeper) that hosts that phone number. Instead of having a VoIP dial peer that points to every Cisco CME system in your network, the Cisco CME has only one dial peer that points to the IP address of the H.323 gatekeeper.

To reference a gatekeeper from a VoIP dial peer, use **ras** as the target instead of a specific IP address:

```
session target ras
```

In most cases, the H.323 gatekeeper gets the appropriate phone number-to-IP address configuration dynamically from the component Cisco CME systems. For each individual phone number that's configured on a Cisco CME system, the Cisco CME system can send a Registration message to the gatekeeper. The Registration message basically says, "I'm an H.323 gateway-like device at IP address x.x.x.x, and I have phone number Y." The gatekeeper aggregates the information from the H.323 Registration messages from all the Cisco CME gateways (and other H.323 gateways) into a composite database that contains all the current locations of all the telephone numbers in the network.

Call Admission Control

In addition to providing simple telephone number-to-IP address resolution, a gatekeeper can provide CAC for your VoIP network. CAC keeps track of the number of simultaneous VoIP calls present at each H.323 gateway and prevents overloading of the gateway's WAN links (and sometimes also provides load balancing for PSTN access ports). Without CAC, if too many calls attempt to use the same WAN link at the same time, either calls will fail in uncontrolled ways, or too many voice packets will try to get sent at the same time, leading to voice quality problems.

The Cisco CME can do a limited amount of CAC itself without a gatekeeper, either by limiting the number of simultaneous calls associated with each dial peer or by using an end-to-end bandwidth reservation protocol called Resource Reservation Protocol (RSVP). However, per-dial peer call counting does not work well if you are using more than one dial peer per WAN link, and the RSVP mechanism requires end-to-end support of the RSVP protocol within your network infrastructure, so the gatekeeper-based CAC approach generally is far superior.

Billing

The gatekeeper keeps track of the number of active calls based on messages from the gateway indicating when individual calls start and stop. Because the gatekeeper knows the start and stop times and the called and calling phone numbers, a gatekeeper can provide a centralized point to connect to a billing service (for the VoIP calls).

This type of billing typically does not know about calls being made by a Cisco CME system using its local PSTN connection. These calls don't involve H.323 VoIP call legs, so the H.323 gatekeeper typically does not see them. You can use the Cisco IOS Voice Gateway Remote Authentication Dial-In User Service (RADIUS) feature in conjunction with a central RADIUS server to track all Cisco CME calls for both H.323 and PSTN for billing purposes.

Using a Gatekeeper as a Proxy for Additional Services

The other major type of gatekeeper to consider is a *Routed Signaling Gatekeeper*. Instead of simply providing phone number-to-IP address resolution, the Routed Signaling Gatekeeper acts as an H.323 proxy device and participates in all the H.323 call signaling. With this type of gatekeeper, the Cisco CME system sends the H.323 call setup directly to the gatekeeper. The gatekeeper then relays the H.323 setup to the final (or next-hop) destination. This is very similar to the tandem hub-and-spoke VoIP call routing described earlier with Cisco CME systems.

The Routed Signaling Gatekeeper approach has two disadvantages:

- You tend to need more Routed Signal Gatekeepers because each individual gatekeeper has more work to do per call. Instead of just being primarily involved in the phone number-to-IP address resolution at the start of the call, a Routed Signaling Gatekeeper stays involved throughout the call. It has to process all the H.323-related messages that pass through it.

- Routed Signaling Gatekeepers tend not to be transparent to the supplementary service ITU-T H.450 messages used for call transfer and forwarding between Cisco CME systems. The presence of a Routed Signaling Gatekeeper may actually prevent you from using H.450 services between Cisco CME systems.

On the other hand, a Routed Signaling Gatekeeper may be able to provide your network with additional services. This is generally truer in an H.323 VoIP network that is used for residential services. In this case, a Routed Signaling Gatekeeper can provide services, such as call forwarding and call waiting, on behalf of H.323 endpoints that (unlike Cisco CME) do not natively support these services. The situation can get more complicated in some service provider networks where the same VoIP infrastructure is used to provide both direct residential and hosted or managed enterprise and small or medium business VoIP services.

Finally, one other point that sometimes favors using Routed Signaling Gatekeepers is in service provider networks, where there is a legal regulatory requirement to support lawful interception of telephone calls for government law enforcement agencies. In the United States this requirement is called Communications Assistance to Law Enforcement Agencies (CALEA). In this case, having the Routed Signaling Gatekeeper present in both the signaling and media path for all calls to the H.323 endpoint allows wiretapping to take place such that it is undetectable to the H.323 endpoint that is having its voice calls monitored. If you are interested in building a private corporate VoIP network, however, you do not need to be concerned with this consideration.

Public and Internal Phone Numbers in an H.323 Network

You have already seen how a Cisco CME system can register its phone numbers to a central H.323 gatekeeper to provide the VoIP network with a phone number-to-IP address directory. Now you must determine which phone numbers to register. In some cases, you may simply want to register all of them. The effect of this is to give all your Cisco CME extensions a direct inward dial (DID) phone number that means that any extension within your Cisco CME system can be called from anywhere in your VoIP network. However, when phone numbers are registered to a gatekeeper, they typically have to be in an appropriate form. In many cases, gatekeepers cannot handle raw (abbreviated) three- or four-digit extension numbers. Extension numbers typically must be converted into a format that looks more like regular PSTN phone numbers. For example, if you have extensions 1000 to 1099 on your CME system, you may need to register them in long form as something like 408-555-1000 to 408-555-1099.

This makes the most sense when your Cisco CME extension numbers also have matching real PSTN phone numbers. In this case, you most likely have a PSTN link that uses an ISDN interface so that the PSTN network signals the calls from the PSTN number by providing you with the full national phone number of the number called. This type of numbering is often called E.164 format after the ITU-T specification that describes the transnational telephone number formatting rules. The term E.164 is often used a little loosely in that strictly using E.164 requires an indication of whether the phone number includes an international access code or otherwise.

One advantage of using E.164 numbers with a gatekeeper is that it simply gives you a larger number space to work with. This means that you are less likely to run out of phone numbers. It also makes it easier to add links to independent external VoIP networks if you need to. A larger number space also means that you can have overlapping extension numbers across different Cisco CME systems. For example, you might have two Cisco CME systems that (for historical reasons) need to use the same extension number range. You could have two Cisco CME systems that both use the extension range 1000 to 1099 but have different E.164 numbers, such as 408-555-1000 and 510-555-1000. Using the full E.164 number helps resolve any potential conflict.

Cisco CME can automatically convert your local extension numbers from two to five digits into E.164 format using the **dialplan-pattern** command. Example 7-5 shows a basic example.

Example 7-5 *Simple **dialplan-pattern** Configuration*

```
Router#show running-config
telephony-service
      dialplan-pattern 1 40855510.. extension-length 4
```

The **dialplan-pattern** command causes the Cisco CME system to attempt to match the extension numbers created by the **ephone-dn** command entries against the defined pattern. Using this example, the extension number 1023 would be matched against the final four digits of the dialplan pattern **10..**, where the **.** characters provide a wildcard match. The extension number 1023 would be expanded to 4085551023, and this number would be registered with the gatekeeper. You can define up to five different dialplan patterns. The 1 immediately following the **dialplan-pattern** command is simply a tag number, 1 to 5, that indicates which of the five **dialplan pattern** entries you are using.

The dialplan-pattern command can also perform leading-digit replacement for cases in which the extension number to E.164 number expansion is not a simple concatenation of a PSTN area code and prefix. Example 7-6 shows a more complex configuration.

Example 7-6 *More Complex **dialplan-pattern** Example*

```
Router#show running-config
telephony-service
    dialplan-pattern 1 51055599.. extension-length 3 extension-pattern 1..
```

Using Example 7-6, extension 123 is expanded to E.164 number 5105559923. The three-digit extension number is matched first against the extension pattern and then is substituted into the E.164 pattern defined. Without this capability, simple truncation of the ten-digit E.164 number to a three-digit extension would result in three-digit extensions in the range 900 to 999, which causes a number plan conflict with the traditional "Dial 9 for an outside line."

The **dialplan-pattern** command allows the Cisco CME's IP phone extension lines to be dialed using both the abbreviated two-to-five-digit extension number and the full E.164 or national phone number. In addition to helping with matching the called number on incoming calls, the **dialplan-pattern** command also promotes the *calling party* number included on outgoing calls from the extension to E.164 format. This is often a requirement on PSTN links using ISDN that usually will not accept abbreviated extension numbers as legitimate calling party identification. You have to choose your extension number range such that it does not conflict with the E.164 area code. For example, if your E.164 phone number is 408555xxxx, you cannot use extension numbers of the form 408x.

NOTE   Using the **dialplan-pattern** command does not require you to use an H.323 gatekeeper.

You can turn off the gatekeeper registration triggered by the **dialplan-pattern** command using the **no-reg** command option at the end of the command.

Registering Individual Telephone Numbers with a Gatekeeper

If you don't want to register all your Cisco CME system's extension numbers with a gatekeeper, you can forgo usage of the global **dialplan-pattern** command, and control registration of each individual extension number from within the **ephone-dn** command that is used to create the extensions (or virtual voice ports).

Each ephone-dn allows you to assign a primary and secondary number to associate with the extension. You then have a choice to register both, either, or neither of these with the gatekeeper using the **no-reg**, **no-reg primary**, or **no-reg both** command options for the **ephone-dn number** command.

If you decide not to use the **dialplan-pattern** command, you can still provide the three-to-five-digit abbreviated number and full E.164 numbering for each ephone-dn by using the **secondary** number option, as shown in Example 7-7.

Example 7-7   *Secondary Number Options*

```
Router#show running-config
ephone-dn 1
       number 1023 secondary 4085551023 no-reg primary
```

Using the secondary number allows incoming calls to the ephone-dn to use either 1023 or 4085551023 as the called number. It also only registers the secondary number 4085551023 to the Cisco CME's gatekeeper. This approach gives you control over what is registered on a per-ephone-dn basis. However, it does use up the secondary number, which prevents you from using the secondary number for call coverage purposes. (Refer to Chapter 5, "Cisco CME Call Processing Features.")

Note that this approach does not modify the default calling party number selected on outgoing calls from the extension. In Example 7-7, the calling party number for outgoing calls is set to 1023. This is normally just fine for internal extension-to-extension calling. If you need to promote the calling party number to E.164 format for the benefit of VoIP or ISDN calls, you can do this using an IOS voice gateway translation rule applied to the call's outgoing dial peer.

You can mix and match the two approaches for controlling gatekeeper registration by using narrower extension pattern matches within the **dialplan-pattern** command. For example, instead of using **extension-pattern 10..** to match all the extensions in the 1000 to 1099 range, you can add multiple (up to five) **dialplan-pattern** commands that have narrow match ranges such as **extension-pattern 102.**, which matches only extension numbers in the 1020 to 1029 range.

If you don't have enough E.164 DID numbers available, but you still need a few extra extension lines, you can assign them to a different range of numbers. You can then use the **dialplan-pattern** command to register E.164 phone numbers in the match range with a gatekeeper. For example, you might give all your employees extension numbers in the 1000 to 1099 range, have these match a **dialplan-pattern** and, thus, register to a gatekeeper, and then simply assign nonemployee phone numbers, such as break room and lobby phones, into a separate range that doesn't have corresponding DID E.164 numbers, as shown in Example 7-8.

Example 7-8   *Dial Plan Configuration*

```
Router#show running-config
telephony-service
       dialplan-pattern 1 40855510.. extension-length 4
ephone-dn 1
       number 1023
       name employee1
ephone-dn 2
       number 1024
       name empolyee2
ephone-dn 3
       number 2001
       name BreakRoom
```

In Example 7-8 the extension numbers 1023 and 1024 are registered with the gatekeeper as 4085551023 and 4085551024. The break room extension 2001 is not registered.

With this approach, one final detail to take care of is deciding what calling party number identification you want to provide for ISDN or VoIP calls placed from the break room phone. The simplest solution is to add a translation rule on the outgoing dial peer for calls from the break room phone to map the calling party number to your main or receptionist E.164 number, such as 4085551000. You may choose to do this for all outgoing calls from all extensions if you don't want the called party to be able to see individual extension numbers.

Internal and External Callers for VoIP

With the **dialplan-pattern** command, you can cause certain incoming VoIP calls to be treated as "internal" calls. By default, calls between IP phones on the same Cisco CME system are treated as internal calls and ring with an internal ringer cadence. All other calls (VoIP and

PSTN) are treated as external calls and ring with a different external call ringer cadence. Analog phones attached to router Foreign Exchange Station (FXS) voice ports also are treated as external calls by default. However, incoming calls that have calling party numbers that match one of the available five **dialplan-pattern** commands are treated as internal calls.

For example, suppose you have two Cisco CME systems linked via VoIP and you use extension numbers 100 to 199 with E.164 numbers 4085550100 to 4085550199 on one system and extension numbers 200 to 299 with E.164 numbers 5105550200 to 5105550299 on the second system. You can create **dialplan-pattern** commands on both systems that provide extension number matches for both systems, as shown in Example 7-9.

Example 7-9 **dialplan-pattern** *Configuration*

```
Router#show running-config
telephony-service
      dialplan-pattern 1 40855501.. extension-length 3
      dialplan-pattern 2 51055502.. extension-length 3
```

Any incoming calls that match either of the dialplan patterns are treated as internal calls, regardless of where the call physically originates. When the incoming calling party number matches the dialplan pattern, the Caller ID displayed for the call is demoted from E.164 format back to abbreviated three-to-five-digit extension number format. Also, the call is presented using the internal ring cadence. This allows you to treat incoming VoIP calls from other Cisco CME systems within your network as internal calls.

To make a call coming from a router FXS voice port appear as an internal call, you need to set the voice port **station-id number** to match the dialplan pattern number range, as shown in Example 7-10.

Example 7-10 *FXS Station ID*

```
Router#show running-config
voice-port 1/0/0
      station-id number 4085550188
      station-id name AnalogPhone
dial-peer voice 408188 pots
      destination-pattern 4085550188
      port 1/0/0
dial-peer voice number 188 pots
      destination-pattern 188
      port 1/0/0
```

This configuration causes calls from the analog phone to have caller ID 4085550188. It also allows the analog phone to be called by dialing either the long form 4085550188 or the abbreviated three-digit extension number 188.

Note that calls from analog phones that are attached to Cisco Analog Telephony Adapters (ATAs) are treated as IP phones and don't need any special treatment.

DTMF Relay for H.323

Dual-tone multifrequency (DTMF) relay is a mechanism for reliably carrying DTMF digits across VoIP connections. If you need to signal the 0 to 9, *, and # keypad digits (DTMF digits) from your IP phone across your VoIP network, you must configure DTMF relay. DTMF digits are also sometimes called *TouchTone digits*.

You should configure DTMF relay if you want to operate a remotely connected voice mail system, use calling card access for PSTN calls placed through a remote VoIP PSTN gateway, or access any kind of DTMF-driven interactive voice response (IVR) system (for example, telephone banking or airline flight information services).

DTMF Digits

DTMF describes a method of encoding telephone digits using two audio tones. For a conventional telephone keypad in which the keys are arranged in three columns by four rows, the first audio tone selects the row of the key, and the second audio tone selects the column. Each row-and-column tone uses a different audio frequency (pitch). This method of telephone digit signaling replaced the old-fashioned loop disconnect (dial pulse) digit dialing used by old rotary-style analog phones.

There are 16 DTMF digits (arranged as four columns by four rows). In addition to the standard 12 keypad digits—0 to 9, *, and #—an additional four digits form an extra fourth column of digits called simply A, B, C, and D. Because the ABCD digits are unavailable on a normal phone keypad, you are unlikely to ever come across these for normal phone calls. They are used occasionally by voice mail systems to operate an intersystem exchange of voice messages between separate voice mail systems using a standard called Analog Message Interchange Standard (AMIS).

Some security-type phones also use the ABCD digits for initial negotiation. You may also see these used in some Cisco CME configuration examples where there is a need to create telephone numbers that can't be directly dialed from a phone keypad. One example of this is if you want to create nondialable phone numbers for intercoms. You normally place an intercom call by pressing a button specifically configured for intercom (this works somewhat like a speed-dial button), so you don't need to be able to enter individual dialed digits.

Transporting DTMF Digits Reliably Using DTMF Relay

In the simple case of analog phones, the phone keypad digits result in the generation of DTMF audio tones. DTMF signaling works fine for analog phones connected directly to PSTN analog subscriber lines that travel only a relatively short distance to reach a central office (CO) telephone exchange. However, when the analog phone is connected to a VoIP system, and telephone calls are made using compressed voice (for example, G.729 at 8 Kbps), there is a substantial risk that the audio tones of the DTMF digits sent through the compressed voice path may become too distorted to be predictably recognized correctly by a remote voice mail system.

Even when you use uncompressed G.711 A-law/μ-law 64 Kbps for VoIP calls, there is still a risk that DTMF digits can get distorted in transit. This is because of the risk of packet loss in the VoIP network. If the network drops an occasional IP packet containing voice, this is usually imperceptible to the human ear. However, if an IP packet is dropped that contains an audio encoding of part of a DTMF tone, this is very likely to keep the DTMF digit detection in the far-end system from detecting the digit (or to make it erroneously detect multiple digits). This is also the reason that other nonvoice audio signals such as fax and data modems need special treatment in VoIP networks.

To work around this issue, you generally have to use some form of DTMF relay. DTMF relay causes the digit press to be detected by the PSTN trunk or analog phone interface on the VoIP gateway. The originating VoIP gateway then signals the digit as an explicit event to the far-end VoIP gateway and removes the audio signal for the DTMF from the voice packet stream. When the far-end VoIP gateway receives the signal for the DTMF event, it regenerates the DTMF audio signal and inserts it into the outgoing audio stream to the PSTN or analog phone.

In the case of the Cisco SCCP IP phones, the digit never exists as an audio signal from the VoIP perspective, because it's directly signaled via the SCCP control protocol. The digit audio that the phone user hears from the phone handset is for the benefit of the phone user only and is not passed to the VoIP connection.

Different Forms of DTMF Relay

In general, there are two main ways to signal DTMF events between VoIP gateways: H.245 digit relay and Real-Time Transport Protocol (RTP)-based DTMF digit relay. This is true for both the H.323 and SIP protocols, although the specific details are different.

The H.245 digit relay option sends a message via the H.323 control channel that is associated with the VoIP call. (This is called H.245 digit relay because it uses the H.245 control channel part of the H.323 protocol to signal the digit event.)

The RTP-based DTMF digit relay method carries the digit event through the voice media channel as a special marked RTP media packet. The problem of possible IP packet drop is overcome by sending multiple redundant copies of the event so that even if one of the copies is lost, there is little chance that all copies will be lost.

H.245 Digit Relay

H.245 digit relay comes in two flavors: signal and alphanumeric. The dial peer commands for these are **dtmf-relay h245-signal** and **dtmf-relay h245-alphanumeric**.

In signal mode, two events are sent: one to indicate the start of the digit and one to indicate the end of the digit. This lets the duration of the keypress on the phone be reflected in the duration of the digit regenerated by the far-end VoIP gateway. This is useful for calling card PSTN access where a long-duration press of the # key is sometimes used to indicate the end of a calling card call plus the intention to place a follow-on call (without needing to re-enter a calling card number and its associated PIN).

Alphanumeric mode has only a single event signal. This results in the regeneration of a fixed-duration DTMF signal (usually 200 milliseconds) by the far-end VoIP gateway. In this mode, the length of the regenerated digit is unrelated to how long you press the keypad button on the phone. Some implementations generate the alphanumeric DTMF signal when you press the phone's keypad button, and others generate the signal when you release the keypad button. You can use this duration-of-press-independent property to tell which type of VoIP DTMF digit relay is being used.

H.245 alphanumeric mode is the one that should be used with Cisco CME's IP phones.

RTP Digit Relay

RTP-based digit relay mode also has two flavors:

- **RFC 2833**—A standards-based mechanism, sometimes called *Named Telephony Events* (*NTE*) or *Named Signaling Events* (*NSE*). The IOS dial peer command for this mode is dtmf-relay rtp-nte. This method is prevalent in SIP VoIP networks.

- **cisco-rtp**—A Cisco-proprietary mechanism that represents an implementation of RTP-based DTMF relay that predates the RFC 2833 standard. The dial peer command for this is **dtmf-relay cisco-rtp**. If you enable the **dtmf-relay** command without specifying an explicit DTMF relay type, you get the cisco-rtp type.

When you press a keypad digit on an IP phone, you hear a tone in the phone handset that corresponds to the digit you press. Although you hear this audio tone, the far-end party that your call is connected to doesn't. The IP phone sends the keypad audio signal only to the phone's handset (or speaker). It does not insert the audio digit indication into the outgoing voice packet stream. When you press the keypad digit on an SCCP-based IP phone, the phone sends a control message to the Cisco CME router via the SCCP protocol. Because the digit press originates from the phone as a control channel message, the SCCP digit message is simply converted into an H.245 alphanumeric message to send this across H.323 VoIP.

The SCCP digit press event does not indicate the duration of the keypad button press. This means that the H.245 signal method cannot be used, because the SCCP phone does not provide digit-start and digit-stop information. Also, the SCCP phones do not natively support either the RFC 2833 or cisco-rtp RTP-based digit relay mechanisms.

For you to signal DTMF keypad digits across H.323, you need to configure your VoIP dial peers as shown in Example 7-11.

Example 7-11 *DTMF Relay Configuration*

```
Router#show running-config
dial-peer voice 510200 voip
      destination-pattern 51055502..
      session target ipv4:10.1.1.1
      dtmf-relay h245-alphanumeric
```

If you are using your Cisco CME system in a SIP network, you have to use the RFC 2833 DTMF relay method where possible. Cisco CME 3.2 (and later) software provides automatic conversion from the SCCP control channel DTMF messages received from the SCCP IP phone into standard SIP RFC 2833 RTP digits.

Call Transfer and Call Forwarding in an H.323 Network Using H.450 Services

The ITU-T H.450 services are a set of standard supplementary services defined for H.323 VoIP networks. H.450 provides services above and beyond basic A to B telephone calls. Cisco CME 3.0 offers only the services related to call transfer (H.450.2) and call forwarding (H.450.3). Cisco CME 3.1 also introduced support for the H.450.12 capabilities discovery protocol to ease interworking issues with non-Cisco CME H.323 systems.

Here's a full list of the H.450.x services, including the date when they became formal ratified ITU-T standards:

- **H.450.1 (2/1998)** — A generic functional protocol that supports supplementary services in H.323 (supported by Cisco CME)
- **H.450.2 (2/1998)** — A call transfer supplementary service for H.323
- **H.450.3 (2/1998)** — A call diversion supplementary service for H.323 (supported by Cisco CME)
- **H.450.4 (5/1999)** — A call hold supplementary service for H.323
- **H.450.5 (5/1999)** — A call park and call pickup supplementary service for H.323
- **H.450.6 (5/1999)** — A call waiting supplementary service for H.323
- **H.450.7 (5/1999)** — An MWI supplementary service for H.323
- **H.450.8 (2/2000)** — A name identification service
- **H.450.9 (11/2000)** — A call completion supplementary service for H.323 (includes callback for a busy subscriber)
- **H.450.10 (3/2001)** — A call offering supplementary service for H.323 (includes camp-on busy subscriber)
- **H.450.11 (3/2001)** — A call intrusion supplementary service for H.323
- **H.450.12 (7/2001)** — A common information additional network feature for H.323 (for H.450.x capabilities discovery, supported by Cisco CME 3.1 and later)

An important thing to note about the dates these standards became available is that many H.323 networks were brought into service before these standards were issued. This means that support of these standards within H.323 networks varies widely, which causes some challenges in deploying these services within multivendor H.323 networks. Even within the overall Cisco voice product line, support of these services is not yet widespread.

H.450.2 and H.450.3 services are present and enabled by default in Cisco IOS 12.3(4)T and later (for voice-enabled images). This allows an IOS voice gateway (without CME configuration) to be used as a VoIP-to-PSTN gateway and to automatically support the forwarded party, transferee, and transfer-to roles when using the standard default voice session application.

The earlier Cisco IOS 12.2(15)T and later software releases can also support H.450.2 and H.450.3 provided that they are configured to use a special Toolkit Command Language (TCL) script (called app_h450_transfer.tcl and available on Cisco.com) in place of the default voice session application.

H.450.12 services are available in Cisco IOS 12.3(7)T. They need to be explicitly enabled using the **supplementary-service** command.

The next sections describe H.450.2 call transfer, H.450.3 call forward, and H.450.12 supplementary services in more detail, including proxying of these services. It also introduces digital signal processor (DSP) farm services that are needed to support some modes of call transfer and call forwarding.

H.450.2 Call Transfer

For call transfer with consultation, the basic operation of the telephone user interface is expected to look like this:

1   The inbound call to the phone is answered. The parties talk.

2   The phone user (transferor) presses the transfer key, gets dial tone, and enters the transfer-to destination. The calling party (transferee) is placed on hold and may hear the music on hold audio feed.

3   The transferor hears the transfer-to phone start to ring.

4   The phone at the transfer-to destination is answered, and a consultation call takes place between the transfer-to and the transferor.

5   The transferor presses the transfer key a second time (or simply hangs up) to execute the transfer.

6   The original caller (the transferee) is connected to the transfer-to party.

The H.450.2 protocol is designed to allow this operation to take place where the transferee, transferor, and transfer-to parties are all associated with different H.323 endpoints, regardless of physical location. This means (for example) that a transferee party originating a call in Paris can place a call to a transferor in Los Angeles and get transferred to a transfer-to destination in London. In a VoIP network that fully supports H.450.2, the resulting post-transfer call between Paris and London is a direct call and does not have to be relayed via the transferor (in Los Angeles). This is an especially important consideration when you consider the network design implications from a voice quality, delay, and scalability point of view. It's an even more important consideration for cases in which a call might need to be transferred multiple times before it reaches its final destination.

Multiple transfer is one area in which VoIP-based networks have considerable superiority over traditional legacy-based TDM networks—if they are implemented to take full advantage of the H.450.2 service.

There are other ways of invoking a call transfer that don't follow the usual user interface steps. One particular example is a three-party conference call where A calls B, B calls C, and then B joins the A–B and B–C calls together as a conference. If the B party conference initiator wants to drop out of the conference and leave the A and C parties connected to each other, this can be implemented as a call transfer where B invokes a transfer of A to C.

The following detailed protocol transactions allow the transfer to take place (see Figure 7-4):

1 The original incoming call is just an ordinary "A calls B" H.323 call between two parties. Of course, the original call doesn't even have to be an incoming call. For example, it could be an outgoing call placed by an assistant on behalf of an executive who is transferred to the executive as soon as the call is successfully connected.

2 The transferring party presses the transfer key. This puts the original call on hold. A second line or call instance is acquired on the transferor's phone, and dial tone is obtained. The transferor dials the phone number of the transfer-to destination using the second line or call instance. This consultation call is also a simple "B calls C" H.323 call between two parties. To the external H.323 network, the A–B and B–C calls are seen as unrelated at this point. At this stage in the process, there is no guarantee that a transfer will actually take place. The B–C call can return a busy indication, and the B (transferor) party can elect to try a different transfer-to destination, D. The B–C call may connect, and a consultation call may take place in which C declines to talk to A. The B–C call can terminate at that point, and the transferor B party may then resume the A–B call. Alternatively, B can place another consultation call B–D.

3 The transferor B decides to commit the transfer either by pressing the transfer button a second time or by hanging up. At this point, a complex sequence of actions takes place in an attempt to transfer the call. First, the transferor B puts the B–C call into a hold state and then sends an H.450.2 message to the transfer-to destination C. This informs C that a transfer will take place and requests that C issue a unique consultation ID to B. This consultation ID is used to identify the call that is being transferred.

4 When B receives the consultation ID from C, it sends an H.450.2 transfer request to A containing the consultation ID. This message includes the phone number for C.

5 When the A party (the transferee) receives the transfer request, it places a direct H.323 call to C using the phone number provided by B. This call includes the consultation ID that was generated by C and passed via B (the transferor). The transfer-to destination receives the A–C call from A. At this point the B–C consultation call is still active. The transfer-to C destination uses the consultation ID from the A–C call to match the B–C call. Because the B–C and A–C calls have the same consultation ID, the transfer-to C party can tell that the A–C call is intended to replace the B–C call.

6 As soon as the transfer-to C has matched up the A–C and B–C calls using the consultation ID, C disconnects the B–C call. When the transferee A gets a successful call response from C so that the A–C call enters the connected state, the transferee A disconnects the A–B call. The transferor B party gets a disconnect indication for both the A–B and B–C calls and drops out of the transferred call.

Figure 7-4 *H.450.2 Call Transfer Protocol*

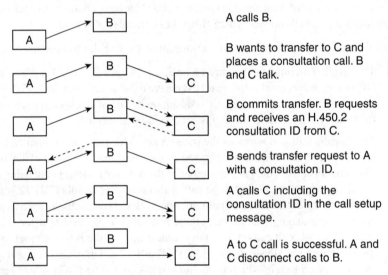

A couple of minor variations on this flow are worth mentioning. The transferor phone user at B can choose to commit the transfer before the B–C consultation call is answered, while the B–C call is still in the alerting (ringing) state. The B to C consultation ID request can take place regardless of whether the B–C consultation call is in the connected or alerting (ringing) state.

The transferor phone B can be configured to invoke a transfer to C without first placing a consultation call. In this case, the B to A call transfer request carries a zero consultation ID. This type of transfer has the disadvantage that B has no guarantee that the A–C transferred call will succeed. It has the advantage that it does not require the transfer-to C destination to support the H.450.2 protocol and the associated B–C-to-A–C call replacement operation. This type of blind transfer is useful when the transfer-to destination is some type of automatic voice system, such as a voice mail device or a call queuing service.

So, as you can see, you can invoke three types of transfers using the H.450.2 call transfer protocol:

- Transfer with consultation with the transfer committed when the B–C call is in the connected state. Cisco CME calls this type *full consult with transfer at connected*.

- Transfer with consultation with the transfer committed when the B–C call is in the alerting (ringing) state. CME calls this type *full consult with transfer at alerting*.

- A blind transfer that does not involve a consultation call. Cisco CME calls this type a full-blind transfer.

Cisco CME lets you mix and match the full-consult and full-blind transfer types at several levels:

- Configure a global default using the **transfer-system** command (under **telephony-service**) and select either **transfer-system full-consult** or **transfer-system** full-blind.

- Override the global transfer system selection for each IP phone line (ephone-dn) using the **transfer-mode** command. You can select either **transfer-mode consult** or **transfer-mode blind**. For example, you might choose to have a receptionist phone that deals with a high volume of calls always perform blind transfers.

- Use the **transfer-pattern** command to force selection of the blind transfer mode for specific transfer-to destination numbers. The **transfer-pattern** command is also used to set up transfer permissions for nonlocal transfer-to destinations. This is useful if you need to prohibit trunk-to-trunk transfers and prevent toll fraud.

Now that you understand the process for H.450.2 call transfer, the next section discusses H.450.3 call forwarding.

H.450.3 Call Forwarding

For call forwarding, similar considerations as with call transfer apply:

1 An inbound call is placed to an IP phone.

2 The IP phone is busy, does not answer, or is configured for unconditional call forwarding (call forward all).

3 The IP phone forwards the call to an alternate destination.

4 The original calling phone may optionally receive a display update to show that the call has been forwarded. This can be an important issue if billing or cost differences depend on the location of the final destination.

5 The IP phone at the alternate destination answers the call or may forward it to another destination. The IP phone that receives the forwarded call receives information that lets it know that the call was forwarded. This may include information about the original called number.

The H.450.3 protocol is designed to allow this operation to take place where the original calling party, forwarding phone, and forward-to party are all associated with different H.323 endpoints, regardless of physical location.

This means, for example, that a calling party originating a call in Paris can place a call to an IP phone in Los Angeles and get forwarded to a destination in London. In a VoIP network that fully supports H.450.3, the resulting forwarded call between Paris and London is a direct call and does not have to be relayed via the forwarder (in Los Angeles).

The H.450.3 forwarding protocol details are quite a bit simpler than the H.450.2 transfer case. When call forwarding takes place on an A to B call, the forwarding party B simply sends an H.450.3 message back to the calling A party to request that A call C (the forward-to destination). Generally, there is no requirement that the C party be aware of the H.450.3 protocol message exchange between A and B. If the A party accepts the call forwarding request, the A party disconnects the original A–B call, as shown in Figure 7-5.

Figure 7-5 *H.450.3 Call Forwarding Protocol*

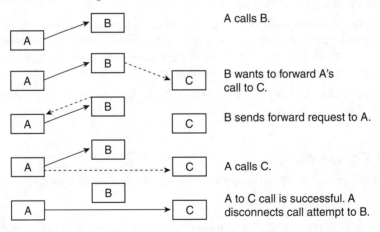

You activate the H.450.3 service using the **call-forward pattern command**. This is designed to let you selectively invoke the end-to-end H.450.3 style of call forwarding based on matching the calling party phone number. To invoke H.450.3 for all possible calling party numbers, you configure **call-forward pattern .T**, where the **.T** pattern parameter provides a wildcard match of any length.

If you do not configure the H.450.3 service, by default you are restricted to forwarding incoming VoIP calls only within the scope of the local Cisco CME system. The local scope includes forwarding to other local IP phones or to voice ports physically connected to the router (including PSTN access).

CAUTION   If you permit call forwarding of incoming PSTN calls into outgoing PSTN calls where your PSTN interface uses simple analog Foreign Exchange Office (FXO) ports, you may have a problem with disconnect supervision. In many cases, your PSTN provider will not have enabled call disconnect signaling on the PSTN subscriber lines connected to your FXO ports. For the case of a PSTN FXO-to-FXO hairpin call path, this can result in hung voice ports, because there is no signaling of disconnect when the remote PSTN parties hang up. If you encounter this problem, you need to contact your PSTN service provider and have it enable disconnect supervision on your PSTN phone lines. Note that for most PSTN hairpin call paths, the caller ID of the original caller is replaced by the caller ID of the outgoing PSTN interface.

H.450.12 Supplementary Services Capabilities

As you've seen, the H.450.2 and H.450.3 protocols can give you a significant degree of flexibility in distributing and moving H.323 calls in your VoIP network irrespective of geographic location considerations. At the same time, this can present a challenge when you attempt to deploy these services into an existing H.323-based network where support of H.450.x is not widespread.

To help you operate H.450.2 and H.450.3 services in a mixed-capability network, the CME 3.1 release introduced support of H.450.12. The formal name for this service is *Common Information Additional Network Feature for H.323*. Basically, this means that H.450.12 provides an H.450.x service capabilities exchange between H.323 endpoints.

The H.450.12 protocol allows Cisco CME to detect the H.450.x service capabilities that are available on a call-by-call basis. This allows the Cisco CME system to safely invoke H.450.2 transfer and H.450.3 forwarding without risk of dropping calls, because one or more of the remote endpoints involved in the call does not support H.450.

If Cisco CME detects that H.450.2 or H.450.3 is not supported for the call, you can configure CME to support the transfer or forwarding by locally bridging together the call legs to form VoIP-to-VoIP hairpin or tandem call paths. The term *hairpin* is used because the call path doubles back on itself in a U shape that resembles a hairpin. You may sometimes see this type of call path called tromboning, because a trombone has a similar U shape.

In the case of a call transfer, this means that the A–B original call and the B C consultation calls are retained and then simply bridged together to create a hairpin or tandem call A to B to C. In the case of a call forward, the call path for A calls B and B forwards to C also becomes A to B to C.

The Cisco CME 3.1 code has the restriction that to successfully hairpin or tandem VoIP calls, the call legs for the A B and B C segments must have compatible properties. This primarily means that the A B and A C call legs must both use the same voice compression codec (either G.729 or G.711). This restriction does not apply in the special case that either A and B or B and C are phones or voice ports connected to the same Cisco CME system.

Cisco CME 3.2 allows you to overcome this single-codec restriction, because it supports SCCP-based digital signal processor (DSP) farms that can be used to provide transcoding of voice packets between the bridged call legs. The DSP farm transcoding service supports conversion of G.711 voice packets to G.729 as needed (as you'll learn in the next section).

With the VoIP-to-VoIP tandem call routing approach, you lose the final call path optimization that you would get if H.450.x were fully supported. Costs associated with this nonoptimal call routing include extra bandwidth used and additional end-to-end delay in the voice path.

DSP Resources for Transcoding

DSP resources is a group of one or more DSPs that are not directly associated with any physical interfaces (such as PSTN voice ports). Instead, the DSPs are available as a pool of signal processing resources that can be used to provide additional processing services for telephony calls. The primary applications that require DSP resource services are transcoding for VoIP hairpin calls and transcoding for G.729 three-party conferencing. Support for DSP resources for transcoding is available in Cisco CME 3.2 and later releases.

The term *transcoding* describes the operation of converting a telephone call that is encoded (compressed) using one type of voice coder-decoder (codec) into another. Specifically, transcoding is used to convert voice packets between the G.711 (64 Kbps) and G.729 (8 Kbps) compression formats.

NOTE　　Cisco CME supports the use of DSP resources for only transcoding services. It does not support DSP resources for conferencing services, even though it does use DSP resources to support three-party conferencing for G.729 VoIP calls. The Cisco CME three-party conferencing service uses software-based audio mixing of G.711 audio streams. When Cisco CME needs to conference three-party G.729 calls, it uses the DSP transcoding service to convert the G.729 audio into G.711 and then applies the G.711 software-based audio mixing to the transcoded G.711 audio. DSP resources require separate physical DSPs for the transcoding-versus-conferencing service. It is generally more cost-effective to support G.729 three-party conferencing via a transcode-plus-software-mixer approach rather than dedicating whole DSPs to support just the conferencing service.

Although the DSPs in a resource pool are not directly associated with physical voice ports, they are hardware devices. If you need DSP resource services, you have to consider how and where you can attach these to your Cisco CME system.

The DSP resource systems that Cisco CME supports are the same as those used by Cisco CallManager. So this is one more place where Cisco provides investment protection in case you ever need to redeploy hardware originally purchased for Cisco CME into Cisco CallManager environments (or vice versa).

You can attach DSPs to Cisco CME systems in a number of ways. The simplest way is to insert DSP modules into the DSP sockets on the motherboards of some of the newer routers, such as the Cisco 2800 and 3800 series Integrated Services Routers (ISRs).

For Cisco routers that do not have motherboard DSP sockets, you can usually overprovision extra DSPs into voice network modules (NM) such as the NM-HDV and NM-HDV2 that are used to provide PSTN interfaces. The extra DSPs in these modules that aren't needed to support the PSTN interface connections can be configured as DSP resource pools.

The DSP resources do not even have to be in the same physical router as Cisco CME. The DSP resources are operated and controlled using the SCCP protocol over TCP/IP. This means that you can use a spare NM slot in a second router (that supports DSP resources) and have it controlled by a Cisco CME in a separate router. In practice, the Cisco CME and DSP resource routers do need to be connected locally over Ethernet or some other high-bandwidth interface.

Because the DSP resources are operated using the SCCP protocol, this means that, just as with the SCCP IP phones, the SCCP DSP resources can be used in support of either H.323 or SIP networks.

The configuration steps for DSP resources are too detailed to include in this book. However, they are covered in detail in the Cisco CME 3.2 System Administrator guide. Look for the command **dspfarm** for configuring the actual DSP resources and the command **sdspfarm** for configuring the Cisco CME to manage the DSP resources.

Configuring H.450.x Services

This section provides a quick look at the Cisco IOS commands that you use to configure H.450 services. To enable basic H.450.2 and H.450.3 call transfer and call forwarding, you use the **transfer-system** and **call-forward pattern** commands, as shown in Example 7-12.

Example 7-12 *Calls Forward Pattern*

```
Router#show running-config
telephony-service
      ip source-address 10.1.1.1 port 2000
      max-ephones 24
      max-dns 48
      transfer-system full-consult
      call-forward pattern .T
      create cnf-files
```

To turn on the H.450.12 service (in Cisco CME 3.1 and above), use the following:

```
voice service voip
        supplementary-service h450.12
```

To permit VoIP-to-VoIP hairpin or tandem call routing to work with remote H.323 endpoints that do not support H.450.x service, use this:

```
voice-service-voip
        allow-connections h323 to h323
```

Older Cisco CME 3.0 and earlier code does not support the H.450.12 service. This means that if you enable H.450.12 on a Cisco CME 3.1 system and place a call from a Cisco CME 3.0 system, the Cisco CME 3.1 system will incorrectly infer that H.450.x services are not supported by the Cisco CME 3.0 system.

To work around this upgrade issue, you can operate the H.450.12 service in advertise-only mode. In this mode, your CME system transmits H.450.12 capability indications for the benefit of remote H.323 systems that are H.450.12-aware, but it does not require receipt of H.450.12 indications from a remote H.323 endpoint. You can then manually disable the H.450.2 and H.450.3 service for each non-H.450-capable VoIP link using per-dial peer configuration, as shown in Example 7-13.

Example 7-13 *Disable H.450.2 and H.450.3*

```
Router#show running-config
voice service voip
        supplementary-service h450.12 advertise-only
        allow-connections h323 to h323
dial-peer voice voip 5000
        destination-pattern 50..
        session target ipv4 10.1.20.1
        no supplementary-service h450.2
        no supplementary-service h450.3
```

With this configuration, no attempt is made to invoke H.450.2 transfer and H.450.3 forwarding for calls using the VoIP dial peer. Instead, VoIP-to-VoIP hairpin or tandem call routing is used.

Cisco CME Local Supplementary Services

Cisco CME is designed to make use of H.450.2 call transfer and H.450.3 call forwarding for all calls that involve one or more VoIP call legs. For example, for an incoming H.323 VoIP call that is internally forwarded from one local IP phone to a second IP phone, Cisco CME sends an H.450.3 response back to the original calling party. This causes the caller to cancel the original H.323 call to the Cisco CME's first phone and creates a new H.323 call back to the Cisco CME using the second phone's number.

At first, this might seem like doing things the hard way. However, the point of doing this is to make sure that the original caller can see that his call has been forwarded. Returning the call to the originator and making him issue a new call allows the calling party system to have full visibility of what is going on and allows the display on the calling phone to be updated accordingly. This is an important feature if you are trying to create a seamless multisite Cisco CME network as part of an internal enterprise-wide phone system.

You can use the **supplementary-service** commands to disable this VoIP end-to-end behavior and invoke hairpin and tandem call handling. For the special case in which the forwarding phone and forward-to phone are part of the same Cisco CME system, the hairpin and tandem call routing mechanism can be used without incurring any real-world penalty. For incoming VoIP calls that are locally forwarded within a single Cisco CME system, the final call and media path are the same, regardless of which mechanism you use to handle call forwarding. Although this example describes only local call forwarding, the same principle applies to call transfer.

Also, it's important to stress that the complexities associated with the H.450.x end-to-end services apply only to calls that involve at least one VoIP call leg. For simple standalone Cisco CME usage, in which all external calls directly use the router's PSTN interfaces, CME operation is more simplified. However, to use call transfer with consultation, you still need to configure **transfer-system full-consult**.

H.450.x and Cisco CallManager

Cisco CallManager (as of release 4.0) does not support H.450.x services, including H.450.12. However, Cisco CME 3.1 (and above) automatically detects a call that involves a Cisco CallManager using special H.323 nonstandard information elements (IEs). Even without an H.450.12 indication, Cisco CME's automatic Cisco CallManager detection can be used to invoke VoIP-to-VoIP hairpin or tandem call routing when needed for call transfer and forwarding. You need to enable the **allow-connections h323 to h323** command to make this work.

Some special configuration of the H.323 interface on Cisco CallManager may also be required, depending on the specific Cisco CallManager software version used. For example, you may be required to configure a Media Termination Point (MTP), disable H.323 Fast, Start, and use Cisco CallManager's H.323 Inter-Cluster Trunk (ICT) mode.

H.450.x Proxy Services

You've seen how you can use Cisco CME to create VoIP-to-VoIP call paths for call forwarding and transfer initiated by IP phones attached to Cisco CME. What may not be obvious is that this same mechanism can be applied to calls that simply need to pass physically through a router. This is true regardless of whether the router is configured as a Cisco CME with IP phones attached. Calls that pass through a router as a result of deliberate H.323 call processing (within the router) are not the same as calls that pass through the router at the basic IP packet routing and IP connectivity level. The distinction being made here is the difference between routing H.323 calls and routing IP packets.

When a call passes through a router and the router is used in onward routing of the called number, this is called *tandem call routing*. In the special case that the tandem call routing results in the call entering and exiting the router on the same VoIP interface, the result is a VoIP-to-VoIP hairpin call.

A Cisco CME system that is deployed at a remote branch office typically has only a single WAN and VoIP interface. This means that all VoIP-to-VoIP call paths created by the CME inevitably are of the hairpin form. Hairpin VoIP-to-VoIP paths are inherently undesirable, because the doubled-back voice path is an inefficient use of scarce WAN bandwidth.

The more general VoIP-to-VoIP tandem case may offer some real advantages. One example is when you choose to use VoIP tandem call routing to provide a proxy for H.450 services.

Consider a VoIP network that connects to a central Cisco CallManager system at a company's headquarters site. Assume that the central site has a single voice mail system. Attached to the central system are a number of remote branches with Cisco CME systems connected over WAN links in a hub-and-spoke arrangement, with the Cisco CallManager site acting as the hub. Because the Cisco CallManager does not support H.450 services, a call from the Cisco CallManager site to a remote Cisco CME system that is forwarded-on-busy to a voice mail system at the central site is VoIP-to-VoIP hairpin routed. This means that the call and media path for the voice mail call extends all the way from the central Cisco CallManager to the remote Cisco CME site and then hairpins back to the central voice mail. This consumes two calls worth of bandwidth on the WAN link and could potentially block other calls from reaching the remote-site Cisco CME.

You can configure a router to act as an H.450 Tandem Gateway, and use it to proxy H.450 service for the Cisco CallManager, and avoid extending the hairpin call path all the way to the remote-branch Cisco CME system.

Calls from the Cisco CallManager to the remote Cisco CME systems are configured to pass through an H.450 Tandem Gateway that is co-located with the Cisco CallManager at the central site. The H.450 Tandem Gateway adds an H.450.12 capabilities indication to the call before it is sent to the remote Cisco CME system. This allows the remote Cisco CME system to invoke H.450.2 transfer or H.450.3 call forwarding on the call. The H.450 Tandem Gateway intercepts any H.450.x service messages sent by the Cisco CME system. If the call path required by the H.450 service invocation requires a VoIP-to-VoIP hairpin, the hairpin is created at the central site, where bandwidth is more plentiful. You still get a VoIP-to-VoIP hairpin path, but the hairpin is located in the central site network instead of the call path going all the way to the remote Cisco CME system at the far end of the WAN link, as shown in Figure 7-6. In this figure, the H.450 Tandem Gateway provides proxy services for H.450 messages coming from the CME systems. Call transfers/forwards are rolled back to the Tandem Gateway instead of hairpinning the call at the remote-branch site.

Consider the case of a call from the Cisco CallManager that goes through the H.450 Tandem Gateway to Cisco CME 1 and is then H.450.3 forwarded to Cisco CME 2. For this case, the H.450.3 forwarding request causes the original call to be rolled back to the H.450 Tandem Gateway and then reoriginated to the second Cisco CME 2. The final call path for the forwarded call is actually optimum for this case. It's the same call path as a direct dialed call from the Cisco CallManager to Cisco CME 2. The physical IP packet path for the call is the same as you would get for a pure H.450.3 case.

Figure 7-6   *H.450 Tandem Gateway*

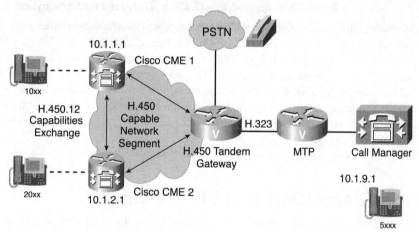

Furthermore, the router you deploy to act as the H.450 Tandem Gateway can also be equipped with physical voice ports. It then can do double duty and act as a PSTN gateway to provide central PSTN access for the Cisco CallManager and also, optionally, for the remote Cisco CME systems.

To configure a router to act as an H.450 Tandem Gateway, you simply create VoIP dial peers to direct incoming VoIP calls to outgoing VoIP links, as shown in Example 7-14.

Example 7-14   *VoIP Dial Peers*

```
Router#show running-config
voice service voip
        supplementary-service h450.12
        allow-connections h323 to h323
```

The same caveats that apply to Cisco CME hairpin routing also apply in the H.450 Tandem Gateway case. The inbound and outbound VoIP call legs need to use the same codec unless you use a DSP farm to provide transcoding.

In the case that you use an H.450 Tandem Gateway to also provide PSTN access, you may need to configure separate dial peers to allow the main site Cisco CallManager-to-PSTN calls to operate using G.711 at the same time Cisco CallManager-to-Cisco CME via tandem calls use G.729.

Cisco CME 3.x and Pre-H.450.x Transfer and Forwarding

As a little history on the software releases that predate H.450.x support, the original Cisco CME code introduced in Cisco IOS 12.2(8)T did not support H.450. At that time, the Cisco CME product was still called *IOS Telephony Services (ITS)*. This code used a Cisco-proprietary H.323 call transfer and forwarding mechanism. It supported only blind transfers and could not perform VoIP-to-VoIP call forwarding. It's included here only because this is the behavior you get with the default configuration, which provides backward compatibility with the older software. This is the transfer and forwarding mechanism you get if you do not configure the **transfer-system** and **call-forward pattern** commands.

Integrating Cisco CME in a SIP Network

Much of what you've read about linking Cisco CME systems over WAN VoIP links for H.323 also applies to SIP, so a lot of the heavyweight detail that's been covered for H.323 is not repeated here. Instead, the following sections focus on some of the differences between SIP and H.323 implementations. This approach also helps you understand some of the issues associated with investment protection for your VoIP network and hopefully provides some reassurance about picking the "right" protocol for intersite calls. Cisco Systems is agnostic about protocols. In that spirit, you'll see how Cisco CME provides you with flexibility and safeguards against protocol dependencies.

A major point that should be made here is that IOS and Cisco CME's support of SIP is primarily for *SIP trunking*, or using SIP as a protocol to connect calls between peer Cisco CME systems over a WAN link. This is primarily a property inherited from the Cisco IOS Voice Infrastructure functionality that underlies Cisco CME. This is quite a different usage case than that of connecting SIP phones directly to Cisco CME.

However, you can host SIP phones directly on Cisco CME 3.0, because the same Cisco IOS 12.3(4)T code also independently includes the Survivable Remote Site Telephony for SIP (SIP-SRST) feature that provides a basic Registrar and Redirect Server. The services and features that you can access from the SIP phones are very limited in comparison to the phone features offered for SCCP-based phones. More significantly, Cisco CME 3.x does not provide any mechanisms to support administration and configuration management for SIP phones.

You can also host H.323-based phones on a Cisco CME system if you use a router image that includes gatekeeper functionality. These services that enable support of H.323 and SIP phones are part of the general IOS Voice Infrastructure functionality and are unrelated to Cisco CME.

You should understand here that although you can concurrently and independently operate the IOS Voice SIP and H.323 phone-hosting capabilities with Cisco CME, this functionality is not integrated and productized in the same way as support for SCCP phones. Cisco CME 3.0, 3.1, and 3.2 are not marketed as providing SIP or H.323 phone support for this reason.

The following sections describe using SIP to interconnect Cisco CME systems.

Two-Node Topology with SIP

You can connect two Cisco CME systems using a pair of VoIP dial peers configured symmetrically on each CME to point to the other CME. This is exactly the same as the H.323 case described in the section "A Simple Two-Node Topology with H.323" near the beginning of this chapter. The only difference is that you must explicitly select the SIP protocol in your dial peer, whereas H.323 is the default VoIP protocol.

For a pair of Cisco CME systems that have extensions 1000 to 1099 on Cisco CME 1 (IP address 10.1.1.1) and 2000 to 2099 on Cisco CME 2 (IP address 10.1.2.1), you need the dial peers shown in Example 7-15.

Example 7-15 *SIP Dial Peers*

```
Cisco CME 1:
Router#show running-config
dial-peer voice 2000 voip
    destination-pattern 20..
    session target 10.1.2.1
    session protocol sipv2
    dtmf-relay sip-notify
    codec g729r8

Cisco CME 2:
Router#show running-config
dial-peer voice 1000 voip
    destination-pattern 10..
    session target 10.1.1.1
    session protocol sipv2
    dtmf-relay sip-notify
    codec g729r8
```

As you can see, switching your simple two-CME system network from H.323 to SIP is easy. All you need to add is **session protocol sipv2** to the dial peers on both systems and it's done. You will also notice that the dtmf-relay method has been changed. (You'll read more about this later, in the section "DTMF Relay and RFC 2833 for SIP.") Note that the sip-notify form of DTMF relay is required for Cisco CME systems that use CME 3.1 or earlier. Cisco CME systems based on CME 3.2 or later should use the **dtmf-relay rtp-nte** form where possible. See Figure 7-7.

Figure 7-7 *Simple Two-Node Cisco CME SIP Network*

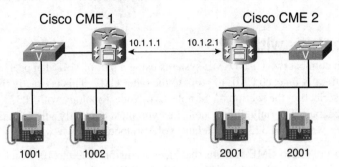

Example 7-16 shows the relevant CME node configurations.

Example 7-16 *CME Node SIP Configurations*

```
Cisco CME 1:
Router#show running-config
dial-peer voice 2000 voip
   destination-pattern 20..
   session target ipv4:10.1.2.1
   session protocol sipv2

Cisco CME 2:
Router#show running-config
dial-peer voice 1000 voip
   destination-pattern 10..
   session target ipv4:10.1.1.1
   session protocol sipv2
```

You face exactly the same issues and options as in the H.323 case in expanding beyond a two-node H.323 CME network to a multinode SIP network. The exception is that Cisco CME does not natively support tandem SIP call routing. However, you can easily buy a non-Cisco SIP proxy or redirect server to do this instead.

The Role of SIP Proxy/Registrar/Redirect Server

In H.323 you saw how you can use an H.323 gatekeeper to provide telephone number-to-IP address resolution. In SIP this same function is often carried out using a SIP registrar and a SIP Redirect Server that are internally linked. The SIP Registrar accepts SIP REGISTER messages from client voice endpoint systems (called user agents [UAs] in the SIP world) and uses them to build a phone number-to-IP address conversion database. Just as CME can generate H.323 gatekeeper registrations, Cisco CME can generate SIP REGISTER messages based on the Cisco CME ephone-dn extension numbers and **dialplan-pattern** command. Cisco CME can maintain concurrent registrations with both an H.323 gatekeeper and SIP Registrar at the same time.

There's a small difference in the protocol flow between the H.323 and SIP cases. In the H.323 case, an explicit address query (ARQ) goes from the Cisco CME to the gatekeeper to obtain the destination IP address from the destination phone number. As soon as that operation is successful, the Cisco CME initiates a call setup. In the SIP case the Cisco CME sends an INVITE call setup message to the combined SIP Registrar/Redirect Server. The Redirect Server responds with a REDIRECT message that guides the Cisco CME to send a second INVITE message to the correct IP address.

The combination of a Registrar and Redirect Server in a single system is often called a SIP proxy, albeit a very basic one. If you look up the word *proxy* in the dictionary, you'll see it defined as something like "the agency, function, or office of a deputy who acts as a substitute for another" and "authority or power to act for another" (Merriam-Webster's Collegiate Dictionary, 11th Edition). So it's actually a fairly broad term. This is also in keeping with the use of the word proxy in the SIP environment, where it can cover a very broad range of proxied services. This is something to note in general when you encounter the term proxy used in the SIP arena, because you often need to look carefully to understand exactly what services are being proxied.

In an alternative implementation, the proxy accepts the initial INVITE sent by the Cisco CME. Instead of responding with a redirect response, the proxy may simply relay the INVITE to its final destination. This is similar to tandem call routing and to the action of a Routed Signaling Gatekeeper in the H.323 context.

To use the services of a SIP proxy with your VoIP dial peers, you can use the configuration shown in Example 7-17.

Example 7-17 *SIP Proxy Dial Peers*

```
Router#show running-config
sip-ua
        sip-server ipv4:10.1.10.2
dial-peer voice 408525 voip
        destination-pattern 408525....
        session target sip-server
```

You can use a DNS name instead of a raw IP address for the sip-server address.

To register your Cisco CME phone numbers with an external SIP registrar, you can use the configuration shown in Example 7-18.

Example 7-18 *SIP Registrar Dial Peers*

```
Router#show running-config
sip-ua
retry invite 3
retry register 3
timers register 150
registrar ipv4:10.1.10.2 expires 3600
```

Public and Internal Phone Numbers in a SIP Network

Just as for H.323, you may need to choose which phone numbers you register with a SIP registrar. You can control this in the same way that you learned for H.323 using the **dialplan-pattern** command and the **no-reg** option for the **ephone-dn number** command.

Although SIP does allow the use of Internet domain names for telephone number scoping purposes, this is not supported by the IOS SIP Voice Gateway software. The IOS SIP Voice Gateway software mostly ignores domain names in SIP messages.

DTMF Relay and RFC 2833 for SIP

The same technical issues and motivations exist for DTMF relay in SIP as in H.323. The first-choice DTMF relay method for most SIP networks is the RTP-based RFC 2833 protocol. Unfortunately, the Cisco SCCP IP phones do not natively support this.

As you saw in the "DTMF Relay for H.323" section, the Cisco SCCP phones only provide out-of-band control channel signaling for DTMF digits. In the H.323 world, this can be easily translated into H.245 alphanumeric signaling events to pass across VoIP over WAN.

The equivalent method in the SIP domain is to use a SIP NOTIFY event. However, this is not well standardized. The original SIP DTMF NOTIFY implemented in the Cisco IOS Voice Gateway software is based on an early draft proposal for this mechanism and, therefore, is not supported on most third-party SIP products. However, this mechanism is adequate provided that you are using only Cisco IOS voice endpoints with Cisco IOS Release 12.3(4)T or later. You also need to transport DTMF keypad events across VoIP to an IOS PSTN voice gateway for regeneration as an audio signal into a PSTN trunk or FXS port.

To enable the SIP NOTIFY for dtmf-relay, add the following command to your SIP VoIP dial peers:

```
dtmf-relay sip-notify
```

Cisco CME 3.2 introduces support for conversion and interworking between the SCCP control channel DTMF digit indications and RTP-based RFC 2833 (for SIP only). This significantly improves CME's ability to work with SIP networks that include non-Cisco SIP-based voice mail systems. To use this RFC 2833 RTP in-band to SCCP out-of-band interworking function for dtmf-relay, you use the following:

```
dtmf-relay rtp-nte
```

NOTE   Cisco Unity Express (Cisco UE) voice mail currently supports only the **sip-notify** format of DTMF relay. When using Cisco CME 3.2 or higher, you still have to use **sip-notify** on the SIP VoIP dial peers used to interconnect Cisco CME with Cisco UE. Even when using the notify method in the SIP VoIP dial peers for interworking with Cisco UE, you can at the same time use the RFC 2833 mechanism on other SIP VoIP dial peers that require it.

Use of RFC 2833 **dtmf-relay rtp-nte** for SIP is recommended where possible.

SIP Supplementary Services

The SIP supplementary services for call transfer and call forwarding enjoy significantly more widespread support across the majority of non-Cisco SIP implementations compared with supplementary services for H.323. These services have been part of the SIP landscape from fairly early on in the development of the SIP protocol set, in contrast with the history of H.323, where these services were defined relatively late.

SIP REFER

Call transfer with the SIP protocol is supported using the SIP REFER method. As its name suggests, it allows one SIP UA, or endpoint, to refer a caller to a different SIP UA. It operates in a manner very similar to H.450.2. It triggers a replacement of the transferor-to-transfer-to consultation call by a transferee-to-transfer-to call. Just as in the H.450.2 case, the original and consultation call legs are treated as unrelated and independent entities until the call transfer is actually committed. Just like H.450.2, three possible transfer scenarios exist:

- Transfer-consult with commit-at-connect
- Transfer-consult with commit-at-alerting
- Blind transfers (without any consultation call)

One difference is that there's no specific consultation ID exchange transaction between the transferor and transfer-to parties, because the basic SIP protocol inherently contains a mechanism to uniquely identify the call being replaced at the transfer-to endpoint.

For the sake of completeness in describing SIP transfers, an older (and less preferred) SIP method called BYE/ALSO exists for executing blind transfers with SIP. As its name suggests, this is a method whereby the transferor terminates the original call from the transferee (BYE) but includes a request in the termination for the transferee to generate a follow-on call (to the transfer-to destination) using the ALSO part. Cisco CME does not use the BYE/ALSO method to initiate transfers, but it does support receipt of this method from other SIP devices. This is the method used by the automated attendant (AA) in Cisco UE, which you will read about in Chapter 9, "Cisco IPC Express Automated Attendant Options."

To enable Cisco CME to send REFER messages for call transfers, you need to configure **transfer-system full-consult** under **telephony-services**. This is the same basic configuration that is needed for H.450.2 transfers.

Unlike the H.450.2-related IOS CLI, there are no configuration commands to directly control usage of the REFER mechanism. This is a reflection of the almost-universal support that exists for REFER. Hence, there is little need to be able to enable and disable it in the same manner as H.450.2.

SIP 3XX Response

Call forwarding in SIP is supported mostly using the 302 moved temporarily in response to an incoming SIP call setup INVITE message. Just like the H.450.3 protocol, this response includes the alternate forward-to destination information (phone number). It requests that the caller cancel the original call and create a new call to the indicated destination. A range of SIP responses in the 3xx value code range includes a 300 multiple-choice response that allows the forwarding party to provide the caller with a range of alternative contacts. The 300-response code is not directly supported in the Cisco CME context. However, the Cisco IOS voice router SIP-SRST feature can generate this under some circumstances that are a little outside the scope of this book. You can find more information on this on Cisco.com by searching for "SIP Survivable Remote Site Telephony" under the SRST 3.2 Feature Guides.

To enable call forwarding using the 302 response, you need to configure **call-forward pattern .T** under **telephony-services**. This is the same basic configuration that is used for H.450.3 call forwarding.

Like the REFER case, no commands in IOS specifically control the generation of 302 response because of the universal support of this message by non-Cisco SIP devices.

SIP Interoperability

Interoperability for basic calls and transfer and forwarding for SIP is generally widespread among multiple SIP offerings from Cisco and non-Cisco products. The one major caveat for this with Cisco CME 3.0 and 3.1 is the lack of RFC 2833 support for DTMF relay. This is solved with the Cisco CME 3.2 release.

The SIP protocol is undergoing very rapid evolution, and many Internet Engineering Task Force (IETF) RFC drafts are in circulation at any given time. This is a good news/bad news situation. On the plus side, it shows that SIP is a flexible and extensible protocol. On the minus side, this situation has a lot of the larger and more conservative VoIP customers in a mode where they are waiting to see some stability before going to large, widespread deployments. By their very nature, large-scale deployments have difficulty absorbing significant and rapid protocol churn. If 100,000 endpoints are deployed in a VoIP network, it is very hard to do frequent upgrades to absorb the latest and greatest new protocol features.

Because Cisco CME is based on top of the H.323 and SIP software that's part of the IOS Voice Gateway code, Cisco CME automatically keeps up with, and benefits from, the best of both protocols. It represents a low-risk approach to VoIP telephony.

Summary

This chapter covered many details of the H.323 and SIP protocols. Choosing between the H.323 and SIP protocols depends on where you are starting from and what you are trying to do. In many cases, your choice is dictated by the nature of your existing voice network. This tends to favor H.323 simply because it is a more mature and well-established protocol. This is certainly the more conservative approach that you may favor if you're looking at immediate deployment of a large-scale VoIP network, and you don't want to get caught up in new technology issues.

If you are just getting started with VoIP trials, if you have no legacy network to worry about, and you are interested in exploring the latest new ideas in VoIP, SIP is a good choice.

In the end, your decision is best based on looking at solid business functions and economic factors. Your VoIP system end users are not likely to care what the underlying protocol is. You should be looking primarily to see which vendors have the best products and user features that are available within your deployment schedule.

In the end, the choice between H.323 and SIP is generally not an irrevocable decision. They are both very good protocols for implementing peer-to-peer voice networks. Cisco CME supports both protocols and will continue to evolve as they do. Many other vendors of VoIP systems are likely to follow a similar dual-track approach to this issue. It's unlikely that any radically new voice telephony features will be available using just one basic protocol. The key innovation is to use VoIP and embrace the concept of a converged voice and data network. You can do this with either H.323 or SIP.

This chapter covers the following topics:

- Basic call interoperability between Cisco CallManager Express (CME) and Cisco CallManager
- Call transfer and forward operation between Cisco CME and Cisco CallManager
- Operation of name display between Cisco CME and Cisco CallManager
- H.450 tandem gateway operation

## CHAPTER 8

Integrating Cisco CME with Cisco CallManager

This chapter covers the deployment of Cisco CallManager Express (CME) for branch offices in conjunction with a Cisco CallManager deployed at a central or head office site. In this situation, the central Cisco CallManager site can act as a hub linking the remote Cisco CME sites. Cisco CME and Cisco CallManager can communicate across IP WAN links using H.323 (or using Session Initiation Protocol [SIP] with Cisco CallManager 4.1 or later versions).

In H.323 networks, Cisco CME provides supplementary service interworking (H.450) using voice over IP (VoIP) hairpin call routing when needed for intersite call transfer and forwarding. The basics of this operation are covered in Chapter 5, "Cisco CME Call Processing Features." Chapter 7, "Connecting Multiple Cisco CMEs with VoIP," covers inter-Cisco CME H.323 network operation. This chapter discusses these services in a network that has both Cisco CME systems and one or more Cisco CallManagers.

Goals of Interoperability

Chapter 2, "Building a Cisco IPC Express Network," covers the choice between centralized architectures (those based solely on Cisco CallManager) and distributed or autonomous site architectures (those based on Cisco CME) for implementing VoIP networks. In many real-world cases, this isn't a simple either/or decision, because many networks include both types of structures, discussed in Chapter 2 as the hybrid network architecture.

Real enterprise VoIP networks that have been designed consistently from the ground up and that adhere to a single uniform architectural approach are rare. The technologies available to network designers have evolved rapidly over the past decade or two. This rapid evolution is likely to continue for some time. It requires organizations to continually rethink their network architectures to take advantage of the latest available enhancements. Not only do the technologies change, but so do the companies trying to make best use of them. Companies split and merge and reinvent themselves in a continuous effort to stay profitable and competitive. This leads to real-world networks made up of a mixture of architectures formed by the ad hoc fusion of components contributed by multiple network designs.

Looking at VoIP networks that incorporate Cisco components, you commonly see both central-site Cisco CallManager networks using Survivable Remote Site Telephony (SRST) at some remote branch offices coupled with Cisco CME systems used at other remote offices. Being able to interconnect these systems is a fairly important consideration. In fact, some businesses deliberately design their networks using both central and distributed models to take into account issues with geographic variation in the availability of WAN services. For example, in the banking industry, central Cisco CallManager designs have been widely used in city branches located in metropolitan areas where adequate bandwidth and quality of service (QoS)-enabled WAN links are fairly readily available. On the other hand, Cisco CME systems have been used in small-town bank branches located in more rural areas where WAN services might be less sophisticated and unable to support voice.

Both Cisco CallManager and Cisco CME support H.323, which you can use to create Cisco CallManager-to-CME links. Cisco CME also supports SIP for VoIP interconnect. SIP is also being introduced as a WAN trunking interface on Cisco CallManager. This chapter focuses only on the H.323 interconnect option, because the SIP interconnect option is still a work in progress as SIP support on successive Cisco CallManager releases evolves. However, you can expect that most of the architectural issues raised in this chapter are also applicable in the SIP context.

The descriptions contained in this chapter apply to the Cisco CME 3.1 and 3.2 releases and the Cisco CallManager 3.3(3) and 4.0 releases. Newer releases may have different behaviors and options than those described here.

Basic Calls Between Cisco CallManager and Cisco CME

Even before the introduction of Cisco CME, Cisco CallManager used Cisco IOS voice routers to provide a Public Switched Telephone Network (PSTN) access gateway for Cisco CallManager's IP phones. Both the H.323 and Media Gateway Control Protocol (MGCP) VoIP protocols can support this function. The choice between these two is partly a historic issue and partly related to the type of PSTN interface used, but this topic is outside the scope of this book.

Direct MGCP integration between Cisco CME's IP phones and Cisco CallManager is not supported. Although this does not preclude the concurrent operation of MGCP (used for the PSTN gateway ports) and H.323-with-CME on the same Cisco IOS voice router, this configuration is not recommended. Using MGCP with Cisco CallManager to control the PSTN voice ports on a Cisco CME system would force PSTN traffic originated by the Cisco CME's IP phones to route through the Cisco CallManager to reach the PSTN. In most cases, this would be inefficient because it would result in the Cisco CME-to-PSTN voice traffic traversing the Cisco CME-to-Cisco CallManager WAN link twice.

Because Cisco CME is built on top of the Cisco IOS voice infrastructure software foundation also used by the Cisco IOS router-based PSTN gateways, Cisco CME inherits most of the H.323 gateway-to-CallManager interoperability. You should be aware of some minor differences, however.

In the simple PSTN gateway case, most of the call progress signaling for calls is performed as in-band audio tones. For example, when an IP phone (hosted by Cisco CallManager) places an outbound call to the PSTN, the ringing tone (also called the *alerting* or *ringback tone*) heard by the caller is usually generated as an audio signal that's passed through end-to-end from the

PSTN trunk. This means that the audio path from the gateway to the IP phone is opened and active before the call is connected.

In the case where a call is placed from a Cisco CallManager IP phone to a Cisco CME IP phone, the ringing tone is provided as an out-of-band H.323 indication from Cisco CME (through H.323 control channel signaling). This means that the Cisco CME system signals to the Cisco CallManager, which in turn instructs the Cisco CallManager's IP phone to generate the ringing tone locally.

The reasons for this difference include the following:

- It saves some bandwidth because the audio path is not opened until the call actually connects.

- The Skinny Client Control Protocol (SCCP)-based IP phones attached to Cisco CME cannot generate in-band ringing tone.

- It avoids issues with shared extension lines, where an inbound H.323 call to Cisco CME may ring multiple phones at the same time. This could create complexity in choosing which phone should physically be required to do the tone generation. Add to this the fact that any of the Cisco CME phones involved might also have calls already in progress, and it should become clear why out-of-band signaling of call progress tones is the preferred approach for Cisco CME.

This issue of ringing-tone signaling causes some specific changes in the H.323 protocol exchange that Cisco CME uses when talking to a Cisco CallManager, compared with H.323 signaling to another Cisco IOS PSTN gateway, for example.

To get Cisco CallManager to provide local ringing-tone generation for outbound calls from Cisco CallManager, the Cisco CME delays negotiation of the media path until the call connects. The Cisco CallManager 3.3 and 4.0 H.323 implementations assume that in-band ringing tone is provided (by the Cisco CME or another H.323 device) on all calls that negotiate the media path (using H.245) before the call is connected. This delayed negotiation can lead to a minor delay (typically about a quarter of a second) in establishing the audio path when the call actually connects. This delay is called the *voice cut-through delay.*

Cisco CME only uses this delayed H.245 media negotiation on calls that go to or from a Cisco CallManager. Cisco CME (3.1 and above) can explicitly identify Cisco CallManager calls based on special nonstandard H.323 information element (IE) messages that Cisco CallManager attaches to its H.323 call setup, proceeding, alerting, and connected messages. See Figure 8-1.

Figure 8-1 *Cisco CallManager-to-Cisco CME 3.1 Basic Call*

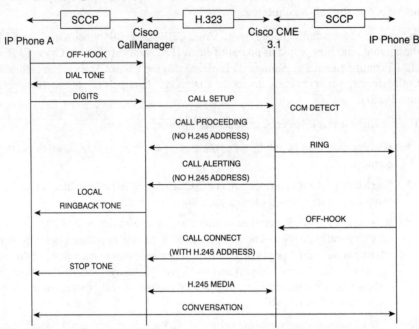

Call Transfer

Cisco CallManager and Cisco CME implement significantly different approaches to handling call transfer. These differences are related to the basic architectural differences that exist between a highly centralized (CallManager) and fully distributed (Cisco CME) VoIP network architecture.

In Cisco CME, the preferred mechanism for handling call transfer is H.450.2. This allows calls to be transferred in a highly optimized fashion not only between phones on the same Cisco CME system, but also between different Cisco CME systems. This is a significant attribute when you consider that Cisco CME-based VoIP networks can include hundreds or thousands of individual CME nodes. Each CME node is a distinct and separate H.323 device with autonomous call processing.

In Cisco CallManager, the call transfer mechanism is designed to allow calls to be transferred between hundreds or thousands of IP phones controlled by the *same* Cisco CallManager (or CallManager cluster). Furthermore, in a Cisco CallManager environment, there is a significant need to separate the H.323 control path from the H.323 media path. Because a single Cisco CallManager server can be required to control approximately 2500 IP phones, it's impossible for the server to play an active intermediary role in the media path for all phone calls. Consider that there's a media packet in each direction every 20 milliseconds (ms) for each call, and then multiply this by 2500 phones. To allow a Cisco CallManager to support this number of phones, the media path for phone-to-phone calls must be directly between the phones whenever possible.

Note that each Cisco CallManager (or CallManager cluster) represents a single H.323 device from the external VoIP network perspective regardless of how many IP phones it supports.

One other issue to examine when comparing Cisco CallManager to Cisco operation CME is that for enterprise telephone systems, the ratio between internal and external call counts is related to the overall size of the phone system. As the number of extensions attached to a phone system increases, so does the relative proportion of internal calls compared to external calls. For example, in a system with only ten phones, almost 100% of phone calls are external calls between a phone and the outside world. In a system with 1000 phones, the external calls may make up only about 10% of the total call volume.

You can view this call transfer difference between Cisco CallManager and Cisco CME as being equivalent to the difference between an internal intra-private branch exchange (PBX) call transfer and an inter-PBX transfer. Viewed from the legacy PBX perspective, you can see that these are fundamentally different problems.

H.323 Call Transfer Using an Empty Capabilities Set

The problem with call transfer becomes more complex when you consider the interaction of Cisco CallManager IP phones with an external H.323 network. When an H.323 call exists between an external H.323 device and a Cisco CallManager IP phone, the preferred arrangement is to have a direct media path between the endpoints that does not pass through the Cisco CallManager server. In some cases, a direct media path is not possible (as described in the section "Call Transfer and the Media Termination Point"). In this case, it is necessary to introduce a Media Termination Point (MTP) into the media path. The MTP acts as a media relay or middleman and relays the Real-Time Transport Protocol (RTP) voice packets between the two terminating endpoints. The call signaling path does pass through the Cisco CallManager server. The H.323 signaling is terminated on the Cisco CallManager server and then is converted into SCCP to talk to the IP phone. The Cisco CallManager is required to participate in this signaling path to provide the needed conversion between H.323 and SCCP.

When there is a call transfer for an H.323 call from one Cisco CallManager IP phone (phone A) to another (phone B), the H.323 signaling path does not change. It remains terminated on the Cisco CallManager server. The Cisco CallManager server establishes a new SCCP signaling path to phone B. Of course, the media path also has to change. Changing the media path on the IP phones is easy. The Cisco CallManager simply sends the appropriate SCCP messages to phone B, telling it to participate in the media connection to the external H.323 endpoint.

To change the media connection on the H.323 side, the Cisco CallManager uses a mechanism known as Empty Capabilities Set (ECS). This mechanism informs the external H.323 device that it should stop sending its media packets to phone A's IP address and should instead send the media packets to phone B's IP address. This mechanism allows the media stream to be redirected to the transfer-to destination phone while preserving the original H.323 control path connection. Figure 8-2 shows the media path before and after the transfer.

Figure 8-2 *Cisco CallManager ECS Transfer*

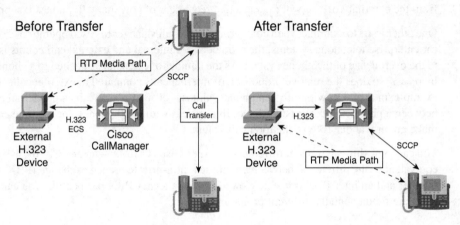

With this arrangement, there is no limit on the number of times the call can be transferred, as long as the call termination point remains within the set of phones controlled by CallManager. This is the behavior you would expect, considering how a legacy time-division multiplexing (TDM)-based PBX works. There's usually no limit on the number of internal chained transfers. Cisco CME (and Cisco IOS-based H.323 PSTN gateways in general) supports receipt of ECS signaling from Cisco CallManager but does not initiate ECS signaling for call transfer.

H.323-to-H.323 Call Transfer

Now consider what happens when the transfer-to destination is not an internal IP phone. In the case of an H.323 endpoint that calls an internal IP phone and then is transferred to a second external H.323 endpoint, the same ECS mechanism can be used. The transferred call has its H.323 signaling path relayed through the Cisco CallManager, but the media path is direct between the two external H.323 endpoints.

This process works fine except in the case where one of the H.323 endpoints wants to further transfer the call (or perform some other media-related operation, such as call hold with music on hold [MOH]). In general, chained H.323 ECS operations do not work well. This is because the attempt to chain-transfer the call results in a very indirect H.323 control path. None of the entities in the H.323 control path is directly connected to *both* of the call media final termination points. This means that the media path negotiations have to pass through two middlemen instead of one.

For example, for the first transfer, A calls B and is transferred to C. The transferor node B is in direct contact with both the A and C points and can help them negotiate a mutually acceptable media path. The H.323 control path is A-to-B-to-C, but the media path is A-to-C.

A problem arises when C wants to transfer the call to D. This would create an A-to-B-to-C-to-D H.323 control path. In this case, neither of the B or C middlemen is in direct contact with both of the A and D final endpoints. This can make successful media negotiation between A and D quite difficult to achieve in practice.

Call Transfer and the Media Termination Point

One way to solve the problem of end-to-end negotiation of the media path is to use an MTP that can provide *transcoding* services. One example of this type of MTP is the digital signal processor (DSP) farms that are supported on Cisco IOS voice-enabled routers. DSP farms are controlled by a Cisco CallManager (or Cisco CME) using the SCCP protocol. The term *transcode* means the ability to convert the media stream from one codec type to another. You may sometimes see this term abbreviated as *xcode*.

If you introduce a transcoding MTP into the media path, there is no need to perform end-to-end media path renegotiation for the chained call transfer case. The use of an MTP simplifies the problem of connecting or transferring a call through multiple H.323 endpoints, because it removes the need to perform a multiparty negotiation and capabilities adaptation between all the H.323 entities involved. Figure 8-3 shows the media path before and after the transfer.

Figure 8-3   *Cisco CallManager Transfer with MTP*

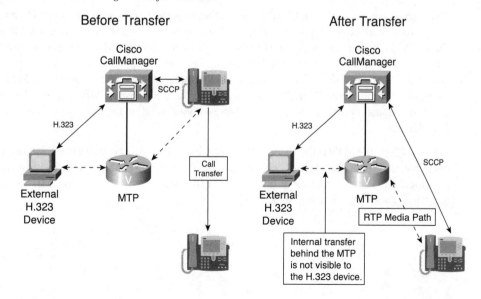

In general, the MTP approach simplifies the set of H.323 signaling operations required and increases the overall compatibility and the ability to interoperate. This is true even in cases where everyone uses the same codec type and actual transcoding of codecs is unnecessary.

The drawback to this approach is the impact on overall scalability, because an MTP channel is needed for every H.323 (external) call. A mitigating factor in this situation (as mentioned earlier, in the section "Call Transfer") is that as the number of IP phones in the Cisco CallManager cluster increases, the fraction of H.323 calls to internal calls decreases. In general, the expense of adding MTPs is worthwhile because of the reduction in H.323 interoperability issues.

Another issue with the chained transfer cases is that each leg in the transfer chain contributes additional delay to both the signaling and media path. If a call is chain-transferred too many times, the resulting delay and voice quality are likely to become unacceptable. In general, end-to-end one-way delays of more than 150 to 200 ms are unacceptable to phone users.

The chained-transfer issues apply only to intersite transfers that are chained across multiple separate H.323 nodes. Transfers within the internal scope of a single H.323 node do not suffer from this problem, because (with an MTP) the transfer is invisible to the other H.323 endpoints involved.

Connecting Cisco CallManager with Cisco CME

This section examines how what you've learned so far in this chapter relates to connecting a Cisco CallManager to a network of Cisco CME systems.

You learned in Chapter 7 that Cisco CME prefers to perform call transfers using H.450.2 but can perform VoIP-to-VoIP hairpin or tandem routing when needed. You also learned that a Cisco CME can automatically detect calls to or from a Cisco CallManager and can use this information to disable its normal H.450.2 behavior. The final piece of this puzzle is to understand that an H.323 call to a Cisco CME IP phone always passes through an MTP-like mechanism within Cisco CME. This arrangement allows the Cisco CME to optionally perform its internal transfers without using H.450.2 and without affecting the H.323 connection to Cisco CallManager.

In Cisco CME, the MTP is the Cisco CME router itself. However, you still need a separate MTP device on the Cisco CallManager side in case the Cisco CallManager phone itself invokes additional call transfer operations on the same call. Figure 8-4 shows Cisco CME connecting to a Cisco CallManager using MTP.

Figure 8-4   *Cisco CallManager and Cisco CME Connected Using MTPs*

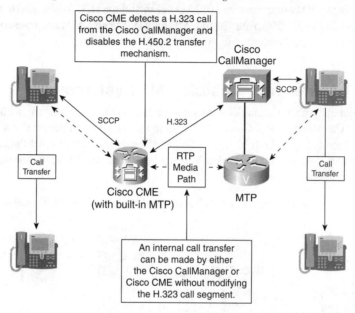

The issue of MTP scalability largely doesn't apply to Cisco CME for two reasons. First, the RTP media stream voice packets have to pass through the Cisco CME router anyway. Even if Cisco CME did not deliberately invoke MTP treatment for the media stream packets, the packets would still need to be routed by the Cisco CME's IP routing function. In many cases, the router might also have to perform other operations on the media stream packets, such as firewall and Network Address Translation (NAT). As a result, no additional real-world penalty is incurred by the MTP treatment; it's more or less free.

Second, the number of IP phones that Cisco CME supports is relatively low compared to a Cisco CallManager. The number of phones supported by a Cisco CME router is scaled according to the overall performance of the specific Cisco IOS router model used. Many different router models are available with IP phone support, which ranges from 24 phones to about 240 phones. This topic is covered in Chapter 1, "Introducing Cisco IPC Express."

The only condition under which the Cisco CME's MTP treatment incurs an additional cost is when you actually need codec transcoding. Even in this case, the additional cost usually is not large, because you almost certainly already have DSP resources included in your Cisco CME router to support its PSTN ports. In many cases, you can meet the MTP transcoding requirement simply by adding DSP chips to your existing voice-port hardware. This is in contrast to the need to explicitly add an entire voice module solely for DSP farm transcoding purposes.

However, in many cases transcoding for call transfer is unneeded, because a Cisco CME has only a single WAN link carrying H.323 calls, and all the H.323 calls tend to use the same codec (either G.711 or G.729). Your Cisco CME may still need DSP farm transcoding services to support three-party conferencing for G.729 calls (see Chapter 7).

Intersite Call Transfer with Multiple CME Systems

The final call transfer scenario you should understand is what happens with a call placed from a Cisco CallManager to a Cisco CME system that is then transferred to a second Cisco CME system (see Figure 8-5). In this case, the first Cisco CME detects that the call is from a Cisco CallManager. As a result, it invokes VoIP-to-VoIP tandem or hairpin routing to provide the call path (see Chapter 7 for details).

Figure 8-5   *Intersite Call Transfer for a Cisco CallManager with Multiple Cisco CME Systems*

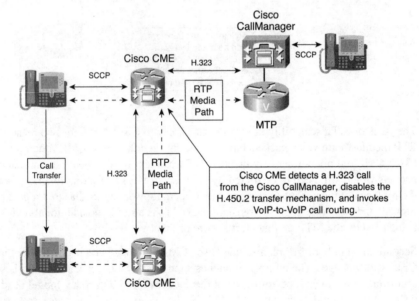

Call Forwarding

Call forwarding (for busy, no-answer, and unconditional forwarding) raises many of the same issues as call transfer. Likewise, these issues can be addressed using an MTP to simplify the H.323 signaling operations.

As you read in Chapter 7, the preferred method of handling call forwarding for Cisco CME is H.450.3. Again, Cisco CME can disable its H.450.3 feature when it detects calls from a Cisco

CallManager. Under these circumstances, the Cisco CME system falls back to using internal call forwarding or VoIP-to-VoIP call routing for intersite call forwarding.

Just like the call-transfer case, an MTP allows internal call forwarding to occur without impact to the H.323 call leg. Of the three types of forwarding—busy, no-answer, and unconditional—the no-answer form generally involves more signaling complexity. When a call forward no-answer occurs, the preliminary call negotiation for the original called phone must be revoked (after the no-answer timeout). It is replaced with a new call to the forward-to destination phone. The forwarded call can potentially require the use of different parameters than those negotiated for the original called phone. The busy and unconditional forms of call forwarding usually don't involve a preliminary call actually reaching the forwarding phone; this tends to simplify the signaling. Figure 8-6 shows call forwarding between a Cisco CME system and a Cisco CallManager using MTP.

Figure 8-6 *Cisco CallManager and Cisco CME Call Forwarding with MTP*

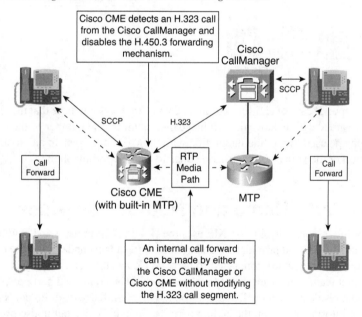

You can see that Figure 8-4, which shows call transfer, and Figure 8-6, which shows call forwarding, are nearly identical. Figure 8-7 shows intersite Cisco CME call forwarding for a call from a Cisco CallManager. Compare it to Figure 8-5 for the equivalent call transfer case.

Figure 8-7 *Cisco CallManager Forwarding with Multiple Cisco CMEs*

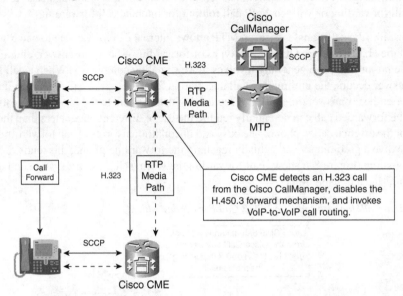

For the special case of call forwarding to a voice mail system, note that the H.323 call setup for the forwarded call includes the original called number (the number of the forwarding phone). This can be used to provide integration with the voice mail system and to allow automatic selection of the voice mailbox that belongs to the forwarding phone.

Connected Party Name and Number Services

One of the reasons why Cisco CME uses the H.450.2 call transfer and H.450.3 call forwarding mechanisms is that it provides a standard means to support updating of the originating phone's display to track who the connected-to party is. Connected party display is often considered an important feature in business telephone networks. The connected party display is broader than the usual residential caller ID display you may be familiar with at home. Not only does it provide information about the calling party for inbound calls, but it also provides information about the called party for outbound calls. The connected party display can show you the name of the person you have called, for example. This is in contrast to simply displaying the number you dialed. Also, the standard caller ID display function provides a one-time indication of who the caller is only at the beginning of an incoming call. The connected party display feature allows for midcall updates of the connected party information that occur when the far end of the call performs a call transfer.

For example, after a caller has been transferred, his phone display can be updated to show the name and number of the extension he has been transferred to. Likewise, when you receive a call transferred to you by someone else, your phone display may initially show the caller ID of the person who is transferring the call to you. After the transfer is complete, your phone's display may update to show the caller ID of the transferee (caller).

When Cisco CME disables the H.450.2/3 mechanisms to interwork with Cisco CallManager, this display update mechanism is unavailable. However, Cisco CallManager has its own mechanism for performing connected party display updates. Cisco CallManager uses H.323 display and information IEs. Cisco CME also supports these IEs for performing connected party display updates.

The H.323 IE messages are carried as part of the H.323 signaling path. They are unaffected by the use of an MTP because they are informational messages only and don't generate changes to the call signaling state. This means that even when a Cisco CallManager performs an internal call transfer hidden behind an MTP, the H.323 information and display IEs are received by the Cisco CME system and are used to provide display updates. Not only can Cisco CME receive display IEs from Cisco CallManager, but it also sends display IEs to Cisco CallManager when Cisco CME performs internal transfer or forwarding.

Cisco CME sends these display IE messages for all H.323 calls regardless of whether a Cisco CallManager is involved in a call. This means that you can still get intersite connected-to party updates in Cisco CME networks where you have chosen to globally disable H.450 services.

Using H.450.x Tandem IP-to-IP Gateway

One final point to understand in planning your Cisco CallManager-to-Cisco CME connections is the advantages that an H.450 Tandem IP-to-IP gateway can provide. You can insert an H.450 Tandem IP-to-IP gateway into the call path between your Cisco CME network and Cisco CallManager, and use it to mitigate some of the issues that arise from the use of VoIP-to-VoIP call paths. If an intersite call transfer or forward initiated by a Cisco CME creates a VoIP hairpin call, you can often use an H.450 Tandem IP-to-IP gateway co-located with your Cisco CallManager to avoid most of the voice path delay caused. Just hairpin the media stream through the Cisco CME system located at the end of a narrow-bandwidth WAN link. Refer to Chapter 7 for more details about IP-to-IP gateways.

Summary

In this chapter, you've learned how to connect a network of Cisco CME systems with a Cisco CallManager using H.323. You've seen how Cisco CME can automatically and intelligently react to the presence of a Cisco CallManager and adapt its behavior accordingly. You've also learned how to optimize call transfers and forwards using H.450 for intersite Cisco CME calls within a fully distributed telephony network that at the same time can interoperate with a central site Cisco CallManager.

This chapter covers the following topics:

- Using an automated attendant (AA) or receptionist in your office
- Understanding the Cisco IP Communications (IPC) Express integrated AA
- The Cisco Unity Express (UE) system AA, including features such as dial-by-number, dial-by-name, business hours, and holiday call routing
- Customizing the Cisco UE AA with prompts and scripts using the Cisco UE AA Editor
- The Cisco UE Greeting Management System (GMS)
- Tasks to set up a Cisco UE AA
- Toolkit Command Language (TCL)-based AA as an alternative to the Cisco UE integrated AA

## CHAPTER 9

Cisco IPC Express Automated Attendant Options

The chapters thus far in Part II, "Feature Operation and Applications," have discussed how to use the Cisco CallManager Express (CME) call processing and IP phone features and operation. Cisco CME provides Cisco IOS router-based call management and control to the IP phones and public switched telephone network (PSTN) trunks defined on the system. An IP telephony package for a small or medium office or enterprise branch office is, for most installations, incomplete without automated attendant (AA) and voice mail functions, even though not everybody needs these features.

An AA is a voice system feature that automatically answers your business's incoming calls with a welcome greeting (for example, "Thank you for calling company x."). It also provides a menu of choices for the caller to select from. The caller presses the appropriate button on the phone. The AA system then interprets the dual-tone multifrequency (DTMF) tones and redirects the call to the chosen destination based on the menu selection.

This chapter discusses the Cisco IP Communications (IPC) Express options for AA functionality, including an integrated AA application and a Toolkit Command Language (TCL)-based AA. The integrated AA option is a Cisco CME application, Cisco Unity Express (Cisco UE), which includes both an AA and a voice mail component. The AA component is covered in this chapter, and the voice mail portion of the application is discussed in Chapter 10, "Cisco IPC Express Integrated Voice Mail."

The Cisco UE AA is a full-featured, customizable AA application offering an easy-to-use graphical user interface (GUI) drag-and-drop interface to change the system's AA menu flow. Cisco UE is cost-effective for small and medium standalone or networked offices, or as a distributed AA (and voice mail system) in branch offices of an enterprise network. Cisco UE offers up to five distinct AAs, each associated with an individual pilot number and one or more scripts that can be fully customized.

The second alternative is a TCL-based AA that leverages Cisco IOS built-in TCL capability. Although it can be customized by someone proficient in the TCL language, it is not typically an end-user interface. Instead, it is a tool used by Cisco and Cisco developers to provide ready-made scripts for your system.

Although choosing and understanding an AA for your system is important, it is also important that you understand how a receptionist and an AA can work together to provide the best services for customers calling your business. This is the first topic in this chapter, followed by in-depth discussions of the two AA technology alternatives.

Using an Automated Attendant or a Receptionist in Your Office

With its AA options, Cisco CME can provide a fully automated front end to calls coming into a small office. All IP phone extensions, the system's voice mail pilot number (the number called to access the voice mail application), and general information such as location, business hours, and driving directions can all be accessed via the AA menu choices. However, many small businesses choose to enhance their customer relationships with a receptionist instead of presenting an AA menu to their callers. For maximum flexibility, both modes of operation can be used. A receptionist can answer calls during normal business hours, and an AA can direct after-hours calls or can be used as a backup if the receptionist is unable to answer the phone.

When deploying an AA in an office, you must first decide how to handle calls into the office, both during business hours and after hours. Next, craft the Cisco CME call routing features, the AA menus, and the digit manipulation done by the Cisco CME system to achieve the desired call routing. Cisco CME call routing capabilities depend in part on how the PSTN trunks are configured and what digit information the PSTN delivers.

Calls to the Main Office Number

For a business with direct inward dial (DID) service, the only calls typically answered by an AA or receptionist are the general calls to the main office number. DID calls are switched automatically to the extension number that the caller dials. For example, extension 3001's PSTN DID number is 222-555-3001, so whenever this number is called, the IP phone for extension 3001 rings automatically without AA or human assistance. DID call routing makes sense for a business such as a lawyers' office, where each lawyer must be individually reached by clients and the DID PSTN phone number appears on the lawyer's business card.

Cisco CME's default operation is to switch calls automatically to the dialed extension (via dial peer matching), provided that dialed digits (DNIS) are available from the PSTN for the call. However, even with DID service, it is still possible to redirect all or certain calls to an AA or receptionist by doing digit manipulation on the dialed digits if you prefer this call routing.

Many small businesses might not desire the cost of DID PSTN service because of either size (the business is too small) or the type of business they conduct. For example, a small charity or restaurant's incoming phone business is of a general nature and can be handled equally well by any employee answering the phone. For these types of businesses, multiple general PSTN lines make more sense.

Calls to multiple general PSTN lines can also be directed to either an AA or receptionist. Or all calls can simply ring on the multiple line appearances (Line 1, Line 2, and so on) on the phones and be answered by any employee at any phone. It is also possible that these PSTN lines appear on one phone only—the receptionist's phone—and that the receptionist then transfers the call to the appropriate extension. All calls not answered directly by employees via these methods must be answered by either a receptionist or an AA.

If you decide that only an AA is required in an office, simply configure all main office PSTN calls to terminate on the AA pilot number. As soon as the AA answers the call, callers can use the dial-by-number or dial-by-name features to reach the extension or service of their choice.

If you decide that a receptionist is required, configure all main office PSTN calls to terminate on the receptionist's extension. The receptionist can then transfer the call to the extension of the employee or group the caller wants to contact. If you want to use the AA to handle calls as a backup to the receptionist, or as an after-hours mechanism, it is possible to call-forward-no-answer (CFNA) the receptionist's extension to the AA.

NOTE   If the receptionist's phone CFNAs to the AA, unanswered calls cannot be directed to a personal voice mailbox, with the result that the receptionist cannot have voice mail. This situation can be circumvented in one of two ways:

- Define a separate private extension for the receptionist that forwards to personal voice mail when not answered. Then define a different public extension for the main office calls that forwards to the AA if not answered. Both extensions appear on the receptionist's phone, but different types of calls are directed to each extension, and they have different CFNA destinations.

- CFNA the receptionist's phone to the AA and then define an AA menu branch where a caller can choose to leave a message for the business. Define a Cisco UE general delivery mailbox (GDM) for this purpose, and configure it to provide a message waiting indicator (MWI) on the receptionist's phone. The definition and use of GDMs are discussed in Chapter 10.

Call Routing Considerations for AA Versus a Receptionist

In addition to the business decisions for call routing covered in the preceding section, you also have to consider Cisco CME/UE feature operation when deciding whether to route calls to an AA or a receptionist. These feature considerations are discussed briefly in the following sections. The discussion draws on concepts such as user and group definitions, which are covered in greater detail in Chapter 10, and AA concepts such as dial-by-number and dial-by-name, which are covered later in this chapter.

Using Dial-by-Name to Reach Group Names

Group and personal extensions can be reached via the Cisco UE AA dial-by-number feature or via a receptionist. Group names, however, cannot be reached via the Cisco UE AA dial-by-name feature—only personal names can. Personal names are those associated with the employees in the office. Group names are associated with functions in your office, such as the help desk or the sales or shipping departments.

Reaching a group by name requires one of the following call routing alternatives:

- A receptionist
- The caller must know the extension associated with the group
- A customized AA menu that leads the caller through the available group choices (such as "Press 1 for sales; press 2 for support") and transfers the call to the appropriate extension

Transferred Calls That Forward to Voice Mail

A call arriving at the AA that is subsequently redirected to the chosen extension (by dial-by-number or dial-by-name) may be forwarded to voice mail if the extension is not answered or is busy. In this call scenario, the Cisco UE AA sets the redirected number field appropriately for the call to enter the called person's mailbox.

Consider an example: A PSTN caller dials 444-555-3000, the business's main office number. This call terminates on the Cisco UE AA (for example, 6801 as the AA pilot number), and the caller chooses extension 3001 from the menu. Extension 3001 rings. When it isn't answered, the call is forwarded to voice mail (for example, 6800 as the voice mail pilot number) and enters the voice mailbox associated to Grace Garrett at extension 3001. At this point, 3001 is the number contained in the call's *redirected number* field when entering voice mail. Therefore, the caller hears Grace's mailbox greeting (for example, "You have reached the desk of Grace Garrett. Please leave a message after the tone.").

Now consider the same call scenario, but with the receptionist answering the call instead of the AA. The PSTN caller dials the main office number, 444-555-3000. The receptionist answers the call and learns that the caller wants to speak to Grace Garrett at extension 3001. The receptionist has two choices when redirecting the call:

- Transfer the call to the Grace's extension, 3001
- Transfer the call directly to voice mail (using the voice mail pilot number, 6800)

The first case works exactly like the AA call flow described earlier, and the call enters Grace's voice mailbox. The second case, though, has the *redirected number* field set to the receptionist's extension, not to extension 3001; therefore, the call does not enter Grace's mailbox, but the receptionist's mailbox instead.

If a receptionist is used to front calls, it is recommended that calls are transferred to the desired extension and not directly to the voice mail pilot number. If the direct transfer method must be implemented, each employee must have an associated phantom directory number (DN) in addition to his or her normal extension. Also, the phantom DN must be associated with the mailbox in the Primary E.164 field of the Cisco UE user definition (you'll read more about this in Chapter 10). In this configuration, the receptionist must transfer calls to the phantom DN for the employee, instead of to his or her normal extension. This phantom DN is then call-forward-all (CFA) to voice mail. This configuration is shown in Figure 9-1.

Figure 9-1   *Transferring a Call Directly to Voice Mail*

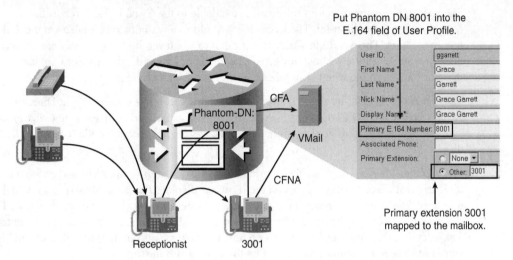

Following the lower set of arrows in Figure 9-1, the receptionist receives a call and chooses to transfer it to Grace's phone (extension 3001). It rings and then forwards to voice mail (pilot number 6800) if it isn't answered.

The upper set of arrows shows the call flow for transferring the call directly to voice mail without first ringing Grace's phone. A phantom DN 8001 is defined for Grace. This secondary extension is configured into the User Profile in the Primary E.164 Number field as shown. In this scenario, the receptionist answers the call, determines that it must be redirected to Grace's voice mail, and transfers the call to extension 8001 (Grace's phantom DN) instead of 3001 (Grace's desk IP phone extension).

Example 9-1 shows the phantom DN configuration required on Cisco CME to support this operation.

Example 9-19 *Creating a Phantom Ephone-dn*

```
router# show running-config
ephone-dn 100
  number 8001
  !choose a number that is easy for the receptionist to remember and that fits
  !well into the dial plan
  call-forward all 6800
  !call forward all calls unconditionally into voice mail pilot number
```

The only configuration to be added to Cisco UE is to enter the phantom DN (8001) into the User Profile Primary E.164 Number field, as shown in Figure 9-1. The option of adding a second DN (8001 in this example) is available only if the Primary E.164 Number field is not already used for the employee's DID number (for example, 222-555-3001). This field and its use for voice mail configuration are further discussed in Chapter 10.

Directory Information

The user or extension directory information available to the Cisco UE AA versus the receptionist may be different. The Cisco UE AA allows any digits to be dialed via the dial-by-number feature. The AA blindly transfers the call to whatever digits the caller entered into the dial-by-number feature without any cross-checks. In other words, the AA does not use a directory to determine whether or where the call can be transferred.

The Cisco UE AA dial-by-name feature, however, uses its built-in Lightweight Directory Access Protocol (LDAP) directory, so only extensions associated with users (not with groups) and with names appropriately configured into the system are accessible via the Cisco UE AA dial-by-name feature.

A receptionist is likely to use either a printed list of extensions (employees and groups) or the directory that Cisco CME provides on the IP phone display. The phone-based Cisco CME directory feature uses the **name** field under the **ephone-dn** configuration as its database. This information is not synchronized with the Cisco UE's LDAP name information, so the entries can potentially be different (depending on how the system was configured and which fields' values have been manually coordinated by the system administrator).

Understanding the Cisco IPC Express Integrated Automated Attendant

The preceding section discussed general considerations with call routing to a receptionist or an AA. Provided that your business requires at least some of its calls to be routed via an AA, the following several sections discuss Cisco UE's AA capabilities in more detail. The features discussed here assume a minimum of Cisco UE 1.1 software. Some features require later releases.

When callers call into the AA number, based on the time of day and the day of the week, the AA may play a different greeting to callers, followed by a menu of options. After the caller selects the desired option, the call is routed to the requested destination, which can be an employee extension or a service such as recorded driving directions or business hours.

One of the many benefits of an AA is that after-hours callers can still receive the information they need to contact your business. It also lowers business expenses and lessens the burden on a receptionist. An AA is especially useful for larger sites where the number of calls to the main office number may overwhelm a receptionist. An AA menu should be carefully designed, because it is the public face of your business to clients. Badly designed menus, menu choices that are ambiguous, or loops within the AA script will frustrate callers.

Cisco UE provides the capability to define up to five different AAs. Each individual AA is a menu script associated with a phone number called a pilot or call-in number. Calls arriving at the pilot number, either internal or PSTN calls, are then handled by the script associated with the pilot number.

Cisco UE ships with a system AA (using system-provided scripts) that requires minimal configuration to set up for your business. You may also use one or more custom scripts that tailor the AA menu options to your business's exact needs. Each pilot number that you associate with an AA script counts as a distinct AA application. Up to five of these AA applications can be active in the Cisco UE system at once.

Which AA is executed depends on which pilot number you direct your calls to; this is entirely flexible. For example, you may have the system AA active, one custom AA that you have written, and one or more test scripts that are not actively taking calls but that are present on Cisco UE as the third or fourth AAs. Or you may have different departments, each with its own direct PSTN number, and each wanting to manage its own AA greeting and menu separate from the other departments. This configuration can be accommodated with two or more separate AAs in the system. Most businesses, however, in addition to an optional receptionist use one of the following:

- The system AA
- A single custom AA (with a dormant system AA, meaning that the system AA is present but no calls are directed to it)

The Cisco UE System AA

The system AA is shipped to ensure that you can set up a working system in a minimal amount of time. You simply configure a small number of parameters, and record a few greetings (called prompts on the Cisco UE system). You do not have to worry about the script itself, because it is fixed and cannot be changed.

The system AA offers the canned menu shown in Example 9-2. The highlighted lines are new features added to the system AA in Cisco UE Release 2.1.

Example 9-20 *Cisco UE System AA Menu*

```
If emergency alternate greeting active
   Play "alternate greeting"
Play "welcome greeting"
If holiday
   Play "holiday greeting"
Else if business open
   Play "business open greeting"
Else
   Play "business closed greeting"
To enter the phone number of the person you are trying to reach, press 1
To enter the name of the person you are trying to reach, press 2
To transfer to the operator, press 0
```

You can change the welcome greeting to your own greeting, such as "Welcome to XYZ Company...." Similarly, you can rerecord the alternate, holiday, business open, and business closed greetings to suit your needs even though the Cisco UE system supplies system default greetings.

The system AA's menu structure cannot be changed. The parameters of the system AA script, such as the welcome greeting and the operator extension, can be configured as shown in Figure 9-2. The list of available prompts (or greetings) present on the system is shown in the drop-down box. The operator extension is set to 3010 in Figure 9-2. The concepts of scripts, variables, and parameters are discussed in more detail in the "Customizing the Cisco UE AA" section later in this chapter.

Figure 9-2 *Setting the System AA Parameters*

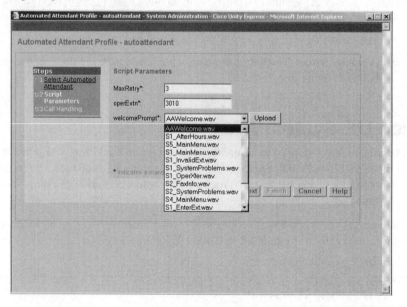

The system AA script contains several general AA features, such as dial-by-number and dial-by-name, that you also can reuse in your customized AA scripts. Before you look at the script editor and the mechanics of writing a script for your AA, the next sections cover some of these general AA features in more detail.

The Dial-by-Number Feature

If the caller selects the dial-by-number option (the "To enter the phone number of the person you are trying to reach, press 1" line from the system AA uses this feature), the caller is prompted to enter the extension followed by the pound (or hash) key. After the caller presses this key (#), a blind transfer attempt is made to the digits the caller enters.

If the transfer is successful, the destination phone rings, and the caller hears ringback. If the destination party does not answer, after the CFNA timeout, the call is redirected to voice mail.

If the transfer is unsuccessful because of a system error or because the caller enters a nonexistent extension, the caller hears an overflow (also called reorder or fast-busy) tone.

The call is transferred (blind transfer) regardless of whether the extension exists or whether the caller entered an extension or a longer number that may translate to a PSTN destination. Cisco UE AA does not check the digits entered and does not consult any directories for the dial-by-number feature. By default, any number that is part of the Cisco CME dial plan can be dialed from the Cisco UE AA.

If you want to restrict the destination numbers that can be reached via the AA dial-by-number feature, use the Class of Restriction (COR) Cisco CME feature to stop calls to undesired destinations.

The Dial-by-Name Feature

If the caller selects the dial-by-name option (the "To enter the name of the person you are trying to reach, press 2" line from the system AA uses this feature), he or she is prompted to spell the person's name (the last name followed by the first name) using the phone's touch-tone keypad. Based on the digits the caller enters, the local directory on Cisco UE is searched to find a match. If multiple matches are found, Cisco UE plays the names for all the matches and prompts, and the caller chooses the correct entry from the list.

When the destination party has been identified, a blind transfer attempt is made to the extension. Before attempting the transfer, a prompt in the format of *calling*: *<spoken name of destination party>* is played. If the destination party does not have a spoken name recorded in the directory, the prompt *calling <extension>* is played instead.

When the transfer is successful, the destination phone rings, and the caller hears ringback. If the destination party does not answer, after the CFNA timeout, the call is redirected to voice mail.

Unlike the dial-by-number feature, the dial-by-name feature can transfer a call only to a valid user configured on the system. Figure 9-3 shows the fields (First Name and Last Name) to configure in the user profile that underpin the directory used by the dial-by-name feature.

Figure 9-3 *Configuring User Names for the Dial-by-Name Feature*

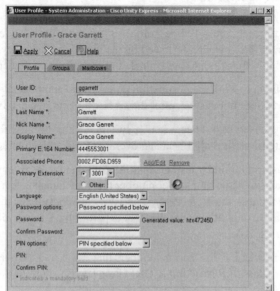

Groups configured on Cisco UE do not have associated name fields and, therefore, do not exist in the directory used for dial-by-name. This means groups cannot be dialed via the dial-by-name feature. Instead, explicit AA menu branches can be built to direct calls to groups. For example, a menu branch such as "For sales, press 2. For support, press 3" may be used to direct calls to groups of people in your organization that support a particular function. This type of AA menu requires a custom AA to be used on your system.

The Transfer to the Operator Feature

The caller is given the option of being transferred to an operator or receptionist by pressing 0 in the system AA via the line "To transfer to the operator, press 0." The operator extension may be any extension in your organization. Upon pressing 0, the caller is transferred to the extension configured in the operExtn parameter, shown earlier in Figure 9-2.

Although the system AA uses this feature specifically for a *transfer to the operator* operation, it uses a generic script component to transfer a call. In a custom script, this element may be used to transfer the call to any destination of your choice, including PSTN locations.

Business Hours Call Routing

A business hours schedule is a popular use of an AA. Callers during business hours get different treatment (greetings and menu options) than after-hours callers.

The system AA (as of Cisco UE Release 2.1) checks for business hours (as shown in Example 9-2). You set this up in the GUI by indicating which days of the week and which hour ranges (in 30-minute increments) within each day represent your business hours.

There is also a business hours script step that you can use in a custom AA to achieve the same functionality.

Holiday Schedule

Cisco UE Release 2.1 introduces a holiday schedule within the system AA. You can use this to provide a different greeting (or menu) on January 1 than on any other day of the year. You can configure up to 26 different dates (over three years) that are considered holidays. When the system date matches any of these dates, callers hear the holiday greeting and menus.

On Cisco UE releases before 2.1 that do not have this built-in holiday schedule capability, you can build similar functionality by using the day-of-week step in a custom script. The system AA in releases up to 2.0 contains no way to provide special holiday treatment.

With a custom script, if, for example, January 1 is a holiday for your business and it falls on Thursday of this week, you can change the AA script on Monday to provide a special menu on Thursday using the day-of-week element. After Thursday, January 1 has passed, you have to change the AA script again (removing the special Thursday menu). Otherwise, the special holiday menu will occur on every Thursday of every week.

Emergency Alternate Greeting

Another popular AA function is an emergency greeting that can be activated remotely in case something unexpected happens, and the AA menu must be changed immediately to inform callers of the situation—for example, that the office will not be open today. Examples of common emergencies include a snowstorm or a natural disaster such as an earthquake, or an illness in a very small business where there may not be other employees to cover for the absent person.

The Cisco UE emergency alternate greeting (EAG) is a system function that is used in the system AA. It also can be included at any place in the menu flow in any custom script. The system AA is set up such that when the EAG exists (if this feature has been activated), it is played out right at the top of the script before the normal welcome greeting. The modified system AA flow was shown in Example 9-2. The EAG might say something like "Due to the heavy snowstorm in New York, the office will be closed until Monday, April 4." After the EAG recording has been played, the normal AA menu is presented to the caller.

The EAG feature is controlled by the existence or absence of an EAG greeting (a .wav file) in the system with the appropriate filename (AltGreeting.wav). If this file exists on the system, the EAG feature is automatically active, and the special greeting is played wherever the AA menu directs it to be played. If the .wav file is deleted, the EAG feature is automatically deactivated (the If test in Example 9-2 is false), and the AA menu reverts to its normal flow. The EAG is a very convenient feature to use. All you have to do is call the system and record the EAG or delete it. When you do that, the EAG feature is automatically turned on or off.

The number to call to record the greeting (to turn on the EAG feature) or to delete it (to turn off the EAG feature) is the Cisco UE pilot number associated with the greeting management system (GMS). It can be accessed from any PSTN location. The GMS aspect of the Cisco UE AA system is discussed in more detail in the later section "The Cisco UE Greeting Management System." Briefly, it allows you to record and manage all the prompts used in your AA via any telephone (a local IP phone or a PSTN phone).

The AA Operator

A call must always be handled to logical completion by an automated system such as an AA. During the AA menu flow, various errors may occur, such as timeouts. Another error can occur when the caller is told to press some keys and he or she either does not have a touch-tone phone, chooses not to respond, or is unable to understand the language spoken by the AA prompt. These calls cannot be left hanging. When the error occurs, the call must be redirected to a default treatment, because it cannot proceed through the AA script.

A typical way to handle these types of errors in an AA menu is to transfer such calls to a person (an operator) who can then speak to the caller. This person can be the receptionist or any of the employees in the business. The system AA script has an operator extension parameter. It is recommended that your custom AA scripts include the same functionality. That way, an extension can be filled into this parameter for the person (extension) who acts as the operator for all calls that cannot proceed to completion through the AA.

Customizing the Cisco UE AA

The system AA is fairly simple, and the menu flow cannot be customized. (The only customization possible is rerecording the greetings, setting the business hours and holiday dates, and setting the operator extension.) If a different AA menu flow is needed, a custom AA script must be placed on the system. Up to five AAs (including the system AA) can be loaded into the Cisco UE system to provide a wide range of flexible AA menus to cover very specific business needs.

This section of the chapter covers how to prepare a custom AA script using the Cisco UE AA Script Editor. You'll explore script elements such as steps, parameters, and variables. You'll learn about operations such as viewing, uploading, downloading, and executing scripts. System limits governing scripts and prompts on your system are also discussed.

AA Scripts, Prompts, Variables, and Parameters

To understand how to build a custom AA script, some programming knowledge is helpful. However, even if you do not have any programming background, customizing an AA script is not a complex task. The Cisco UE Script Editor provides a graphical drag-and-drop interface for easily rearranging the steps in a script. An AA script is essentially a computer program, which means that it is a list of steps executed for every call that arrives at the system. The sequence of these steps is specified at a very high level with an easy-to-use icon-based GUI interface.

An AA script is an ordered, logical sequence of actions called *steps*. Each step signifies a task or operation to be performed on the call, such as playing a prompt, collecting DTMF digits, or redirecting a call to another destination. Each script step has one or more attributes associated with it, such as the Menu step in which the attributes describe what should be done when the caller presses 1 or 2 or any other DTMF digit on the phone keypad.

The following elements make up an AA script:

- **Steps**—Programming steps in the script perform actions such as answering the call, playing prompts, receiving DTMF digits from the caller, making conditional choices based on time-of-day or any other internal value, transferring a call, looking up a username in a directory, and many more.

- **Prompts**—Scripts use short sections of recorded voice to interact with the caller, such as "Please enter the extension of the person you want to reach," "Press 1 for sales," or "Our business hours are 8 a.m. to 5 p.m. Monday through Friday." Each of these recorded voice segments is called a *prompt* and is referenced by the script as a variable. A prompt is physically stored in a .wav file on the system.

- **Variables**—A variable is a label or tag representing a value that may change during the life of the script. For example, *retry_limit* may be a variable referenced in a script. This tag has a value of three or five, indicating how many times you want to retry a prompt after a timeout.

- **Parameters**—A parameter is a variable whose value can be changed while the script is running on the Cisco UE system. In other words, you can change the value without editing the script and reuploading it to the system. For example, *operExtn* is a parameter that can be populated with extension 3001 on Monday and 3002 on Tuesday and so on without the need to edit the script. Not all script variables have to be parameters. Only those that you want to change without editing the script are assigned the property of *parameter*.

Preparing a Script Using the Cisco UE AA Editor

Custom AA scripts are executed on the Cisco UE system, but they are prepared offline on a Windows PC platform by using the Cisco UE AA Editor. Follow these steps, which are shown in Figure 9-4, to prepare and install a custom Cisco UE AA script:

Step 1   Install the Cisco UE AA Editor software (from CD or by downloading it from Cisco.com) onto a Windows 2000/XP PC or server.

Step 2   Open the Cisco UE Editor to create or edit an AA script. After all the editing changes have been made, validate the script to ensure that no logic errors exist in it.

Step 3   Record the prompts used by the script either offline in a recording studio, with standard PC .wav file recording equipment, or via any telephone connected to the Cisco UE system.

Step 4   Upload the script to the Cisco UE system. If prompts were recorded offline, these too must be uploaded to the Cisco UE system.

Step 5   Assign values to all script parameters. Associate the script with a phone number (pilot number) so that callers can reach the script.

Figure 9-4   *Preparing a Custom Cisco UE AA Script*

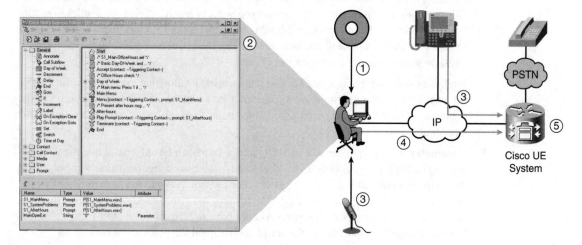

The Cisco UE AA Editor has several window panes that allow you to construct different aspects of the script, such as the steps, variables, and parameters. Instead of opening an empty file and creating a script from scratch, you may find it easier to reuse several sample scripts available on Cisco.com. The sample scripts can expedite your construction of a custom script. You can open the sample scripts in the Editor, and then copy and paste script segments that you want in your AA menu flow rather than creating a completely new script.

The Cisco UE AA Editor Panes

After you have downloaded and installed the Cisco UE AA Editor onto your PC and have downloaded the sample scripts from Cisco.com, you can open the script files in the Editor application. As with any other Windows application, you can launch the Editor, and then choose files to open. Or you can simply double-click an existing .aef (script) file to launch the Editor automatically (provided that your PC is set up to associate the Editor application with .aef files). Figure 9-5 shows what the Cisco UE Editor screen looks like with an open script.

Figure 9-5   *Cisco UE Editor Screen*

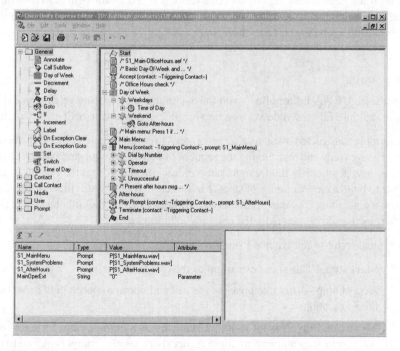

The Cisco UE Editor window consists of the following four panes:

- **Palette pane**—This is the top-left pane shown in Figure 9-5. It includes the palette of icons (representing the steps) that can be used in a script.

- **Design pane**—The top-right pane shows the script's content. This is where the steps are sequenced to form the design or flow of the script under construction.

- **Variable pane**—The bottom-left pane shows the variables defined in the script. Columns show the type, current value, and attributes of each variable. The last variable shown in Figure 9-5, *MainOperExt*, has an attribute of Parameter. The variable pane is where variables are marked as parameters such that as soon as the script is installed on a Cisco UE system, the value of a parameter variable can be viewed and controlled without editing the script.

- **Debug pane**—When a script is validated, any error or warning messages are shown in this window pane.

The Cisco UE Editor uses a simple and intuitive GUI. Expert users can create sophisticated AA scripts using multilevel nesting and conditional statements. Novice users may find it easiest to start with an existing script, such as one of the sample scripts covered in the "Using Sample Scripts" section later in this chapter, and merely adjust it slightly to suit their needs rather than writing a script from scratch.

After it has been edited and validated, a script is saved to the local hard disk on the PC as an .aef file. It can then be uploaded to Cisco UE (using the GUI or command-line interface [CLI]) to be installed and executed as the system's AA.

Constructing a Script

The Cisco UE AA Editor allows you to have multiple script files open at one time, or you can have multiple Editor windows open on your PC, each viewing a single script file.

A script is constructed by using a series of steps to control a call's flow. You can start by opening an existing script and rearranging the sequence of steps, copying and pasting steps from another file to new positions in the Design Pane, or dragging steps from the Palette Pane to the Design Pane to build a new sequence of steps. Many steps have attributes that must be checked or filled in on a dialog box. You can access these attributes by right-clicking the step in the Design Pane and selecting Properties from the resulting Windows menu.

A typical script is constructed from the following components:

- **Start step**—This starts execution of the call in the script.

- **Accept step**—This step answers the call and opens a speech path between the caller and the application.

- **Menu and Play Prompt steps**—Usually a series of these steps form the main body of the AA script. A menu (with multiple choices) or a single prompt is played to the caller. After that, the script waits for input on the caller's selection from the menu.

- **Call Redirect step**—This step transfers the call to a selected destination, of which the value is usually kept in a variable in the script that was filled in during an earlier step.

- **Call Subflow step**—An optional step to pass control of the call to another script. When it finishes executing that script, the phone call returns to executing in the calling script.
- **Goto and If steps**—Unconditional or conditional branching within the script steps to control the flow of execution based on variable values or input from the caller.
- **End**—This terminates the script and ends processing of this call.

A full explanation of every step and step attribute that you can use in a script is beyond the scope of this chapter. The Cisco UE Editor is based on the Cisco Customer Response Solutions (CRS) Editor. Therefore, you can use the Cisco Customer Response Applications Developer's Guide (available at Cisco.com) as reference material for a detailed explanation of each step and its attributes. The Cisco UE Editor supports fewer steps than the full Cisco CRS Editor used with some other Cisco products.

The Cisco UE Editor uses several categories of steps to perform AA tasks. These categories are shown in the Palette Pane of the Cisco UE Editor window and include the following:

- General steps
- Contact steps
- Call Contact steps
- Media steps
- User steps
- Prompt steps

The following tables list the exact steps in each category available in the Cisco UE Editor.

NOTE   The term *step* is used here to denote the individual actions you are building into a script. No sequence is implied in the steps listed in the following tables; instead, they are listed alphabetically. You can use these steps in almost any sequence you like in a script. (Obviously steps such as *Start* and *End* will occupy a certain logical position within the script, but steps such as *Menu* and *Redirect* can be used anywhere.) When you build the content of the script in the design pane of the Editor is when you apply your preferred sequencing to the steps.

Table 9-1 lists the steps in the general category.

Table 9-1   *General Steps*

Step Name	Description
Annotate	Comments in the script (similar to the C language /* */ comments).
Business Hours	Configures the business hours schedule for each of the seven days in a week.
Call Subflow	Invokes a subflow (one script passing control to another script).

continues

Table 9-1 *General Steps (Continued)*

Step Name	Description
Day of Week	Used to branch, depending on the current day of the week.
Decrement	Decreases the value of an integer variable by one.
Delay	Pauses the script's execution for a specified number of seconds.
End	Ends the script and frees all the allocated resources.
Goto	Causes script execution to branch to the specified Label step.
Holiday	Specifies a list of dates to be treated by the system as holidays. A maximum number of 26 holidays can be entered into the list.
If	A branch based on the evaluation of a Boolean expression.
Increment	Increases the value of an integer variable by one.
Label	Inserts a label into a script as a target for the Goto step.
On Exception Clear	Removes an exception set by the previous On Exception Goto step.
On Exception Goto	Catches an exception or problem during script execution and handles it.
Set	Changes the value of a variable (assignment operator).
Start	Start of the script.
Switch	Causes script execution to branch to one of a number of cases.
Time of Day	Used to branch, depending on the current time of day.

Table 9-2 lists the steps in the contact and call contact categories.

Table 9-2 *Contact and Call Contact Steps*

Step Name		Description
Contact	Accept	Answers a call.
	Get Contact Info	Extracts information from a contact and stores it in script variables.
	Set Contact Info	Modifies the context information associated with a contact.
	Terminate	Disconnects a call.
Call Contact	Call Redirect	Redirects a call to another extension.
	Get Call Contact Info	Accesses call-specific information and stores it in script variables.

Table 9-3 lists the steps for the media category.

Table 9-3   *Media Steps*

Step Name	Description
Explicit Confirmation	Confirms an explicit response to a prompt—DTMF 1 for yes and 2 for no.
Get Digit String	Collects DTMF digits in response to a prompt.
Implicit Confirmation	Confirms an action without asking a question.
Menu	Provides a menu from which the caller can choose from a series of options.
Name To User	Collects DTMF and tries to match it to a person's name.
Play Prompt	Plays a specified prompt to the caller.

Table 9-4 lists the steps for the user and prompt categories.

Table 9-4   *User and Prompt Steps*

Step Name		Description
User	Get User Info	Accesses user attributes.
Prompt	Create Conditional Prompt	Creates one of two prompts based on the evaluation of a Boolean expression.
	Create Container Prompt	Combines multiple prompts into a larger prompt.
	Create Generated Prompt	Creates prompt phrases from intermediate variables—for example, number, currency, and so on.

Example 9-3 shows the logic of one of the sample AA scripts you can download from Cisco.com. It illustrates how the steps are sequenced in a script to determine the flow of the AA menu for a caller. This simple script illustrates how to build a basic office hours-based AA menu. During office hours, a menu (dial-by-number or transfer to the operator) is given to the caller. After hours a recorded prompt is given, telling the caller when the office is open.

Example 9-3 is not meant to be an example of a complete AA script. It is merely a script fragment illustrating the use of the time-of-day and day-of-week steps to build a branch into a script based on office hours. In a complete AA script, the office hours menu choices, the after-hours caller options, and the error-handling script instructions would be much more comprehensive.

Example 9-21 *Sample AA Script*

```
Start
/* S1_Main-OfficeHours.aef */
/* Basic Day-Of-Week and ... */
Accept (contact: --Triggering
/* Office Hours check */
```

continues

Example 9-21 *Sample AA Script (Continued)*

```
Day of Week
        Weekdays
                Time of Day
                        Work hours
                                Goto Main Menu
                        After hours
                                Goto After-hours
        Weekend
                Goto After-hours
/* Main menu: Press 1 if ... */
Main Menu:
Menu (contact: --Triggering Contact--, prompt: S1_MainMenu)
        Dial by Number
                Call Subflow -- S1_DialbyExtension.aef
                End
        Operator
                Call Subflow -- S1_XfertoOper.aef
                End
        Timeout
                Play Prompt (contact: --Triggering Contact--, prompt: S1
                        _SystemProblems)
                Terminate (contact: --Triggering Contact--)
                End
        Unsuccessful
                Play Prompt (contact: --Triggering Contact--, prompt: S1
                        _SystemProblems)
                Terminate (contact: --Triggering Contact--)
                End
/* Present after hours msg ... */
After-hours:
Play Prompt (contact: --Triggering Contact--, prompt: S1_AfterHours)
Terminate (contact: --Triggering Contact--)
End
```

Figure 9-6 shows the same script open in the Cisco UE Editor, where the graphical representation of the steps can be seen.

Figure 9-6   *Sample AA Script*

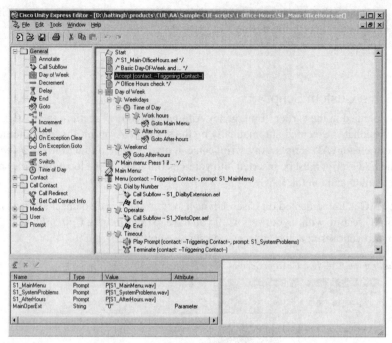

Using Sample Scripts

The Cisco UE Editor and scripting design offers maximum flexibility to customize the system to your individual business needs. However, it can be somewhat daunting to write your first script, especially if you are unfamiliar with programming.

For this reason, a number of sample scripts, or script fragments, have been developed to help you cut and paste to build an AA script from known elements, rather than requiring you to develop it from scratch. These sample scripts are posted on Cisco.com and can be accessed from the Software Center, where Cisco UE software is downloaded.

The contents of these sample scripts may change over time, but in general they offer script fragments or examples of the following functions:

- A dial-by-number component
- A dial-by-name component
- Call transfer to an operator or a given extension
- An office hours menu using time-of-day and day-of-week branching
- A loop that repeats a menu three times, in case no input is received from the caller
- An office directory (a menu that has a branch for each individual in the office)

- A branch that gives the caller the office location and directions

- A branch that gives the caller the option of leaving a message (not for an individual employee, but for the business in general)

- The EAG

Using the EAG in a Custom Script

As explained in the earlier "Emergency Alternate Greeting" section, the EAG is a system function that is executed automatically by the system AA script. It is not automatic, however, in your custom AA scripts. Any script can call on this system function, but a *Call Subflow* step to the EAG script must be inserted into your custom script at the location in the sequence where you want to call out the EAG.

The EAG is implemented on Cisco UE as a system script called checkaltgreet.aef. To activate the EAG feature within your script, all you have to do is insert a *Call Subflow checkaltgreet.aef* step into your script at the appropriate spot, as shown in Figure 9-7.

Figure 9-7 *Including the EAG in a Custom Script*

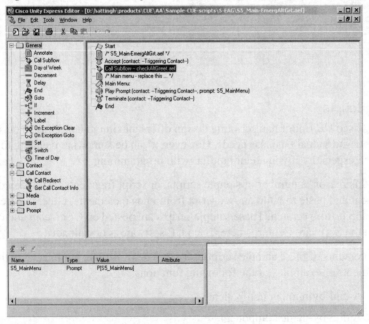

The general EAG feature operation has not changed; it is still activated by the existence or absence of the actual greeting. It is stored in a .wav file called AltGreeting.wav, just as it operates with the system AA. But now you have incorporated the EAG feature into your own custom script.

Validating a Script

Before a script can be uploaded to Cisco UE for execution, you should validate it in the Editor. This function is found on the Tools menu on the Editor's Windows toolbar.

Validating a script is a necessary but insufficient step to ensure correct operation of your custom AA script. It is a *necessary* step because any syntax or flow errors caught by the validation step will prevent the script from executing properly. All validation errors must therefore be fixed before the script is uploaded to Cisco UE. However, it is an *insufficient* step, because the Cisco UE Editor cannot check runtime error conditions that may occur when the script executes. It also cannot check for missing prompts (missing .wav files) referenced by the script, because the Editor has no access to the script's runtime environment. These types of errors can be found only during script execution.

Viewing Scripts and Prompts in the System

You can use the Cisco UE GUI or CLI to manage AA scripts and prompts. Scripts cannot be edited on the Cisco UE system; they are edited offline on a PC with the Cisco UE Editor. You can manage the AA scripts on the Cisco UE system, including operations such as

- Listing the scripts present in the system
- Deleting a script
- Uploading or downloading a script
- Associating a script with a phone (pilot) number
- Setting a script's parameter values

Figure 9-8 shows an example of a Cisco UE system with a number of scripts installed. You can access this screen by selecting **Voice Mail > Scripts** from the GUI menu.

Figure 9-8 *Listing the AA Scripts in a Cisco UE System*

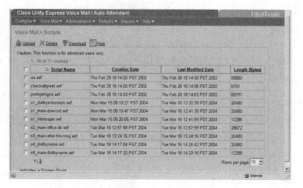

Scripts that have a checkbox to the left and grayed out are system scripts. The others are custom scripts. A script can call another script (using the *Call Subflow* step), so not each of these scripts is an AA. Some of the scripts are associated with a phone (pilot) number and therefore constitute an AA. The other scripts are merely subflows (subroutines) called by the main AA script(s) to make the logic easier to understand and to allow you to craft reusable functions, such as the EAG, which you can use in many AA scripts. This relationship between the scripts cannot be seen in Figure 9-8. You have to open a script in the Cisco UE Editor to see which other scripts (subflows) are called from the script you are viewing.

You can see a list of prompts present on a Cisco UE system by selecting **Voice Mail > Prompts** from the GUI menu, as shown in Figure 9-9.

Figure 9-9 *AA Prompts in a Cisco UE System*

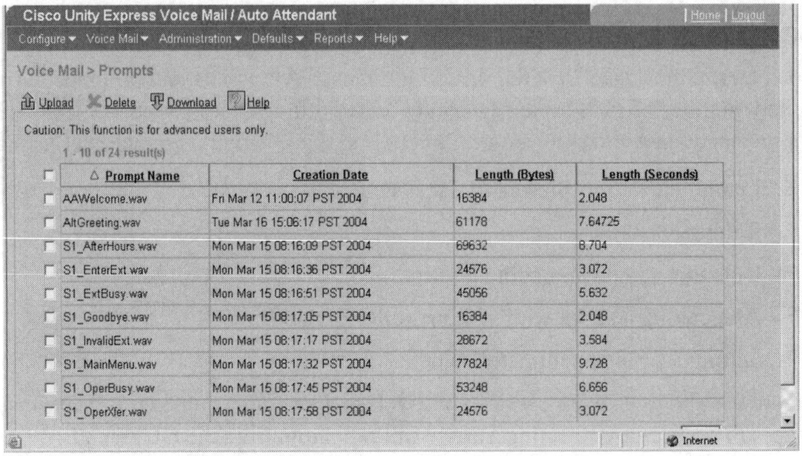

The scripts and prompts present on the system can also be seen from the CLI of the Cisco UE system. Example 9-4 presents the CLI command and output to show all the scripts available on the system. Each script is shown (the name of the script file is highlighted), followed by its parameters. The CLI doesn't indicate whether a script is a system or custom script.

Example 9-22 *CLI That Shows Scripts on a Cisco UE System*

```
cue>show ccn application
Name:                              autoattendant
Description:                       autoattendant
Script:                            aa.aef
ID number:                         2
Enabled:                           yes
Maximum number of sessions:        8
MaxRetry:                          3
operExtn:                          0
welcomePrompt:                     AAWelcome.wav
```

Example 9-22 *CLI That Shows Scripts on a Cisco UE System (Continued)*

```
Name:                                promptmgmt
Description:                         promptmgmt
Script:                              promptmgmt.aef
ID number:                           3
Enabled:                             yes
Maximum number of sessions:          1

Name:                                main-dow-tod
Description:                         main-dow-tod
Script:                              s1_main-dow-tod.aef
ID number:                           4
Enabled:                             yes
Maximum number of sessions:          8
MainOperExt:                         6001

Name:                                s2-office-dir
Description:                         s2-office-dir
Script:                              s2_main-office-dir.aef
ID number:                           5
Enabled:                             yes
Maximum number of sessions:          8
Mary:                                6001
Mike:                                6012
Bruce:                               6020
S2_OfficeDir:                        S2_OfficeDir.wav
S2_FaxInfo:                          S2_FaxInfo.wav
Candice:                             6007
S2_LocationInfo:                     S2_LocationInfo.wav
John:                                6005
Janet:                               6008
S2_MainMenu:                         S2_MainMenu.wav

Name:                                s4-dial-by-name
Description:                         s4-dial-by-name
Script:                              s4_main-dialbyname.aef
ID number:                           7
Enabled:                             yes
Maximum number of sessions:          8

Name:                                s5-emerg-alt-grt
Description:                         s5-emerg-alt-grt
Script:                              s5_main-emergaltgrt.aef
ID number:                           6
Enabled:                             yes
Maximum number of sessions:          8
```

Uploading and Downloading Scripts

After a script is edited and validated on an offline PC, it is uploaded to the Cisco UE system to be associated with a pilot phone number and, thus, to run as an active AA. Also, if you need to change a script, download it from Cisco UE to your PC, where you can view its content, edit it, and revalidate the new script. Upload the new version to Cisco UE to make the change active.

You can upload a script by clicking the **Upload** button on the **Voice Mail > Scripts** GUI screen. The resulting screen is shown in Figure 9-10. There is a **Download** button on the same **Voice Mail > Scripts** screen to start a download operation.

Figure 9-10 *Uploading an AA Script to the Cisco UE System*

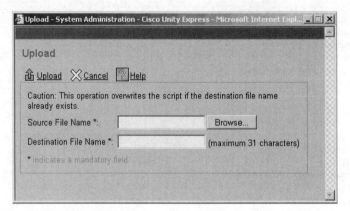

NOTE The Cisco UE system scripts cannot be uploaded, downloaded, viewed, or deleted. Custom scripts can be fully controlled.

Executing a Script

The AA in Cisco UE runs as a Workflow script. It interacts with the Workflow engine and various subsystems to perform the operations specified in the AA script. (The basic architecture of the Cisco UE system is covered in Chapter 3, "Cisco IPC Express Architecture Overview.") A *Workflow* is a Cisco-developed scripting format that can be executed by an engine. This Workflow format is used in a variety of Cisco products. Cisco UE is also used to run the system's GMS and voice mail components. Understanding the script execution environment is necessary only for troubleshooting purposes.

When a call is placed to the AA pilot number, the Workflow engine is notified of the incoming call by the underlying call control subsystem. Based on the configuration, the engine recognizes that this particular phone number is associated with the AA (as opposed to the GMS or voice mail scripts), so it starts (triggers) the appropriate AA Workflow script and starts executing it. The engine starts from the first step in the script. Based on the output of each individual step, the execution either moves on to the next step or branches to some other location in the script to continue execution there.

For the execution of each step, the engine communicates with either a library or an underlying subsystem to perform the actual operation. For example, the engine communicates with the media termination library to play a specific prompt to the caller, and the prompt is streamed out by the media termination library. Similarly, the engine communicates with the call control subsystem to redirect the call. Based on the results reported by the subsystem, it carries on with the execution of the next step in the script.

System Limits on Scripts and Prompts

Many more scripts and prompts may exist on the Cisco UE system than are actively executed as part of the AA. As explained in the earlier section "Viewing Scripts and Prompts in the System," not every script is an AA. An AA is a phone number associated with a script that is the main entry point for that AA. This script may call on other scripts with the Call *Subflow* step to handle sections of the AA menus.

The Cisco UE hardware platform has limited storage space for scripts and prompts. Table 9-5 lists the system limits on custom scripts and prompts for Cisco UE 1.1, 2.0, and 2.1 software. Consult Cisco.com for changes in these limits that may become effective in later software releases.

Table 9-5   *System Limits for Scripts and Prompts*

Hardware Platform	Maximum Number of Stored Scripts	Maximum Number of Stored Prompts
NM-CUE	8	50
AIM-CUE	4	25

The limits shown in Table 9-5 do not apply to or include system scripts or prompts. There is no limit on the size of an individual script, the number of steps per script, or the number of nesting levels within a script. Script complexity and readability become limiting factors before the software limits these attributes.

A prompt may have a maximum file size of 1 Mb, which represents about 2 minutes of recording time.

The Cisco UE Greeting Management System

Cisco UE is a low-end entry-level system that does not assume that you have sophisticated offline recording facilities or a studio available to create your AA prompts. You can certainly use such facilities if you have them and upload the resulting professionally created prompts to the system. Cisco UE also offers a built-in facility to record and manage prompts via any telephone that can call into the system (a local IP phone or PSTN phone). This feature is called the GMS.

Like the AA and voice mail pilot numbers, the GMS also has a pilot number assigned. When calls arrive at the GMS pilot number, the caller is put into an interactive session where you can listen to existing prompts and record new ones.

Calling into the GMS requires an extension and personal identification number (PIN) for security authorization. The extension/PIN combination is the same one used for your mailbox access authorization. Any user defined on the Cisco UE system with a mailbox can, therefore, theoretically access the GMS. However, actual access is restricted to users who also have administrative privileges on the Cisco UE system (those who belong to the administrators group). This is much more likely to be just one or two of the users defined on the system.

The GMS itself runs a Workflow script within the Cisco UE system and can, therefore, be seen when a listing of all the system scripts is given (the script is called promptmgmt.aef). The GMS offers two main features related to the Cisco UE AA, as discussed in the following sections:

- Recording or deleting the EAG
- Recording and listening to custom prompts

Prompts on the Cisco UE system must be a specific .wav file format to be played correctly. You can record prompts with the GMS or offline with a PC or studio sound equipment and then upload them to Cisco UE. You can download prompts already resident on Cisco UE to your PC as .wav files. Uploading and downloading prompts works just like uploading and downloading scripts, as discussed earlier, in the section "Uploading and Downloading Scripts."

Recording or Deleting the EAG

You can record the EAG via the GMS. Calling into the GMS guides the administrator through the process of recording or deleting the alternate greeting:

Step 1   The script prompts the caller (administrator) to enter his or her extension and PIN to determine if the caller has administrative rights on the system.

Step 2   After the caller is authenticated, the script checks to see if an EAG exists on the system. If it does not, the script prompts the administrator to record one.

Step 3   As soon as the EAG is recorded and saved, it becomes active, and new callers to the AA start hearing the EAG before the regular welcome prompt.

If the EAG already exists on the system, the script prompts the administrator to delete the existing greeting. If the administrator deletes it, the EAG is deleted from the system, and new callers into the AA hear only the regular welcome greeting as their first prompt.

The system has no default EAG. If the EAG exists, it must have the filename AltGreeting.wav. If you record the EAG via the GMS, it automatically has this filename. If you record it on an offline system and upload it to the Cisco UE system, you must ensure manually that the .wav file has this name so that it will be recognized by the Cisco UE system as the EAG.

Example 9-5 shows the GMS conversation for managing the EAG.

Example 9-23 *GMS Menu Flow for Managing the EAG*

```
Please enter your Extension
Please enter your PIN Number
Welcome to the Greeting Management System
Press 1 to administer Automated Attendant Alternate Greeting
   If (Alternate Greeting exists)
       The Alternate Greeting is currently active
       Press 1 to hear the Alternate Greeting
       Press 2 to re-record the Alternate Greeting
          Record the Alternate Greeting at the beep. To finish recording,
          press the # key
          Press 1 to save and activate the Alternate Greeting
          Press 2 to hear the Alternate Greeting
          Press 3 to re-record the Alternate Greeting
       Press 3 to deactivate the Alternate Greeting. Deactivating the Alternate
       Greeting will delete it from the system
   else
       Press 1 to record the Alternate Greeting
          Record the Alternate Greeting at the beep. To finish recording,
          press the # key
          Press 1 to save and activate the Alternate Greeting
          Press 2 to hear the Alternate Greeting
          Press 3 to re-record the Alternate Greeting
Press 2 to administer custom prompts
...
```

Recording and Listening to Custom Prompts

Similar to the EAG, all other prompts used by the AA scripts can be managed via the GMS. From the GMS, an administrator can listen to, record, and delete any prompt used by the system. After a prompt is recorded, it is given a filename in the format UserPrompt_*mmddyyyyhhmmss.wav*, where *mmddyyyyhhmmss* shows the system date and time that the prompt was recorded. The file shows up in the prompt list when viewed via the GUI or CLI.

To assign more meaningful names to the prompt files, you can download the prompt to a PC, change the filename, and then upload the file back to Cisco UE.

CAUTION   If you change the name of a prompt file while an AA script already refers to the prompt filename, be sure to change the script parameter (the one referring to the prompt file) to the new prompt filename before you delete the old prompt file. Otherwise, you will introduce a script runtime error.

Example 9-6 shows the GMS conversation for managing the prompts.

Example 9-24 *GMS Menu Flow for Managing Prompts*

```
Please enter your Extension
Please enter your PIN Number
Welcome to the Prompt Management System
Press 1 to administer Automated Attendant Alternate Greeting
      ...
Press 2 to administer custom prompts
      Press 1 to record a new prompt
            If limit reached
                  Sorry you have already recorded <<x>> prompts
            Else
      Record a new prompt at the beep. To finish recording, press the # key.
            ...
            You have recorded the new prompt as follows
            Play recorded prompt
            Press 2 to save the prompt, Press 3 to delete it
      Press 2 to play previously recorded custom prompts
            There are <<x>> recorded prompts
            In a loop {
                  Prompt <<i>>
                  Play prompt <<i>>
                  To delete it, press 3, to skip it, press #
                  If 3 pressed, delete the prompt
            }
```

Prompt File Format

All prompts on the Cisco UE system must meet the following .wav file format requirements to be able to play correctly:

- G.711 μ-law
- 8 kHz
- 8-bit
- Mono

Prompts recorded via the GMS are automatically of this type. Prompts recorded offline and uploaded to the Cisco UE system must be manually checked to ensure they are of this type, or they will not play properly. No system format checking occurs when prompts are uploaded into the system. If they are of the wrong format, they simply do not play correctly.

Setting Up a Cisco UE Automated Attendant

In the preceding sections, you learned the reasons to use an AA; general features of the Cisco UE AA, such as dial-by-number; and how to customize an AA script.

This section walks you through building the actual AA. Just having written the script is not enough. It is the biggest step, but now the script, the prompts, and the AA pilot number must be linked to form a working AA application on your Cisco UE system. This is not a difficult task, but it takes a few steps to accomplish:

Step 1 Determine whether the system AA is sufficient.

Step 2 Prepare a custom script.

Step 3 Upload the script.

Step 4 Record the prompts.

Step 5 Select a script.

Step 6 Set the script parameters.

Step 7 Assign a pilot number.

Determining Whether the System AA Is Sufficient

The first question to consider is whether you have to write a custom AA at all. Have a good look at the Cisco UE system AA, shown earlier in Example 9-2. Even though it's simple, it might be sufficient for your AA needs. If so, you only have to associate an AA pilot number with this script, customize the greeting, and insert your business hours and holidays, and you're done.

If the Cisco UE system AA is insufficient, you should continue using the sample AA functions illustrated in the various sample scripts in this chapter to put together a script that is tailor-made for your business.

Preparing a Custom Script

Follow these steps to prepare a custom script:

Step 1 Ensure that the Cisco UE Editor is installed on your PC. If it isn't, download it from Cisco.com and install it.

Step 2 Download the sample AA scripts from Cisco.com, and load them onto your PC.

Step 3 Draw a rough diagram of the flow of menus and prompts you want for your AA.

Step 4 Copy the sample script that is closest to your needs to a new file, and open it using the Cisco UE Editor.

Step 5 Adjust (edit) the script to match your drawing from Step 3 by copying and pasting steps from other sample scripts, rearranging the existing steps, or dragging new steps from the Editor's Palette Pane.

Step 6 Ensure that all the variables you defined and that you want to control via the Cisco UE GUI while the script is running are tagged with the parameter attribute. Also ensure that all the variables you want to control are defined in the top-level script and not in any subflows. Subflow parameters are inaccessible via the Cisco UE GUI to change their values.

Step 7 Validate the script, resolve all warning and errors until it validates clean, and manually ensure that the steps will execute the call flow you want.

Uploading the Script

There are two places from where you can initiate a script upload:

* If you want to upload the script before you enter the AA Setup Wizard, select the **Voice Mail > Scripts** menu in the Cisco UE GUI, and click the **Upload** button. Follow the dialog box instructions to upload the script to the Cisco UE system.

* The second place where the upload function appears is in the AA Setup Wizard itself. To navigate to the wizard, select the **Voice Mail > Auto Attendant** menu, and then click the **Add** button. This step is discussed further in the upcoming section "Selecting a Script."

Recording the Prompts

Dial into the Cisco UE GMS, and record all the prompts needed by the script(s), or record them offline. If they were recorded via the GMS, download the prompts to your PC, rename them to have filenames that make it easy for you to recognize the content of each prompt, upload the new files to the Cisco UE system, and delete the old prompts.

If you are using prompts recorded offline, upload the prompt files to the Cisco UE system. Uploading of prompt files can be initiated from the **Upload** button on the **Voice Mail > Prompts** GUI menu.

Selecting a Script

Enter the AA Setup Wizard by selecting the **Voice Mail > Auto Attendant** GUI menu and then clicking the **Add** button. The screen that results from this, the first screen of the AA Setup Wizard, is shown in Figure 9-11.

In the drop-down box corresponding to the Select Automated Attendant Script, choose the name of the script you previously uploaded. If you have not yet done so, you can upload it now by clicking the **Upload** button.

Figure 9-11   *Selecting the AA Script*

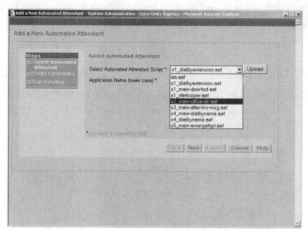

Setting the Script Parameters

Click **Next** and proceed to Step 2 of the AA Setup Wizard. In this screen, shown in Figure 9-12, all variables tagged as parameters during the script preparation show up, and you can set their values. The prompt variables indicate whether the system has found the corresponding .wav files on the storage medium. If it hasn't, you can upload them now, or choose a different filename from the drop-down box next to each prompt variable.

Figure 9-12   *Setting the Script Parameters*

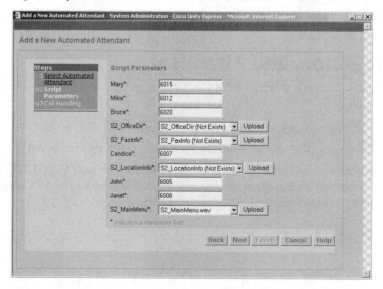

Figure 9-12 shows a sample screen to set a script's parameters, but this screen is dynamically formatted for each script based on the variable parameters present in that script. This screen, therefore, looks different for every script you view.

Assigning a Pilot Number

Click **Next** and proceed to Step 3 of the AA Setup Wizard, where the call handling parameters are set up. Here you associate the AA pilot number with the script you chose in Step 1 of the AA Setup Wizard, as shown in Figure 9-13.

Figure 9-13 *Setting the AA Pilot Number*

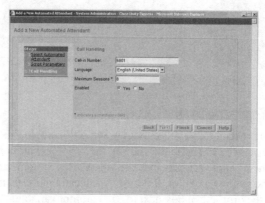

As soon as you have completed this step, click Finish. You now have a working Cisco UE AA application on your system.

TCL-Based Automated Attendant

As discussed at the beginning of this chapter, Cisco CME offers two options for an AA application:

- The integrated AA application, which is part of Cisco UE, as discussed in this chapter
- Leveraging the router's TCL scripting capabilities to provide an AA

Both schemes are adequate to provide AA functionality for your Cisco CME. However, when you're deciding which of these two mechanisms to use for your business, you should keep in mind several considerations, as listed in Table 9-6.

Table 9-6 *Considerations When Choosing a Cisco CME AA*

Consideration	TCL-Based AA	Cisco UE AA
Where the scripts execute	Scripts run on the router's processor and, therefore, have a small impact on the router's performance.	Scripts execute on the dedicated Cisco UE module. Therefore, they use the dedicated module CPU and do not affect the router's performance.
Memory	Scripts are loaded into the router's DRAM, so memory is allocated regardless of whether the script is being used.	Scripts are loaded into the dedicated Cisco UE module's storage and, therefore, do not use any router memory.
Scripting expertise	Requires a working knowledge of TCL programming and uses a text-based editor.	Uses an easy-to-use web-based graphical editor. Knowledge of logic and call processing steps is still helpful.
Error checking	The editor has no script validation or error checking.	The Cisco UE Editor has a *validation* function.
Script management	Requires an offline editor. Scripts are installed by copying the script to the router's Flash via Trivial File Transfer Protocol (TFTP).	Requires an offline editor. Scripts are installed by using a GUI *Upload* function that browses your PC file system.
Prompt management	Prompts are recorded offline as .au files and are copied to the router's Flash using TFTP.	Prompts can be recorded online using the Cisco UE GMS (from any phone). Prompts also can be recorded offline as .wav files and *Uploaded* via the GUI.
Hardware required	Router-based capability that does not require any extra hardware in addition to your Cisco CME router, although it may require an increase in router Flash memory size.	Cisco UE AA runs on the Cisco UE network module (NM) or advanced integration module (AIM) hardware blade that you slide into a slot on your Cisco CME router chassis.
Customization	Should be customized only by knowledgeable TCL developers.	Can be customized using the Cisco UE Editor and GUI.
Sample scripts	No sample scripts are available to use as a starting point.	Sample scripts are posted on Cisco.com. You can use them as is or copy from them to customize your own scripts.
Script activation	You activate a script by attaching it to a router dial peer using the router's CLI.	You activate a script by associating it with a pilot number using the Cisco UE GUI.

continues

Table 9-6 *Considerations When Choosing a Cisco CME AA (Continued)*

Consideration	TCL-Based AA	Cisco UE AA
TFTP/FTP	Scripts are copied to the router from a TFTP server.	Cisco UE script upload requires only IP connectivity between your PC browser and the Cisco CME router.
Router knowledge and access	Scripts reside in router Flash. Therefore, they require router login access and some knowledge of router CLI commands (for example, the Cisco IOS CLI commands used to get, view, or show a file in router Flash).	Requires only IP connectivity (an IP address or DNS host name), an Internet Explorer (IE) browser window, and a Cisco UE GUI login. No router knowledge is required.

In summary, the Cisco CME TCL AA is an option if you are comfortable with router CLI and the TCL language or if you have easy access to someone with these skills. The Cisco UE AA is much easier for the general person to use, requires no router internal knowledge, and is much easier to customize. However, you must add extra hardware to your Cisco CME router system.

NOTE   A TCL-based AA and Cisco UE should not be used at the same time on the same Cisco CME system. If Cisco UE is present, use its AA facilities. Use the TCL-based AA features only when a pure router-based solution is required and Cisco UE is not present.

Now that you understand the trade-offs, the next sections describe TCL-based AA in more detail.

TCL Scripts

TCL scripts reside on the router's Flash. When activated, the TCL script responds according to the predetermined steps included in the script. TCL is a general call processing scripting technology that isn't particular to an AA. Building an AA is only one of many different types of call processing functions that can be carried out with TCL.

Example 9-7 shows an extract from the Cisco CME 3.0 TCL AA script. (For the full script listing, download the script file from the Software Center for Cisco CME on Cisco.com.) It is a simple dial-by-number AA that plays a welcome greeting and then allows the caller to enter the digits of the extension to reach. It also has an operator transfer function if the caller enters

0 or if an error condition occurs. The flow of the Cisco CME TCL AA script (partly shown in Example 9-7) is as follows:

Step 1 Set up the global parameters.

Step 2 Check whether the AA pilot number and operator number have been configured.

Step 3 Check whether caller ID and DNIS information is available for the call.

Step 4 Play the welcome prompt (en_welcome.au).

Step 5 Prompt (en_enter_dest.au) the caller to enter the desired extension.

Step 6 If the caller does not dial any number or dials 0, transfer the call to the operator.

Step 7 If the caller dials an invalid extension number, prompt (en_reenter_dest.au) the caller to re-enter the extension number (this loop is repeated up to three times).

Step 8 If the caller dials a valid extension number, connect the call to that extension.

Step 9 If the caller dials a valid extension number, but that number is busy or unreachable, play the appropriate prompt (en_dest_busy.au or en_dest_unreachable.au), and ask the caller to re-enter an extension number.

Example 9-25 *Cisco CME TCL AA Script*

```
# Script Version: 2.0.1.0
# Copyright  2001 by cisco Systems, Inc.
# All rights reserved.
#-----------------------------------------------------------------
#
# Description:
#       This is a TCL IVR script for the IOS Telephony Service and
#       Call Manager (CM) offload scenario. The IVR script plays a
#       welcome prompt to the user and prompts the user to enter a
#       destination number when the user dials the auto-attendant number
#       (aa-pilot configured in the CLI). The script collects the digits that
#       the user has entered and hands the call to the enhanced session
#       application (named Default).  The session application
#       returns once there is a disconnect (if the call is established)
#       or if a call setup problem occurs.
#       The operator support is also included. If the user does not dial
#       any number or enters "0" the user will be transferred to an operator
#       (if operator number is configured in the CLI). If the user enters
#       an invalid number, the user will be prompted again to re-enter
#       the number for up to 3 times before disconnecting the call.
#-----------------------------------------------------------------
proc init { } {
    global param1
    global selectCnt
    global callInfo
```

continues

Example 9-25 *Cisco CME TCL AA Script (Continued)*

```
        global legConnected

        set param1(interruptPrompt) true
        set param1(abortKey) *
        set param1(terminationKey) #

        set selectCnt 0
        set legConnected false
}

proc init_ConfigVars { } {
    global destination
    global aaPilot
    global oprtr

# aa-pilot is the IVR number configured on the gateway to be used by the customer
# operator is the operator number for assisted calling
    if [infotag get cfg_avpair_exists aa-pilot] {
        set aaPilot [string trim [infotag get cfg_avpair aa-pilot]]
    } else {
        set aaPilot "NONE"
    }
    if [infotag get cfg_avpair_exists operator] {
        set oprtr [string trim [infotag get cfg_avpair operator]]
    } else {
        set oprtr "NONE"
    }
}
...
proc act_Setup { } {
...
   if { ($dnis == "") || ($dnis == $aaPilot) } {
...
        media play leg_incoming _welcome.au %s1000 _enter_dest.au
          } else {
            set fcnt 6
          leg setupack leg_incoming
          handoff callappl leg_incoming default "DESTINATION=$dnis"
          fsm setstate HANDOFF
        }
```

The Cisco CME TCL script refers to several prompts (two of which are shown in Example 9-7), including the following:

- **en_welcome.au**—Welcome greeting

- **en_dest_busy.au**—Played if the chosen extension is busy

- **en_reenter_dest.au**—Played to ask the caller to re-enter the destination if an invalid destination was detected

- **en_disconnect.au**—Informs the user that the call will be disconnected under an error condition

- **en_dest_unreachable.au**—Played to inform the user that the chosen extension is unreachable

Recording the Prompts

The prompts referenced by the script must be recorded and made available for use by the script. Prompts are recorded offline with computer-based recording tools and then are uploaded to the Cisco CME router. The router's Flash stores the prompts for a TCL script with the script. This may require additional Flash in the router if many TCL scripts and prompts are needed.

Prompts used by the TCL script are audio files stored as .wav or .au files in the router's Flash. The Cisco UE GMS cannot be used to record these prompt files. Example 9-8 shows the TCL AA files, including the prompts and the script itself, installed into a router's Flash.

Example 9-26 *TCL AA Installed into Router Flash*

```
router>show flash
-#- --length-- -----date/time------ path
...
36            0 Oct 20 2003 17:33:18 aa
37        42484 Oct 20 2003 17:47:08 aa/en_dest_busy.au
38        26376 Oct 20 2003 17:47:10 aa/en_dest_unreachable.au
39        14352 Oct 20 2003 17:47:10 aa/en_disconnect.au
40        19512 Oct 20 2003 17:47:10 aa/en_enter_dest.au
41        17167 Oct 20 2003 17:47:10 aa/en_reenter_dest.au
42        17486 Oct 20 2003 17:47:10 aa/en_welcome.au
43         6627 Oct 20 2003 17:47:10 aa/its-CISCO.2.0.1.0.tcl
  < Readme file is not required
```

Developing TCL Scripts

TCL scripting is a mature technology that is widely used to provide automated response and other types of call processing applications. Carefully plan the script logic by mapping out the steps required for the call flow, and then translate that into script steps. Depending on the features needed in the AA, the scripts can be lengthy, and script development can be a long process.

TCL is very powerful and can perform many functions, but at the same time, it requires skill and programming experience to develop well structured and fully functional scripts. Great care should be taken with AA menus and call flows, because the AA is a caller's first introduction to a business. An ill-structured AA can frustrate potential customers just as easily as a well-structured AA can improve customer service and increase satisfaction.

Implementing TCL Scripts

The TCL scripts are composed external to the router. The number of features used in the scripts adds to the development and maintenance complexity.

After the script is composed and debugged, it is uploaded to the router's Flash using TFTP or FTP. The copy commands in Cisco IOS allow you to transfer TCL scripts from a TFTP or FTP server to the router's Flash memory. The Cisco CME TCL AA script file its-CISCO.2.0.1.0.tcl, present in router Flash, was shown in Example 9-7.

If changes or new features are required, the TCL scripts must be modified, recomposed, and then uploaded again to the router's Flash memory to replace the outdated scripts.

After the scripts and prompts have been loaded into the router's Flash memory, you can use a phone to dial the AA, step through the preprogrammed features, and verify that the scripts and prompts have been created correctly.

Setting Up the Cisco CME TCL AA

A TCL script is activated by attaching it to a dial peer. The Cisco CME TCL AA is supported only for incoming PSTN calls, so it must be attached to the plain old telephone service (POTS) dial peer handling your PSTN calls. (It cannot be attached to an ephone-dn, which represents an IP phone.)

Example 9-9 shows the Cisco IOS router commands necessary to configure the TCL application.

Example 9-27 *Commands to Configure the TCL AA*

```
router>show running-config
call application voice cmeaa flash:/aa/its-CISCO.2.0.1.0.tcl
call application voice cmeaa operator 3001
call application voice cmeaa aa-pilot 6801
call application voice cmeaa language 1 en
call application voice cmeaa set-location en 0 flash:/aa/
```

Example 9-10 shows a PSTN (POTS) dial peer with the TCL AA application attached.

Example 9-28 *TCL AA Application Attached to the PSTN Dial Peer*

```
router>show running-config
dial-peer voice 2 pots
 application cmeaa
 incoming called-number 6801
 direct-inward-dial
 port 2/0:23
```

TCL Developer Support

TCL enjoys wide industry support. If you want to use TCL scripts, you can either develop your own scripts or obtain help from seasoned TCL developers to tailor scripts for your requirements. Cisco has a developer support group that designs and implements customized TCL scripts. You can also select TCL-independent script developers to develop your scripts. You can find more information about TCL developer support on Cisco.com.

Summary

In this chapter, you learned ways to provide an AA for a Cisco CME system. You have two options: using the AA that is a component of Cisco UE or using a TCL-based AA.

At the start of this chapter, you looked at general considerations when deploying an AA feature or using a receptionist for your business. You explored how to use both functions to offer personalized service to your clients and accessibility after hours or when the office is closed.

You learned about the Cisco UE AA—how to set it up, how to customize the scripts to suit your business needs, and how to work with the Cisco UE AA Editor. The end of the chapter provided information on the Cisco CME TCL AA. Trade-offs between using the Cisco UE AA and TCL AA were discussed.

Although Cisco UE is not the only means of offering AA with a Cisco CME system, it is by far the most integrated and comprehensive solution.

This chapter covers the following topics:

- Cisco Unity Express (UE) voice mail application
- Subscriber voice mail features
- Caller voice mail features
- Administrative voice mail features
- Call redirection into voice mail
- Working with users and names
- Dialplan considerations
- Voice mail networking
- Voice mail deployment considerations

## CHAPTER 10

Cisco IPC Express Integrated Voice Mail

In Part I, "Cisco IP Communications Express Overview," you learned about Cisco Unity Express and its contribution to the Cisco IP Communications (IPC) Express solution. Cisco UE offers an automated attendant (AA) and a voice mail application integrated with the Cisco CallManager Express (CME) call processing software.

Chapter 9, "Cisco IPC Express Automated Attendant Options," covered the Cisco IPC Express AA options in detail, including the AA offered by Cisco UE. This chapter explores Cisco UE's voice mail capabilities in greater depth. Alternative voice mail options that can be used with Cisco CME are covered in Chapter 11, "Cisco CME External Voice Mail Options."

Cisco UE is a typical voice mail system that includes all the common features you would expect from a low-end voice mail system, including personal mailboxes; subscriber login control; sending, listening to, saving, deleting, and forwarding voice messages; recording greetings and a spoken name for each mailbox; and directing calls to voice mail after the user's phone has rung for a configurable number of cycles.

Additionally, Cisco UE offers voice mail networking between different sites in your network, broadcast messaging, and distribution lists. Cisco UE also provides a number of general delivery mailboxes (GDMs) that you can use for functions in your organization (such as the factory or the sales desk) as opposed to being assigned to an individual employee.

Cisco UE Voice Mail Overview

Cisco UE is a small-to-medium office or enterprise branch office voice mail system that you can use with either Cisco CME or Cisco CallManager as the call control agent for directing the calls and managing the IP phones. When deployed with Cisco CME, Cisco UE is a local, collocated voice mail system integrated into the same router chassis as Cisco CME. With Cisco CallManager, Cisco UE represents a distributed voice mail system with a centralized call control agent in the network. Because this book focuses on Cisco CME, this chapter covers only Cisco CME network deployments and operation in detail. If you are interested in how you can use Cisco UE voice mail in Cisco CallManager networks, consult Cisco.com for more information (http://www.cisco.com/go/cue). Cisco UE's voice mail capabilities are the same for both deployment choices.

Cisco UE is offered in two hardware form factors: a Network Module (NM-CUE) and an Advanced Integration Module (AIM-CUE). The Cisco UE hardware provides for a fully self-contained software and hardware system with an onboard CPU and operating system, memory, and storage capacity (a hard disk on the NM and compact Flash [CF] on the AIM). This relieves the router's processing of the tasks required to execute and manage AA menus and voice mail messaging. For this reason Cisco UE does not impact the router's performance at all.

The Cisco UE hardware draws power from the router chassis. All communication between the router and Cisco UE software is carried across the router's backplane. The Cisco UE module is inserted into the router, an IP address is assigned, and the system is active. This complete integration means that Cisco UE requires no external servers or cabling and only minimal configuration and setup to deploy as a fully functional voice mail system. Cisco UE provisioning and installation are covered in detail in Chapters 13 and 14.

Cisco UE requires a minimum of Cisco IOS software release 12.3.4T (Cisco CME 3.0) on the router, using the IP Plus or IP Voice minimum software image. The AIM-CUE was introduced later and requires Cisco IOS software release 12.3.7T (Cisco CME 3.1) or later. It is recommended that Cisco UE deployments use Cisco CME 3.2 (12.3.11T) or later.

The following sections further explain the following aspects of Cisco UE:

- The mailbox licensing structure and how application parameters are controlled by licensing
- The types of mailboxes offered by Cisco UE, including personal and GDMs
- The concepts of users and groups, which underlie Cisco UE mailbox definition and operation

Cisco UE Licensing

Cisco UE offers an entry-level voice mail system that is cost-effective for offices requiring up to 120 total mailboxes. You can purchase mailbox licenses at the 12, 25, 50, and 100 personal mailbox levels. Future enhancements in Cisco UE releases beyond 2.1 may offer higher mailbox levels. The mailbox license you purchase equals the number of personal mailboxes on the Cisco UE system. In addition, you get a small number of GDMs with the license (the difference between the 100-mailbox license and getting 120 total mailboxes on the system). GDMs are discussed in more detail in the next section. Table 10-1 summarizes the Cisco UE system parameters controlled by the system license for Cisco UE software releases up to 2.0.

Table 10-1   *Cisco UE Voice Mail Licensed Parameters for Cisco UE Up to Release 2.0*

Hardware Form Factor	Parameters	12-Mailbox License	25-Mailbox License	50-Mailbox License	100-Mailbox License
NM-CUE	Personal mailboxes	12	25	50	100
	GDM	5	10	15	20
	Total mailboxes	17	35	65	120
	Hours of storage	100	100	100	100
	Ports	4	4	8	8
	Default mailbox size (minutes)	352	171	92	50
AIM-CUE (512 MB)	Hours of storage	8	8	8	—
	Ports	4	4	4	
	Default mailbox size (minutes)	28	13	7	
AIM-CUE (1 GB)	Hours of storage	14	14	14	—
	Ports	4	4	4	
	Default mailbox size (minutes)	49	23	13	

As of Cisco UE release 2.1, several changes have occurred in the licensing parameters, and therefore to the information shown in Table 10-1:

- The number of ports is no longer associated with the license. Instead, it depends only on the hardware module (NM-CUE or AIM-CUE) and the router platform where the module is housed.

- There is no longer a fixed separation between the number of personal mailboxes and GDMs allowed per license. Instead, the total number of mailboxes per license remains the same as shown in Table 10-1 (for example, 120 for a 100-mailbox license), but you can configure any combination of personal mailboxes and GDMs up to that total.

- An additional NM-CUE type (NM-CUE with 512 MB dynamic random-access memory [DRAM]) is introduced with more memory (DRAM) than the existing one (NM-CUE with 256 MB DRAM) for higher-end applications.

Table 10-2 summarizes the number of ports supported on the various hardware modules as of Cisco UE release 2.1.

Table 10-2 *Cisco UE 2.1 Port Support*

Hardware Form Factor	Platform	Number of Ports
NM-CUE (256 MB DRAM)	All	8
NM-CUE (512 MB DRAM)	All	16
AIM-CUE (512 MB and 1 GB CF)	Cisco 2600XM series and the Cisco 2691	4
AIM-CUE (512 MB and 1 GB CF)	Cisco 2800, 3700, and 3800 series	6

A valid license file must be present on the system at all times to determine the system parameters and identity controlled by licensing.

NOTE   The features described in this chapter are generally applicable to Cisco UE release 2.1, except where noted. Not all of these features are present in earlier releases. Consult the Cisco UE documentation on Cisco.com (http://www.cisco.com/go/cue) for details on features in various releases.

Licenses are installed on Cisco UE using *package* (.pkg) files. Chapter 13, "Cisco IPC Express General Administration and Initial System Setup," discusses how these are used during the installation process. In summary, the following are the package files corresponding to the licenses available for Cisco UE release 2.0:

- cue-vm-license_12mbx_cme_2.0.1.pkg
- cue-vm-license_25mbx_cme_2.0.1.pkg
- cue-vm-license_50mbx_cme_2.0.1.pkg
- cue-vm-license_100mbx_cme_2.0.1.pkg
- cue-vm-license_12mbx_ccm_2.0.1.pkg
- cue-vm-license_25mbx_ccm_2.0.1.pkg
- cue-vm-license_50mbx_ccm_2.0.1.pkg
- cue-vm-license_100mbx_ccm_2.0.1.pkg

Separate license files exist for Cisco UE used with Cisco CME (the license files that contain *cme* in the name) and Cisco UE used with Cisco CallManager (the license files that contain *ccm* in the name).

Personal and General Delivery Mailboxes

Cisco UE voice mail lets subscribers defined on the system receive voice messages when they are unavailable to answer calls, because they are busy or away from the phone when the call arrives. The voice mail system allows subscribers to access each voice message and then skip it, play it, save it, or delete it, or reply to the sender. Subscribers can also compose and send messages to other subscribers on the same voice mail system or across the network to a voice mail system at another location.

A *personal mailbox* is associated with an individual subscriber. Only this person can access the mailbox to review the voice messages. The subscriber logs into the mailbox with a personal identification number (PIN) to retrieve or compose voice messages or change personal parameters, such as a greeting or spoken name. Calls to the subscriber's phone are forwarded using the call forward busy (CFB), call-forward-no-answer (CFNA), or call-forward-all (CFA) Cisco CME features to the voice mail pilot number.

A *general delivery mailbox* (GDM) is associated with a group of subscribers. It allows callers to leave messages for a function of your business, such as your customer service desk or the sales department. The caller does not know any employees within that business function and does not care who in the group responds to the voice mail as long as the matter he or she is calling about is taken care of. For example, suppose you own or manage a grocery store and a customer calls the bakery with an order for a birthday cake. Any employee in the bakery can retrieve the message, enter the order into your computer system, and return the customer's call or send an e-mail to confirm the order. The employee's identity is unimportant to the caller.

Any subscriber who is a member of the group associated with the GDM, has equal rights to access the GDM to retrieve, reply to, forward, save, or delete the messages left in the GDM. When a member of the group saves a message, it is available for other members of the group to hear (as a *saved* message). If a member deletes a voice message, no one else has a chance to listen to it. Messages in the GDM are not sent to everyone's individual mailbox. The GDM is not a broadcast mechanism; it is a shared mailbox.

A subscriber does not log into a GDM directly. To access a GDM, a subscriber must be a member of the group associated with the mailbox. The subscriber logs into his or her personal mailbox first. From there a special menu branch (menu item 9) allows the subscriber to access messages in all the GDMs of which he or she is a member. A single subscriber can be a member of multiple GDMs and can select the appropriate GDM from a menu list. To prevent multiple subscribers from trying to listen to and delete the same message, only one subscriber at a time can be active inside a GDM.

Up to Cisco UE release 2.0, the maximum number of GDMs on the system is defined by the license installed on the system, as shown earlier in Table 10-1. As of release 2.1, only the total number of mailboxes is counted against the system license, and any number of personal and GDMs up to the total can be defined.

A physical phone need not be associated with a GDM, but an extension must be associated with the mailbox to forward calls to voice mail. If the GDM's extension appears on any phone (perhaps as a secondary button on the phones of the employees in the department associated with the GDM), message waiting indicator (MWI) is set on this phone (or phones) when new messages are left in the GDM. A GDM does not automatically turn on MWI on every group member's phone, unless all group members have an appearance of the GDM's extension on their phones.

Users and Groups

Cisco UE defines a user profile to contain the parameters of a voice mail subscriber. A user is associated with a personal mailbox. Figure 10-1 shows a typical user profile defining the user's name, extension, and password.

Figure 10-1 *Subscriber User Profile*

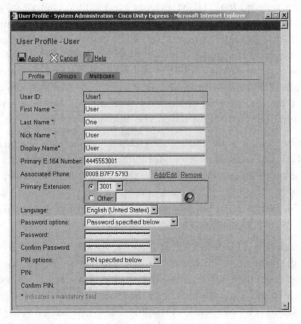

Using the tabs across the top of the screen, you can see the user's profile, the groups he belongs to, and his mailbox definition, as shown in Figure 10-2.

Figure 10-2 *Subscriber Mailbox Definition*

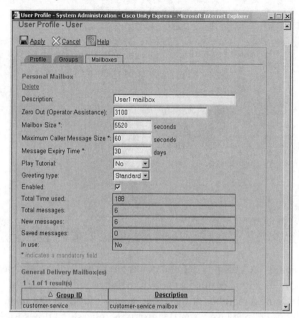

Cisco UE defines a group as lists of users or members. If a mailbox is associated with a group, it is a GDM. Only one member can log into a particular mailbox, including a GDM, at any one time. Groups can have multiple members and multiple owners, and these designations afford an employee different privileges. The same employee might be both a member and an owner of the group.

- A group *member* can log into the GDM and manage its voice message content.
- A group *owner* can make changes to the group membership.

For example, assume that the customer service hotline in your office is extension 3050 (mapping to a Public Switched Telephone Network [PSTN] number of 444.555.3050). User1 and User2 are the employees who staff this function—one on the morning shift and the other on the afternoon shift. User1's personal extension is 3001, and User2's is 3002. The customer service group profile is shown in Figure 10-3.

Figure 10-3 *Group Profile*

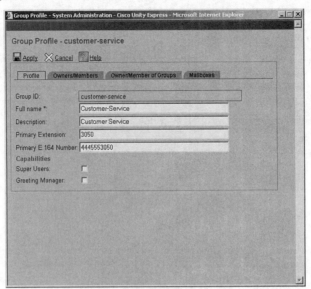

The customer service group is defined containing User1 and User2 as well as User10, who is the supervisor. User10 is defined as both a member and an owner of the group, as shown in Figure 10-4. Being a member of the group means that User10 can staff the customer service function if required, because User10's group membership allows login access to the GDM associated with extension 3050. Being an owner of the group means that User10 also has access rights to change the group's membership.

NOTE   The terms *user* and *subscriber* are used largely interchangeably in this chapter. In general, the term *user* is preferred, because that is how the Cisco UE graphical user interface (GUI) and command-line interface (CLI) address the profiles of people who are configured on the system. The term *subscriber* is used in this chapter to specifically indicate someone who has a mailbox on the Cisco UE system. *User* is a more generic term that includes subscribers, but it also includes people who have user definitions on Cisco UE but do not necessarily have mailboxes.

Figure 10-4   *Group Membership Definition*

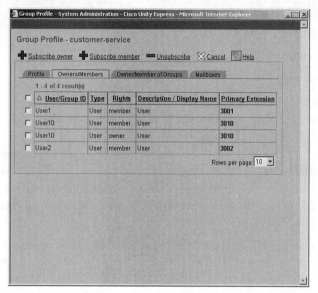

Subscriber Features

A subscriber is the person who owns the voice mailbox. A subscriber can access the voice mailbox, listen to the messages in it, and take action on these messages using the Telephony User Interface (TUI). Cisco UE is not a unified messaging system and, therefore, does not allow access to voice messages by any means other than the TUI.

The following voice mail features are available to a subscriber:

- Mailbox login and PIN
- Mailbox tutorial
- Personal greeting
- Alternate greeting
- Spoken name
- Message management
- Message playback control
- Message waiting indicator
- Mailbox-full notification
- Message reply and forward
- Private or urgent messages

- Envelope information
- Message playout sequence
- Zero-out destination
- Local and remote nondelivery notifications
- Distribution lists
- GUI access

The following sections describe each of these functions in detail.

Mailbox Login and PIN

PINs are mandatory; subscribers must enter a valid PIN to log into their mailboxes. The administrator assigns the PIN when the mailbox is created and tells the subscriber what it is. The system default may be a blank PIN.

When a subscriber logs into the TUI for the first time, she is prompted (forced) to change her system-assigned default PIN to a private PIN. Only the subscriber knows this private PIN (the administrator cannot see or access this value) and can change it through either the TUI or GUI.

If a subscriber forgets her PIN, she must contact her administrator to have it reset. Administrator control over PINs is discussed further in the section "Setting Subscriber PINs and Passwords."

If the caller ID on an incoming call to the voice mail system matches a subscriber's extension, the subscriber is prompted only to enter his or her PIN for login. This caller ID may be his or her local extension (for example, 3001) or a PSTN number (for example, a home phone number). Only a single extension can be associated with a mailbox, but an alternate field—the Primary E.164 Number field, as shown in Figure 10-5—can contain a PSTN number or an alternate extension that is also matched to this mailbox.

You can use the Primary E.164 Number field to enter a PSTN phone number to enable the subscriber mailbox login from home (you're prompted for the PIN only, not the extension number and PIN). However, this is unlikely to be the most effective use of this field. Usually, as shown in Figure 10-5, this field is set to the subscriber's direct inward dial (DID) number (444.555.3001 for a subscriber at extension 3001) so that both local and PSTN callers can leave the subscriber a message. If you use this field to direct DID calls (which is likely), a subscriber calling from home to retrieve his messages must log in with both his extension and PIN to access his mailbox, instead of being prompted for only his PIN. On the other hand, if you don't need to direct DID numbers to mailboxes, you can use this field for a PSTN number for mailbox login purposes.

NOTE	Note that the extension used to transfer from an AA or for MWI is always the Primary Extension field, not the Primary E.164 Number field.

Figure 10-5 *Primary E.164 Field Associated with a Mailbox*

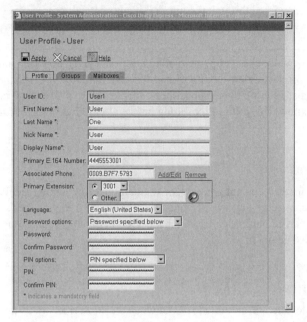

If the caller ID on an incoming call to the voice mail system does not match any subscriber's extension, the voice mail system plays the "Please enter your ID" prompt, which is followed by a prompt for the PIN.

If a subscriber (for example, User1) calls into voice mail from a neighbor's phone (User2, who is also a subscriber on the system), the system matches the caller ID to User2's mailbox and prompts User1 only for the PIN. User1 must press the star (*) button to exit this prompt, and the system reverts to the "Please enter your ID" prompt to allow User1 to log in from any phone on the system.

Mailbox Tutorial

A mailbox tutorial is automatically enabled for any new mailbox created on the system, unless you specifically choose to bypass this feature. The tutorial walks subscribers through basic setup options the first time they log into the voice mailbox, including the following:

- Recording a spoken name (this is optional and can be bypassed by pressing the # key)
- Recording a standard greeting (this is optional and can be bypassed by pressing the # key)
- Changing the PIN for the mailbox from the system-assigned PIN to a private user-assigned PIN

You can also reenable the tutorial for an existing voice mailbox. As soon as the subscriber has logged in and worked through the tutorial, it automatically turns off.

NOTE When a new mailbox is set up, the mailbox tutorial can be accessed only if the subscriber logs in from the primary extension associated with the mailbox. If first-time logins from other locations must be available to subscribers, set the PIN to a nonblank value, and ensure that the subscriber knows this initial PIN setting before attempting to log in for the first time.

Personal Greeting

A caller hears the personal greeting, or standard greeting, upon reaching the voice mailbox. A subscriber can record her own personal greeting. If she does not, the Cisco UE standard system greeting is played out to a caller. After it is recorded, the greeting cannot be deleted, but it can be rerecorded at any time.

Alternate Greeting

The alternate personal greeting is useful when the subscriber wants to set a special notification to callers, such as a vacation notification. The original personal (standard) greeting is still stored but is inactive. The subscriber can switch between the standard personal greeting and alternate personal greeting without erasing either of the recordings. Both the TUI and GUI have a toggle where the subscriber can activate either the standard or alternate personal greeting for the mailbox. The current setting for User1's mailbox is shown in Example 10-1.

Example 10-1 *Mailbox Parameters*

```
cue#show voicemail detail mailbox User1
Description:                    User1 mailbox
...
New Message Count:              6
Saved Message Count:            0
Expiration (days):              30
Greeting:                       standard
```

Either of the two greetings can also be rerecorded at any time.

Spoken Name

When a subscriber logs into the TUI for the first time, he is allowed to record a spoken name to identify himself as the mailbox's owner. The subscriber can change the spoken-name recording at any time but cannot delete it. The system plays the spoken name as verification when another subscriber sends a message, or in the AA if the caller chooses the subscriber's extension. If a spoken name is not recorded for a mailbox, the system plays a default announcement including the extension number.

Message Management

A subscriber can log into his or her mailbox and manage messages as follows:

- Play and replay
- Save
- Forward
- Reply
- Delete and undelete
- Skip
- Send and edit (or rerecord)

When a subscriber sends a message, he or she can address it either by extension or by dial-by-name. If the recipient is local, spoken-name confirmation is played during the addressing step. If spoken name is unavailable because the recipient has not recorded it, the system reads the recipient's extension. If the recipient is remote, spoken-name confirmation is played if available in the system local directory or cache (both of which can be disabled if this functionality is not desired). Otherwise, the location and extension are read.

If a subscriber deletes a message during a voice mail login session, the message is marked for deletion. An option under the Listen to Saved Messages TUI menu allows a subscriber to undelete any message deleted during the current session before logging out. When a subscriber logs out of the mailbox, all messages marked for deletion are physically deleted from the system and can no longer be recovered. The undelete feature requires a minimum of Cisco UE release 2.1.

Message Playback Controls

When listening to messages, a subscriber can fast-forward (advance), pause, or rewind a message. Cisco UE currently does not support speed acceleration or deceleration controls. The rewind and fast-forward actions skip by 3-second increments within the message.

Message pause halts playout of the current message. The subscriber is prompted every 50 seconds to restart the message playout, up to a maximum of 2.5 minutes, at which point the call is disconnected. In pause mode, the subscriber can take the following actions:

- **Rewind and resume**—Rewinds 3 seconds and restarts message playout
- **Resume**—Restarts message playout
- **Fast-forward and resume**—Skips forward by 3 seconds and restarts message playout

At any time during message playout, a subscriber can press 7 (rewind) to repeat the last 3 seconds of the voice message. This is useful if the caller left his or her phone number and the subscriber wants to repeat this segment.

Message Waiting Indicator

When a new message is left in a personal mailbox, the message waiting indicator (MWI) is turned on for the subscriber's phone. When the last new message is either saved or deleted, MWI is turned off. All the phones with an appearance of a subscriber's extension receive MWI.

If a manager and his or her assistant both have an appearance of the manager's extension on their phones, MWI comes on for both phones when a new message is left in the mailbox.

NOTE   The MWI may take the form of a light or a flashing envelope in the phone display, depending on the extension's particular line appearance.

Mailbox-Full Notification

If the subscriber's mailbox is full, he or she is notified of this situation upon login to his or her mailbox. The Cisco UE system calculates the percentage of space used in a mailbox every time the subscriber accesses it. If the use level exceeds 90% of the allocated space in the mailbox, the following system prompts are given:

- If mailbox use exceeds 90% but is less than 100%, the subscriber hears "Your mailbox is almost full. Please delete some messages."

- If mailbox use reaches 100%, the subscriber hears "Your mailbox is full. Please delete some messages."

If a subscriber attempts to send or forward a message to a recipient whose mailbox is full, the sender hears "Sorry. Your message *xxx* cannot be delivered to extension *yyy*. To send another message...." (The Cisco UE system plays your current voice message where *xxx* appears and reads the recipient's extension where *yyy* appears.) The sending subscriber can rerecord a shorter message because the mailbox may have a little bit of space left, but not enough for the longer message he or she first attempted to send.

If a subscriber sends a message to several other subscribers, all recipients receive the message if at least one recipient's mailbox has sufficient space to contain the message.

NOTE   The mailbox's MWI is not used to alert a subscriber to a message-full situation.

An administrator cannot delete messages from a subscriber's mailbox (unless he has the PIN from the subscriber and can log into the mailbox himself). But the administrator can see from the system statistics that the mailbox is full and can tell the subscriber by other means (perhaps an e-mail) to delete some messages. Or the administrator can delete the entire mailbox from the system, thus deleting all messages in the mailbox.

Message Reply and Forward

A subscriber can reply to or forward messages to other local subscribers in the Cisco UE system or another site. When replying or forwarding messages to local recipients, the subscriber can hear spoken-name confirmation of the receiving mailbox if that account has a spoken name recorded.

A subscriber can also forward a message with an introduction to other subscribers.

Private or Urgent Messages

When forwarding a message to another subscriber or sending a voice message, a subscriber can designate the message as urgent or private.

The recipient of a private message cannot forward the message to other subscribers. An urgent message is played at a higher priority than normal messages in the recipient's mailbox.

Message Playout Sequence

Messages in a subscriber's mailbox are played in the following sequence of priority. If a message of a higher priority does not exist, the next priority is the first to be played:

1 **Broadcast messages**—Can be played, replayed, saved, and deleted.

2 **Expired messages**—Can be played, replayed, saved, and deleted.

3 **Urgent messages**—Are played before other new personal messages, regardless of when they arrived.

4 **New personal messages**—Can be skipped, played, replayed, saved, deleted, replied to, and forwarded. These are sequenced based on arrival time.

5 **Archived messages**—Can be skipped, played, replayed, saved, deleted, replied to, and forwarded.

Subscribers can interrupt playback of all messages except broadcast messages by pressing the pound key (#) on the phone keypad.

Envelope Information

Messages received by a subscriber contain an envelope with information, such as the time of day and the sender's name or extension. Envelope information is played to the subscriber when retrieving the message.

Zero-Out Destination

Upon hearing a subscriber's greeting, a caller may choose not to leave a voice mail, but instead to press 0 to contact the subscriber at an alternate, preconfigured number. The subscriber can configure this zero-out destination number (perhaps a cell phone number, a home phone number, or an alternate extension in a lab in the building) where he or she can be reached.

Nondelivery Notification

Subscribers can send or forward voice messages to other subscribers who are on the same Cisco UE system (a local destination) or on another Cisco UE or Cisco Unity system at other sites in the network (a remote, or network, destination).

A send or forward operation to a local subscriber fails during the addressing step while the message is sent because the local system can do immediate error checking on the state of the recipient's mailbox. Sending or forwarding a message to a remote destination, however, does not fail immediately, because the checking does not happen until the message arrives at the destination system. In this case, the subscriber sends or forwards the message blindly and later receives a notification if an error should be detected by the receiving system.

Local Nondelivery Notification

If an internal caller sends or forwards a message to another local subscriber that is longer than the remaining space in the recipient's mailbox, the sender hears a system message announcing that the voice message cannot be delivered because the recipient's mailbox is full. The sender can choose to rerecord a shorter message.

A similar system message is played if the subscriber attempts to send or forward a message to a local recipient mailbox that does not exist.

Network Nondelivery Notification

The Network Nondelivery Notification feature is also called Nondelivery Receipt (NDR). If a voice message is sent or forwarded to a subscriber at another site, the originating subscriber gets an NDR if the message cannot be delivered.

The voice message may be undeliverable for various reasons:

- A network outage or connectivity problem
- A problem with the addressing of the message
- A configuration problem at either the local or remote site
- The recipient's mailbox is full
- The recipient's mailbox does not exist

The NDR feature is discussed further in the section "Voice Mail Networking."

Distribution Lists

Distribution lists allow subscribers to build lists of other subscribers, so they can send or forward a single voice message to multiple coworkers at the same time. This is particularly useful if you want to address the same group of coworkers repeatedly, such as the other employees in your group or everyone involved in a particular project.

Cisco UE defines two types of distribution lists:

- **Private**—Private distribution lists are maintained by a subscriber and are available only for his or her own use.
- **Public**—Public distribution lists are system-defined, maintained by the administrator, and visible to all subscribers.

Subscribers create their own private distribution lists. The administrator cannot create them on behalf of the subscriber. Private distribution lists are inaccessible to other subscribers.

GUI Access

In addition to the TUI, subscribers can access their user and mailbox account parameters through the GUI and can review and change account information. The optional GUI access gives the subscriber flexibility and keeps the voice mail system administrator from having to make personal changes. Figure 10-6 shows an example of the GUI subscriber screen (which is different from the view an administrator sees). The subscriber can change only certain user profile and mailbox parameters, which appear as white boxes as opposed to being grayed out.

Figure 10-6 *Subscriber GUI Screen*

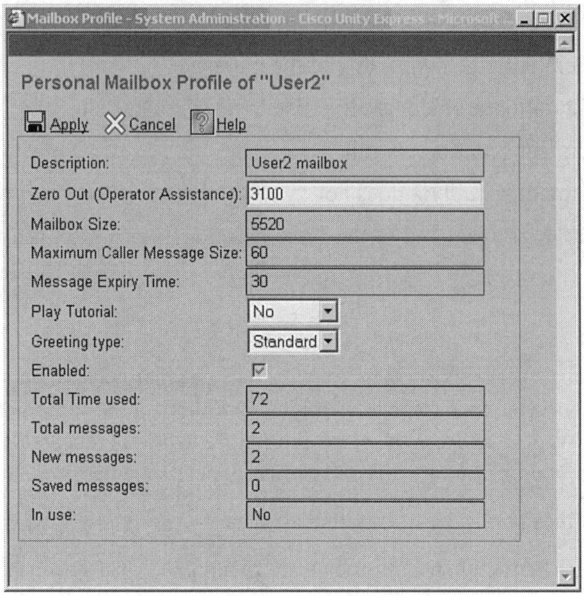

Caller Features

Two types of callers interact with a voice mail system:

- A customer or vendor who calls your business. The person he or she wants to speak to is unavailable or is already busy on the phone, and the call forwards to voice mail. The caller hears the greeting of the person he or she called and then leaves a voice message for that person.

- An employee of your business who calls into the voice mail system to check or retrieve his or her messages.

All callers interact with the voice mail system by using the TUI only. The following features are available to the first type of caller (the person calling to leave a message) and are covered in this section:

- Outbound greeting bypass
- Message editing
- Urgent messages
- Mailbox-full indication
- Message leaving and mailbox login
- Zero-out destination or revert to AA

The second type of caller is a subscriber. Features available to this type of caller were covered in the section "Subscriber Features."

Outbound Greeting Bypass

If callers are not interested in listening to the outgoing greeting of the mailbox reached, they can bypass the greeting and proceed immediately to the beep, where they can leave a message. The caller can bypass the outgoing greeting of a voice mailbox by pressing # on the phone keypad at any time during the greeting playout.

Message Editing

After recording a message, a caller can listen to, edit, rerecord, or delete the message before sending. Or he or she can simply hang up, and the message is automatically sent.

Urgent Messages

If a caller hangs up after leaving a voice message for a subscriber, the message is sent with normal priority. If a caller presses the # key to end recording of a message, the Cisco UE voice mail system provides a menu where the caller can choose to tag the message as urgent (among other options, such as rerecording the message, deleting it, or listening to the message before sending).

Urgent messages are played at higher priority in the recipient's mailbox so that a subscriber hears urgent messages before normal messages when he or she logs into his or her mailbox.

Mailbox-Full Indication

If the recipient's mailbox is almost full (less than 5 seconds of available space), the caller is notified before recording a message and is not allowed to proceed. The caller hears "Sorry. The mailbox you're trying to reach is currently full. Please try again later." After this prompt, the caller is transferred to the voice mail operator (typically the AA) for further choices.

If the recipient's mailbox has available space, a new message from a caller is limited to the minimum of the following:

- The remaining space available in the mailbox
- The maximum caller message size parameter set for the mailbox

Message Leaving and Mailbox Login

Cisco UE has a single voice mail pilot number for both types of callers. If a call is redirected (by CFA, CFNA, or CFB), Cisco UE treats the call as if the person called to leave a message and plays the mailbox greeting. The appropriate mailbox is selected from the last redirected number in the call information delivered to Cisco UE. If the call was not redirected, Cisco UE treats the call as if a subscriber is calling in to retrieve messages. The mailbox is selected from the calling number information delivered to Cisco UE.

Zero-Out Destination or Revert to AA

When a caller leaves a message for a subscriber and does not hang up afterwards (you can press # and get a menu from the Cisco UE voice mail system to, for example, tag a message as urgent), a caller can press 0 and have the call transferred to a preconfigured destination. This is called the *zero-out* destination for the mailbox or the *revert to AA* feature.

By default, the zero-out destination for all mailboxes is the system voice mail operator number, discussed in the later section "Voice Mail Operator." The default for this operator number, in turn, is the Cisco UE AA pilot number. If a caller leaves a message for one subscriber in your business and wants to try to connect with another employee (who may be in the office), he or she can do so without redialing across the PSTN. For long-distance or international calls, this feature can be of significant benefit to avoid the inconvenience and expense of dialing into the called number multiple times.

If the AA is not the desired transfer destination, the zero-out number can be customized by the subscriber or administrator, per mailbox, as of Cisco UE release 1.1. The zero-out destination can be any destination that can be dialed within the Cisco CME system's dialplan, including PSTN locations.

Administrator Features

As the system administrator, you can use the GUI or CLI to manage voice mail system parameters and voice mail subscriber accounts. The GUI is more user-friendly for individual operations, and the CLI lends itself better to scripting from another management system for faster configuration.

The voice mail-related features available to a Cisco UE system administrator include the following:

- Voice mail pilot number
- Mailbox management
- MWI
- Mailbox storage allocation

- Maximum message size
- Message expiry
- Subscriber PINs and passwords
- Broadcast messaging
- Voice mail operator
- Distribution lists
- Language support
- System reports and status

Chapter 14, "Configuring and Managing Cisco IPC Express Systems," covers the configuration steps of the Cisco UE voice mail system in greater detail. This section discusses the features themselves and how they operate.

Voice Mail Pilot Number

The voice mail pilot number is the number subscribers call to retrieve their voice messages (typically triggered by pressing the messages button on the phone), as well as the number IP phones are call forwarded to so that callers can leave a voice message.

NOTE   For Cisco UE, the voice mail pilot number is always different from the AA pilot number. The same pilot number cannot be used for both applications. You can, however, define multiple pilot numbers for voice mail, as well as multiple numbers for the AA.

Cisco UE uses a single voice mail pilot number for both types of calls. Whether the voice mail system plays a subscriber's mailbox greeting or prompts for subscriber login depends on whether the call has been redirected before entering the voice mail system. How Cisco UE makes this decision depends on the last redirected number and Calling Number fields of the incoming voice call. This process was explained earlier, in the sections "Mailbox Login and PIN" and "Message Leaving and Mailbox Login."

The following Cisco IPC Express configuration elements must match for the voice mail pilot number to work correctly:

- A SIP dial peer must be defined on Cisco CME to direct calls to the pilot number to Cisco UE. Ensure that calls to both the local extension pilot number (for example, 3105) and PSTN calls to the DID pilot number (for example, 444.555.3105) are all directed to Cisco UE. Multiple dial peers can be defined—one for the extension, and another for the E.164 DID number—or digit manipulation can be used to translate the DID number to the extension.

- The **voicemail** parameter within Cisco CME **telephony-service** configuration must be set to the pilot number to ensure that pressing the message button on an IP phone calls the correct number.

- The IP phones must be configured to call forward calls to the voice mail pilot number to ensure that callers reach the voice mail greeting.

Example 10-2 shows the Cisco CME and Cisco UE configuration parameters relevant to the voice mail pilot number (3105, in this example). You can configure the Cisco UE voice mail pilot number in the GUI by navigating to the **Voice Mail > Call Handling** screen. The configuration in Example 10-2 uses Cisco IOS translation rules (as explained in Chapter 6, "Cisco CME PSTN Connectivity Options") to translate the E.164 PSTN number to the pilot number extension. Translation profile to_aavm is attached to SIP dial peer 3100. The to_aavm profile, in turn, refers to translation rule 10 (applicable to *called* numbers only), where rule 2 substitutes a called number of 4445553105 with the digits 3105. Alternatively, you could also define a second SIP dial peer with a **destination-pattern 44455531..** statement.

Example 10-2 *Voice Mail Pilot Number Operation*

```
router#show running-config
voice translation-rule 10
 rule 1 /4445553100/ /3100/
 rule 2 /4445553105/ /3105/
!
voice translation-profile to_aavm
 translate called 10
!
dial-peer voice 3100 voip
 description VM-AA
 translation-profile outgoing to_aavm
 destination-pattern 31..
 session protocol sipv2
 session target ipv4:172.19.153.37
!
telephony-service
 ip source-address 10.10.1.100 port 2000
 voicemail 3105
!
ephone-dn  1
 number 3001
 description User1
 call-forward busy 3105
 call-forward noan 3105 timeout 10

cue#show running-config
ccn trigger sip phonenumber 3105
 application "voicemail"
 maxsessions 8
 end trigger
```

Under the ephone-dn configuration for each extension, calls are forwarded on busy or no-answer (with a ringing timeout of 10 seconds) to extension 3105, which is the voice mail pilot number, defined by the **voicemail 3105** statement under **telephony-service**.

In the last few lines of Example 10-2, the Cisco UE CLI configuration is shown, where the voice mail pilot number 3105 is defined as a SIP *trigger* to the application. This means that when a call arrives at this number, it *triggers* the voice mail application.

Mailbox Management

The administrator can create mailboxes up to the maximum number of mailboxes supported by the license installed on the Cisco UE system. When you create a mailbox, you must associate it with an existing user or group. You can modify mailbox parameters in the Mailbox Profile screen in the GUI. You can navigate to this screen either by going to **Voice Mail** > **Mailboxes** and clicking the appropriate mailbox or by going to the **Configure** > **Users** or **Configure** > **Groups** screens, clicking the appropriate user or group, and then selecting the **Mailbox** tab from the user or group profile.

GDMs cannot be reused as personal mailboxes, because logging into a GDM requires that the member (subscriber) also have a personal mailbox. However, as mentioned earlier, in the "Cisco UE Licensing" section, as of Cisco UE release 2.1 any number of personal mailboxes or GDMs can be defined, up to the maximum number of mailboxes allowed by the Cisco UE license. An existing personal mailbox cannot be converted to a GDM (or the other way around) and keep the existing messages in the mailbox. Making such a configuration change requires you to delete the mailbox and redefine it as the new type, which means that the mailbox will be created new and will be empty of messages.

You may change mailbox parameters at any time, and you also may delete a mailbox. The user definition (information associated with the subscriber) is separate from that of the mailbox, and the user definition may exist without an associated mailbox. However, a mailbox may not exist without being associated with either a user or group.

Parameters such as mailbox size, expiry time, and maximum caller message size are assigned at mailbox creation time. The default mailbox size is calculated based on the hardware form factor and license you are using, as given earlier in Table 10-1. Unless you override the values in the Configuration screen, the system default values are automatically applied. If you change the system defaults, these changes apply only to mailboxes you create after the defaults have changed. Existing mailboxes continue to have the parameter values assigned to them at creation time.

If you foresee that your business will grow, you probably want to set the mailbox size defaults to be smaller than the system defaults. The reason for this is that the total system storage space is determined by the hardware form factor. For example, the NM-CUE provides 100 hours of storage, regardless of the mailbox license installed. If you first purchase your NM-CUE system with 50 mailboxes, the default system mailbox size allocates all 100 hours equally across the

50 mailboxes. If you later upgrade to the 100-mailbox license, there is still only 100 hours of storage in total, and there may not be enough unallocated storage space left to define the new mailboxes. To alleviate this situation, you have to go into the existing mailboxes and make them smaller to release space for the new mailboxes you can now add to the system. The recommendation is to set the default mailbox size to the actual mailbox size you foresee using in your business, as opposed to simply using the system defaults.

MWI

The MWI on the IP phone is turned on when a new message is waiting in the mailbox associated with the extension that appears on the phone. MWI is turned off when the last new message in the mailbox is saved or deleted. Several topics related to MWI operation are discussed in the next sections:

- Understanding when each of the two MWI mechanisms on an IP phone (either a red lamp on the handset or a flashing envelope in the phone display) is used
- Controlling MWI on multiple phones for a single mailbox
- Controlling MWI for GDMs
- Understanding how MWI directory numbers (DNs) operate
- Refreshing MWI for an individual phone or the entire system if the indications should become unsynchronized with the mailbox message content

Lamp or Flashing Envelope MWI

Cisco IP phones offer two types of MWI alerts: the red lamp on the handset and a flashing envelope icon that appears on the phone display next to a particular button. Not all phone models provide both types of indicators, but phones with multiple buttons (or lines) do.

Cisco CME and Cisco UE do not offer a direct configuration option where you can select which type of MWI alert you want on the phone. The selection is based on where the extension associated with the mailbox appears on the phone's buttons. The red lamp MWI is used when the extension appears on button 1 of the phone. The flashing envelope MWI is used for extensions that appear on any button *except* button 1. Therefore, you can indirectly control the type of MWI by selecting the sequence in which extensions appear on a phone.

MWI on Multiple Phones for the Same Mailbox

MWI is turned on per extension, not per phone. A mailbox is associated with a user, the user is associated with an extension (the Primary Extension field in the Cisco UE user profile), and the extension is associated with a button on one or more phones. All phones with extension appearances associated with the mailbox receive MWI. The type of MWI is determined individually per phone, as explained in the preceding section.

For example, assume that User1 is a manager at extension 3001 and User5 is the manager's assistant. Extension 3001 appears on button 1 of User1's phone and on button 2 of User5's phone. When a caller leaves a new message for User1, the red lamp MWI comes on for User1's phone, and the flashing icon MWI comes on for User5's phone. If you want the assistant to also receive a red lamp MWI for the manager's messages, the manager's extension (3001) must be moved to button 1 of the assistant's phone.

MWI for GDMs

MWI for GDMs works exactly the same way as MWI for personal mailboxes. A GDM is associated with a group, a group is associated with an extension, and an extension appears on button 1 or higher of one or more phones.

For example, suppose User1 (3001) and User2 (3002) work in the customer service department of your business. Their manager is User10 (3010). The extension associated with customer service is 3050. The customer service group is associated with extension 3050 and has a GDM so that callers can leave a message for help, regardless of which employee is currently on shift. Both employees (User1 and User2) and their manager (User10) belong to the customer service group, so they all have access to the GDM to check for messages.

You want the customer service employees (User1 and User2) to receive a red lamp MWI for the GDM, because responding to customer service calls is their primary responsibility. The manager (User10) must receive a red lamp MWI for User10's personal mailbox, but the manager also wants to monitor the state of the GDM to respond to customer service messages if the employees in the group should be overloaded or unavailable.

The way to achieve this is to put the customer service group extension 3050 on button 1 of User1 and User2's phones, as shown in Figure 10-7. On the manager's (User10) phone you put the manager's own extension (3010) on button 1 and an appearance of 3050 on button 2 (or higher) so that the manager can see a flashing icon for the GDM message status.

Figure 10-7 *MWI for General Delivery Mailboxes*

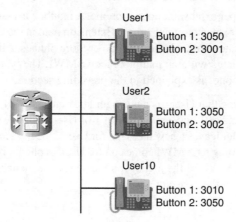

You can use the Cisco CME silent ring option so that calls to extension 3050 do not disturb the manager while still allowing the manager to monitor message status for the GDM. This configuration is shown in Figure 10-8 in the Ring Type/Mode field.

Figure 10-8 *Silent Ring for GDM Monitoring*

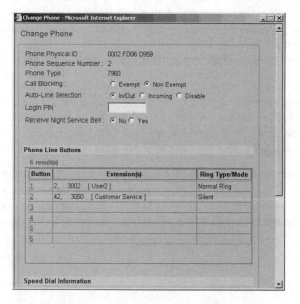

MWI DN Operation

Cisco UE has no direct control mechanism over the IP phones and triggers MWI on a phone via the Cisco CME call control engine. When a new voice message is left in a subscriber's mailbox, Cisco UE originates a call to a special extension type, an MWI DN or extension. Two separate MWI DNs must be defined on Cisco CME: an MWI ON DN and an MWI OFF DN. The Cisco CME configuration of the MWI DNs is shown in Example 10-3.

Example 10-3 *MWI ON and OFF Control*

```
Router#show running-config
ephone-dn  51
 number 8000....
 mwi on
!
ephone-dn  52
 number 8001....
 mwi off
```

A call terminating on one of these DNs is handled by Cisco CME call control and results in a message sent to the IP phone of the extension matched by the wildcards in the MWI DN definition.

To illustrate how Cisco UE triggers MWI, consider an example in which a new voice message is left for User1 at extension 3001. The MWI DN definition shown in Example 10-3 is configured on the Cisco CME system. The sequence of events that follow is illustrated in Figure 10-9:

1 A new voice message is left for User1 at extension 3001.

2 Cisco UE originates a SIP call to destination number 80003001. 8000 is the MWI ON DN defined in the configuration, and 3001 is the extension where the lamp must be turned on. The call to 80003001 matches the ephone-dn definition for number 8000...., and Cisco CME extracts the wildcard portion of this match (that is, 3001) to determine which phone is to be controlled. The DN type matched by the SIP call destination number (MWI ON or MWI OFF) determines the type of control. In this case, 8000 is the MWI ON DN.

3 Cisco CME sends a Skinny Client Control Protocol (SCCP) message to every IP phone that has an appearance of extension 3001 defined to turn on its MWI.

Figure 10-9 *MWI with Cisco CME*

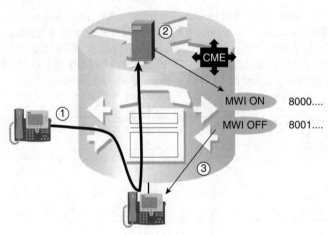

Similarly, when User1 has listened to this message and the lamp must be turned off on the phone, Cisco UE originates a call to extension 80013001. Extension 8001 is the MWI OFF DN defined in the configuration. Therefore, Cisco CME knows to send an SCCP message to turn off the MWI on every IP phone with an appearance of extension 3001.

NOTE   It is important that the MWI ON and MWI OFF DN definitions contain enough wildcards (the dots) to match the extension length of the phones defined on the system. For example, if four-digit extensions are defined on the system, the MWI ON and MWI OFF DNs must contain four trailing dots. If the MWI DN is defined only as 8000, instead of 8000...., a call originated by Cisco UE to 80003001 cannot match any ephone-dn, and MWI will not work. This process does not work in the same way as Cisco Unity MWI control. The MWI configurations for Cisco Unity and Cisco UE are different.

MWI Refresh

If users complain that their MWI alerts are out of synchronization with the message content of their voice mailboxes, you can force a manual refresh of MWI either for an individual user, selected users, or the entire system. You can refresh MWI from the **Voice Mail > Message Waiting Indicators > Refresh** GUI screen. When refreshing MWI for the entire system, Cisco UE sends one MWI update every 4 seconds until all MWIs on all extensions have been updated.

Getting out of synchronization can happen in some situations when phones are disconnected from the network (and therefore powered off) or are rebooted, and Cisco UE does not know that MWI was lost on the phone. If the phone was not moved or rebooted, getting out of synchronization usually indicates a software error. The Cisco UE MWI refresh ability allows you to synchronize MWI for your users immediately, either individually or for the entire system. However, you should follow the troubleshooting techniques described in Chapter 21, "Troubleshooting Cisco UE Voice Mail Features," to determine the root cause of the problem.

Mailbox Storage Allocation

Cisco UE stores voice messages and greetings in G.711 μ-law format. This means that every second of stored voice consists of 64,000 bits. You can calculate the size of the audio file representing a voice message with the following formula:

1 minute of stored voice = 60 seconds * 64000 bits = 3840 Kb = 480 KB

This is a good minimum estimate of the size of your Cisco UE backups. If you have 200 minutes of stored voice mail, your backup is at least 96,000 KB, or 96 MB, in size. You can see the total amount of voice mail storage allocation in your Cisco UE system by using the **show voicemail usage** command, as shown in Example 10-4. You can see the same information in the GUI by navigating to the **Reports > Voice Mail** screen.

Example 10-4   *Total Voice Mail Storage Use*

```
cue#show voicemail usage
personal mailboxes:                    20
general delivery mailboxes:            1
capacity of voicemail (minutes):       6000
allocated capacity (minutes):          1562.0
message time used (seconds):           1469
message count:                         25
average message length (seconds):      58.76
greeting time used (seconds):          149
greeting count:                        19
```

Cisco UE does not provide any disk usage or disk statistics counters. Voice mail storage allocation is always reflected with respect to the number of hours of storage allowed by the license installed on your system.

If your Cisco UE system's storage capacity starts filling up, you will see log file messages issued at 90% usage and 95% usage. Above 95% storage usage, you see another log file message at every additional 1% usage, reminding you that subscribers must start deleting voice messages to keep the system from running out of space.

Storage Allocation Per Mailbox

The administrator can specify, in seconds, the amount of message storage available independently for each individual subscriber's mailbox. This can be done at mailbox creation time or after the mailbox has been created. The total amount of storage allocated for all mailboxes cannot exceed the amount of message storage available on the Cisco UE system. By default, all mailboxes created on a Cisco UE system are the same size. The actual size depends on the hardware form factor (NM-CUE or AIM-CUE) and the mailbox license level on your system. Table 10-1 in the earlier section "Cisco UE Voice Mail Overview" provided the different system defaults.

If you want to change the message storage size for a subscriber after the mailbox already has some messages stored, the new mailbox size cannot be less than the current used space.

System Settings and Defaults

You can configure your own default mailbox message storage size in the **Defaults > Mailbox** GUI screen, which is used whenever a new mailbox is created.

The GUI screen under **Reports > Voice Mail** shows you how much storage space has already been allocated to existing mailboxes and how much of the allocated space is used by existing messages in the system. This is shown in Figure 10-10.

Figure 10-10   *Voice Mail Storage Allocation Summary*

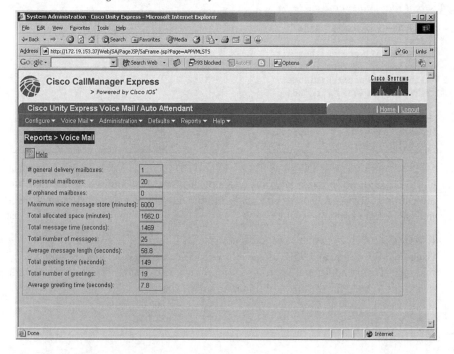

In the GUI screen **Defaults > Voice Mail,** you see the parameter maximum voice message store. This is the total amount of storage (in minutes) you have on your system, and this value depends on the Cisco UE hardware platform you have. You can make this value smaller if you want to, but you cannot make it larger.

Maximum Message Size

Cisco UE defines a maximum message size for both outbound (message send) and inbound (caller leaving a message) messages. These are independent values with defaults that you can control by setting your own desired system value.

Inbound Message Size

The inbound message size is the maximum size message a caller can leave in a mailbox. This maximum size prevents calls from maliciously or accidentally filling the voice mail system's storage with a single errant message. This inbound maximum message size is a system-wide parameter you can find in the **Defaults > Mailbox GUI** screen called Maximum Caller Message Size. You can control this parameter individually per mailbox, as shown in Figure 10-11, or you can leave the system default intact for all mailboxes.

Figure 10-11   *Maximum Message Size Per Mailbox*

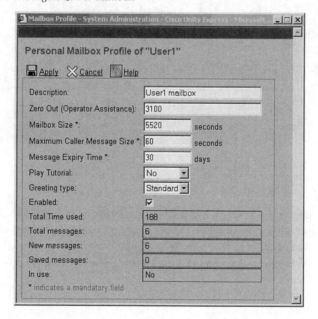

Outbound Message Size

The outbound message size is the maximum size message a subscriber can record and send to another mailbox. You cannot control this value individually per mailbox, but you can set the system default value to a value you desire. This single value applies to all subscribers on the system.

You can find this parameter in the **Defaults > Voice Mail** GUI screen, in a field called Maximum Subscriber Recording Size (see Figure 10-12).

Figure 10-12 *Maximum Subscriber Recording Size*

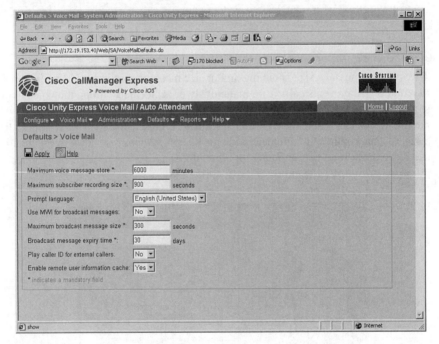

Message Expiry

You can configure each mailbox individually to specify the maximum duration for which messages are stored in the mailbox before they expire. Or you can choose to have the single system-defined default (30 days) apply to all mailboxes. You can find this parameter in the **Defaults > Mailbox** GUI screen, in a field called Message Expiry Time (see Figure 10-13).

Figure 10-13 *Message Expiry Time*

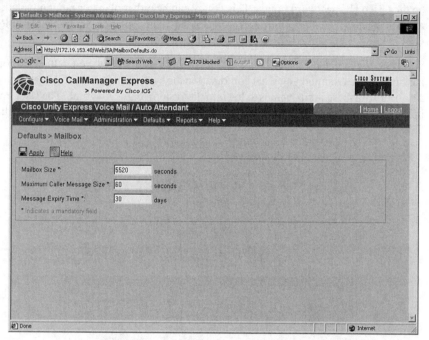

When a message, whether new or saved, has been in the mailbox for the specified expiry duration, it is automatically marked as expired. Cisco UE does not automatically delete messages from a subscriber's mailbox.

When the subscriber next logs into his or her mailbox, a system prompt announces that one or more messages have expired and that some action is necessary. The subscriber is prompted to either keep the message (which resets the message's expiry time) or delete the message.

Setting Subscriber PINs and Passwords

The administrator sets the initial value of a subscriber's PIN and password when the user profile is created. The administrator can reset the PIN or password to a known value if the subscriber forgets his or her PIN or password, but the administrator can never display the user-chosen values. After you have reset the forgotten PIN or password, the subscriber can log in again and change the PIN or password to a new private value.

Cisco UE uses its own underlying user administration and authentication functions to keep track of a subscriber's PIN or password. External authentication mechanisms such as authentication, authorization, and accounting (AAA) cannot be used by Cisco UE up to release 2.1. PINs and passwords are stored in a one-way encrypted form and cannot be displayed or read in any way.

When you create a new user on Cisco UE, a PIN and password are automatically assigned based on the Cisco UE password policy. This policy can be either blank or randomly generated PINs and passwords (the latter policy is recommended). This policy is set in the **Defaults > User GUI** screen.

The system-generated PIN and password for a new user are displayed in the GUI for you (as an administrator) to remind you what combination the system assigned to the user. You provide the new user with these initial values to log into the system for the first time. The User Profile screen in Figure 10-14 shows that a new user's password is assigned as act772113, and the PIN as 5678.

Figure 10-14 *PIN and Password for a Newly Created User*

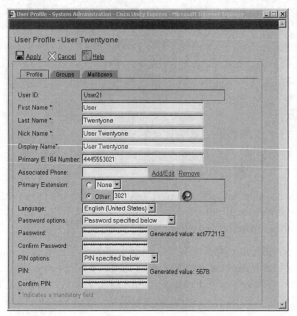

After the user logs on and changes his or her PIN or password, these values are never again displayed or viewable. You, as the administrator, can always reset the values of both fields, but you can never see the values the user chose. Figure 10-15 shows the User Profile screen after User21 has changed the password and PIN. Through the User Profile screen, you can tell whether a user has reset the PIN or password or whether the user is still using the system-assigned defaults.

Figure 10-15   *A User Who Has Changed His or Her PIN and Password*

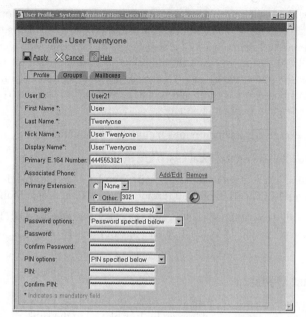

PINs

PINs are mandatory in all releases of Cisco UE. They are used to log into a mailbox. Until Cisco UE release 2.0, PINs were 3 to 16 digits long, numeric only, and did not expire. As of release 2.1, the administrator can configure a PIN's minimum length (the system default remains three digits) and assign an expiry time in days.

Passwords

Passwords are mandatory in all releases of Cisco UE. Passwords are used to log into the GUI using a web browser. Until Cisco UE release 2.0, PINs were 3 to 32 characters long, case-sensitive, allowed alphabetic and numeric characters, and did not expire. As of release 2.1, the administrator can configure a password's minimum length (the system default is four characters) and assigns an expiry time in days.

Broadcast Messaging

Broadcast messaging is a common voice mail system function. Broadcast capability requires Cisco UE release 2.1 or later software. This section describes sending and receiving broadcast messages.

Sending a Broadcast Message

Only users with broadcast privileges can send a broadcast message. Normal subscribers cannot send broadcast messages. You compose a broadcast message by using the Cisco UE TUI Administration Via Telephony (AVT) (also called the Greeting Management System [GMS] in Cisco UE releases before release 2.1) and selecting option 3 from the menu. Logging into the AVT requires the same user ID and PIN as your personal mailbox login. Therefore, you require a personal mailbox on the system and broadcast privileges assigned to your user ID to have access to sending a broadcast message.

Broadcast message addressing options include the following:

- Send to all users on the local Cisco UE system.
- Send to all users at selected networked Cisco UE locations by choosing the systems' location IDs. (This is explained further in the section "Voice Mail Networking.")
- Send to all users at the local site, and select networked Cisco UE locations. This requires selection of the local Cisco UE site as one of the networked location IDs.

Receiving a Broadcast Message

A broadcast message is sent to all subscribers on any of the Cisco UE systems (local or networked) the message was addressed to. It is played to the subscribers, as explained in the earlier section "Message Playout Sequence."

You can configure MWI for broadcast messages if you are the Cisco UE system administrator. Whether MWI is turned on for broadcast messages is a property of the receiving Cisco UE system; it is turned off by default. The same broadcast message sent to multiple destination Cisco UE systems can, therefore, cause the MWI to light up in one destination Cisco UE system and not on another Cisco UE system, based on the broadcast MWI configuration in each recipient system.

Voice Mail Operator

Cisco UE defines a system voice mail operator where calls are redirected if a caller does not respond to voice mail menus or does not hang up after leaving a voice message for a subscriber. The voice mail "operator" is triggered when the following voice mail prompt is reached: "If you have a mailbox on the system, please press #, or you will be transferred to the operator."

By default, the Cisco UE voice mail operator is set to the Cisco UE AA pilot number. Alternatively, you can set this to the extension of any employee in your office or a PSTN location. To change this attribute, on the **Voice Mail > Call Handling** GUI screen, change the Voice Mail Operator Number field, as shown in Figure 10-16. (It's set to extension 1100, which is the AA pilot number.)

Figure 10-16 *Voice Mail Operator Number*

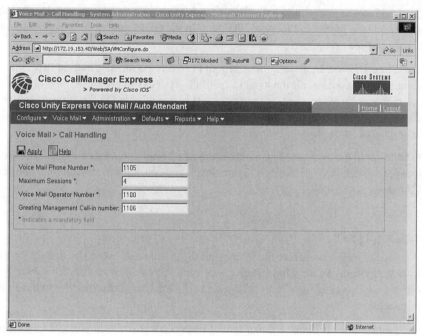

Distribution Lists

As covered in the earlier section "Subscriber Features," Cisco UE defines two types of distribution lists: private and public. As the system administrator, you maintain public distribution list definition and membership. Distribution lists may have as one or more of the following as members:

- A group
- A subscriber
- A GDM
- Other public distribution lists

Distribution lists have the following properties:

- If a user is removed from the Cisco UE system, he or she is also removed as a member from all the public and private distribution lists in the system.
- A list is identified by a unique number or name.
- A list may contain a mix of local and networked Cisco UE destinations.
- A spoken name may be recorded by the owner of a list for easier addressing.

Public Distribution Lists

If a voice message is sent to a distribution list that has all the member elements just described, the message is placed in the user's mailbox, in the GDM, and in the personal mailbox of each member of the group.

The Cisco UE system has a system default *everyone* public distribution list. This list automatically contains all the local users of the system (no groups or GDMs are included) and is automatically maintained by the system. If a user is added to the system, that person is automatically also added to the *everyone* distribution list. Members cannot be manually added to or deleted from the *everyone* list.

In addition to the *everyone* list, a maximum of 15 public distribution lists can be defined irrespective of Cisco UE mailbox license level. You can define a total of 1000 public distribution list entries per Cisco UE system.

Private Distribution Lists

When you delete a user from the system, all the private lists owned by that user are also deleted from the system. As the administrator, you cannot create private lists for subscribers, but you can see the lists (and members) belonging to a particular subscriber if you have viewing privileges.

Each subscriber can define a maximum of five private distribution lists and a total of 50 private distribution list entries.

Automatic Gain Control

Cisco UE contains Automatic Gain Control (AGC) code. This means that differences in volume levels between internal calls and PSTN locations are automatically compensated for when callers leave messages.

AGC is active on all calls into Cisco UE and ensures that all messages recorded are of the same volume level. Incoming voice streams are normalized to a standard input value, and the adjusted audio is stored. You have no configuration control over these settings.

Language Support

Before Cisco UE release 2.0, the only language supported by Cisco UE was U.S. English. As of release 2.0, support for Spanish (European), German, and French (European) was introduced. Only a single language may exist on Cisco UE at any one time. Cisco UE does not yet support multiple simultaneous languages. You choose the language for your system during the Cisco UE installation when language-specific prompts are installed and the appropriate language files are downloaded to the system.

Language customization on Cisco UE affects only the voice mail and AA system prompts. The GUI, CLI, and system monitoring and debugging tools, such as log file messages, are always supported in English only.

Your own customized AA prompts and voice mail greetings can be recorded in any language you like, regardless of the system language installed on Cisco UE. Clearly, it would make sense to have the system and custom prompts in the same language, but no Cisco UE system knowledge forces this coordination. For example, your opening AA welcome greeting may be bilingual and lets callers choose which language to use to interact with the remaining AA menus. But if they should encounter any system AA or voice mail prompts during this interaction, the system prompts are provided only in the system language currently installed on your system. You cannot rerecord the system prompts or translate them.

System Reports and Status

Cisco UE up to release 2.1 does not include formal reports, but you can use various GUI screens and CLI **show** commands to provide system status and statistics to monitor system use and performance:

- Cisco CME call detail records (CDRs)

- Cisco IOS router displays, such as **show voice call status** and **show voice call summary**

- Summary voice mail space usage displayed by the **show voicemail usage** Cisco UE command or by the **Reports > Voice Mail** GUI screen

- Summary voice mail space usage showing individual mailbox usage levels displayed by the **show voicemail mailboxes** Cisco UE command

- Individual mailbox usage statistics displayed by the **show voicemail detail mailbox** *xxx* Cisco UE command (where *xxx* is the user ID) or the mailbox profile displayed in the GUI by clicking a specific user ID in the **Voice Mail > Mailboxes** screen

- System statistics such as memory usage (**show memory** and **show proc memory**) and CPU usage (**show proc cpu**)

Call Redirection into Voice Mail

As mentioned in the section "Message Leaving and Mailbox Login," Cisco UE uses the last Redirected Number field in the call information to select the mailbox greeting to play to a caller. This field can be seen in the Diversion header in the SIP INVITE message delivering the call to Cisco UE, as shown in Example 10-5. In this example, 6800 is the voice mail pilot number, extension 7010 originates a call to extension 5010, and the call is redirected to voice mail by CFNA.

Example 10-5 *SIP INVITE for a Call Forwarded to Cisco UE*

```
router#debug ccsip messages
INVITE sip:6800@1.3.6.179:5060 SIP/2.0
Via: SIP/2.0/UDP  1.3.6.4:5060
From: "7010" <sip:7010@1.3.6.4>;tag=691AE6E4-223C
To: <sip:6800@1.3.6.179>
Call-ID: E5D39E6A-8FC011D7-9025DAEC-459632B0@1.3.6.4
CSeq: 101 INVITE
Max-Forwards: 6
Remote-Party-ID: <sip:7010@1.3.6.4>;party=calling;screen=no;privacy=off
Timestamp: 1054070868
Contact: <sip:7010@1.3.6.4:5060>
Diversion: <sip:5010@1.3.6.4>;reason=no-answer;counter=1
```

Correct voice mailbox selection depends on the redirection information delivered with the call, which is extension 5010 in Example 10-5. A call can be redirected to voice mail in numerous ways, and these ways may populate the redirection information differently. The following sections explore some common ways for calls to be redirected to voice mail and their dependencies on voice mailbox selection and operation.

Call Forward into Voice Mail

CFNA, CFB, and CFA are the typical ways to divert a call to voice mail. If a call is redirected multiple times before reaching voice mail, the value in the last Redirected Number field always selects the voice mail greeting that Cisco UE plays to the caller. For example, if extension 3001 calls extension 3061, which CFAs to extension 5001, which in turn CFNAs to voice mail, the caller at extension 3001 hears the voice mail greeting of the subscriber associated with extension 5001.

Some voice mail systems use the original called Number Field for voice mailbox selection. In the call flow just described, that would be extension 3061. This field does not change, regardless of how many times the call is subsequently diverted before reaching voice mail. Some voice mail systems, including Cisco UE, use the last Redirected Number field. Other systems allow you to configure which field to use.

Transfer and Conference

Other possible ways for a call to enter a voice mail system are by using call modification features such as transfer and conference. Call transfer to voice mail is fairly common, but call conference is perhaps less so.

If your business has a receptionist or administrative assistant answering calls, a caller may choose to transfer to the employee's voice mail instead of waiting to speak to the person. This scenario is discussed in detail in Chapter 9 in the section "Transferred Calls That Forward to Voice Mail."

When a call is transferred to voice mail, the extension initiating the transfer is the *last redirected number,* and this extension's mailbox is selected. For example, suppose a PSTN caller calls the receptionist at extension 3001. The caller wants to speak to User5 at extension 3005. If the receptionist transfers the call to voice mail, extension 3001's mailbox is selected. Chapter 9 describes a workaround configuration that allows your receptionist to transfer a call without ringing the destination extension (3005) while having the caller hear extension 3005's voice mail greeting.

Conferencing with voice mail being one of the endpoints usually happens when you are talking to a caller and you want to add another employee to the call. You initiate a conference to the extension, but that person is unavailable, and your conference consultative call forwards to voice mail. You can choose to drop the consultative call at that point, and return to the original caller. Or you can complete the conference and have both of you leave a combined voice message for the unavailable person. If you decide to leave a combined message, you must hang up at the end of the voice mail session, because there is no manual way to disconnect the voice mail endpoint from your conference call while preserving the other conference participants.

Transcoding

Cisco UE voice mail supports only G.711 voice streams. If you have a multisite network with voice over IP (VoIP) calling between the sites, it is likely that you are using G.729 between the sites to conserve bandwidth on your IP network. Figure 10-17 shows a call from extension 2010 at a remote site calling to extension 3001 at your site. The call uses G.729 as it crosses your WAN backbone. If extension 3001 does not answer and the call forwards to Cisco UE voice mail, the call must use G.711 for the caller to hear the voice mail greetings and prompts correctly. For this you need a transcoder device, as shown in Figure 10-17. Transcoding with Cisco CME is covered in greater detail in Chapter 7, "Connecting Multiple Cisco CMEs with VoIP" in the section "DSP Resources for Transcoding."

Figure 10-17 *Transcoding Calls into Voice Mail*

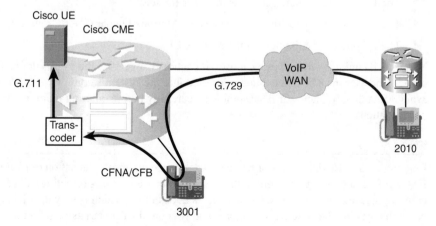

Transcoding can be classified as a call modification in the sense that the call is split into two call legs, each using a different codec. Each leg is terminated by a digital signal processor (DSP) hardware device. Yet transcoding is not a call modification in the same sense as the call forward, transfer, and conference features discussed earlier in this section. Transcoding a call does not alter the dialplan in any way and does not cause the last Redirected Number field to be changed. Therefore, it does not affect voice mailbox selection.

Working with Users and Names

The Cisco CME and Cisco UE configurations include various username fields. Understanding which Name field controls which aspect of your system helps you configure your Cisco IPC Express system, including voice mail, to the best benefit for your business.

Names are associated primarily with users, but also, in some specific cases, with phones. Cisco CME and Cisco UE mutually identify a user by a unique user ID field. Before discussing the various Name fields in more detail, it is necessary to understand how a Cisco IPC Express system handles user IDs.

User ID

A *user ID* is a tag the system uses to track and identify a user and his or her associated configuration. Cisco CME and Cisco UE use the user ID tag to coordinate configuration information about a specific user between the router's configuration (Cisco CME) and the configuration information stored on Cisco UE's local disk or Flash unit.

The user ID is a single configuration field, but it shows up in various locations in a Cisco IPC Express system configuration:

- The **Configure > Phones** screen as the Login Name field
- The **Configure > Users** screen as the User ID field
- The **Voice Mail > Mailboxes** screen as the Mailbox Owner (User/Group ID) field
- The ephone Username field in the router CLI

This user ID uniquely identifies each user. It cannot change after the user is defined. If it *must* change, the user must be deleted and reinserted into the system's configuration. You want to avoid doing this, so plan user ID assignments carefully before entering them into the system configuration.

CAUTION   Deleting a user also deletes his or her associated voice mailbox. The action of *changing* a user ID, therefore, amounts to redefining the user's mailbox and losing (deleting) all of the user's current voice mailbox contents. Clearly this is undesirable, which is why user IDs typically never change after the system is configured and your employees start using it for their daily tasks.

If a user preexists in the Cisco CME configuration before Cisco UE is installed and configured, this user ID is automatically imported from the Cisco CME configuration into the Cisco UE Initialization Wizard. (This wizard is further discussed in Chapter 13.)

NOTE   If the Cisco CME CLI **ephone-dn username** configuration is changed by using the router's CLI, and the Cisco UE GUI is then synchronized with the latest changes, a new user is created and shows up in the configuration. The mailbox associated with the old user definition cannot be moved to the new user.

Name Fields

You can configure various Name fields associated with a user or a phone. This information is contained in multiple fields so that you can control different aspects or features of your Cisco IPC Express system independently, because the features often serve different purposes. However, it is instructive to know which fields affect which features so that you know what part of the configuration to change to activate the feature you are interested in. The different name fields and how they are used are discussed in the following sections.

Name Display on an On-Hook Phone

A username is displayed in the top-right corner of an idle IP phone display. This name is associated with the user's extension, which appears on button 1 of that phone. The Name field shows the phone number (extension) by default, but it can be configured to show the name of the person at that phone. This field shows up in the following locations in the system configuration:

- The **Extension > Description** GUI screen
- The **ephone-dn description** configuration in the router CLI

Example 10-6 shows an ephone-dn configuration that shows Joe Blow on the display of his IP phone when the phone is idle. The phone display uses the **description** configuration to control the display, not the **name** configuration. Joe's extension is 3005. The fact that the **name** configuration is set to *Jonathan Bloe* does not affect the idle IP phone display. The **name** configuration affects other aspects of the system's operation, but it is not relevant to the name displayed on an idle phone.

Example 10-6 *Idle IP Phone Name Display*

```
router#show running-config
ephone-dn  5
 number 3005
 description Joe Blow
```

continues

Example 10-6 *Idle IP Phone Name Display (Continued)*

```
name Jonathan Bloe
call-forward busy 3105
call-forward noan 3105 timeout 10
```

Caller ID Name

When a call is ringing on an IP phone, the caller's name appears in the top-left corner of the called party's phone display. This field shows up in the following locations in the system configuration:

- The **Extension > Name** GUI screen
- The **ephone-dn name** field in the router CLI

Looking back at the configuration shown in Example 10-6, if the employee at extension 3005 calls you, you see *Jonathan Bloe* displayed on your ringing phone.

Extension Label

Extensions are associated with one or more buttons on your IP phone. By default, the extension number associated with each button is displayed on the idle phone console. Typically, this is your own extension on button 1 and additional extensions you monitor on higher-numbered buttons. You can configure a text string to be associated with a button. This field shows up in the following locations in the system configuration:

- The **Extension > Label** GUI screen
- The **ephone-dn label** field in the router CLI

Example 10-7 shows a configuration in which User2 has his own extension, 3002, on button 1 of his phone and extension 3050 on button 2. Extension 3002 (**ephone-dn 2**) has no label configured, so it shows up as 3002 on the phone display. Extension 3050 has a Customer Service label assigned, so this text string shows up next to button 2 on the phone.

Example 10-7 *IP Phone Button Labels*

```
router#show running-config
ephone-dn  2  dual-line
 number 3002
 name User2
 call-forward busy 3105
 call-forward noan 3105 timeout 10
!
ephone-dn  42
 number 3050 secondary 4445553050
 label Customer Service
 description Customer Service
 name Cust Svc
 call-forward busy 3501
 call-forward noan 3105 timeout 10
```

Example 10-7 *IP Phone Button Labels (Continued)*

```
!
ephone  2
  mac-address 0002.FD06.D959
  speed-dial 4 3100 label "AA"
  button  1:2 2:42
```

Dial-by-Name for Subscribers

The Cisco UE AA has a dial-by-name feature in which a caller can spell the name of the user he or she wants to reach, and the system looks up the associated extension. The same feature is available when a voice mail subscriber composes (or *sends*) a message to another subscriber. The message addressing can be done by using the Cisco UE dial-by-name feature. The Name field for this feature shows up in the following locations in the system configuration:

- The **User > First Name** GUI screen
- The **User > Last Name** GUI screen
- The **user fullname first** and **user fullname last** fields in the Cisco UE CLI

Example 10-8 shows the Cisco UE Dial-By-Name fields for User5.

Example 10-8 *Cisco UE Dial-by-Name Fields*

```
cue#show user detail username User5
Full Name:       Joey Blow
First Name:      Joey
Last Name:       Blow
Phone:           3005
Phone(E.164):    4445553005
```

Cisco UE's dial-by-name feature matches the Last Name field. If that field isn't unique, Cisco UE proceeds to match the First Name field in the configuration. This sequence cannot be changed or customized.

However, if the system operation desired is to have First Name and then Last Name matching, the fields in the configuration can simply be reversed. These fields are not used for any other features, so no name displays or phone displays are altered by transposing the First Name and Last Name fields underlying the dial-by-name feature.

NOTE   Note that the dial-by-name prompt in the system AA script continues to ask for the last name followed by the first name. This system prompt cannot be changed or customized. If you want to change the AA prompt as well, you have to write a custom AA script and record your own prompt, as covered in Chapter 9.

For example, suppose Joey (first name) Blow (last name) works for the company. In the normal configuration, dial-by-name matches Blow (the *last* name in the configuration) and then Joey (the *first* name in the configuration). If instead you want to have Joey matched first and then Blow in the dial-by-name applications, *Joey* has to be configured as the last name and *Blow* as the first name, as shown in Example 10-9.

Example 10-9 *Customizing the Cisco UE Dial-by-Name Fields*

```
cue#show user detail username User5
Full Name:        Joey Blow
First Name:       Blow
Last Name:        Joey
Phone:            3005
Phone(E.164):     4445553005
```

Dial-by-Name for Nonsubscribers

Your office may have users or employees who do not need a voice mailbox but who should be available via the dial-by-name feature in the AA. If so, you can enter these employees in the Cisco UE configuration as users without mailboxes. By virtue of the user profile (and its associated extension and phone), the employees appear in the Cisco UE Lightweight Directory Access Protocol (LDAP) directory and, therefore, are recognized by the dial-by-name feature in the AA. Note that without a mailbox defined, a user cannot have a spoken name recorded (because this configuration parameter is part of the mailbox definition). However, the names can be spelled via the dial-by-name facility and found in the database. If a spoken name does not exist, the system reads back the extension as confirmation to the caller.

NOTE   Users without a mailbox defined do not count against the Cisco UE license. However, the number of users allowed to be defined on the Cisco UE system is derived from the number of licensed mailboxes, and this may change over different software releases. Currently, in Cisco UE the number of users allowed to be defined on a system is set to twice the number of mailboxes specified by the license. For example, if a 12-mailbox license is installed on the Cisco UE system, a maximum of 24 user profiles can be defined in the configuration.

Spoken Name

When a call rings on an extension and then forwards into voice mail, the greeting may say, "Sorry. Joe Blow is unavailable," and then the caller can leave a message. If the user's spoken name is not recorded in the system, the greeting instead says, "Sorry. Extension 3005 is unavailable." The Spoken Name field shows up in the voice mailbox login as the option Spoken Name in the subscriber TUI menu. This field cannot be entered, viewed, or controlled via either the GUI or the CLI.

A subscriber can record a spoken name only if he or she has a mailbox on the Cisco UE system. Users who are accessible using the dial-by-name feature therefore might not have spoken names (because they do not necessarily have mailboxes). On the other hand, a user who has a spoken name must have a mailbox and, therefore, must have a user profile and must be accessible in the dial-by-name feature.

Dial Plan Considerations

Cisco UE deployed with Cisco CME requires that the IP phones that have mailboxes all have extensions of the same length. The specific length of the extension does not matter: the length of the extensions can be anywhere between one and 16 digits (as supported by Cisco CME). What is important is that all extensions with mailboxes must be of the *same* length on a particular Cisco CME and Cisco UE system.

Chapter 7 covered various ways in which you can manipulate digits on dialed numbers to translate PSTN numbers (E.164 numbers) into local extensions:

- Cisco IOS dial peer commands
- Cisco IOS translation rules
- Cisco CME dial plan pattern commands

Another way to configure the mapping from PSTN numbers to internal extensions is by using the E.164 number configuration of Cisco CME and Cisco UE. These fields essentially associate a second number—the fully qualified E.164 number—with the extension or mailbox so that dialing either number terminates on the correct extension or mailbox.

Cisco CME has a Secondary Number field, as shown in Example 10-10. You can access this same field by using the GUI by navigating to the **Configure > Extensions** screen. Filling in the Secondary Number field on that screen associates an additional number with the extension so that calls dialing the extension directly (likely other IP phones) and calls dialing the DID number (likely PSTN callers) terminate on the phone without further dialing plan assistance.

Example 10-10 *Cisco CME Secondary Number Field*

```
Router#show running-config
ephone-dn  1
 number 6001 secondary 5103953001
 description Grace Garrett
 name Grace Garrett
 call-forward busy 6800
 call-forward noan 6800 timeout 10
```

The effect of configuring the Secondary Number field is that an E.164 PSTN number can terminate directly on an extension without digit manipulation of the called digits. If this call forwards into Cisco UE voice mail, the Called Digits field still contains the full E.164 number, which must be recognized by Cisco UE as a mailbox owner. This requires the configuration of the Cisco UE E.164 field.

Cisco UE has a Primary E.164 Number field that you can also access by navigating to the Configure > Users screen in the GUI and clicking a specific user to highlight that person's parameters. Filling in this field associates an additional number with the user (and therefore the user's mailbox) so that calls dialing this number directly can enter the mailbox for the correct user.

Voice Mail Networking

Cisco UE release 2.0 introduced basic voice mail networking between systems using blind addressing, and release 2.1 enhances this functionality with spoken-name and limited dial-by-name addressing using a local directory and cache. You can network voice mail messaging between Cisco UE systems at different sites, as well as with Cisco Unity systems, using Voice Profile for Internet Mail (VPIM) connectivity between the systems. Cisco UE does not support networking with any voice messaging systems other than Cisco UE and Cisco Unity systems.

You can configure Cisco UE networking using either Domain Name System (DNS) host names or explicit IP addressing. If you are networking with a Cisco Unity system, you must use a DNS configuration.

The following sections provide a brief overview of Cisco UE voice mail networking operation, including the following topics:

- Applicable standards
- Definition of network locations
- Voice mail network location addressing
- Directories
- Network broadcast messaging
- Message formats
- Nondelivery notification

Standards

Voice mail networking uses the following Internet Engineering Task Force (IETF) standards:

- RFC 3801, *Voice Profile for Internet Mail - Version 2 (VPIMv2)*
- RFC 2821, *Simple Mail Transfer Protocol (SMTP)*
- RFCs 2045–2049, *Multipurpose Internet Mail Extensions (MIME) Part One: Format of Internet Message Bodies*
- RFC 822, *Standard for the Format of ARPA Internet Text Messages*

The Simple Mail Transfer Protocol (SMTP) and Multipurpose Internet Mail Extension (MIME) protocols are the basic protocols used to send and receive e-mail. Voice mail networking leverages the exact same protocols and infrastructure. The primary attributes of a voice mail (compared to an e-mail) are the address (voice mail uses a phone number and e-mail uses a user ID) and the message's payload type (voice mail uses an encoded form of a .wav file, and e-mail uses other formats, including text).

Cisco Unity is a unified messaging system and provides both voice mail and e-mail networking. Cisco UE (up to release 2.1) is only a voice messaging system. It does not provide any way to address, send, or receive e-mail messages.

Although Cisco UE's voice mail networking implementation is compliant with the VPIM standard, the entire RFC is not supported. Cisco UE and Cisco Unity also implement some extensions to VPIM to provide features such as broadcast messaging between sites that are not specified by the standard.

You can find more information on Internet Engineering Task Force (IETF) standards at http://www.ietf.org/.

Locations

You can enable voice mail networking by configuring the parameters of the locations in the network, including the local location and all remote locations that this site can exchange messages with. The network has no central directory or proxy location. Each Cisco UE site must be configured with the identities of the other locations in the network that it can send messages to or receive messages from. For security reasons, Cisco UE does not accept (receive) messages from any sites other than those configured in its database as a valid networking location.

Each location is defined in the Cisco UE configuration with the following parameters:

- **ID**—A unique one- to seven-digit numeric identifier assigned to each site. The location ID is a sequence of digits that must be dialed before the extension when addressing a message to a remote site via the TUI. It is only locally significant (to select which remote site is being addressed) and is not sent with the VPIM message.

- **Abbreviation**—A one- to five-character alphanumeric abbreviated name for the location. This is spelled to the user as part of address confirmation if a spoken name for the location was not recorded or is unavailable.

- **Name**—A one- to five-character descriptive name for the location. Used only for human readability of the configuration information.

- **Extension Length**—The number of digits in extensions at this location. Used for a level-of-error checking in blind addressing.

- **Domain Name of IP Address**—This part of the address appears after the @ when messages are addressed. For example, for the VPIM address 34001@site2.xyz.com, site2.xyz.com is the domain name. This can be a DNS host name or an explicit IP address.

- **Phone Number Prefix (optional)**—A digit prefix added to the extension number to ensure that VPIM addresses are unique in the network. If your extensions are already unique (nonoverlapping), you generally do not have to configure this field. You can use the field to do a limited amount of digit manipulation on the extension portion of the VPIM address. Phone prefixes are prepended to the extension by the sending location and are removed from the address by the receiving location. Phone prefixes apply to both the To and From address fields in the VPIM header.

- **Spoken Name (optional)**—Specifies whether to send the spoken name of the voice mail originator as part of the VPIM message. If the spoken name is sent, it is played as the first part of the message envelope to the recipient. This feature is enabled by default.

- **Message Encoding (optional)**—Configures the encoding method used to send voice mail messages to this location. This is discussed further in the later section "Message Formats."

As soon as you have defined all the locations in the configuration, you indicate which one of these locations represents your local system by configuring the local location ID to match one of the locations in the list. A configuration with five sites is shown in Example 10-11. You can view this same configuration in the GUI by navigating to the **Administration > Networking Locations** screen. The local location is ID 888. This exact same configuration also appears in sites 222, 333, 444, and 666, except that their local location IDs are indicated as 222, 333, 444, and 666, respectively.

Example 10-11 *Network Location Configuration*

```
cue#show network locations
ID        NAME                        ABBREV DOMAIN
222       'Site2'                     S2     site2.xyz.com
333       'Site3'                     S3     site3.xyz.com
444       'Site4'                     S4     site4.xyz.com
666       'Site6'                     S6     site6.xyz.com
888       'Site8'                     S8     site8.xyz.com
Local location id: 888
```

Example 10-12 shows the full configuration parameters of site 888 from the configuration summary in Example 10-11.

Example 10-12 *Site8 Networking Parameters*

```
cue#show network detail local
Location Id:                        888
Name:                               Site8
Abbreviation:                       S8
Email domain:                       site8.xyz.com
Minimum extension length:           4
Maximum extension length:           4
Phone prefix:
VPIM encoding:                      dynamic
Send spoken name:                   enabled
```

Example 10-12 *Site8 Networking Parameters (Continued)*

```
Send vCard:                  enabled
State:                       enabled
VPIM broadcast ID:           vpim-broadcast
```

Up to 500 sites may be defined on a Cisco UE system for voice mail networking.

Addressing

A voice message to another site can be addressed in one of the following methods:

- **Blind addressing**—The sender explicitly specifies the location ID and the recipient's extension at that location.

- **Spell-by-name**—The spell-by-name message sends facility searches for matches in both the local Cisco UE user directory and the remote user information available in the sender's local system directory, as described in the next section.

- **Spell-by-location**—If a sender uses the spell-by-name feature, but the name spelled matches a location name instead of the name of subscriber, the sender is prompted to add the recipient's extension digits to complete the addressing.

As the Cisco UE system administrator, you can record spoken names for remote locations so that when a subscriber addresses a message to a remote location, the address confirmation is not just simply numeric or the spelled-out abbreviation you configured, but plays the recorded name associated with that location. For example, if a sender on Site2 addresses a message to extension 4001 at Site4, the address confirmation he or she hears says "San Jose" as opposed to just "444" or "S-4." You can record these spoken names to make it as easy as possible for your subscribers to address messages correctly.

Directories

Cisco UE keeps a small amount of information on remote users to aid in spoken-name confirmation during message addressing at the sending location. The Cisco UE system reads the remote user's location ID and extension by default as the address confirmation to the local sender during the message addressing step. If a spoken name has been recorded for the remote location, it is played instead of the location ID. If the remote user's spoken name exists in the networking directory on the sender's local system, it is played instead of the extension.

A Cisco UE system keeps the following two local directories of information about remote users to provide spell-by-name and spoken-name confirmation support during a subscriber message send activity:

- **Static directory**—This directory is populated explicitly by the administrator with the names and extensions of frequently addressed remote users. You can enter this configuration by using the **Configure > Remote Users GUI** screen or the **remote username** CLI command.

- **Cache**—A least-recently-used (LRU) cache of entries is kept, dynamically populated by the names on the incoming voice messages received by this Cisco UE system.

Messages sent by Cisco UE contain vCard information. On the receiving system, the Vcard information on an incoming voice message is used to populate or refresh the information in the local and LRU cache directories.

The static directory and the LRU cache each have a capacity of 50 user entries on an NM-CUE and 20 entries on an AIM-CUE.

Network Broadcast Messages

Cisco UE supports sending broadcast messages to remote sites. All remote sites or a subset of remote sites can be selected in the addressing of a broadcast message. If a broadcast message is sent to a remote site, all users at that site receive the message.

Message Formats

The VPIM specifies G.726 (32K adaptive differential pulse code modulation [ADPCM]) encoding. Cisco UE supports two formats of message encoding, which can be selected in the configuration of each site:

- **G.726**—Messages are converted to G.726 for transmission to a remote system. Although this format uses half the bandwidth of the G.711 format, VPIM voice messages are sent like e-mails (which means best-effort, non real-time-sensitive traffic), and bandwidth typically is not a concern.

- **G.711**—Messages are sent as .wav file format to the remote system. This format reduces the overhead of encoding and decoding messages between systems. This format is used when exchanging messages between two Cisco UE systems.

When you configure the message encoding for a Cisco UE site, you can choose either of the two methods explicitly, or you can use the default setting, which is dynamic. This was shown earlier in Example 10-12 as the VPIM encoding field. The dynamic option means that Cisco UE automatically determines which of the two formats to use. If the destination system is another Cisco UE, it uses the G.711 format. If the destination system is a Cisco Unity system, it uses the G.726 format.

If you configure the encoding method explicitly, Cisco UE always sends messages in the configured format to the corresponding remote site. When configured with the dynamic option, Cisco UE sends messages based on the capabilities advertised by the remote system in the SMTP session setup.

Nondelivery Notification

Cisco UE attempts to send a message to a remote destination immediately. If it isn't successful, it retries every 15 minutes for 6 hours. If a message cannot be delivered during this time, a notification is returned to the sender and is placed in the sender's voice mailbox. This notification appears as a new message and informs the sending subscriber of a delayed delivery. Similarly, if the message cannot be delivered for reasons such as the recipient's mailbox is full, does not exist, or is disabled, an NDR is placed in the sender's mailbox along with a copy of the original message. When the subscriber plays the NDR, he or she can readdress and resend the message or delete it.

If Cisco UE is unable to create an SMTP session for one day to deliver remote messages, an NDR message is returned to the message sender, as well as to the administrator's mailbox to inform him or her of a networking problem.

Voice Mail Deployment Considerations

Cisco IPC Express deployment options were covered in Chapter 2, "Building a Cisco IPC Express Network." Three primary deployment models with Cisco CME and voice mail using Cisco UE were discussed:

- Standalone office
- Multisite business or enterprise
- Service provider managed multisite network

You can deploy Cisco CME without Cisco UE, either completely without an AA or voice mail, or with alternate voice mail solutions, as covered in Chapter 11. However, Cisco UE was specifically designed to provide these applications with Cisco CME. It offers the greatest breadth of features and the highest level of integration.

You can choose to deploy Cisco UE at only some sites in your network, while the remaining sites have either no voice mail or have voice mail provided by Cisco Unity or an alternate system. As explained in the preceding section, Cisco UE can network voice messages with other Cisco UE sites as well as with Cisco Unity sites.

Before Cisco UE release 2.0, if Cisco UE and Cisco CME were deployed together at a site, they had to be present in the same router chassis. As of Cisco UE release 2.0, you can house Cisco UE on a router that is physically separate from the one that provides Cisco CME call processing services to your site. This is not a likely or preferred deployment option, but in some cases, you may have an existing router you want to redeploy, and it does not have enough slots to add Cisco UE into the chassis. In this case, you can run Cisco CME on one router and physically house Cisco UE on a different router at the same site.

Ensure that LAN connectivity exists between the two routers, however, as opposed to low-speed serial connectivity. Also, Cisco UE can provide voice mail to only a single Cisco CME site. You cannot "centralize" one Cisco UE system to provide voice mail to multiple remote Cisco CME sites, as you can do with a Cisco Unity system.

Summary

This chapter discussed the voice mail capabilities provided by the Cisco UE aspect of the Cisco IPC Express solution. The operation of the voice mail features was discussed from a subscriber, caller, and administrator point of view. System-level features such as storage options, as well as typical voice mail activities, such as sending and addressing messages, were also covered.

This chapter explained how to configure Name fields in Cisco CME and Cisco UE to tailor the phone displays, dial-by-name options, and directories in your office. The configuration and operation of voice mail networking between sites was discussed to help you network your sites into a cohesive business.

You should now have a good understanding of the features Cisco UE provides and how to tailor the system to your needs for call flows, name displays, and the general operation of your office. The internals of the application and how to troubleshoot potential problems are covered later in this book.

This chapter covers the following topics:

- Cisco Unity voice mail
- Stonevoice voice mail
- Analog voice mail
- Public Switched Telephone Network (PSTN)-based voice mail

## CHAPTER 11

Cisco CME External Voice Mail Options

Cisco Unity Express (UE) voice mail was covered in Chapter 10, "Cisco IPC Express Integrated Voice Mail." It represents the integrated voice mail system recommended for use with Cisco CallManager Express (CME). However, you also have the option to deploy one of several external voice mail systems with Cisco CME. You might want to consider one of these voice mail options for your office in the following situations:

- If you are using a Cisco CME platform, such as the Cisco 1760-V, that does not support Cisco UE (although you could use a separate router to house Cisco UE as of release 2.0)

- If your Cisco CME router platform does not have any available slots to add the Cisco UE hardware

- If you require features such as unified messaging that are not yet available with Cisco UE

- If you want to deploy a centralized voice mail system to support multiple Cisco CME sites instead of a distributed voice mail option at each site

- If you have an existing legacy voice mail system that you want to continue to use

This chapter briefly reviews the external voice mail options available for use with Cisco CME. These options include the Cisco Unity voice mail system and several non-Cisco systems that integrate with Cisco CME via either H.323 voice over IP (VoIP) or an analog phone interface.

Cisco Unity Voice Mail

Cisco Unity is a Windows 2000 server-based IP unified messaging system. Cisco Unity scales up to several thousand users and typically is deployed in a central or campus site of an enterprise network with a Cisco CallManager providing the call control.

| NOTE | Note that Cisco Unity and Cisco UE are two different voice mail systems. Cisco UE is a hardware module installed inside the Cisco CME router scaling up to 100 voice mailboxes, whereas Cisco Unity is a separate Windows server platform scaling up to thousands of users. |

Cisco Unity's unified messaging capabilities allow you to integrate voice mail, e-mail, and faxes into the same end-user mailbox. The mailbox operation is highly customizable via call handlers. Cisco Unity provides options for integrating with the Microsoft Outlook or Lotus Notes mail architectures. Cisco Unity leverages Active Directory to access your network's user and location directory.

Although Cisco Unity's unified messaging features provide many productivity-enhancing applications such as Cisco Personal Assistant and text-to-speech support, you can also choose to deploy it as a voice mail-only system. Cisco Personal Assistant is a telephony application suite that streamlines communications by helping users manage how and where they can be reached.

Different levels of licensing are available with Cisco Unity for a voice mail-only deployment or a full unified messaging system. Cisco Unity is a sophisticated messaging system with robust failover and networking options. A full discussion of its capabilities is beyond the scope of this book, but you can consult Cisco.com and search for "Cisco Unity" to find more information.

Cisco Unity uses IP as the transport and Skinny Client Control Protocol (SCCP) for call control, appearing to Cisco CME as an IP phone (SCCP) endpoint. Cisco Unity can support a single Cisco CME in a standalone deployment or can be deployed at a central site in your network with multiple Cisco CMEs at remote sites in a centralized voice mail scenario. These architectures are discussed further in the following sections.

NOTE Cisco CME is Cisco IOS-based, whereas Cisco Unity is a Windows 2000-based application; therefore, users considering this combination of applications should have a good working knowledge of both operating systems. Cisco Unity uses Microsoft Exchange (5.5, 2000, and 2003) or Lotus Domino mail stores, so familiarity with these technologies is also beneficial.

Standalone Cisco CME System with Cisco Unity

You can connect a standalone Cisco CME with a dedicated Cisco Unity system to provide unified or voice mail services to a single site. Though technically feasible, this is often not a cost-effective way to deploy Cisco Unity. Cisco Unity is an application designed to support large numbers of users, whereas Cisco CME can support only up to 240 users. Figure 11-1 shows how Cisco CME is connected to the Cisco Unity system.

Although Cisco CME functions as the call control system for taking care of IP phone and PSTN calls, Cisco Unity provides the voice mail services. Cisco Unity communicates with Cisco CME using the SCCP protocol emulating IP phone endpoints.

Figure 11-1 *Standalone Cisco CME with Cisco Unity Messaging*

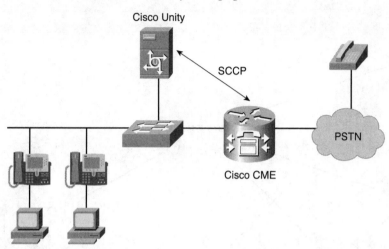

Multiple Cisco CME Systems with a Centralized Cisco Unity

A much more typical and cost-effective model of using Cisco Unity with Cisco CME is as a centralized messaging system to several remote Cisco CME sites. Figure 11-2 shows multiple Cisco CME systems distributed across several smaller sites connected to a shared, centralized Cisco Unity system. A Cisco CME system at the central site collocated with the Cisco Unity server is required. This Cisco CME relays both voice and Message Waiting Indicator (MWI) to the remote sites.

A centralized Cisco Unity system offers several advantages:

- It eases the management and provisioning of voice mail.

- It provides a single integrated user directory that eases sending voice mail and setting up distribution lists across users physically located at different sites.

- It facilitates forwarding and replying to voice messages without requiring networking of the distributed voice mail systems between the individual sites.

- It conserves valuable bandwidth by not forwarding and replying to voice mails between users resident at different sites.

Configuring Cisco CME for Cisco Unity

Cisco Unity integrates with Cisco CME as SCCP-controlled IP phone endpoints. Each voice mail port on Cisco Unity is configured as an ephone on Cisco CME, and the voice mail pilot number is configured as an ephone-dn that appears on each of the phones (ports).

Figure 11-2   *Multiple Cisco CME Systems with Cisco Unity Messaging*

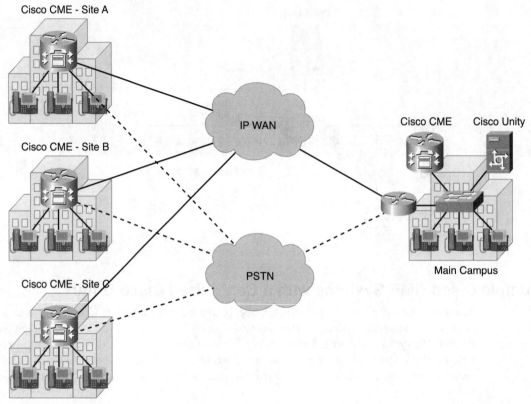

The Cisco Unity ports register with the Cisco CME router using a voice mail device ID (vm-device-id) such as Cisco UM-VI2. Example 11-1 shows the Cisco CME configuration for connecting to a four-port Cisco Unity voice mail system.

Example 11-1   *Cisco CME Configuration for Cisco Unity Ports*

```
router#show running-config
telephony-service
 voicemail 6800
!
ephone-dn 32
 number 6800
 name "VM Port 1"
 preference 0
 no huntstop
!
ephone-dn 33
 number 6800
 name "VM port 2"
```

Example 11-1 *Cisco CME Configuration for Cisco Unity Ports (Continued)*

```
 preference 1
 no huntstop
!
ephone-dn  34
 number 6800
 name "VM port 3"
 preference 2
 no huntstop
!
ephone-dn  35
 number 6800
 preference 3
 name "VM Port 4"

ephone  5
 vm-device-id CiscoUM-VI1
 button  1:32
!
ephone  6
 vm-device-id CiscoUM-VI2
 button  1:33
!
ephone  7
 vm-device-id CiscoUM-VI3
 button  1:34
!
ephone  8
 vm-device-id CiscoUM-VI4
 button  1:35
```

The **voicemail 6800** command defines the voice mail pilot number as extension 6800. You can define an ephone-dn for each of the four ports; these definitions control call routing to Cisco Unity. All the ephone-dns have 6800 as the extension and are tagged with **preference 0** to **preference 3**. You need four individual ephone-dns, one per port, to route and deliver four calls to the Cisco Unity system simultaneously. From Cisco CME's point of view, four IP phones have an appearance of extension 6800; therefore, four individual calls to 6800 can be busy at the same time.

The **preference** and **no huntstop** designations ensure that the Cisco CME system hunts across the available phones if some of them are busy.

Each of the physical ports is defined as an ephone. To Cisco CME, Cisco Unity ports look like an IP phone, and they register as such. The vm-device-id (for example, Cisco UM-VI2) defined for each ephone must match the device ID configured in the Cisco Unity configuration.

You configure call forwarding to voice mail on your employee's IP phones exactly as you would for Cisco UE, as shown in Example 11-2.

Example 11-2 *Call Forwarding to Cisco Unity Voice Mail*

```
router#show running-config
ephone-dn  1
 number 6001
 call-forward busy 6800
 call-forward noan 6800 timeout 10
```

With the configurations given in the previous examples, users on your system can press the messages button on their IP phones to retrieve their voice mail. They can also call the voice mail pilot number 6800 directly—for example, from the PSTN—to access their voice mail.

MWI

MWI with Cisco Unity is accomplished via outdial directory numbers (DNs), similar to the architecture with Cisco UE (but not configured in exactly the same way). Cisco CME defines two MWI DNs, one for turning on MWI and another for turning it off. Cisco Unity outdials to one of these numbers to control the phone's MWI state. This configuration is shown in Example 11-3.

Example 11-3 *MWI Configuration for Cisco Unity Voice Mail*

```
router#show running-config
ephone-dn  30
 number 8000
 mwi on
!
ephone-dn  31
 number 8001
 mwi off
```

The extension for which MWI must be turned on or off is derived from the caller ID (the number of the call's originator) provided in the SCCP message received by Cisco CME. Cisco Unity populates the appropriate caller ID in the SCCP message sent to Cisco CME when it initiates the call to one of the MWI DNs. Cisco CME then uses this caller ID to determine which IP phone on the system should receive MWI and sends a separate SCCP message to the phone(s) to turn its MWI on or off.

The MWI configuration for Cisco Unity differs from that of Cisco UE in two important ways:

- For Cisco UE, the MWI DN requires wildcard dots following the MWI extension number (as many dots as you have digits in your extensions). For four-digit extensions, the MWI DN for Cisco UE would specify **number 8000....** instead of the **number 8000** command used for Cisco Unity.

- For Cisco UE, the IP phone extension for which MWI must be turned on or off is derived from the digits that match the dots just described—that is, from the *called number* of the outgoing call to the MWI DN. For Cisco Unity, the IP phone extension is derived from the *calling number* of the outgoing call to the MWI DN.

MWI Relay

Cisco Unity physically integrates only with the single Cisco CME that is collocated with it. All the Cisco Unity ports register with this Cisco CME system. To get Cisco Unity to support voice mail for users of Cisco CME systems at remote sites, certain information must be relayed via the central Cisco CME that is physically connected to Cisco Unity.

Calls to Cisco Unity to leave or retrieve messages can be freely routed across your network between the sites based on your dial plan. The relay mechanism comes into play only for getting MWI notifications to an IP phone at a remote site.

Cisco CME contains an MWI relay mechanism that is configured at the central Cisco CME (the one with the MWI DNs that Cisco Unity dials). The central Cisco CME cannot send an SCCP message directly to an IP phone that is registered with a different Cisco CME system. Instead, it uses a Session Initiation Protocol (SIP) subscribe/notify mechanism to notify the remote Cisco CME of an MWI change. The remote Cisco CME system (where the IP phone is registered) then sends an SCCP message to the phone to change its MWI state. This configuration is shown in Figure 11-3.

Figure 11-3   *MWI Relay with Cisco Unity*

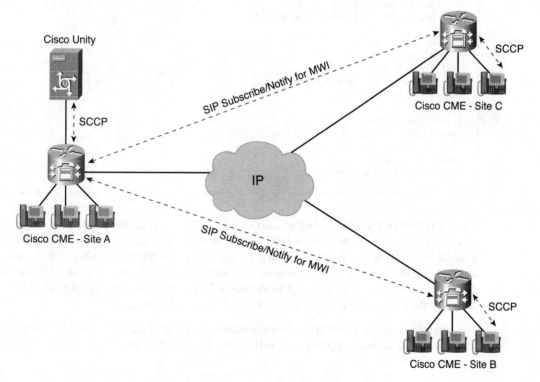

The MWI relay configuration at the central Cisco CME (site A) is shown in Example 11-4.

Example 11-4 *MWI Relay Configuration for the Central Site*

```
router#show running-config
telephony-service
   ip source-address 10.10.10.1
   mwi relay
   mwi expires 99999
   voicemail 6800
```

The **mwi relay** command lets the Cisco CME router relay the MWI information to a remote IP phone. The **mwi expires** command sets the expiry timer for the SIP subscribe/notify registration.

The MWI relay configuration at one of the remote Cisco CME sites (for example, site B) is shown in Example 11-5.

Example 11-5 *MWI Relay Configuration for a Remote Site*

```
router#show running-config
telephony-service
   ip source-address 20.20.20.10
   mwi sip-server 10.10.10.1 transport tcp
!
ephone-dn 1
   number 2000
   mwi sip
   call-forward noan 6800 timeout 10
   call-forward busy 6800
!
dial-peer voice 101 voip
   destination-pattern 6800
   session target ipv4:10.10.10.1
   codec g711ulaw
   dtmf-relay h245-alphanumeric
   no vad
```

The **mwi sip-server** command instructs the Cisco CME at site B to subscribe to the SIP server on Cisco CME site A (IP address 10.10.10.1 in Example 11-4). Each of the ephone-dns at sites B and C must contain the **mwi sip** command to ensure that the controlling Cisco CME system knows that this phone's MWI is controlled via a SIP notification from another site. As soon as the configuration is entered, the **show mwi relay clients** command at the site A Cisco CME shows all the extensions subscribed to the Cisco CME site A SIP server.

The dial peer shown in Example 11-5 ensures that users at site B can dial 6800 (the voice mail pilot number). The call is routed across VoIP to site A, where the Cisco Unity system is located.

Stonevoice Voice Mail

Cisco CME can integrate with various non-Cisco voice mail systems using H.323. One of the H.323 voice systems supported by Cisco CME is the Stonevoice Switch Answering Machine (SSAM), a unified messaging system designed to provide access to and control over software-based voice mail services.

SSAM is a Windows 2000-based application that runs on an external PC. All traffic between Cisco CME and SSAM uses H.323. Figure 11-4 shows how the Stonevoice SSAM application integrates with Cisco CME.

Figure 11-4   *Cisco CME with Stonevoice SSAM Voice Mail*

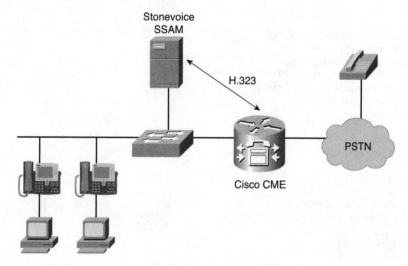

When integrated with CME, SSAM supports the following:

- Direct access to voice mail
- Call forward no answer (CFNA) or call forward busy (CFB) to a personal greeting
- MWI

For more information on the SSAM system, go to http://www.stonevoice.com/.

The following sections provide more details on integrating a Stonevoice system with Cisco CME, including

- Configuring Cisco CME for Stonevoice
- MWI from Stonevoice

Configuring Cisco CME for Stonevoice

Communication between Cisco CME and SSAM is via H.323, so you have to configure an H.323 dial peer to direct calls into the SSAM system. You must configure a voice mail pilot number (for example, 9999) on SSAM for message retrieval and an individual voice mail number for each extension (ephone-dn). Because the original called number (the IP phone extension) is not preserved when the call is forwarded to SSAM via H.323, you must embed this information in the called number (the call forward number) delivered to SSAM.

Example 11-6 shows a sample Cisco CME configuration defining a voice mail pilot number of 9999 (used when you press the messages button on your IP phone), voice mail number 9001 for extension 1001, and 9002 for extension 1002.

Example 11-6 *Configuring Cisco CME for SSAM*

```
router#show running-config
dial-peer voice 100 voip
 destination-pattern 9...
 session target ipv4:172.19.153.120
 dtmf-relay h245-alphanumeric
 codec g711ulaw
 no vad
!
telephony-service
 voicemail 9999
!
ephone-dn  1
 number 1001
 call-forward busy 9001
 call-forward noan 9001 timeout 10
!
ephone-dn  2
  number 1002
  call-forward busy 9002
  call-forward noan 9002 timeout 10
```

The voice dial peer command **destination-pattern 9**... ensures that all calls to 9999, 9001, and 9002 are directed to SSAM via H.323. The IP address 172.19.153.120 in this example belongs to the SSAM system.

The **voicemail 9999** command under **telephony service** is the voice mail pilot number used when you press the messages button on your IP phone. This number must match the "Voicemail number" parameter on the SSAM Modify IP Telephony System page.

Individual voice mail forwarding numbers are defined for each extension. These are used in the **call-forward busy** and **call-forward noan** fields of the ephone-dn Cisco CME configuration. These numbers must be configured on the SSAM system for each individual user. For example, for the person on ephone-dn 1, you configure his or her extension (1001) in the "First extension number" field, and configure 9001 in the "Voicemail number" field of the SSAM Account Management page for this user.

MWI

MWI is controlled by the SSAM system outdialing with H.323 to a Cisco CME MWI DN. The extension for which the MWI must be turned on or off is embedded in the dialed number. The Cisco CME configuration for this is shown in Example 11-7.

Example 11-7   *Configuring MWI for SSAM*

```
router#show running-config
ephone-dn  11
 number 8000*....*1 secondary 8000*....*2
 mwi on-off
 no huntstop
 !
ephone-dn  12
 number 8000*....*1 secondary 8000*....*2
 mwi on-off
 preference 1
```

You should configure as many of these MWI ephone-dns as you have "ports" on the SSAM system so that the maximum number of simultaneous calls can be handled correctly. Use the Cisco CME **preference** and **no huntstop** command designations to make sure the Cisco CME system hunts across any available MWI ephone-dns.

When the SSAM system makes an outgoing call to Cisco CME, the MWI information is embedded in the called party's telephone number—for example, 8000*1001*1 or 8000*1001*2. The 8000 is the MWI DN's number, and the asterisks are used as delimiters. The extension for which MWI should be turned on or off is contained between the asterisks, and the final digit in the string specifies whether MWI is on (1) or off (2).

The notation 8000*....*1 in the ephone-dn definition accepts any extension number and represents the extension digits that Cisco CME extracts to determine for which IP phone to turn MWI on or off. The MWI on (ending in digit 1) and MWI off (ending in digit 2) strings are given on the same ephone-dn as the primary and secondary extensions on that ephone-dn, as shown in Example 11-7.

Analog Voice Mail

You can integrate Cisco CME with analog systems to provide voice mail services, as shown in Figure 11-5. In general, these systems connect to the Cisco CME via Foreign Exchange Station (FXS) analog phone interfaces. Each port is configured as a normal plain old telephone service (POTS) dial peer in Cisco CME.

Figure 11-5 *Cisco CME with Analog Voice Mail*

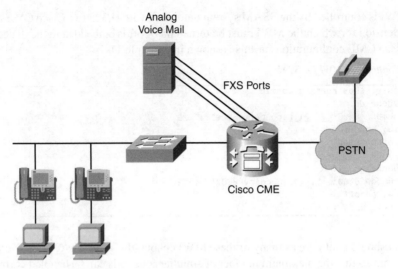

Cisco CME interacts with the analog voice mail system via inband dual-tone multifrequency (DTMF) tones. All call routing and MWI information exchanged between Cisco CME and the voice mail system also occurs via DTMF tones.

When integrated with Cisco CME, an analog voice mail system provides the following:

- Direct access to voice mail
- CFNA or CFB to a personal greeting
- MWI

Many types of analog voice mail systems are available. The Octel system from Avaya and the Reception system from Active Voice, LLC are two of the more popular models. The following sections discuss Cisco CME integration with these systems.

Octel

Integrating the Octel voice mail system with Cisco CME requires configuration on both systems. The configuration sample in Example 11-8 shows how to configure the CME.

Example 11-8 *Cisco CME Configuration for Octel Analog Integration*

```
router#show running-config
call application voice bator flash:app-h450-transfer.2.0.0.9.tcl
call application voice bator language 1 en
call application voice bator set-location en 0 flash:/prompts
!
voice-port 1/0/0
```

Example 11-8 *Cisco CME Configuration for Octel Analog Integration (Continued)*

```
 caller-id enable
 !
 voice-port 1/0/1
  caller-id enable
 !
 dial-peer voice 5000 pots
  application bator
  destination-pattern 5000.....
  port 1/0/0
 !
 telephony-service
  voicemail 5000
  transfer-system full-consult
 !
 vm-integration
  pattern direct 2 CGN
  pattern ext-to-ext no-answer 5 CGN * FDN
  pattern ext-to-ext busy 7 CGN * FDN
  pattern trunk-to-ext no-answer 5 CGN * FDN
  pattern trunk-to-ext busy 7 CGN * FDN
 !
 ephone-dn  1
  number 1000
  call-forward busy 5000
  call-forward noan 5000 timeout 5
  application bator
  no huntstop
 !
 ephone-dn  2
  number 1001
  call-forward busy 5000
  call-forward noan 5000 timeout 5
  application bator
 !
 ephone-dn  100
  number 3000*....*
  mwi on
 !
 ephone-dn  101
  number 3001*....*
  mwi off
```

The Toolkit Command Language (TCL) application (called bator in the preceding configuration) is used to support a hookflash operation on the FXS ports. FXS port 1/0/0 is used for voice mail access, so the POTS dial peer points to this port. Port 1/0/1 is used for MWI operation.

The series of **vm-integration** commands specifies the DTMF digit strings to be generated to the analog voice mail system to control feature operation, such as selecting which greeting (external or internal, or busy or no answer) to play to the caller. The MWI DNs have asterisk delimiters surrounding the wildcards that match the extension number for which MWI must be turned on or off.

Note the following restrictions when integrating an Octel system with Cisco CME:

- One FXS port must be dedicated for MWI operation.

- The Octel system must have analog ports and must be configured for analog DTMF integration. Digital and Simplified Message Desk Interface (SMDI) integration with CME is not supported.

- The Octel system does not distinguish between extension-to-extension and trunk-to-extension transfers. Thus, you must configure the DTMF patterns for these transfers with the same values on the Cisco CME system.

- The MWI ephone-dn must use the . wildcard rather than the T wildcard to specify the exact extension length. Also, you must use an asterisk before and after configuring the called party ID (for example, **number 3000*....***).

Active Voice Reception

The Reception system from Active Voice, LLC is another popular voice mail system. To allow calls to be forwarded to the Reception system, you must configure Cisco CME with four different DTMF patterns for the following four possible call flows:

- Extension-to-extension no answer

- Extension-to-extension busy

- Extension-to-trunk no answer

- Extension-to-trunk busy

When the Reception system receives the DTMF pattern, it plays the corresponding voice mail prompt.

Example 11-9 shows how to configure Cisco CME to work with the Reception voice mail system.

Example 11-9 *Cisco CME Configuration for Reception Analog Integration*

```
router#show running-config
voice-port 1/0/0
 caller-id enable
!
voice-port 1/0/1
 caller-id enable
!
dial-peer voice 5000 pots
 application bator
 destination-pattern 6800.....
 port 1/0/0
!
```

Example 11-9   *Cisco CME Configuration for Reception Analog Integration (Continued)*

```
telephony-service
 voicemail 6800
!
vm-integration
 pattern direct 2 CGN *
 pattern ext-to-ext no-answer 5 FDN * CGN *
 pattern ext-to-ext busy 7 FDN * CGN *
 pattern trunk-to-ext no-answer 4 FDN * CGN *
 pattern trunk-to-ext busy 6 FDN * CGN *
!
phone-dn  2
 number 3002
 call-forward busy 6800
 call-forward noan 6800 timeout 10
!
ephone-dn  25
 number A1.....*
 mwi on
!
ephone-dn  26
 number A2.....*
 mwi off
```

PSTN-Based Voice Mail

Another option for voice mail with Cisco CME is through your PSTN provider. The call flows to the voice mail from your PSTN provider are controlled by the central office (CO) PSTN switch. If the lines to your business are busy or don't answer, the voice mail system at the CO picks up and stores the senders' voice messages at the voice mail storage located at the CO. You do not need to configure Cisco CME for this type of voice mail. You do need to configure MWI, however.

CO-based voice mail systems signal MWI by using stutter dial tone. When you go off-hook on your phone, you hear the tone and know you have a message. This works well if you use an analog phone directly connected to the CO and you, therefore, get dial tone from the CO. If you have a Cisco CME system in your office with IP phones on, however, dial tone comes from the Cisco CME system, not from the CO.

To hear stutter dial tone provided by a CO-based voice mail system, you can use the Cisco CME 3.2 FXO Trunk Line Select feature by pressing a button on your IP phone. It directly selects a CO Foreign Exchange Office (FXO) line, which gets dial tone from the CO, and you can hear stutter dial tone.

Example 11-10 shows how to use the **trunk** command to create a direct connection to a CO line on an IP phone.

Example 11-10 *FXO Trunk Command*

```
router#show running-config
voice-port 1/0/0
   connection plaropx 1082
dial-peer voice 82 pots
   destination-pattern 82
   port 1/0/0
   forward-digits 0
ephone-dn 10
   number 1010
   name manager
ephone-dn 11
   number 1082
   name private-line
   trunk 82
ephone 1
   button 1:10 2:11
```

Example 11-10 shows the following sequence of events:

- You press the softkey 2 on your phone, and it automatically triggers the configuration for ephone-dn 11.

- ephone-dn 11 initiates a call to 82, which matches the dial peer that points to FXO line 1/0/0.

- When line 1/0/0 goes off-hook (as if you had picked up an analog phone set directly connected to the CO), it does not dial any digits. The effect is that you can hear the dial tone provided by the CO.

Summary

In this chapter, you learned about several external voice mail options you can use with your Cisco CME system if you choose not to use the integrated voice mail application provided by Cisco UE.

The Cisco Unity unified messaging system provides a very good voice mail alterative, especially if you have a multisite network that has a larger location with several smaller locations, and you want to centralize voice mail for all locations at one site.

Non-Cisco voice mail solutions, such as Stonevoice, provide voice mail applications that integrate via H.323 with Cisco CME. Another alternative to integrate with some popular voice mail systems, such as Octel and Active Voice Reception, is to use analog connectivity and DTMF interaction between Cisco CME and the voice mail system. Using PSTN-based voice mail is also an option.

This chapter covered the trade-offs of the different methods and provided brief configuration information on how to set up your Cisco CME system to interwork with external voice mail systems.

This chapter covers the following topics:

- Telephony Application Programming Interface (TAPI) and XML application architecture
- TAPI applications
- XML applications

## CHAPTER 12

Additional External Applications with Cisco CME

In addition to the voice mail and automated attendant (AA) applications discussed in Chapters 9, 10, and 11, Cisco CallManager Express (CME) can provide even more capabilities by integrating with external applications offered by Cisco and other vendors. This chapter briefly reviews the external applications that you can integrate with Cisco CME, such as applications that use the Telephony Application Programming Interface (TAPI) and Extensible Markup Language (XML) interfaces.

Some external applications integrate with Cisco CME by using Skinny Client Control Protocol (SCCP) connections. This chapter does not discuss these application because they appear to Cisco CME as IP phones (SCCP endpoints) and not as an application using an application interface, such as TAPI or XML. SCCP applications register with Cisco CME as IP phones do and communicate with the Cisco CME call processing features via SCCP messages as any IP phone would. Applications in this category include softphone PC applications such as the Cisco IP Communicator and IP Blue Software Solutions' softphone. More information about IP Blue can be found at http://www.ipblue.com/.

TAPI and XML Application Architecture

TAPI applications interface directly with the Cisco CME call processing software to control the call processing signaling events that apply to an IP phone. For example, a TAPI application can answer a call on behalf of a phone, make the phone go off-hook, or disconnect a call. Windows-based screen-pop applications typically use TAPI.

XML applications interface directly with the IP phone and leverage its HTTP capabilities. The phone has one or more URLs as part of its software load that it accesses when buttons such as the services or directory keys are pressed. The XML application renders some text or graphics on the phone's display. Cisco CME call processing is not involved in this application interchange. XML applications control the phone display while the phone is idle (that is, not on a call).

Figure 12-1 shows how TAPI and XML applications interface with Cisco CME and its IP phones. The left side of the figure depicts a TAPI application. An employee has an IP phone and PC on the desktop. The PC runs a productivity application, such as a contact management application, that provides a screen pop based on caller ID whenever a call starts ringing. All messaging between the application and the phone passes through Cisco CME and is interpreted by the Cisco CME software. On the right side of the figure is an XML application. The phone has a URL that points to a server. The server application writes to the phone display using HTTP.

Figure 12-1 *TAPI and XML Application Architecture*

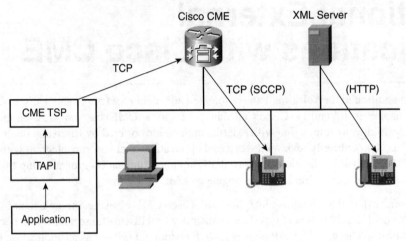

TAPI Applications

TAPI is a Microsoft software application interface for integrating-telephony-services into Windows-based PC applications. Cisco CME provides telephony services via a TAPI Service Provider (TSP) interface to applications.

The TSP allows TAPI-based applications such as Microsoft Outlook and Microsoft Customer Relationship Management (CRM) to provide call control to the IP phones connected to Cisco CME. Other TAPI-based applications are available in the industry, such as automatic dialers. You can use these applications to control an IP phone to make and receive calls via a computer or to trigger database lookups based on caller ID.

The following sections describe TAPI in more detail, including the following topics:

- The Cisco CME TAPI Light implementation and capabilities
- Cisco CME TSP functions
- Cisco CRM Communications Connector

Cisco CME TAPI Light

Cisco CME offers a TAPI Light capability, which is not a full TAPI implementation but a selection of the applicable components for Cisco CME. The implementation consists of two parts: one part resides on the Windows platform, and the other part resides in Cisco CME's Cisco IOS software.

The interface between the TSP in the Windows application and Cisco CME uses SCCP over TCP. Cisco CME listens on a standard TCP port, while the TAPI client authenticates to Cisco CME by providing a username and password unique for each IP phone on Cisco CME. The Windows application's TSP must have the same username, password, and port number configured to be able to connect successfully with Cisco CME and exert phone and call control. The username and password authentication provides a layer of security to Cisco CME to enable authorized application development.

Example 12-1 shows the configuration of the username and password associated with the IP phone on Cisco CME. This information must be quoted by the TAPI application during login to be able to control the phone. The **telephony-service ip source-address** command specifies the port number used for communication between Cisco CME and the TAPI application.

Example 12-1 *IP Phone Configuration*

```
router#show running-config
telephony-service
  ip source-address 172.19.153.129 port 2000
!
ephone-dn  1
 number 3001
 description User1
 name User1
 call-forward busy 3105
 call-forward noan 3105 timeout 10
!
ephone  1
 username "User 1" password user1
 mac-address 0009.B7F7.5793
 speed-dial 4 3100 label "AA"
 button  1:1
```

You can verify IP phone TAPI application login status with the **show ephone login** Cisco CME command.

Cisco CME TSP Functions

The Cisco CME TSP provides the following functions:

- It allows multiple addresses on a single line.
- It makes calls using address book dialing from applications.
- It answers or rejects calls.
- It holds calls using screen pop-ups.
- It provides caller ID information to applications.

- It places calls on hold and switches between active calls.

- It transfers calls.

When using TAPI applications with Cisco CME, consider the following restrictions:

- Media or voice termination is not supported. Media or voice traffic is sent to the phone. The TAPI application has access only to signaling events.

- TAPI clients can operate on only one phone line at a time.

- Multiple users and call handling of multiple calls on a single client are not supported.

- Java TAPI (JTAPI) is not supported.

Cisco has partnered with independent TAPI developers to provide support for TAPI development.

Table 12-1 lists the TAPI and TSP functions supported in the Cisco CME TSP.

Table 12-1 *Supported Cisco CME TAPI/TSP Functions*

TAPI Function	TSP Function	Description
lineAnswer	TSPI_lineAnswer	Answers the specified offered call.
lineBlindTransfer	TSPI_lineBlindTransfer	Performs a blind or single-step transfer of the specified call to the specified destination address.
lineClose	TSPI_lineCloseCall	Closes the specified open line device after completing or aborting all outstanding calls and asynchronous operations on the device.
lineCompleteTransfer	TSPI_lineCompleteTransfer	Completes the transfer of the specified call to the party connected in the consultation call.
lineDial	TSPI_lineDial	Dials the specified dialable number on the specified call.
lineDrop	TSPI_lineDrop	Drops or disconnects the specified call.
lineGetAddressID	TSPI_lineGetAddressID	Returns the address identifier associated with the address in a different format on the specified line.
	TSPI_lineGetCallAddressID	Retrieves the address identifier for the indicated call.
lineGetCallInfo	TSPI_lineGetCallInfo	Returns detailed information about the specified call.

Table 12-1   *Supported Cisco CME TAPI/TSP Functions (Continued)*

TAPI Function	TSP Function	Description
lineGetCallStatus	TSPI_lineGetCallStatus	Returns the current status of the specified call.
lineGetDevConfig	TSPI_lineGetDevConfig	Returns a data structure object, the contents of which are specific to the line (service provider [SP]) and device class, giving the current configuration of a device associated one-to-one with the line device.
	TSPI_lineGetExtensionID	Returns the extension identifier that the SP supports for the indicated line device.
lineGetID	TSPI_lineGetID	Returns a device identifier for the specified device class associated with the selected line, address, or call.
	TSPI_lineGetNumAddressIDs	Retrieves the number of address identifiers supported on the indicated line.
lineHold	TSPI_lineHold	Places the specified call on hold.
lineMakeCall	TSPI_lineMakeCall	Places a call on the specified line to the specified destination address.
lineNegotiateExtVersion	TSPI_lineNegotiateExtVersion	Returns the highest extension version number the service provider can operate under for this device, given the range of possible extension versions.
	TSPI_lineNegotiateTSPIVersion	Returns the highest service provider interface (SPI) version the service provider can operate under for this device, given the range of possible SPI versions.
lineOpen	TSPI_lineOpen	Opens the line device whose device identifier is given, returning the service provider's handle for the device.
lineSetCallParams	TSPI_lineSetCallParams	Sets certain parameters for an existing call.
	TSPI_lineSetDefaultMedia Detection	Tells the service provider the new set of media types to detect for the indicated line, replacing any previous set.

continues

Table 12-1   *Supported Cisco CME TAPI/TSP Functions (Continued)*

TAPI Function	TSP Function	Description
lineSetStatusMessages	TSPI_lineSetStatusMessages	Lets TAPI specify which notification messages the service provider should generate for events related to status changes for the specified line or any of its addresses.
lineSetupTransfer	TSPI_lineSetupTransfer	Initiates a transfer of a call.
lineUnhold	TSPI_lineUnhold	Retrieves the specified held call.

Cisco CRM Communications Connector

The Cisco CRM Communications Connector (CCC) integrates Cisco CME with the Microsoft Business Solution Customer Relationship Management (Microsoft CRM) application. Cisco CCC provides an easy-to-use IP phone application using Microsoft Outlook or Internet Explorer as the PC client software for managing tasks and contacts.

Cisco CCC offers the following application capabilities:

- **Screen pop**—Opens a contact record and creates a new phone call activity record as a call arrives. Creates screen pops from click-to-dial calls as well as from manually dialed outbound calls.

- **Click-to-dial**—Allows the user to click a field on the PC screen and have the PC automatically dial a number. This feature is available from a Microsoft CRM contact record on your desktop.

- **Call duration tracking**—Tracks the duration of a phone call and associates it with the phone activity record.

- **Call information capture**—Captures incoming and outgoing call information, including calling number, called number, and call start and end times.

- **Customer record creation**—Creates a new CRM customer record when a new customer call arrives.

Two pieces of software must be installed to activate the CRM application: one on the Microsoft CRM Server (Cisco CCC server software), and the other on each CRM client PC (Cisco CCC client software). In addition, the Cisco CME TSP driver is installed on each client. The Microsoft CRM Client can use Microsoft Outlook or an HTML interface as the client software.

For further information on Cisco and Microsoft solutions, go to http://www.cisco.com/go/ciscomicrosoftsmb.

For information on the CRM Express Solution Specialization, visit http://www.cisco.com/go/specialization.

For more information on the installation of Cisco CCC, go to Cisco.com, and search for "Cisco CRM Communications Connector for Cisco CallManager Express."

Extensive Markup Language Applications

XML is a text markup language designed to control web-based documents. With XML, you can create web pages customized for specific application requirements.

This section briefly discusses the XML applications applicable to Cisco CME IP phones. For more information on developing XML applications, go to http://www.cisco.com/en/US/products/svcs/ps3034/ps5408/ps5418/serv_home.html, or go to Cisco.com and search for "Developer Support Central."

General XML Phone Services

XML services on Cisco IP phones give you another way to perform or access more business applications. Some examples of XML-based services on IP phones are user direct-dial directory, announcements, and advertisements.

The IP phones are equipped with a pixel-based display that can display full graphics instead of just text on the screen. The pixel-based display capabilities allow you to use sophisticated graphical presentations for applications on Cisco IP phones and make them available at any desktop, counter, or location. In addition, you can select prepackaged applications. A sample phone display with applications is shown in Figure 12-2.

Figure 12-2   *XML Application on a Cisco IP Phone Display*

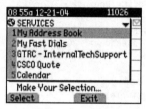

Cisco CME XML Phone Services

In a Cisco CME application, XML between an XML server and the IP phones provides customized phone displays and services. The interaction between the IP phone and the XML server includes the following events:

1 The IP phone sends an HTTP request to the application server.

2 The server renders an XML document and sends it to the IP phone.

3 The IP phone parses the XML document and renders the screen graphics on the IP phone display.

You can build applications particular to your business, such as a store inventory or stock quote lookup capability. These applications are especially useful to employees who do not have PCs or do not work at desks. You can also write more general applications, such as displaying a large-numbered clock on the IP phone (that displays when the phone is idle), and use this in conference rooms, lobbies, or break rooms instead of a wall clock.

You can find more information about XML-based IP phone services and productivity applications at the Cisco Applications Central web portal. To get to this site, go to Cisco.com and search for "IP Communications Applications Central." This site also has application partner information and discussion forums.

XML Application Example

Cisco CME runs standards-based XML scripts developed by any XML developer. This flexibility allows you to customize XML scripts for your specified requirements and enable applications for your particular environment.

Example 12-2 shows an XML script that provides a system-wide speed-dial feature on an IP phone. When you press the appropriate keys on the IP phone, the display shows the corresponding directory page of the desired party. You can dial the phone number by simply pressing a predefined button.

Example 12-2 *XML Script of an IP Phone Directory Application*

```
- <IPPhoneDirectory>
    <Title>XYZ Corp User Speed Dials</Title>
    <Prompt>Record 1 to 6 of 6</Prompt>
  - <DirectoryEntry>
     <Name>Directory Assistance</Name>
     <Telephone>95551212</Telephone>
   </DirectoryEntry>
  - <DirectoryEntry>
     <Name>XYZ Paging</Name>
     <Telephone>918007654321</Telephone>
   </DirectoryEntry>
  - <DirectoryEntry>
     <Name>Alan Anderson</Name>
     <Telephone>2001</Telephone>
   </DirectoryEntry>
  - <DirectoryEntry>
     <Name>Bill Brandy</Name>
     <Telephone>2003</Telephone>
   </DirectoryEntry>
  - <DirectoryEntry>
     <Name>Charles Cramer</Name>
     <Telephone>3214</Telephone>
   </DirectoryEntry>
  - <DirectoryEntry>
     <Name>Donna Davis</Name>
     <Telephone>3721</Telephone>
   </DirectoryEntry>
  </IPPhoneDirectory>
```

Cisco CME Configuration for XML Applications

The XML application interacts directly with the IP phone. You can activate the application in one of three ways:

- By pressing the services button on the phone
- By pressing the directory button on the phone
- By specifying an idle URL that activates when the phone has been idle for a short time

Example 12-3 shows the **telephony-service url** command you use to configure the URL accessed by each of the three modes of activating an XML application. This URL is resident on your XML server and can be any application or code of your choice.

Example 12-3 *Cisco CME Configuration for XML Applications*

```
router(config)#telephony-service
router(config-telephony)#url ?
  authentication   authentication url
  directories      directories url
  idle             idle url
  information      information url
  proxy-server     proxy-server url
  services         services url

router#show running-config
telephony-service
 load 7960-7940 P00303020214
 ...
 ip source-address 10.10.1.100 port 2000
 system message CUE System 2691
 create cnf-files version-stamp 7960 Jul 15 2003 13:48:12
```

You can have a services button, a directory button, and an idle phone application configured at the same time. Cisco CME creates phone loads for the IP phones by using the **create cnf-files** command, shown in Example 12-3. This pulls the URLs specified in the **telephony-service url** configuration into the phone load and allows the IP phone to access the correct URL immediately when the appropriate button is pressed on the keypad. If URL settings are changed, you must reset the phones for the changes to take effect.

Summary

This chapter provided a brief overview of the external TAPI and XML applications you can use with Cisco CME. With these applications you can tailor the native capabilities of Cisco CME IP phones much more closely to your own business environment. This chapter discussed the architecture necessary to activate the applications, the required Cisco CME configuration, and some examples of applications.

PART III

Administration and Management

This chapter covers the following topics:

- An overview of administrative access to a Cisco IP Communications (IPC) Express system
- System installation and initial setup
- Cisco CallManager Express (CME) graphical user interface (GUI) customization via XML
- Cisco Zero Touch deployment

Cisco IPC Express General Administration and Initial System Setup

The chapters in Part II, "Feature Operation and Applications," discussed Cisco IP Communications (IPC) Express system capabilities and features to implement a complete IP communications system for your office. The chapters in Part III, "Administration and Management," look at the configuration and administration of a Cisco IPC Express system.

This chapter focuses on the administration methods and access to the system, as well as the installation and initial setup of a new system. Chapter 14, "Configuring and Managing Cisco IPC Express Systems," offers a more in-depth view of configuring the system's features. Chapter 15, "Cisco IPC Express System Configuration Example," takes you through a step-by-step configuration setup of a sample system.

Cisco IPC Express is composed of four major components, as described in Chapter 1, "Introducing Cisco IPC Express":

- The router platform, which provides IP connectivity to the network and connectivity to the Public Switched Telephone Network (PSTN)
- Cisco CallManager Express (CME), which provides call processing capabilities
- Cisco Unity Express (UE), which provides automated attendant (AA) and voice mail capabilities
- IP phone endpoints

In this chapter, the IP endpoints are considered part of Cisco CME and, therefore, are covered in the Cisco CME sections along with the call processing features provided on the phones.

NOTE   Cisco Unity Express (UE) is an optional part of your system. If you do not have this component installed, you can skip the sections in this chapter particular to Cisco UE.

A comprehensive, detailed discussion of all Cisco IPC Express system administration capabilities would take a book in itself. Therefore, this chapter introduces the salient aspects of Cisco IPC Express system administration interfaces, installation, and setup.

Administrative Access Overview

Cisco IPC Express is a converged office communications system deployed by several different types of businesses:

- Small and medium businesses with one or more sites (using the standalone or multisite deployment scenarios, as discussed in Chapter 2, "Building a Cisco IPC Express Network")

- A branch office of an enterprise network of any size (also using the standalone or multisite deployment scenarios)

- A customer premises equipment (CPE) solution offered by service providers (SPs) as a managed service

These different ways in which you can deploy Cisco IPC Express require different types of administrative interfaces and different levels of access. For that reason, a Cisco IPC Express system offers a full command-line interface (CLI), a browser-based graphical user interface (GUI) for the key features, and several setup wizards to expedite system initialization tasks.

System installation and setup always require CLI access to install and provision enough of the system to be able to drive a GUI. You can set up the general call processing, AA, and voice mail features using either the CLI or the GUI. End-user interaction with voice mailboxes uses a Telephony User Interface (TUI), which means that users use a phone to interact with the system.

User IDs, logins, and passwords are defined at various levels. Different types of administrator accounts exist to partition access to different aspects of the system.

Cisco CME also offers several application programming interfaces (APIs) to interface with external applications for monitoring, configuration, and end-user phone applications.

Command-Line Interface

CLI is typically preferred by large enterprises and managed services networks where hundreds or thousands of systems must be provisioned. These are often scripted by higher-level network management systems centralized in a data center or a network operations center (NOC). Resellers and system integrators often use the CLI for initial system setup before they bring the system to your office. For the expert user, CLI access is often more expeditious than using a GUI.

The CLI for Cisco CME is part of the Cisco IOS router CLI. Access to the Cisco UE CLI requires that you log into the router CLI and then open a session to the Cisco UE application's CLI, which is modeled on Cisco IOS CLI but is not exactly the same. If you're a system administrator and are familiar with Cisco IOS and CLI commands, you can Telnet to the Cisco CME router (or use the console port), access the Cisco UE service engine from the same Cisco CME router, and perform all the setup and configuration tasks by using CLI commands.

Users unfamiliar with CLI in general and Cisco IOS router CLI in particular might find it much more intuitive to perform day-to-day moves, adds, and changes using the system GUI after an administrator or system reseller has set up the initial system for you and created a GUI account.

The following sections briefly summarize the Cisco CME and Cisco UE CLI commands.

Cisco CME CLI Command Summary

General Cisco CME CLI commands are under the **telephony-service** command on the router. Other key Cisco CME commands are **ephone** and **ephone-dn**, where many of the phone and call processing features are configured. You can find a more in-depth description of all the Cisco CME commands in the Cisco CME Administrator and Command Reference Guides on Cisco.com (http://www.cisco.com/go/ccme under "Feature Guides").

Example 13-1 shows the parameters of the **telephony-service** command.

Example 13-1   *Summary of the Cisco CME **telephony-service** Command*

```
router(config)#configure terminal
router(config)#telephony-service
router(config-telephony)#?
Cisco Call Manager Express configuration commands.
For detailed documentation see:
www.cisco.com/univercd/cc/td/doc/product/access/ip_ph/ip_ks/index.htm
  after-hours       define after-hours patterns, date, etc
  application       The selected application
  auto              Define dn range for auto assignment
  call-forward      Configure parameters for call forwarding
  caller-id         Configure caller id parameters
  calling-number    Replace calling number with local for hairpin
  create            create cnf for ethernet phone
  date-format       Set date format for IP Phone display
  default           Set a command to its defaults
  dialplan-pattern  Define E.164 telephone number prefix
  directory         Define directory naming order or add an entry
  dn-webedit        enable Edit DN through Web
  exit              Exit from telephony-service configuration mode
  fxo               FXO port support option in ITS
  ip                Define IP address and port for Telephony-Service/Fallback
  keepalive         Define keepalive timeout period to unregister IP phones
  load              Select the IP phone firmware load file
  log               Define log table parameters
  login             set the login timeouts
  max-conferences   Define max number of 3 party G.711 conferences
  max-dn            Maximum directory numbers supported
  max-ephones       Define max number of IP phones
  max-redirect      Define max number of redirect per call
  moh               Define music-on-hold filename
  multicast         Configure ip multicast parameters
  mwi               Define IP address and port for MWI Server
  network-locale    Define ephone network locale
```

continues

Example 13-1 *Summary of the Cisco CME* **telephony-service** *Command (Continued)*

```
night-service      define night-service options
no                 Negate a command or set its defaults
reset              reset ethernet phone
restart            restart ethernet phone
secondary-dialtone configure the secondary dial tone
service            Service configuration in ITS
system             Define system message
time-format        Set time format for IP Phone display
time-webedit       enable Edit Time through Web
timeouts           Define timeout value for IP phone
transfer-pattern   Define valid call transfer destinations
transfer-system    Define call transfer system: blind/consult and
                   local/end-to-end
url                Define Ephone URL's
user-locale        Define ephone user locale
voicemail          Set the voicemail access number called when the MESSAGES
                   IP phone button is pressed
web                define username for admin user
xmlschema          Command for setting xml schema
xmltest            Command for testing xml apis
xmlthread          Command for setting xml thread
```

Example 13-2 displays the parameters of the **ephone-dn** command.

Example 13-2 *Summary of the Cisco CME* **ephone-dn** *Command*

```
router(config)#ephone-dn 100
router(config-ephone-dn)#?
Ephone DN configuration commands - configure phone lines for ephone
For detailed documentation see:
www.cisco.com/univercd/cc/td/doc/product/access/ip_ph/ip_ks/index.htm
  application    The selected application
  call-forward   Define E.164 telephone number for call forwarding
  caller-id      Configure port caller id parameters
  cor            Class of Restriction on dial-peer for this dn
  default        Set a command to its defaults
  description    dn desc, for DN Qualified Display Name
  exit           Exit from ephone-dn configuration mode
  feed           set live feed multicast stream mode
  hold-alert     Set Call On-Hold timeout alert parameters
  huntstop       Stop hunting on Dial-Peers
  intercom       Define intercom/auto-call extension number
  label          dn label, for DN Display text
  loopback-dn    Define dn-tag to create loopback dn pair with this ephone-dn
  moh            set live-feed music-on-hold mode (with optional multicast)
  mwi            set message waiting indicator options (mwi)
  name           Define dn user name
  night-service  Define night-service bell
  no             Negate a command or set its defaults
  number         Define E.164 telephone number
  paging         set audio paging mode
```

Example 13-2 *Summary of the Cisco CME **ephone-dn** Command (Continued)*

```
park-slot       set ephone-dn as park slot
pickup-group    set the call pickup group number for the DN
preference      Preference for the attached dial-peer for the primary dn number
transfer-mode   Define call transfer mode: blind vs. consult
translate       Translation rule
```

Example 13-3 shows the parameters of the **ephone** command.

Example 13-3 *Summary of the Cisco CME **ephone** Command*

```
router(config)#ephone 40
router(config-ephone)#?
Ethernet phone configuration commands
For detailed documentation see:
www.cisco.com/univercd/cc/td/doc/product/access/ip_ph/ip_ks/index.htm
  after-hour     ephone exempt from after-hour blocking
  auto-line      Automatically select the most appropriate phone line when the
                 telephone handset is lifted offhook for both incoming and
                 outgoing calls. The 'no' form of this command requires the
                 phone user to always explicitly select the phone line to use
                 by pressing the appropriate phone Line button
  button         Assign ephone-dn phone lines to phone using format with
                 feature options.
  default        Set a command to its defaults
  exit           Exit from ephone configuration mode
  fastdial       Define ip-phone fastdial number
  keepalive      Define keepalive timeout period to unregister IP phone
  keyphone       Identify an IP phone as keyphone
  mac-address    define ethernet phone MAC address
  night-service  Define night-service bell
  no             Negate a command or set its defaults
  paging-dn      set audio paging dn group for phone
  pin            Define 4-8 digit personal identification number
  reset          reset ethernet phone
  restart        restart ethernet phone
  speed-dial     Define ip-phone speed-dial number
  type           Define ip-phone type
  username       define username to access ethernet phone from Web
  vm-device-id   define voice-mail id string
```

Cisco UE CLI Command Summary

You access the Cisco UE CLI by using the **service-module service-engine** *x/y* **session** command on the router (where *x/y* denotes the slot number where Cisco UE is present on your system).

You can find a more in-depth description of the Cisco UE CLI commands in the Cisco UE Administrator Guide on Cisco.com (http://www.cisco.com/go/cue under "Administration Guides").

Example 13-4 briefly lists the general Cisco UE CLI administration commands.

Example 13-4 *Summary of Cisco UE Basic CLI Commands*

```
router#service-module service-engine 1/0 session
Trying 172.19.153.38, 2033 ... Open
cue>
cue#?
  ccn         Telephony application
  configure   Enter configuration mode
  copy        Copy data from one location to another
  disable     Turn off privileged commands
  echo        print the arguments
  enable      enter privileged mode
  erase       Erase a configuration
  exit        quit the cli
  groupname   Group descriptions and accounts
  mwi         Message Waiting Indicator
  no          Negate a command
  offline     Change the system to administration mode
  ping        Send echo messages
  reload      Reboot the system
  remote      commands associated with remote info
  show        Show running system information
  shutdown    Halt the system
  terminal    Configure this session's terminal
  trace       Enable trace events for debugging
  username    User descriptions and accounts
  voicemail   voicemail application
  web         define username for GUI user
  write       Write running configuration to memory or terminal
```

Example 13-5 shows the Cisco UE configuration commands.

Example 13-5 *Summary of Cisco UE Configuration CLI Commands*

```
cue#configure terminal
cue(config)#?
  backup      Save data to a server
  calendar    Configure calendar schedule information
  ccn         Telephony application
  clock       software clock
  default     Return a configuration value to its default
  end         Exit from configure mode
  exit        Exit configuration mode
  groupname   Group descriptions and accounts
  hostname    set the system name
  ip          internet protocol
  list        Public Distribution List
  log         System event messages
  network     network application
  no          delete configuration command
  ntp         Network Time Protocol
  privilege   Privileges
```

Example 13-5   *Summary of Cisco UE Configuration CLI Commands (Continued)*

```
remote          Remote info.
security        Configure security features
username        User descriptions and accounts
voicemail       voicemail application
```

Example 13-6 summarizes the Cisco UE **show** commands.

Example 13-6   *Summary of Cisco UE **show** CLI Commands*

```
cue#show ?
arp             ARP table
backup          Print backup utility configuration
calendar        Print calendar schedule information
ccn             Telephony Application
clock           Display the system clock
configuration   Contents of Non-Volatile memory
crash           Show kernel crash information
debugging       State of each debugging option
errors          Print statistics about system events
exception       Exception information
group           Print information about a single group
groups          Print list of known group names
hosts           IP domain-name, lookup style, nameservers,  and host table
interfaces      Show interface status and configuration
ip              IP application
list            Print information about a single distribution list
lists           Distribution lists
log             Print recent system event messages
logging         Show console logging options
logs            List the logs
memory          Memory statistics
network         Networking application
ntp             Network time protocol
packets         Network traffic
privilege       Print information about a single privilege
privileges      Print list of known privileges
processes       Application subsystem state
remote          Commands associated with remote info
running-config  Current operating configuration
security        Print information about a security settings
software        Program and Options
startup-config  Contents of startup configuration
sysdb           System configuration database
tech-support    Summary of diagnostic information for Cisco TAC
trace           Show trace information
user            Print information about a single user
users           Print list of known usernames
version         System hardware and software status
voicemail       Telephony application
web             GUI interface
```

Browser-Based GUI

The GUI is helpful to users interested in doing ongoing maintenance on the system, such as day-to-day moves, adds, and changes. For example, you might use the GUI when a new employee joins your company and needs a phone, extension, and mailbox, or when you want your AA menu to change to provide location information to callers to your business.

By using the GUI, you can accomplish configuration tasks without having the expert-level understanding of the system that is often required by the CLI. You cannot access all the Cisco IPC Express features and capabilities via the GUI. Most notably, installation, upgrading, and troubleshooting always require CLI access. You can access most other features via either the CLI or GUI.

The Cisco IPC Express GUI integrates Cisco CME and Cisco UE features and allows you to add, delete, and configure IP phones, extensions, and some of the Cisco CME system-wide dial plan and phone-based features, such as call-forward-no-answer (CFNA) destination. The GUI also lets you set up the Cisco UE subscriber voice mail, group voice mail, and the AA.

The Cisco CME GUI uses HTTP to transfer information between the Cisco CME router and the administrator's computer or a user's phone. The Cisco UE GUI also uses an HTTP server that resides on the Cisco UE module itself. Therefore, the integrated Cisco IPC Express GUI is implemented using HTTP servers and by proxying requests between the two.

The following sections cover the GUI's highlights and introduce how to set up the GUI for a Cisco CME system.

Cisco IPC Express GUI Highlights

You can configure and change many of the general system features via the GUI. These include viewing, adding, changing, and deleting IP phones, extensions, voice mailboxes, AA scripts, and AA voice prompts. Call processing features, such as hunting and speed dials, can also be administered via the GUI.

Access to administering system features is based on the administrator's access level. The section "Levels of Administrative Access" discusses this in more detail.

Setting Up a System for GUI Access

The Cisco IPC Express system requires Microsoft Internet Explorer (IE) 6.0 or later. The Netscape browser is not supported because of its lack of support for some of the standard HTML 4.0 tags and attributes that cause the back and forward buttons to work correctly. You must enable JavaScript in the browser.

If you have a Cisco CME system where Cisco UE is not installed, to access the Cisco CME GUI, go to http://*router_ipaddr*/ccme.html, where *router_ipaddr* is the IP address of your Cisco CME router. For example, if the IP address of your Cisco CME router is 172.19.153.129, you would enter http://172.19.153.129/ccme.html in your browser. You can also use HTTP over SSL (HTTPS) to administer Cisco CME.

NOTE Cisco UE up to release 2.1 does not support HTTPS access.

Figure 13-1 shows the login pop-up menu you use to log into the system.

Figure 13-1 *Cisco CME Login Screen*

Enter Network Password
Please type your user name and password.
Site: 172.19.153.129
Realm its_access
User Name
Password
Save this password in your password list
OK
Cancel

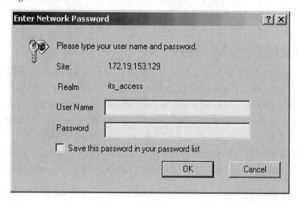

If you have an integrated Cisco CME and Cisco UE system, go to http://*CUE_ipaddr*/ to access the Cisco IPC Express GUI, where *CUE_ipaddr* is the IP address of your Cisco UE module. For example, if the IP address of your Cisco UE module is 172.19.153.40, you would go to http://172.19.153.40/.

Figure 13-2 shows the login pop-up menu you use to log into the combined Cisco CME and Cisco UE systems.

Figure 13-2 *Cisco IPC Express Login Screen*

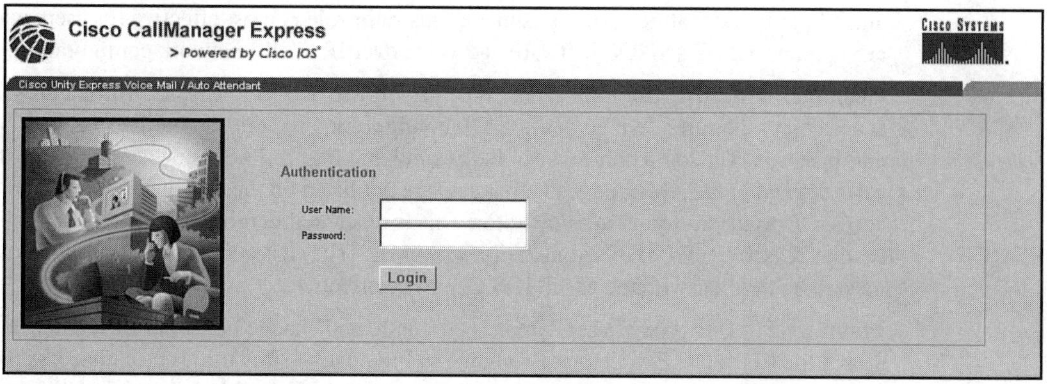
Cisco CallManager Express
> Powered by Cisco IOS
Cisco Systems
Cisco Unity Express Voice Mail / Auto Attendant
Authentication
User Name:
Password:
Login

Telephony User Interface

Systems with an integrated Cisco UE offer a TUI, which is used to access AA and voice mail. A TUI means that you interact with the system from a phone and press digits on the keypad in response to menus or prompts spoken by the system.

Callers use the TUI to interact with your business's AA and to leave voice mail for your employees. End users (subscribers) use it to access their voice mail, and administrators use it to set up and change AA greetings.

Levels of Administrative Access

Cisco IPC Express CLI access offers no user ID or password control beyond that which is already offered by the Cisco IOS router. In other words, access to the CLI is controlled by normal router methods. All the tools to restrict access to certain commands or to configure authentication, authorization, and accounting (AAA)/Remote Authentication Dial-In User Service (RADIUS) authentication for CLI access can be reused for Cisco CME and UE. Access to the **service-module service-engine** *x/y* **session** command to access Cisco UE from the router CLI requires enable mode on the router and, hence, requires **enable** password access.

Cisco IPC Express GUI access is controlled by defining user IDs and passwords that must be provided on the web login screens shown in Figures 13-1 and 13-2. The features available to you in the GUI after you are logged in depend on the access level of the user ID you entered.

The next sections describe access levels for Cisco CME and Cisco UE.

Cisco CME Access Levels

Cisco CME implements three levels of access and shows the appropriate screen based on the login name and password entered:

- **System administrator**—This user type, shown in Figure 13-3, has access to all system and phone-based features. The system administrator role is most effective for users who are familiar with Cisco IOS software and voice over IP (VoIP) network configuration.

- **Customer administrator**—This user type has limited access to Cisco CME features according to the rules defined in the XML configuration file created by the system administrator. The login home screen looks similar to Figure 13-3. However, based on the rules defined in the XML file, some features are not listed on the screen and, thus, are not accessible to the customer administrator. This is discussed in more detail in the later section "Cisco CME GUI Customization Via XML." The customer administrator does not need to be familiar with the Cisco IOS CLI to be effective.

- **Phone user**—This type of user can only configure and change his or her own phone and search the Cisco CME directory. As shown in Figure 13-4, this user type can access the Configure, Search, and Help menus but cannot access the Voice Mail, Administration, and Reports menus available to the system administrator. The phone user does not need any knowledge of or familiarity with the Cisco IOS CLI to be effective.

Figure 13-3   *Cisco CME GUI Home Page with System Administrator Privileges*

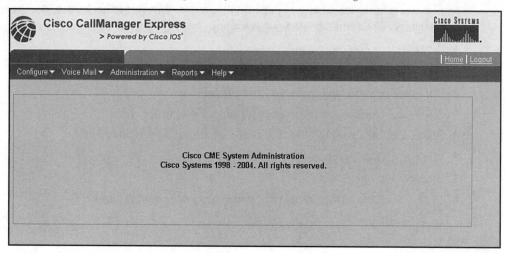

Figure 13-4   *Cisco CME GUI Home Page with Phone User Privileges*

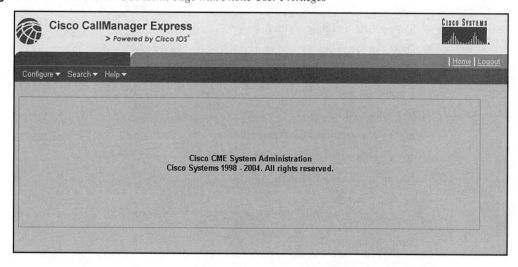

The system administrator can access all the Cisco CME GUI functions, whereas the customer administrator is limited to what the system administrator allows his or her login to do. Only an administrator can perform the following functions:

- View, add, change, and delete IP phones
- View, add, change, and delete phone extensions
- View, add, change, and delete system configuration
- View, add, change, and delete an administrator's login account
- View, add, change, and delete a customer administrator's login account
- View a call history report
- Launch help information
- Add, delete, and change certain call processing and system features:
  — Speed dial
  — Page trunks
  — Intercom
  — Call park slots
  — Hunt group settings and huntstop channels
  — Ephone-dn labels
  — Call blocking
  — System date and time format
  — Dial plan patterns
  — Directory service
  — Extension login clearing
  — IP phone URLs
  — Maximum number of IP phones
  — Night service bell configuration
  — Secondary dial tone pattern
  — System message
  — System time
  — Timeout setting
  — Transfer patterns
  — IP phone loads
  — Music on hold (MOH) file

A customer administrator might have access to all or a subset of the features the system administrator can access. On the Cisco CME system, you can configure which features the customer administrator can access. Doing so is further discussed in the later section "Cisco CME GUI Customization Via XML."

A phone user login (where the username and password are configured in ephone configuration mode) is granted limited access rights to perform certain operations:

- Viewing or changing the phone (the user's own phone) configuration, such as adding or removing speed-dial numbers or changing the user's password
- Viewing or changing user information (the user's own information)
- Searching the local directory
- Launching help information

Cisco UE Access Levels

Cisco UE implements two levels of access and shows the appropriate screen based on the login name and password entered:

- **System administrator**—This user type, shown in Figure 13-5, has access to all Cisco CME GUI screens as well as the Cisco UE AA and voice mail features.
- **Subscriber**—This type of user, shown in Figure 13-6, can only configure and change his or her own phone and voice mailbox.

Figure 13-5   *Cisco UE GUI Home Page with System Administrator Privileges*

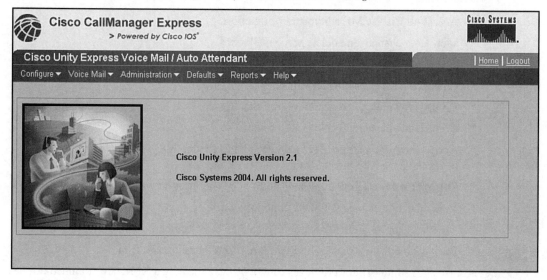

Figure 13-6 *Cisco UE GUI Home Page with Subscriber Privileges*

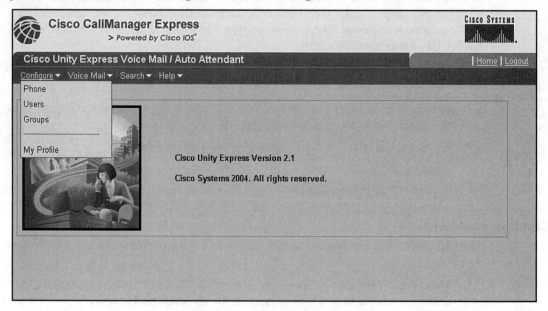

The Cisco UE system administrator can carry out all the GUI functions, including the following:

- Access all Cisco CME administrator functions
- View, add, change, and delete voice mailboxes
- Change the voice mail user and system parameters
- Change AA script parameter values
- Upload, download, and delete AA scripts
- Upload, download, and delete AA prompts
- Access the Administrator Management TUI to change AA prompts and features, such as the Emergency Alternate Greeting (EAG) for the AA
- Refresh the Message Waiting Indicator (MWI) per user or system-wide
- View, add, and change the MWI configuration
- View, add, and change the AA and voice mail pilot numbers
- Back up and restore the AA and voice mail configuration and data

The Cisco UE administrator privileges cannot be customized via XML. An administrator has full access to all system features available in the GUI.

A subscriber login is granted limited access rights to perform operations such as

- Viewing and changing mailbox (the user's own mailbox) configuration, such as changing the active greeting and the PIN on the account
- Obtaining limited access to the group the user is a member of

User Login Authentication

User and administrator access to both Cisco CME and Cisco UE requires a login/password combination and, therefore, a user authentication cycle. However, Cisco CME and Cisco UE use different methods of login authentication, as discussed in the following sections.

Cisco CME

Before gaining access to the Cisco CME GUI, all users are required to log in and are authenticated. The Cisco CME GUI provides a login dialog box for local authentication via HTTP 1.1 and the Cisco IOS HTTP login infrastructure. The Cisco CME router must be configured as an HTTP server.

Cisco CME logins for the system administrator can be configured to use AAA. The customer administrator and normal phone user logins are authenticated against local accounts on the router and are clear-text-based.

You can configure Cisco CME login accounts for the system administrator and customer administrator under the telephony-service configuration modes via the CLI. You can configure a phone user under the ephone CLI. These commands are shown in Example 13-7.

Example 13-7   *Cisco CME Login Account Sample Configuration*

```
router#show running-config
telephony-service
 web admin system name admin password admpswd
 web admin customer name custadmin password custpswd
 !
ephone  1
 username "user1" password user1-pswd
 mac-address 000D.BC50.DEC6
 type 7960
 button  1:1
```

You might also configure or change the customer administrator and phone user login accounts via the Cisco CME GUI. From the **Configure > System Parameters** menu, choose Administrator's Login Account. The resulting screen is shown in Figure 13-7.

You can change the phone user login accounts from the **Configure > Phone** menu. Select and click the phone to which the normal user has been assigned, and then scroll down to Login Account, as shown in Figure 13-8.

Figure 13-7 *Configuring and Changing the Customer Administrator's Login Account*

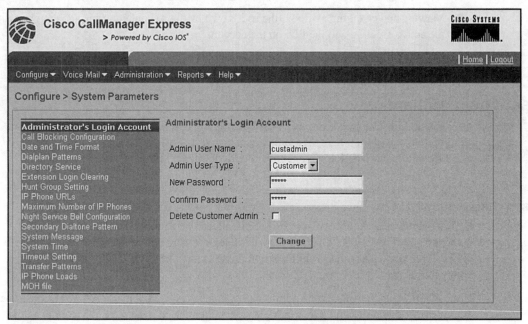

Figure 13-8 *Configuring and Changing the Normal Phone User Login Account*

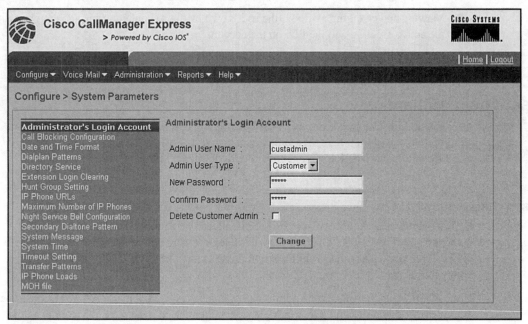

NOTE	To prevent a phone user from accidentally gaining access to system administrator pages by having the same password as the router enable password, Cisco CME must have **ip http authentication aaa** or **ip http authentication local** configured. As soon as Cisco CME has either of these commands configured, the user must have privilege level 15 router access in local configuration or in the AAA server (in case the **ip http authentication aaa** command is used) to access system administrator pages. Refer to Cisco IOS documentation on Cisco.com for more information on router enable password and privilege level 15 access if you are unfamiliar with these router capabilities.

Cisco UE

Cisco UE logins for the system administrator are stored in the local Lightweight Directory Access Protocol (LDAP) directory on Cisco UE. They cannot be authenticated with any external directory.

First configure login accounts for Cisco UE system administrators as normal users on the Cisco UE system, and then add them as members of the administrators group. This group membership awards administrator privileges to the user account. A subscriber does not have this group membership. These commands are shown in Example 13-8.

Example 13-8   *Cisco UE Login Account Sample Configuration*

```
cue#show running-config
username ggarrett create
username admin create
username ggarrett phonenumberE164 "4445553001"
groupname Administrators member admin
```

You might also configure and change the system administrator and subscriber accounts via the Cisco UE GUI. From the **Configure > Users** menu, choose the user ID of the account to change. The resulting screen is shown in Figure 13-9.

At this level of configuration, there is no difference between a Cisco UE administrator and subscriber. The screen shown in Figure 13-9 looks the same for both types of accounts. The attribute that awards administrator privileges to a user ID on the Cisco UE system is its membership in the administrators group, as shown in Figure 13-10.

Figure 13-9 *Configuring and Changing the Cisco UE Administrator Login Account*

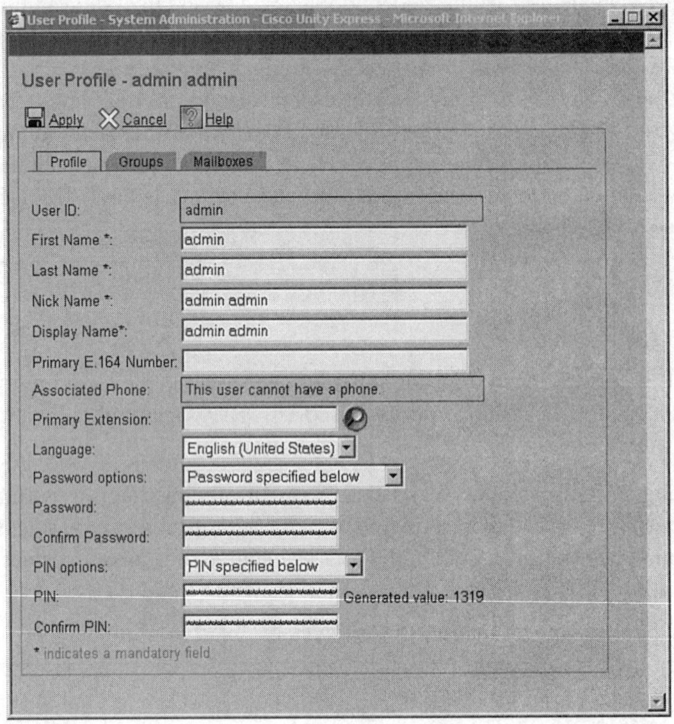

Figure 13-10 *Configuring and Changing the Cisco UE Administrator Login Account*

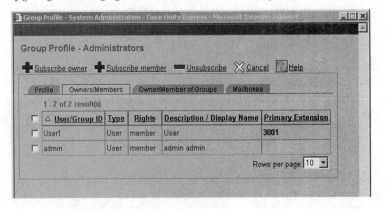

Application Programming Interfaces

Several programming interfaces to Cisco CME let management applications interface with the system. CME supports the following:

- XML cascading style sheets (files with a .css suffix) to customize the customer administrator browser GUI display. This is further discussed in the later section "Cisco CME GUI Customization Via XML."

- Integration with other network management applications via the XML Layer (AXL) application programming interface (API). This API provides a mechanism for inserting, retrieving, updating, and removing data from the Cisco CallManager database using an XML Simple Object Access Protocol (SOAP) interface. This is further discussed in Chapter 14.

Cisco UE with Cisco CME deployments does not support any programmatic interfaces at this time.

System Installation and Initial Setup

When you order a new Cisco IPC Express system, both the router and the Cisco UE hardware come preinstalled with the software and licensing you purchased. You do not need to do a software installation for a new system unless you have to upgrade the software levels from what was originally ordered. This section provides a high-level overview of the software installation and initial system setup process.

Although you do not need to install software on a new system, you must configure the system to make it functional. Several setup utilities can help you with these first-time tasks and these utilities, as discussed in the following sections.

Software Installation

Cisco CME software is part of the general Cisco IOS router software. You need an IP voice or greater Cisco IOS image to get voice features, including Cisco CME. In addition to the Cisco IOS software, you purchase the following licenses based on the number of users at your site, as covered in Appendix A, "Cisco IPC Express Features, Releases, and Ordering Information":

- Cisco CME seat licenses for the number of IP phones
- Cisco UE voice mail licenses for the number of mailboxes

NOTE If you are upgrading an existing router to become a Cisco CME system, you have to follow a full software installation procedure. Also, if you are upgrading an existing Cisco UE module to a new level of licensing or software, a software installation is required. Refer to Cisco.com for more detailed step-by-step instructions on router, Cisco CME, and Cisco UE software installation procedures.

Cisco CME Router Software Installation

Installing Cisco CME is exactly the same as installing your router with software. In summary, here are the steps:

Step 1 Download the correct Cisco IOS software image and release level from the Cisco.com Software Center at http://www.cisco.com/go/software. Note that you have to be a registered Cisco.com user to access the Software Center.

Step 2 Place these files on a Trivial File Transfer Protocol. (TFTP) or FTP server at your site.

Step 3 Use the Cisco IOS router CLI to load the software image into router Flash.

Step 4 Reboot the router.

In addition to loading the Cisco IOS software image, several processes apply to Cisco CME installation:

- Download the phone images into the router Flash.
- Download the GUI files into the router Flash. (You can use the **archive** command on the router to extract the contents of the entire .tar file with a single step into the router Flash.)
- Optionally, copy any TCL scripts needed by your configuration into router Flash.
- Optionally, copy any MOH files needed by your configuration into router Flash.

Cisco UE Installation

You can download Cisco UE software from the Cisco.com Software Center at http://www.cisco.com/go/software. Follow the links to Voice Software and Cisco UE. Cisco UE also ships with a set of CD-ROMs containing the software.

The Cisco UE application software resides on the storage medium of the Cisco UE hardware and has to be loaded separately from the router's software. The Cisco UE software files from Cisco.com or the CD-ROMs must be loaded onto an FTP server. From there the Cisco UE module itself is loaded via FTP from the server to the hard disk or compact Flash unit.

NOTE The installation procedure for Cisco UE changed significantly between releases 1.1 and 2.0. Before release 2.0, Cisco UE did not have an onboard installer and required an additional TFTP step to load the installer before proceeding to the FTP step that installed the system software. As of release 2.0, the TFTP step is no longer required.

Cisco UE is an embedded Linux-based application. Although neither the operating system nor the file system is accessible to the administrator, it is instructive to know this to understand the methods of loading and troubleshooting the system.

The following files constitute the software components for a particular software release of Cisco UE—in this example, release 2.0.1. The package and manifest files control the installation, and the .prt1 file is the actual software image. The exact files that constitute a release might differ slightly from one release to another. Before release 2.0 there was also a manifest file component.

- cue-installer.2.0.1
- cue-vm-full.2.0.1.pkg
- cue-vm-full.2.0.1.prt1

In addition to the software files, a license (or package) file must be installed on the Cisco UE system to determine the system parameters and identity controlled by licensing. One of the files listed next, corresponding to the license purchased for the system, must be installed on the application. The installation procedure is very similar to that of a software installation.

- cue-vm-12-license.2.0.1.cme.pkg
- cue-vm-25-license.2.0.1.cme.pkg
- cue-vm-50-license.2.0.1.cme.pkg
- cue-vm-100-license.2.0.1.cme.pkg
- cue-vm-12-license.2.0.1.ccm.pkg
- cue-vm-25-license.2.0.1.ccm.pkg
- cue-vm-50-license.2.0.1.ccm.pkg
- cue-vm-100-license.2.0.1.ccm.pkg

The Cisco UE application ships preinstalled from the Cisco factory, so there is no default license file and software download, and installation is required only for upgrading the system after the initial order. License installation is required only if a change is made to the system's licensing—for example, if a 25-mailbox system is upgraded to a 50-mailbox system. As shown in the file list, separate license files exist for Cisco UE deployed with Cisco CME (filename ending in .cme.pkg) or with Cisco CallManager (filename ending in .ccm.pkg). These license files control the Cisco UE GUI pages that allow configuration parameters for the appropriate call control engine. Ensure that if you are using Cisco UE with a Cisco CME system you have the correct version of the license installed.

Installing Cisco UE is very similar to a router software installation. Always consult the appropriate release notes first for any software installation. You can find the release notes at the same Cisco.com location where you download the software.

In summary, here are the software installation steps:

Step 1   Download the correct Cisco UE software image and release level from the Cisco.com Software Center (at http://www.cisco.com/go/software), or use the software files from your CD-ROM.

Step 2 Download the Cisco UE license files (if they are changing from what is already installed on the system) from the same site.

Step 3 Place these files on a server at your site set up for both TFTP and FTP.

Step 4 If you are upgrading an existing Cisco UE system, you must do a backup before you start the software installation. An installation reformats the storage medium (disk or Flash) on your Cisco UE module.

Step 5 Log into the router and shut down the Cisco UE module using the **reload** command at the Cisco UE CLI prompt. You also can use the **service-module service-engine** *x/y* **reload** command from the router CLI, where x/y is the slot in your router where the Cisco UE module is inserted.

Step 6 During the Cisco UE bootup sequence, interrupt the normal automatic startup with three asterisks when prompted. (You see the message "Please enter '***' to change boot configuration: ***" on the screen. You have a few seconds to interrupt the bootup sequence and get to the Cisco UE bootloader prompt ServicesEngine bootloader>.)

Step 7 Enter the required configuration at the bootloader prompt (such as the IP address of the FTP server where the software is loaded from).

Step 8 Ping the FTP server to ensure that there is contact between the router and the server.

Step 9 Enter the software load command, such as **software install package url ftp:/ /10.10.10.1/cue-vm-full.2.0.1.pkg user ftpuser**, to install Cisco UE software release 2.0.1 from the FTP server at IP address 10.10.10.1 using the **ftpuser** login. The FTP server prompts you for a password, which you can then enter. This command starts the software installation, which takes several minutes. It requires no manual intervention, so it can be left unattended as long as you are making a log of the output in case any errors occur.

If you are also changing the licensing on Cisco UE, follow all the preceding steps exactly as if you are doing a software installation. However, in Step 9 you specify a license package filename instead of the software package file (cue-vm-full.2.0.1.pkg).

A sample license installation command is **software install package url ftp://10.10.10.1/cue-vm-25-license.2.0.1.cme.pkg user ftpuser**. This installs a 25-mailbox Cisco CME license on your Cisco UE system.

If you are upgrading an existing system, you must now do a restore from backup to reinstate the configuration and voice mail messages that were present on the Cisco UE system before the software installation.

Initial System Setup

As soon as the system is installed with all its software and licensing information, you must enter the basic configuration to make the system functional enough to drive the GUI so that you can do additional feature configuration. (You also can do this using the CLI if you choose.) Several Cisco CME and Cisco UE utilities help you with these tasks:

- Cisco CME Auto-Registration Utility
- Cisco CME Setup Utility
- Cisco UE Post-Installation Setup
- Cisco UE Initialization Wizard

The following sections describe each of these utilities.

Cisco CME Auto-Registration Utility

Your Cisco CME system can automatically detect and register new IP phones added to the network. With this capability, you no longer have to manually associate the Media Access Control (MAC) address of the IP phone and bind buttons to the ephone-dn definition.

IP phones added to the Cisco CME network register automatically. The Auto-Registration utility assigns an extension number (ephone-dn) on a first-come, first-served basis as long as a pool of extension numbers is preconfigured and available to use. Example 13-9 automatically assigns ephone-dns 1 to 8 for Cisco 7960 IP Phones newly discovered by the Cisco CME router. It also auto configures call forwarding for these ephone-dns, with calls forwarded to extension 59000 on busy or when they are not answered within 10 seconds.

Example 13-9   *Configuration Sample for Auto-Registration Using CLI*

```
telephony-service
 auto assign 1 to 8 type 7960 cfw 59000 timeout 10
 create cnf-files
!
ephone-dn  1
 number 59001
!
ephone-dn 2
 number 59002
...
ephone-dn  8
 number 59008
```

If the configuration shown in Example 13-9 is not done on the Cisco CME system, newly added IP phones complete the boot and registration process with no button or extension number (ephone-dn) associated. They also cannot make or receive calls until manual configuration has been entered into the system. Be sure that the Example 13-9 configuration is in place if you want newly connected IP phones to be automatically registered and configured.

When automatically registering and configuring newly connected IP phones using the Cisco CME Auto-Registration utility, keep the following points in mind:

- Shared-line appearances on multiple phones can't be automatically set up by using the configuration shown in Example 13-9.

- *Auto-registration* isn't available on the Cisco 7914 Expansion Modules.

- Automatically assigned ephone-dn tags are normal ephone-dns (extensions). They are not the specialized directory number (DNs) needed for paging, intercom, MOH, and MWI.

- All the ephone-dns in an automatic assignment set must be in either single-line or dual-line mode; they cannot be mixed.

- Manual CLI commands are required to remove the configuration created by automatic assignment.

Cisco CME Setup Utility

The Cisco CME Setup Utility allows you to set up a CME system and its IP phones during a single session by providing a dialog box interface with a series of questions. This utility is extremely useful when you set up or install a Cisco CME system for the first time. Cisco CME automatically builds its configuration based on the selections and answers to the questions. As soon as all the phones have been registered, you must manually save the autogenerated configuration using the router **write** command.

You must enter **telephony-service setup** at the router prompt to trigger the Setup Utility. If a previous Cisco CME configuration exists, enter the **no telephony-service** command to remove the existing configuration, and then use the Setup Utility to create a new configuration.

The following is a list of parameters and fields queried during the Setup Utility. Your selections and answers to these allow Cisco CME to build a configuration automatically:

- DHCP service
- IP source address and Skinny Client Control Protocol (SCCP) port
- Number of phones
- Dual line or single line
- Language
- Call progress tones
- First extension number
- Direct inward dial (DID) service
- Forward calls
- Voice mail number

If you enter the **telephony-service setup** command on a system with a previous CME configuration, you see the prompts shown in Example 13-10.

Example 13-10 *Cisco CME Setup Utility Configuration Sample*

```
router(config)#telephony-service setup
--- Cisco IOS Telephony Services already configured. ---
- Please do "no telephony-service" to cleanup & run Setup again -
router(config)#no telephony-service
```

If you enter the **telephony-service setup** command again, you see the prompts shown in Example 13-11.

Example 13-11 *Cisco CME Setup Utility Prompts*

```
router(config)#telephony-service setup
 --- Cisco IOS Telephony Services Setup ---
Do you want to setup DHCP service for your IP Phones? [yes/no]: y
Configuring DHCP Pool for Cisco IOS Telephony Services :
  IP network for telephony-service DHCP Pool: 192.168.1.0
  Subnet mask for DHCP network: 255.255.255.255.0
  TFTP Server IP address (Option 150): 192.168.1.1
  Default Router for DHCP Pool: 192.168.1.1
Do you want to start telephony-service setup? [yes/no]: y
Configuring Cisco IOS Telephony Services:
  Enter the IP source address for Cisco IOS Telephony Services: 192.168.1.1
  Enter the Skinny Port for Cisco IOS Telephony Services: [2000]: 2000
  How many IP phones do you want to configure: [0]: 3
  Do you want dual-line extensions assigned to phones? [yes/no]: y
  What Language do you want on IP phones:
      0  English
      1  French
      2  German
      3  Russian
      4  Spanish
      5  Italian
      6  Dutch
      7  Norwegian
      8  Portuguese
      9  Danish
      10  Swedish
 [0]: 0
  Which Call Progress tone set do you want on IP phones:
      0  United States
      1  France
      2  Germany
      3  Russia
      4  Spain
      5  Italy
      6  Netherlands
      7  Norway
      8  Portugal
      9  UK
      10  Denmark
      11  Switzerland
      12  Sweden
```

continues

Example 13-11 *Cisco CME Setup Utility Prompts (Continued)*

```
        13  Austria
        14  Canada
   [0]: 0
     What is the first extension number you want to configure: [0]: 1001
   Do you have Direct-Inward-Dial service for all your phones? [yes/no]: n
   Do you want to forward calls to a voice message service? [yes/no]: y
     Enter extension or pilot number of the voice message service: 57777
     Call forward No Answer Timeout: [18]: 10
   Do you wish to change any of the above information? [yes/no]: n
   ---- Setup completed config ---
   router(config)#
   Jan  9 17:50:24.069: %LINK-3-UPDOWN: Interface ephone_dsp DN 1.1, changed statep
   Jan  9 17:50:24.069: %LINK-3-UPDOWN: Interface ephone_dsp DN 1.2, changed statep
   Jan  9 17:50:24.069: %LINK-3-UPDOWN: Interface ephone_dsp DN 2.1, changed statep
   Jan  9 17:50:24.069: %LINK-3-UPDOWN: Interface ephone_dsp DN 2.2, changed statep
   router(config)#
   Jan  9 17:50:55.467: %IPPHONE-6-REG_ALARM: 16: Name=SEP000DBC50DEC6 Load=3.2(2.d
   Jan  9 17:50:55.467: %IPPHONE-6-REGISTER_NEW: ephone-1:SEP000DBC50DEC6 IP:192.1.
   router(config)#
   reseting 000D.BC50.DEC6
   Jan  9 17:50:57.499: %IPPHONE-6-UNREGISTER_NORMAL: ephone-1:SEP000DBC50DEC6 IP:.
   router(config)#
   Jan  9 17:51:14.220: %IPPHONE-6-REG_ALARM: 21: Name=SEP00036B7FFF59 Load=5.0(3.P
   Jan  9 17:51:14.220: %IPPHONE-6-REGISTER_NEW: ephone-2:SEP00036B7FFF59
    IP:192.168.1.13
   reseting 0003.6B7F.FF59
   Jan  9 17:51:16.517: %IPPHONE-6-UNREGISTER_NORMAL: ephone-2:SEP00036B7FFF59 IP:.
   router(config)#
   Jan  9 17:52:01.296: %IPPHONE-6-REG_ALARM: 22: Name=SEP000DBC50DEC6 Load=3.2(2.t
   Jan  9 17:52:01.296: %IPPHONE-6-REGISTER: ephone-2:SEP000DBC50DEC6 IP:192.168.1.12
   router(config)#end
   router#show ephone register
   ephone-1 Mac:000D.BC50.DEC6 TCP socket:[7] activeLine:0 REGISTERED
   mediaActive:0 offhook:0 ringing:0 reset:0 reset_sent:0 paging 0 debug:0
   IP:192.168.1.13 51378 Telecaster 7960  keepalive 16 max_line 6
   button 1: dn 1  number 1001 CH1 IDLE      CH2 IDLE
   ephone-2 Mac:0003.6B7F.FF59 TCP socket:[9] activeLine:0 REGISTERED
   mediaActive:0 offhook:0 ringing:0 reset:0 reset_sent:0 paging 0 debug:0
   IP:192.168.1.12 50922 Telecaster 7960  keepalive 15 max_line 6
   button 1: dn 2  number 1002 CH1 IDLE      CH2 IDLE
```

The Setup Utility automatically generates the configuration commands shown in Example 13-12.

Example 13-12 *Commands Created by the Cisco CME Setup Utility*

```
   ! when DHCP service is selected
   ip dhcp pool ITS
      network 192.168.1.0 255.255.255.0
      option 150 ip 192.168.1.1
      default-router 192.168.1.1
   ! auto-generated telephony-service commands
```

Example 13-12 *Commands Created by the Cisco CME Setup Utility (Continued)*

```
telephony-service
 load 7910 P00403020214
 load 7960-7940 P00303020214
 max-ephones 3
 max-dn 3
 ip source-address 192.168.1.1
 port 2000
 auto assign 1 to 3
 create cnf-files version-stamp 7960 Jan 09 2004 17:50:24
 voicemail 57777
 max-conferences 8
! Note that Setup tool uses auto-assign command to assign ephone-dns to the phones
ephone-dn  1   dual-line
 number 1001
 call-forward busy 57777
 call-forward noan 57777 timeout 10
!
ephone-dn  2  dual-line
 number 1002
 call-forward busy 57777
  call-forward noan 57777 timeout 10
!
ephone  1
 mac-address 000D.BC50.DEC6
 type 7960
 button  1:1
!
ephone  2
 mac-address 0003.6B7F.FF59
 type 7960
 button  1:2
```

Cisco UE Post-Installation Setup

After you have completed a software installation on Cisco UE, the software automatically starts up. During the first startup, the software detects that no configuration has been entered yet. It asks you a series of questions to set up a Domain Name System (DNS), a Network Time Protocol (NTP) time server, the system's time zone, and an initial administrator account (user ID and password) that you will use later to log into the GUI. Example 13-13 shows this exchange.

Example 13-13 *Cisco UE Post-Installation Setup*

```
********** rc.post_install ****************
IMPORTANT::   Welcome to Cisco Systems Service Engine
IMPORTANT::    post installation configuration tool.
IMPORTANT:: This is a one time process which will guide
IMPORTANT:: you through initial setup of your Service Engine.
IMPORTANT:: Once run, this process will have configured
IMPORTANT:: the system for your location.
```

continues

Example 13-13 *Cisco UE Post-Installation Setup (Continued)*

```
IMPORTANT:: If you do not wish to continue, the system will be halted
IMPORTANT:: so it can be safely removed from the router.
Do you wish to start configuration now (y,n)? y
Are you sure (y,n)? y
Enter Hostname: cue-site6
Enter Domain Name (mydomain.com, or enter to use localdomain):
IMPORTANT:: DNS Configuration:
IMPORTANT:: This allows the entry of hostnames, for example foo.cisco.com, instead
IMPORTANT:: of IP addresses like 1.100.10.205 for servers used by CUE.  In order
IMPORTANT:: to configure DNS you must know the IP address of at least one of your
IMPORTANT:: DNS Servers.
Would you like to use DNS for CUE (y,n)?n
WARNING: If DNS is not used CUE will require the use
WARNING: of IP addresses.
Are you sure (y,n)? y
Enter IP Address of the Primary NTP Server (IP address, or enter for
 171.19.153.38):
Found server 171.19.153.38
Enter IP Address of the Secondary NTP Server (IP address, or enter to bypass):
Please identify a location so that time zone rules can be set correctly.
Please select a continent or ocean.
1) Africa          4) Arctic Ocean    7) Australia       10) Pacific Ocean
2) Americas        5) Asia            8) Europe
3) Antarctica      6) Atlantic Ocean  9) Indian Ocean
#? 2
Please select a country.
 1) Anguilla            18) Ecuador             35) Paraguay
 2) Antigua & Barbuda   19) El Salvador         36) Peru
 3) Argentina           20) French Guiana       37) Puerto Rico
 4) Aruba               21) Greenland           38) St Kitts & Nevis
 5) Bahamas             22) Grenada             39) St Lucia
 6) Barbados            23) Guadeloupe          40) St Pierre & Miquelon
 7) Belize              24) Guatemala           41) St Vincent
 8) Bolivia             25) Guyana              42) Suriname
 9) Brazil              26) Haiti               43) Trinidad & Tobago
10) Canada              27) Honduras            44) Turks & Caicos Is
11) Cayman Islands      28) Jamaica             45) United States
12) Chile               29) Martinique          46) Uruguay
13) Colombia            30) Mexico              47) Venezuela
14) Costa Rica          31) Montserrat          48) Virgin Islands (UK)
15) Cuba                32) Netherlands Antilles 49) Virgin Islands (US)
16) Dominica            33) Nicaragua
17) Dominican Republic  34) Panama
#? 45
Please select one of the following time zone regions.
 1) Eastern Time
 2) Eastern Time - Michigan - most locations
 3) Eastern Time - Kentucky - Louisville area
 4) Eastern Standard Time - Indiana - most locations
 5) Central Time
 6) Central Time - Michigan - Wisconsin border
 7) Mountain Time
```

Example 13-13 *Cisco UE Post-Installation Setup (Continued)*

```
 8) Mountain Time - south Idaho & east Oregon
 9) Mountain Time - Navajo
10) Mountain Standard Time - Arizona
11) Pacific Time
12) Alaska Time
13) Alaska Time - Alaska panhandle
14) Alaska Time - Alaska panhandle neck
15) Alaska Time - west Alaska
16) Aleutian Islands
17) Hawaii
#? 11
The following information has been given:
        United States
        Pacific Time
Therefore TZ='America/Los_Angeles' will be used.
Local time is now:     Wed Sep  1 05:40:16 PDT 2004.
Universal Time is now: Wed Sep  1 12:40:16 UTC 2004.
Is the above information OK?
1) Yes
2) No
#? 1
Configuring the system. Please wait...
...
IMPORTANT::         Administrator Account Creation
IMPORTANT:: Create an administrator account. With this account,
IMPORTANT:: you can log in to the Cisco Unity Express GUI and
IMPORTANT:: run the initialization wizard.
Enter administrator user ID: (user ID): admin
Enter password for admin:
Confirm password for admin by reentering it:
SYSTEM ONLINE
cue-site6>
cue-site6> show software version
Installed Packages:
 - Core  2.0.0.6
 - Auto Attendant  2.0.0.6
 - Global  2.0.0.6
 - Voice Mail  2.0.0.6
Installed Languages:
 - US English  2.0.0
cue-site6> show software license
Core:
 - application mode: CCME
 - total usable system ports: 4
Voicemail/Auto Attendant:
 - max system mailbox capacity time: 480
 - max general delivery mailboxes: 15
 - max personal mailboxes: 50
Languages:
 - max installed languages: 1
max enabled languages: 1
```

As shown in Example 13-13, the post-installation setup asks you a series of questions that help you set up the host name, DNS entries, and time zone information for the Cisco UE system. The last two commands shown in Example 13-13, **show software version** and **show software license**, are not part of the post-installation setup. However, they are handy commands to use to check that the system has been installed with the software and license you intended.

Cisco UE Initialization Wizard

If you set up your entire system using the CLI, you never need or see the Cisco UE Initialization Wizard. On the other hand, if you are setting up a newly installed Cisco UE system for the first time, the GUI Initialization Wizard is a handy way to set up the basic configuration for the system in a few successive GUI screens.

The Cisco UE Initialization Wizard comes up automatically the first time you log into the GUI of a newly installed Cisco UE system. After you finish working through the Cisco UE Initialization Wizard, you can never run it again. The only way to access it again is to reinstall the software on the Cisco UE system. However, everything you can do from the Cisco UE Initialization Wizard can also be done later using the normal GUI screens. The Cisco UE Initialization Wizard simply lays it out in an easy-to-use sequence for setting up a system that has no prior configuration to make sure you configure all the system's basic aspects.

To get the best results from the Cisco UE Initialization Wizard, configure your Cisco CME IP phones and extensions before you enter the Wizard. The Cisco UE Initialization Wizard walks you through several steps (each on a separate screen) that request basic system configuration information:

- **Cisco CME Login**—This screen asks for the Cisco CME administrator login (configured using the **web admin** command under **telephony-service** on the router). This is used to coordinate configuration information between Cisco CME and Cisco UE.

- **Import Users**—In this step, the Cisco UE software imports all the users (IP phones, their extensions, and the usernames) found in the router configuration. This screen allows you to select which ones you want to import. You can also choose which users get a mailbox and which users get administrator privileges assigned to the user ID.

- **System Defaults**—This step allows you to set the password and PIN generation policy for the system and the mailbox size and expiry defaults to be used for mailbox creation.

- **Call Handling**—This step allows you to set the pilot numbers for voice mail, AA, and administrator TUI access, as well as the MWI DNs for the system.

The final screens summarize the configuration you have entered, allow you to go back and make changes, and commit the configuration to the system.

After you have completed the Cisco UE Initialization Wizard, the system logs you out, and you have to log back in using the administrator login. At this point, you see the normal system login screen.

Prerequisites to Using the GUI

Before you set up the GUI features, you should be familiar with the prerequisites for using the GUI, including the following:

- Copy all the GUI files into the Cisco CME router's Flash.
- Configure the Cisco CME router to act as an HTTP server and to service the HTML GUI files.
- Use Microsoft IE version 6.0 or later.
- Limit the size of the XML file to 4000 bytes or smaller if you plan on using an XML configuration file to create a customized administrator login.

NOTE   You might change the password of the system administrator, customer administrator, and phone user via the GUI.

GUI File Installation

The GUI and xml.template files supporting the Cisco CME GUI are bundled into a single archive, such as cme-gui-*x.x.x*.tar, where *x.x.x* indicates the Cisco CME software release that this file pertains to. You can download this .tar file from the Cisco.com Software Center by looking for Voice Software and then for Cisco CME under Voice Applications Software.

Each release of Cisco IOS software is shipped with a unique version of the Cisco CME GUI file set. Therefore, you should be sure that the files matching the Cisco IOS release on your router are installed in the Cisco CME router Flash to ensure that the GUI features function properly. When upgrading a Cisco CME router from one version of Cisco IOS software to another, you must erase the old GUI files from Flash, and replace them with the new set matching the software release now installed on the router.

To copy and extract the contents of the cme-gui-*x.x.x*.tar file to the router's Flash, follow these steps:

Step 1   Download the appropriate cme-gui-*x.x.x*.tar file to a TFTP server, substituting the Cisco CME release you're using for *x.x.x*.

Step 2   Log on to privileged EXEC mode on the router.

Step 3   Enter the **archive** command to extract the contents of the .tar file to the router's Flash memory:

```
router#archive tar /xtract tftp://ip-address/cme-gui-x.x.x.tar flash:
```

For example, to extract the contents of cme-gui-3.0.3.tar from the TFTP server at IP address 192.168.1.1 to the router's Flash, enter the following command:

```
router#archive tar /xtract tftp://192.168.1.1/cme-gui-3.0.3.tar flash:
```

The files extracted to Flash include

- CiscoLogo.gif
- dom.js
- normal_user.js
- Delete.gif
- downarrow.gif
- sxiconad.gif
- Plus.gif
- ephone_admin.html
- telephony_service.html
- Tab.gif
- uparrow.gif
- admin_user.html
- logohome.gif
- xml-test.html
- admin_user.js
- normal_user.html
- xml.template

Setting up the Router for HTTP

After the Cisco CME GUI files have been extracted to the router's Flash, you must configure the Cisco CME router to act as an HTTP server, set the base path for the HTML files, and enter a Cisco CME administrator account username and password, as shown in Example 13-14.

Example 13-14 *Enabling the Cisco CME Router as an HTTP Server*

```
router#show running-config
ip http server
ip http path flash:
...
telephony-service
 web admin system name admin1 password admin1pswd
 web admin customer name admin2 password admin2pswd
 dn-webedit
 time-webedit
```

The following commands are needed to allow an IP phone user to log in and use the GUI to manage his or her own phone, and perform some basic configuration tasks:

```
router#ephone 1
router#username user1 password user1pswd
```

At this point, you can access the Cisco CME GUI pages by pointing your browser to the following link:

```
http://ip-address of your router/ccme.html
```

If you also have Cisco UE installed on your router (and it already has an IP address assigned, as discussed in the following section), you can access the integrated system GUI by pointing your browser to the following link:

```
http://ip-address of your CUE module/
```

NOTE   You must enable IP routing on the Cisco CME router for the Cisco UE GUI to connect correctly.

Router Prerequisite Configuration for Cisco UE

The Cisco UE GUI provides access to configure AA and voice mail application features. If you have just installed a brand new system, you must perform some basic router configuration before the CLI or GUI can access the Cisco UE module for application-level configuration. The prerequisite router configuration for access to Cisco UE is discussed in the following sections.

Service-Engine Interface

The Cisco UE hardware shows up on the router as a service-engine interface, as shown in Example 13-15.

Example 13-15   *Router Service-Engine Interface for Cisco UE*

```
router#show version
Cisco IOS Software, 2600 Software (C2691-IPVOICE-M), Version 12.3(8)T3, RELEASE
  SOFTWARE (fc1)
...
2 FastEthernet interfaces
1 terminal line
1 cisco service engine(s)
DRAM configuration is 64 bits wide with parity disabled.
```

IP Connectivity

To be able to communicate with the Cisco UE module, you must assign it an IP address. The most common way to configure the Cisco UE module is by using the unnumbered IP address method. An **ip unnumbered** configuration, shown in Example 13-16, allows the Cisco UE module to consume an IP address in the subnet of the network associated with a particular router egress port, such as FastEthernet 0/0 or a loopback interface. The router interface that the Cisco UE interface is associated with must be in an up state at all times for Cisco UE to communicate.

NOTE	The **ip unnumbered** method of IP addressing for Cisco UE requires the configuration of a static route to the service-engine interface.

Example 13-16 *IP Unnumbered Configuration*

```
router#show running-config
interface FastEthernet0/0
 ip address 171.68.10.1 255.255.255.0
!
interface Service-Engine4/0
 ip unnumbered FastEthernet0/0
 service-module ip address 171.68.10.10 255.255.255.0
 service-module ip default-gateway 171.68.10.1
!
ip route 171.68.10.10 255.255.255.255 Service-Engine4/0
```

The IP address of the Cisco UE module in Example 13-16 is 171.68.10.10. The default gateway on the service-engine interface must be set to the IP address of the Ethernet interface on the router that the unnumbered statement refers to (171.68.10.1 in the example). The default gateway setting for Cisco UE must be the Cisco CME router. You can also use a subinterface or a loopback interface as the **ip unnumbered** parameter—for example, by replacing **ip unnumbered FastEthernet0/0** with an **ip unnumbered Loopback0** statement.

It is also possible to assign Cisco UE its own IP subnet. This configuration does not require a static route. In this configuration the IP address must be routable such that the TFTP or FTP server used for software installation or backup knows how to reach the Cisco UE module. This is shown in Example 13-17.

Example 13-17 *Stub Network Configuration*

```
router#show running-config
interface FastEthernet0/0
 ip address 171.68.10.1 255.255.255.0
!
interface Service-Engine4/0
 ip address 171.68.20.1 255.255.255.0
 service-module ip address 171.68.20.10 255.255.255.0
 service-module ip default-gateway 171.68.20.1
```

The last variation that you can use for Cisco UE is to configure its IP address as a VLAN (virtual LAN). This method is typically used if a LAN switch module is integrated into the Cisco CME router instead of using an external LAN switch. This configuration, shown in Example 13-18, is very similar to the **ip unnumbered** configuration given previously and also requires a static route.

Example 13-18 *VLAN Configuration*

```
router#show running-config
interface VLAN1
 ip address 171.68.10.1 255.255.255.0
!
interface Service-Engine4/0
 ip unnumbered VLAN1
 service-module ip address 171.68.10.10 255.255.255.0
 service-module ip default-gateway 171.68.10.1
!
ip route 171.68.10.10 255.255.255.255 Service-Engine4/0
```

Date and Time

Cisco UE's date and time are controlled by two configurations on the system:

- Time zone and geographic area
- NTP source

Although the Cisco UE module has its own onboard clock, you cannot set the clock using the GUI or CLI. The Cisco UE clock is controlled entirely via NTP (which is in Coordinated Universal Time [UTC]). The system's time zone setting (shown earlier in Example 13-13) controls the offset from UTC to local time. The clock is synchronized with the NTP source during Cisco UE software startup and ongoing synchronization checks while the application is running. Therefore, it is important to insert a valid NTP configuration to ensure that the Cisco UE clock is set correctly.

The following Cisco UE module configuration is required to set the clock's NTP source:

```
ntp server 171.19.153.31
```

NOTE   On a Cisco CME system with Cisco UE, the GUI clock set capability on the **Configure > System Parameters > System Time** GUI screen displays and controls the Cisco CME router clock, not the Cisco UE module clock. Setting the router's clock has no effect on Cisco UE, unless the router is also defined as the NTP source for Cisco UE.

Call Routing to the AA and Voice Mail Pilot Numbers

Cisco UE is logically an application across a LAN segment from the Cisco CME router. It just so happens that the LAN segment physically runs across the backplane of the router chassis. No IP packets can reach Cisco UE unless IP routing is enabled on the router, the Cisco UE module has a valid IP address, and some call routing statements exist on the router to direct calls via VoIP to Cisco UE.

The Cisco CME router, as well as any other PSTN gateways that might exist in your office, must have dial peers configured to route calls to the Cisco UE AA and voice mail pilot numbers.

The Cisco CME router hosting Cisco UE must have a Session Initiation Protocol (SIP) dial peer for AA and voice mail calls with the following parameters:

- Disable VAD (voice activity detection)
- G.711 codec
- SIP-Notify dual-tone multifrequency (DTMF) relay

You can define a single wildcard dial peer for both your AA and voice mail pilot numbers, or you can define separate, more explicit dial peers for each pilot number individually. Example 13-19 shows a combined SIP dial peer applicable to a sample AA pilot number of 6800 and a voice mail pilot of 6801. The IP address of the Cisco UE, in this example, is 171.68.10.10. The dial peer example shown here assumes that your office has no other extensions starting with 680. If you do, you have to use a more explicit destination pattern in the dial peer for Cisco UE calls.

Example 13-19 *SIP Dial Peer for Cisco UE*

```
dial-peer voice 3100 voip
 description VM-AA
 destination-pattern 680.
 session protocol sipv2
 session target ipv4: 171.68.10.10
 dtmf-relay sip-notify
 codec g711ulaw
 no vad
```

If your PSTN trunks are integrated into your Cisco CME router, you do not need any further configuration to route calls to Cisco UE. The SIP dial peer shown in Example 13-19 is sufficient to route both IP phone and PSTN calls to Cisco UE. On the other hand, if you are using a separate router for your PSTN trunks and there is an IP network segment (LAN or WAN) between the PSTN gateway router and the Cisco CME router, you must configure H.323 dial peers on the PSTN gateway to route calls to Cisco CME (and Cisco UE).

Cisco CME GUI Customization Via XML

You can customize Cisco CME GUI features to provide a customer administrator login. This Cisco CME facility is used if you as a reseller are setting up a system for your end customer and that person wants to perform certain administrative functions on the system while you remain responsible for other items. You can use the system administrator login and access all system GUI features. You can limit the items your end customer sees in the GUI (using the customer administrator login) to those he or she is responsible for managing.

The following sections discuss how to customize the Cisco CME GUI features, and change the look and feel of the GUI pages with a sample XML file. The Cisco UE GUI cannot be customized in this manner.

The Cisco CME system administrator defines what a customer administrator can do by defining and setting the tags in an XML file. The XML file can be read in through the CLI to control the set of GUI functions allowed for a customer administrator.

Based on the existing Cisco CME XML Schema Template file, you might create a sample.xml and copy it to your router's Flash. In the sample.xml file, you can use tags with values of Show or Hide to allow or deny the customer administrator access to the corresponding GUI features.

If a tag item is missing from the XML file, the default behavior is to show. The customer administrator's access is equivalent to the system administrator under the following circumstances:

- No XML file exists in Flash
- After a **no web customize load** command is executed on the router (this command can be written to nonvolatile RAM [NVRAM])

You configure Cisco CME to allow GUI customization using the sample.xml file as shown in Example 13-20.

Example 13-20 *Using an XML File for GUI Customization*

```
telephony-service
    web admin system name admin password admin
    web admin customer name Cisco password Cisco
    web customize load sample.xml
```

Cisco CME XML Schema Template

The Cisco CME XML Schema Template is shown in Example 13-21. This sample template lists all the GUI features available to be customized using XML tags. You can select each to hide or show. By default, all features are shown in the GUI pages if neither Hide nor Show is specified.

Example 13-21 *Cisco CME XML Schema Template*

```
<Presentation>
  <MainMenu>
      <!-- Take Higher Precedence over CLI "dn-wed-edit" -->
      <AddExtension> [Hide | Show] </AddExtension>
      <DeleteExtension> [Hide | Show] </DeleteExtension>
      <AddPhone> [Hide | Show] </AddPhone>
      <DeletePhone> [Hide | Show] </DeletePhone>
  </MainMenu>
  <Extension>
      <!-- Control both view and change, and possible add or delete -->
      <SequenceNumber> [Hide | Show] </SequenceNumber>
      <Type> [Hide | Show] </Type>
      <Huntstop> [Hide | Show] </Huntstop>
      <Preference> [Hide | Show] </Preference>
      <HoldAlert> [Hide | Show] </HoldAlert>
      <TranslationRules> [Hide | Show] </TranslationRules>
      <Paging> [Hide | Show] </Paging>
```

continues

Example 13-21 *Cisco CME XML Schema Template (Continued)*

```
        <Intercom> [Hide | Show] </Intercom>
        <MWI> [Hide | Show] </MWI>
        <MoH> [Hide | Show] </MoH>
        <LBDN> [Hide | Show] </LBDN>
        <DualLine> [Hide | Show] </DualLine>
        <Reg> [Hide | Show] </Reg>
        <PGroup> [Hide | Show] </PGroup>
        <CallPark> [Hide | Show] </CallPark>
        <CFNA> [Hide | Show] </CFNA>
        <CFB> [Hide | Show] </CFB>
        <CFA> [Hide | Show] </CFA>
        <Label> [Hide | Show] </Label>
        <SecondaryN attr=[Both | Change]> [Hide | Show] </SecondaryN>
        <Overlay> [Hide | Show] </Overlay>
    </Extension>
    <Phone>
        <!-- control both view and change, and possible add and delete --->
        <SequenceNumber> [Hide | Show] </SequenceNumber>
        <CallBlockExpt> [Hide | Show] </CallBlockExpt>
        <AutoLineSel> [Hide | Show] </AutoLineSel>
        <LoginPin> [Hide | Show] </LoginPin>
        <RecNightBell> [Hide | Show] </RecNightBell>
        <ExtAssign> [Hide | Show] </ExtAssign>
    </Phone>
    <System>
      <!-- Control View Only -->
      <PhoneURL> [Hide | Show] </PhoneURL>
      <PhoneLoad> [Hide | Show]</PhoneLoad>
      <CallHistory> [Hide | Show] </CallHistory>
      <MWIServer> [Hide | Show] </MWIServer>
      <!-- Control Either View and Change or Change Only -->
      <TransferPattern attr=[Both | Change]> [Hide | Show] </TransferPattern>
      <VoiceMailNumber attr=[Both | Change]> [Hide | Show] </VoiceMailNumber>
      <MaxNumberPhone attr=[Both | Change]> [Hide | Show] </MaxNumberPhone>
      <DialplanPattern attr=[Both | Change]> [Hide | Show] </DialplanPattern>
      <SecDialTone attr=[Both | Change]> [Hide | Show] </SecDialTone>
      <Timeouts attr=[Both | Change]> [Hide | Show] </Timeouts>
      <CallBlock attr=[Both | Change]> [Hide | Show] </CallBlock>
      <HuntGroup attr=[Both | Change]> [Hide | Show] </HuntGroup>
      <NightSerBell attr=[Both | Change]> [Hide | Show] </NightSerBell>
      <DateTime attr=[Both | Change]> [Hide | Show] </DateTime>
      <DirService attr=[Both | Change]> [Hide | Show] </DirService>
      <ExtLoginClr attr=[Both | Change]> [Hide | Show] </ExtLoginClr>
      <SysMessage attr=[Both | Change]> [Hide | Show] </SysMessage>
      <MoHFile attr=[Both | Change]> [Hide | Show] </MoHFile>
      <!-- Control Change Only -->
      <!-- Take Higher Precedence over CLI "time-web-edit" -->
      <Time> [Hide | Show] </Time>
    </System>
    <Function>
      <AddLineToPhone> [No | Yes] </AddLineToPhone>
```

Example 13-21 *Cisco CME XML Schema Template (Continued)*

```
            <DeleteLineFromPhone> [No | Yes] </DeleteLineFromPhone>
            <NewDnDpCheck> [No | Yes] </DpDnCrossCheck>
            <MaxLinePerPhone> [1-6] </MaxLinePerPhone>
        </Function>
    </Presentation>
```

Guidelines for GUI Customization

You can customize the GUI with the XML file shown in Example 13-21 any way you like based on the requirements you and your end customer have for using the GUI. This section explains some general guidelines for what is best to do when customizing the GUI.

Generally, you should not allow the customer administrator to do the following:

- Add or delete a line
- Add or delete an extension
- Add or delete a phone

You might use the Hide tag for the following:

- Paging
- Intercom
- Call history

On the View Extension menu, you might use the Hide tag for the following items:

- Sequence Number (including both the Search-by page and the Extension Information page)
- Extension Type
- Huntstop
- Preference
- Hold-Alert
- Translation Rules

On the View Phone menu, you might use the Hide tag for the following items:

- Paging
- Display Maximum Number of four lines

On the Change Extension menu, you might use the Hide tag for the following items:

- Normal DN
- Sequence Number
- Extension Type

- Huntstop
- Hold-Alert
- Preference
- Translation Rules
- Paging DN
- IP Multicast Address and Port

On the Change Phone menu, you might use the Hide tag for the following items:

- Phone Sequence Number
- Paging Information

On the View System Configuration menu, you might use the Hide tag for the following items:

- IP Phone URL
- IP Phone Loads
- Transfer Pattern
- Voice Mail Number
- Call History Information
- Maximum Number of IP Phones
- MWI Server Setting

On the Change System Parameter Configuration menu, you might use the Hide tag for the following items:

- Dialplan Patterns
- Transfer Patterns
- System Time
- Voicemail Number
- Maximum Number of IP Phones

GUI Customization Sample File (sample.xml)

By default, the customer administrator has full access to the Cisco CME GUI. The customer administrator can be limited to certain GUI features by a GUI customization file defined by the system administrator. Using the XML template given in Example 13-21, Example 13-22 shows a sample GUI customization file (sample.xml).

Example 13-22 *Sample GUI Customization File*

```
<Presentation>
        <MainMenu>
                <AddExtension> Hide </AddExtension>
                <DeleteExtension> Hide </DeleteExtension>
        </MainMenu>
        <Extension>
        <SequenceNumber> Hide </SequenceNumber>
                <Type> Show </Type>
                <Huntstop> Hide </Huntstop>
                <Preference> Hide </Preference>
                <HoldAlert> Hide </HoldAlert>
                <TranslationRules> Hide </TranslationRules>
                <Paging> Show </Paging>
                <Intercom> Hide </Intercom>
        </Extension>
</Presentation>
```

Features not specified in the sample.xml file are shown in the GUI by default. Thus, every feature you want to hide must be explicitly stated in the file. After the sample.xml file shown in Example 13-22 is installed on a Cisco CME system, the customer administrator can no longer access the following features, because they are tagged with Hide in the XML file:

- Add Extension
- Delete Extension
- Sequence Number
- Huntstop
- Preference
- Hold-Alert
- Translation Rules
- Intercom

Figure 13-11 shows that the add and delete buttons and the Sequence Number column are hidden from the customer administrator GUI (limited access). Compare it to Figure 13-12, which shows all the hidden features for a system administrator who has full access to the GUI.

Figure 13-11 *GUI Customization (Limited Access)*

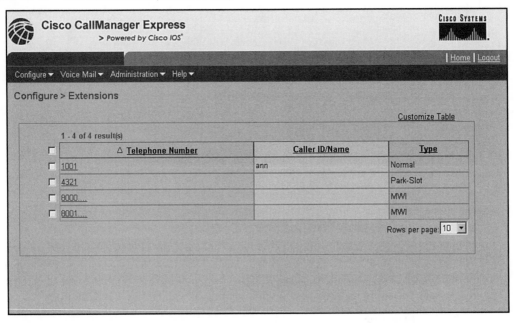

Figure 13-12 *GUI Customization (Full Access)*

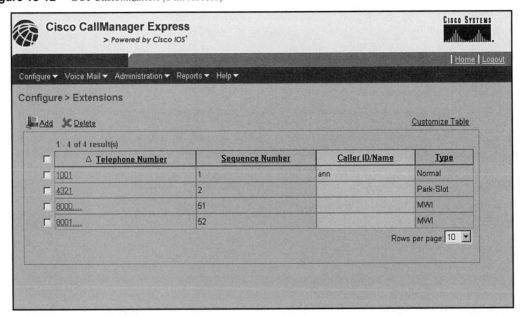

Style Sheet

Cisco CME supports a style sheet to make it easier for you to customize the GUI's look and feel by controlling the font, size, and alignment of GUI HTML pages. You can specify multiple style sheets. The style sheet is not limited to the hard-coded filename in Cisco IOS. Cisco CME also uses all feedback, error messages, and action state strings from an HTML file. This allows you to customize the GUI's look and feel to your own style and with international language support if needed.

If you are a service provider offering Cisco CME as a hosted customer premises equipment (CPE) solution, or a reseller offering your customers the option to own or brand the systems you provide, this is a Cisco CME facility you can put to good use to customize the GUI to look like *your* system. Large enterprises that have IT conventions on what application GUIs should look like can also use this facility to customize the GUI to fit better within your own conventions.

The customizable HTML capability opens the code for you to view and change GUI frames. Here are some examples:

- Add your own logo along with the Cisco logo
- Customize the set of functions provided to your customers (useful for a service provider)
- Develop a localized version of the GUI that fits your country's style and language

The Cisco CME style sheet template is part of the Cisco CME GUI files loaded in the router's Flash and can be modified to suit your needs. Note that any GUI customization implemented might be specific to an individual Cisco CME software release and might need to be modified if the Cisco CME release is changed.

NOTE   The Cisco Technical Assistance Center (TAC) does not support customized and localized GUI files.

Cisco Zero Touch Deployment

Cisco Networking Services (CNS) technology provides the infrastructure for automated configuration of large numbers of network devices. Based on CNS event and configuration agents, it eliminates the need for an on-site technician to initialize the devices. The CNS Zero Touch feature provides a deployment solution in which the router contacts a CNS CE to retrieve its full configuration automatically. This capability is made possible through a single generic bootstrap configuration file common across all service provider end customers subscribing to the services. Within the CNS framework, customers can create this generic bootstrap configuration without device-specific or network-specific information, such as interface type or line type.

Understanding Cisco Zero Touch Deployment Components

Cisco Zero Touch deployment consists of the following three components:

- Cisco Configuration Express (CX)
- Cisco CNS Configuration Engine (CNS CE)
- Cisco CNS Agent built into Cisco IOS software

Cisco Configuration Express

Cisco Configuration Express (CX) is an online ordering system and customizable inline manufacturing process that lets SPs easily deploy customer premises equipment (CPE)-based managed services to their small-to-medium sized business and enterprise customers. When ordering Cisco products, SPs use CX to specify the shipping instructions, including the Cisco IOS software version and a bootstrap configuration, which are configured, tested, and shipped with the CPE. The resulting fully configured CPE is shipped either directly to the end customer site or to the service provider's warehouse.

The bootstrap configuration integrates with Cisco CNS CE the moment the CPE devices are plugged into the network at the end-customer site.

Cisco CNS Configuration Engine

Cisco CNS CE runs on the Cisco CNS 2100 series Intelligence Engine (CNS IE 2100) hardware platform as well as customer UNIX servers. It is a secure and scalable deployment and configuration management application that provides an intelligent network interface to applications and users supporting up to 5000 Cisco CPE devices.

Cisco CNS CE includes the Configuration Service and Configuration Server. The Configuration Server communicates with the CNS Configuration Agent running on the managed Cisco CME via HTTP and transfers data in XML format parsed by the CNS Configuration Agent on the Cisco CME router using its own parser.

The CNS Configuration Service delivers device and service configurations to Cisco IOS devices for initial configuration and mass reconfiguration by logical groups. Routers receive their initial configuration from the CNS Configuration Service when they start up on the network the first time. The CNS Configuration Service uses the CNS Event Service to send and receive events required to apply configuration changes and to send success and failure notifications.

The templates created on the CNS CE are automatically pushed to the CPE devices running the bootstrap configuration.

For more information on Cisco CNS CE, go to Cisco.com, and search for "Cisco Configuration Engine."

Figure 13-13 shows how a Cisco CNS IE 2100 is used for Zero Touch deployment on a multisite Cisco CME network.

Figure 13-13 *Zero Touch Deployment for Multisite Cisco CME Networks*

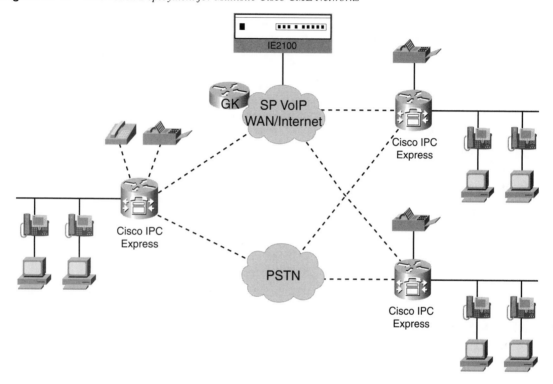

Cisco CNS Agent

The Cisco CNS Agent is built into Cisco IOS devices to provide intelligence to connect to the Cisco CNS CE. Using its bootstrap configuration, the CPE device, such as Cisco CME, polls the network and provides inventory to the Cisco CNS CE.

Zero Touch Deployment for Cisco CME Systems

Whether you're managing a standalone system or a multisite Cisco CME network, Zero Touch deployment is often used by SPs and large enterprises.

The following sections explain how you might use the three Cisco CNS components to auto-provision a Cisco CME configuration. This includes provisioning the Cisco CME, the EtherSwitch module in the same Cisco CME router chassis, and IP phones. You can accomplish subsequent changes to the IP phone configuration by modifying the Cisco CME configuration through the CNS CE system. After you modify the Cisco CME configuration, the phones automatically reset to accept the new configuration.

NOTE   The Cisco CNS components cannot yet be used to autoprovision Cisco UE.

Bootstrap Configuration

Example 13-23 shows a sample bootstrap configuration requested via the Cisco CE when ordering the CPE devices.

Example 13-23   *Sample Bootstrap Configuration*

```
cns config connect-intf serial ping-interval 10 retries 3
!Sets the unique event-id or config-id router ID
cns config initial 135.15.254.10 80 event syntax-check no-persist
!Sets CNS CE ip address to 135.15.254.10
cns id hostname
cns id hostname event
cns event 135.15.254.10 11011
```

Example 13-24 shows a sample bootstrap configuration for a Cisco 3725 router with a built-in EtherSwitch module and Cisco UE.

Example 13-24   *Sample Cisco 3725 Bootstrap Configuration*

```
enable password cisco
!
interface FastEthernet0/0
 mac-address 0002.2ccf.6900
 ip address 172.24.109.146 255.255.255.248
 duplex auto
 speed auto
!
interface Service-Engine2/0
 ip unnumbered Vlan1
 service-module ip address 192.168.1.21 255.255.255.0
 service-module ip default-gateway 192.168.1.1
!
interface Vlan1
 ip address 192.168.1.1 255.255.255.0
!
ip classless
ip route 0.0.0.0 0.0.0.0 172.24.109.145
ip route 192.168.1.21 255.255.255.255 Service-Engine2/0
!
cns config initial 192.168.94.163 80 event no-persist
cns id string EBCDEMO
cns id string EBCDEMO event
```

Example 13-24   *Sample Cisco 3725 Bootstrap Configuration (Continued)*

```
cns event 192.168.94.163 11011
!
line 65
 flush-at-activation
 no activation-character
 no exec
 transport preferred none
 transport input all
line aux 0
line vty 0 4
 password cisco
 login
```

Deployment Workflow

The deployment Workflow is described in the following steps:

Step 1   The Cisco CME is powered on at the customer site.

Step 2   The CNS agents locate the first interface type identified in the generic
bootstrap configuration, and apply the following CLI command:

> **cns config connect-intf** *type number* [**ping-interval** *seconds*] [**retries**
> *number*]

Step 3   The Cisco CME router gets its IP address from the aggregator of service
provider networks using Serial Line Address Resolution Protocol (SLARP).
The IP address for the CPE device becomes the aggregator's IP address plus
one. Note that SLARP is supported only on high-level data link control
(HDLC) links.

Step 4   The bootstrap configuration of the Cisco CME router lets the device connect
to the Cisco CNS CE.

Step 5   The CNS agents publish the Cisco CME router's physical inventory
information to the Cisco CNS CE in XML format when a successful ping
occurs. If the ping fails, the Cisco CNS agents retry for the number of retries
specified as an optional value entered using the **cns config connect-intf**
command.

Step 6   Using the inventory data, the Cisco CNS CE system substitutes interface and
line card information with the correct slot number.

Step 7   The complete configuration is pushed and stored on the Cisco CME router.

Using the Cisco CNS Configuration Engine

This section describes how to use the Cisco CNS CE for Cisco CME configuration and provisioning. Before an initial deployment starts, you must create a template that holds the common Cisco IOS commands for each device, and enter the attribute value that is unique to each device. You must also create the device objects to be deployed, and associate each device with a template. Follow these steps to automate the initial deployment of a Cisco CME router:

Step 1 Log into the Cisco CNS CE.

Step 2 Create a template for each network module.

Step 3 Create a template for the main device.

Step 4 Add a subservice for each network module.

Step 5 Add a main device.

Step 6 Verify and troubleshoot the initial configuration deployment.

Step 7 Make incremental configuration changes (if needed).

The following sections provide detailed instructions for each of these steps.

Logging into the CNS Configuration Engine

Open your web browser and enter the following to access the CNS CE on IE 2100:

```
http://ip-address-of-ie2100.cisco.com/config/login.html
```

Enter the user ID and password for the Cisco CNS CE. Figure 13-14 shows the main page after you have successfully logged into the system.

Creating and Adding Templates

After you are logged in, choose **Tools > Template Manager** to create a template or subtemplate for each device or network module. Do not use your browser's back and forward buttons when in the Cisco CNS CE. Use only the options within the Cisco CNS CE GUI. Figure 13-15 shows the Cisco CNS CE Template Manager options.

Figure 13-14   *Cisco CNS Configuration Engine Main GUI Page*

Figure 13-15   *Cisco CNS Configuration Engine Template Manager*

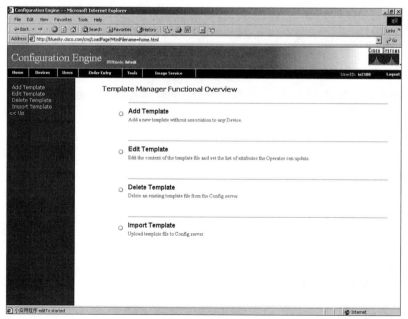

Choose Add Template, and then fill in the details to add a template, as shown in Figure 13-16.

Figure 13-16 *Adding a Template*

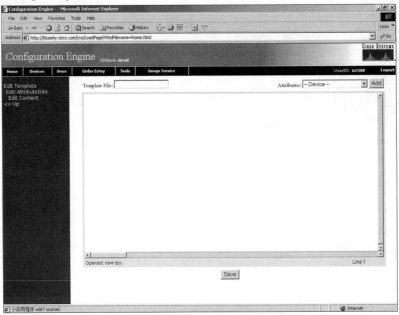

Figure 13-17 *Importing a Configuration into a Template*

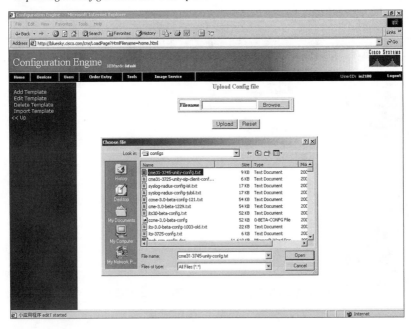

Enter the template name in the Template File field and click **Save**. You might enter CLI commands directly in the text box or import the configuration from a file using the import template button, as shown in Figure 13-17. Click **Browse** to select the file, and then click **Upload**.

Figure 13-18 shows the configuration successfully uploaded as a template.

Figure 13-18 *File Uploaded as a Template*

Adding a Main Device

To add a main device, choose **Devices > Add-device** from the Cisco CNS CE GUI to associate the main device with a main template. Click **Add**. The window shown in Figure 13-19 appears.

Figure 13-19 *Adding a Main Device—First Page*

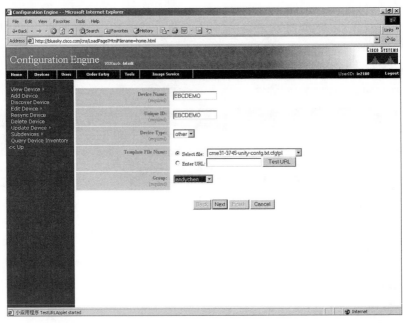

Figure 13-20 *Adding a Main Device—Second Page*

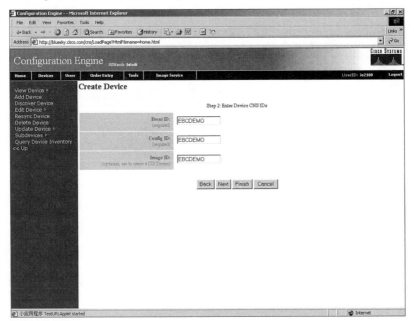

On the screen shown in Figure 13-20, fill in the Event ID, Config ID, and Image ID fields, and then click **Next**.

Click Finish. You see the window shown in Figure 13-21 when the device is added successfully.

Figure 13-21   *Device Added Successfully*

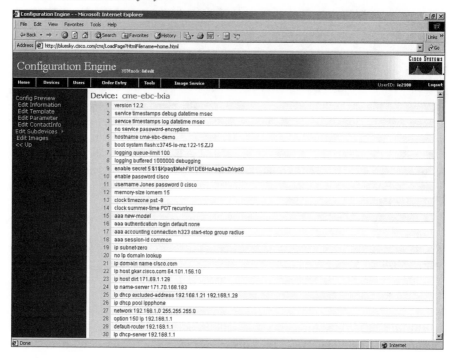

You might edit parameters in the **Device** > **Edit Device** pane, as shown in Figure 13-22. Locate the right device, and then make the changes needed.

Figure 13-22 *Edit Device*

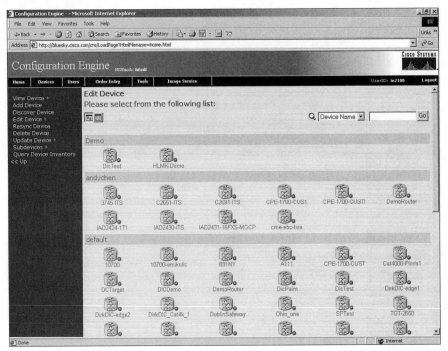

Verify the Configuration

Choose **Config Preview** to verify that your configuration is correct. Monitor the messages between your configuration server and the event gateway. Telnet to the Cisco CNS CE, and enter the following:

```
/opt/COSCOcnsie/tools/cns-listen "cisco.cns.>"
```

Check the event log file to see whether your initial deployment was successful.

Making Incremental Configuration Changes

Incremental configuration changes can be pushed to the partial configuration agent or pulled from the Cisco CNS CE system by the partial configuration agent. In the push model, the event message delivers the configuration data to the partial configuration agent. In the pull model, the event message triggers the partial configuration agent to pull the configuration data from the Cisco CNS CE system.

For more information, refer to the Cisco CNS CE Documentation on Cisco.com.

Summary

This chapter reviewed the administrative interfaces to a Cisco IPC Express System, including CLI and GUI capabilities. Several types of logins control administrator and end-user privileges and access to the system. You can also customize the Cisco CME via XML files and style sheets to fit your business model.

Cisco CME and Cisco UE system installation and various setup tools and utilities were discussed. For SPs or large enterprises managing hundreds or thousands of systems, the Cisco Zero Touch deployment mechanism with Cisco IE 2100 was covered.

This chapter covers the following topics:

- Cisco IP Communications (IPC) Express system graphical user interface (GUI) overview
- Configuring the router
- Configuring IP phones and extensions
- Configuring Public Switched Telephone Network (PSTN) interfaces
- Configuring extensions and the dial plan
- Configuring Cisco CallManager Express (CME) call processing features
- Configuring the Cisco Unity Express (UE) automated attendant (AA)
- Configuring Cisco UE voice mail
- Configuring the Cisco UE Administration via Telephony (AVT)
- Configuring Cisco UE Backup and Restore
- Configuring Cisco CME interconnection with other sites
- Security best practices for Cisco CME
- Security best practices for Cisco UE
- Configuring and monitoring via network management systems using XML Layer (AXL)/Simple Object Access Protocol (SOAP)
- Managing Cisco IPC Express systems by managed services and enterprises
- Cisco voice network management solutions
- Managing Cisco IPC Express with Cisco partner applications

Configuring and Managing Cisco IPC Express Systems

Chapter 13, "Cisco IPC Express General Administration and Initial System Setup," described general Cisco IP Communications (IPC) Express administration. It introduced the command-line interface (CLI) and graphical user interface (GUI) interfaces and the types of logins and access privileges you can use with the system.

This chapter discusses configuring and monitoring the system in greater detail, as well as how to configure your system for general security aspects.

Cisco UE is an optional part of your system. If you have not installed this component, you can skip the sections in this chapter particular to Cisco UE.

Cisco IPC Express System GUI Overview

The overall aspects of a Cisco IPC Express system that you must configure include the following, many of which are optional:

- Router
- IP phones and lines
- Public Switched Telephone Network (PSTN) interfaces
- Extensions and the dial plan
- Cisco CallManager Express (CME) call processing features such as intercom and hunting
- automated attendant (AA)
- Personal mailboxes and general delivery mailboxes (GDMs)
- Message waiting indicator (MWI)
- Voice mail networking
- Backup and restore

The Cisco IPC Express GUI does not provide access to all the system's components. You must configure many basic router features (such as IP routing, Dynamic Host Configuration Protocol [DHCP], and virtual LAN [VLAN]), the PSTN trunk interfaces, many dial plan aspects, intersite interconnection, and security features on the router itself. The router leverages the Cisco IOS general and voice infrastructure software discussed in Chapter 3, "Cisco IPC Express Architecture Overview."

You can configure components such as IP phones, extensions, AA, and voice mailboxes via the Cisco IPC Express GUI. This section briefly introduces the GUI. Later sections provide a configuration overview of each system component.

Figure 14-1 shows the following main menu items of the Cisco IPC Express GUI:

- Configure
- Voice Mail
- Administration
- Defaults
- Reports
- Help

Figure 14-1 *Cisco IPC Express Main Menu*

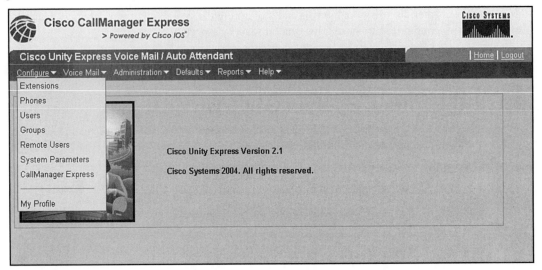

The next sections describe the submenus that make up each main menu, assuming that you logged into the system as an administrator. Note that to access the Cisco IPC Express GUI main menu shown in Figure 14-1, you have to point the browser to Cisco UE's IP address so that voice mail options are included.

Configure Menu

Under the Configure menu, you see the following submenus:

- **Extensions**—Extensions correspond to the directory numbers (DNs) in the Cisco CME configuration. The extension can be either an actual number assigned to the IP phone or a virtual number for special features such as controlling the MWI.

- **Phones**—This submenu shows the IP phones configured on Cisco CME. The list shows all the available IP phones with their corresponding Media Access Control (MAC) addresses. You can check if an extension is assigned to the appropriate phone.

- **Users**—Users are the Cisco UE administrators and subscribers. Note that users in the voice mail system do not require phones, but they do need extensions. An example is mobile workers. They do not need a physical phone, but they do need a phone number so that people can leave them messages.

- **Groups**—Groups are formed by building lists of members (users). A mailbox associated with a group is a GDM. It allows a voice mailbox to be shared among individuals working in the same organization or function so that any member of the group can act on incoming voice messages.

- **Remote Users**—This information is the (optional) static directory of remote users defined for Cisco UE voice mail networking.

- **System Parameters**—These are the Cisco CME features and system configuration parameters.

- **CallManager Express**—This submenu shows the Cisco CME system that the Cisco UE voice mail is working with. As of Cisco UE release 2.0, the Cisco CME and Cisco UE making up your Cisco IPC Express system no longer have to be housed in the router.

Voice Mail Menu

Under the Voice Mail menu, you see the following submenus:

- **Mailboxes**—This submenu lists voice mailboxes. An administrator can modify the parameters in each mailbox.

- **Distribution Lists**—This submenu lets you configure public and private voice mail distribution lists.

- **Message Waiting Indicators**—This submenu provides two options: refresh and number. Use the refresh option to initiate a manual refresh of all MWI lights. The number option shows the current MWI DNs defined by Cisco CME.

- **Auto Attendant**—This submenu allows you to access the AA definitions to upload or download prompts or scripts, change script parameters, and change the AA pilot number.

- **Call Handling**—This submenu shows the voice mail and Administration Via Telephony (AVT) Telephony User Interface (TUI) pilot numbers and the voice mail operator number.

- **Prompts**—This submenu shows a list of prompts used by the system and by the customized AA scripts. It allows you to upload, delete, and download the .wav files.

- **Scripts**—This submenu shows a list of system and customized AA scripts.

- **Business Hours Settings**—This submenu allows you to customize the business hours used by the system AA.

- **Holiday Settings**—This submenu allows you to customize the list of holidays used by the system AA.

Administration Menu

Under the Administration menu, you see the following submenus:

- **Synchronize Information**—This submenu allows you to force a synchronization of databases between Cisco CME and Cisco UE. As configurations change, Cisco CME and Cisco UE perform periodic updates between the two systems. The synchronization does not require a system reboot, but it also is not performed each time you make a configuration change. Thus, for a brief period the router's configuration (Cisco CME) might be out of step with the Cisco UE configuration for items such as extensions that appear in both databases. If you have made configuration changes, it is recommended that you synchronize the databases before writing the configurations to permanent storage.

- **Backup/Restore**—This submenu sets up the FTP server and directory information for Cisco UE Backup and Restore. You can also invoke a backup or restore operation from here.

- **Domain Name Settings (DNS)**—This submenu shows the current DNS settings. Changes are allowed.

- **Network Time and Time Zone Settings**—This submenu shows the current settings. Changes are allowed.

- **Control Panel**—This submenu allows you to save the Cisco CME configuration (the router's configuration), save the Cisco UE's configuration, or initiate a reload of Cisco UE.

- **Traces**—This submenu allows you to enable debug traces on the Cisco UE system. When the system is active, traces are collected on the designated file or server. You cannot read the traces from the GUI; you can only start and stop them. CLI access is required to read trace information.

- **Networking Locations**—This submenu allows you to configure sites in the network, including the local site, for voice mail networking.

Defaults Menu

Under the Defaults menu, you see the following submenus:

- **User**—Here you configure password and PIN defaults for new accounts, as well as password expiry and minimum length policies.

- **Mailbox**—This submenu lets you configure the default mailbox and message sizes for new accounts.

- **Voice Mail**—This submenu lets you configure the system defaults for the message store, message sizes, broadcast message MWI and expiry, caller ID for external callers, and enabling or disabling the voice mail networking cache.

Reports Menu

Under the Reports menu, you see the following submenus:

- **Voice Mail**—This submenu summarizes voice mail parameters such as the number of mailboxes and how much time is used.

- **System**—This submenu shows information about hardware on the Cisco UE system.

- **Backup History**—This submenu lists past Cisco UE backups; the IDs, dates, and times; and the characteristics of the backup choices.

- **Restore History**—This submenu lists past restores; the IDs, dates, and times; and the characteristics of the restore choices.

- **Network Time Protocol**—This submenu shows the IP address of the Network Time Protocol (NTP) server and the time difference between the host and Cisco UE.

- **Call History**—This submenu shows the history of Cisco CME calls over the past 24 hours.

Help Menu

The Help menu provides access to online help. The About menu gives system configuration information such as the router platform you are using.

Configuring the Router

Cisco IPC Express is based on the router architecture. Many aspects of the system require certain router and LAN switch components to be configured and operational:

- IP interfaces such as Ethernet, serial WAN, or internetworking interfaces

- IP addressing and routing

- DHCP

- Router login and password accounts and security measures (such as authentication, authorization, and accounting [AAA]/Remote Authentication Dial-In User Service [RADIUS])

- NTP for clock coordination

- Network Trivial File Transfer Protocol (TFTP) access to install and reload the router

- Voice and data virtual LANs (VLANs) and inline power (if supported and used)

- Security features such as network address translation (Network Address Translation [NAT]) and firewall

In addition to these items, you must configure the basic aspects of Cisco IPC Express:

- Turn on Cisco CME with the **telephony-service** command.
- If Cisco UE is present, configure the service engine interface.
- Configure HTTP access for the GUI.
- Install the Cisco CME GUI files into the router Flash.

Configuring IP Phones and Extensions

The features and configuration discussed thus far can be configured only via the router CLI because they cannot be accessed through the GUI. Cisco CME IP phones and extensions (lines) are the first features available using the GUI. After you successfully log into the Cisco CME GUI (as covered in Chapter 13), you might add, change, and remove ephone-dns, ephones, and speed-dial lists and perform other configuration tasks.

NOTE   Not all the Cisco CME features can be configured via the GUI. Some features might require router configuration (CLI), and others might depend on the privilege level granted with your login.

The following sections provide some highlights of the GUI configuration:

- Adding an extension
- Adding a phone
- Assigning an extension to a phone
- Changing or deleting an extension
- Changing or deleting a phone

For configuration details on more GUI features, choose **Help > Configuration** to launch the online GUI help, or access the Cisco CME and Cisco UE Administration Guides on Cisco.com.

Adding an Extension

An extension in the GUI maps to an ephone-dn in the router CLI. It is best to add the extensions before configuring the phones, because the phone's buttons have extensions assigned to them. Therefore, you can't complete the phone configuration until the extensions have been defined.

To add an extension to your system, choose **Configure > Extensions** and then click **Add**, as shown in Figure 14-2.

Figure 14-2   *Adding an Extension*

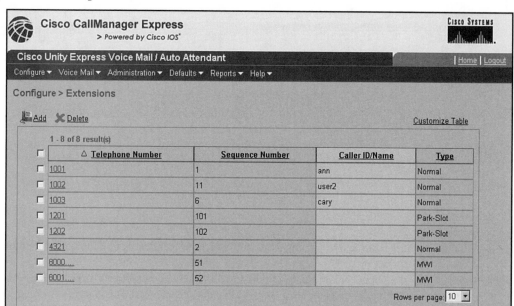

The system automatically assigns the Sequence Number field and maps to the ephone-dn number in the router configuration.

Adding a Phone

A phone in the GUI maps to an ephone in the router CLI. To see a list of the phones on your system, choose **Configure > Phones**. Cisco CME automatically detects the MAC address and type of phones connected to your router and assigns a phone sequence number to each (the **ephone** *x* configuration in the router CLI). With the GUI you cannot manually enter a MAC address for a phone that is not registered with the Cisco CME router. The phone must register first, and then its MAC address automatically shows up in the GUI for selection. Chapter 16, "Troubleshooting Basic Cisco IPC Express Features," discusses troubleshooting phone registrations. If your phones' MAC addresses do not show up in the GUI because they do not register with Cisco CME, follow the troubleshooting steps described in Chapter 16 to correct this.

To add an IP phone on your system, follow these steps:

Step 1   Select **Add a phone** from the **Configure > Phones** menu.

Step 2   Select the phone's MAC address from the Phone Physical ID drop-down list, as shown in Figure 14-3.

Figure 14-3 *Adding a Phone*

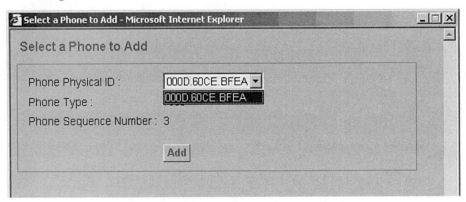

For testing or lab purposes, you can enter fictitious MAC addresses into the configuration for phones that do not exist. This might be useful if you want to preconfigure the system, and you do not have the phones with you (but you know the MAC addresses). Or perhaps you want to set up a lab configuration for training or experimentation purposes, and you want to enter more phones into the configuration than are physically available in your lab.

You can enter an ephone definition into the router CLI configuration with a fictitious MAC address, as shown in Example 14-1. The MAC address 0002.FFFF.1040 does not belong to any real phone; it was simply entered as a string of characters into the CLI prompt. If you then log into the GUI (or refresh the page if you are already logged in), this new phone shows up on the **Configure > Phones** menu.

Example 14-1 *Entering a Nonexistent Phone into the Configuration*

```
Router#show running-config
ephone   40
 username "User40"
 mac-address 0002.FFFF.1040
```

Assigning an Extension to a Phone

Extensions appear on the buttons of an IP phone. To add an extension to a phone, follow these steps:

Step 1   Select a phone from the **Configure > Phones** menu by clicking its MAC address. The Change Phone window appears, as shown in Figure 14-4.

Figure 14-4 *Change Phone Window*

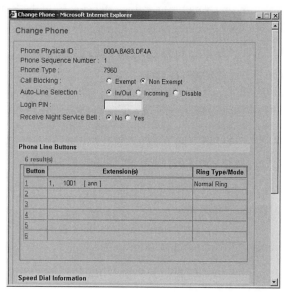

Step 2 In the phone line buttons layout, select the button to which you want to add the extension. The Button window pops up, as shown in Figure 14-5 (button 2 is selected).

Figure 14-5 *Adding an Extension to a Phone*

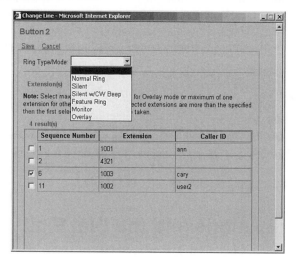

Step 3   Select an extension from the list to add it to the button on the phone. You might also select a ring type for this extension from the Ring Type/Mode drop-down list. Click **Save** to save the change.

Changing or Deleting an Extension

To change or delete an extension, follow the same steps as given previously for adding an extension to a phone. In the Change Phone window, instead of selecting a button with no extension assigned, as you did to add an extension, you select a button with the extension to change or delete. In the subsequent Button window, you can select a new extension (to change it) or deselect the existing assigned extension (to delete it).

Changing or Deleting a Phone

To change a phone, select the MAC address from the **Configure > Phones** menu, and change the desired parameters in the subsequent windows.

To delete a phone, select the phone(s) to delete from the **Configure > Phones** menu, and click **Delete** at the top of the screen.

Configuring PSTN Interfaces

You cannot configure the PSTN trunks of your Cisco CME system in the GUI. This requires CLI configuration on the router. The types of trunks and interfaces you can add to the system to connect to the PSTN or fax machines in your office were covered in Chapter 6, "Cisco CME PSTN Connectivity Options." Numerous configuration examples were also given in Chapter 6.

Adding PSTN connectivity involves the following configuration:

- The voice interface that connects to your PSTN trunks, analog phones, or fax machines
- The dial plan that directs calls to these interfaces

You might review the examples in Chapter 6 for more details on configuring a Foreign Exchange Office (FXO), Foreign Exchange Station (FXS), T1 Channel Associated Signaling (CAS), and Primary Rate Interface (PRI) Public Switched Telephone Network (PSTN) trunks and the dial plans to direct calls to these ports and trunks.

Configuring Extensions and the Dial Plan

The dial plan of your Cisco CME system is composed of the following components:

- Plain old telephone service (POTS) dial peers
- Voice over IP (VoIP) dial peers

- Extensions
- Digit manipulation features

The following sections describe configuring these components.

POTS Dial Peers

POTS dial peers are router configuration structures that point calls to a particular voice interface based on whether the dialed number matches certain criteria (as specified in the dial peer's **destination-pattern**). The voice interface can be a PSTN trunk, an analog phone, a fax machine, or an IP phone. Example 14-2 shows several sample POTS dial peers, including some for PSTN trunks and one for an analog phone or fax machine.

Example 14-2 *POTS Dial Peer Examples*

```
router#show running-config
!11-digit long-distance PSTN dialing with an access code of 9
dial-peer voice 1 pots
 preference 1
 destination-pattern 91..........
 port 2/0:23
 forward-digits 11
!
!7-digit local PSTN dialing with an access code of 9
dial-peer voice 4 pots
 destination-pattern 9[2-9]......
 port 2/0:23
 forward-digits 7
!
!Analog phone or fax machine
dial-peer voice 2701 pots
 destination-pattern 2701
 port 2/0/0
```

VoIP Dial Peers

VoIP dial peers are router configuration structures that point calls to a particular IP interface based on the same criteria that are used for POTS dial peers (that is, matching the dialed number to the dial peer's **destination-pattern**). IP interfaces can be H.323 or Session Initiation Protocol (SIP). Example 14-3 shows an H.323 dial peer that directs calls to another site where all the extensions start with three.

Example 14-3 *VoIP Dial Peer Examples*

```
router#show running-config
dial-peer voice 3000 voip
 destination-pattern 3...
 session target ipv4:172.19.153.41
 dtmf-relay h245-alphanumeric
 codec g711ulaw
 no vad
```

Extensions

You can configure the extensions defined for your IP phones either by using the GUI or directly on the router using the **ephone-dn** command. As covered in Chapter 5, "Cisco CME Call Processing Features," an ephone-dn has two components:

- A virtual POTS dial peer for directing calls to the phone
- A virtual voice port

NOTE   The voice ports and dial peers automatically generated by ephone-dns do not appear on the Cisco CME running configuration. They can be seen only using more specific show commands.

Example 14-4 shows the definition on an ephone-dn and its associated POTS dial peer and voice port.

Example 14-4   *Ephone-dn Dial Peer Example*

```
router#show running-config
ephone-dn  1
 number 3001
 description User1
 name User1
 call-forward busy 3105
 call-forward noan 3105 timeout 10
!
router#show telephony-service dial-peer
dial-peer voice 20001 pots
 destination-pattern 3001
 huntstop
 call-forward busy 3105
 call-forward noan 3105
!
router#show telephony-service voice-port
voice-port 50/0/1
 station-id number 3001
 station-id name User1
 timeout ringing 10
 progress_ind setup enable 3
 port 50/0/1
```

Digit Manipulation Features

Having an internal dial plan such as calling from one IP phone to another using a short extension of three or four digits, while also calling the outside world through the PSTN using fully qualified E.164 numbers, requires a certain amount of digit manipulation to add or subtract leading digits to or from an extension.

Typically, you have a *trunk access* code for an IP phone user to specify that a call should be routed to the PSTN as opposed to another extension. This access code must be translated to a PSTN-recognizable number before delivering the call to the PSTN. In Example 14-2 you saw 9 used as the PSTN access code. Because this number matches the dial peer **destination-pattern** explicitly, it is deleted from the digit string forwarded to the PSTN. You can also see **forward-digits** commands in those POTS dial peers. These control how many of the numbers dialed by the IP phone user are forwarded to the PSTN, thereby offering simple digit manipulation within the dial peer statement itself.

Chapter 6 covered more sophisticated digit manipulation features available in Cisco CME, such as **dialplan-patterns** and Cisco IOS translation rules.

Other Cisco CME Dial Plan Features

Various other types of DNs or extensions also make up part of your dial plan in the sense that defining these features requires the definition of digits to dial to activate the feature. These features include speed dial, intercom, call park, and paging.

There are also other special types of numbers, such as the AA and voice mail pilot numbers, as well as MWI DNs. The **transfer-pattern** feature also plays a role in your dialing plan, because this definition determines what numbers your IP phone users can transfer calls to.

Class of Restriction (COR) and call blocking are features that determine which numbers might *not* be dialed on the system.

NOTE	Dial plans are a wide topic that extends well beyond the scope of Cisco CME. All the different ways you can configure dial plans are beyond the scope of this book.

Configuring Cisco CME Call Processing Features

Chapter 5 discussed numerous Cisco CME call processing features. The following sections discuss how to configure the most common of these features. For further information, refer to the Cisco CME Administration and Configuration Guides on Cisco.com. You can configure all the features discussed in the following sections by using the GUI or CLI.

Configuring Speed Dial

On the **Configure > Phones** menu, scroll down to the speed-dial information. Here you might add or change the speed dials assigned to this phone, as shown in Figure 14-6.

Figure 14-6 *Adding and Changing Speed-Dial Information*

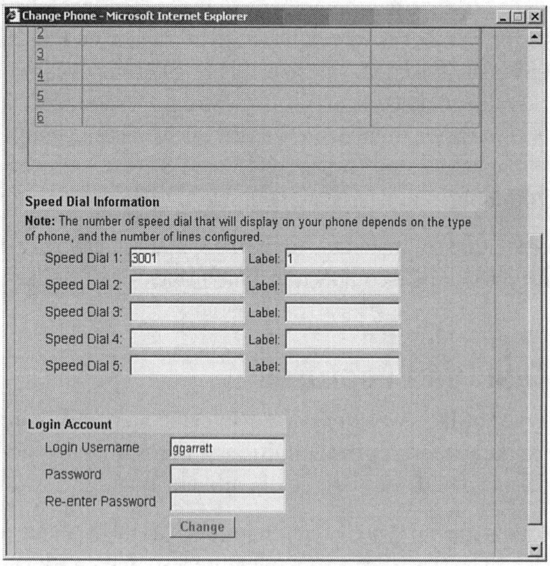

Configuring Call Blocking Toll Bar Override with a PIN

From the **Configure > System Parameters** menu, select **Call Blocking Configuration**, as shown in Figure 14-7. You might add, change, or delete a block pattern (for example, 1900), and block date and day so that no calls to extension 1900 can be made during the date and time configured.

On the **Configure > Phones** menu, select the phone to which you want to apply the call blocking pattern, and then select **Exempt** or **Non Exempt**. If you select Non Exempt, you need to enter a **PIN** for toll bar override if you want the user to be able to log in to remove the call blocking. This is shown in Figure 14-8.

Figure 14-7   *Configuring Call Blocking*

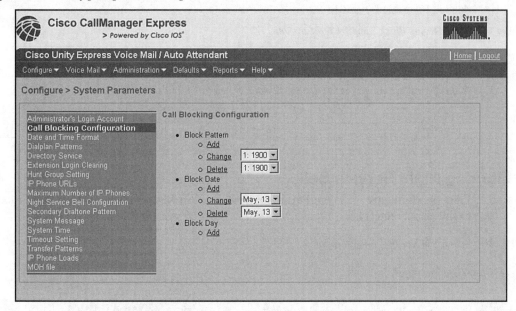

Figure 14-8   *Configuring Phone Call Blocking and Toll Bar Override with a PIN*

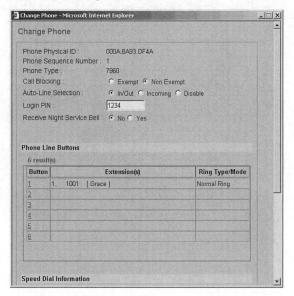

The configuration commands shown in Example 14-5 are created as a result of the configuration done in Figures 14-7 and 14-8.

Example 14-5   *After-Hours Block Sample Configuration*

```
Router#show running-config
telephony-service
after-hours block pattern 1 1900 7-24
 after-hours date might 13 00:00 23:00
 !
 ephone 1
 pin 1234
```

Configuring Night Service Bell

From the **Configure > System Parameters** menu, select **Night Service Bell Configuration**, as shown in Figure 14-9.

Figure 14-9   *Night Service Bell Configuration*

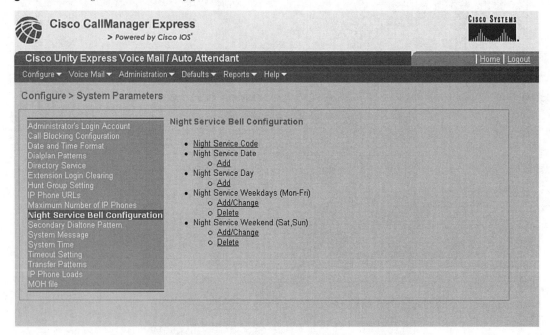

To configure Night Service Bell, follow these steps:

Step 1   To configure the periods of time for weekdays or weekends when you want the Night Service Bell to be active, click **Night Service Weekdays (Mon-Fri) or Night Service Weekend (Sat, Sun)**. Click the add button to add a new time period, or change the **Start Time** and **End Time** fields to make changes to the currently defined time period, as shown in Figure 14-10.

Figure 14-10   *Configuring Night Service Weekday*

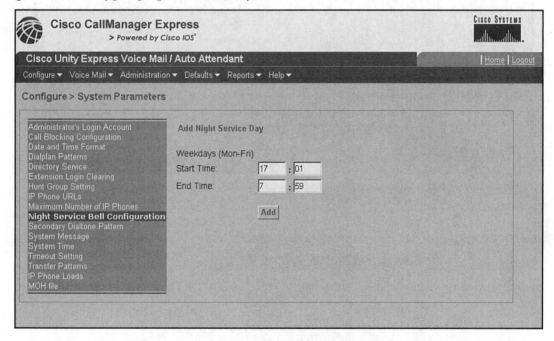

Step 2   Configure the code that triggers Night Service to become active by clicking the **Night Service Code** field on the screen shown in Figure 14-9. Use an asterisk (*) as the prefix to the other digits, as shown in Figure 14-11, and then click the **Change** button.

Step 3   Configure the extension to which to apply the **Night Service Bell** in the **Configure > Extensions** menu. Select the appropriate extension, as shown in Figure 14-12 (where extension 1001 is selected as an example). Select the **Yes** radio button next to **Receive Night Service Bell**, and click the **Change** button.

Figure 14-11 *Configuring Night Service Code*

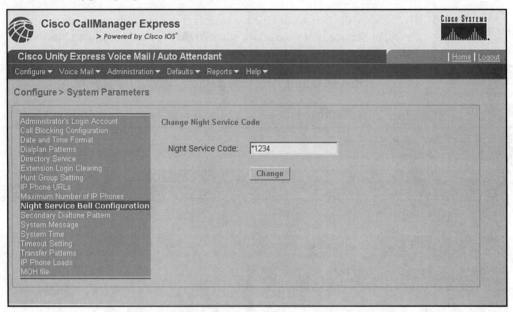

Figure 14-12 *Configuring an Extension with Night Service Bell*

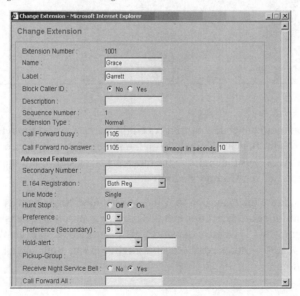

Step 4   Configure the phone for the Night Service Bell by choosing **Configure >
Phones**. Then select the phone needed for the Night Service Bell, as shown
in Figure 14-13 (where ephone 1 is selected). Select the Yes radio button next
to the **Receive Night Service Bell** field, and then scroll down the window to
click the **Change** button at the bottom. This means that the IP phone
associated with ephone 1 receives the Night Service Bell notification when
extension 1001 is called during the time configured for night service.

Figure 14-13   *Configuring an IP Phone with Night Service Bell Notification*

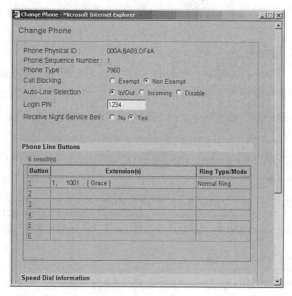

Step 5   When you are done with the changes in GUI, choose **Administration >
Update System** Info (if you have a Cisco CME system) or **Administration
> Synchronize Information** (if you have a combined Cisco CME and Cisco
UE system). This ensures that all the changes are put into effect.

The Cisco CME CLI configuration commands shown in Example 14-6 are created as a result
of the preceding GUI configuration.

Example 14-6   *Night Service Bell Configuration*

```
Router#show running-config
telephony-service
  night-service code *1234
  night-service day Mon 17:01 07:59
  night-service day Tue 17:01 07:59
  night-service day Wed 17:01 07:59
  night-service day Thu 17:01 07:59
  night-service day Fri 17:01 07:59
```

continues

Example 14-6 *Night Service Bell Configuration (Continued)*

```
!
ephone-dn  1
 number 1001
 night-service bell
!
ephone  1
 username "ggarrett" password cisco
 mac-address 000A.8A93.DF4A
 button  1:1
 night-service bell
```

Configuring Hunt Groups

You might add, delete, or change hunt groups in the **Configure > System Parameters** menu by selecting **Hunt Group Setting**.

You can select one of three hunt group types when adding a hunt group:

- **Sequential**—Call hunting always starts with the first extension in the group.

- **Peer**—Call hunting starts with the extension immediately after the one that just took the previous call.

- **Longest Idle**—Presents the call to the extension with the longest idle time, according to the time stamp of the most recent call taken by that extension. If the first extension selected is unavailable, the search continues to the next extension in the group.

NOTE   You should use the huntstop channel feature on any dual-line extensions in the hunt group for calls to these extensions to be routed to the first idle extension within the hunt group, rather than presenting the call as a call-waiting call on an extension that is already in use.

Follow these steps to add a hunt group:

Step 1   Choose **Configure > System Parameters**.

Step 2   Select **Hunt Group Setting**. The Hunt Group Configuration window appears.

Step 3   Click **Add**.

Step 4   Enter the data in the fields shown in Figure 14-14.

Figure 14-14   *Adding Hunt Groups*

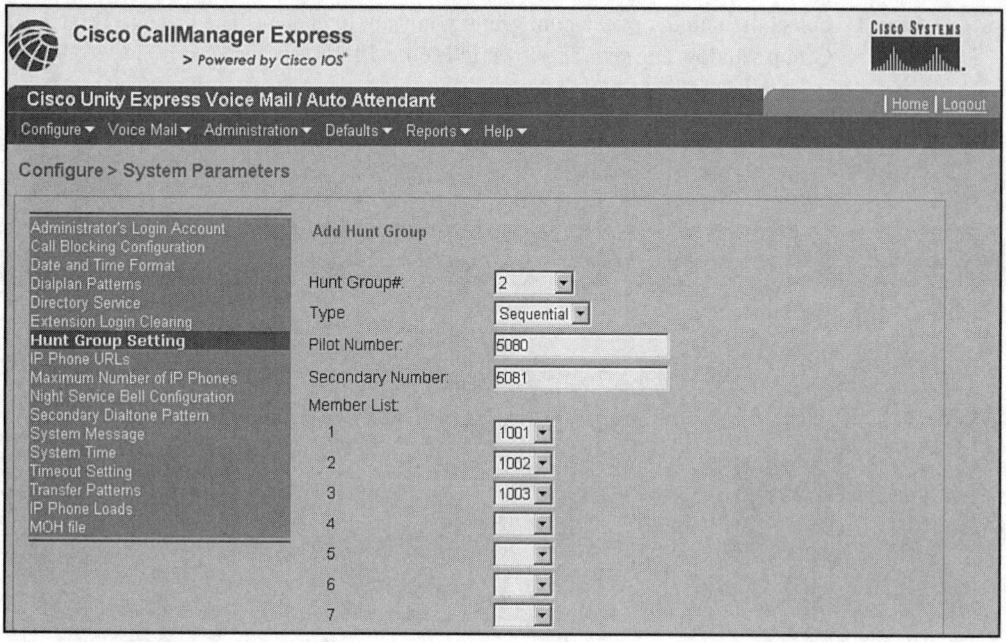

Step 5   To save the information, click **Add**.

Step 6   Click **OK** to save changes.

The Cisco CME CLI configuration commands shown in Example 14-7 are created as a result of the preceding GUI configuration.

Example 14-7   *Hunt Group Configuration*

```
Router#show running-config
ephone-hunt 2 sequential
 pilot 5080 secondary 5081
 list 1001, 1002, 1003
 final 5222
 preference 0 secondary 7
```

Follow these steps to delete a hunt group:

Step 1   Select the group and click **Delete**.

Step 2   Click **OK** to delete, and click **OK** again at the information prompt.

Follow these steps to change a hunt group:

Step 1   Select the number of the hunt group you want to change. The Change Hunt Group window appears, as shown in Figure 14-15.

Figure 14-15   *Changing Hunt Groups*

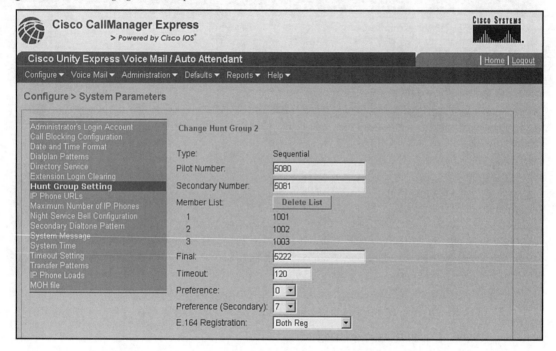

Step 2   Enter your changes to the fields in the table. Scroll down to the bottom of the screen and click **Change**.

Step 3   Click **OK** to save changes.

Configuring Transfer Patterns

Transfer patterns allow phone users to transfer calls to off-net (PSTN) numbers, non-SCCP voice mail such as Cisco UE, or on-net numbers of extensions at other sites. You must explicitly configure these numbers in a transfer pattern to be allowed to transfer to these destinations by the system. By default, all local IP phone extension numbers can transfer from one extension to another, but not to the PSTN or extensions at other sites.

Follow these steps to configure transfer patterns:

Step 1   Choose **Configure > System Parameters**.

Step 2   Select **Transfer Patterns**. The Transfer Patterns window appears, as shown in Figure 14-16.

Figure 14-16   *Configuring Transfer Patterns*

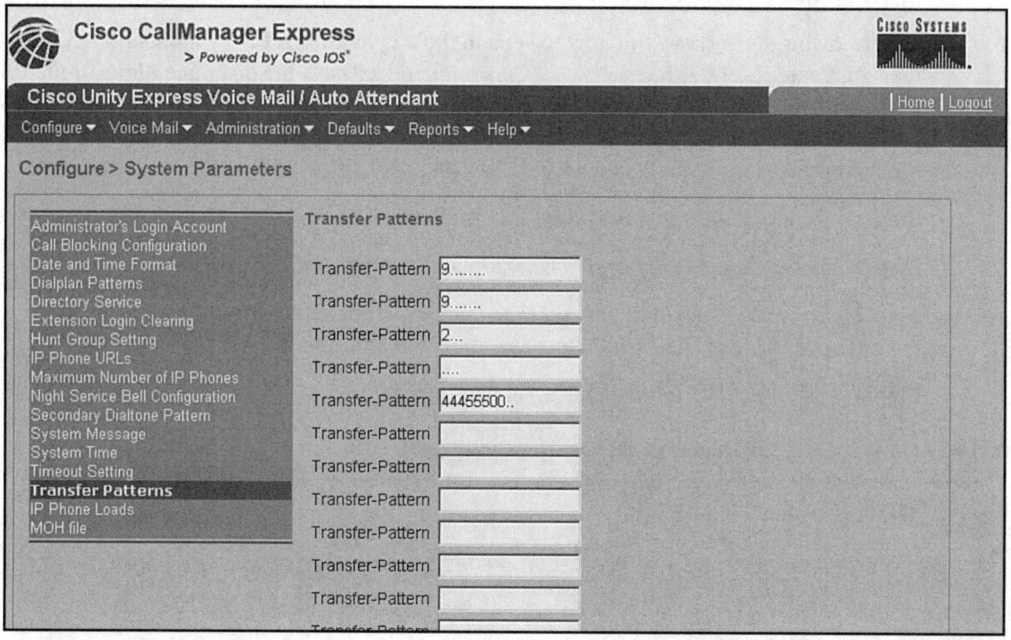

Step 3   In the **Transfer-Pattern** fields, enter the numbers to which calls are allowed to be transferred. Use wildcards to allow transfers to a range of numbers. For example, set 40855500.. to allow calls to be transferred to numbers in the range 4085550001 to 4085550099, as shown in Figure 14-16.

Step 4   After entering the information, click **Set** and then click **OK** to save.

The Cisco CME CLI configuration commands shown in Example 14-8 are created as a result of the preceding GUI configuration.

Example 14-8   *Transfer Patterns Configuration*

```
Router#show running-config
telephony-service
transfer-pattern 9.......
 transfer-pattern 9.......
 transfer-pattern 2...
 transfer-pattern ....
 transfer-pattern 44455500..
```

Configuring Dial Plan Patterns

The dial plan pattern specifies a global prefix for expanding abbreviated extension numbers into fully qualified E.164 PSTN numbers. Set the prefix information if your PSTN connection supports Direct Inward Dial (DID).

The following steps show you how to set a dial plan pattern for PSTN number 3335550... to a four-digit extension starting with 1.... The command extracts the last three digits of the PSTN DID number to form the last three digits of the extension number. You can use this command to keep DID numbers such as 333-555-0111 from resulting (after translation) in four-digit extensions that start with 0 (such as 0111).

Step 1 Choose **Configure > System Parameters**.

Step 2 Select Dialplan Patterns. The Dialplan Patterns window appears.

Step 3 To create a new dial plan pattern, click the **<not set>** field to the right of a pattern. The Dialplan Pattern **number** window appears.

Step 4 Enter the data in the fields as shown in Figure 14-17.

Figure 14-17 *Cisco CME Configure System Parameter Dial Plan Patterns*

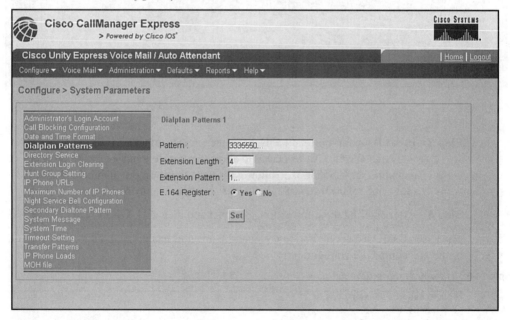

Step 5 Click **Set** to save the information, and then click **OK** to confirm.

The Cisco CME CLI configuration commands shown in Example 14-9 are created as a result of the preceding GUI configuration.

Example 14-9   *Dial Plan Patterns Sample Configuration*

```
Router#show running-config
telephony-service
dialplan-pattern 1 3335550... extension-length 4 extension-pattern 1...
```

Music on Hold

This feature supports .au and .wav files. Music on hold (MOH) works only for G.711 on-net VoIP calls and PSTN calls. Calls between local Cisco CME phones do not hear MOH; instead, they get tone on hold.

A sample MOH file, music-on-hold.au, is included in the CME.zip or .tar file that you can download from Cisco.com. Place the MOH file on a TFTP server in your network, and then copy it to the Cisco CME router's Flash using the command **copy tftp://ip address/music-on-hold.au flash:**. **ip address** is the TFTP server's IP address. Be sure to enter **n** when prompted to erase Flash.

The MOH file is configured using the **moh music-on-hold.au** command under **telephony-service**. The MOH file can also be configured via the GUI, as shown in Figure 14-18.

Figure 14-18   *Cisco CME Configure > System Parameters MOH*

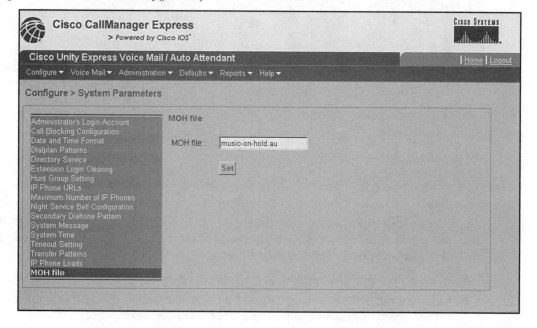

Configuring the Cisco UE AA

You set up the Cisco UE system-provided AA when you worked through the Initialization Wizard (see the section "Cisco UE Initialization Wizard" in Chapter 13). The configuration needed for the system AA includes the business hours, holiday list, operator extension, AA pilot number, and a few prompts spoken to callers by the system AA.

Configuring the System AA

Figure 14-19 shows the customization of the Cisco UE system AA. You start in the **Voice Mail > Auto Attendant** menu, and then click **autoattendant** in the list of AA scripts. This opens the AA Configuration Wizard. Go to the second step, Script Parameters, and set the parameter operExtn to the extension in your office where you want calls transferred when a caller chooses to speak to the operator. Figure 14-19 shows the operator extension set to extension 1001.

Figure 14-19   *Cisco UE System AA Configuration*

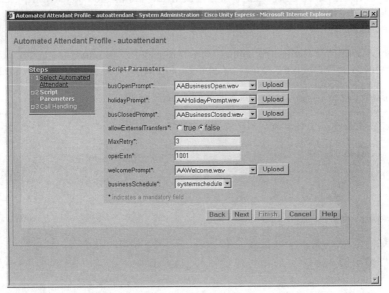

To replace the system-provided prompts (shown in Figure 14-19), log into the AVT TUI (called the Greeting Management System [GMS] in Cisco UE releases before release 2.1), and record the following customized prompts for your office:

- **welcomePrompt**—The welcome greeting spoken when the AA answers a call.

- **busOpenPrompt**—The prompt following the welcome prompt, spoken if your office is currently open (based on the system time when the call arrives).

- **busClosedPrompt**—The prompt following the welcome prompt, spoken if your office is currently closed (based on the system time when the call arrives).

- **holidayPrompt**—The prompt following the welcome prompt, spoken if the current system date is listed as a holiday in the system.

The business hours and holiday list configurations that the system AA consults to determine which prompt to play to a caller are general Cisco UE system configurations. They are not particular to the system AA. All system and customized AA scripts can use these business hours and holiday definitions to branch appropriately within an AA script. The following two sections discuss configuring the business hours and holidays for your office.

Configuring Business Hours

You can define several business hours schedules in your Cisco UE system. A default schedule (named systemschedule) ships with Cisco UE software. You can add others or customize the system default.

Figure 14-20 shows the customized system default business hours schedule. You access this configuration by navigating to the **Voice Mail > Business Hours Settings** screen. The office is open Monday through Friday from 07:00 to 18:00 and Saturday from 10:00 to 15:00 and is closed on Sunday. The column titles have scrolled off the screen, but Monday is on the far left and Sunday is on the far right.

Figure 14-20   *Cisco UE Business Hours Configuration*

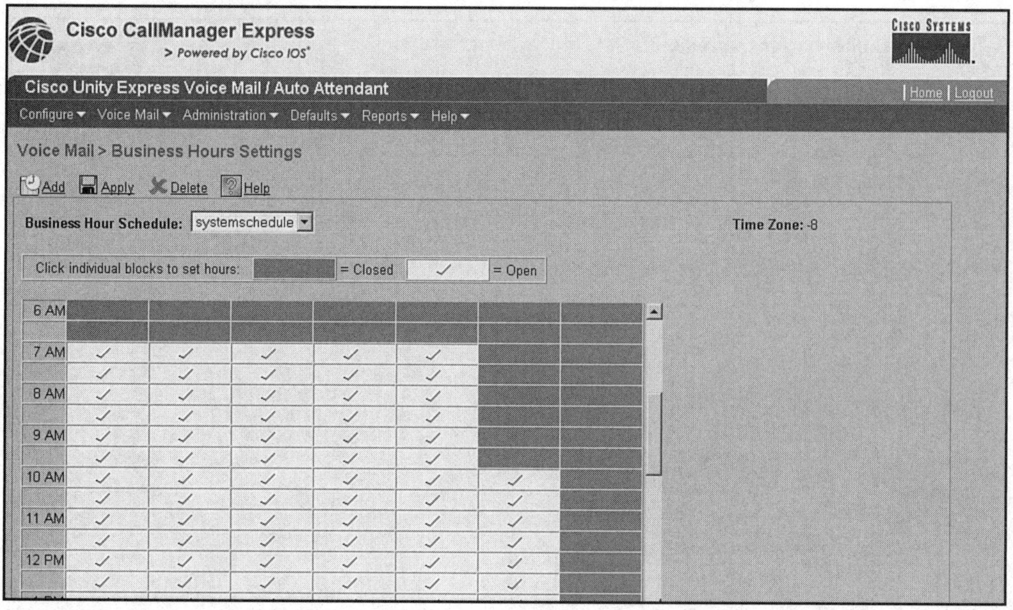

The Cisco UE CLI configuration commands shown in Example 14-10 are created as a result of the preceding GUI configuration. Day 1 corresponds to Sunday.

Example 14-10   *Business Hours Customization Configuration*

```
CUE#show running-config
calendar biz-schedule systemschedule
 closed day 1 from 00:00 to 24:00
 open day 2 from 07:00 to 18:00
 open day 3 from 07:00 to 18:00
 open day 4 from 07:00 to 18:00
 open day 5 from 07:00 to 18:00
 open day 6 from 07:00 to 18:00
 open day 7 from 10:00 to 15:00
 end schedule
```

Configuring Holidays

You can define up to 26 holidays per year in your Cisco UE system. The system ships with no holidays predefined.

Figure 14-21 shows a list of holidays configured for the year 2005. You access this configuration by navigating to the **Voice Mail > Holiday Settings** screen. If the system date matches any of these days, the system AA automatically speaks the holiday greeting you recorded in your system. Your custom AA scripts might also use the holiday list definition to branch to special menus.

Figure 14-21   *Cisco UE Holiday List Configuration*

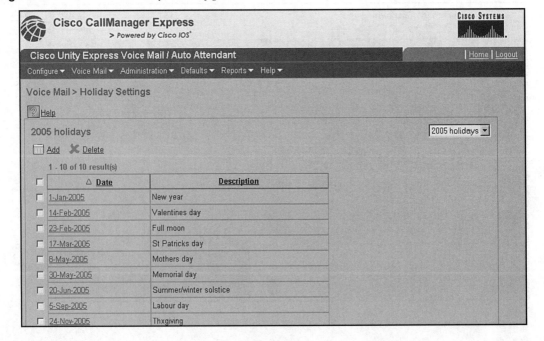

The Cisco UE CLI configuration commands shown in Example 14-11 are created as a result of the preceding GUI configuration.

Example 14-11 *Holiday List Customization Configuration*

```
CUE#show running-config
  calendar holiday date 2005 01 01 description "New year"
  calendar holiday date 2005 05 30 description "Memorial day"
  calendar holiday date 2005 09 05 description "Labour day"
  calendar holiday date 2005 11 24 description "Thxgiving"
  calendar holiday date 2005 12 21 description "Summer/winter solstice"
  calendar holiday date 2005 02 23 description "Full moon"
  calendar holiday date 2005 02 14 description "Valentines day"
  calendar holiday date 2005 03 17 description "St Patricks day"
  calendar holiday date 2005 05 08 description "Mothers day"
  calendar holiday date 2005 06 20 description "Summer/winter solstice"
```

Creating a Custom AA

Chapter 9, "Cisco IPC Express Automated Attendant Options," covered the AVT and a step-by-step approach to setting up a custom AA.

Cisco UE lets you define up to five different AAs, each with an individual pilot number. The system shown in Figure 14-22 has three AAs defined:

- The system AA, titled autoattendant, which is associated with 1100 as the pilot number. It cannot be changed or deleted, so it always shows up.

- A custom AA titled officehours, associated with 1102 as the pilot number.

- A custom AA titled salesmtg05, associated with 1101 as the pilot number.

NOTE	If an AA consists of multiple scripts (the main script and some subflows called by the main script), only the script parameters defined in the main script can be seen and the values changed in the Script Parameters window of the AA Configuration Wizard. This window was shown in Figure 14-19. (This is just an example. Remember that the screen is different for every script because the parameters for every script differ.) Parameters defined in subflows do not show up in the Script Parameters window.

Viewing the List of AA Scripts

Each AA might use one or more scripts. You can see all the scripts in the system by selecting **Voice Mail > Scripts**, as shown in Figure 14-23.

Figure 14-22 *Defining Multiple Custom AAs*

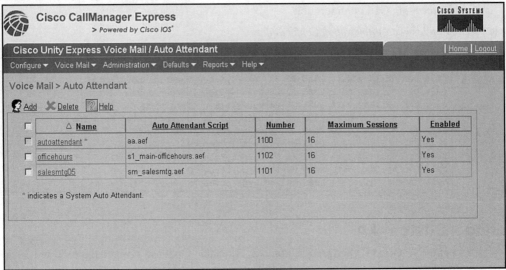

Figure 14-23 *AA Scripts*

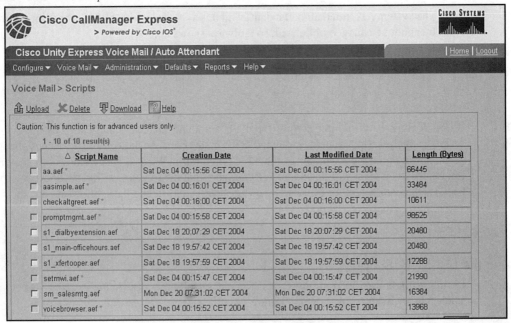

The list of scripts shown in Figure 14-23 includes a number of system scripts (denoted by an asterisk following the name) and several custom AA scripts.

System scripts might not be uploaded, downloaded, or deleted. You might perform these operations on any custom scripts you have loaded on the system by selecting the script and clicking the appropriate button at the top of the screen, as shown in Figure 14-23.

You can upload a maximum of four custom scripts on the AIM-CUE and eight on the NM-CUE. Scripts support an unlimited number of steps and nesting levels so that you can build very sophisticated AA menus with the Cisco UE AA application.

Recording and Deleting AA Prompts

The AVT allows you to record and delete prompts used by your AA scripts. You can also record the prompts offline and upload them to Cisco UE. However, if you do not have a recording facility, or you just want to test the system before you do the professional recordings, you can use the AVT. The functionality of the GMS was covered in Chapter 9.

To log into the AVT, you must define a user on the Cisco UE system who has administrative privileges (that is, a user who is a member of the administrators group). This user must also have a mailbox defined. The PIN for the mailbox is used as the login authentication for the AVT.

If you record prompts by using the AVT, the system assigns automatic filenames to the prompts. You cannot change these filenames on the Cisco UE system, but you can download the prompt file to your PC, rename it there, and then upload it to the Cisco UE system. Associate this new filename with your script, and delete the original prompt file. Figure 14-24 shows a list of the prompts in your Cisco UE system, which you can see by going to the **Voice Mail > Prompts** GUI menu.

The AVT has a pilot number associated with it, just like the AA and voice mail pilot numbers. This is the number you call when you want to log into the AVT to change AA prompts. You define the pilot number in the **Voice Mail > Call Handling** GUI window.

Figure 14-24 *AA Prompts*

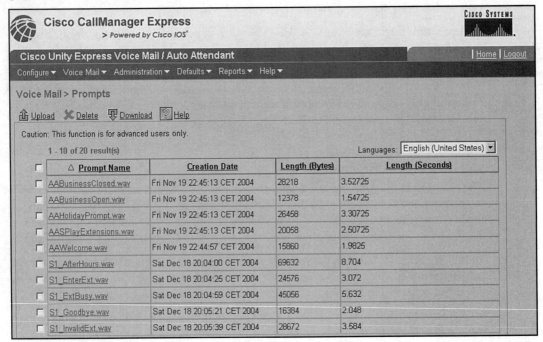

Configuring Cisco UE Voice Mail

Cisco UE offers both personal and GDMs, as covered in Chapter 10, "Cisco IPC Express Integrated Voice Mail." The following sections cover configuring the Cisco UE voice mail system, personal mailboxes, GDMs, and MWI. You also learn how to delete a mailbox.

Configuring the Voice Mail System

You have to set several system-level voice mail configuration parameters, including system attributes such as the voice mail pilot number, voice mail operator number, and mailbox system defaults. You also define individual mailboxes for users and groups.

Pilot Number

The voice mail pilot number is the extension subscribers call when they want to retrieve their voice mail. It is also the number that IP phones are forwarded to so that callers are deflected into voice mail to leave a message. The configuration of the pilot number is shown in Figure 14-25.

Figure 14-25   *Voice Mail Pilot Number Configuration*

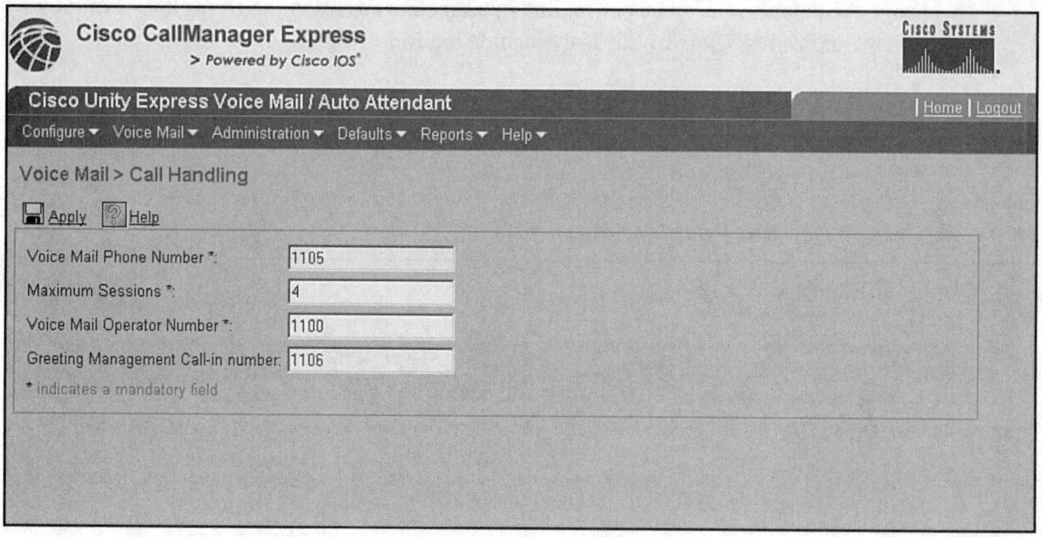

Voice Mail Operator

The voice mail operator is the extension number where callers are deflected if they leave a voice mail and do not hang up. This configuration is shown in Figure 14-25. The default voice mail operator is the AA.

System and Mailbox Defaults

When you create a new mailbox for an existing user, or when you add a user at the same time as the mailbox, you can use the default system mailbox parameters. As the administrator, you can override the values of these parameters for each mailbox at creation time or later, or you can reset the system defaults so that all newly created mailboxes are assigned the same parameters.

You should set the per-mailbox parameters carefully before creating a large number of user mailboxes. When the system defaults are changed, existing mailboxes are unaffected. The default settings apply only to creating new mailboxes. For example, if the message expiry time default parameter is set to 30 days, all mailboxes created are assigned a 30-day expiry time. If you create 25 mailboxes before deciding that the expiry time should instead be 60 days, you then have to change each of the 25 existing mailboxes individually to reset the expiry time to

60 days. Changing the default value to 60 days affects only new mailboxes you create after you change the default value. The per-mailbox parameters are set in the **Defaults > Mailbox** window, shown in Figure 14-26. They include the following:

- Mailbox size in seconds
- Maximum caller message size
- Message expiry time

Figure 14-26 *Mailbox Parameter Default Configuration*

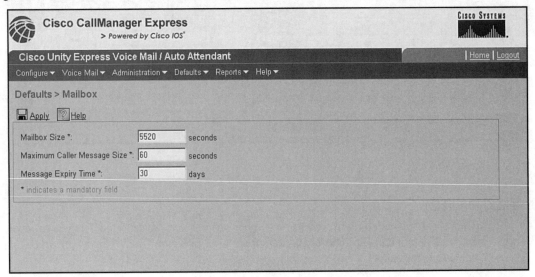

You set the system-level voice mail parameters in the **Defaults > Voice Mail** window, as shown in Figure 14-27.

Configuring Personal Mailboxes

Mailboxes cannot exist without being associated with a user. You typically add a user and his or her mailbox at the same time, as shown in Figure 14-28. You add a user in the **Configure > Users** window. When the Add a New User window appears, fill in all the user-related parameters, and then click the **Create Mailbox** checkbox at the bottom of the window.

Figure 14-27   *Mailbox System Default Configuration*

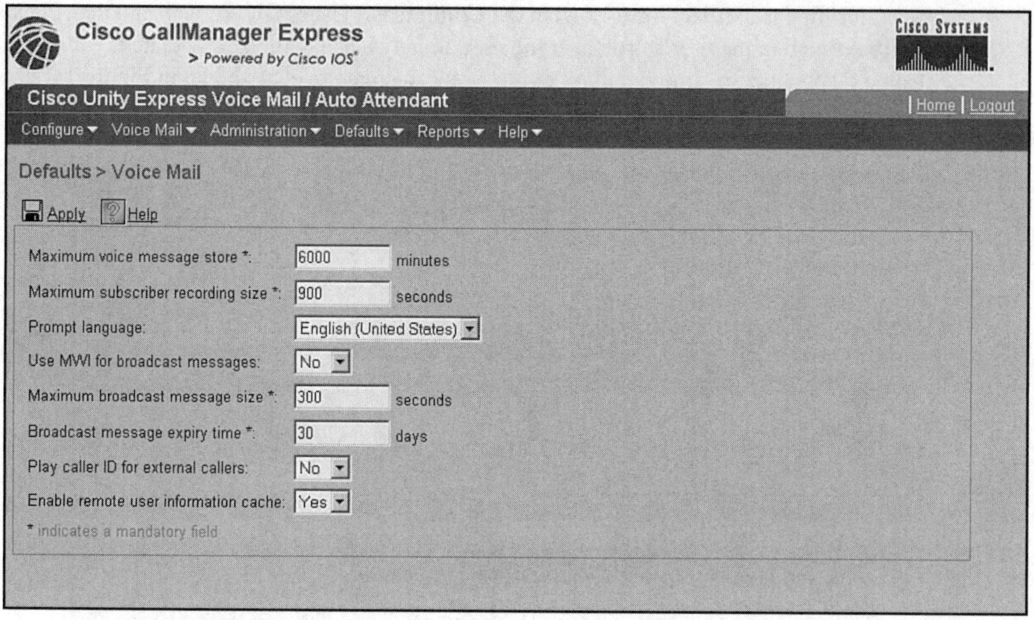

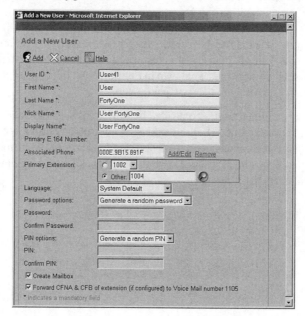

Figure 14-28   *User and Mailbox Configuration*

You can also later add a mailbox to an existing user definition. You can do this in one of two ways. The first is to select the user from the **Configure > Users** GUI screen, and then click the **Mailboxes** tab in the user's profile. If the user already has a mailbox associated, you see the mailbox's parameters. If no mailbox exists, you can create one, as shown in Figure 14-29.

Figure 14-29 *Adding a Mailbox from the User Profile*

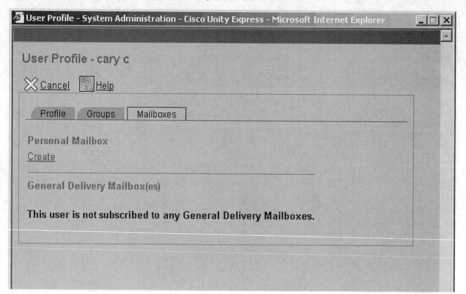

The second way to add a mailbox to an existing user definition is to look at a list of existing mailboxes in the **Voice Mail > Mailboxes** window, and click **Add** on this screen. The Add a New Mailbox window appears, as shown in Figure 14-30. It lets you define the mailbox's owner (the associated user) and the mailbox parameters.

MWI for a personal mailbox is controlled by the extension associated with the user (and, by implication, with the mailbox). If the extension appears on button 1 of a phone (any phone or multiple phones), the lamp is lit on that phone for MWI. If the extension appears on button 2 or higher of a phone (again, any phone or multiple phones), a flashing envelope is displayed next to the extension appearance.

Figure 14-30   *Adding a Mailbox from the Mailbox List*

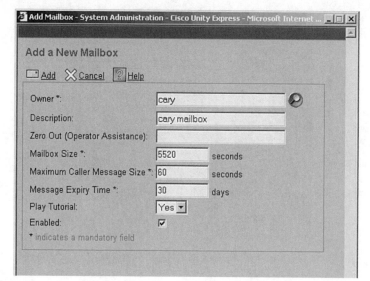

Configuring General Delivery Mailboxes

A GDM is a mailbox associated with a group as opposed to an individual user. In most respects, it works just like an individual mailbox, except that multiple people (all members of the group) have access to the mailbox. Also, you cannot log into a GDM itself, because no PIN is associated with it. Members of the group log into their personal mailboxes first (where system authentication occurs), and then choose number nine from their mailbox menu to gain entry to all GDMs they have access to.

Like a personal mailbox, you can define the mailbox at the same time as the group, as shown in Figure 14-31. Or you can go to the **Voice Mail > Mailboxes** window, click **Add** on this screen, and then define the owner of the new mailbox as a group in the Add a New Mailbox window.

The customer service group defined in the system shown in Figure 14-31 has three members. Any of these three people can log into the GDM to retrieve messages. Each of the three has a personal mailbox and PIN used to log into and then access the GDM from there. The group definition is shown in Figure 14-32.

Figure 14-31 *Group and GDM Configuration*

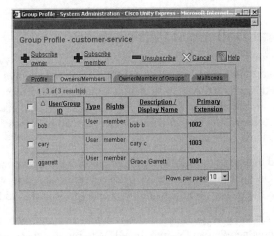

Figure 14-32 *Group Member Configuration*

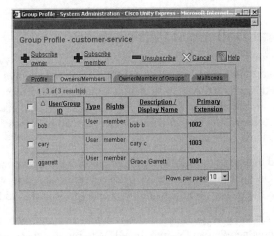

NOTE   *Members* of a group can access the GDM to retrieve messages. A group's *owner* can change the group's configuration (the membership list). Unless the owner is also specified as a member of the group, he or she cannot log into the GDM.

MWI for GDMs works just like MWI for personal mailboxes. If the extension associated with the group appears on the button of any phone, that phone's lamp is lit when a message is left in the GDM. (The lamp is not lit automatically for every member of the group; it is lit only if the group's extension appears on the phone.) If the extension appears on button 2 or higher of a phone, a flashing envelope icon appears. If the extension does not appear on any phone, no MWI exists for the GDM.

Grace Garrett is a member of the customer service group, as shown in Figure 14-32. The extension associated with customer service is 1050. Extension 1050 appears on button 2 of Grace's phone (whose own extension is 1001), so Grace sees a flashing envelope icon as an indication of MWI for messages in the GDM. Grace's phone button layout is shown in Figure 14-33.

Figure 14-33   *Phone Configuration for GDM MWI*

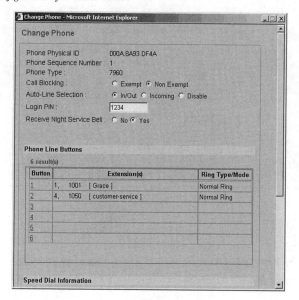

Deleting a Mailbox

One way to delete a mailbox (but keep the subscriber definition) is to select the mailbox(es) to be deleted from the mailbox list shown in the **Voice Mail > Mailboxes** screen, and click the delete button at the top of the screen.

A more common way is to delete the subscriber from the **Configure > Users** window. When you do that, the subscriber's associated mailbox is automatically deleted as well.

In the GUI, a mailbox is deleted when the subscriber is deleted. This is not true for the CLI. In the CLI, deleting a subscriber leaves the mailbox intact. That mailbox is not associated with any subscriber. Therefore, it shows up as an orphaned mailbox in the listing, as shown in Figure 14-34.

Figure 14-34 *Orphaned Mailbox*

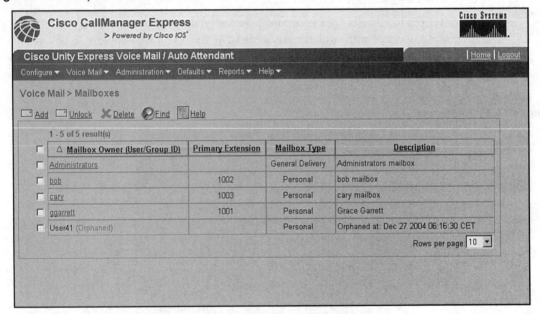

Configuring MWI

You define the MWI DNs on the Cisco CME system as ephone-dns. You see them in the GUI in the **Voice Mail > Message Waiting Indicators > Numbers** window, as shown in Figure 14-35.

Figure 14-35   *MWI Configuration*

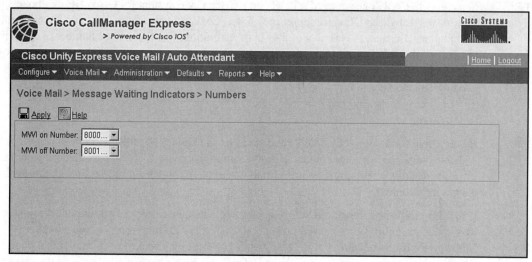

MWI is controlled using two special-purpose DNs: an MWI-on DN and an MWI-off DN. You can also see the MWI DNs in the **Configure > Extensions** window. The router CLI definitions for the MWI DNs are shown in Example 14-12.

Example 14-12   *MWI DN Definition*

```
router#show running-config
ephone-dn  51
 number 8000....
 mwi on
!
ephone-dn  52
 number 8001....
 mwi off
```

The dots in the preceding definitions are critical. MWI does not work if the dots are not configured correctly. You must have one dot for each digit in your extension dialing plan, so the definitions shown in Example 14-12 are applicable to a four-digit extension number dialing plan.

NOTE   You can define only one set of MWI DNs on a Cisco CME system for Cisco UE mailboxes. This means that Cisco UE can support only Cisco CME configurations that have fixed-length dialing plans. Because the number of dots in the definitions must match the number of digits in the dialing plan, MWI does not work if the extensions are a different length than the number of dots. Because you can specify only one set of MWI DNs, Cisco UE cannot support MWI for variable-length extension dialing plans.

If everything works correctly, MWI lamp states on the phones should always be synchronized with the mailboxes' message content. However, through moving phones around, turning phones off, and changing configurations, it is possible to get lamp states out of synchronization with the mailbox content.

If MWI needs to be resynchronized, you can force a manual refresh of an individual phone's MWI or of the entire system's MWI (all phones). You can do this from the **Voice Mail > Message Waiting Indicators > Refresh** window. Select the checkboxes of individual phones where you want to reset MWI, or click the **Refresh All** button to reset all phones on the system, as shown in Figure 14-36.

Figure 14-36   *MWI Refresh*

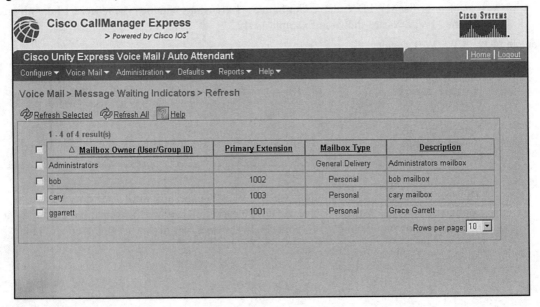

The refresh all function resets all phones in a serial manner at the rate of one MWI every 4 seconds, so for a system with 100 mailboxes, a full MWI refresh might take up to 7 minutes.

Configuring Voice Mail Networking

Voice mail networking allows you to send and forward messages between multiple Cisco UE or Cisco Unity sites in your network using Voice Profile for Internet Mail (VPIM). At a particular Cisco UE site, every location in the network that you want to send messages to or receive messages from must be defined on the local system. Therefore, every networked location contains voice mail networking definitions for itself (the local location) and all the remote locations you want to be able to network to from this site.

Configure voice mail networking locations by navigating to the **Administration > Networking Locations** screen, shown in Figure 14-37. You can access the same functionality by using the **network location** Cisco UE CLI command. In Figure 14-37, five sites are configured, and the local location is Site8.

Figure 14-37 *Configuring Voice Mail Network Locations*

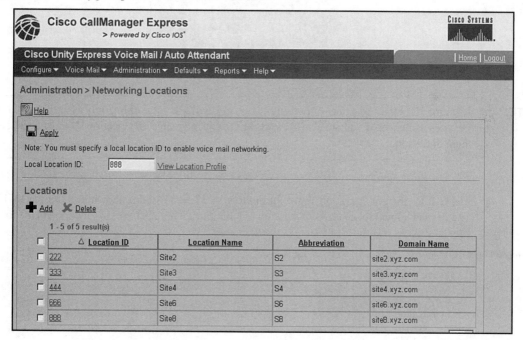

To see the configuration of a particular location (both local and remote sites), click the site's location ID. The resulting screen for Site3 (location 333) is shown in Figure 14-38. You see the individual networking parameters for the selected site.

Figure 14-38 *Networking Parameters for Location Site3*

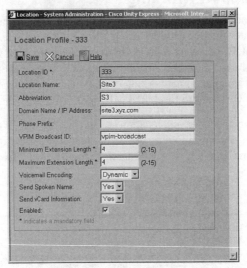

NOTE Location IDs might be a one- or two-digit number if you are networking only a handful of Cisco UE sites. However, if you are also networking Cisco Unity sites, the location ID must be at least three digits long.

The CLI for the configuration shown in Figures 14-37 and 14-38 is shown in Example 14-13. The **network local location id 888** command identifies which networking location is the local site.

Example 14-13 *Configuring Voice Mail Network Locations*

```
cue#show running-config
ip name-server 172.19.2.133
network location id 222
 abbreviation "S2"
 email domain site2.xyz.com
 name "Site2"
 voicemail extension-length 4
```

Example 14-13 *Configuring Voice Mail Network Locations (Continued)*

```
 end location

network location id 333
 abbreviation "S3"
 email domain site3.xyz.com
 name "Site3"
 voicemail extension-length 4
 end location

network location id 444
 abbreviation "S4"
 email domain site4.xyz.com
 name "Site4"
 voicemail extension-length 4
 end location

network location id 666
 abbreviation "S6"
 email domain site6.xyz.com
 name "Site6"
 voicemail extension-length 4
 end location

network location id 888
 abbreviation "S8"
 email domain site8.xyz.com
 name "Site8"
 voicemail extension-length 4
 end location

network local location id 888
```

If domain names are used for networking, as shown in this configuration example, ensure that a DNS server is configured where Cisco UE can resolve the domain names to IP addresses. Figure 14-39 shows the GUI screen for configuring a DNS server.

Cisco UE networking uses blind addressing by default, which means you address a voice message to a remote location with numbers only, using the location ID followed by the extension at the remote site. For example, a message from local Site8 to extension 2444 at remote Site2 is addressed as 2222444. The address confirmation heard by the sending subscriber says "extension 2444 at site S2," using the abbreviation S2 of Site2 to construct the confirmation.

Figure 14-39 *DNS Server Configuration*

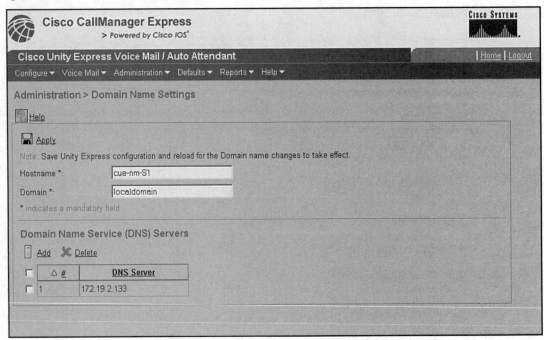

You can provide a limited amount of spoken-name address confirmations on Cisco UE by configuring the following options:

- You can record spoken names for all remote locations, such as "Vancouver" instead of "S2" for Site2. You can record the names associated with the remote location IDs by using the Cisco UE AVT.

- You can use the static directory to configure certain remote users who are frequently addressed in voice mails, and record spoken names for them.

- You can turn on the dynamic directory cache so that vCard information from messages received from remote sites is available for use if a subscriber addresses one of these subscribers or clicks **Reply** on the received message.

The Cisco UE static directory of remote users is populated using the **Configure > Remote Users** screen, as shown in Figure 14-40. You can use the AVT to record initial spoken names associated with these users (until a message is received and the spoken name is updated with the subscriber's real name).

Figure 14-40   *Remote User Static Directory*

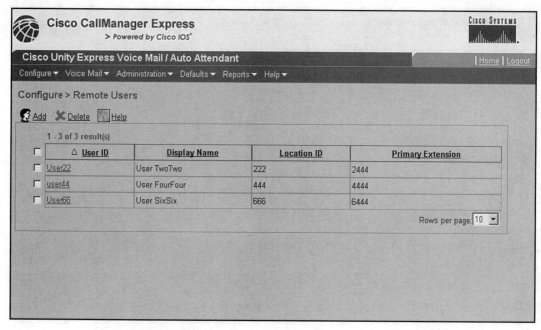

Example 14-14 shows the Cisco UE CLI resulting from this GUI configuration.

Example 14-14   *Configuring the Remote User Static Directory*

```
cue#show running-config
remote username User22 location 222 create
remote username User66 location 666 create
remote username user44 location 444 create
remote username User22 phonenumber 2444
remote username User66 phonenumber 6444
remote username user44 phonenumber 4444
```

The Cisco UE dynamic cache keeps a least recently used (LRU) cache of remote user information based on messages received from other networking locations. The cache is of limited size, so entries age out of this cache based on usage statistics. The cache is turned on by default, as shown in Figure 14-41 (see the parameter **Enable remote user information cache**). You can disable this operation by turning off this parameter.

Figure 14-41 *Enabling the LRU Cache*

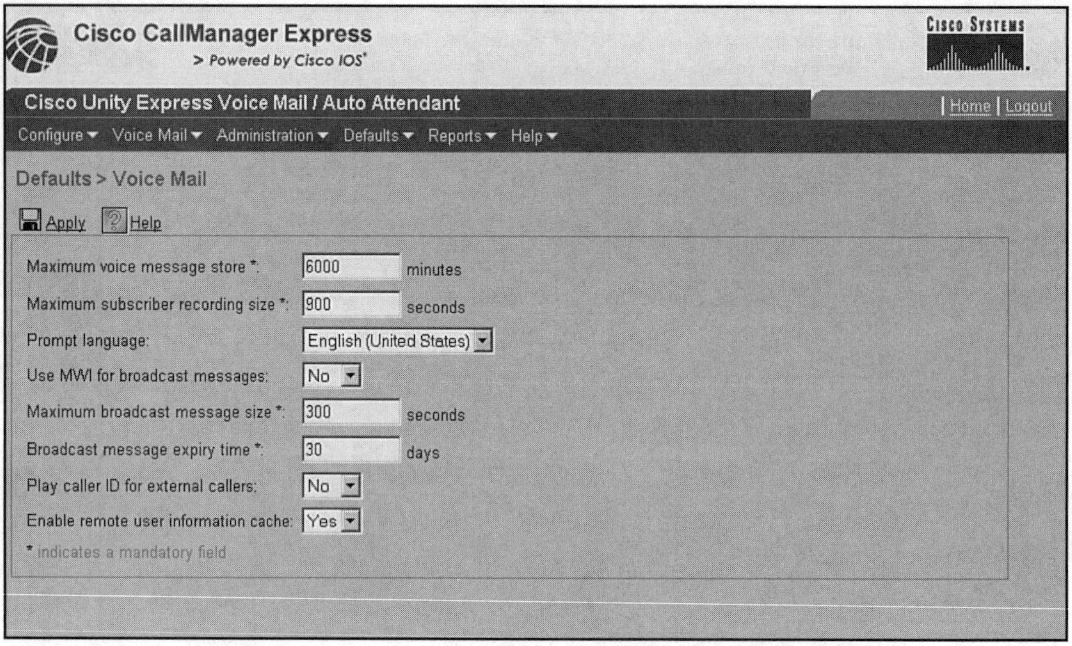

Configuring the AVT

You can manage Cisco UE AA prompts, broadcast messaging, spoken names for remote users and location, and the Emergency Alternate Greeting (EAG) by using the TUI. This means that the administrator can dial in on a phone and make small changes to the system. The AVT requires an extension and a PIN to log in. It authenticates users based on the extension/mailbox PIN combination. It also checks that the user associated with the extension/PIN combination has administrative privileges on the system.

Configuring Cisco UE Backup and Restore

Cisco UE runs on a hardware module that contains storage media separate from that of the router. The NM-CUE has a hard disk, and the AIM-CUE uses onboard compact Flash for storage. The configuration of Cisco UE AA and voice mail—including the AA prompts, user greetings, spoken names, and voice messages—is stored on this disk or Flash unit. Backing up the router configuration, therefore, is insufficient to preserve the Cisco UE application configuration in the event of a disaster (for example, a hard disk failure) or to restore the system's operational data after an application upgrade.

NOTE   A Cisco UE software upgrade reformats the hard disk or Flash unit. To preserve the application configuration and voice messages over an upgrade, you must perform a backup before the upgrade and a restore afterwards.

Cisco UE includes a Backup and Restore facility that uses an FTP server as the backup's destination device. You cannot use Flash or other types of media for backup and restore. You might locate the FTP server anywhere in the network, and you do not need to collocate it with the Cisco UE system being backed up. An FTP server login and password provide secure access to the backup and restore operations.

Backups are invoked manually from the Cisco UE system, using either the CLI or GUI interface. The system must be offline during a backup; therefore, no calls might be active in the system when a backup is being done. After a restore operation, you must restart the application.

Although the Cisco UE system has no mechanism to schedule unattended backups, the backup functionality is available through the CLI. Therefore, it is possible for you to develop a script on another server that automatically (for example, based on time of day) logs into the Cisco UE system's CLI and initiates a backup. If you do scheduled backups in this manner, consider the following:

- A backup requires the system to be offline, and taking the system offline disconnects all calls in progress. If the backup is triggered by a script where the warnings about call disconnection are not seen (because of a scripted interface), backups during normal daytime system use disrupt the system's operation. Write your script to initiate backup during a time of day when no calls are expected to be active.

- If any errors occur, ensure that your script includes a notification to an administrator so that the errors can be investigated.

Several aspects important to configuring backups are discussed in the following sections:

- Specifying a directory path for backup
- Backing up multiple Cisco UEs in a network
- Including configuration and data in the backup
- Configuring multiple generations of backups
- Determining backup file sizes
- Determining backup bandwidth
- Best practices

Specifying a Directory Path for Backup

A backup from a Cisco UE system is done to a configured FTP server. The directory location specified in the configuration cannot be the root path of the FTP system. Figure 14-42 shows a sample configuration in which ftp://172.19.153.33/CUE-site6 is the backup path. A value of ftp://172.19.153.33/ is unacceptable. To enter the backup server path, the FTP server must be in contact with Cisco UE. This means that the FTP location must exist and that Cisco UE validates the location during configuration entry.

Figure 14-42 *Backup FTP Server Configuration*

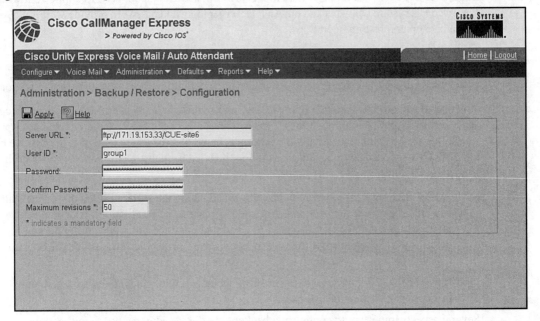

| NOTE | The backup path location is relative to the default FTP path for the user account logging in. |

The configuration shown in Figure 14-42 is shown in Example 14-15 in CLI. Note that the password is not printed in either the GUI or the CLI for security purposes. It is strongly recommended that the FTP server user account you use for backups be password protected. Cisco UE does not encrypt the backup files.

Example 14-15 *Backup FTP Server Configuration*

```
cue#show backup
Server URL:                          ftp://172.19.153.33/CUE-site6
User Account on Server:              group1
Number of Backups to Retain:         50
```

Cisco UE logs into the FTP server with the account user ID specified in the configuration. In Example 14-15, this is group1. The backup directory specified in the configuration (CUE-site6) is, therefore, a subdirectory from the home location of the user ID on the server. In this example, the subdirectory is

```
/home/group1/CUE-site6
```

Backing Up Multiple Cisco UEs in a Network

Backups done from one Cisco UE system have no knowledge of backups or server paths used by other Cisco UE systems in the same network. If multiple Cisco UE sites are configured to back up to the same FTP server, use a separate directory for each site, and name the directories in a recognizable manner. For example, you can use site numbers or geographic tags of sites, as follows:

- ftp://172.19.153.33/CUE-site6
- ftp://172.19.153.33/CUE-site7
- ftp://172.19.153.33/CUE-site8

Using separate, well-named directories is important because nothing in the actual backup file naming indicates what site this backup belongs to. All sites' filenames are the same as those shown in Example 14-16. If multiple Cisco UE systems point their backups to the same directory location on the FTP server, they interfere with each other, and the backup does not succeed. Also, the administrator is unable to tell which backup belongs to which Cisco UE system, making restore operations unsuccessful.

Example 14-16 *Backup Filenames*

```
[backup-server]$ cd /home/group1/CUE-site6
[backup-server]$ ls -l
total 40
drwxr-xr-x    2 cue      cue      4096 Mar 11 19:42 Configuration_1
drwxr-xr-x    2 cue      cue      4096 Mar  6 19:00 Configuration_2
drwxr-xr-x    2 cue      cue      4096 Mar 19 11:38 Configuration_3
drwxr-xr-x    2 cue      cue      4096 Mar 19 12:52 Configuration_4
drwxr-xr-x    2 cue      cue      4096 Mar  5 17:00 Data_1
drwxr-xr-x    2 cue      cue      4096 Mar  6 18:58 Data_2
drwxr-xr-x    2 cue      cue      4096 Mar 13 21:15 Data_3
drwxr-xr-x    2 cue      cue      4096 Mar 19 11:38 Data_4
-rw-r--r--    1 cue      cue      5178 Mar 19 13:15 history.log
```

Selecting Configuration and Data in the Backup

The router configuration is not backed up or restored; only the Cisco UE application configuration and data are backed up and restorable. Use your normal Cisco IOS methods to back up the router's configuration.

A Cisco UE backup provides a choice of configuration or data categories or both. Configuration information includes

- System configuration
- Voice mail configuration
- User information and spoken names
- AA scripts and prompts

Data information includes

- Voice mail greetings
- Voice mail message content

NOTE   License data is not backed up. A backup must be restored to a system already installed with a license of the same type (the same number of mailboxes and for the same type of system, either Cisco CME or Cisco CallManager) that was on the system when it was backed up.

For a large system (many mailboxes and many messages in them), the *data* information is the bulk of the information to be backed up, and the configuration is small in comparison. The *data* is also what changes most frequently and what must be backed up daily. Therefore, there is little incentive to back up one set of information without the other. It is recommended that you back up configuration and data daily during a time when no voice calls are likely to be active in the system. Doing both categories together at all times also makes restore operations simpler, because it ensures that the configuration (of mailboxes) and the voice messages (content of the mailboxes) coincide.

Because the system's configuration is part of the backup, it is important to back up from, and restore to, the same system. If a backup is done from Site1 and is restored onto Site2, the Site2 system assumes Site1's identity and all its characteristics, including DNS settings, host name, and IP address settings, which is undesirable.

Although you can choose to back up configuration or data or both, this facility does not provide a selective backup capability. The Backup and Restore feature in Cisco UE is designed as a disaster protection mechanism. Therefore, a backup or restore operation is per system, not per mailbox or per message. It is not designed to facilitate moving a subscriber's mailbox from one system to another as he or she moves between sites. Nor is there any way to restore a message a subscriber accidentally deleted.

Configuring Multiple Generations of Backups

The Cisco UE Backup and Restore facility keeps up to 50 generations of backups (if configured to do so; the default is 10). When a backup is done that exceeds the configured maximum number of generations, the oldest backup is automatically deleted. The number of generations of backups the system keeps, such as 15, is a moving window of the most recent 15 backups done on the system.

There is no date/time stamp in the backup itself or in the filenames used, so ensure that the clock is set correctly on the FTP server where the backups are stored. This way, file time stamps will accurately indicate the date when a backup was done. The backup history on the Cisco UE system does contain a time and date stamp for when the backup was done. Example 14-17 shows sample output for the CLI **backup history** command. You can find the same information by using the GUI and navigating to the **Administration > Backup/Restore > Configuration** screen.

Example 14-17 *Backup History*

```
cue#show backup history
#Start Operation
Category:      Configuration
Backup Server: ftp://172.19.153.33/CUE-site6
Operation:     Backup
Backupid:      1
Description:   Site 6
Date:          Sun Apr 21 06:42:34 PDT 2004
Result:        Success
Reason:
#End Operation
#Start Operation
Category:      Data
Backup Server: ftp://172.19.153.33/CUE-site6
backups
Operation:     Backup
Backupid:      1
Description:   Site 6
Date:          Sun Apr 21 06:42:41 PDT 2004
Result:        Success
Reason:
#End Operation
```

If more than 50 generations of backups must be kept (or 50 days, assuming that backups are run daily), this can be accomplished by using a succession of different directories for backups. For example, ftp://172.19.153.33/CUE-site6 could be the backup directory configured for the first 50 backup days, and then the configuration can be changed to ftp://172.19.153.33/CUE-site6-2. This lets another 50 backups be stored in the second directory without affecting the ones in the initial directory.

The backup generations are controlled by the history.log file stored in the backup directory, shown earlier in Example 14-16. This file controls the number of backups and which ones should be deleted if the maximum number of generations is exceeded. This file also controls the restore view (in the GUI, navigate to **Administration > Backup/Restore > Start Restore**) should you select to do a restore. The restore view is built from the current directory configured for backups, so by changing the configuration (temporarily), you can get a view of an older directory and select a restore from there.

NOTE   Do not move or change individual files within a backup directory (for example, CUE-site6). Doing this invalidates the history.log control file and, therefore, the ability to restore any of the backups from this directory. The entire directory can be moved or copied (or encrypted with an offline utility), but do not perform such operations on individual files within the directory.

Determining Backup File Sizes

The largest contribution in size to a typical Cisco UE backup is the actual voice mail message content. Messages are stored in G.711, which is a 64-Kbps codec, so the size can be calculated as 64000 / 8 = 8000 bytes per second, which is 8 KB per second of recorded voice. This factor applies to mailbox greetings, spoken names, and voice message content.

The components of a Cisco UE system that determine the backup file size include

- The base system configuration
- User and mailbox definitions, including spoken names and greetings
- Voice message content
- Custom AA scripts and prompts

If the following attributes of the system are known, the backup size can be estimated:

- AA script and prompt sizes
- Greeting time per user (in seconds)
- Spoken name time per user (in seconds)
- Number of users
- Total voice mail minutes

All the non-AA information, with the exception of spoken name time, is available from the Cisco UE system, as shown in Example 14-18. You can see the same information in the GUI by navigating to the **Reports > Voice Mail** screen. Spoken name time can be estimated at 3 seconds per mailbox.

Example 14-18 *Cisco UE System Summary*

```
cue#show voicemail usage
personal mailboxes:                 40
general delivery mailboxes:         0
orphaned mailboxes:                 0
capacity of voicemail (minutes):    6000
allocated capacity (minutes):       3310.0
message time used (seconds):        2400
message count:                      33
average message length (seconds):   72.72727272727273
greeting time used (seconds):       308
greeting count:                     40
average greeting length (seconds):  7.7
total time used (seconds):          2708
total time used (minutes):          45.13333511352539
percentage used time (%):           1
```

You can derive the size of AA information from the file sizes given in the **Voice Mail > Prompts** and **Voice Mail > Scripts** GUI screens. Similarly, you can use the **show ccn prompts** and **show ccn scripts** CLI commands to see the same information.

You can estimate the backup file size of a particular Cisco UE system with the following calculations (the figures given here are based on Cisco UE release 1.2 and might vary for other releases) and by adding together all the components:

- Base system configuration: Assume 400 to 500 KB

- Users and mailboxes: (average greeting time(s) * 8 KB) + (average spoken name time(s) * 8 KB) * number of mailboxes

- Voice messages: (voice message time(s) * 8 KB) + 5% overhead factor

- AA: (script + prompt files sizes) + 5% overhead factor

Determining Backup Bandwidth

FTP is a protocol that uses all the bandwidth it can get to communicate between the two systems. The more bandwidth that is available, the quicker the FTP session will be. It is recommended that you insert a quality of service (QoS) policy on the WAN link of the router that carries the Cisco UE backup traffic to regulate the bandwidth available to FTP traffic. As soon as this available bandwidth is determined, and you have an estimate of the backup size for a particular site (using the information given in the preceding section), you can estimate how long a typical backup will take. Cisco UE does not do incremental backups; it does a full backup of all information every time.

If you have LAN connectivity between the Cisco UE system and the FTP server, a typical backup takes 2 to 3 minutes.

Best Practices

The following list provides the best practices for configuring and doing backups on a Cisco UE system:

- Ensure that the running configuration is written to the startup configuration before a backup is done. From the Cisco UE CLI, use the **write** command, or from the GUI, go to Administration > Control Panel and click the **Save Unity Express Configuration** button.

- Restore onto the same system that was backed up from.

- If you have to restore onto a different system, it is best to do so on a system that has been newly installed (that is, it has no preexisting configuration) with a license that matches that of the system that created the backup.

- License mismatches when restoring onto a different system than was backed up from might cause unpredictable results. Backups from a Cisco UE configured for a Cisco CME system cannot be restored onto a Cisco UE configured for a Cisco CallManager system, or vice versa.

- Do a backup at the end of the business day when users are no longer using the system and incoming calls are at a minimum.

- Back up both configuration and data daily.

- Back up each system in a network to a uniquely named directory on the FTP server.

- Ensure that the clock is set correctly on the FTP server before initiating a backup.

- Ensure that there is enough disk space on the FTP server for the backups to complete successfully.

- Do not modify or delete individual files within a backup directory.

Configuring Interconnection with Other Sites

You might use Cisco IPC Express as a standalone system, or you might interconnect multiple Cisco CME sites. You might also use a centralized Cisco Unity for voice mail. For these types of networks, you have to configure not only the Cisco IPC Express system itself, but also the interconnectivity between the sites.

The topics of site interconnection and examples of the salient aspects of Cisco IPC Express system configuration were covered in other chapters:

- Chapter 7, "Connecting Multiple Cisco CMEs with VoIP"

- Chapter 8, "Integrating Cisco CME with Cisco CallManager"

- Chapter 10, "Cisco IPC Express Integrated Voice Mail"

- Chapter 11, "Cisco CME External Voice Mail Options"

Security Best Practices for Cisco CME

Cisco IPC Express provides integrated IP communications on Cisco IOS routers. Therefore, the same security best practices recommended for all Cisco IOS voice-enabled routers also apply to Cisco CME. In addition, you should implement Cisco CME-specific security practices to provide additional security protection.

This section explains how you can set up the Cisco CME using the CLI to prevent users from intentionally or accidentally gaining system-level control from the GUI as well as local or remote CLI access.

Securing GUI Access

A Cisco IOS router authenticates an administrator CLI login against the enable password only, and the default setting for HTTP access is **ip http authentication enable**. If the system administrator, customer administrator, or phone user has the same password as the router's enable password, he or she can gain level 15 EXEC privilege access to Cisco IOS via HTTP. A normal IP phone user can then accidentally change the Cisco CME configuration, erase Flash, or reload the router when logging on to this URL:

```
http://cme-ip-address/
```

You should configure the following commands for Cisco CME to use AAA or local authentication to prevent a normal user from gaining access to the enable password and therefore having access to the system administrator page:

```
ip http authentication aaa
```

or

```
ip http authentication local
```

NOTE   Note that authentication, AAA is applied only to the system administrator login. Local authentication, which is clear-text-based, is applied to both the customer administrator and phone user logins.

Using HTTPS for Cisco CME GUI Management

HTTP over SSL (HTTPS) provides Secure Socket Layer (SSL) version 3.0 support for the HTTP 1.1 server and HTTP 1.1 client within Cisco IOS software. SSL provides server authentication, encryption, and message integrity to allow secure HTTP communications. SSL also provides HTTP client authentication. This feature is supported only in Cisco IOS software images that include the SSL feature. Specifically, SSL is supported in the Advanced Security, Advanced IP Services, and Advanced Enterprise Services images. Use the Advanced IP Services or Advanced Enterprise Services Cisco IOS images to get both the Cisco CME and SSL features.

Currently IP phones do not serve as HTTPS clients. If HTTPS is enabled on the Cisco CME router, IP phones still attempt to connect to HTTP using port 80. Because the SSL default port is 443, the phones cannot display local directory and system speed dials. IP phones using HTTP can work with a system configured for SSL by enabling both HTTP and HTTPS, as shown in Example 14-19.

Example 14-19 *Enabling HTTP Secure Server Sample Configuration*

```
router#show running-config
ip http server
ip http secure-server
ip http secure-port port_number
!if https port is changed from default 443
ip http authentication AAA I TACACS I local
```

Use the following command to generate an RSA usage key pair with a length of 1024 bits or greater:

```
crypto key generate rsa usage 1024
```

If you do not generate an RSA usage key pair manually, an RSA usage key pair with a length of 768 bits is generated automatically when you connect to the HTTPS server for the first time. These auto generated RSA keys are not saved to the startup configuration; therefore, they are lost when the device is rebooted unless you save the configuration manually. For more information on RSA, refer to Cisco IOS documentation on Cisco.com.

You should obtain an X.509 digital certificate with digital signature capabilities for the device from a certification authority (CA). If you do not obtain a digital certificate in advance, the device creates a self-signed digital certificate to authenticate itself.

If you change the device host name after obtaining a device digital certificate, HTTPS connections to the device *fail* because the host name does not match the host name specified in the digital certificate. Obtain a new device digital certificate using the new host name to fix this problem.

The **ip http secure-server** command prevents clear-text passwords from traveling across the network when a Cisco CME administrator logs into the Cisco CME GUI. However, communications between the phone and router remain in clear text.

The following are the suggested best practices for using HTTP interactive access to the Cisco CME router:

- Use the **ip http access-class** command to allow only specified IP addresses to access the Cisco CME GUI, thus restricting unwanted IP packets from connecting to Cisco CME.

- Use the **ip http authentication** command with a central TACACS+ or RADIUS server for authentication purposes. Configuring authentication for the HTTP and HTTPS servers adds security to communication between clients and the HTTP and HTTPS servers on the device.

- Do not use the router enable password as a Cisco CME login password (to prevent a regular user from gaining administrator privileges).

Setting Local and Remote System Access

When in EXEC mode, the **configure terminal** and **telephony-service** commands take a user into Cisco CME configuration mode. The **show running-config** and **show telephony-service** commands show all registered phones and users, extension numbers, usernames, and passwords for Cisco CME GUI access. So the first step to security control is at the system access level. Password encryption, user authentication, and command auditing are all critical to prevent security breaches.

Using the **enable secret** Command

The enable password is shown in clear text by default. To provide access control to EXEC mode on the router, use the **enable secret** command to encrypt the enable password, as shown in Example 14-20.

Example 14-20 *Enable Secret*

```
router#show running-config
service password-encryption
enable secret <removed>
no enable password
```

Restricting Access to tty

You can allow only certain users and locations to Telnet to the router by using its terminal (tty) or virtual terminal (vty) lines. Define and apply an access list for permitting or denying remote Telnet sessions to your Cisco CME router as shown in Example 14-21.

Example 14-21 *Restricting Access to vty*

```
router#show running-config
line vty 0 4
 access-class 10 in
 access-list 10 permit 10.1.1.0 0.0.0.255
```

Using AAA to Secure Access

Example 14-22 shows how to use AAA for login and command auditing.

Example 14-22 *Using AAA for Login and Command Auditing*

```
router#show running-config
aaa new-model
aaa authentication login default tacacs+ enable
aaa authentication enable default tacacs+ enable
aaa accounting exec start-stop tacacs+
aaa accounting exec start-stop tacacs+
!
ip tacacs source-interface Loopback0
tacacs-server host 215.17.1.2
```

continues

Example 14-22   *Using AAA for Login and Command Auditing (Continued)*

```
tacacs-server host 215.17.34.10
tacacs-server key CKr3t#

Sample command log:
Wed Jun 25 03:46:47 1997 172.16.25.15 fgeorge tty3 5622329430/4327528 stop
task_id=3 service=shell priv-lvl=1 cmd=show version <cr>
Wed Jun 25 03:46:58 1997 172.16.25.15 fgeorge tty3 5622329430/4327528 stop
task_id=4 service=shell priv-lvl=1 cmd=show interfaces Ethernet 0 <cr>
Wed Jun 25 03:47:03 1997 172.16.25.15 fgeorge tty3 5622329430/4327528 stop
task_id=5 service=shell priv-lvl=1 cmd=show ip route <cr>
```

When the AAA server cannot be reached in the network, the router should always require login, as shown in Example 14-23.

Example 14-23   *Using a User Account on the Router*

```
router#show running-config
username joe password 7 045802150C2E
username jim password 7 0317B21895FE
!
line vty 0 4
  login local
```

Configuring SSH Access

Example 14-24 shows you how to configure secure shell (SSH) access on your Cisco CME router.

Example 14-24   *Configuring SSH*

```
router(config)#crypto key generate rsa
line vty 0 4
transport input telnet ssh
```

Using ACLs for SNMP Access

You might use access control lists (ACLs) to permit or deny SNMP access, as shown in Example 14-25.

Example 14-25   *Using ACLs for SNMP Access*

```
router#show running-config
access-list 10 remark SNMP filter
access-list 10 permit 10.1.1.0 0.0.0.255
snmp-server community changeme-rw RW 10
snmp-server community changeme-ro RO 10
```

Change the community strings to words different from *read* and *write*, because these are two common community strings for read and write access, respectively.

Disabling CDP

Cisco Discovery Protocol (CDP) automatically discovers the neighboring network devices that also support CDP. In an untrusted domain, disable CDP so that Cisco CME routers do not automatically show up in the CDP tables of other devices. This is shown in Example 14-26.

Example 14-26 *Disabling CDP*

```
router#show running-config
no cdp run
!If cdp is needed then consider disabling cdp on a per interface basis.
interface FastEthernet0/0
  no cdp enable
```

Configuring COR for Incoming and Outgoing Calls

One of the ways to restrict unauthorized incoming and outgoing calls is to use the COR commands. The configuration shown in Example 14-27 defines two groups of users: *user* and *superuser. Superuser* is allowed to make any calls, including local, long-distance, 411 directory lookup, and 911 calls. *User* is restricted from making 900, 411, and international calls.

Example 14-27 *Configuring COR for Toll Fraud*

```
router#show running-config
dial-peer cor custom
 name 911
 name 1800
 name local-call
 name ld-call
 name 411
 name int-call
 name 1900
!
dial-peer cor list call911
 member 911
!
dial-peer cor list call1800
 member 1800
!
dial-peer cor list calllocal
 member local-call
!
dial-peer cor list callint
 member int-call
!
dial-peer cor list callld
 member ld-call
!
dial-peer cor list call411
 member 411
!
dial-peer cor list call1900
 member 1900
```

continues

Example 14-27 *Configuring COR for Toll Fraud (Continued)*

```
!
dial-peer cor list user
 member 911
 member 1800
 member local-call
 member ld-call
!
dial-peer cor list superuser
 member 911
 member 1800
 member local-call
 member ld-call
 member 411
 member int-call
 member 1900
!
dial-peer voice 9 pots
 corlist outgoing callld
 destination-pattern 91..........
 port 1/0
 prefix 1
!
dial-peer voice 911 pots
 corlist outgoing call911
 destination-pattern 9911
 port 1/0
 prefix 911
!
dial-peer voice 11 pots
 corlist outgoing callint
 destination-pattern 9011T
 port 2/0
 prefix 011
!
dial-peer voice 732 pots
 corlist outgoing calllocal
 destination-pattern 9732.......
 port 1/0
 prefix 732
!
dial-peer voice 800 pots
 corlist outgoing call1800
 destination-pattern 91800.......
 port 1/0
 prefix 1800
!
dial-peer voice 802 pots
 corlist outgoing call1800
 destination-pattern 91877.......
 port 1/0
 prefix 1877
!
dial-peer voice 805 pots
```

Example 14-27 *Configuring COR for Toll Fraud (Continued)*

```
 corlist outgoing call1800
 destination-pattern 91888.......
 port 1/0
 prefix 1888
!
dial-peer voice 411 pots
 corlist outgoing call411
 destination-pattern 9411
 port 1/0
 prefix 411
!
dial-peer voice 806 pots
 corlist outgoing call1800
 destination-pattern 91866.......
 port 1/0
 prefix 1866

ephone-dn  1
 number 2000
 cor incoming user

ephone-dv 2
 number 2001
 cor incoming superuser
```

Restricting Outgoing Calling Patterns

You might use the **after-hours block** command to restrict incoming or outgoing calls after
certain hours. You can also use after-hours blocking to restrict calls to numbers or area codes
known to be fraudulent calling patterns. The commands shown in Example 14-28 block all calls
at all times for patterns 2 to 6. Pattern 7 is blocked only during the configured after-hours
period.

Example 14-28 *Using After-Hours Blocking to Restrict Outgoing Calling Patterns*

```
router#show running-config
telephony-service
after-hours block pattern 2 .1264 7-24
after-hours block pattern 3 .1268 7-24
after-hours block pattern 4 .1246 7-24
after-hours block pattern 5 .1441 7-24
after-hours block pattern 6 .1284 7-24
after-hours block pattern 7 9011
after-hours day Sun 19:00 07:00
after-hours day Mon 19:00 07:00
after-hours day Tue 19:00 07:00
after-hours day Wed 19:00 07:00
after-hours day Thu 19:00 07:00
after-hours day Fri 19:00 07:00
after-hours day Sat 19:00 07:00
```

Configuring IP Phone Registration Control

You should configure Cisco CME to allow IP phones in a trusted domain for registration. Assuming that the local LAN segment is a trusted domain, use the **strict-match** option on the **ip source-address** command so that only locally attached IP phones can register to the Cisco CME router and get IP telephony-services:

```
router(config-telephony)#ip source-address 1.1.1.1 port 2000 strict-match
```

Block port TCP 2000 access from the WAN or Internet side to prevent external SCCP phones from registering with the Cisco CME system. Use the following ACL to block TCP port 2000 access from WAN or Internet interfaces:

```
router(config-t)#access-list 101 deny tcp any any eq 2000
```

NOTE   Unknown phones or phones that are not configured in Cisco CME are allowed to register with Cisco CME by default for ease of management, but they do not get dial tone until you configure them by associating the buttons with ephone-dns or by configuring **auto assign dns** under **telephony-service**.

Security Best Practices for Cisco UE

You should consider various additional aspects of network security to protect against unauthorized access to Cisco UE. This section covers Cisco UE security best practices related to system access, remote access, and other security parameters applicable to the application environment.

System and Remote Access

Cisco UE hardware does not have external interfaces (physically, there is a Fast Ethernet interface port, but it is disabled in software and unusable). All Cisco UE system access must pass through the host Cisco CME router. Cisco UE CLI access has no login access or password control in addition to that of the router that houses Cisco UE. Therefore, it is imperative that the router's configuration parameters for local access (the console port) and remote access (Telnet) are set according to your security needs.

Local Access

The only local access to a Cisco UE system is via the host Cisco CME router's console interface into the router CLI. You then open a session to the Cisco UE CLI by using the following command:

```
router#service-module service-Engine x/y session
```

Entering this command on the router requires enable mode and, therefore, is protected by the router's enable login and password settings. Although the Cisco UE CLI also has an enable mode, it has no user ID or password capability. Any network administrator who has access to enable mode on the router also has access to the Cisco UE CLI. Access is controlled via the router, so if logging is required, set up the router with AAA/RADIUS monitoring of login access.

GUI access via a browser to Cisco UE is considered remote access, because it is across an IP segment from the router.

Remote Access—Telnet

Routers typically are geographically dispersed in your network and are seldom accessed locally via the console port. Remote access via Telnet across the IP network is much more typical. Use the IP configuration shown in Example 14-29 as a reference for the discussion in this section.

Example 14-29 *IP Reference Configuration*

```
router#show running-config
interface FastEthernet0/0
 ip address 172.19.153.41 255.255.255.0
 no ip mroute-cache
 duplex auto
 speed auto
!
interface Service-Engine1/0
 ip unnumbered FastEthernet0/0
 service-module ip address 172.19.153.37 255.255.255.0
 service-module ip default-gateway 172.19.153.41
```

Direct Telnet access to the Cisco UE IP address is disabled, as shown in Example 14-30.

Example 14-30 *Cisco UE Telnet Access Disabled*

```
pc>telnet 172.19.153.37
Trying 172.19.153.37...
telnet: Unable to connect to remote host: Connection refused
```

Remote CLI access to Cisco UE is possible only by using Telnet to the router (172.19.153.41) and then using the **session** command to get access to the Cisco UE CLI. That way, all the security protections built into Telnet access on your router automatically also protect access to Cisco UE. Example 14-31 shows a Telnet session to the router followed by a session into Cisco UE.

Example 14-31 *Telnet Access to Cisco UE*

```
pc>telnet 172.19.153.41
Trying 172.19.153.41...
Connected to 172.19.153.41.
Escape character is '^]'.
User Access Verification
Password:
lab-2691>en
Password:
lab-2691#service-module service-Engine 1/0 session
Trying 172.19.153.41, 2033 ... Open
```

Although direct Telnet access to the Cisco UE IP address is blocked, you can Telnet to the router's IP address followed by the explicit tty port number allocated to Cisco UE, as shown in Example 14-32. This indirect type of Telnet access is not blocked and can provide undesirable access to Cisco UE.

Example 14-32 *Telnet Access with an Explicit Port Number*

```
pc>telnet 172.19.153.41 2033
Trying 172.19.153.41...
Connected to 172.19.153.41.
Escape character is '^]'.
```

To protect against this kind of access, insert a login/password configuration on the tty port (in this example, the port number is 2033) leading to Cisco UE, as shown in Example 14-33.

Example 14-33 *Login/Password on Telnet Access*

```
router#show running-config
line 33
 password 7 02050D480809
 login
 no exec
```

Cisco UE CLI access via the router tty port does not time out by default. The connection stays up until it is disconnected by the user who initiated it. If an inactivity timeout on remote access to Cisco UE CLI is required, you can use the **session-timeout** command on the router tty configuration to disconnect the session after a configured number of minutes of inactivity. This is shown in Example 14-34.

Example 14-34 *Inactivity Timeout on Cisco UE CLI Access*

```
router#show running-config
line 33
 session-timeout 5
 password 7 02050D480809
 login
```

Remote Access—SSH

For secure CLI access to Cisco UE, enable SSH on the router and use an SSH-enabled remote-access application, such as the SSH Windows application. Cisco UE itself does not support SSH (but neither does it support Telnet access). However, communication between the router and Cisco UE is via the router backplane and, therefore, is not exposed to any external interfaces or IP segments. SSH access to the router is sufficient to protect remote access to Cisco UE.

Remote Access—HTTPS

Cisco UE does not yet support HTTPS for browser access. Although login to the GUI is password-protected, the login ID and password currently travel in clear text across the IP network.

You can protect GUI access in Cisco UE by using IPSec tunnels on the routers between the nearest router to where the browser is located and the router hosting the Cisco UE module. You can use virtual private network (VPN) technology to protect the segment between the client PC and the nearest router where IPSec is available. Alternatively, you can use VPN technology all the way from the client PC to the host router.

Application Environment

Cisco UE is an IP application and therefore communicates with its environment via various TCP and UDP protocols and ports. Open port numbers are typical security attack targets. Therefore, traffic to the open TCP and UDP port numbers should be protected by ACLs as much as possible to allow only desired traffic from known endpoints into the application.

Protocols and Port Numbers

To construct suitable ACLs and other security mechanisms that monitor traffic (and deny undesired traffic), it is important to know which ports are open and used by an application such as Cisco UE. Table 14-1 lists the protocols and port numbers that Cisco UE uses.

Table 14-1   *Cisco UE Protocols and Port Numbers*

Protocol	Protocol and Port Number
DNS	TCP/UDP 53
TFTP	UDP 69
FTP	TCP 20 (data), TCP 21 (control)
HTTP	TCP 80
NTP	UDP 123
Syslog	TCP 514

continues

Table 14-1 *Cisco UE Protocols and Port Numbers (Continued)*

Protocol	Protocol and Port Number
SIP	UDP 5060
RTP	UDP 16384–32767
SMTP	TCP 25

Suggested ACLs

This section provides best-practice suggestions for ACLs to protect the open ports on your Cisco UE system. Use the following IP configuration information as a reference for this section. Substitute your network's configuration for these values when you customize the ACLs for your implementation.

- Cisco UE service module IP default gateway — 172.19.153.41
- Cisco UE service module IP address — 172.19.153.37
- FTP server for software backup and download — 10.10.1.150
- Admininstration subnet — 10.10.1.0/24
- IP phone and PSTN gateway subnet — 10.10.2.0/24
- Syslog server — 10.10.1.160
- DNS — 10.10.1.170

The ACLs shown in Example 14-35 are recommended to be used with Cisco UE. You should apply these ACLs on the Cisco UE service-engine interface on the router.

Example 14-35 *Recommended ACLs for Cisco UE*

```
router#show running-config
!Inbound:
access-list 101 remark Filter Outbound Traffic from CUE - Apply Inbound on
  Interface ServiceEngine
access-list 101 remark Restrict DNS to only 10.10.1.170, add additional dns
  servers as required
access-list 101 permit udp host 172.19.153.37 host 10.10.1.170 eq domain
access-list 101 permit tcp host 172.19.153.37 host 10.10.1.170 eq domain
access-list 101 remark Restrict TFTP to only the host router
access-list 101 permit udp host 172.19.153.37 host 172.19.153.41 eq tftp
access-list 101 remark Restrict FTP traffic to only a single server
access-list 101 permit tcp host 172.19.153.37 host 10.10.1.150 eq ftp
access-list 101 permit tcp host 172.19.153.37 host 10.10.1.150 eq ftp-data
access-list 101 remark Restrict NTP traffic to only the host router
access-list 101 permit udp host 172.19.153.37 host 172.19.153.41 eq ntp
access-list 101 remark Restrict Syslog traffic to single server
access-list 101 permit tcp host 172.19.153.37 host 10.10.1.160 eq syslog
access-list 101 remark Restrict SIP signaling to host router
access-list 101 permit tcp host 172.19.153.37 host 172.19.153.41 eq 5060
access-list 101 permit udp host 172.19.153.37 host 172.19.153.41 eq 5060
```

Example 14-35   *Recommended ACLs for Cisco UE (Continued)*

```
access-list 101 remark Restrict RTP to IP phone and GW segment plus router
access-list 101 permit udp host 172.19.153.37 10.10.1.0 0.0.0.255 range 16384
  32767
access-list 101 permit udp host 172.19.153.37 host 172.19.153.41 range 16384
  32767
!Outbound:
access-list 102 remark Filter Traffic to CUE - Apply Outbound on Interface
  ServiceEngine
access-list 102 remark Restrict http access to management and phone segment
access-list 102 permit tcp 10.10.1.0 0.0.0.255 host 172.19.153.37 eq www
access-list 102 permit tcp 10.10.2.0 0.0.0.255 host 172.19.153.37 eq www
access-list 102 remark Restrict SIP signaling to host router
access-list 102 permit tcp host 172.19.153.41 host 172.19.153.37 eq 5060
access-list 102 permit udp host 172.19.153.41 host 172.19.153.37 eq 5060
access-list 102 remark Restrict RTP to IP phone and GW segment plus router
access-list 102 permit udp 10.10.1.0 0.0.0.255 host 172.19.153.37 range16384
  32767
access-list 102 permit udp host 172.19.153.41 host 172.19.153.37 range 16384
  32767
```

Attach the ACLs to the service-engine interface as shown in Example 14-36.

Example 14-36   *Attaching ACLs to the Service-Engine Interface*

```
interface Service-Engine1/0
 ip unnumbered FastEthernet0/0
 ip access-group 101 in
 ip access-group 102 out
 service-module ip address 172.19.153.37 255.255.0.0
 service-module ip default-gateway 172.19.153.41
```

Cisco UE Security Best Practices

Follow the recommendations in this section to secure access to your Cisco UE system:

- Assign an enable password to the Cisco CME router hosting the Cisco UE module.

- Restrict Telnet access to the Cisco CME router.

- Enable login and password control on the Cisco CME router tty port connecting to Cisco UE.

- Configure an inactivity timeout on the Cisco CME router tty port connecting to Cisco UE.

- Enable SSH on the Cisco CME router to protect Telnet traffic, and use only SSH-capable Telnet client software.

- Use VPN/IPSec router technology to protect HTTP web access into Cisco UE.

- Use ACLs to restrict SIP signaling traffic into Cisco UE to be sourced only by the Cisco CME router that hosts Cisco UE. No other source in the network should be able to send SIP traffic to Cisco UE.

- Protect the FTP server used for software installation with login and password control.

- Protect the FTP server used for backup and restore with login and password control.

- During a Cisco UE software install or upgrade, do not provide the FTP password on the install command line. Let the installer prompt for it.

- Maintain the Cisco UE system with the generate random password/PIN user access policy.

- Mailbox PINs do not expire in Cisco UE releases before release 2.1. Upgrade to release 2.1 to get the ability to have passwords expire.

- Set the minimum length of Cisco UE passwords and PINs (this feature requires release 2.1 or later) to the lengths demanded by your security policies.

Configuring and Monitoring Via Network Management Systems Using the Cisco CME AXL/SOAP Interface

You can integrate Cisco CME with network management applications by using the Cisco CME XML Layer (AXL) application programming interface (API). The AXL API provides a mechanism for inserting, retrieving, updating, and removing data from the Cisco CallManager database using an XML SOAP interface. The AXL API allows programmatic access to Cisco CallManager data in XML form instead of using a binary library or a Dynamic Link Library (DLL). The AXL API methods, or requests, are performed using a combination of HTTP and SOAP. The HTTP payload is encapsulated in SOAP, which is essentially an XML remote procedure call protocol. User requests send XML data to the Cisco CallManager server, which returns an AXL response encapsulated in a SOAP message.

Cisco CME extends the AXL/SOAP capabilities by providing XML APIs for monitoring and configuring IP phones and extensions. A Network Management System (NMS) might use the Cisco CME AXL/SOAP APIs to poll the Cisco CME network elements (NEs), including IP phones and extensions. As with the AXL protocol, communication between an NMS and Cisco CME is based on an HTTP data exchange and can be initiated only by polling from the NMS. However, Cisco CME can enable or disable the sending of data, as well as control the polling interval.

NOTE   AXL/SOAP APIs for NMS configuration and monitoring are supported only by Cisco CME, not by Cisco UE.

The next sections describe the features supported by the Cisco CME AXL/SOAP APIs and a test procedure to check if your Cisco CME is set up properly to respond to the AXL/SOAP queries.

The Cisco CME AXL/SOAP Interface

The Cisco CME AXL/SOAP APIs provide many capabilities for monitoring and configuring IP phones and extensions.

For monitoring, Cisco CME AXL/SOAP APIs support the following:

- Getting static information
  - ISgetGlobal—Gets global information
  - ISgetDevice—Gets device information
  - ISgetExtension—Gets extension information
- Getting dynamic information
  - ISgetEvtCounts—Gets the number of events recorded in the buffer
  - ISgetDevEvts—Gets device events if IP phones are in the register, unregister, or decease state
  - ISgetExtEvts—Gets extension events (the virtual voice port is up or down)
- Setting information (configuring) and executing CLI
  - ISsetKeyPhones—Sets the "key" phone
  - ISexecCLI—Executes the CLI

The following are supported CLI commands that can be executed by the ISexecCLI API. You might execute all the subcommands under each of these configuration mode commands with the ISexecCLI API.

- **telephony-service**
- **ephone**
- **ephone-dn**
- **vm-integration**
- **ephone-hunt**
- **dial-peer voice**
- **call application voice interactive voice response (IVR)**

You might get more information on supported Cisco CME AXL/SOAP APIs by going to Cisco.com and searching for "XML Developer Guide for Cisco CME."

Testing the Cisco CME AXL/SOAP Interface

You might use the test page (xml-test.html) that is available with the Cisco CME GUI files to verify that the Cisco CME router is set up correctly to respond to AXL/SOAP requests. The following are the steps to set up and run the test page:

Step 1 Load xml-test.html into Flash.

Step 2 Configure the following on the Cisco CME router:

```
router(config)#ip http server
router(config)#ip http path:flash
router(config)#telephony-service mode
router(config)#log password abcd
router(config)#xmltest
```

Step 3 Enter the following URL in the browser:

```
http://ip-address of router/ISApi/AXL/V1/soapisapi.is
```

Step 4 When the Login window opens, log on as follows:

```
username: any non-empty string
password: abcd
```

Step 5 In the test page, input content into the form. The XML request is written to the form at the bottom. Go to the bottom of the page and click **Submit**.

Step 6 Try the preceding steps on your system. If you receive any errors, the following debugs on the router might help:

```
router#debug ip http appinout
router#debug ip http appdetail
```

The xml-test.html file is a test program for you to check that the Cisco CME router can respond to AXL/SOAP requests. You must disable the test program when polling from an NMS using the Cisco CME AXL APIs with the following configuration:

```
router(config)#telephony-service
router(config-telephony)#no xmltest
```

NOTE A polling request from an NMS must be sent in clear-text format.

For developer services support, go to the Cisco Developer Support site at http://www.cisco.com/cgi-bin/dev_support/access_level/product_support. You must be a Cisco.com registered user to access this site.

Monitoring Cisco IPC Express

You might monitor the Cisco IPC Express system with Syslog messages and Simple Network Management Protocol (SNMP) Management Information Base (MIB). You also can monitor call activity information through Syslog messages and Call Detail Records (CDRs).

Monitoring IP Phones Using Cisco CME Syslog Messages

Cisco CME 3.0 introduced type 6 Syslog messages, as shown in Example 14-37, for IP phone registration and deregistration events. These Syslog messages are useful for a central NMS to manage Cisco CME systems and IP phones.

Example 14-37 *Type 6 Syslog Messages*

```
%IPPHONE-6-REG_ALARM
%IPPHONE-6-REGISTER
%IPPHONE-6-REGISTER_NEW
%IPPHONE-6-UNREGISTER_ABNORMAL
%IPPHONE-6-REGISTER_NORMAL

Example Message:
 %IPPHONE-6-REGISTER_NEW: ephone-3:SEP003094C38724 IP:1.4.170.6 Socket:1
  DeviceType:Phone has registered.
```

The IPPHONE-6-REGISTER_NEW message shown in Example 14-37 indicates that a phone has registered and that it is not part of the explicit router configuration. In other words, the ephone configuration has not yet been created. Cisco CME allows unconfigured phones to register to make provisioning of the Cisco CME system more convenient. By default, phones designated as new are not assigned phone lines; therefore, they cannot make calls until they are configured into the system.

Enable the Cisco IOS logging capability to log all the Syslog events into the buffer on the Cisco CME router, or send the Syslog messages to a Syslog server for offline management, as shown in Example 14-38.

Example 14-38 *Enabling Syslogging*

```
telephony-service#(config)#service timestamps log datetime msec localtime
telephony-service #(config)#aaa new-model
telephony-service #(config)#aaa authentication login default none
telephony-service #(config)#aaa accounting connection H.323 start-stop radius
telephony-service #(config)#gw-accounting syslog
telephony-service #(config)#logging 10.10.10.1
!!! 10.10.10.1 is the ip address of syslog server, multiple servers might also be
  specified
```

To synchronize your Cisco CME system to an external NTP server, use the following:

```
ntp server ip-address
  !!! ip address - IP address of the time server providing the clock
  synchronization
```

If there is no external NTP time source, use the internal router clock as the time source:

```
ntp master
```

To ensure that the time stamps are correct, set the router clock to the correct time:

```
clock set 15:15:00 might 31 2001
```

You can specify multiple Syslog servers for redundancy, because Syslog uses UDP as the underlying transport mechanism and data packets are unsequenced and unacknowledged.

In addition to the Syslog messages from Cisco CME, you can also set up Cisco UE for logging to an external Syslog server in addition to logging a message locally to its own storage. Use the following command:

```
cue(config)#log server 10.10.10.1
```

Monitoring Call Activity

NMS systems can retrieve CDRs and call history information in any of the following ways:

- Cisco CME GUI
- Syslog or RADIUS servers
- SNMP CISCO-DIAL-CONTROL-MIB and CISCO-VOICE-DIAL-CONTROL-MIB
- Voice performance statistics from Cisco CME

The next sections describe how you can monitor call activities, CDR logs, billing records, and voice performance statistics in more detail.

Monitoring Cisco CME Call History

The Cisco CME GUI provides call history information in the **Reports > Call History** window so that a network administrator can monitor for unknown callers or disallowed calling activities based on calling patterns. Configure the call history log to perform any forensics and accounting to track down fraudulent calling patterns, as shown in Example 14-39.

Example 14-39 *Configuring Call History*

```
router#show running-config
dial-control-mib retain-timer 10080
dial-control-mib max-size 500
!
gw-accounting syslog
logging 10.10.10.1
```

Logging CDR to External Servers

You might follow the same method discussed earlier in the section "Monitoring IP Phones Using Cisco CME Syslog Messages" to allow Syslog messages to be logged to an external server and to log CDRs to an external server. Cisco CME allows you to log CDRs for accounting or billing purposes to an external AAA server (RADIUS or TACACS). This provides CDR logging, post call record processing, and a billing report generation facility. You can use a MindCTI (http://www.mindcti.com/) RADIUS server or a Cisco Secure Access Control Server (ACS) to provide billing support and view CDR details.

To configure RADIUS on your Cisco CME router, perform the following tasks:

- Use the **aaa new-model** global configuration command to enable AAA. You must configure AAA if you plan to use RADIUS.

- Use the **aaa authentication** global configuration command to define method lists for RADIUS authentication.

- Use the **line** and **interface** commands to allow the defined method lists to be used.

Example 14-40 is a sample configuration that allows the Cisco CME router to generate and send VoIP CDRs to an external RADIUS server.

Example 14-40   *Logging CDR to a RADIUS Server*

```
router#show running-config
aaa new-model
aaa authentication login default group radius
!! Login Authentication using RADIUS server
aaa authorization config-commands
aaa authorization exec default if-authenticated group radius
aaa authorization network default group radius
!! Authorization for network resources
aaa authorization configuration default group radius
!! Authorization for global config mode
aaa accounting send stop-record authentication failure
!! Start-Stop Accounting services
aaa accounting update periodic 1
aaa accounting network default start-stop group radius
!! For local Authentication
aaa accounting connection default start-stop group radius
!! For local Authentication
aaa accounting connection h323 start-stop group radius
!! For Voice Call Accounting
aaa accounting system default start-stop group radius
aaa accounting resource default start-stop group radius
aaa session-id common
!
gw-accounting h323
!!  H.323 gateway Accounting
gw-accounting syslog
!! Optional - for system log information
gw-accounting voip
!! VoIP call Accounting
```

continues

Example 14-40 *Logging CDR to a RADIUS Server (Continued)*

```
!
Router RADIUS Server configuration:
radius-server host 11.11.11.1 auth-port 1645 acct-port 1646
!! RADIUS Server host address
radius-server retransmit 30
!!  RADIUS messages update interval
radius-server key cisco
!! RADIUS server secure key
```

Using Account Codes for Billing

Cisco CME provides account code support into CDRs, which a RADIUS server or customer billing server then can use for the billing process. The Cisco 7960 and 7940 IP Phones support an acct softkey so that users can enter an account code from an IP phone during the call ringing (alerting) or active (connected) states. This account code is also added to the Cisco-VOICE-DIAL-CONTROL-MIB SNMP MIB.

You can view the Account Code field in the **show call active voice** log, as shown in Example 14-41.

Example 14-41 *Viewing the Account Code*

```
router#show call active voice
Telephony call-legs: 2
SIP call-legs: 0
H.323 call-legs: 0
MGCP call-legs: 0
Total call-legs: 2
!
GENERIC:
SetupTime=97147870 ms
Index=1
PeerAddress=2001
!
TELE:
AccountCode 1234
```

Note that this Account Code field can also be added to the Vendor-Specific Attribute (VSA) fields for CDR. For more information on Cisco VSA, go to Cisco.com and search for "Cisco VSA Implementation Guide."

Monitoring Voice Performance Statistics

If you are running Cisco IOS release 12.3(4)T or later, you might take advantage of the Cisco Voice Performance Statistics to collect voice call signaling statistics and VoIP AAA accounting statistics based on user-configured time ranges. The statistics can be displayed on your console or can be formatted and archived to an FTP or Syslog server. This feature can help you diagnose performance problems on the network, and identify impaired voice equipment.

Example 14-42 shows an example of the amount of memory used for accounting and signaling call statistics records (CSRs) by fixed interval and since a reset or reboot. It also shows the estimated memory allocated for future use.

Example 14-42 *Call Statistics Record Memory Allocation*

```
router#show voice statistics memory-usage csr
*** Voice Call Statistics Record Memory Usage ***
        Fixed Interval Option -
                CSR size: 136 bytes
                Number of CSR per interval: 9
                Used memory size (proximate): 0
                Estimated future claimed memory size (proximate): 10
        Since Reset Option -
                CSR size: 136 bytes
                Total count of CSR: 9
                Used memory size (proximate): 1224

*** Voice Call Statistics Accounting Record Memory Usage ***
        Fixed Interval Option -
                ACCT REC size: 80 bytes
                Number of ACCT REC per interval: 1
                Used memory size (proximate): 0
                Estimated future claimed memory size (proximate): 25
        Since Reset Option -
                ACCT REC size: 80 bytes
                Total count of ACCT REC: 1
                Used memory size (proximate): 80
```

For more information, you can refer to the Cisco IOS 12.3(4)T documentation and read about "Voice Performance Statistics on Cisco Gateways."

Using Cisco CME Supported SNMP MIBs

You might leverage Cisco SNMP router MIBs for Cisco CME management. The following are examples of supported MIBs:

- **CISCO-DIAL-CONTROL-MIB**—Contains information for CDRs and call history
- **CISCO-VOICE-DIAL-CONTROL-MIB**—Extends call detail information to telephony and VoIP dial peers/call legs
- **CISCO-VOICE-IF-MIB**—Allows access to voice interface parameters such as loss and gain values and echo cancellation status
- **CISCO-CDP-MIB**—Lets you manage CDP
- **CISCO-SYSLOG-MIB**—Allows access to Syslog messages

Managing Cisco IPC Express Systems by Managed Services and Enterprises

As described in earlier chapters, Cisco IPC Express is ideal if you have data connectivity requirements and also need IP telephony in the office. SPs normally deploy Cisco IPC Express systems as one of the following:

- Standalone, single-site managed services
- Large-scale, multisite managed services

A managed-services solution with Cisco CME offers two opportunities for value-added services:

- The customer premises equipment (CPE) router
- Network management support

SPs offer their customers the Cisco IPC Express systems at the end customer's site. They also install, set up, maintain, and manage the systems.

Most of the NMSs used by SPs to deploy Cisco IPC Express in a managed-services model also apply to enterprise networks. The difference between a managed-services model and an enterprise model is who offers, owns, and manages the core network.

Note that this chapter covers only management capabilities for Cisco IPC Express systems, not for the larger IP telephony solutions and products offered by Cisco in general. The next sections describe how you can manage standalone or multisite Cisco IPC Express systems. They also cover some general information on the typical Cisco Voice Network Management Solutions that are applicable to Cisco IPC Express.

Managing a Standalone Cisco IPC Express System

Figure 14-43 shows a deployment in which a single Cisco IPC Express system in a branch office connects to a SP's VoIP network. All voice and data traffic can be routed over the SP's network, or calls can be routed via the PSTN if the destination (called party) cannot be reached via the SP's IP network.

Figure 14-43   *Managing a Standalone Cisco IPC Express System*

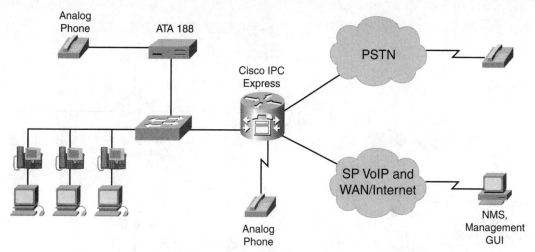

To manage a standalone Cisco IPC Express system, you might provision or configure the system by using the CLI, the Cisco CME setup utility, or the Cisco IPC Express GUI. This is sufficient for simple moves, adds, changes to the phones, and basic configuration changes for a standalone or single-site deployment. However, you might also use the Zero Touch deployment, monitoring, accounting, and billing management capabilities for multisite Cisco IPC Express deployments.

Managing Multisite Cisco IPC Express Networks

You can also deploy Cisco IPC Express in large-scale enterprise networks or in managed-services networks, as described in Chapter 2, "Building a Cisco IPC Express Network." Figure 14-44 shows multiple small and medium business or enterprise branch office Cisco IPC Express sites connected to the SP's VoIP network.

Figure 14-44 *Managing a Multisite Cisco IPC Express Network*

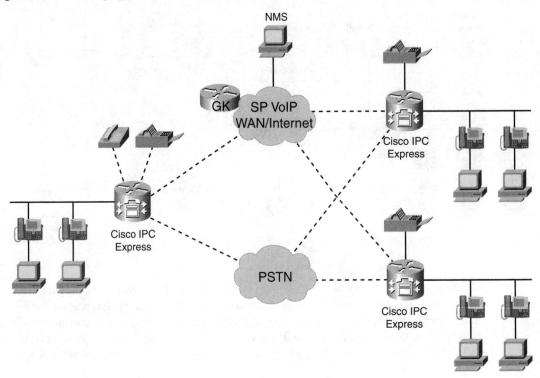

When deploying Cisco IPC Express systems in a multisite environment, provisioning, configuring, and managing only one Cisco IPC Express system at a time is insufficient. The Cisco Zero Touch deployment method described in Chapter 13 can be used to deploy large-scale Cisco IPC Express networks.

Cisco Voice Network Management Solutions

This section describes what Cisco network management applications you can use to manage Cisco IPC Express systems. Some of these solutions might not manage Cisco IPC Express features directly but might facilitate the management of the underlying voice network.

Cisco offers management tools that dramatically reduce the cost of operating a network. By providing tools that reduce human intervention in the initial deployment of network hardware and ongoing maintenance, network management helps decrease human error and increases the total number of devices that a single person can manage. Cisco provides network management tools to help SPs and enterprise customers manage their data and voice networks. The network management options are via either the CLI for standalone sites or automated NMSs for large networks.

The NMS solution is an automated service deployment option that uses integrated network management devices to provide fault, configuration, accounting, performance, and security (FCAPS) management support. Because a Cisco IPC Express system runs as part of the Cisco IOS voice-enabled router, all the existing Cisco Voice Network Management systems are applicable, including the following:

- CiscoWorks QoS Policy Manager (QPM)
- CiscoWorks Resource Manager Essentials (RME)
- Internetwork Performance Monitor
- Cisco Voice Manager and Telemate

The next sections describe each of these systems in more detail.

CiscoWorks QoS Policy Manager

CiscoWorks QoS Policy Manager (QPM) is a management tool for QoS policy creation, deployment, and monitoring. It provides rules-based policy guidance plus templates (designed by Cisco or customized by users) to streamline QoS management. It improves efficiencies by administering QoS for IP telephony across the entire network using step-by-step wizards and templates based on Cisco design recommendations. CiscoWorks QPM enforces network-wide services such as low latency, as well as fast response for VoIP, video, and other applications, such as SAP, Oracle, and PeopleSoft.

CiscoWorks Resource Manager Essentials

CiscoWorks Resource Manager Essentials (RME) is an infrastructure tool for full-service branch management. It helps streamline a network's daily operations. The CiscoWorks RME browser interface allows easy access to information critical to network uptime and simplifies time-consuming administrative tasks. The Management Connection feature in CiscoWorks RME adds web integration of other management tools from Cisco and partner companies. Therefore, you can use these tools and applications to create a seamless central point of network administration. CiscoWorks RME includes the following components:

- **Inventory Manager**—Manages inventory of the devices
- **Change Audit**—Tracks changes made to each managed device
- **Device Configuration Manager**—Manages device configuration
- **Software Image Manager**—Manages software images installed on devices
- **Availability Manager**—Displays device availability
- **Syslog Analyzer**—Analyzes Syslog messages
- **Cisco Management Connection**—Allows integration with other management tools

CiscoWorks Internetwork Performance Monitor

CiscoWorks Internetwork Performance Monitor (IPM) is a network response time and availability troubleshooting application. It lets network engineers proactively troubleshoot network-wide performance to diagnose congestion and latency problems using real-time and historic statistics.

As enterprise networks continue to grow in size, scope, and strategic importance, network managers face numerous challenges in maintaining their networks' performance and availability. Furthermore, as enterprises deploy new network applications and services, such as VoIP and streaming video, measurements of network performance must be able to recognize different levels of service based on these different types of network traffic.

CiscoWorks IPM helps meet these challenges by performing proactive network response-time measurement. With CiscoWorks IPM, network managers have the tools they need to isolate performance problems, locate bottlenecks, diagnose latency and jitter, and perform trend analysis of network response time. Furthermore, CiscoWorks IPM can perform path and hop performance analysis between virtually any two points in an IP-based network. IPM removes the guesswork from response-time problem diagnosis, thereby helping network managers be proactive in providing the appropriate level of network response time to their users.

Cisco Voice Manager and Telemate

The International Telecommunication Union (ITU) standard G.113 specifies how to measure voice quality by calculating the Calculated Planning Impairment Factor (ICPIF) value.

Cisco IOS voice-enabled routers can calculate an ICPIF value for every call, and log it in the CDR records and the CISCO-VOICE-DIAL-CONTROL-MIB. In addition, the routers can send a quality of voice (QoV) trap via SNMP if a call's ICPIF value exceeds a preset value. This means that the voice-enabled routers have built-in voice quality measurement abilities. An NMS can then collect these measurements, and analyze the data to identify trends. VoIP voice quality is mainly affected by network QoS. Therefore, the call analysis focuses on identifying voice quality problems on a per-site basis. If you can identify sites that have a large number of calls with poor voice quality, you can focus on any QoS issues in the network path to and from those sites.

Cisco Voice Manager (CVM) and Telemate provide monitoring and reporting capabilities for voice quality in large-scale IP networks. Voice quality reporting uses the ICPIF value calculated by the Cisco IOS voice-enabled routers for each call, which allows the network manager to identify sites that suffer from poor voice quality and take appropriate steps to correct them.

Cisco CVM and Telemate are two separate applications. Cisco CVM is a Cisco developed product, and Telemate is a product by a separate vendor that Cisco bundles with Cisco CVM. Cisco CVM collects CDRs from the router and receives QoV SNMP traps from the gateways. Cisco CVM then sends this information to Telemate, which processes this information and stores it in a Microsoft SQL database, listing calls with their respective details, including the ICPIF value. You can run various reports against the database, including QoV reports. You can use Telemate's Packet Voice Calls with a Quality of Service Traps report listing all calls for which the gateway generated a QoV trap to identify which site suffers from voice quality issues.

Managing Cisco IPC Express with Cisco Partner Applications

In addition to the Cisco management solutions discussed in the previous sections, some Cisco partners offer management solutions. This section describes two of these solutions:

- NetIQ Vivinet Manager
- Stonevoice

NetIQ Vivinet Manager

NetIQ's Vivinet Manager allows you to gain access to Cisco CME data, and then analyze and manage Cisco CME Systems. With NetIQ Vivinet Manager for Cisco CME, you gain easy access to a new set of tools you can leverage to gather a wide range of diagnostic and management data, which can help prevent outages and keep things running smoothly.

NetIQ Vivinet Manager for Cisco CME is an add-on module to NetIQ Vivinet Manager version 2.1. Equipped with Cisco CME AXL/SOAP API support, you can use Knowledge Scripts included in Vivinet Manager for Cisco CME to create jobs that monitor the health, availability, and performance of key devices. These scripts allow you to monitor and manage crucial device properties at a depth unparalleled by any other solution. You can configure each Knowledge Script to send an alert, collect data for reporting, and perform automated problem management when an event occurs.

The Vivinet Manager Knowledge Scripts let you monitor phone status (registered, unregistered, and deceased), reset IP phones, specify key phones, monitor for duplicate extensions, and show inventory information for phones attached to Cisco CME systems. The following are the supported Knowledge Scripts for the Cisco CME module:

- **CiscoCME_Device_Reset**—Resets Cisco CME IP phones for reasons such as troubleshooting or picking up new default firmware. Use this script in conjunction with CiscoCME_Device_Status to ensure that the selected phones have upgraded successfully.
- **CiscoCME_Device_Status**—Monitors the status of key Cisco CME phones.
- **CiscoCME_Extension_Check**—Monitors for duplicate phone extension numbers. This script looks for all phones configured in Cisco CME, regardless of whether they are registered.
- **CiscoCME_Phone_Inventory**—Generates an inventory of the phone details for phones that are attached to Cisco CME.
- **CiscoCME_Set_Key_Phones**—Designates one or more "key" phones. After you designate key phones, you can choose to monitor only key phones.

The following features are provided by NetIQ Vivinet Manager for Cisco CME:

- It discovers Cisco CMEs with CME version and device information.

- It provides Knowledge Scripts for day-to-day and diagnostic monitoring.

- It monitors Cisco CME resources, including CPU, memory, Flash memory, power supplies, and temperature sensors.

- It supports Cisco CME version 3.0 and later.

- It monitors and reports scripts in the Network Device module in addition to the scripts created especially for the Cisco CME module.

NetIQ for Cisco CME is an add-on module to the NetIQ Vivinet Manager. Get the installation CD-ROM from NetIQ (http:/www.netiq.com/products/vm/) for Cisco CME, and install it to the NetIQ Vivinet Manager. Refer to the NetIQ Vivinet Manager for Cisco CME documentation for installation and setup information.

Example 14-43 shows the required configuration on a Cisco CME system.

Example 14-43   *Cisco CME Configuration for NetIQ*

```
router#show running-config
snmp-server community public RO
! Set up the community string
!
telephony-service
   log password abcd
   no xmltest
   ! doesn't show when "no xmltest" is configured
   no xmlschema
   ! doesn't show when "no xmlschema" is configured
```

Figure 14-45 shows the operator console of NetIQ Vivinet Manager for Cisco CME.

The following sections provide some highlights of how you can use the NetIQ Vivinet Manager for Cisco CME.

Discovery of Cisco CME

You might use the Discovery script (Discovery_CiscoCME) found on the Discovery tab of the Knowledge Script pane to discover the Cisco CME managed object on a device in the TreeView pane of the Operator Console.

From the Discovery tab of the Knowledge Script pane, drag and drop the Discovery_CiscoCME script onto a proxy computer in the TreeView pane. Set the Values tab parameters, as shown in Figure 14-46.

Figure 14-45   *NetIQ Vivinet Manager Operator Console for Cisco CME*

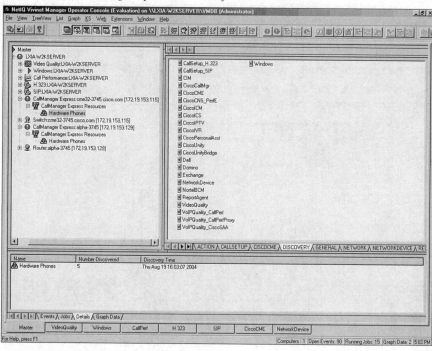

Figure 14-46   *Discovery Property*

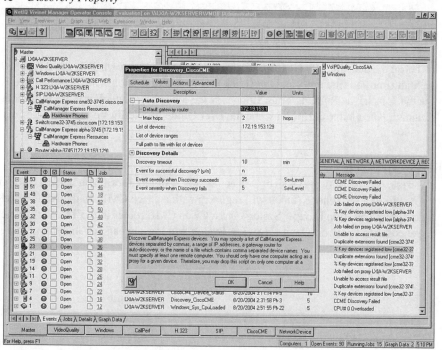

To arrange when you want to run the Discovery script, click the Schedule tab. You see the screen shown in Figure 14-47.

Figure 14-47 *Scheduling a Job*

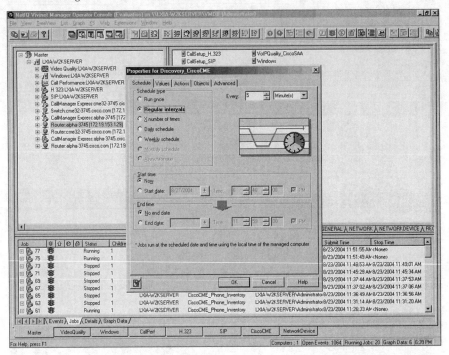

Choose the Schedule type to run once, at regular intervals, or on a daily/weekly schedule. Select a Start time and End time, and then click **OK** to schedule a job. The job scheduled is displayed in the Jobs tab as Running or as Stopped if the job is complete. For more information about running Knowledge Script jobs, see the User Guide for NetIQ Vivinet Manager.

Monitoring New Phones

You can use the NetworkDevice_Device_Syslog script to inform you when a configured phone (known) or a new phone (unknown) registers with a Cisco CME. In the NETWORKDEVICE pane, drag and drop Device_Syslog onto a Cisco CME router in the TreeView panel. The Properties for NetworkDevice_Device_Syslog window appears, as shown in Figure 14-48.

Figure 14-48 *Device Syslog Setup*

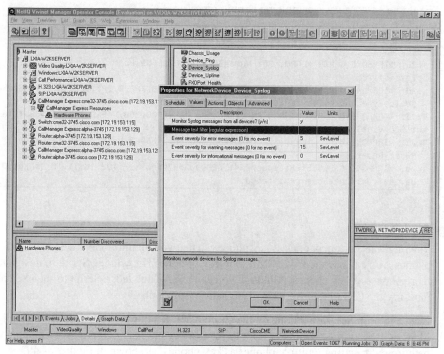

In the Values tab, change the value for Monitor Syslog messages from all devices? (y/n) to y, and change other values if needed. You might configure an action to be taken (in the Actions tab) when events or errors occur.

As described in the section "Monitoring IP Phones Using Cisco CME Syslog Messages," a Syslog message is generated when an IP phone registers with Cisco CME. In addition, a different Syslog message is generated when a new or unknown phone requires Cisco CME to create an ephone configuration entry. You can configure NetworkDevice_Device_Syslog to watch for these entries and to generate events as needed.

In Example 14-44, a new phone registers with Cisco CME. Cisco CME creates an ephone entry and then forces a reset of the new phone. When the phone restarts, a normal register message is generated, because the phone now has a configuration entry. When a new phone registers and has no ephone configuration entry, the register message is IPPHONE-6-REGISTER_NEW.

When a configured phone registers, the register message is simply IPPHONE-6-REGISTER. Example 14-44 gives a sample registration message.

Example 14-44 *Monitoring New Phones with Syslog Messages*

```
router#
1w2d: %IPPHONE-6-REG_ALARM: 25: Name=SEP00036B7FFF59 Load=3.2(2.14)Last=
  Initialized
1w2d: %IPPHONE-6-REGISTER_NEW: ephone-4: SEP00036B7FFF59 IP:192.168.1.16 Socket:3
  DeviceType:Phone has registered. Reseting SEP00036B7FFF59
1w2d: %IPPHONE-6-UNREGISTER_NORMAL: ephone-4: SEP00036B7FFF59 IP:192.168.1.16 Soc
ket:3 DeviceType:Phone has unregistered normally.
1w2d: %IPPHONE-6-REG_ALARM: 22: Name=SEP00036B7FFF59 3 Load=3.2(2.14)Last=
  Reset-Reset
1w2d: %IPPHONE-6-REGISTER: ephone-4: SEP00036B7FFF59 IP:192.168.1.16 Socket:3
  DeviceType:Phone has registered.
```

Managing Key Phones

You might set certain phones as key phones so that you monitor only a selected set of important phones. You can use the CiscoCME_Set_Key_Phones Knowledge Script to designate one or more phones as key phones. Although you can use a Knowledge Script to set a key phone, you must use the CLI to remove a key designation from a phone.

Drag and drop Set_Key_Phone on the Cisco CME Resource in the TreeView. Configure the MAC address of the phone you want to set as a key phone, or configure a filename with a full path if you're setting multiple phones as key phones, as shown in Figure 14-49.

For more information on NetIQ Vivinet Manager Applications, go to http://www.netiq.com.

Stonevoice

Stonevoice, a business unit of Computer Design in Italy, offers an application suite for Cisco CME IP Telephony Solutions with the following capabilities:

- **Switch Answering Machine (SSAM)**—Manages voice mail integration with Cisco CME via H.323. Refer to Chapter 11 for more information about configuring Cisco CME for SSAM.

- **Billy**—A call accounting and reporting tool based on CDR records.

- **IVR Manager**—Equipped with canned scripts and prompts.

- **Concerto**—An MOH server to change a music file on-the-fly.

- **Speedy**—A directory manager that lets users add, delete, or modify public and personal directories.

- **CallBarring**—Call blocking and restriction based on time and day.

- **Service Manager**—An embedded tool to manage XML services and user subscriptions.

- **Idle URL Manager**—Displays text and images on the phone display when the phone is idle.

Figure 14-49   *Setting Key Phones*

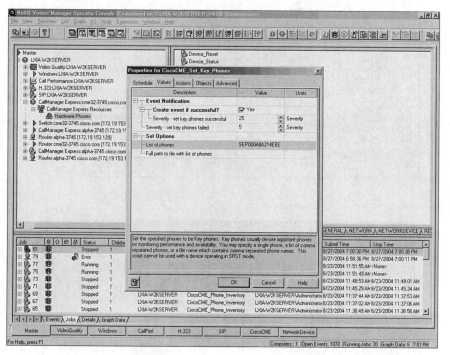

The Billy accounting application is shown in Figure 14-50.

Figure 14-51 shows the IVR Manager screen where you can set up different system behaviors.

Figure 14-50 *Billy: View Call Report*

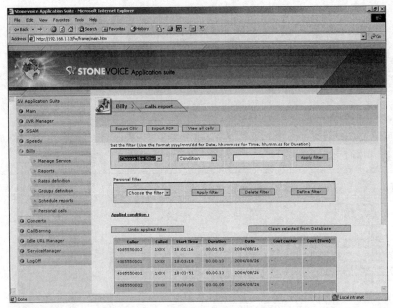

Figure 14-51 *IVR Manager: Setup Behaviors*

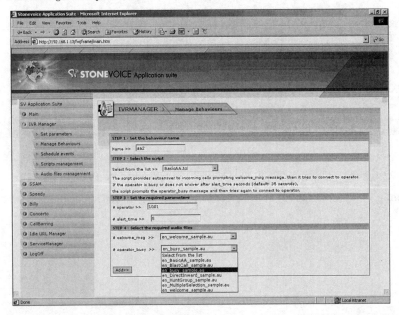

Figure 14-52 shows the IVR Manager screen where you see the TCL scripts in your system and where you can run a particular TCL script.

Figure 14-52 *IVR Manager: Running the TCL scripts*

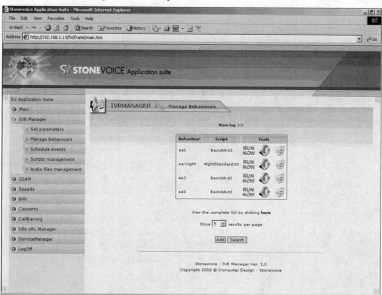

Figure 14-53 shows the IVR Manager screen where you can manage the TCL scripts on your system.

Figure 14-53 *IVR Manager: Managing TCL scripts*

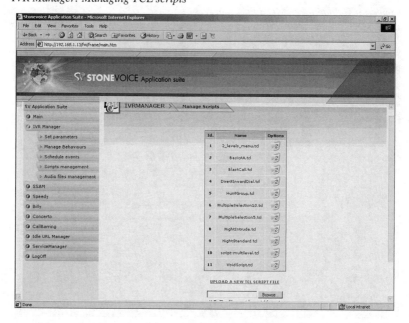

Figure 14-54 shows the IVR Manager screen where you can manage .wav and .au audio files on your system.

Figure 14-54 *IVR Manager: Managing Audio Files*

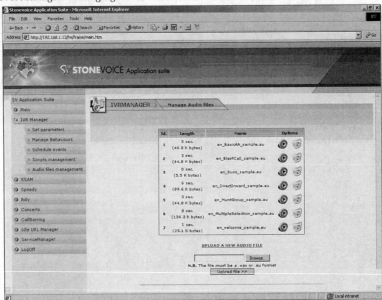

Figure 14-55 shows the Concerto MOH management application.

Figure 14-55 *Concerto: Uploading an MOH file*

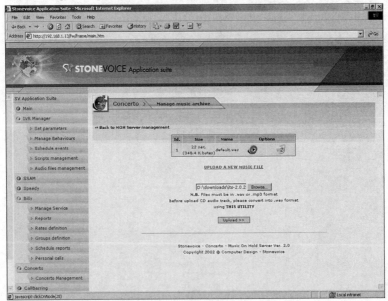

Figure 14-56 shows the CallBarring application, which lets you set up digit strings that might not be called.

Figure 14-56   *CallBarring: Setting Up Call Blocking*

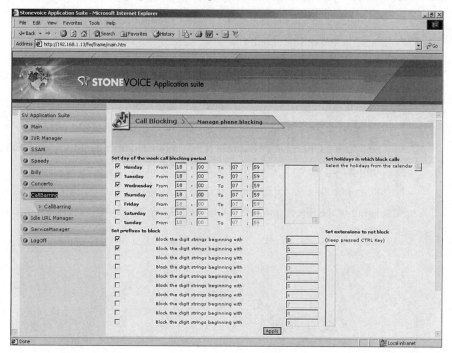

Summary

This chapter covered how many of the different features of a Cisco IPC Express system are configured, including Cisco CME phone and call processing features, as well as Cisco UE AA and voice mail features.

It also gave an overview of the network management applications available for Cisco voice (IP telephony) solutions for small and medium businesses and enterprise branch offices. It covered managing Cisco IPC Express when deployed as a managed service CPE by a SP. This chapter also covered details on using the Cisco partner applications NetIQ Vivinet Manager with Cisco CME (interfacing via Cisco CME's SOAP AXL APIs) and Stonevoice.

This chapter covers the following topics:

- Configuring a two-site sample Cisco IP Communications (IPC) Express system
- Planning and offline staging
- Basic router setup
- Initial Cisco CallManager Express (CME) system setup
- Configuring extensions and phones
- Configuring the Public Switched Telephone Network (PSTN) interface
- Configuring Cisco Unity Express (UE) automated attendant (AA) and voice mail
- Configuring Cisco CME call processing features
- Interconnecting multiple Cisco IPC Express systems
- Listing of the Site A and Site B Cisco CME and Cisco UE configurations built in this chapter

## CHAPTER 15

Cisco IPC Express System Configuration Example

This chapter provides a step-by-step configuration guide to help you set up your Cisco IP Communications (IPC) Express system. System configuration and setup topics, features, and details were discussed in depth in Chapter 13, "Cisco IPC Express General Administration and Initial System Setup," and Chapter 14, "Configuring and Managing Cisco IPC Express Systems." This chapter helps you understand that information by walking you through configuring a newly ordered system to create a working system for your office. Not every feature is covered again in this chapter. Instead, it focuses on the steps you should follow and draws on the previous chapters for many of the details.

This chapter uses a two-site sample network, as shown in Figure 15-1. This chapter walks through the setup and configuration of Site A, the primary site. Site B has a very similar basic configuration and is used to illustrate what extra configuration to do (as soon as you have the standalone system running with Site A) to connect two Cisco IPC Express sites.

Figure 15-1 *Cisco IPC Express Network with Two Sites*

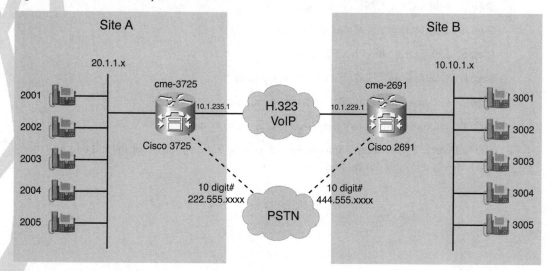

Site A uses the following hardware components:

- PSTN—VWIC-2MFT-T1 and AIM-ATM-VOICE-30 (WIC slot 0)
- Router—Cisco 3725 router
- NM-CUE—Cisco UE R2.0 (NM Slot 1)
- PSTN interface—NM-HD-2V and VIC2-2FXO (NM slot 2)
- IOS image—Cisco IOS Release 12.3(11)T2 IP Voice
- IP phones—Two real Cisco 7960 IP Phones and three virtual phones

Site B uses the following hardware components:

- Router—Cisco 2691 router
- NM-CUE—Cisco UE R2.0 (slot 1)
- IOS image—Cisco IOS Release 12.3(11)T2 IP Voice
- IP phones—Two real Cisco 7960 IP Phones and three virtual phones

Site A's numbering plan starts with two, and Site B's extensions start with three. Both sites use a four-digit extension numbering plan.

The next sections work through the following steps for configuring a Cisco IPC Express system:

Step 1 Planning and offline staging

Step 2 Basic router setup

Step 3 Initial Cisco CME system setup

Step 4 Configuring extensions and phones

Step 5 Configuring the PSTN interface

Step 6 Configuring Cisco UE AA and voice mail

Step 7 Configuring Cisco CME call processing features

Step 8 Interconnecting multiple Cisco IPC Express systems

The last part of this chapter, "Sample System Configurations," provides the full configurations of Sites A and B built during these steps.

Step 1: Planning and Offline Staging

Before building a configuration for a Cisco IPC Express system, you should note the parameters of the configuration you want to put in place. This includes such information as the names of the employees in your office, the extension numbering scheme you want to use, the Public Switched Telephone Network (PSTN) numbers your office has assigned, where PSTN calls should be routed, what type of phone each employee and room will have, what the IP addressing of your office is, and where the Trivial File Transfer Protocol (TFTP) server is located.

You can proceed from here in two ways, depending on whether you have the equipment ready in your office or lab:

- If you have already ordered the equipment and it has been delivered, or if you are reusing existing routers and IP phones, move on to Step 2, Basic Router Setup.

- If you have no equipment readily available, but you want to start building a configuration for staging purposes, read about offline staging in this section before moving on. The rest of this chapter cannot be executed without access to the equipment.

A Cisco CME Installation Configuration Tool (ICT) is an offline HTML tool available as a shareware application provided for Cisco Partners and Resellers. You can download the tool from the Cisco.com software center for Cisco CME, and use it to set up the basic telephony-service, IP phone, and voice mail configuration for all Cisco CME supported platforms.

You fill in basic fields about the system's desired configuration and scan in the phones' Media Access Control (MAC) addresses (if they are available). The tool output provides the router configuration (command-line interface [CLI]) as well as the Cisco UE configuration, which you can cut and paste into the equipment when that arrives.

Bring up a Microsoft Internet Explorer (IE) browser with the expresso.htm file. Note that expresso.htm is the only file that serves as an entrance to the tool. Figure 15-2 shows this tool's main screen, where you enter the number of phones, the IP addressing, whether you have voice mail, and, if so, the pilot numbers for AA and voice mail.

Figure 15-2 *Cisco CME ICT System Parameters*

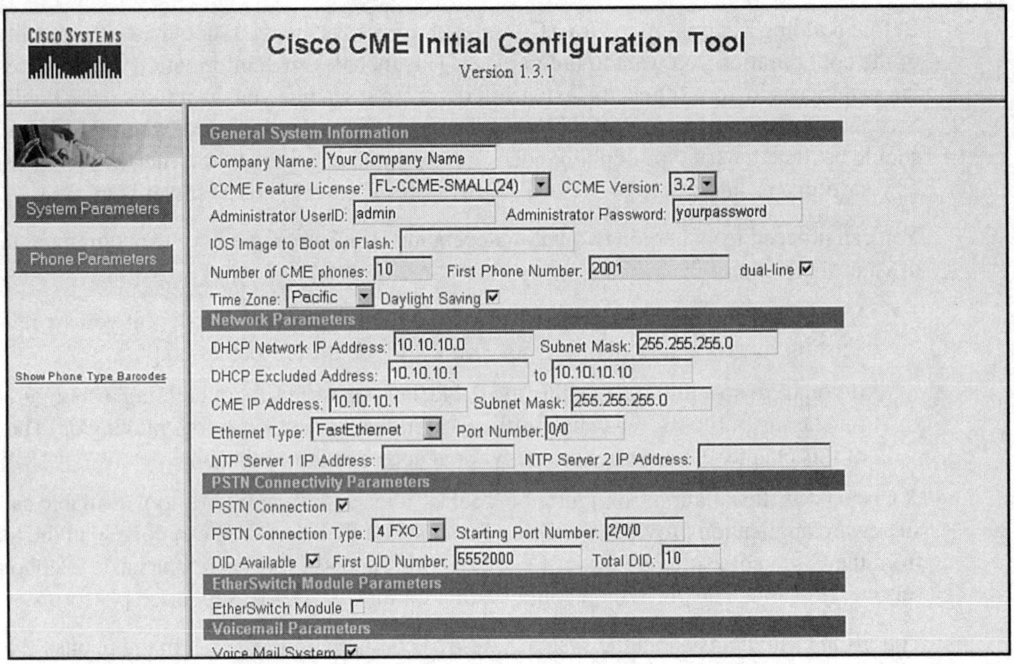

Click the **Phone Parameters** tab on the left panel to go to the next screen, shown in Figure 15-3, where you can enter or scan in the phones' MAC addresses. Using a barcode scanner is an effective method to add phones to a configuration with the ICT tool. The Flic scanner from http://www.flicscanner.com has been tested with the ICT tool.

Click the **show cli** button on the left panel after filling in the phone parameters to generate both the Cisco CME and Cisco UE CLI configurations for the given parameters. This is a flat text file that you can cut and paste into a document and ultimately into the console or a Telnet session into the router CLI to enter the configuration into the system.

Figure 15-3   *Cisco CME ICT Phone Parameters*

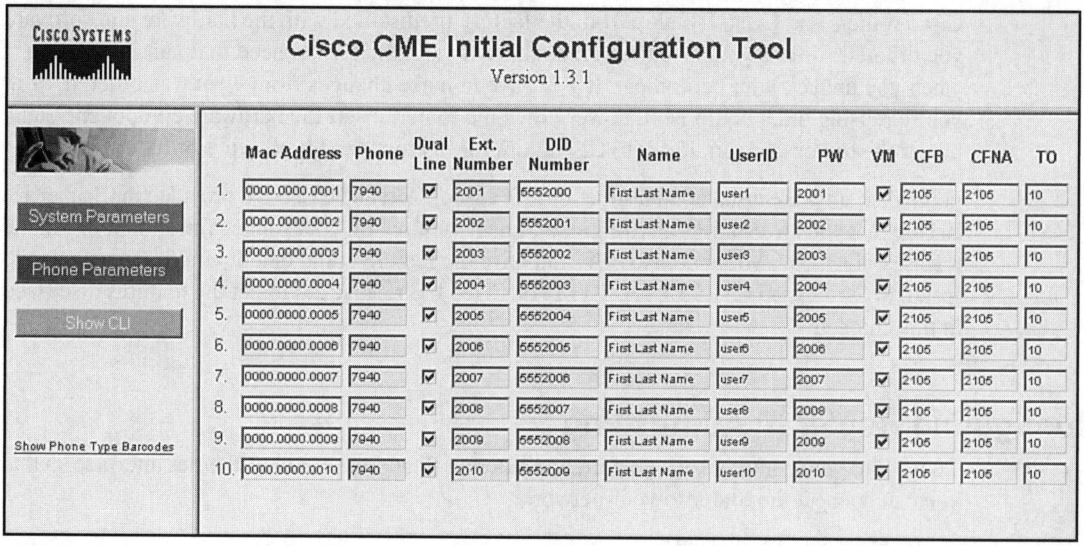

	Mac Address	Phone	Dual Line	Ext. Number	DID Number	Name	UserID	PW	VM	CFB	CFNA	TO
1.	0000.0000.0001	7940	☑	2001	5552000	First Last Name	user1	2001	☑	2105	2105	10
2.	0000.0000.0002	7940	☑	2002	5552001	First Last Name	user2	2002	☑	2105	2105	10
3.	0000.0000.0003	7940	☑	2003	5552002	First Last Name	user3	2003	☑	2105	2105	10
4.	0000.0000.0004	7940	☑	2004	5552003	First Last Name	user4	2004	☑	2105	2105	10
5.	0000.0000.0005	7940	☑	2005	5552004	First Last Name	user5	2005	☑	2105	2105	10
6.	0000.0000.0006	7940	☑	2006	5552005	First Last Name	user6	2006	☑	2105	2105	10
7.	0000.0000.0007	7940	☑	2007	5552006	First Last Name	user7	2007	☑	2105	2105	10
8.	0000.0000.0008	7940	☑	2008	5552007	First Last Name	user8	2008	☑	2105	2105	10
9.	0000.0000.0009	7940	☑	2009	5552008	First Last Name	user9	2009	☑	2105	2105	10
10.	0000.0000.0010	7940	☑	2010	5552009	First Last Name	user10	2010	☑	2105	2105	10

Cisco CME Initial Configuration Tool — Version 1.3.1. Navigation: System Parameters, Phone Parameters, Show CLI, Show Phone Type Barcodes.

Step 2: Basic Router Setup

As soon as you have the equipment on hand, the configuration of the real system can start. You can do this either by copying and pasting the staging configuration you built in the preceding section or by working through the following sections to set up the basic router and then the Cisco CME and Cisco UE parameters. Even if you use the staging configuration, it is still recommended that you scan the steps in this chapter. This will help you make sure that the parameters in the staged configuration are, in fact, the values you want for your real system configuration. It also helps you make any adjustments along the way to tailor the system for your use.

Installing Hardware and Software

Cisco routers and Cisco UE ship from the factory preinstalled with the hardware and software you ordered. Unless you have to upgrade the software, there is no need to do an installation when you unpack your equipment. If you have to make changes from what was ordered, or if you're reusing older equipment, power down the router, insert the hardware components, and power the router back up. Refer to Cisco.com for instructions for all types of hardware.

Follow the software installation instructions for Cisco CME and Cisco UE provided in Chapter 13. Ensure that you have an IP Voice or greater image running on your router. You should install the releases of Cisco CME and Cisco UE that have the feature complement you're interested in. Install at least Cisco CME 3.2 (12.3.11T) or Cisco UE release 2.0 to get the features discussed in this chapter.

Configuring Router IP Addressing

Connect to your router's console port, and enter an IP address for the Ethernet interface so that you can connect the router to your network:

```
interface FastEthernet0/0
  ip address 10.1.235.1 255.255.0.0
```

Also, set your router's host name to a descriptive string. For Site A, the name is cme-3725:

```
hostname cme-3725
```

Setting the Router Clock

Ensure that the clock is set correctly on your router, for example:

```
cme-3725#clock set 10:00:00 19 Aug 2004
```

You might also set the router clock using Network Time Protocol (NTP). The details are given in the section "Configuring NTP."

Setting Up the LAN Switch

You can use either an external LAN switch or an internal EtherSwitch housed inside the router chassis. You should define virtual LAN (VLAN) for both voice and data traffic.

External LAN Switch

For an external LAN switch, to enable separate VLANs for voice and data on a single router port, configure a trunk between the Cisco CME router and the LAN switch. The Cisco Catalyst 3550 and 3560 support autodetection of the VLAN type for IP phones (voice VLAN) and PCs (data VLAN). VLAN configuration varies between LAN switch types. Consult the appropriate documentation for the LAN switch model you are using.

Internal EtherSwitch

You can use several internal EtherSwitch network modules on a Cisco CME router, such as the NM-16ESW-PWR. If you need only one voice VLAN, the simplest configuration is to use the default VLAN 1 for all the IP phones connected to the same EtherSwitch, as shown in Example 15-1. The configuration in Example 15-1 shows an internal EtherSwitch module, but the actual Site A configuration in the full configurations being built in this chapter uses an external LAN switch.

Example 15-1 *Internal EtherSwitch Module Configuration*

```
Router#show running-config
ip dhcp excluded-address 192.168.1.1
!
ip dhcp pool ipphone
   network 192.168.1.0 255.255.255.0
   option 150 ip 192.168.1.1
   default-router 192.168.1.251
   dns-server 171.70.168.183
!
ip dhcp-server 192.168.1.1
!
interface Vlan1
 ip address 192.168.1.1 255.255.255.0
 no shutdown
!
interface FastEthernet4/0
 no ip address
!
interface FastEthernet4/1
 no ip address

interface FastEthernet4/2
 no ip address

 interface FastEthernet4/3
 no ip address

 interface FastEthernet4/4
 no ip address
!output omitted for brevity
```

Connecting Phones

Connect your IP phones to the LAN switch, and verify that they are powered. Confirm that there is connectivity between the router and the LAN switch.

Connecting the TFTP Server

Confirm that your TFTP server can be reached across the network by doing a **ping** from the router to the server's IP address.

Downloading and Extracting Cisco CME Files

Download the Cisco CME GUI files from http://www.cisco.com/cgi-bin/tablebuild.pl/ip-iostsp, and extract them into the router Flash memory. This process is described in Chapter 13 in the section "GUI File Installation."

Step 3: Initial Cisco CME System Setup

You have now set up the basic routing and LAN switching. The next task to accomplish is to start setting up the basic Cisco CME configuration. You can accomplish this in several ways:

- Use the Cisco CME Setup Utility
- Copy and paste the configuration, or segments thereof, from the staging configuration (if you used that tool)
- Configure the commands individually on Cisco CME

In the next section, you use the Cisco CME Setup Utility to do the basic Cisco CME configuration. If you are not using this utility, check the resulting CLI from the sections following the discussion of the Setup Utility, and compare that to the CLI that exists in your configuration to ensure that all the different parameters are set to the desired values.

Refer to the related sections in Chapter 13 for details on the configuration for different features.

Running the Cisco CME Setup Utility

Example 15-2 provides a log of running the Cisco CME Setup Utility (discussed in Chapter 13) to build the Site A basic configuration.

Example 15-2 *Cisco CME Setup Utility for Site A*

```
cme-3725(config)#telephony-service setup
 --- Cisco IOS Telephony Services Setup ---
Do you want to setup DHCP service for your IP Phones? [yes/no]: yes
Configuring DHCP Pool for Cisco IOS Telephony Services :
  IP network for telephony-service DHCP Pool:20.1.1.0
  Subnet mask for DHCP network :255.255.255.0
  TFTP Server IP address (Option 150) :20.1.1.100
  Default Router for DHCP Pool :20.1.1.100
Do you want to start telephony-service setup? [yes/no]: yes
Configuring Cisco IOS Telephony Services :
```

Example 15-2 *Cisco CME Setup Utility for Site A (Continued)*

```
        Enter the IP source address for Cisco IOS Telephony Services :20.1.1.100
        Enter the Skinny Port for Cisco IOS Telephony Services :  [2000]:
        How many IP phones do you want to configure :  [0]:_5
        Do you want dual-line extensions assigned to phones? [yes/no]: yes
        What Language do you want on IP phones [0]: 0
        Which Call Progress tone set do you want on IP phones [0]:
        What is the first extension number you want to configure : 2001
Do you have Direct-Inward-Dial service for all your phones? [yes/no]: no
Do you want to forward calls to a voice message service? [yes/no]: yes
        Enter extension or pilot number of the voice message service: 2105
        Call forward No Answer Timeout : [18]: 10
Do you wish to change any of the above information? [yes/no]: no
---- Setup completed config ---
cme-3725(config)#
2w3d: %LINK-3-UPDOWN: Interface ephone_dsp DN 1.1, changed state to up
2w3d: %LINK-3-UPDOWN: Interface ephone_dsp DN 1.2, changed state to up
2w3d: %LINK-3-UPDOWN: Interface ephone_dsp DN 2.1, changed state to up
2w3d: %LINK-3-UPDOWN: Interface ephone_dsp DN 2.2, changed state to up
2w3d: %LINK-3-UPDOWN: Interface ephone_dsp DN 3.1, changed state to up
2w3d: %LINK-3-UPDOWN: Interface ephone_dsp DN 3.2, changed state to up
2w3d: %LINK-3-UPDOWN: Interface ephone_dsp DN 4.1, changed state to up
2w3d: %LINK-3-UPDOWN: Interface ephone_dsp DN 4.2, changed state to up
2w3d: %LINK-3-UPDOWN: Interface ephone_dsp DN 5.1, changed state to up
2w3d: %LINK-3-UPDOWN: Interface ephone_dsp DN 5.2, changed state to up
```

Configuring Router Parameters for Cisco CME

You must set a number of options to configure the IP environment to ensure that Cisco CME has access to devices such as TFTP servers and IP phones:

- TFTP for phone firmware download
- Dynamic Host Configuration Protocol (DHCP) to provide automatic IP addresses for the IP phones
- NTP for clock synchronization
- HTTP for the GUI to function correctly

Configuring TFTP

Cisco CME phone loads must be available for TFTP download, as shown in Example 15-3. Note that the **tftp-server** command parameters are case-sensitive; specifying filenames in lowercase does not work. The **tftp-server** commands must be configured manually for phone types, including the Cisco ATA, 7905, 7912, 7935, 7936, 7920, and 7970 IP Phones, even if the Cisco CME Setup Utility is used. The Cisco 7970 IP IP Phone requires multiple phone load files to be served by **tftp-server** commands, whereas other phones require only one phone load.

Example 15-3 *TFTP Phone Loads*

```
Router#show running-config
tftp-server flash:P00303020214.bin
tftp-server flash:P00303020209.bin
tftp-server flash:P00305000200.bin
tftp-server flash:P00305000300.bin
```

Configuring DHCP

Basic DHCP was configured during the Cisco CME Setup Utility. If you chose not to configure DHCP there and now you want to add it, or you want to make changes to the basic DHCP configuration, follow the information in this section.

You must define a DHCP pool for IP address assignment to the IP phones. If you use separate VLANs for voice and data, you need two DHCP pools to assign IP addresses dynamically to the IP phones and the data devices. On the voice DHCP pool, Option 150 should be the LAN interface address. You may also define a DHCP pool to map IP addresses statically to phone MAC addresses. If existing devices use static IP addresses in the same range defined in the DHCP pools, these addresses must be excluded from the DHCP pool to avoid addressing conflicts. You can use the **show ip dhcp binding** command to verify the addresses assigned to the IP phones. Example 15-4 shows a sample two-VLAN configuration. Note that you may use the **ip dhcp exclude-address** command to exclude individual or multiple addresses from the DHCP pool.

Example 15-4 *Voice and Data VLAN Configuration*

```
Router#show running-config
ip dhcp excluded-address 100.0.0.1
ip dhcp excluded-address 200.0.0.1
!
ip dhcp pool data
   network 100.0.0.0 255.255.255.0
   default-router 100.0.0.1
!
ip dhcp pool voice
   network 200.0.0.0 255.255.255.0
   option 150 ip 200.0.0.1
   default-router 200.0.0.1
!
ip dhcp-server 100.0.0.1
ip dhcp-server 200.0.0.1

Router#show ip dhcp binding
Bindings from all pools not associated with VRF:
IP address        Hardware address       Lease expiration        Type
200.0.0.2         0100.3094.c2a3.c5      Mar 02 1993 06:58 AM    Automatic
200.0.0.3         0100.3094.c289.a9      Mar 02 1993 06:27 AM    Automatic
```

Configuring NTP

You must configure NTP (even if the Cisco CME Setup Utility is used) to ensure that clocks are synchronized and voice mail time stamps are correct. If you have a Cisco UE module in your system, be sure to reboot it at some point after the NTP configuration is complete so that it can pick up the correct time stamps before you start day-to-day operation on your system.

Configuring HTTP

The Cisco CME router must be set to be an HTTP server (even if the Cisco CME Setup Utility is used) for the Cisco IPC Express GUI to function. Enter the following statements in configure terminal mode on the router:

```
ip http server
ip http path flash
```

Configuring Cisco CME GUI Administrators

If you plan to use Cisco CME GUI access, configure a system administration account and password with the **web admin** command, as shown in Example 15-5. (Replace admin and **cisco** with your choices.) Also set the **dn-webedit** and **time-webedit** commands to make sure you can access directory numbers (DNs), and set the router clock from the GUI.

Example 15-5 *Configuring Cisco CME GUI System Administrator Access*

```
Router#show running-config
telephony-service
 web admin system name admin password cisco
 dn-webedit
 time-webedit
```

If you are a Cisco Partner or Reseller and you plan to customize GUI access for your end customer, enter a customer administrator account, as shown in Example 15-6. (Replace **custlogin** and **custpswd** in the **web admin command** with your choices.)

Example 15-6 *Configuring Cisco CME GUI System Administrator Access for a Customer*

```
Router#show running-config
telephony-service
 web admin customer name custlogin password custpswd
 web customize load sample.xml
```

You may now point your browser to the following URL to access the Cisco CME GUI, and log in with your configured username and password:

```
http://ip-address-of-cme/ccme.html
```

Adjusting Basic Cisco CME Parameters

A few parameters control system Cisco CME operation:

- Source address and TCP port
- Maximum phone and maximum DN parameters
- Phone loads

The first two parameters were set during the Cisco CME Setup Utility, but you may want to adjust the values.

The *source address* is the IP address associated with Cisco CME. You typically use the IP address of the interface where the local IP phones are connected. Port 2000 is the default TCP port. Use the following commands to set these values:

```
telephony-service
ip source-address 20.1.1.100 port 2000
```

The maximum phone and maximum DN parameters were set to the default values during the Cisco CME Setup Utility. This setting may not have the values you want for your system. Reset these values if needed to numbers that are comfortably more than the actual number of phones and DNs you foresee using, but that are less than or equal to the Cisco CME seat license you purchased. Use the following commands to set these values:

```
telephony-service
 max-ephones 20
 max-dn 120
```

In addition to the **tftp-server** commands given earlier, you have to specify the phone load to use for the IP phones. Only specify the loads that are actually used. Do not use the .bin or .sbn extensions in the **load** command. The **create cnf-files** command generates an XML phone configuration file. Use commands similar to this one to specify phone loads for particular IP phone types:

```
load 7960G-7940G P00305000301
create cnf-files
```

After you've completed the configuration up to this point, IP phones that are powered on and that have received an IP address via DHCP automatically register with Cisco CME and download firmware from the router. It may take up to 5 minutes for the phones to register. All Cisco 7960G IP Phones registered with Cisco CME show "Cisco CME" on the lower portion of the phone display.

At this point, your router and basic Cisco CME system are operational. But you cannot yet make calls between IP phones, because no extensions have been defined or assigned to any buttons on the phones, nor do the phones have dial tone.

Step 4: Configuring Extensions and Phones

On Cisco CME you normally configure DNs (ephone-dns) before configuring the phones (ephones). This is different from Cisco CallManager, where phones must register before you configure extensions. On Cisco CME, you can configure extensions regardless of whether the phones are registered. The following sections walk you through setting up phones and extensions on this chapter's sample system.

Defining Extensions

The Cisco CME Setup Utility has already created basic DN and phone definitions for the number of phones you specified. For the Site A setup, five phones were specified.

One of the Setup Utility questions that inquires about dual-line phones is, "Do you want dual-line extensions assigned to phones?" For Site A, the reply was yes (refer to Example 15-2). A dual-line configuration is needed for features such as call transfer, call waiting, and call conferencing. A dual-line configuration uses one line with two channels so that a second call to the same line can be put in call waiting mode, or a call transfer or conference call can be initiated using the second channel.

You cannot change a nondual-line ephone-dn to dual-line mode. You have to insert the ephone-dn with this mode. If you chose dual-line mode in the Setup Utility, as in Example 15-2, you're all set. If not, you may have to delete the ephone-dns created by the utility. (Use the command **no ephone-dn** *x,* where *x* is the number of the ephone-dns.) Reenter them in dual-line mode using the **ephone-dn** *x* **dual-line** command.

Example 15-7 shows the first two of the five ephone-dns created by the utility log shown in Example 15-2. Because the replies in the utility also specified that a voice mail system existed and that the pilot number was 2105, the call forward CLI has already been entered for the ephone-dns.

Example 15-7 *Ephone-dns Created by the Setup Utility*

```
cme-3725#show running-config
ephone-dn  1  dual-line
 number 2001
 call-forward busy 2105
 call-forward noan 2105 timeout 10
!
ephone-dn  2  dual-line
 number 2002
 call-forward busy 2105
 call-forward noan 2105 timeout 10
```

You can create additional ephone-dns using the CLI, or you can log into the GUI at this point and add extensions via the **Configuration > Extensions** screen.

Many types of DNs and different ephone-dn features exist. The configuration done so far in this section provides only the basic extension (DN) configuration necessary to make calls, but you have not yet configured the phones. The following section shows you how to complete some basic phone configuration.

Assigning Extensions to IP Phones

The Cisco CME Setup Utility shown in Example 15-2 has already entered ephone definitions into the configuration. They show up as a single line only in the CLI, as shown here, until the phones are powered, connected, and registered with Cisco CME:

```
ephone  1
ephone  2
```

As soon as the phones are powered and registered (setup steps completed in the earlier sections "Connecting Phones" and "Adjusting Basic Cisco CME Parameters"), the MAC addresses of the IP phones are known to Cisco CME and are automatically populated into the configuration, as shown in Example 15-8.

Example 15-8   *Ephones Created by the Setup Utility*

```
cme-3725#show running-config
ephone  1
 mac-address 0003.6BAA.D1F8
 type 7960
!
ephone  2
 mac-address 0003.6BAA.D362
 type 7960
```

Next, you have to assign extensions (ephone-dns) to the phones by using the **button** CLI command, as shown in Example 15-9, or by going to the **Configuration > Phones** GUI screen and configuring the extensions on each phone's buttons. The number following the colon in the **button** command refers to the ephone-dn (the extension) attached to this button.

Example 15-9   *Basic Button Mappings for the Ephones*

```
cme-3725#show running-config
ephone  1
 mac-address 0003.6BAA.D1F8
 type 7960
 button  1:1
!
ephone  2
 mac-address 0003.6BAA.D362
 type 7960
 button  1:2
```

You can set up a Cisco CME system in Key System mode or in private branch exchange (PBX) mode. In Key System mode, you normally configure two or more lines per phone, so buttons 1 and 2 (and more) on each phone are each mapped to an individual extension. In PBX mode, there is usually only one line per phone, so you configure only button 1 with an extension on each phone.

If you did not use the Cisco CME Setup Utility to create initial ephone definitions, you can discover the MAC addresses of the phones connected to Cisco CME by using the **show ephone** command, as shown in Example 15-10, and then use the MAC addresses shown in the output to configure your ephone definitions.

Example 15-10   *Discovering IP Phone MAC Addresses*

```
router#show ephone
ephone-1 Mac:0008.218C.05D8 TCP socket:[-1] activeLine:0 UNREGISTERED
mediaActive:0 offhook:0 ringing:0 reset:0 reset_sent:0 paging 0 debug:0
IP:0.0.0.0 0 Unknown 0  keepalive 0 max_line 0
```

Resetting or Restarting Phones

Configuration changes on an IP phone or its associated DNs usually require a phone restart or reset to take effect. Note that when a PC is connected to the LAN from the access port on an IP phone, the PC temporarily loses network connectivity while the phone resets. It may take up to 5 minutes for the PC to regain network connectivity.

- The **restart** command performs a softphone reboot without contacting the DHCP and TFTP servers. If you have a PC connected to the IP phone being restarted, this PC doesn't lose network connectivity during the time the phone is being restarted.

- The **reset** command performs a complete phone reboot that includes contacting the DHCP and TFTP servers for the latest configuration information.

You may **reset** or **restart** an individual IP phone or globally **reset all** or **restart all** the IP phones connected to the same Cisco CME system.

The **restart all** or **reset all** commands cause the router to pause for 15 seconds between the reseting of each successive phone. See Example 15-11.

Example 15-11   *Resetting or Restarting All the IP Phones*

```
cme-3725(config-telephony)#reset all ?
  <0-60>  time interval in seconds between each phone reset
cme32-3745(config-telephony)#restart all ?
cme32-3745(config-telephony)#reset sequence-all
```

The **sequence-all** option on the **reset** command causes the router to wait until one phone's reset is complete before resetting the next phone.

Example 15-12 shows how to restart or reset phone 1 or globally reset or restart all the phones connected to the Cisco CME system.

Example 15-12 *Resetting and Restarting Phones*

```
cme-3725#show running-config
telephony-service
ephone 1
restart

telephony-service
ephone 1
reset

telephony-service
reset all

telephony-service
restart all
```

Making Calls Between IP Phones

At this point in the configuration, you can make calls from one IP phone to another. You should also see the extension mapped to each of the phone buttons appear on the phone's display. Calls can also be transferred and conferenced (because of the dual-line configuration used earlier) between IP phones.

You can use the following **debug** commands for troubleshooting if your system does not allow you to make calls or if your phones have not registered correctly. You may also refer to Chapter 16, "Troubleshooting Basic Cisco IPC Express Features," for more details on troubleshooting.

- **debug ephone error**
- **debug ephone register**
- **debug ephone detail**
- **debug tftp events**
- **debug dhcp detail**
- **debug ip dhcp server event**

Step 5: Configuring the PSTN Interface

The next step in Cisco CME system configuration is to route PSTN calls into your office to the extensions on the IP phones, and to allow IP phones to make outgoing PSTN calls. The following sections cover voice port and PSTN trunk configurations necessary to route PSTN calls to IP phones.

Configuring Voice Ports

Chapter 6, "Cisco CME PSTN Connectivity Options," explained the various hardware options you have on Cisco CME for connecting to the PSTN and also provided several configuration examples for different trunk types. The following sections build examples of basic PSTN connectivity for both an analog Foreign Exchange Office (FXO) and a digital T1 Primary Rate Interface (PRI) trunk. It is likely that your office will use one or the other, but not both.

If analog hardware is present in your Cisco CME system, ports show up automatically in the router configuration as follows:

```
voice-port 2/0/0
voice-port 2/0/1
```

To add caller ID to analog FXS or FXO ports, use the **caller-id** command, as shown in Example 15-13.

Example 15-13   *Configuring Caller ID on FXS or FXO Ports*

```
cme-3725#show running-config
voice-port 2/0/0
 caller-id enable
!
voice-port 2/0/1
 caller-id enable
```

Digital ports do not show up in the configuration simply because the hardware is present in your router. All you see by default is the **controller** statement alerting you that T1 or E1 port hardware is present. On the newer controller cards that allow software configuration for either T1 or E1 operation on the same hardware, the controller doesn't show up in the configuration until you configure the port type to be either T1 or E1 operation. Use the **card type** command to accomplish this.

Example 15-14 shows the configuration for a T1 PRI trunk type with the 5ESS switch type. Which switch type you should use depends on the central office you connect to and varies between geographic locations, as well as for T1 compared to E1 ports. The voice port, 0/0:23 in Example 15-13, is created automatically by the **pri-group** configuration, as is the D channel interface (interface Serial0/0:23 in Example 15-13). If you have T1 Channel Associated Signaling (CAS) or E1 R2 connectivity to the PSTN, you use the **ds0-group** command instead of the **pri-group** command.

Example 15-14   *Configuring a T1 PRI PSTN Trunk*

```
cme-3725#show running-config
network-clock-participate wic 0
network-clock-participate aim 0
isdn switch-type primary-5ess
!
controller T1 0/0
 pri-group timeslots 1-24
!
interface Serial0/0:23
```

continues

Example 15-14 *Configuring a T1 PRI PSTN Trunk (Continued)*

```
 no ip address
 isdn switch-type primary-5ess
 isdn incoming-voice voice
 no cdp enable
!
voice-port 0/0:23
```

As covered in Chapter 6, you can use various hardware cards on the router to provide a digital T1 or E1 connection to the PSTN. The configuration shown in Example 15-14, with the exception of the **network-clock-participate** commands, is generic to all T1/E1 trunks and does not vary based on which hardware you are using.

Routing PSTN Calls to IP Phones

FXO analog lines deliver no dial-in digits (discussed in Chapter 6), so it is necessary to configure an autoterminate destination for these PSTN calls. Ultimately, you should direct these calls to the AA, but because you have not set up the AA for Site A yet, the configuration in this section terminates the calls on extension 2001 for the time being. This is sufficient to test that PSTN calls into your Cisco CME system work properly. In the "Configuring the AA" section later in this chapter, the configuration changes to terminate the PSTN calls onto the AA.

The **connection plar opx** option does not provide answer supervision (connect) to the PSTN if the Cisco CME IP phone does not answer the call. Thus, it does not generate billing until the call is answered. The **connection plar** option, on the other hand, generates answer supervision to the PSTN (and therefore starts billing) the moment the router accepts the call, whether or not the call is answered by an IP phone.

The autoterminate destination for calls on the FXO port is configured under the **voice-port**, as shown in Example 15-15. All calls arriving on voice port 2/0/0 automatically start ringing on extension 2001.

Example 15-15 *Configuring FXO Trunks*

```
cme-3725#show running-config
voice-port 2/0/0
 connection plar opx 2001
```

PSTN calls arriving on the FXO port can now terminate on extension 2001, but calls arriving on the PRI trunk cannot yet ring any phone. All trunks other than FXO provide dialed digits, so the router can switch the calls based on the digits received from the PSTN. However, the digits delivered by the PSTN do not yet match any Cisco CME extension, so the calls receive overflow tone. Some digit manipulation is required. The current ephone-dn for extension 2001 is

```
 ephone-dn  1  dual-line
  number 2001
```

The PSTN number for dialing this phone is 222.555.2001, so you need to change the longer PSTN (E.164) number to 2001 so that it can match the ephone-dn configuration. Digit manipulation can be done in various ways, as explained in Chapter 6. The most straightforward way is simply to configure a secondary number associated with the ephone-dn so that calls to 2001 and calls to 222.555.2001 terminate on the same phone. This is shown in Example 15-16.

Example 15-16   *Configuring a Secondary Number*

```
cme-3725#show running-config
ephone-dn  1  dual-line
 number 2001 secondary 2225552001
```

Calls coming in from the PSTN to extension 2001 now ring the IP phone and can be answered. You can also use dial plan patterns to accomplish this.

Routing IP Phone Calls to the PSTN

Your employees most likely are used to dialing an access code to get a PSTN line. Assuming that this access code is 9, the dial plan entered into the configuration should direct calls dialed with a leading 9 to the PSTN trunks. Because the Site A system currently has both a PRI and analog FXO trunks to the PSTN, you likely want to give the PRI preference, and use the FXO as a backup only if no timeslots are available. You can achieve this by putting preferences on the dial peers.

The dial plan must also take care of local PSTN calls (9 + seven digits) and long-distance calls (9 + 11 digits). You may also want to add more dial peers to allow (or disallow) international PSTN dialing. The dial plan (and dial peers supporting it) can become very sophisticated. Example 15-17 shows just the basic plain old telephone service (POTS) dial peers necessary on the voice ports to route seven-digit and 11-digit PSTN calls to the PRI trunk first and to the FXO trunk second. The **forward-digits** command instructs the router to deliver a certain number of digits to the PSTN. In this example, it suppresses the "9" access code and forwards the rest of the digits the IP phone user dialed. You can add any number of digits to or delete any number of digits from the original string, or send completely different digits to the PSTN from what was dialed by the IP phone.

Example 15-17   *Configuring POTS Dial Peers for the PSTN*

```
cme-3725#show running-config
dial-peer voice 1000 pots
 destination-pattern 91..........
 port 0/0:23
 forward-digits 11
!
dial-peer voice 1001 pots
 preference 1
 destination-pattern 91..........
 port 2/0/0
!
```

continues

Example 15-17 *Configuring POTS Dial Peers for the PSTN (Continued)*

```
dial-peer voice 1002 pots
 destination-pattern 9[2-9]......
 port 0/0:23
 forward-digits 7
!
dial-peer voice 1003 pots
 preference 1
 destination-pattern 9[2-9]......
 port 2/0/0
```

As soon as you enter this configuration, IP phones can call 914445551212 (11-digit) or 95551212 (seven-digit) and have these calls routed to the PSTN.

Step 6: Configuring Cisco UE AA and Voice Mail

If your system does not have Cisco UE installed, you can skip this section and proceed to Step 7. The following sections step you through setting up the basic Cisco UE configuration necessary to use the AA and voice mail on your system.

Setting Up the Router for Cisco UE

Before you can configure and use Cisco UE applications such as AA and voice mail, you must set up the following basic IP connectivity parameters to ensure that the Cisco UE software can communicate with its environment:

- IP addressing
- Call routing to Cisco UE
- H.323-to-Session Initiation Protocol (SIP) call routing
- Message Waiting Indicator (MWI)

IP Addressing

The Cisco UE hardware module must be configured with an IP address on the router. This setup is covered in Chapter 13. Following the information provided there, the resulting configuration for the Cisco UE module for Site A is shown in Example 15-18.

Example 15-18 *Service-Engine Interface for Cisco UE*

```
cme-3725#show running-config
interface Service-Engine1/0
 ip unnumbered FastEthernet0/0
```

Example 15-18 *Service-Engine Interface for Cisco UE (Continued)*

```
service-module ip address 10.1.235.128 255.255.0.0
service-module ip default-gateway 10.1.235.1
ip route 10.1.235.128 255.255.255.255 Service-Engine1/0
```

You can show the status of the Cisco UE module by using the command shown in Example 15-19. You can also **ping** the IP interface (10.1.229.128 in this example) to ensure that IP connectivity is established.

Example 15-19 *Showing the Status of the Cisco UE Module*

```
cme-3725#service-module service-engine 1/0 status
Service Module is Cisco Service-Engine1/0
Service Module supports session via TTY line 33
Service Module is in Steady state
Getting status from the Service Module, please wait..
cisco service engine 1.1
```

Call Routing to Cisco UE

Cisco CME and Cisco UE communicate using a SIP interface. Therefore, Cisco CME uses SIP dial peers to determine which calls must be routed to Cisco UE. The AA pilot number for Site A is 2100, and the voice mail pilot is 2105. Example 15-20 shows the SIP dial peers necessary to route calls to these pilot numbers from Cisco CME to Cisco UE.

Example 15-20 *SIP Dial Peers Needed for Call Routing*

```
cme-3725#show running-config
dial-peer voice 2100 voip
 destination-pattern 21..
 session protocol sipv2
 session target ipv4:10.1.235.128
 dtmf-relay sip-notify
 codec g711ulaw
 no vad
```

H.323-to-SIP Call Routing

If you have multiple sites to connect to each other, such as Site B in the sample topology used in this chapter, calls between sites use H.323, and calls to Cisco UE use SIP. This requires an H.323-to-SIP translation on the Cisco CME router. The following CLI enables this function (available with Cisco CME 3.2 and later):

```
voice service voip
 allow-connections h323 to sip
```

Message Waiting Indicator

Chapter 10, "Cisco IPC Express Integrated Voice Mail," explains the mechanism for turning MWI on and off from Cisco UE voice mail to Cisco CME phones. The MWI definitions shown in Example 15-21 are necessary to enable MWI for Site A.

Example 15-21 *MWI DN Definition*

```
cme-3725#show running-config
ephone-dn  51
 number 8000....
 mwi on
!
ephone-dn  52
 number 8001....
 mwi off
```

You are now ready to point a browser to Cisco UE (http://10.1.235.128/ for Site A) to run through the Cisco UE Initialization Wizard. This is covered in the next section.

Configuring Basic Cisco UE

The Cisco UE Initialization Wizard, covered in Chapter 13, allows you to import the configuration (primarily phones and extensions) already done on your Cisco CME system into Cisco UE, create mailboxes for the users, and define the pilot numbers for the AA and voice mail.

Importing Users from Cisco CME

Figure 15-4 shows how the six Site B users already defined on the router are imported into Cisco UE in the first Initialization Wizard screen.

Check the boxes in the Mailbox column for all six users to automatically create personal mailboxes for all six users at the end of the Initialization Wizard.

Setting System Defaults

In the System Defaults screen, you set attributes such as the PIN and password generation policy for new accounts. Figure 15-5 shows the settings and selections made for the Site B configuration.

Figure 15-4   *Importing Users*

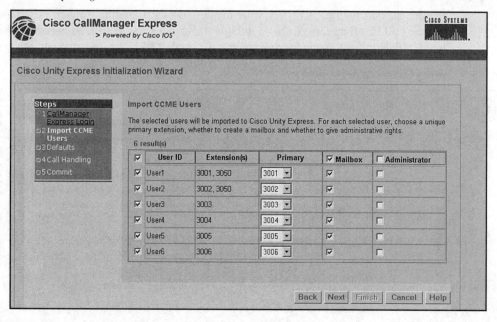

Figure 15-5   *Setting System Defaults*

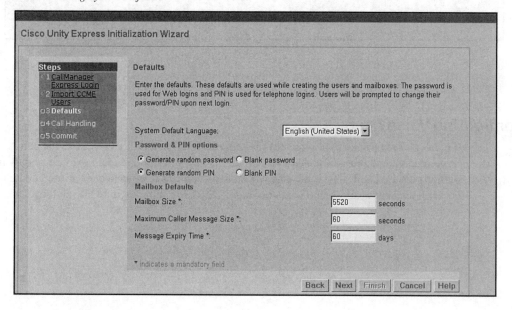

Setting Call Handling Parameters

The pilot numbers for the AA (3101), voice mail (3105), and the administration TUI (3106) are set in the Call Handling screen, shown in Figure 15-6. Also, the MWI DNs imported from the Cisco CME definitions entered earlier (refer to Example 15-21) are imported into this screen.

Figure 15-6 *Setting Call Handling Parameters*

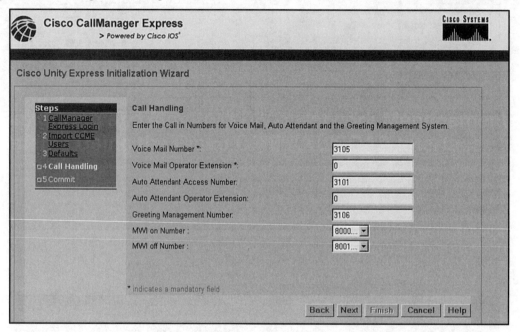

At this point in the system setup, you can call into the system AA and voice mail.

Configuring Voice Mail

Figure 15-7 shows the final screen of the Initialization Wizard. It summarizes the auto-generated system passwords and PINs for all the user profiles and mailboxes created by the Initialization Wizard. This is a handy screen to preserve as a screenshot or printout to help you let each user know his default password and PIN for first-time login to his mailbox.

Figure 15-7   *Cisco UE User Passwords and PINs*

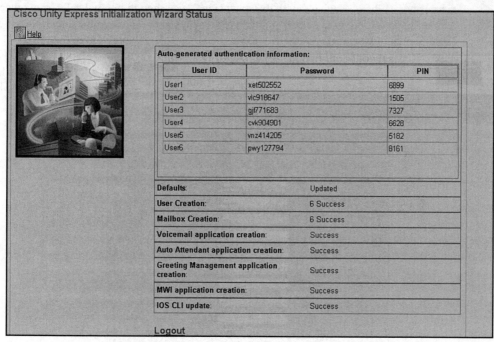

All users have mailboxes with the tutorial set to yes. When you notify users of their default system-assigned PINs, they can log into their mailboxes and work through the setup tutorial. The tutorial helps them record a spoken name and an outgoing greeting and forces them to change their PIN to a private setting not known to you as the system administrator.

Calls to your employees' phones automatically forward into voice mail, where the caller hears the standard system greetings until your employees have logged in to customize their mailbox greetings. Call forwarding was set up in Step 3, earlier in this chapter, by the Cisco CME Setup Utility. Example 15-22 shows the call forwarding setup for ephone-dns. If you want to change this call forward destination, go to the **Configure > Extensions** GUI screen or use the **ephone-dn** command in the CLI.

Example 15-22   *Call Forward Setup for Ephone-dns*

```
cme-3725#show running-config
ephone-dn  1  dual-line
 number 2001 secondary 2225552001
 call-forward busy 2105
 call-forward noan 2105 timeout 10
```

In the current configuration, PSTN calls cannot get into voice mail. Instead, callers hear, "Sorry, there is no mailbox associated with this extension," even though internal calls from other IP phones get into voice mail correctly. One way to address this is to add the direct inward dial (DID) number associated with the extension (and therefore the mailbox) to the Primary E.164 Number field in the **Configure > Users** screen, as shown in Figure 15-8. Now PSTN calls also work into voice mail. Alternatively, you can use Cisco IOS translation rules or Cisco CME dial plan patterns to translate the DID numbers to extensions before the calls enter voice mail.

Figure 15-8 *Configuring the DID Number for a Mailbox*

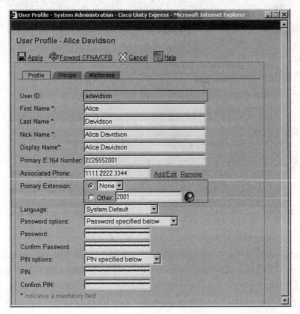

If you did not add mailboxes in the Initialization Wizard, go to the **Configuration > Users** GUI screen to add user definitions and mailboxes for the employees on your system.

At this point, basic voice mail is set up and working. Example 15-23 summarizes the mailboxes defined on the system and the time used in each.

Example 15-23 *Mailbox Summary*

```
cue-3725#show voicemail mailboxes
OWNER             MSGS NEW  SAVED  MSGTIME MBXSIZE  USED
"adavidson"       1    0    1      13      5520     1 %
"awilkins"        1    0    1      9       5520     1 %
"awyant"          0    0    0      5       5520     1 %
"amcdougal"       0    0    0      5       5520     1 %
"acoley"          0    0    0      5       5520     1 %
```

Configuring the AA

Cisco UE ships with a system AA that is very easy to set up. It offers callers dial-by-extension, dial-by-name, and transfer-to-the-operator choices. You can also install a fully customized AA into Cisco UE so that you can tailor the AA menus and choices to your own business needs.

Setting Up the System AA

If your office intends to use only the Cisco UE system AA, follow the steps in this section; otherwise, proceed to the next section.

The system AA is set up by default and is working already with the AA pilot number you assigned during the Cisco UE Initialization Wizard. Dial-by-extension from the system AA works without any further setup, but dial-by-name requires that you configure the names of your employees in their user profiles. In the **Configure > Users** GUI screen, click each user to see his or her profile, and fill in the First Name and Last Name fields with the strings you want to be used for matching in the AA dial-by-name feature.

The last remaining field to set up in the system AA is to customize your company's AA welcome greeting. Record this greeting offline on a PC, and upload the .wav file to Cisco UE. You also can record the greeting by using the administrative TUI (extension 2106 for Site A or 3106 for Site B) on Cisco UE. Associate the .wav file with the system AA.

The sample system setup in this chapter uses Cisco UE 2.0, and you have now configured all the system AA parameters for this release. If you are using Cisco UE release 2.1 (or later), a few more parameters need to be customized, as discussed in Chapter 14.

Setting Up a Custom AA

If your business requires a more sophisticated AA than the Cisco UE system AA, use the guidelines in this section to set up your custom AA. Chapter 9, "Cisco IPC Express Automated Attendant Options," explained how to customize an AA script on Cisco UE. Assume at Site B that you require only the system AA, whereas a custom AA is necessary at Site A.

For example, the script written for Site A is named S1_Main-OfficeHours.aef, and it calls two subflows: S1_DialbyExtension.aef and S1_XfertoOper.aef. You can download these scripts and the prompts they use from Cisco.com by going to the Software Center for Cisco UE. The S1_Main-OfficeHours script includes nine different prompts that you record on a PC or in a studio as a .wav file. Upload all three scripts (.aef files) and nine prompts (.wav files) from your PC to Cisco UE, as shown in Figure 15-9.

Figure 15-9 *Uploading Scripts and Prompts to Cisco UE*

Cisco Unity Express Voice Mail / Auto Attendant				Home	Logout

Configure ▼ Voice Mail ▼ Administration ▼ Defaults ▼ Reports ▼ Help ▼

Voice Mail > Prompts

⬆ Upload   ✖ Delete   ⬇ Download   ⬚ Help

Caution: This function is for advanced users only.

1 - 10 of 10 result(s)   Languages: English (United States) ▼

	△ **Prompt Name**	**Creation Date**	**Length (Bytes)**	**Length (Seconds)**
☐	AAWelcome.wav	Tue Aug 24 12:52:26 PDT 2004	15860	1.9825
☐	S1_AfterHours.wav	Wed Sep 29 11:01:44 PDT 2004	69632	8.704
☐	S1_EnterExt.wav	Wed Sep 29 11:01:53 PDT 2004	24576	3.072
☐	S1_ExtBusy.wav	Wed Sep 29 11:02:06 PDT 2004	45056	5.632
☐	S1_Goodbye.wav	Wed Sep 29 11:03:38 PDT 2004	16384	2.048
☐	S1_InvalidExt.wav	Wed Sep 29 11:02:14 PDT 2004	28672	3.584
☐	S1_MainMenu.wav	Wed Sep 29 11:02:21 PDT 2004	77824	9.728
☐	S1_OperBusy.wav	Wed Sep 29 11:02:30 PDT 2004	53248	6.656
☐	S1_OperXfer.wav	Wed Sep 29 11:02:37 PDT 2004	24576	3.072
☐	S1_SystemProblems.wav	Wed Sep 29 11:02:47 PDT 2004	61440	7.68

Rows per page: All ▼

As soon as the scripts and prompt files are available on the Cisco UE system, you have to add a custom AA to the system. Start this activity by going to the **Voice mail > Auto Attendant** GUI screen, and choose **Add**. Select the S1_Main-OfficeHours.aef script for the AA, as shown in Figure 15-10. Insert a name for the AA (the example uses **custom-aa**).

Figure 15-10 *Selecting a Script for the Custom AA*

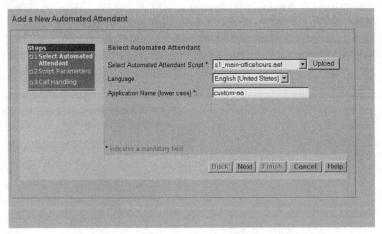

Add a New Automated Attendant

Steps
□1 **Select Automated Attendant**
□2 Script Parameters
□3 Call Handling

Select Automated Attendant

Select Automated Attendant Script *: [s1_main-officehours.aef ▼] [Upload]

Language: [English (United States) ▼]

Application Name (lower case) *: [custom-aa]

* indicates a mandatory field

[Back] [Next] [Finish] [Cancel] [Help]

Assign a pilot number for the AA, as shown in Figure 15-11. Because your real AA pilot number, extension 2100, is already assigned to the system AA, you cannot choose that. For the time being, choose 2101.

Figure 15-11   *Choosing a Pilot Number for the Custom AA*

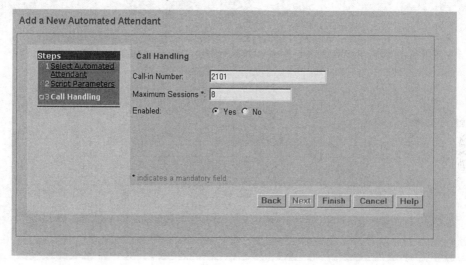

After you add the AA, you see custom-aa show up in the **Voice mail > Auto Attendant** GUI screen. To switch around the pilot numbers, assuming that 2100 is the actual AA pilot number your business wants to use, click the system AA (**autoattendant**), and change its pilot number to a different extension (for example, 2102). Click **custom-aa** and change its pilot number to 2100. The resulting configuration is shown in Figure 15-12. Your custom AA is now operational.

At this point, internal calls from the IP phones to the AA (extension 2100) work, but PSTN DID calls to the AA don't work. PSTN calls arrive at 222.555.2001, and this DID number must be mapped to the AA. Insert the Cisco IOS translation rule (or its equivalent), shown in Example 15-24, into the Cisco CME router, and attach it to the dial peer in Cisco UE that matches PSTN trunk calls. This same translation rule includes translations to allow calls into your voice mail (2105) and administrative TUI (2106) pilot numbers from the PSTN.

Figure 15-12 *Correcting the Pilot Number for the Custom AA*

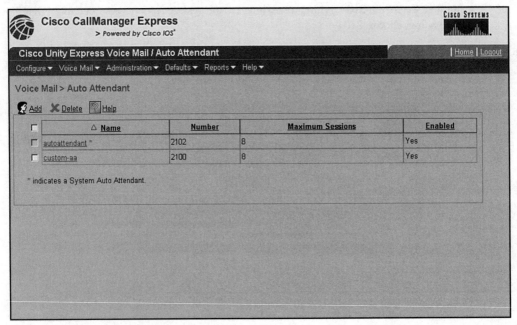

Example 15-24 *Translation Rule to Route PSTN Calls to the AA*

```
cme-3725#show running-config
voice translation-rule 10
 rule 1 /2225552100/ /2100/
 rule 2 /2225552105/ /2105/
 rule 3 /2225552106/ /2106/
!
voice translation-profile to_cue
 translate called 10
!
dial-peer voice 2100 voip
 destination-pattern 21..
 session protocol sipv2
 session target ipv4:10.1.235.128
 dtmf-relay sip-notify
 codec g711ulaw
 no vad
!
dial-peer voice 2101 voip
 description VM-AA-PSTN
 translation-profile outgoing to_cue
 destination-pattern 22255521..
 session protocol sipv2
 session target ipv4:10.1.235.128
```

Example 15-24 *Translation Rule to Route PSTN Calls to the AA (Continued)*

```
dtmf-relay sip-notify
codec g711ulaw
no vad
```

In the section "Routing PSTN Calls to IP Phones," the FXO PSTN trunk was set up to ring employee extension 2001, because the AA was not yet implemented. Now that the AA is fully configured, the routing of the FXO calls should be changed to the AA (extension 2100) instead of IP phone 2001:

```
voice-port 2/0/1
 connection plar opx 2100
```

Step 7: Configuring Cisco CME Call Processing Features

Your Cisco IPC Express system is fully operational after the completion of Step 6 for all basic features. However, you probably want to configure numerous additional Cisco CME call processing features to better tailor the system to your business needs. The next sections describe configuring the following:

- Phone and user features
- System features such as music on hold (MOH) and paging
- Call forward, transfer, and conference
- Phone applications

Configuring Phone and User Features

In this section, you configure several phone and user-related features:

- Caller ID name display
- Phone name display
- Phone button label customization
- Shared lines
- Hunt group
- Local directory
- Speed dial
- Local speed dial
- Personal speed dial
- Localization

- Autoline selection
- IP phone softkey customization
- Direct FXO trunk line select
- Overlay DN

Caller ID Name Display

Caller ID is the name associated with the calling party's extension when a call is ringing on an IP phone. To customize this field, set the Name field on the ephone-dn, as shown in Example 15-25. The calling name appears only on IP phone-to-IP phone calls.

Example 15-25 *Customizing the Caller ID Name*

```
cme-3725#show running-config
ephone-dn  1  dual-line
 number 2001 secondary 2225552001
 name Alice
!
ephone-dn  2  dual-line
 number 2002 secondary 2225552002
 name Aaron
```

Phone Name Display

The top line of an idle IP phone display can show the name of the extension or the phone's owner. To show a name in this field, set the Description field on the ephone-dn, as shown in Example 15-26. Note that top-line display customization is supported only on Cisco 7960 and 7940 IP Phones.

Example 15-26 *Customizing the Phone Name*

```
cme-3725#show running-config
ephone-dn  1  dual-line
 number 2001 secondary 2225552001
 description Alice Davidson
```

Phone Button Label Customization

The IP phone displays the extension configured on each button next to the button. For example, on Alice's phone, 2001 is displayed by default next to button 1. To customize this display to a different string, set the Label field on the ephone-dn, as shown in Example 15-27.

Example 15-27 *Customizing the Button Display*

```
cme-3725#show running-config
ephone-dn  1  dual-line
 number 2001 secondary 2225552001
 label Alice
```

Shared Lines

A shared line is an extension that appears on multiple phones. There are different ways of defining shared lines, depending on the operation you want.

To define a shared line that rings on several phones simultaneously, define a single ephone-dn, and place it as a button appearance on multiple phones.

Another way to define a shared line is to have the extensions ring in succession. For example, assume that two employees, Anne (2004) and Alan (2005), work in your office as receptionists. Reception is extension 2060. Anne is the main receptionist, and Alan fills in for Anne while she is not at her desk.

Example 15-28 shows how to configure this. Two ephone-dns are defined with the same extension number (2060). The first has **no huntstop** configured, and the second has **preference 1**. A call to extension 2060 is first routed to ephone-dn 6, which appears on button 1 of Anne's phone. If Anne (ephone-dn 6) is busy, the call is routed to Alan's phone (ephone-dn 7 on button 1 of ephone 5). If Alan (ephone-dn 7) is also busy, the calling party hears busy tone. Note that **preference 0** is the default configuration on an ephone-dn and does not show in the CLI.

Example 15-28 *Configuring Reception as a Shared Line*

```
cme-3725#show running-config
ephone-dn  6
 number 2060
 label Reception
 name Reception
 no huntstop
!
ephone-dn  7
 number 2060
 label Reception
 name Reception
 preference 1
!
ephone  4
 mac-address 0003.AAAA.0004
 button  1:6
!
ephone  5
 mac-address 0003.AAAA.0005
 button  1:7
```

Hunt Group

The hunt group feature redirects incoming calls to a hunt pilot number on busy or *no answer* from one ephone-dn to another based on a list defined in the **ephone-hunt** group. The calling party's number is displayed on IP phones with Cisco CME 3.2 or later. There are three types of hunt groups:

- **Sequential**—The ephone-dns ring from first to last in the list specified. If the call is not answered, the call is redirected to the final destination configured.

- **Peer**—In this configuration, the list of ephone-dns in the hunt group are rung in a round-robin manner. The next ephone-dn to ring is the number in the list to the right (as you read the CLI configuration from left to right) of the last ephone-dn that rang when the hunt pilot number was last called. Ringing proceeds in a circular manner through the list, first to last, for the number of hops specified in the hunt group. If the call is not answered in the specified number of hops, it is redirected to the final destination configured.

- **Longest-idle**—A new incoming call is directed to the ephone-dn that has been idle for the longest time. The longest-idle time is determined from the last time a phone registered, reregistered, or went on-hook.

Site B has two employees (User2 at extension 3002 and User3 at 3003) who take customer service calls. The number called internally for customer service is 3050 and 444.555.3050 from the PSTN. To distribute calls equitably across the two employees, a longest-idle hunt group is defined as shown in Example 15-29.

Example 15-29   *Configuring a Hunt Group for Customer Service*

```
cme-2691#show running-config
ephone-hunt 1 longest-idle
 pilot 3050 secondary 4445553050
 list 3002, 3003
 final 3105
```

The final destination is defined as the voice mail pilot number (3105) so that a caller can leave a message if neither of the customer service employees is available. User2 and User3 are members of a customer service group defined on Cisco UE. A general delivery mailbox (GDM) is associated with extension 3050, as shown in Figure 15-13.

Figure 15-13   *GDM for Customer Service*

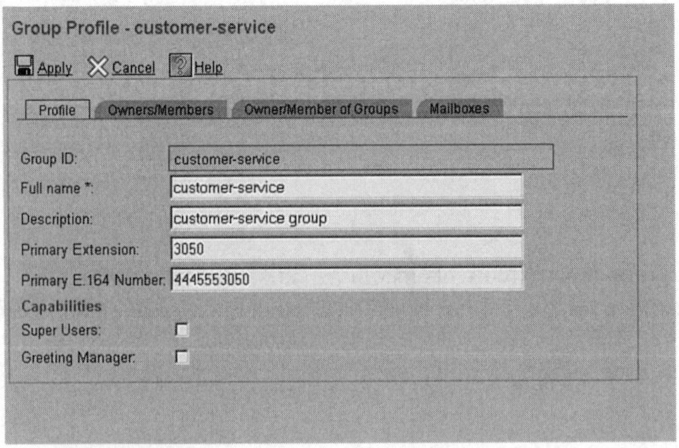

Local Directory

A local directory of names and phone numbers is automatically built using the Name and Number fields under the ephone-dn configuration, as shown in Example 15-30. You can configure the local directory to show directory information in *first name, last name* format or *last name, first name* format. Phones have to be reset for directory changes to take effect.

NOTE   The **directory** command does not automatically reorder names entered under the ephone-dn. If you change the directory format, you also have to manually change all the names under the ephone-dns to match the directory format.

Example 15-30   *Local Directory*

```
cme-3725#show running-config
telephony-service
 directory last-name-first
 !
ephone-dn  1   dual-line
 number 2001 secondary 2225552001
 name Alice Davidson
 !
ephone-dn  2   dual-line
 number 2002 secondary 2225552002
 name Aaron Wilkins
```

Speed Dial

You may define a number of speed-dial buttons for each IP phone, limited by the number of buttons supported on the phone. This configuration is shown in Example 15-31. If more speed-dial buttons are configured than the number of available buttons on the phone, the extra speed-dial configurations are ignored. If speed dials are mapped to buttons with DNs assigned, speed-dial configurations are ignored. Speed dials cannot appear between buttons with DNs assigned. For example, on a Cisco 7960 IP Phone with six buttons, if button 1 and button 6 have an ephone-dn defined, the entire speed-dial configuration is ignored, even if buttons 2 to 5 are unassigned.

You can configure up to four speed-dial buttons on a Cisco 7960G IP Phone. The following example shows speed dials on buttons 2 and 3.

Example 15-31   *Speed Dials*

```
cme-3725#show running-config
ephone  1
 mac-address 0003.6BAA.D1F8
 speed-dial 1 2005 label "Alan"
 speed-dial 2 3050 label "Customer Svc"
 type 7960
 button  1:1
```

Local Speed Dial

To work around the number of speed-dial entries limited by the number of buttons per phone, you may create a speeddial.xml file, as shown in Example 15-32 to list all the speed-dial entries. The local speed-dial Cisco CME feature provides a system-wide list of frequently called numbers (up to 32) accessible from the directory button on the phone.

Example 15-32 *Speed-Dial XML File*

```
<CiscoIPPhoneDirectory>
<Title>Speed Dials</Title>
<Prompt>Record 1 to 2 of 2 </Prompt>
 <DirectoryEntry>
 <Name>Directory Assistance</Name>
 <Telephone>95551212</Telephone>
 </DirectoryEntry>
 <DirectoryEntry>
 <Name>Your friends at Cisco</Name>
 <Telephone>4085264000</Telephone>
 </DirectoryEntry>
</CiscoIPPhoneDirectory>
```

After you have created the XML file, place the speeddial.xml file in the Cisco CME router's Flash memory by using the **copy tftp flash** command:

```
Router(config)#copy tftp://ip address/speeddial.xml flash:speeddial.xml
```

The local speed-dial menu appears when you select **Local Speed Dial** from the phone's **Directory** menu.

Personal Speed Dial

The Personal Speed Dial feature adds personal speed-dial entries, on a per-phone basis, to the system-wide speed-dial directory (discussed in the preceding section).

You create personal speed-dial entries by using the **fastdial** command under an ephone definition, as shown in Example 15-33. Phone users access personal speed-dial numbers through the **Directories > Local Services > Personal Speed Dial** menu. Personal speed-dial numbers appear in the order in which they are entered into the configuration.

NOTE The **fastdial** command is supported only on the Cisco 7940 and 7960 IP Phones.

Example 15-33 *Personal Speed Dials*

```
cme-3725#show running-config
ephone 2
 username "awilkins"
```

Example 15-33 *Personal Speed Dials (Continued)*

```
mac-address 0003.6BAA.D362
fastdial 1 3001 name User1
fastdial 2 3002 name User2
fastdial 3 2001 name Alice
fastdial 4 2005 name Alan
speed-dial 1 2004 label "Anne"
type 7960
button  1:2
```

Localization

Cisco CME supports country-specific language displays and call progress tones for IP phones. All phones on a Cisco CME system must use the same language settings. You can't configure multiple languages on a single CME router. The default language is set to English/U.S. Example 15-34 shows how to configure a system for Italian. (Both Sites A and B in the sample configuration are configured for U.S. English.)

Example 15-34 *Localization*

```
router#show running-config
telephony-service
 user-locale IT
 network-locale IT
 reset all
```

Autoline Selection

Up to Cisco CME release 3.1, the first available line is automatically selected to make or answer a call on an IP phone. Since release 3.1, Cisco CME supports four different modes for selecting the line to answer on an incoming call or to select an extension (by pressing a button) to make an outgoing call:

- autoline
- no autoline
- autoline incoming
- autoline button number

You can find details on these modes in the Cisco CME Command Reference on Cisco.com.

For most of the phones at Site A and Site B, the default (autoline) is sufficient. The exception is the two receptionists, where you want incoming calls to select a line automatically, but you want outgoing calls to explicitly press a button (choosing between their own extension or the receptionist's extension) before making the call. Example 15-35 shows this configuration for Anne's phone.

Example 15-35 *Autoline Selection*

```
router#show running-config
ephone  4
 mac-address 0003.AAAA.0004
 auto-line incoming
 button  1:6 2:4
```

IP Phone Softkey Customization

You can change or disable the display order of softkeys on the Cisco 7960, 7940, 7905, and 7912 IP Phones using the **ephone-template** command. The template can specify softkey order settings for phone states including alerting, connected, idle, and seized, as shown in Example 15-36. You must restart an IP phone to make the changes in the template take effect. You can define up to five templates.

Example 15-36 *Softkey Customization*

```
cme-3725#show running-config
ephone-template  1
 softkeys idle  Redial Pickup Dnd Login Gpickup
 softkeys seized  Pickup Redial Endcall Gpickup
!
ephone  1
 ephone-template 1
```

Direct FXO Trunk Line Select

Cisco CME can automatically seize an FXO trunk line when you press a line button or lift the handset. This allows you to hear stutter dial tone from the central office (CO) when you lift the handset if you get voice mail service from your PSTN provider. The **destination-pattern** configured in the trunk's dial peer must match the trunk code defined on the ephone-dn.

Aaron, at extension 2002, is the manager at your Site A office, and you want him to have direct access to a CO line for emergency 911 access. Button 2 on his phone should be labeled "911." When pressed, this button must select dial tone directly from the CO for outside dialing. The configuration shown in Example 15-37 achieves this by making an automatic connection between button 2 on Aaron's phone and the second FXO line (port 2/0/1) on the Cisco CME system. When Aaron goes off-hook on button 2, his phone gets dial tone from the CO. The following things happen behind the scenes:

- Aaron goes off-hook on button 2, which automatically activates ephone-dn 10.

- Ephone-dn 10 has a **trunk** statement that automatically originates a call to the 911 trunk access code.

- The 911 access code dialed matches POTS dial peer 1004, which connects the outgoing call to FXO port 2/0/1.

- FXO port 2/0/1 goes off-hook and draws dial tone from the CO.

Example 15-37 *FXO Line Select*

```
cme-3725#show running-config
voice-port 2/0/1
!
dial-peer voice 1004 pots
 destination-pattern 911
 port 2/0/1
 forward-digits all
!
ephone-dn  10
 number 2999
 label 911
 trunk 911 timeout 5
!
ephone  2
 type 7960
 button  1:2 2:10
```

Overlay DN

To overcome the button limitation on certain phone types and to support more extensions on a phone, you can use overlay DNs to associate multiple ephone-dns to a single button on a phone. That way the phone can receive calls to multiple extensions on the same button.

As the manager of Site A, Aaron has a special extension (2020) where you can reach him directly, but other employees in the office do not know this number. Because he seldom receives calls on this number, Aaron does not want to dedicate a button on this phone just for this number. Instead, he wants these calls to come in on button 1, where his regular calls to extension 2002 also ring. Example 15-38 shows this configuration using overlay DNs.

Example 15-38 *Overlay DN*

```
cme-3725#show running-config
ephone-dn  30
 number 2020
!
ephone  2
 button  1o2,30 2:10 3:21
```

Configuring System Features

In this section, you configure several general system features:

- Music on hold (MOH)
- On-hold call notification
- Interdigit timeout
- Intercom

- Paging
- Ringing timeout
- Call park
- Time and date format

Music on Hold

The music on hold (MOH) feature supports the .au and .wav file formats. MOH applies only to G.711 intersite VoIP calls and PSTN calls. All other calls, including local calls between Cisco CME phones on the same system, hear tone on hold.

A sample MOH file, music-on-hold.au, is included in Cisco CME as a .zip or .tar file. It also can be downloaded from the Cisco.com Software Center. You normally download the MOH file to a TFTP server in the network, and then copy the file into Flash from the Cisco CME system CLI by using the following:

```
copy tftp://ip address/music-on-hold.au flash:
```

where *ip address* is the TFTP server's address. Be sure to enter **n** when prompted to erase Flash. Example 15-39 shows the content of the Flash and the configuration necessary to enable MOH.

Example 15-39 *Enabling MOH*

```
cme-3725#show flash
-#- --length-- -----date/time------ path
...
11       496521 Apr 02 2002 11:27:06 -08:00 music-on-hold.au

cme-3725#show running-config
telephony-service
 moh music-on-hold.au
```

On-Hold Call Notification

The on-hold call notification feature sends an audible notification on Cisco CME phones to alert the user that a call is on hold. This feature is typically used when multiple lines are configured and the user might forget that a call on a secondary line is still on hold. Three types of on-hold notifications can be configured:

- Idle
- Originator
- Shared

Example 15-40 shows a configuration of an on-hold call notification on Ashley's phone (extension 2003).

Example 15-40   *On-Hold Call Notification*

```
cme-3725#show running-config
ephone-dn  3  dual-line
 number 2003 secondary 2225552003
 hold-alert 15 originator
```

Interdigit Timeout

The interdigit timeout specifies how many seconds the system waits between the initial and subsequent digit presses on the phone keypad when a caller dials a call. This is shown in Example 15-41. If the timeout expires before the destination is identified, a fast-busy is given, and the call ends.

Example 15-41   *Interdigit Timeout*

```
cme-3725#show running-config
telephony-service
 timeouts interdigit 20
```

The initial timeout, which specifies how many seconds Cisco CME waits before the caller enters the initial digit, cannot be configured and is set to 10 seconds. Phones have to be reset to make the configuration take effect.

Intercom

The intercom feature allows one-way, autoanswer voice connections. Specially configured speed-dial buttons allow a call to be placed to the selected extension. On the destination phone, the call is automatically answered in speakerphone mode with mute enabled. To respond to the intercom call and open two-way voice, the recipient can deactivate the mute button (or, in the case of a Cisco 7910 IP Phone, lift the handset). Intercom lines cannot be used in shared-line configurations. There are three types of intercom features:

- Dedicated intercom
- Intercom to PBX phone
- Dialable intercom

At Site A, Alice is Aaron's assistant. Their phones must be linked via the intercom feature so that Alice can announce a visitor's arrival to Aaron, or Aaron can easily ask Alice something without having to dial a call. The configuration shown in Example 15-42 builds a dedicated intercom facility between button 3 on each of the two phones.

Example 15-42 *Intercom*

```
cme-3725#show running-config
ephone-dn  20
 number A2222
 name Intercom from Alice
 intercom A2223
!
ephone-dn  21
 number A2223
 name Intercom from Aaron
 intercom A2222
!
ephone  1
 button  1:1 3:20
!
ephone  2
 button  1:2 2:10 3:21
```

Paging

The paging feature operates in a similar fashion to intercom, but it provides only one-way voice broadcast. Only idle phones receive paging announcements. Paging defines an extension that can be called to broadcast an audio page to a group of idle Cisco CME phones participating in the paging group.

The paging mechanism uses audio distribution using IP Multicast, replicated unicast, and a mixture of both. Therefore, multicast is used where possible, and unicast is allowed on specific phones that cannot be reached through multicast.

The recommended configuration of paging groups is to use a multicast address. If multicast is not configured, IP phones are paged individually using IP Unicast (to a maximum of ten IP phones). When multiple paging extensions are configured, each extension must use a unique IP Multicast address.

At Site A, you want to configure paging to all five employees' phones so that they can make announcements to the entire office staff by dialing extension 2010. This configuration is shown in Example 15-43.

Example 15-43 *Paging*

```
cme-3725#show running-config
ephone-dn  25
 number 2010
 name All Office
 paging ip 224.0.1.20 port 2000
!
ephone  1
 paging-dn 25
```

Ringing Timeout

You may define how long a phone can ring with no answer before returning disconnect tone to the caller. This timeout is used only for extensions that do not have call-forward-no-answer (CFNA) configured. The ringing timeout, shown here, keeps calls from ringing forever over interfaces such as FXO that do not have forward-disconnect supervision:

```
telephony-service
 timeouts ringing 120
```

Call Park

After you answer a call, you may press the **call park** softkey on the phone to park a call to one of the following two types of park slots:

- A slot with the same last two digits as the extension the call is on
- Randomly to any configured or designated park slot

The phone display shows where the call is parked so that you, or another employee, may pick up the call again. You can create a call park slot reserved for use by one extension by assigning that slot a number whose last two digits are the same as the last two digits of the extension number. When an extension starts to park a call, the system first searches for a call park slot that shares the same final two digits as the extension. If no such call park slot is found, the system then chooses any other available call park slot.

Example 15-44 defines a park slot for each of the five extensions at Site A so that each employee has a dedicated park slot. Note that in the call park ephone-dns 101, 102 to 105 map to ephone-dns 1, 2 to 5 that have extensions with the same last two digits 01, 02 to 05. Each park slot 101, 102 to 105 is reserved for use by ephone-dns 1, 2 to 5, respectively.

Example 15-44   *Call Park*

```
cme-3725#show running-config
ephone-dn 1
 number 2001
ephone-dn 2
 number 2002
ephone-dn 3
 number 2003
ephone-dn 4
 number 2004
ephone-dn 5
 number 2005
ephone-dn  101
 number 7401
 park-slot timeout 30 limit 10
!
ephone-dn  102
 number 7402
 park-slot timeout 30 limit 10
!
```

continues

Example 15-44 *Call Park (Continued)*

```
ephone-dn  103
 number 7403
 park-slot timeout 30 limit 10
!
ephone-dn  104
 number 7404
 park-slot timeout 30 limit 10
!
ephone-dn  105
 number 7405
 park-slot timeout 30 limit 10
```

To pick up a call from the same phone where the call was parked, simply press the **pickup** softkey and dial *. To pick up the call from any other phone, press the **pickup** softkey, and dial the extension of the call park slot shown on the phone display.

Time and Date Format

Cisco CME phones use time and date information from the router, which in turn is set up using NTP. You can customize the format in which the date and time are shown as follows:

```
telephony-service
 time-format 24
 date-format dd-mm-yy
```

Configuring Conference Call, Call Transfer, and Call Forward

In this section, you configure several call transfer and conference-related features:

- G.711 conferencing
- Call transfer
- Call forward
- Call forward all restrictions

G.711 Conferencing

G.711 conferencing is the default operation on Cisco CME and requires no configuration. All parties in a conference call must use either the G.711 μ-law codec or G.711 a-law codec. No other codec is supported for conferencing. G.729A endpoints can be supported via transcoding to G.711. Conferencing requires at least two lines configured on the phone initiating the conference. The dual-line configuration entered on the extensions in the earlier section "Defining Extensions" is sufficient to enable conferencing.

Cisco CME also supports conference cascading so that up to a maximum of eight or 16 conference sessions can be supported based on the platform you are using. The maximum number of G.711 conferences supported by Cisco CME varies by platform. If you want to adjust the maximum number of conference sessions, you may use the following CLI:

```
telephony-service
 max-conferences 8
```

Call Transfer

Call transfer was discussed in Chapter 5, "Cisco CME Call Processing Features." The various releases of Cisco CME have different functionality with respect to the transfer operation. As of Cisco CME 3.2, the following methods of transfer are supported:

- **transfer-system blind**—Performs blind call transfers (without consultation) with a single phone line using a Cisco-proprietary method.

- **transfer-system full-blind**—Performs call transfers without consultation using the H.450.2 or SIP REFER standard methods.

- **transfer-system full-consult**—Performs H.450.2 or SIP call transfers with consultation using a second phone line if available. This method falls back to full blind if a second line is unavailable. This is the recommended mode for most systems. Also use the **supplementary-service** command under the **voice service voip** and **dial-peer** commands for call transfer between multiple Cisco CME and non-H.323 endpoints.

- **transfer-system local-consult**—Performs Cisco-proprietary call transfers with local consultation using a second phone line if available. This method falls back to blind for nonlocal transfer targets.

Example 15-45 shows Site A set up for full-consult transfers between Sites A and B. If transfers to PSTN destinations must also be allowed, you must also define transfer patterns matching PSTN dial plan patterns.

Example 15-45 *Call Transfer*

```
cme-3725#show running-config
telephony-service
 transfer-system full-consult
 transfer-pattern 3...
 transfer-pattern 2...
```

Cisco CME allows you to configure a transfer mode for each ephone-dn to override the global transfer mode set for all phones.

NOTE	Transferring an incoming PSTN call to another PSTN destination can cause FXO ports to remain connected after both call parties disconnect. For you to avoid this problem, your PSTN provider must support one of the following disconnect methods on analog lines:

- Battery reversal

- Ground start signaling

- Power denial

- Supervisory tone disconnect

Call Forward

You can configure forwarding calls using the **call-forward busy**, **call-forward noan**, or **call-forward-all** commands for an ephone-dn. Cisco CME can forward calls using either a proprietary method or an H.450.3 standard method. If a **forward-pattern** is configured, as shown here, calls *from* the pattern (such as 2001, the calling number, not the called number) are forwarded using H.450.3, and all other calling parties are forwarded using the Cisco CME-proprietary forwarding method:

```
telephony-services
 forward-pattern 2...
```

Call Forward All Restrictions

You may restrict the maximum number of digits that can be entered by using the **cfwdall** softkey, as shown in Example 15-46. Note that call forward restrictions apply only to destinations entered from the phone keypad, not to destinations entered using the CLI or GUI.

Example 15-46 *Call Forward Restrictions*

```
cme-3725#show running-config
ephone-dn  1  dual-line
 number 2001 secondary 2225552001
 call-forward max-length 4
!
ephone-dn  2  dual-line
 number 2002 secondary 2225552002
 call-forward max-length 8
```

Enabling Applications

In this section, you configure the following features used to enable applications:

- Idle URL

- XML services

Idle URL

The Idle URL feature lets you access a URL, and display its content on idle IP phones. As a general rule, the Idle URL page should be hosted on an external web server. Cisco CME does not support the Idle URL for files stored in router Flash. Use the configuration shown in Example 15-47 to turn on this feature.

Example 15-47   *Idle URL*

```
cme-3725#show running-config
telephony-service
 url idle http://1.1.1.1/idle.asp
```

XML Services

Each Cisco CME system allows you to configure a single URL for services hosted from a separate server:

```
telephony-service
 url services http://10.10.10.4/CCMUser/123456/urltest.xml
```

However, the referenced service page urltest.xml can itself contain multiple URLs pointing to other services. Example 15-48 shows a sample urltest.xml file.

Example 15-48   *XML Services*

```
cme-3725#show running-config
<CiscoIPPhoneMenu>
  <Title>Services</Title>
  <Prompt>Select an option</Prompt>
  <MenuItem>
    <Name>App1</Name>
    <URL>http://10.10.10.4/CCMUser/123456/app.asp1</URL>
  </MenuItem>
  <MenuItem>
    <Name>App2</Name>
    <URL>http://10.10.10.4/CCMUser/123456/app2.asp</URL>
  </MenuItem>
</CiscoIPPhoneMenu>
```

Step 8: Interconnecting Multiple Cisco IPC Express Systems

In the preceding seven steps, you set up the entire Cisco IPC Express system at Site A with examples of the most commonly deployed features you will require for your office. Although the Site B configuration was not discussed step by step, its configuration is very similar to that for Site A, with extensions starting at 3001 instead of 2001.

You cannot yet make calls between Sites A and B, because there is no dial plan to route calls between the sites. To achieve this, first ensure IP routing between the sites. In the sample configuration being built in this chapter, Site A has an IP address of 10.1.235.1 (with a netmask of 255.255.0.0), and Site B has an IP address of 10.1.229.1 (with a netmask of 255.255.0.0), so these systems can easily reach each other. If your sites' IP addressing is more sophisticated, do the necessary configuration to achieve IP routing between your sites. Ensure that you see routes between the IP addresses of your sites with a **show ip route** command on each site's router. You should also be able to **ping** one site from the other.

Interconnecting Sites Via H.323

As soon as you have IP connectivity between the sites, the next step is to add dial peers to route calls between the sites. From Site A, if someone dials an extension that starts with 3, the call must be routed to Site B. Similarly, if someone at Site B dials an extension starting with 2, the call must be routed to Site A. If your dialing plan is less uniform than the sample network in this chapter, you may need multiple dial peers to route all calls. Also, if only one site has PSTN access, and DID numbers for both the 2*xxx* and 3*xxx* ranges arrive on one PSTN trunk, more dial peers are needed to route all calls correctly.

For the sample network, the dial peers to route calls between the sites are shown in Example 15-49.

Example 15-49 *Sites A and B Dial Peers*

```
! Site A (2xxx extension) dial-peers to direct calls to Site B (3xxx extensions)
cme-3725#show running-config
dial-peer voice 3000 voip
 destination-pattern 3...
 session target ipv4:10.1.229.1
 dtmf-relay h245-alphanumeric
 codec g711ulaw
 no vad
!
! Site B (3xxx extension) dial-peers to direct calls to Site A (2xxx extensions)
cme-2691#show running-config
dial-peer voice 2000 voip
 destination-pattern 2...
 session target ipv4:10.1.235.1
 dtmf-relay h245-alphanumeric
 codec g711ulaw
 no vad
```

At this point, the sites can call each other by simply dialing the extensions of the IP phones. One more configuration must be added to ensure that you can transfer calls between the sites. Add the **transfer-patterns** shown in Example 15-50 to both sites' configurations.

Example 15-50 *Sites A and B Transfer Patterns*

```
cme-3725#show running-config
telephony-service
 transfer-system full-consult
 transfer-pattern 3...
 transfer-pattern 2...
```

In the preceding configuration setup, G.711 is used for all calls, including those between sites. To conserve bandwidth on the link between your sites, it is likely that you want to use G.729 on those calls instead. If so, remove the **codec g711ulaw** statement from the dial peers in Example 15-49.

You can specify G.729 explicitly (by using the **codec g729r8** command), or you can simply delete the G.711 statement, because G.729 is the default codec for a VoIP dial peer. Whether the actual codec used is G.729 or G.729A depends on the codec complexity configuration of the PSTN trunk voice card. It doesn't matter for call connectivity, because G.729 and G.729A are fully compatible with each other.

Transcoding

Transcoding is required when part of a call must use the G.711 and another part of the same call must use G.729. When you use G.729 for calls between sites, and calls forward into voice mail, these calls currently fail on the configuration, because Cisco UE voice mail supports only G.711. To fix this, configure transcoding resources on both sites to terminate G.729 calls, and transcode them locally to G.711 before they enter voice mail.

Example 15-51 gives a sample transcoding configuration. Ensure that you have enough digital signal processor (DSP) resources on the voice cards in your system to support this. If you don't, add more DSPs.

Example 15-51 *Transcoding*

```
router#show running-config
voice-card 2
 dsp services dspfarm
!
interface Loopback1
 ip address 10.32.153.45 255.255.255.252
 h323-gateway voip interface
 h323-gateway voip bind srcaddr 10.32.153.45
!
sccp local Loopback1
sccp ccm 10.32.153.45 identifier 1
sccp
sccp ccm group 1
 bind interface Loopback1
 associate ccm 1 priority 1
 associate profile 1 register MTP000e833595e0
 keepalive retries 5
dspfarm profile 1 transcode
 codec g711ulaw
 codec g711alaw
 codec g729ar8
 codec g729abr8
 codec gsmfr
 codec g729br8
 codec g729r8
```

continues

Example 15-51 *Transcoding (Continued)*

```
maximum sessions 10
associate application SCCP

telephony-service
 ip source-address 10.32.153.45 port 2000
 sdspfarm units 1
 sdspfarm transcode sessions 30
 sdspfarm tag 1 MTP000e833595e0
```

Transcoding is required to support the following call flows:

- Conference with one or more G.729 participants

- Call transfer or forward of a G.729 call into Cisco UE AA or voice mail

- Playing MOH streams to G.729 calls for call on hold, call park, and consult transfer

SIP RFC 2833 DTMF Relay

You need SIP DTMF relay if you are using SIP trunking between sites. If you have Cisco UE integrated on your sites, as in the sample configurations built in this chapter, you must use H.323 trunking between the sites. SIP trunking is not yet supported with Cisco UE release 2.1. Note, however, that a SIP dial peer is required to route IP phone and PSTN calls to Cisco UE.

If you are using AA and voice mail solutions other than Cisco UE with Cisco CME, or a future Cisco UE software release that may support this feature, you can use SIP trunking between sites. In a SIP trunking configuration, the out-of-band DTMF relay to the SCCP IP phones must be converted to in-band RFC 2833 DTMF relay on the SIP trunk. This is done using the configuration sample shown in Example 15-52.

Example 15-52 *DTMF Relay for SIP Trunking*

```
router#show running-config
dial-peer voice 2000 voip
 destination-pattern 8005551212
 session protocol sipv2
 session target ipv4:1.1.1.2
 dtmf-relay rtp-nte
```

Sample System Configurations

This section provides the full configurations of Site A and Site B built during the steps in this chapter.

Site A Cisco CME Router Configurations

Site A is a Cisco 3725 router with extensions in the 2*xxx* range. Figure 15-1, at the beginning of the chapter, summarized the site layout. This section provides the Cisco CME configuration.

The **show version** Output

Example 15-53 provides the **show version** output for the Site A Cisco CME router.

Example 15-53   **show version** *Output for the Site A Router*

```
cme-3745#show version
Cisco IOS Software, 3700 Software (C3745-IPVOICE-M), Version 12.3(11)T2, RELEASE
  SOFTWARE (fc1)
Technical Support: http://www.cisco.com/techsupport
Copyright (c) 1986-2004 by Cisco Systems, Inc.
Compiled Fri 29-Oct-04 06:38 by cmong
ROM: System Bootstrap, Version 12.2(8r)T2, RELEASE SOFTWARE (fc1)
cme32-3745 uptime is 2 weeks, 2 days, 4 hours, 39 minutes
System returned to ROM by reload at 15:40:35 PST Wed Dec 8 2004
System restarted at 14:05:42 PST Wed Dec 8 2004
System image file is "flash:c3745-ipvoice-mz.123-11.T2"

Cisco 3725 (R7000) processor (revision 0.1) with 111616K/19456K bytes of memory.
Processor board ID JAB0606800M
R7000 CPU at 240MHz, Implementation 39, Rev 3.3, 256KB L2 Cache
2 FastEthernet interfaces
31 Serial interfaces
2 terminal lines
2 Channelized T1/PRI ports
1 ATM AIM
2 Voice FXS interfaces
2 cisco service engine(s)
DRAM configuration is 64 bits wide with parity disabled.
55K bytes of NVRAM.
31360K bytes of ATA System CompactFlash (Read/Write)
```

The **show running-config** Output

Example 15-54 provides the **show running-config** output for the Site A Cisco CME router.

Example 15-54   **show running-config** *Output for the Site A Router*

```
cme-3725#show running-config
Building configuration...
Current configuration : 8014 bytes
! Last configuration change at 22:13:14 PST Sat Oct 2 2004
! NVRAM config last updated at 21:35:27 PST Sat Oct 2 2004
!
version 12.3
service timestamps debug uptime
service timestamps log uptime
```

continues

Example 15-54 **show running-config** *Output for the Site A Router (Continued)*

```
no service password-encryption
!
hostname cme-3725
!
boot-start-marker
boot system flash: c3745-ipvoice-mz.123-11.T2

boot-end-marker
!
enable secret 5 $1$4dpj$Ta3tjuFSq/pehqZy0VAd.1
enable password cisco
!
memory-size iomem 15
clock timezone PST -8
network-clock-participate wic 0
network-clock-participate aim 0
voice-card 3
 dspfarm
!
no aaa new-model
ip subnet-zero
ip cef
!
ip dhcp pool ITS
   network 20.1.1.0 255.255.255.0
   option 150 ip 20.1.1.100
   default-router 20.1.1.100
!
no ip domain lookup
no ftp-server write-enable
isdn switch-type primary-5ess
!
voice service voip
 allow-connections h323 to sip
!
voice translation-rule 10
 rule 1 /2225552100/ /2100/
 rule 2 /2225552105/ /2105/
 rule 3 /2225552106/ /2106/
!
voice translation-profile to_cue
 translate called 10
!
controller T1 0/0
 pri-group timeslots 1-24
!
controller T1 0/1
!
interface FastEthernet0/0
 ip address 10.1.235.1 255.255.0.0
 duplex auto
```

Example 15-54   **show running-config** *Output for the Site A Router (Continued)*

```
 speed auto
 no cdp enable
!
interface Serial0/0:23
 no ip address
 isdn switch-type primary-5ess
 isdn incoming-voice voice
 no cdp enable
!
interface FastEthernet0/1
 ip address 20.1.1.100 255.255.0.0
 speed auto
 half-duplex
 no cdp enable
!
interface Service-Engine1/0
 ip unnumbered FastEthernet0/0
 service-module ip address 10.1.235.128 255.255.0.0
 service-module ip default-gateway 10.1.235.1
 hold-queue 60 out
!
router ospf 100
 log-adjacency-changes
 network 10.1.0.0 0.0.255.255 area 0
!
ip classless
ip route 10.1.235.128 255.255.255.255 Service-Engine1/0
ip route 10.1.235.228 255.255.255.255 Service-Engine0/0
ip route 128.107.0.0 255.255.0.0 FastEthernet0/0
ip route 223.255.254.0 255.255.255.0 10.1.0.1
ip route 223.255.254.0 255.255.255.0 FastEthernet0/0
!
ip http server
ip http path flash:
ip pim bidir-enable
!
tftp-server flash:P00303020214.bin
tftp-server flash:P00303020209.bin
tftp-server flash:P00305000200.bin
tftp-server flash:P00305000300.bin
!
voice-port 0/0:23
!
voice-port 2/0/0
 connection plar opx 2100
 caller-id enable
!
voice-port 2/0/1
 connection plar opx 2100
 caller-id enable
!
```

continues

Example 15-54 show running-config *Output for the Site A Router (Continued)*

```
dial-peer cor custom
!
dial-peer voice 2100 voip
 destination-pattern 21..
 session protocol sipv2
 session target ipv4:10.1.235.128
 dtmf-relay sip-notify
 codec g711ulaw
 no vad
!
dial-peer voice 1000 pots
 destination-pattern 91..........
 port 0/0:15
 forward-digits 11
!
dial-peer voice 1001 pots
 preference 1
 destination-pattern 91.........
 port 2/0/0
!
dial-peer voice 1002 pots
 destination-pattern 9[2-9]......
 port 0/0:15
 forward-digits 7
!
dial-peer voice 1003 pots
 preference 1
 destination-pattern 9[2-9]......
 port 2/0/0
!
dial-peer voice 2101 voip
 description VM-AA-PSTN
 translation-profile outgoing to_cue
 destination-pattern 22255521..
 session protocol sipv2
 session target ipv4:10.1.235.128
 dtmf-relay sip-notify
 codec g711ulaw
 no vad
!
dial-peer voice 3000 voip
 destination-pattern 3...
 session target ipv4:10.1.229.1
 dtmf-relay h245-alphanumeric
 codec g711ulaw
 no vad
!
dial-peer voice 1004 pots
 destination-pattern 911
 port 2/0/1
!
```

Example 15-54 **show running-config** *Output for the Site A Router (Continued)*

```
telephony-service
 load 7960-7940 P00303020214
 max-ephones 50
 max-dn 120
 ip source-address 20.1.1.100 port 2000
 time-format 24
 date-format dd-mm-yy
 auto assign 1 to 5
 timeouts interdigit 20
 timeouts ringing 120
 create cnf-files version-stamp 7960 Sep 27 2004 12:31:02
 voicemail 2105
 max-conferences 8
 moh music-on-hold.au
 web admin system name admin password cisco
 web admin customer name custlogin password custpswd
 dn-webedit
 time-webedit
 transfer-system full-consult
 transfer-pattern 3...
 transfer-pattern 2...
 directory last-name-first
!
ephone-template  1
 softkeys idle  Redial Pickup Dnd Login Gpickup
 softkeys seized  Pickup Redial Endcall Gpickup
!
ephone-dn  1  dual-line
 number 2001 secondary 2225552001
 label Alice
 description Alice Davidson
 name Alice Davidson
 call-forward max-length 4
 call-forward busy 2105
 call-forward noan 2105 timeout 10
!
ephone-dn  2  dual-line
 number 2002 secondary 2225552002
 label Aaron
 description Aaron Wilkins
 name Aaron Wilkins
 call-forward max-length 8
 call-forward busy 2105
 call-forward noan 2105 timeout 10
!
ephone-dn  3  dual-line
 number 2003 secondary 2225552003
 label Ashley
 description Ashley Coley
 name Ashley Coley
 call-forward max-length 4
```

continues

Example 15-54 **show running-config** *Output for the Site A Router (Continued)*

```
 call-forward busy 2105
 call-forward noan 2105 timeout 10
 hold-alert 15 originator
!
ephone-dn  4  dual-line
 number 2004 secondary 2225552004
 label Anne
 description Anne Wyant
 name Anne Wyant
 call-forward max-length 4
 call-forward busy 2105
 call-forward noan 2105 timeout 10
!
ephone-dn  5  dual-line
 number 2005 secondary 2225552005
 label Alan
 description Alan McDougal
 name Alan McDougal
 call-forward max-length 4
 call-forward busy 2105
 call-forward noan 2105 timeout 10
!
ephone-dn  6
 number 2060
 label Reception
 name Reception
 no huntstop
!
ephone-dn  7
 number 2060
 label Reception
 name Reception
 preference 1
!
ephone-dn  10
 number 2999
 label 911
 trunk 911 timeout 5
!
ephone-dn  20
 number A2222
 name Intercom from Alice
 intercom A2223
!
ephone-dn  21
 number A2223
 name Intercom from Aaron
 intercom A2222
!
ephone-dn  25
 number 2010
```

Example 15-54   **show running-config** *Output for the Site A Router (Continued)*

```
 name All Office
 paging ip 224.0.1.20 port 2000
!
ephone-dn  30
 number 2020
!
ephone-dn  51
 number 8000....
 mwi on
!
ephone-dn  52
 number 8001....
 mwi off
!
ephone-dn  101
 number 7401
 park-slot timeout 30 limit 10
!
ephone-dn  102
 number 7402
 park-slot timeout 30 limit 10
!
ephone-dn  103
 number 7403
 park-slot timeout 30 limit 10
!
ephone-dn  104
 number 7404
 park-slot timeout 30 limit 10
!
ephone-dn  105
 number 7405
 park-slot timeout 30 limit 10
!
ephone  1
 ephone-template 1
 username "adavidson"
 mac-address 0003.6BAA.D1F8
 fastdial 1 3001 name User1
 fastdial 2 2060 name Reception
 fastdial 3 2002 name Aaron
 speed-dial 1 2005 label "Alan"
 speed-dial 2 3050 label "Customer Svc"
 paging-dn 25
 type 7960
 button  1:1 3:20
!
ephone  2
 ephone-template 1
 username "awilkins"
 mac-address 0003.6BAA.D362
```

continues

Example 15-54   **show running-config** *Output for the Site A Router (Continued)*

```
 fastdial 1 3001 name User1
 fastdial 2 3002 name User2
 fastdial 3 2001 name Alice
 fastdial 4 2005 name Alan
 speed-dial 1 2004 label "Anne"
 paging-dn 25
 type 7960
 button  1o2,30 2:10 3:21
 !
ephone  3
 ephone-template 1
 username "acoley"
 mac-address 0003.AAAA.0003
 speed-dial 2 3050 label "Customer Svc"
 paging-dn 25
 button  1:3
 !
ephone  4
 ephone-template 1
 username "awyant"
 mac-address 0003.AAAA.0004
 speed-dial 2 3050 label "Customer Svc"
 paging-dn 25
 auto-line incoming
 button  1:6 2:4
 !
ephone  5
 ephone-template 1
 username "amcdougal"
 mac-address 0003.AAAA.0005
 speed-dial 2 3050 label "Customer Svc"
 paging-dn 25
 auto-line incoming
 button  1:7 2:5
 !
line con 0
 exec-timeout 0 0
 password cisco
line 33
 no activation-character
 no exec
 password cisco
 login
line aux 0
line vty 0
 exec-timeout 0 0
 password cisco
 login
 !
```

Example 15-54 show running-config *Output for the Site A Router (Continued)*

```
ntp clock-period 17181154
ntp master
ntp server 10.1.100.1
```

Site A Cisco UE AA and Voice Mail Configurations

This section provides the configuration for Cisco UE at Site A.

The show software version and show software licenses Output

Example 15-55 provides the **show software version** and **show software licenses** output for the Site A Cisco UE.

Example 15-55 show software version *and* show software licenses *Output for the Site A Cisco UE*

```
cue-3725#show software version
Installed Packages:
 - Core  2.0.1
 - Auto Attendant  2.0.1
 - Global  2.0.1
 - Voice Mail  2.0.1

Installed Languages:
 - US English  2.0.0

cue-3725#show software licenses
Core:
 - application mode: CCME
 - total usable system ports: 8
Voicemail/Auto Attendant:
 - max system mailbox capacity time: 6000
 - max general delivery mailboxes: 15
 - max personal mailboxes: 50
Languages:
 - max installed languages: 1
 - max enabled languages: 1
```

The show running-config Output

Example 15-56 provides the **show running-config** output for the Site A Cisco UE system.

Example 15-56 show running-config *Output for the Site A Cisco UE*

```
cue-3725#show running-config
Generating configuration:
clock timezone America/Los_Angeles
hostname cue-3725
ip domain-name localdomain
ntp server 10.1.100.1
```

continues

Example 15-56 **show running-config** *Output for the Site A Cisco UE (Continued)*

```
software download server url "ftp://10.1.231.201/ftp" credentials hidden
  "6u/dKTN/hsEuSAEfw40XlF2eFHnZfyUTSd8ZZNgd+Y9J3xlk2B35j0nfGWTYHfmPSd8ZZNgd+Y9J3
  xlk2B35jwAAAAA="
!
groupname Administrators create
groupname Broadcasters create
groupname Sales create
username adavidson create
username awilkins create
username acoley create
username awyant create
username amcdougal create
username admin create
!
groupname Sales phonenumberE164 "2225552050"
groupname Sales phonenumber "2050"
!
username adavidson phonenumberE164 "2225552001"
username awilkins phonenumberE164 "2225552002"
username acoley phonenumberE164 "2225552003"
username awyant phonenumberE164 "2225552004"
username amcdougal phonenumberE164 "2225552005"
username adavidson phonenumber "2001"
username awilkins phonenumber "2002"
username acoley phonenumber "2003"
username awyant phonenumber "2004"
username amcdougal phonenumber "2005"
!
groupname Administrators member admin
groupname Sales member acoley
groupname Sales member awilkins
groupname Administrators privilege superuser
groupname Administrators privilege ManagePrompts
groupname Broadcasters privilege broadcast
!
backup server url "ftp://10.1.231.201/pod12nm_27jul04/" credentials hidden
  "xxOaioWv/uC5WSZLs/L2XY/frZzvmJ2MSd8ZZNgd+Y9J3xlk2B35j0nfGWTYHfmPSd8ZZNgd+Y9J3
  xlk2B35jwAAAAA="
!
ccn application autoattendant
 description "autoattendant"
 enabled
 maxsessions 8
 script "aa.aef"
 parameter "MaxRetry" "3"
 parameter "operExtn" "0"
 parameter "welcomePrompt" "AAWelcome.wav"
 end application
!
ccn application ciscomwiapplication
 description "ciscomwiapplication"
```

Example 15-56   **show running-config** *Output for the Site A Cisco UE (Continued)*

```
 enabled
 maxsessions 8
 script "setmwi.aef"
 parameter "strMWI_OFF_DN" "8001"
 parameter "strMWI_ON_DN" "8000"
 parameter "CallControlGroupID" "0"
 end application
!
ccn application custom-aa
 description "custom-aa"
 enabled
 maxsessions 8
 script "s1_main-officehours.aef"
 parameter "MainOperExt" "2001"
 end application
!
ccn application promptmgmt
 description "promptmgmt"
 enabled
 maxsessions 1
 script "promptmgmt.aef"
 end application
!
ccn application voicemail
 description "voicemail"
 enabled
 maxsessions 8
 script "voicebrowser.aef"
 parameter "logoutUri" "http://localhost/voicemail/vxmlscripts/mbxLogout.jsp"
 parameter "uri" "http://localhost/voicemail/vxmlscripts/login.vxml"
 end application
!
ccn subsystem sip
 gateway address "10.1.235.1"
 end subsystem
!
ccn trigger sip phonenumber 2100
 application "custom-aa"
 enabled
 locale "en_US"
 maxsessions 8
 end trigger
!
ccn trigger sip phonenumber 2102
 application "autoattendant"
 enabled
 locale "en_US"
 maxsessions 8
 end trigger
!
ccn trigger sip phonenumber 2105
```

continues

Example 15-56 show running-config *Output for the Site A Cisco UE (Continued)*

```
 application "voicemail"
 enabled
 idletimeout 5000
 locale "en_US"
 maxsessions 8
 end trigger
!
ccn trigger sip phonenumber 2106
 application "promptmgmt"
 enabled
 idletimeout 5000
 locale "en_US"
 maxsessions 1
 end trigger
!
voicemail default broadcast expiration time 30
voicemail default expiration time 30
voicemail default language en_US
voicemail default mailboxsize 5520
voicemail recording time 900
voicemail default messagesize 60
voicemail operator telephone 2001
voicemail capacity time 6000
voicemail mailbox owner "Sales" size 5520
 description "Sales mailbox"
 zerooutnumber "2100"
 end mailbox
!
voicemail mailbox owner "acoley" size 5520
 description "acoley mailbox"
 zerooutnumber "2100"
 end mailbox
!
voicemail mailbox owner "adavidson" size 5520
 description "adavidson mailbox"
 zerooutnumber "2100"
 end mailbox
!
voicemail mailbox owner "amcdougal" size 5520
 description "amcdougal mailbox"
 zerooutnumber "2100"
 end mailbox
!
voicemail mailbox owner "awilkins" size 5520
 description "awilkins mailbox"
 zerooutnumber "2100"
 end mailbox
!
voicemail mailbox owner "awyant" size 5520
```

Example 15-56 **show running-config** *Output for the Site A Cisco UE (Continued)*

```
description "awyant mailbox"
zerooutnumber "2100"
end mailbox
```

Site B Cisco CME Router Configurations

Site B is a Cisco 2691 router with extensions in the 3*xxx* range. Figure 15-1, at the beginning of the chapter, summarized the site layout. This section provides the Cisco CME configuration.

The **show version** Output

Example 15-57 provides the **show version** output for the Site B Cisco CME router.

Example 15-57 **show version** *Output for the Site B Router*

```
cme-2691#show version
Cisco IOS Software, 2600 Software (C2691-IPVOICE-M), Version 12.3(11)T2
  RELEASE SOFTWARE (fc1)
Technical Support: http://www.cisco.com/techsupport
Copyright (c) 1986-2004 by Cisco Systems, Inc.
Compiled Fri 29-Oct-04 06:38 by cmong
ROM: System Bootstrap, Version 12.2(8r)T2, RELEASE SOFTWARE (fc1)
cme-2691 uptime is 1 day, 16 hours, 27 minutes
System returned to ROM by reload at 16:00:52 PST Fri Dec 1 2004
System restarted at 16:00:44 PST Fri Dec 1 2004
System image file is "flash:c2691-ipvoice-mz.123-11.T2"
Cisco 2691 (R7000) processor (revision 0.1) with 111616K/19456K bytes of memory.
Processor board ID JMX0635L1MF
R7000 CPU at 160MHz, Implementation 39, Rev 3.3, 256KB L2 Cache
2 FastEthernet interfaces
1 terminal line
1 cisco service engine(s)
DRAM configuration is 64 bits wide with parity disabled.
55K bytes of NVRAM.
31360K bytes of ATA System CompactFlash (Read/Write)
```

The **show running-config** Output

Example 15-58 provides the **show running-config** output for the Site B Cisco CME router.

Example 15-58 **show running-config** *Output for the Site B Router*

```
cme-2691#show running-config
Building configuration...
Current configuration : 4712 bytes
! Last configuration change at 08:27:56 PST Sun Oct 3 2004
! NVRAM config last updated at 08:27:57 PST Sun Oct 3 2004
!
version 12.3
```

continues

Example 15-58 show running-config *Output for the Site B Router (Continued)*

```
service timestamps debug uptime
service timestamps log uptime
no service password-encryption
!
hostname cme-2691
!
boot-start-marker
boot system flash:c2691-ipvoice-mz.123-11.T2
boot-end-marker
!
no logging console
enable secret 5 $1$/UXs$yVeHaiJawV557ni62uZqb.
!
memory-size iomem 15
clock timezone PST -8
no aaa new-model
ip subnet-zero
ip cef
!
ip dhcp excluded-address 10.10.1.100 10.10.1.200
!
ip dhcp pool 1
   network 10.10.1.0 255.255.255.0
   option 150 ip 10.10.1.100
   default-router 10.10.1.100
!
no ip domain lookup
!
voice service voip
 allow-connections h323 to sip
!
voice translation-rule 10
 rule 1 /4445553100/ /3100/
 rule 2 /4445553105/ /3105/
 rule 3 /4445553106/ /3106/
!
voice translation-profile to_cue
 translate called 10
!
interface FastEthernet0/0
 ip address 10.1.10.1.229.1 255.255.0.0
 no ip mroute-cache
 load-interval 30
 duplex auto
 speed auto
!
interface FastEthernet0/1
 ip address 10.10.1.100 255.255.0.0
 no ip mroute-cache
 duplex auto
 speed auto
```

Example 15-58   **show running-config** *Output for the Site B Router (Continued)*

```
!
interface Service-Engine1/0
 ip unnumbered FastEthernet0/0
 service-module ip address 10.1.10.1.229.128 255.255.0.0
 service-module ip default-gateway 10.1.10.1.229.1
!
ip classless
ip route 10.1.10.1.229.128 255.255.255.255 Service-Engine1/0
!
ip http server
ip http path flash:
!
tftp-server flash:P00303020214.bin
!
dial-peer cor custom
!
dial-peer voice 3100 voip
 description VM-AA
 destination-pattern 31..
 session protocol sipv2
 session target ipv4:10.1.229.128
 dtmf-relay sip-notify
 codec g711ulaw
 no vad
!
dial-peer voice 3101 voip
 description VM-AA-PSTN
 translation-profile outgoing to_cue
 destination-pattern 44455531..
 session protocol sipv2
 session target ipv4:10.1.229.128
 dtmf-relay sip-notify
 codec g711ulaw
 no vad
!
dial-peer voice 2000 voip
 destination-pattern 2...
 session target ipv4:10.1.235.1
 dtmf-relay h245-alphanumeric
 codec g711ulaw
 no vad
!
telephony-service
 load 7960-7940 P00303020214
 max-ephones 48
 max-dn 192
 ip source-address 10.10.1.100 port 2000
 system message CUE System 2691
 create cnf-files version-stamp 7960 Jul 15 2003 13:48:12
 voicemail 3105
 max-conferences 8
```

continues

Example 15-58 **show running-config** *Output for the Site B Router (Continued)*

```
web admin system name admin password cisco
dn-webedit
time-webedit
transfer-system full-consult
transfer-pattern 3...
transfer-pattern 2...
!
ephone-dn  1  dual-line
 number 3001
 description User1
 name User1
 call-forward busy 3105
 call-forward noan 3105 timeout 10
!
ephone-dn  2  dual-line
 number 3002
 description User2
 name User2
 call-forward busy 3105
 call-forward noan 3105 timeout 10
!
ephone-dn  3
 number 3003
 description User3
 name User3
 call-forward busy 3105
 call-forward noan 3105 timeout 10
!
ephone-dn  4
 number 3004
 description User4
 name User4
 call-forward busy 3105
 call-forward noan 3105 timeout 10
!
ephone-dn  5
 number 3005
 description User5
 name User5
 call-forward busy 3105
 call-forward noan 3105 timeout 10
!
ephone-dn  6
 number 3006
 description User6
 name User6
 call-forward busy 3105
 call-forward noan 3105 timeout 10
!
ephone-dn  51
 number 8000....
```

Example 15-58   **show running-config** *Output for the Site B Router (Continued)*

```
 mwi on
!
ephone-dn  52
 number 8001....
 mwi off
!
ephone  1
 username "User1" password null
 mac-address 0009.B7F7.5793
 speed-dial 1 2001 label "Alice"
 speed-dial 2 3050 label "Customer Svc"
 speed-dial 4 3100 label "AA"
 button  1:1
!
ephone  2
 username "User2" password null
 mac-address 0002.FD06.D959
 speed-dial 1 2003 label "Ashley"
 speed-dial 2 2005 label "Alan"
 button  1:2
!
ephone  3
 username "User3" password null
 mac-address 0002.FFFF.1000
 speed-dial 4 3100 label "AA"
 button  1o3,5
!
ephone  4
 username "User4" password null
 mac-address 0002.FFFF.1004
 speed-dial 4 3100 label "AA"
 button  1:4
!
ephone  5
 username "User5" password null
 mac-address 0002.FFFF.1005
 speed-dial 4 3100 label "AA"
 button  1:5
!
ephone  6
 username "User6" password null
 mac-address 0002.FFFF.1006
 speed-dial 4 3100 label "AA"
 button  1:6
!
ephone-hunt 1 longest-idle
 pilot 3050 secondary 4445553050
 list 3002, 3003
 final 3105
!
line con 0
```

continues

Example 15-58 show running-config *Output for the Site B Router (Continued)*

```
 exec-timeout 0 0
line 33
 exec-timeout 0 0
 password cisco
 login
 no activation-character
 no exec
 transport preferred none
 transport input all
 transport output all
line aux 0
line vty 0 4
 exec-timeout 0 0
 password cisco
 login
!
ntp master
ntp server 10.1.100.1
```

Site B Cisco UE AA and Voice Mail Configurations

This section provides the configuration for Cisco UE at Site B.

The show software version and show software licenses Output

Example 15-59 provides the **show software version** and **show software licenses** output for the Site B Cisco UE.

Example 15-59 show software version *and* show software licenses *Output for the Site B Cisco UE*

```
cue-2691#show software version
Installed Packages:
 - Core  2.0.1
 - Auto Attendant  2.0.1
 - Bootloader (Primary)  1.0.18
 - Bootloader (Secondary)  2.0.0
 - Global  2.0.1
 - Voice Mail  2.0.1
Installed Languages:
 - US English  2.0.0


cue-2691#show software licenses
Core:
 - application mode: CCME
 - total usable system ports: 8
Voicemail/Auto Attendant:
 - max system mailbox capacity time: 6000
 - max general delivery mailboxes: 15
 - max personal mailboxes: 50
```

Example 15-59   **show software version** *and* **show software licenses** *Output for the Site B Cisco UE (Continued)*

```
Languages:
  - max installed languages: 1
  - max enabled languages: 1
```

The **show running-config** Output

Example 15-60 provides the **show running-config** output for the Site B Cisco UE system.

Example 15-60   **show running-config** *Output for the Site B Cisco UE*

```
cue-2691#show running-config
Generating configuration:
clock timezone America/Los_Angeles
hostname cue-2691
ip domain-name localdomain
ntp server 10.1.100.1
software download server url "ftp://127.0.0.1/ftp" credentials hidden "6u/dKTN/
    hsEuSAEfw40XlF2eFHnZfyUTSd8ZZNgd+Y9J3xlk2B35j0nfGWTYHfmPSd8ZZNgd+Y9J3xlk2B35jw
    AAAAA="
groupname Administrators create
groupname customer-service create
username admin create
username User1 create
username User2 create
username User3 create
username User4 create
username User5 create
username User6 create
!
groupname customer-service phonenumberE164 "4445553050"
groupname customer-service phonenumber "3050"

username User1 phonenumber "3001"
username User2 phonenumber "3002"
username User3 phonenumber "3003"
username User4 phonenumber "3004"
username User5 phonenumber "3005"
username User6 phonenumber "3006"
!
groupname Administrators member admin
groupname customer-service member User2
groupname customer-service member User3
groupname Administrators privilege superuser
groupname Administrators privilege ManagePrompts
!
backup server url "ftp://10.1.231.201/SiteA" credentials hidden "EWlTygcMhYmjazX
    hE/VNXHCkplVV4KjescbDaLa4fl4WLSPFvv1rWUnfGWTYHfmPSd8ZZNgd+Y9J3xlk2B35jwAAAAA="
!
ccn application autoattendant
 description "autoattendant"
 enabled
```

continues

Example 15-60 **show running-config** *Output for the Site B Cisco UE (Continued)*

```
 maxsessions 8
 script "aa.aef"
 parameter "MaxRetry" "3"
 parameter "operExtn" "0"
 parameter "welcomePrompt" "AAgreeting.wav"
 end application
!
ccn application ciscomwiapplication
 description "ciscomwiapplication"
 enabled
 maxsessions 8
 script "setmwi.aef"
 parameter "strMWI_OFF_DN" "8001"
 parameter "strMWI_ON_DN" "8000"
 parameter "CallControlGroupID" "0"
 end application
!
ccn application promptmgmt
 description "promptmgmt"
 enabled
 maxsessions 1
 script "promptmgmt.aef"
 end application
!
ccn application voicemail
 description "voicemail"
 enabled
 maxsessions 8
 script "voicebrowser.aef"
 parameter "logoutUri" "http://localhost/voicemail/vxmlscripts/mbxLogout.jsp"
 parameter "uri" "http://localhost/voicemail/vxmlscripts/login.vxml"
 end application
!
ccn subsystem sip
 gateway address "10.1.229.1"
 end subsystem
!
ccn trigger sip phonenumber 3100
 application "autoattendant"
 enabled
 maxsessions 8
 end trigger
!
ccn trigger sip phonenumber 3105
 application "voicemail"
 enabled
 maxsessions 8
 end trigger
!
ccn trigger sip phonenumber 3106
 application "promptmgmt"
```

Example 15-60   show running-config *Output for the Site B Cisco UE (Continued)*

```
  enabled
  maxsessions 1
  end trigger
 !
 voicemail default expiration time 60
 voicemail default language en_US
 voicemail default mailboxsize 5520
 voicemail recording time 900
 voicemail default messagesize 60
 voicemail operator telephone 0
 voicemail capacity time 6000
 voicemail mailbox owner "User1" size 5520
  end mailbox
 !
 voicemail mailbox owner "User2" size 5520
  end mailbox
 !
 voicemail mailbox owner "User3" size 5520
  end mailbox
 !
 voicemail mailbox owner "User4" size 5520
  end mailbox
 !
 voicemail mailbox owner "User5" size 5520
  end mailbox
 !
 voicemail mailbox owner "User6" size 5520
  end mailbox
 !
 voicemail mailbox owner "customer-service" size 5520
  description "customer-service mailbox"
  zerooutnumber "3101"
  end mailbox
```

Summary

This chapter walked you step-by-step through a sample setup of a two-site network. The system at Site A was configured from the start to a fully operational system. Additionally, a number of key Cisco CME call processing and phone features were configured on Site A. Site B's configuration was not explored in such great detail. It was used primarily to illustrate the configuration necessary to connect two sites and route calls between them. For the most part, Site B's configuration mirrors that of Site A but is less sophisticated in Cisco CME features containing just the basics to get the system operational.

After working through this chapter, you should be able to configure your own system, and customize it to your or your customer's needs. The content in this chapter solidifies all the feature and management explanations contained in the chapters in Part III. Part IV, starting with the next chapter, is dedicated to troubleshooting and maintaining a Cisco IPC Express system.

PART IV

Maintenance and Troubleshooting

This chapter covers the following topics:

- Understanding the phone bootup sequence
- Understanding the messages on the phone display
- Debugging virtual LAN (VLAN), Dynamic Host Configuration Protocol (DHCP), Trivial File Transfer Protocol (TFTP), and other registration issues
- Upgrading phone loads with signed and unsigned loads
- Troubleshooting basic call setup and teardown issues
- Troubleshooting Cisco IP Communications (IPC) Express graphical user interface (GUI) issues

## CHAPTER 16

Troubleshooting Basic Cisco IPC Express Features

Parts II and III of this book covered Cisco IP Communications (IPC) Express features, applications, and management. In Part IV the focus turns to troubleshooting tools and techniques for Cisco IPC Express. The first three chapters of Part IV focus on Cisco CallManager Express (CME), and the last three concentrate on Cisco Unity Express (UE).

Cisco CME provides a range of troubleshooting tools to isolate the cause of problems that might occur. Issues can range from simple situations, such as getting a phone registered to Cisco CME to more complex scenarios, such as overlay-dns and huntgroup configurations not operating correctly. Quite often you can correct problems with small configuration changes or by adjusting the system's operation to be closer to the expected behavior.

Troubleshooting a Cisco CME system requires an understanding of the following:

- The Cisco CME system architecture and its integration with the Cisco IOS voice architecture. This was covered in Chapter 3, "Cisco IPC Express Architecture Overview."
- The phone registration process.
- Cisco CME **debug** commands.

This chapter explores some basic troubleshooting topics, such as phone bootup and registration, VLAN configurations, Trivial File Transfer Protocol (TFTP) and call setup and teardown, and GUI issues. Subsequent chapters take a closer look at specific features and applications of the system.

Troubleshooting Phone Registration

This section examines the phone's behavior during registration, describes common problems encountered during registration, and illustrates the tools you use to troubleshoot these problems.

The IP phone registration process is fundamental to solving many problems encountered during initial Cisco CME setup. A good understanding of the phone bootup and registration process, phone display messages, and relevant debugs can help you troubleshoot most of these types of problems.

Understanding the Phone Bootup Sequence

When powered on, a phone goes through various states before it attempts to register with a Cisco CME. This section provides an overview in which you learn the correct behavior of an IP phone when it boots up and registers with Cisco CME. The next section provides a step-by-step explanation of the states the phone goes through and what the messages on the phone display mean. The section "Debugging VLAN, DHCP, TFTP, and Registration Issues" discusses problems and issues that may arise when phones don't register correctly.

The following steps summarize the phone bootup sequence; the rest of this section describes the process in more detail:

1 The phone sends out Cisco Discovery Protocol (CDP) messages to discover the voice virtual LAN (VLAN) information from the switch.

2 If the LAN switch is configured with voice VLAN information, the phone receives its voice VLAN information from the switch.

3 The IP phone broadcasts a Dynamic Host Configuration Protocol (DHCP) request to the LAN.

4 The DHCP server responds to the DHCP request with IP address, default gateway, and TFTP server information.

5 The IP phone requests a file named SEP*xxxxyyyyzzzz*.cnf.xml, where *xxxxyyyyzzzz* denotes the IP phone's Media Access Control (MAC) address from the TFTP server.

6 The TFTP server sends the requested file to the IP phone. The file also contains the IP address of the Cisco CME router.

7 The IP phone sends a registration request to the Cisco CME router.

8 The Cisco CME router sends the phone configuration to the IP phone.

When powered on, an IP phone issues a CDP request to discover its VLAN information from the LAN switch. It then broadcasts a DHCP request to obtain an IP address. An IP phone's default operation is to broadcast for DHCP. If you want to, you can manually disable this operation.

You can configure a DHCP server on the LAN or across the WAN at another site. The DHCP server responds to the DHCP request with the IP address, default gateway, and TFTP server information if configured. It is recommended that the TFTP server be the Cisco CME router. Upon receiving its IP information, the IP phone downloads a file named SEP*xxxxyyyyzzzz*.cnf.xml, where *xxxxyyyyzzzz* denotes the IP phone's MAC address from the TFTP server. Some of the important information contained in this file includes

- IP address of the Cisco CME router
- Phone load
- Network locale
- User locale

Example 16-1 shows a sample phone configuration file.

Example 16-1   *Contents of the SEPDefault.cnf.xml File*

```
<devicePool>
<callManagerGroup>
<members>
<member  priority="0">
<callManager>
<ports>
<ethernetPhonePort>2000</ethernetPhonePort>
</ports>
<processNodeName>10.1.0.3</processNodeName>
</callManager>
</member>
</members>
</callManagerGroup>
</devicePool>
<versionStamp>{7960 Dec 23 2004 14:43:07}</versionStamp>
<loadInformation></loadInformation>
<userLocale>
<name>English_United_States</name>
<langCode>en</langCode>
</userLocale>
<networkLocale>United_States</networkLocale>
<idleTimeout>0</idleTimeout>
<authenticationURL></authenticationURL>
<directoryURL>http://10.1.0.3:80/localdirectory</directoryURL>
<idleURL></idleURL>
<informationURL></informationURL>
<messagesURL></messagesURL>
<proxyServerURL></proxyServerURL>
<servicesURL></servicesURL>
</device>
```

At this point, the phone has enough information to register with the Cisco CME router, and it sends a registration request. The Cisco CME router verifies the phone's configuration against the router's running configuration. If it is correct, the phone registration succeeds. An exception to this registration sequence is when an upgrade of the phone load is required. When the IP phone downloads the SEP*xxxxyyyyzzzz*.cnf.xml file from the router during the registration process, the phone compares the load mentioned in this file with the load already installed. If these differ, the phone tries to upgrade its firmware before it sends the registration request to the Cisco CME router. This is explained in the following sections.

Understanding the Messages on the Phone Display

The display on the phone is a very useful tool in debugging problems encountered during phone registration. A unique message is shown on the phone display for each step in the registration process. With correct configurations in place, a phone registration takes between 60 and 180 seconds to complete. Some of the key messages explained in the following sections are

- Configuring VLAN
- Configuring IP
- Configuring CM
- Registering
- Cisco CME
- Upgrading Firmware (if necessary)

Before each of these messages is described in more detail, the next section explains what to do when no message appears on the screen.

No Message Appears on the Phone Display

No message on the phone display means that the phone isn't powered. Therefore, it must be plugged into a power outlet or an Ethernet-powered LAN port. As soon as it is powered on and plugged into a LAN switch's Ethernet port, the phone immediately starts booting. The three LED buttons on the bottom right of the phone—the speakerphone, mute, and headset buttons— light in sequence for a period of 1 or 2 seconds. This indicates that the phone is getting power. A blank display a few seconds after power-on means that the phone's Ethernet connection is not fully functional. The following are some of the possible problems that might cause this situation:

- The Ethernet cable is plugged into the wrong Ethernet port for the phone. The cable should be plugged into the first Ethernet port.
- The LAN switch port is administratively shut down.
- You are using the wrong cable, or the cable is not plugged in properly. Hence, the connector's pins are not making proper contact with the phone or switch port.
- The switch port does not support inline power; an external phone power supply is required.

The "Configuring VLAN" Message

If the physical and data-link layers on the Ethernet connection are operational, the phone multicasts Cisco Discovery Protocol (CDP) packets on the LAN. The phone shows the "Configuring VLAN" message on its display for a short time during this process. If the LAN switch is configured with the appropriate voice VLAN configuration, it responds to the CDP query from the phone, and the phone configures itself accordingly.

If the phone is connected to a device that does not support CDP, the CDP query times out, and the phone moves on to the next step in the registration sequence. Therefore, even if the LAN switch is not configured with voice VLAN information, the phone should still get registered.

The "Configuring IP" Message

The next step in the phone registration process is configuring Layer 3 parameters such as the IP address and default gateway the phone should use. To achieve this, the phone broadcasts a DHCP request on the LAN. The message on the phone display changes to "Configuring IP."

Phones shipped from the Cisco factory are configured to obtain Layer 3 parameters via DHCP. If the "Configuring VLAN" message was previously displayed on the phone, you should now see the "Configuring IP" message.

NOTE   You can also manually configure Layer 3 parameters on the phone by turning off the DHCP feature.

The "Configuring IP" message alone doesn't guarantee that the phone's Layer 3 configuration is correct. If configured properly, the phone acquires its Layer 3 parameters and moves on to the next step in the registration process. If this doesn't happen because of an incorrect configuration, the phone continues to display the "Configuring IP" message indefinitely. This stage of the registration should not take more than approximately 60 seconds. If your phone display appears stuck at the "Configuring IP" message for longer than this, inspect the DHCP configuration on the router.

Simply obtaining an IP address and related parameters doesn't mean that the configuration is correct. An incorrect subnet mask or a wrong TFTP server IP address can prevent the phone from successfully registering with the Cisco CME router. It is a good practice to always check the configurations on the phone. This saves time by helping you identify potential problems faster.

After the phone has obtained its correct Layer 3 parameters, it is a fully functional IP endpoint. The next step in the registration sequence is to download the SEP*xxxxyyyyzzzz*.cnf.xml file to obtain the Cisco CME IP address and other related parameters. Incorrect configurations can cause this file to have the wrong information, which prevents the phone from registering or operating correctly. Not executing the **create-cnf** command keeps the file from being present on the system, so the phone can never register properly.

The "Configuring CM" Message

If the XML configuration file is present on the router and the phone downloads it successfully via TFTP, the phone display changes to "Configuring CM." At this point, the phone has the IP address of its call controller and the information necessary to register with it.

The "Registering" and "Cisco CME" Messages

The phone sends a registration request to the Cisco CME router. If the Cisco CME router is configured correctly, a successful registration takes place.

During the registration process, the message on the phone display changes to "Registering." Upon successful registration, you should see "Cisco CME" displayed on the phone, with the extension number(s) assigned next to the appropriate buttons. An exception to this is if a phone firmware upgrade is required.

The "Upgrading Firmware" Message

If a phone firmware upgrade is required during the registration process, the phone downloads the new firmware from the Cisco CME router before registering with Cisco CME. After the phone downloads the SEP*xxxxyyyyzzzz*.cnf.xml file, the display on the phone changes to "Upgrading Firmware." The phone goes through the bootup sequence again after downloading the new firmware.

Understanding SCCP Endpoint Registration

Figure 16-1 shows the message exchange involved in registering an Skinny Client Control Protocol (SCCP) IP phone with Cisco CME. You can see most of the registration messages by turning on **debug ephone register** during phone registration. To view all the registration messages, turn on **debug ephone detail** in addition to **debug ephone register**.

Figure 16-1 *SCCP Phone Registration Sequence*

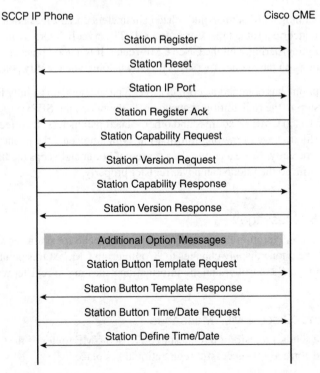

Sample output of a **debug ephone register** command is shown in Example 16-2. These debugs can be useful in troubleshooting registration as well as other problems.

Example 16-2   *Output of* **debug ephone register**

```
Router#debug ephone register
Mar  1 02:53:11.327: ephone-(1)[1] StationRegisterMessage (0/0/24) from 10.1.1.101
*Mar  1 02:53:11.327: ephone-(1)[1] Register StationIdentifier DeviceName
  SEP000DBDBEF372
*Mar  1 02:53:11.327: ephone-(1)[1] StationIdentifier Instance 1    deviceType 7
*Mar  1 02:53:11.327: ephone-1[-1]:stationIpAddr 10.1.1.101
*Mar  1 02:53:11.327: ephone-1[-1]:maxStreams 0
*Mar  1 02:53:11.327: ephone-1[-1]:phone-size 616 dn-size 208
*Mar  1 02:53:11.327: ephone-(1) Allow any Skinny Server IP address 10.1.1.1
*Mar  1 02:53:11.327: ephone-1
*Mar  1 02:53:11.327: Skinny Local IP address = 10.1.1.1 on port 2000

*Mar  1 02:53:11.327: Skinny Phone IP address = 10.1.1.101 51664
*Mar  1 02:53:11.327: ephone-1[1]:RegisterAck sent to ephone 1: keepalive period 30
*Mar  1 02:53:11.327: ephone-1[1]:CapabilitiesReq sent
*Mar  1 02:53:11.327: ephone-1[1]:Skinny IP port 53449 set for socket [1]
*Mar  1 02:53:11.579: ephone-1[1]:CapabilitiesRes received
*Mar  1 02:53:11.579: ephone-1[1]:Caps list 7
G711Ulaw64k   40 ms
G711Alaw64k   40 ms
G729  60 ms
G729AnnexA  60 ms
G729AnnexB  60 ms
G729AnnexAwAnnexB  60 ms
Unrecognized Media Type 25   120 ms

*Mar  1 02:53:11.579: ephone-1[1]:ButtonTemplateReqMessage
*Mar  1 02:53:11.579: ephone-1[1]:CheckAutoReg
*Mar  1 02:53:11.579: ephone-1[1]:AutoReg skipped: phone already has DN 1
*Mar  1 02:53:11.579: ephone-1[1]:Setting 6 lines 0 speed-dials on phone
  (max_line 6)
*Mar  1 02:53:11.579: ephone-1[1]:First Speed Dial Button location is 0 (0)
*Mar  1 02:53:11.579: ephone-1[1]:Configured 0 speed dial buttons
*Mar  1 02:53:11.579: ephone-1[1]:ButtonTemplate lines=6 speed=0 buttons=6
  offset=0
*Mar  1 02:53:11.831: ephone-1[1]:StationSoftKeyTemplateReqMessage
*Mar  1 02:53:11.831: ephone-1[1]:StationSoftKeyTemplateResMessage
*Mar  1 02:53:12.083: ephone-1[1]:StationSoftKeySetReqMessage
*Mar  1 02:53:12.083: ephone-1[1]:StationSoftKeySetResMessage
*Mar  1 02:53:12.335: ephone-1[1]:StationLineStatReqMessage from ephone line 6
*Mar  1 02:53:12.335: ephone-1[1]:StationLineStatReqMessage from ephone line 6
                     Invalid DN -1
*Mar  1 02:53:12.335: ephone-1[1]:StationLineStatResMessage sent to ephone
  (1 of 6)
*Mar  1 02:53:12.587: ephone-1[1]:StationLineStatReqMessage from ephone line 5
*Mar  1 02:53:12.587: ephone-1[1]:StationLineStatReqMessage from ephone line 5
                     Invalid DN -1
*Mar  1 02:53:12.587: ephone-1[1]:StationLineStatResMessage sent to ephone
  (2 of 6)
```

continues

Example 16-2 *Output of* **debug ephone register** *(Continued)*

```
*Mar  1 02:53:12.839: ephone-1[1]:StationLineStatReqMessage from ephone line 4
*Mar  1 02:53:12.839: ephone-1[1]:StationLineStatReqMessage from ephone line 4
                      Invalid DN -1
*Mar  1 02:53:12.839: ephone-1[1]:StationLineStatResMessage sent to ephone
  (3 of 6)
*Mar  1 02:53:13.091: ephone-1[1]:StationLineStatReqMessage from ephone line 3
*Mar  1 02:53:13.091: ephone-1[1]:StationLineStatReqMessage from ephone line 3
                      Invalid DN -1
*Mar  1 02:53:13.091: ephone-1[1]:StationLineStatResMessage sent to ephone
  (4 of 6)
*Mar  1 02:53:13.343: ephone-1[1]:StationLineStatReqMessage from ephone line 2
*Mar  1 02:53:13.343: ephone-1[1]:StationLineStatReqMessage from ephone line 2
                      Invalid DN -1
*Mar  1 02:53:13.343: ephone-1[1]:StationLineStatResMessage sent to ephone
  (5 of 6)
*Mar  1 02:53:13.595: ephone-1[1]:StationLineStatReqMessage from ephone line 1
*Mar  1 02:53:13.595: ephone-1[1]:StationLineStatReqMessage ephone line 1
  DN 1 = 1001 no desc
*Mar  1 02:53:13.595: ephone-1[1]:StationLineStatResMessage sent to ephone
  (6 of 6)
*Mar  1 02:53:13.595: ephone-1[1]:SkinnyCompleteRegistration
```

Debugging VLAN, DHCP, TFTP, and Registration Issues

An incorrect VLAN, DHCP, TFTP, or Cisco CME (telephony-service) configuration can prevent the IP phones from registering with Cisco CME. Before you troubleshoot any other configuration issues, however, you must fix physical layer problems, as described in the next section.

Physical Layer Problems

Troubleshooting network problems generally starts at the lower layers of the OSI reference model. This same principle holds true for an IP phone, because it is a fully functional IP endpoint. Therefore, it is important to make sure that your physical layer is intact before attempting to troubleshoot problems at higher layers.

Some of the common physical layer problems are as follows:

- The phone doesn't get powered.
- The phone gets powered but doesn't go through the bootup sequence.

These problems can be caused by one of the following:

- The LAN switch port to which the phone is connected is shut down.
- The LAN switch or switch module does not support inline power.
- A faulty or wrong cable is used.
- The cable is connected to the wrong port on the IP phone.

It's easy to see when a phone isn't getting power. If the phone is not getting powered on, chances are good that the LAN switch is not providing or cannot provide inline power. The first thing to do is check that your LAN switch supports inline power for IP phones. If the switch supports inline power but the phone is not getting power, the cause could be a faulty cable, a shut-down port, a cable connected to the wrong IP phone port, or a faulty phone or port (which is rare). You can isolate the problem by doing one or more of the following:

- Plug the phone into a different port to isolate a faulty port.
- Plug a different phone into the same port to isolate a faulty phone.
- Plug a known working phone into the same port to isolate a faulty phone.
- Plug a phone into a known working port to isolate a faulty port.
- Use a cable known to be good.

The preceding actions should eliminate faulty hardware. If the problem persists, the cause might be a configuration issue. Make sure that the LAN switch port is not shut down, and check the configuration to see if inline power is disabled.

Example 16-3 shows a configuration in which switchport fa0/1 is in a shutdown state, inline power is disabled for switchport fa0/2, and switchport fa0/3 is the only port correctly providing inline power to an attached IP phone.

Example 16-3 *Switchports with the Wrong Configuration*

```
Switch#show running-config
Building configuration...

Current configuration:
!
version 12.0
no service pad
service timestamps debug uptime
service timestamps log uptime
no service password-encryption
service internal
!
hostname Aprilia_Switch
!
no logging console

ip subnet-zero
!
interface FastEthernet0/1
 shutdown
 switchport access vlan 100
 switchport voice vlan 110
!
interface FastEthernet0/2
 switchport access vlan 100
 switchport voice vlan 110
 power inline never
```

continues

Example 16-3 *Switchports with the Wrong Configuration (Continued)*

```
!
interface FastEthernet0/3
 switchport access vlan 100
 switchport voice vlan 110
```

VLAN

If the physical layer is intact, the phone should be getting power and should start booting up. The next thing to look for is any possible issues related to VLAN. A wrong VLAN configuration prevents the phone from getting its DHCP information or causes it to get the wrong DHCP configuration.

When the phone boots up, it sends three CDP messages requesting the voice VLAN information. If CDP is disabled on the LAN switch or on a particular interface, the phone cannot get its voice VLAN information. If you have configured a voice VLAN for your network, make sure that CDP is also enabled on the router or at least on the ports that are configured for the voice VLAN. Also, make sure that your VLAN configurations are correct.

DHCP

With step-by-step instructions for troubleshooting Cisco CME, DHCP configuration is the next item on the list after VLAN-related problems. A faulty DHCP configuration prevents the phone from having IP connectivity with other equipment on the LAN. Although the DHCP server can be on the LAN or across the WAN, only issues related to DHCP configuration on a LAN are covered here because this is the typical configuration. You can find more information about configuring a DHCP remotely at Cisco.com. Some of the key areas for troubleshooting DHCP are as follows:

- **Subnet mask**—The subnet mask in the DHCP configuration and the one in the network interface should match.

- **MAC address**—The MAC address should be prefixed with 01.

- **TFTP server address**—The TFTP server IP address should be configured. It is also important that there is IP connectivity to the TFTP server.

Example 16-4 shows an extract of a router configuration for DHCP. The Cisco CME router is configured to be the DHCP server for the phones. At first glance the configuration seems fine, but if you look at the phone's network configuration, you can see that the phone has not received an IP address, subnet mask, or TFTP server address.

Example 16-4 *Erroneous DHCP Configuration*

```
Router#show running-config
Building configuration...
!
ip dhcp pool Phone2
```

Example 16-4 *Erroneous DHCP Configuration (Continued)*

```
  host 10.0.0.10 255.0.0.0
  client-identifier 0007.8513.136c
  default-router 10.0.0.1
  option 150 ip 10.0.0.1
 !
interface Ethernet0/0
 ip address 10.0.0.1 255.0.0.0
 half-duplex
```

You can verify an IP phone's network configuration by pressing the **settings** phone button and selecting the **Network configuration** option from the menu. You can turn on **debug ip dhcp server packets** to see the DHCP messages to understand why the phone is not receiving its IP network configuration.

Example 16-5 shows the output of **debug ip dhcp server packets**. A close look at the configuration and the debugs reveal that the MAC address configured on the router and the MAC address of the IP phone broadcasting the DHCP request are not the same. As a result, the phone is unable to get an IP address via DHCP. If you take a closer look at the MAC address shown in Example 16-4 and the debug output shown in Example 16-5, you can see that the MAC address in the debug output contains two extra digits. In fact, the MAC address in the show output is the MAC address in the configuration prefixed with 01.

Example 16-5 *Output of* **debug ip dhcp server packets** *with the Wrong MAC Address Configured*

```
CME_Router#debug ip dhcp server packets
*Mar  1 00:24:46.459: DHCPD: DHCPDISCOVER received from client 0100.0785.1313.6c
  on interface Ethernet0/0.
*Mar  1 00:24:54.459: DHCPD: DHCPDISCOVER received from client 0100.0785.1313.6c
  on interface Ethernet0/0.
```

When configuring the **client-identifier** (MAC address) for IP phones, you should prefix the actual phone's MAC address with 01. The correct configuration is shown in Example 16-6.

Example 16-6 *Correct DHCP Configuration*

```
Router#show running-config
Building configuration...
!
ip dhcp pool Phone2
   host 10.0.0.10 255.0.0.0
   client-identifier 0100.0785.1313.6c
   default-router 10.0.0.1
   option 150 ip 10.0.0.1
!
interface Ethernet0/0
 ip address 10.0.0.1 255.0.0.0
 half-duplex
```

Example 16-7 shows the debugs with a correct configuration. Comparing the debug text in Example 16-6 with that shown in Example 16-7, you can see that the router is not responding to the DHCP request, because it doesn't have an IP address assigned for the MAC address.

Example 16-7 *Output of* **debug ip dhcp server** *for a Working Configuration*

```
CME_Router#debug ip dhcp server
*Mar  1 05:06:35.074: DHCPD: DHCPDISCOVER received from client 0100.0785.1313.6c
  on interface Ethernet0/0.
*Mar  1 05:06:35.074: DHCPD: Sending DHCPOFFER to client 0100.0785.1313.6c
  (10.0.0.10).
*Mar  1 05:06:35.074: DHCPD: broadcasting BOOTREPLY to client 0007.8513.136c.
*Mar  1 05:06:35.078: DHCPD: DHCPREQUEST received from client 0100.0785.1313.6c.
*Mar  1 05:06:35.078: DHCPD: Sending DHCPACK to client 0100.0785.1313.6c
  (10.0.0.10).
*Mar  1 05:06:35.078: DHCPD: broadcasting BOOTREPLY to client 0007.8513.136c.
```

The network configuration menu on the phone is one of the ways you can verify that the phone is getting the right configuration. You can view the IP address, subnet mask, TFTP server address, and Cisco CME IP address from this menu.

You can also erase the current phone configuration, and disable the DHCP option from the same menu. If a user reports that a phone is not working and debugging shows that there is no DHCP broadcast from the phone, it is likely that the DHCP option was accidentally or intentionally disabled from the Network Configuration menu. In the configuration shown in Example 16-4, the DHCP server assigns an IP address based on the phone's MAC address. Another way of configuring DHCP is to have an open pool of address space. This method potentially eliminates the missing 01 prefix problem described previously, but the disadvantage is that the router responds to a DHCP request from any IP endpoint on the network.

TFTP

The phone uses TFTP to download files required during the registration process, such as the following:

- SEP*xxxxyyyyzzzz*.cnf.xml file
- Phone firmware (if an upgrade or downgrade is necessary)
- Network and user locale files
- Language files

All these files are created and stored in the Cisco CME system memory when you issue the **create-cnf files** command. An exception to this is the phone firmware, which must be copied onto flash and placed on the TFTP server using the command **tftp-server flash:filename**. You can see the files on the system memory by issuing the command **show telephony-service**

tftp-bindings. A sample output of this command is shown in Example 16-8. You can see that individual SEP*xxxxyyyyzzzz*.cnf.xml files are an alias of the XMLDefault7960.cnf.xml file.

Example 16-8 *Output of* **show telephony-service tftp-bindings**

```
CME_HQ#show telephony-service tftp-bindings
tftp-server system:/its/SEPDEFAULT.cnf
tftp-server system:/its/SEPDEFAULT.cnf alias SEPDefault.cnf
tftp-server system:/its/XMLDefault.cnf.xml alias XMLDefault.cnf.xml
tftp-server system:/its/ATADefault.cnf.xml
tftp-server system:/its/XMLDefault7960.cnf.xml alias SEP000DBDBEF372.cnf.xml
tftp-server system:/its/united_states/7960-tones.xml alias United_States/
  7960-tones.xml
tftp-server system:/its/united_states/7960-font.xml alias English_United_States/
  7960-font.xml
tftp-server system:/its/united_states/7960-dictionary.xml alias
  English_United_States/7960-dictionary.xml
tftp-server system:/its/united_states/7960-kate.xml alias English_United_States/
  7960-kate.xml
tftp-server system:/its/united_states/Skinny-dictionary.xml alias
  English_United_States/Skinny-dictionary.xml
```

Registration can fail if these files are either unavailable or not placed on the router's TFTP server. Understanding TFTP **debug** commands is very useful in troubleshooting these problems. One of the most useful TFTP **debug** commands is **debug tftp events**. Example 16-9 shows the output of **debug tftp events** during a successful phone registration. From the debugs you can see that the phone is looking for various files and obtains these files via TFTP.

Example 16-9 *Output of* **debug tftp events** *During a Successful Registration*

```
CME_HQ#debug tftp events
*Jul 20 15:17:50.785: TFTP: Looking for OS79XX.TXT
*Jul 20 15:17:50.785: TFTP: Looking for SEP000DBDBEF372.cnf.xml
*Jul 20 15:17:50.785: TFTP: Opened system:/its/XMLDefault7960.cnf.xml, fd 0,
  size 775 for process 131
*Jul 20 15:17:50.789: TFTP: Finished system:/its/XMLDefault7960.cnf.xml,
  time 00:00:00 for process 131
*Jul 20 15:17:55.813: TFTP: Looking for P00303020200.bin
*Jul 20 15:17:58.129: TFTP: Looking for SEP000DBDBEF372.cnf.xml
*Jul 20 15:17:58.129: TFTP: Opened system:/its/XMLDefault7960.cnf.xml, fd 0,
  size 775 for process 131
*Jul 20 15:17:58.133: TFTP: Finished system:/its/XMLDefault7960.cnf.xml,
  time 00:00:00 for process 131
```

Registration Problems

In this section, you learn how to interpret the output of the **show ephone** command, and then tackle a phone registration problem. Example 16-10 shows the output of the relevant portion of the running configuration of a Cisco CME router.

Example 16-10 *Configuring the CME Router*

```
CME_HQ#show running-config
ip dhcp pool phoneA
   host 10.10.10.141 255.255.255.0
   client-identifier 0100.07eb.4629.9e
   default-router 10.10.10.1
   option 150 ip 10.10.10.1
!
ip dhcp pool phoneB
   host 10.10.10.142 255.255.255.0
   client-identifier 0100.03e3.7376.fb
   option 150 ip 10.10.10.1
   default-router 10.10.10.1

telephony-service
 load 7910 P00403030401
 load 7960-7940 P00303020214
 max-ephones 24
 max-dn 24
 ip source-address 10.10.10.1 port 2000
 create cnf-files version-stamp Jan 01 2002 00:00:00
 max-conferences 8
!
ephone-dn  1  dual-line
 number 1001
 huntstop channel
!
ephone-dn  2
 number 1002
 name CS Engineer2
!
ephone-dn  5
 number 1005
 name CS Engineer5
!
ephone  1
 mac-address 0007.EB46.299E
 type 7960
 button  1:1 2:2
!
ephone  2
 mac-address 0003.E373.76FB
 button  1:2
```

Example 16-11 gives the **show ephone** output for the same configuration. The output provides a lot of useful information about the phone's current state. This information includes the phone's MAC address, IP address, and whether the phone is registered.

Example 16-11 *Output of* **show ephone**

```
CSE_HQ#show ephone

ephone-1 Mac:0007.EB46.299E TCP socket:[4] activeLine:0 REGISTERED
mediaActive:0 offhook:0 ringing:0 reset:0 reset_sent:0 paging 0 debug:0
IP:10.10.10.141 49654 Telecaster 7960  keepalive 1 max_line 6
button 1: dn 1  number 1001 CH1    IDLE        CH2    IDLE
button 2: dn 2  number 1002 CH1    IDLE        shared

ephone-6 Mac:0003.E373.76FB TCP socket:[3] activeLine:0 REGISTERED
mediaActive:0 offhook:0 ringing:0 reset:0 reset_sent:0 paging 0 debug:0
IP:10.10.10.142 52023 Telecaster 7960  keepalive 1 max_line 6
button 1: dn 2  number 1002 CH1    IDLE        shared
```

One important point to note from the configuration shown in Example 16-10, and the **show ephone** output shown in Example 16-11, is the ephone tag (the number next to **ephone**). The tag for the ephone with MAC address 0007.EB46.299E (ephone1) is the same in the configuration and the **show ephone** output, but the tag for the ephone with MAC address 0003.E373.76FB (ephone-2) is different. The tag for the second ephone is 6 in the **show ephone** output and 2 in the configuration. This is very important when troubleshooting, because if you look for the phone by its configuration tag, chances are you are looking at the wrong phone. You should always look up the phone by MAC address in the **show** output.

The last two lines of the ephone 1 output (the lines starting with **button**) tell you which ephone-dns are attached to the ephone.

For ephone 1, button 1 is attached to ephone-dn 1 (button 1: dn 1, 1001) and button 2 is attached to ephone-dn 2 (button 2: dn 2, 1002). In the case of the ephone-dn, the tag shown on the **show** output and the configuration are the same as that in the configuration (unlike the tags for the ephones). The extension numbers configured for the ephone-dn are also shown in this output. Another useful piece of information available on the same line is the status of the virtual voice port attached to this ephone-dn.

Ephone-dn 1 is a dual-line DN and, hence, has two channels (CH1 and CH2 in Example 16-11) associated to the same voice port. Ephone-dn 2 is a single-line DN and, hence, has only a single channel (CH1) associated with it. All the voice channels shown in Example 16-11 are in the IDLE state, which means that the phones are on-hook. Some of the other channel states you may see include

- SEIZED (off-hook)
- RINGING
- HOLD

You can also see from Example 16-11 that ephone 1 and ephone 2 share the same ephone-dn 2 (extension 1002) on buttons 2 and 1 of the phones, respectively.

The second lines of the debug for each ephone in Example 16-11 show the parameters **mediaActive**, **offhook**, **ringing**, **reset**, and others with a 0 or 1 next to them. A 0 next to the parameter means no, and 1 means yes. For example, **offhook: 1** means that the phone is off-hook. Similarly, **ringing: 0** means that the phone is not ringing. These extra details make troubleshooting Cisco CME much easier.

At this point, a new phone is added to the existing configuration, and the relevant portion of the new configuration is shown in Example 16-12.

Example 16-12 *CME Configuration After a New Phone Is Added*

```
CME_HQ#show running-config
ip dhcp pool phoneA
    host 10.10.10.141 255.255.255.0
    client-identifier 0100.07eb.4629.9e
    default-router 10.10.10.1
    option 150 ip 10.10.10.1
!
ip dhcp pool phoneB
    host 10.10.10.142 255.255.255.0
    client-identifier 0100.03e3.7376.fb
    option 150 ip 10.10.10.1
    default-router 10.10.10.1

ip dhcp pool phoneC
    host 10.10.10.143 255.255.255.0
    client-identifier 0100.0dbd.bef3.72
    default-router 10.10.10.1
    option 150 ip 10.10.10.1


telephony-service
 load 7910 P00403030401
 load 7960-7940 P00303020214
 max-ephones 24
 max-dn 24
 ip source-address 10.10.10.1 port 2000
 create cnf-files version-stamp Jan 01 2002 00:00:00
 max-conferences 8
!
ephone-dn  1   dual-line
 number 1001
 huntstop channel
!
ephone-dn  2
 number 1002
 name CS Engineer2
!
ephone-dn  3
 number 1003
```

Example 16-12   *CME Configuration After a New Phone Is Added (Continued)*

```
 name CS Engineer3
!
ephone-dn  4
 number 1004
 name CS Engineer4
!
ephone-dn  5
 number 1005
 name CS Engineer5
!
ephone  1
 mac-address 0007.EB46.299E
 type 7960
 button  1:1 2:2
!
ephone  2
 mac-address 0003.E373.76FB
 button  1:2
!
ephone  3
 mac-address 000B.BDBE.F372
 type 7910
 button  1:4
```

The **show ephone** output for the same configuration is shown in Example 16-13.

Example 16-13   *Output of* **show ephone** *After a New Phone Is Added*

```
CME_HQ#show ephone
ephone-1 Mac:0007.EB46.299E TCP socket:[2] activeLine:0 REGISTERED
mediaActive:0 offhook:0 ringing:0 reset:0 reset_sent:0 paging 0 debug:0
IP:10.10.10.141 52800 Telecaster 7960  keepalive 25 max_line 6
button 1: dn 1  number 1001 CH1   IDLE         CH2   IDLE
button 2: dn 2  number 1002 CH1   IDLE         shared

ephone-6 Mac:0003.E373.76FB TCP socket:[1] activeLine:0 REGISTERED
mediaActive:0 offhook:0 ringing:0 reset:0 reset_sent:0 paging 0 debug:0
IP:10.10.10.142 51595 Telecaster 7960  keepalive 26 max_line 6
button 1: dn 2  number 1002 CH1   IDLE         shared

ephone-3 Mac:000B.BDBE.F372 TCP socket:[-1] activeLine:0 UNREGISTERED
mediaActive:0 offhook:0 ringing:0 reset:0 reset_sent:0 paging 0 debug:0
IP:10.10.10.143 52243 Unknown 0  keepalive 0 max_line 0

ephone-4 Mac:000D.BDBE.F372 TCP socket:[3] activeLine:0 REGISTERED
mediaActive:0 offhook:0 ringing:0 reset:0 reset_sent:0 paging 0 debug:0
IP:10.10.10.143 50898 Telecaster 7960  keepalive 23 max_line 6
```

A quick look at the configuration indicates that only three phones are configured, but four phones show up in the **show ephone** output. When the debugs were done, only three phones were plugged into the network, so where did the fourth phone come from?

You can also see from the output shown in Example 16-13 that three of the four phones are in REGISTERED state but the fourth one is in UNREGISTERED state. The ephone with tag 3 (in Example 16-13) is in UNREGISTERED state. This phone also doesn't have a line number next to its buttons, so you cannot make a call from this phone. This problem is caused by having entered an incorrect MAC address.

The actual MAC address of ephone-3 is 000D.BDBE.F372. If you look at the configuration, however, you can see that the fourth digit is wrong (B instead of D). This is the reason why ephone-3 (in Example 16-13) is in the UNREGISTERED state—because such a phone does not exist in the configuration used for this example. If a phone with such a MAC address doesn't exist, it cannot register with the router, so that accounts for ephone-3 being in UNREGISTERED state. Now if you look at the MAC address of ephone-4 (in Example 16-13), it matches the correct MAC address.

The phone is registered even though it was never configured. Cisco CME lets a phone register by default as long as the phone is a supported model, and the system has not exceeded its max-ephone limit. However, even though the phone is in REGISTERED state, you can see that no lines are assigned to the ephone (compare it to the output of ephone 1 and ephone 6 in Example 16-13). The reason is that no line was assigned to the phone (with the correct MAC address) in the configuration. This explains the missing line number on the physical phone.

If you try to fix the problem by entering the correct MAC address for ephone 3, the router doesn't accept it. Instead, it displays an error message, as shown in Example 16-14.

Example 16-14 *Error Output When the MAC Address Is Changed*

```
CME_HQ(config)#ephone 3
CME_HQ(config-ephone)#mac-address 000d.bdbe.f372
ePhone slot is already registered with 000b.bdbe.f372.
Can not change MAC address.
CME_HQ(config-ephone)#
```

From the router's perspective, you are trying to assign ephone 3 (in the configuration as well as the **show** output) the MAC address of ephone 4 (in the **show** output), which is already in REGISTERED state. Therefore, this is unacceptable.

The solution for this problem is to remove ephone 3 from the configuration, and add ephone 4 with the correct MAC address, as shown in Example 16-15.

Example 16-15 *Correcting the Faulty MAC Address*

```
CME_HQ(config-ephone)#no ephone 3
CME_HQ(config)#ephone 4
CME_HQ(config-ephone)#mac-address 000D.BDBE.F372
CME_HQ(config-ephone)#button 1:3
CME_HQ(config-ephone)#restart
```

Missing create-cnf file Command

A missing **create-cnf** command can be another reason why the phone does not register successfully with the Cisco CME router. As covered earlier, in the section "Understanding the Phone Bootup Sequence," you can see that the phone gets the Cisco CME router's IP address from the SEP*xxxxyyyyzzzz*.cnf.xml file and that this file is, in turn, created by the command create-cnf. Thus, if the command is not part of the configuration, the SEP*xxxxyyyyzzzz*.cnf.xml file is not created. Therefore, the phone cannot download it from the router. Actually, the file is created even if you don't issue the **create-cnf file** command, but the file is not populated. So technically, an empty SEP*xxxxyyyyzzzz*.cnf.xml file is in the system memory.

In addition to the SEP*xxxxyyyyzzzz*.cnf.xml file created by the **create-cnf file** command, this command creates the files necessary for the user locale and network locale. The user locale defines the language used by the phone on its display. The network locale defines the values for call progress tones for various geographic regions of the world. By default, the user locale and network locale are set to U.S. (United States).

The display on the phone is the most visible indication of a problem with the files created by the **create-cnf file** command: The phone's display switches between "Configuring IP" and "Configuring CM." If you scroll through the Network Configuration menu, you can see that the Call Manager field is not populated.

An exception to this display behavior is if the phone was registered to another Cisco CME system in the past. In this case, the phone still has its previous CME address populated in the Call Manager field, even if it cannot download a valid SEP*xxxxyyyyzzzz*.cnf.xml file from the current system. This happens because the phone remembers the last Cisco CME it was successfully registered with.

You can view the files created using **create-cnf file** by using the command **show telephony-service tftp-bindings**. Also, you can view the file contents by issuing the **more** command followed by the filename with a path to the location.

Example 16-16 shows the output of the **show telephony-service tftp-bindings** command for a configuration without the **create-cnf file** command. You can see that the output shown in Example 16-16 does not have the localization files. Also, the output of **more system:/its/** XMLDefault7960.cnf.xml returns nothing, which means that the file is empty.

Example 16-16 **show** *Output Without the* **create-cnf-file** *Command*

```
CME_HQ#show telephony-service tftp-bindings
tftp-server system:/its/SEPDEFAULT.cnf
tftp-server system:/its/SEPDEFAULT.cnf alias SEPDefault.cnf
tftp-server system:/its/XMLDefault7960.cnf.xml alias SEP000DBDBEF372.cnf.xml

CME_HQ#
CME_HQ#more system:/its/XMLDefault7960.cnf.xml
CME_HQ#
```

Example 16-17 shows the output of the **show telephony-service tftp-bindings** command, which indicates that all the necessary files are present on the system. Also, the file has all the necessary information required for the phone to register.

Example 16-17   **show** *Output with the* **create-cnf-file** *Command Present*

```
CME_HQ#show telephony-service tftp-bindings
tftp-server system:/its/SEPDEFAULT.cnf
tftp-server system:/its/SEPDEFAULT.cnf alias SEPDefault.cnf
tftp-server system:/its/XMLDefault7960.cnf.xml alias SEP000DBDBEF372.cnf.xml
tftp-server system:/its/XMLDefault.cnf.xml alias XMLDefault.cnf.xml
tftp-server system:/its/ATADefault.cnf.xml
tftp-server system:/its/united_states/7960-tones.xml alias United_States/
  7960-tones.xml
tftp-server system:/its/united_states/7960-font.xml alias English_United_States/
  7960-font.xml
tftp-server system:/its/united_states/7960-dictionary.xml alias
  English_United_States/7960-dictionary.xml
tftp-server system:/its/united_states/7960-kate.xml alias English_United_States/
  7960-kate.xml
tftp-server system:/its/united_states/Skinny-dictionary.xml alias
  English_United_States/Skinny-dictionary.xml

CME_HQ#more system:/its/XMLDefault7960.cnf.xml
<device>
<devicePool>
<callManagerGroup>
<members>
<member  priority="0">
<callManager>
<ports>
<ethernetPhonePort>2000</ethernetPhonePort>
</ports>
<processNodeName>10.1.1.1</processNodeName>
</callManager>
</member>
</members>
</callManagerGroup>
</devicePool>
<versionStamp>{Jan 01 2002 00:00:00}</versionStamp>
<loadInformation>P00303020214</loadInformation>
<userLocale>
<name>English_United_States</name>
<langCode>en</langCode>
</userLocale>
<networkLocale>United_States</networkLocale>
<idleTimeout>0</idleTimeout>
<authenticationURL></authenticationURL>
<directoryURL>http://10.1.1.1:80/localdirectory</directoryURL>
<idleURL></idleURL>
<informationURL></informationURL>
<messagesURL></messagesURL>
<proxyServerURL></proxyServerURL>
<servicesURL></servicesURL>
</device>
```

If you turn on **debug tftp events** on the Cisco CME router, you can see that the phone repeatedly tries to download the SEP*xxxxyyyyzzzz*.cnf.xml file via TFTP. Because the file is empty without **create-cnf file** configured, even though it downloads the file, the phone can't get the necessary Cisco CME IP address to register with, and it attempts to download the file again. This is shown in Example 16-18.

Example 16-18 *Output of* **debug tftp events** *Without the* **create-cnf file** *Command*

```
CME_HQ#debug tftp events
TFTP Event debugging is on
CME_HQ#
*Jul 23 11:05:04.399: TFTP: Looking for OS79XX.TXT
*Jul 23 11:05:04.399: TFTP: Looking for SEP000DBDBEF372.cnf.xml
*Jul 23 11:05:04.399: TFTP: Opened system:/its/XMLDefault7960.cnf.xml, fd 0, size
  0 for process 172
*Jul 23 11:05:04.399: TFTP: Finished system:/its/XMLDefault7960.cnf.xml, time
  00:00:00 for process 172
CME_HQ#
*Jul 23 11:05:07.219: TFTP: Looking for OS79XX.TXT
*Jul 23 11:05:07.219: TFTP: Looking for SEP000DBDBEF372.cnf.xml
*Jul 23 11:05:07.219: TFTP: Opened system:/its/XMLDefault7960.cnf.xml, fd 0, size
  0 for process 172
*Jul 23 11:05:07.219: TFTP: Finished system:/its/XMLDefault7960.cnf.xml, time
  00:00:00 for process 172
CME_HQ#
```

Upgrading IP Phone Firmware

The **load** command specifies the firmware for each type of phone supported on the system. It is important to distinguish between this load file and the SEP*xxxxyyyyzzzz*.cnf.xml file. The file referred to in the load command is the firmware load used by each type of IP phone, such as the Cisco 7940 or 7960. On the other hand, the SEP*xxxxyyyyzzzz*.cnf.xml file is a unique system-generated file for each phone configured on the system.

Factory-shipped IP phones have a default firmware load installed. The firmware load required for each release of Cisco CME is different. It is possible that your IP phones were shipped with firmware that is incompatible with the version of Cisco CME on your router. Refer to the Cisco.com documentation for the correct version of IP phone firmware for the version of Cisco CME you are using. (Go to the Software Center, choose Voice Software, Cisco CallManager Express, and the release of Cisco CME you are interested in, and then look for the document "Specifications for All Versions of Cisco CallManager Express.")

When the IP phone downloads the SEP*xxxxyyyyzzzz*.cnf.xml file from the router during the registration process, the phone compares the load mentioned in this file with the load already installed in it. If these differ, the phone tries to upgrade its firmware by downloading the new file from the TFTP server, which in this scenario is the Cisco CME router. Therefore, for this firmware upgrade operation to be successful, the new phone load mentioned in the Cisco CME configuration must be present on the TFTP server given in the DHCP configuration.

NOTE	The firmware change can be an upgrade or a downgrade, depending on the load installed on the phone. If you are upgrading to a signed load, you cannot change your phone load afterward to an unsigned phone load again. Similarly, if the phone already has a signed phone load installed, you cannot downgrade your phone load to an unsigned load; you have to remain on a signed load.

This section discusses upgrading the firmware mentioned in Example 16-8 to a new firmware load named P00303020214.bin. The sample configuration shown in Example 16-19 shows the relevant portions of the modified configuration.

Example 16-19 *Configuration for Upgrading the Phone Firmware*

```
CME_Router#show running-config
Building configuration...
!
ip dhcp pool Phone2
   host 10.0.0.10 255.0.0.0
   client-identifier 0007.8513.136c
   default-router 10.0.0.1
   option 150 ip 10.0.0.1
!
interface Ethernet0/0
 ip address 10.0.0.1 255.0.0.0
 half-duplex

Telephony-service
 ip source-address 10.0.0.1
 max-dn 10
 max-ephone 10
 load 7940-60 P00303020214.bin
 create cnf-files

CME_Router#show flash
P00303020214.bin
```

The output from the **show flash** command in Example 16-19 shows that the new firmware is available on the router flash memory. If the phone is reset, you expect the phone to upgrade its firmware to the new firmware mentioned in the configuration, but when doing this operation, you see the error message "File not found" on the phone display. With Cisco CME 3.0 and later versions, the phone is registered with the error message "Error verifying configuration." In this situation, even though the phone is registered, the correct feature operation is not guaranteed because of the error.

The problem giving rise to these errors is that even though the new firmware has been copied to the router's flash memory, it is still unavailable from the TFTP server. The command **tftp-server flash:load_name** must be configured (using configuration mode) on the router to make these flash-based files available to the TFTP server. This is a basic Cisco IOS command that is not specific to Cisco CME.

Upgrading Phone Loads to a Signed Load

With Cisco CME 3.1 and later, the Cisco 7960, 7940, and 7910 IP Phones support signed phone loads. The unsigned loads come with a .bin extension file, and the signed load carries an .sbn extension. A phone with an unsigned load always looks for a file with a .bin extension when it tries to download a phone load. This prevents the phone from upgrading from an unsigned phone load with a .bin extension to a signed phone load with an .sbn extension.

NOTE	A signed phone load allows the phone to support additional security features.

To get around this problem for every version of a signed load, two files are available: one with a .bin extension and another with an .sbn extension. The .bin extension file is actually the signed load (the .sbn) with a wrapper around it so that the phone reads it as a .bin file. To upgrade a phone from an unsigned load to a signed load, the Cisco CME router should have both .bin and .sbn files for the new load. The phone downloads the file with the .bin extension, but it actually gets the signed load.

This is necessary only if you are upgrading from an unsigned load to a signed load. If the phone is already using a signed load, it automatically looks for the file with the .sbn extension when it downloads a new load.

NOTE	After the phone installs a signed load, it can never be downgraded to an unsigned load again. It is possible to upgrade or downgrade to any other signed load, but not to an unsigned load.

Understanding SCCP and Call Flow Debugging

This section describes the SCCP and H.323 messages during call setup and debugging problems related to call setup. Understanding call flow is very useful in troubleshooting call control-related problems.

SCCP to SCCP Call

Figure 16-2 shows a sample exchange of messages between two SCCP clients (IP phones) during call setup. The messages are self-explanatory. You can view the SCCP call control messages by turning on the **debug ephone** detail command.

Figure 16-2 *SCCP to SCCP Call Setup Messages*

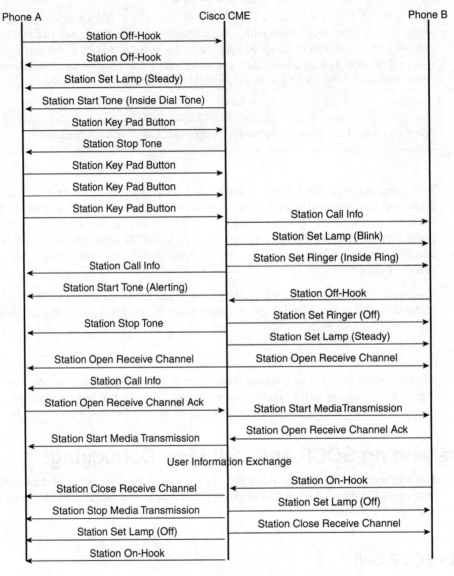

Phone A — Cisco CME — Phone B

- Station Off-Hook (Phone A → Cisco CME)
- Station Off-Hook (Cisco CME → Phone A)
- Station Set Lamp (Steady) (Cisco CME → Phone A)
- Station Start Tone (Inside Dial Tone) (Cisco CME → Phone A)
- Station Key Pad Button (Phone A → Cisco CME)
- Station Stop Tone (Cisco CME → Phone A)
- Station Key Pad Button (Phone A → Cisco CME)
- Station Key Pad Button (Phone A → Cisco CME)
- Station Key Pad Button (Phone A → Cisco CME)
- Station Call Info (Cisco CME → Phone B)
- Station Set Lamp (Blink) (Cisco CME → Phone B)
- Station Set Ringer (Inside Ring) (Cisco CME → Phone B)
- Station Call Info (Cisco CME → Phone A)
- Station Start Tone (Alerting) (Cisco CME → Phone A)
- Station Off-Hook (Phone B → Cisco CME)
- Station Stop Tone (Cisco CME → Phone A)
- Station Set Ringer (Off) (Cisco CME → Phone B)
- Station Set Lamp (Steady) (Cisco CME → Phone B)
- Station Open Receive Channel (Cisco CME → Phone A)
- Station Open Receive Channel (Cisco CME → Phone B)
- Station Call Info (Cisco CME → Phone A)
- Station Open Receive Channel Ack (Phone A → Cisco CME)
- Station Start MediaTransmission (Cisco CME → Phone B)
- Station Open Receive Channel Ack (Phone B → Cisco CME)
- Station Start Media Transmission (Cisco CME → Phone A)
- User Information Exchange
- Station On-Hook (Phone B → Cisco CME)
- Station Close Receive Channel (Cisco CME → Phone A)
- Station Set Lamp (Off) (Cisco CME → Phone B)
- Station Stop Media Transmission (Cisco CME → Phone A)
- Station Close Receive Channel (Cisco CME → Phone B)
- Station Set Lamp (Off) (Cisco CME → Phone A)
- Station On-Hook (Cisco CME → Phone A)

NOTE	The output of **debug ephone detail** is quite verbose and shouldn't be turned on for a Cisco CME in a production environment with large call volumes. Doing so can degrade the router's performance considerably. You can turn on the debugs for specific phones by adding the **mac-address** option to the debug, thus limiting the debug output.

Examples 16-20 to 16-23 show the output of **debug ephone detail** for a call between ephone 1 and ephone 2 connected to a Cisco CME at various states. The directory numbers of ephone 1 and ephone 2 are 1001 and 1002, respectively. The call control messages are highlighted for ease of reading.

Example 16-20 shows ephone 1 going off-hook and dialing the extension number of ephone 2. When the phone goes off-hook, the display on the phone changes to reflect the phone's current status. Also, the Cisco CME router instructs the phone to play dial tone when the phone goes off-hook. Each number dialed by the phone is shown as a KeypadButtonMessage followed by the number dialed. When the first digit is dialed, Cisco CME signals the phone to stop playing dial tone.

Example 16-20 *Ephone 1 Dialing Ephone 2*

```
CME_HQ#debug ephone detail
*Jun  6 15:25:18.623: ephone-1[2]:OFFHOOK
*Jun  6 15:25:18.623: SkinnyGetCallState for DN 1 chan 1 IDLE
*Jun  6 15:25:18.623: called DN -1 chan 1, calling DN -1 chan 1 phone -1 s2s:0
*Jun  6 15:25:18.623: ephone-1[2]:SIEZE on activeLine 0 activeChan 1
*Jun  6 15:25:18.623: SkinnyGetCallState for DN 1 chan 1 IDLE
*Jun  6 15:25:18.623: called DN -1 chan 1, calling DN -1 chan 1 phone -1 s2s:0
*Jun  6 15:25:18.623: ephone-1[2]:Sieze auto select line 1 chan 1
*Jun  6 15:25:18.623: ephone-1[2]:UpdateCallState DN 1 chan 1 state 2 calleddn -1
  chan 1
*Jun  6 15:25:18.623: ephone-1[2]:Binding ephone-1 to DN 1 chan 1 s2s:0
*Jun  6 15:25:18.623: Assign Call Ref 3 to DN 1 chan 1
*Jun  6 15:25:18.623: Skinny Call State change for DN 1 chan 1 SIEZE from IDLE
*Jun  6 15:25:18.623: ephone-(1) DN 1 chan 1 calledDn -1 chan 1 callingDn -1 chan
  1 0.0.0.0 port=0
*Jun  6 15:25:18.623: SkinnyUpdateCstate DN 1 chan 1 state 1
*Jun  6 15:25:18.623: SkinnyGetCallState for DN 1 chan 1 SIEZE
*Jun
*Jun  6 15:25:18.623: called DN -1 chan 1, calling DN -1 chan 1 phone 1 s2s:0
*Jun  6 15:25:18.623: ephone-1[2][SEP000DBDBEF372]:SkinnyUpdateCState line 1 chan
  1 DN 1
*Jun  6 15:25:18.623: ephone-1[2]:SetCallState line 1 DN 1 chan 1 ref 3 TsOffHook
*Jun  6 15:25:18.623: ephone-1[2]:ClearCallPrompt line 1 ref 3
*Jun  6 15:25:18.623: ephone-1[2]:SelectPhoneSoftKeys set 4 mask FFFF for line 1
  ref 3
*Jun  6 15:25:18.623: SkinnyGetCallState for DN 1 chan 1 SIEZE
*Jun  6 15:25:18.623: called DN -1 chan 1, calling DN -1 chan 1 phone 1 s2s:0
*Jun  6 15:25:18.623: ephone-1[2]:SetLineLamp 1 to ON
*Jun  6 15:25:18.623: SkinnyGetCallState for DN 1 chan 1 SIEZE
*Jun  6 15:25:18.623: called DN -1 chan 1, calling DN -1 chan 1 phone 1 s2s:0
```

continues

Example 16-20 *Ephone 1 Dialing Ephone 2 (Continued)*

```
*Jun  6 15:25:18.623: ephone-1[2]:Check Plar Number
*Jun  6 15:25:18.627: SetDnCodec DN 1 chan 1 codec 4:G711Ulaw64k  vad 250 size 160
*Jun  6 15:25:18.627: DN 1 chan 1 Voice_Mode
*Jun  6 15:25:18.627: SkinnyGetCallState for DN 1 chan 1 SIEZE
*Jun  6 15:25:18.627: called DN -1 chan 1, calling DN -1 chan 1 phone 1 s2s:0
*Jun  6 15:25:18.627: dn_tone_control DN=1 chan 1 tonetype=33:DtInsideDialTone
  onoff=1 pid=156
!output omitted for brevity
*Jun  6 15:25:18.627: Skinny StartTone 33 sent on  ephone socket [2]
  DtInsideDialTone
*Jun  6 15:25:19.635: ephone-1[2]:KeypadButtonMessage 1
!output omitted for brevity
*Jun  6 15:25:19.635: ephone-1[2]:Store ReDial digit: 1
*Jun  6 15:25:19.635: ephone-1[2]:SkinnyTryCall to 1 instance 1 start at 0
  secondary 0

*Jun  6 15:25:19.635: dn_tone_control DN=1 chan 1 tonetype=0:DtSilence onoff=0
  pid=156
!output omitted for brevity
*Jun  6 15:25:20.391: ephone-1[2]:KeypadButtonMessage 0
!output omitted for brevity
*Jun  6 15:25:20.391: ephone-1[2]:Store ReDial digit: 10
*Jun  6 15:25:20.391: ephone-1[2]:SkinnyTryCall to 10 instance 1 start at 0
  secondary 0
*Jun  6 15:25:20.643: ephone-1[2]:KeypadButtonMessage 0
!output omitted for brevity
*Jun  6 15:25:20.643: ephone-1[2]:Store ReDial digit: 100
*Jun  6 15:25:20.643: ephone-1[2]:SkinnyTryCall to 100 instance 1 start at 0
  secondary 0
*Jun  6 15:25:20.895: ephone-1[2]:KeypadButtonMessage 2
!output omitted for brevity
*Jun  6 15:25:20.895: ephone-1[2]:Store ReDial digit: 1002
```

Example 16-21 shows the Cisco CME router trying to set up a call to the number dialed (1002). As soon as the matching destination is found, the calling phone (1001) is updated with the destination's caller ID details. The called phone (1002) is set to ringing mode and is also updated with the caller ID of the calling phone.

Example 16-21 *Cisco CME Setting Up a Call to Ephone 2*

```
CME_HQ#debug ephone detail
*Jun  6 15:25:20.895: ephone-1[2]:SkinnyTryCall to 1002 instance 1 start at 0
  secondary 0
SkinnyTryCall to 1002 instance 1 match DN 2
!output omitted for brevity
*Jun  6 15:25:20.895: Skinny Call State change for DN 1 chan 1 ALERTING from SIEZE
!output omitted for brevity
*Jun  6 15:25:20.895: ephone-1[2]:SetCallState line 1 DN 1 chan 1 ref 3 TsRingOut
*Jun  6 15:25:20.895: ephone-1[2]:DialedNumber: 1002 DN 1 line 1 ref 3
*Jun  6 15:25:20.895: ephone-1[2][SEP000DBDBEF372]:CallPrompt line 1 ref 3: Ring
  Out
*Jun  6 15:25:20.895: ephone-1[2]:SelectPhoneSoftKeys set 8 mask FFFF for line 1
```

Example 16-21   *Cisco CME Setting Up a Call to Ephone 2 (Continued)*

```
  ref 3
*Jun  6 15:25:20.895: SkinnyGetCallState for DN 1 chan 1 ALERTING
*Jun  6 15:25:20.895: called DN 2 chan 1, calling DN -1 chan 1 phone 1 s2s:0
*Jun  6 15:25:20.895: ephone-1[2]:SetLineLamp 1 to ON
*Jun  6 15:25:20.895: SetCallInfo calling dn 1 chan 1 dn 1 chan 1
calling [1001] called [1002] calling name Alex Anders called name Bill Bryce
*Jun  6 15:25:20.895: SetCallInfo DN 1 chan 1 is not Skinny-to-Skinny
*Jun  6 15:25:20.895: SkinnyGetCallState for DN 1 chan 1 ALERTING
*Jun  6 15:25:20.895: called DN 2 chan 1, calling DN -1 chan 1 phone 1 s2s:0
*Jun  6 15:25:20.895: ephone-1[2]:DisplayCallInfo outgoing call
*Jun  6 15:25:20.895: ephone-1[2]:SkinnyTryCall to 1002 instance 1 start at 0
  secondary 0
SkinnyTryCall to 1002 instance 1 match DN 2
*Jun  6 15:25:20.895: ephone-1[2]:Call Info DN 1 line 1 ref 3 called 1002 calling
  1001 origcalled 1002 calltype 2
*Jun  6 15:25:20.895: ephone-1[2]:Call Info for chan 1
*Jun  6 15:25:20.895: ephone-1[2]:Original Called Name Bill Bryce
*Jun  6 15:25:20.895: ephone-1[2]: Alex Anders calling
*Jun  6 15:25:20.895: ephone-1[2]: Bill Bryce
*Jun  6 15:25:20.899: SkinnyUpdateDnState by EFXS_PROCEEDING
  for DN 1 chan 1 to state ALERTING
!output omitted for brevity
*Jun  6 15:25:20.899: SetCallInfo calling dn 1 chan 1 dn 2 chan 1
calling [1001] called [1002] calling name Alex Anders
!output omitted for brevity
*Jun  6 15:25:20.899: SkinnyUpdateDnState by EFXS_RING_GENERATE
  for DN 2 chan 1 to state RINGING
!output omitted for brevity
*Jun  6 15:25:20.903: DN 2 chan 1 ephone-2 state set to 4
*Jun  6 15:25:20.903: ephone-2[1]:SetCallState line 1 DN 2 chan 1 ref 4 TsRingIn
*Jun  6 15:25:20.903: ephone-2[1][SEP000B5FF93258]:CallPrompt line 1 ref 4: : 1001
*Jun  6 15:25:20.903: ephone-2[1]:SelectPhoneSoftKeys set 3 mask FFFF for line 1
  ref 4
*Jun  6 15:25:20.903: SkinnyGetCallState for DN 2 chan 1 RINGING
*Jun  6 15:25:20.903: called DN -1 chan 1, calling DN 1 chan 1 phone -1 incoming
  s2s:1
*Jun  6 15:25:20.903: ephone-2[1]:DisplayCallInfo incoming call
*Jun  6 15:25:20.903: ephone-2[1]:SkinnyTryCall to 1002 instance 1 start at 0
  secondary 0
SkinnyTryCall to 1002 instance 1 match DN 2
*Jun  6 15:25:20.903: ephone-2[1]:Call Info DN 2 line 1 ref 4 called 1002 calling
  1001 origcalled 1002 calltype 1
*Jun  6 15:25:20.903: ephone-2[1]:Call Info for chan 1
*Jun  6 15:25:20.903: ephone-2[1]:Original Called Name Bill Bryce
*Jun  6 15:25:20.903: ephone-2[1]: Alex Anders calling
*Jun  6 15:25:20.903: ephone-2[1]: Bill Bryce
*Jun  6 15:25:20.903: ephone-2[1]:Internal RINGING
*Jun  6 15:25:20.903: ephone-2[1]:Ringer Inside Ring On
*Jun  6 15:25:20.903: SkinnyGetCallState for DN 2 chan 1 RINGING
*Jun  6 15:25:20.903: called DN -1 chan 1, calling DN 1 chan 1 phone -1 incoming
  s2s:1
*Jun  6 15:25:20.903: ephone-2[1]:SetLineLamp 1 to BLINK
```

Example 16-22 shows phone 2 answering the call. When it does so, the Cisco CME router sends an "Open Receive Channel" message to both the phones, specifying the codec and packet size. The phones acknowledge this message by sending an "Open Receive Channel Ack" message specifying the port number to start the media transmission. You can see that ephone 1 and ephone 2 send the "Open Receive Channel Ack" message specifying the port numbers 30148 and 29062, respectively. As soon as Cisco CME knows the port numbers for both the phones, a "StartMedia" message is sent to the phones, specifying the port numbers of the other phones to send media to. At this point, the phones start sending media to each other.

Example 16-22 *Establishing Media*

```
CME_HQ#debug ephone detail
*Jun  6 15:25:23.423: ephone-2[1]:OFFHOOK
*Jun  6 15:25:23.423: ephone-2[1]:Disable Ringer line 1
*Jun  6 15:25:23.423: ephone-2[1]:STOP RINGING
*Jun  6 15:25:23.423: ephone-2[1]:Ringer Off
*Jun  6 15:25:23.423: SkinnyGetCallState for DN 2 chan 1 RINGING
*Jun  6 15:25:23.423: called DN -1 chan 1, calling DN 1 chan 1 phone -1 incoming
  s2s:1
*Jun  6 15:25:23.423: ephone-2[1][SEP000B5FF93258]:Auto select answer line 1 dn -1
  chan 1
*Jun  6 15:25:23.423: ephone-2[1]:ANSWER call
*Jun  6 15:25:23.423: Calling DN 1 chan 1 from Called DN 2 chan 1 explicit
*Jun  6 15:25:23.423: SkinnyGetCallState for DN 1 chan 1 ALERTING
*Jun  6 15:25:23.423: called DN 2 chan 1, calling DN -1 chan 1 phone 1 s2s:0
*Jun  6 15:25:23.423: ephone-1[2][SEP000DBDBEF372]:Calling ephone-1 is bound to
  Calling DN 1 chan 1
*Jun  6 15:25:23.423: ephone-2[1][SEP000B5FF93258]:Answer Incoming call from
  ephone-(1) DN 1 chan 1
!output omitted for brevity
*Jun  6 15:25:23.423: Skinny Call State change for DN 2 chan 1 CONNECTED from RINGING
!output omitted for brevity
*Jun  6 15:25:23.423: ephone-2[1]:SelectPhoneSoftKeys set 1 mask FFDF for line 1
  ref 4
*Jun  6 15:25:23.423: SkinnyGetCallState for DN 2 chan 1 CONNECTED
*Jun  6 15:25:23.423: called DN -1 chan 1, calling DN 1 chan 1 phone 2 incoming
  s2s:1
*Jun  6 15:25:23.423: ephone-2[1]:SetLineLamp 1 to ON
!output omitted for brevity
*Jun  6 15:25:23.423: ephone-1[2]:SelectPhoneSoftKeys set 1 mask FFDF for line 1
  ref 3
!output omitted for brevity
*Jun  6 15:25:23.427: ephone-2[1]:SkinnyTryCall to 1002 instance 1 start at 0
  secondary 0
SkinnyTryCall to 1002 instance 1 match DN 2
*Jun  6 15:25:23.427: ephone-2[1]:Call Info DN 2 line 1 ref 4 called 1002 calling
  1001 origcalled 1002 calltype 1
*Jun  6 15:25:23.427: ephone-2[1]:Call Info for chan 1
*Jun  6 15:25:23.427: ephone-2[1]:Original Called Name Bill Bryce
*Jun  6 15:25:23.427: ephone-2[1]: Alex Anders calling
*Jun  6 15:25:23.427: ephone-2[1]: Bill Bryce
*Jun  6 15:25:23.427: ephone-2[1]:Discard duplicate DisplayCallInfo for ref 4
```

Example 16-22 *Establishing Media (Continued)*

```
*Jun  6 15:25:23.427: ephone-1[2]:OpenReceive DN 1 chan 1 codec 4:G711Ulaw64k
  duration 20 ms bytes 160
*Jun  6 15:25:23.427: ephone-2[1]:OpenReceive DN 2 chan 1 codec 4:G711Ulaw64k
  duration 20 ms bytes 160
!output omitted for brevity
*Jun  6 15:25:23.431: ephone-1[2]:Tone Off ignored - already sent
*Jun  6 15:25:23.431: dn_support_g729 true DN 1 chan 1 ephone-1
*Jun  6 15:25:23.431: dn_support_g723 false DN 1 chan 1 ephone-1
*Jun  6 15:25:23.431: dn_support_g729 true DN 2 chan 1 ephone-2
*Jun  6 15:25:23.431: dn_support_g723 false DN 2 chan 1 ephone-2
*Jun  6 15:25:23.431: DN 1 chan 1 End Voice_Mode
*Jun  6 15:25:23.431: SetDnCodec clear_defer media start
*Jun  6 15:25:23.431: SetDnCodec DN 1 chan 1 codec 4:G711Ulaw64k  vad 0 size 160
*Jun  6 15:25:23.431: Skinny clear media defer_start
*Jun  6 15:25:23.431: DN 1 chan 1 Voice_Mode
*Jun  6 15:25:23.431: SkinnyGetCallState for DN 1 chan 1 CONNECTED
*Jun  6 15:25:23.431: called DN 2 chan 1, calling DN -1 chan 1 phone 1 s2s:1
*Jun  6 15:25:23.431: SkinnyUpdateDnState by MSG_RX_VOICE_MODE
  for DN 1 chan 1 to state CALL_START
!output omitted for brevity
*Jun  6 15:25:23.431: ephone-1[2]:Call Start ignored - mediaActive set
*Jun  6 15:25:23.431: SkinnyUpdateDnState by EFXS_OPEN_VOICE_PATH
  for DN 1 chan 1 to state CALL_START
*Jun  6 15:25:23.431: ephone-1[2]:UpdateCallState DN 1 chan 1 state 12 calleddn 2
  chan 1
*Jun  6 15:25:23.431: ephone-1[2]:Binding ephone-1 to DN 1 chan 1 s2s:1
*Jun  6 15:25:23.431: Binding calledDn 2 chan 1 to DN 1 chan 1
*Jun  6 15:25:23.431: ephone-1[2]:Call Start ignored - mediaActive set
*Jun  6 15:25:23.431: SetDnCodec DN 2 chan 1 codec 4:G711Ulaw64k  vad 0 size 160
*Jun  6 15:25:23.431: DN 2 chan 1 Voice_Mode
*Jun  6 15:25:23.431: SkinnyGetCallState for DN 2 chan 1 CONNECTED
*Jun  6 15:25:23.431: called DN -1 chan 1, calling DN 1 chan 1 phone 2 incoming
  s2s:1
*Jun  6 15:25:23.431: SkinnyUpdateDnState by MSG_RX_VOICE_MODE
  for DN 2 chan 1 to state CALL_START
*Jun  6 15:25:23.431: ephone-2[1]:UpdateCallState DN 2 chan 1 state 12 calleddn -1
  chan 1
*Jun  6 15:25:23.431: ephone-2[1]:Binding ephone-2 to DN 2 chan 1 s2s:1
*Jun  6 15:25:23.431: ephone-2[1]:Call Start ignored - mediaActive set
*Jun  6 15:25:23.431: SkinnyUpdateDnState by EFXS_OPEN_VOICE_PATH
  for DN 2 chan 1 to state CALL_START
*Jun  6 15:25:23.431: ephone-2[1]:UpdateCallState DN 2 chan 1 state 12 calleddn -1
  chan 1
*Jun  6 15:25:23.431: ephone-2[1]:Binding ephone-2 to DN 2 chan 1 s2s:1
*Jun  6 15:25:23.431: ephone-2[1]:Call Start ignored - mediaActive set
*Jun  6 15:25:23.435: SkinnyGetCallState for DN 1 chan 1 CONNECTED
*Jun  6 15:25:23.435: called DN 2 chan 1, calling DN -1 chan 1 phone 1 s2s:1
*Jun  6 15:25:23.435: SkinnyGetCallState for DN 1 chan 1 CONNECTED
*Jun  6 15:25:23.435: called DN 2 chan 1, calling DN -1 chan 1 phone 1 s2s:1
*Jun  6 15:25:23.435: dn_callerid_update DN 1 number= 1002 name= Bill Bryce in
  state CONNECTED
```

continues

Example 16-22 *Establishing Media (Continued)*

```
*Jun  6 15:25:23.435: dn_callerid_update (outgoing) DN 1 info updated to
*Jun  6 15:25:23.435: calling= 1001 called= 1002 origCalled=
*Jun  6 15:25:23.435: callingName= Alex Anders, calledName= Bill Bryce,
  redirectedTo =
*Jun  6 15:25:23.435: ephone-1[2][SEP000DBDBEF372]:refreshDisplayLine for line 1
  DN 1 chan 1
*Jun  6 15:25:23.435: SkinnyGetCallState for DN 2 chan 1 CONNECTED
*Jun  6 15:25:23.435: called DN -1 chan 1, calling DN 1 chan 1 phone 2 incoming
  s2s:1
*Jun  6 15:25:23.435: dn_callerid_update DN 2 number= 6502811001 name= Alex Anders
  in state CONNECTED
*Jun  6 15:25:23.435: dn_callerid_update (incoming) DN 2 info updated to
*Jun  6 15:25:23.435: calling= 1001 called= 1002 origCalled=
*Jun  6 15:25:23.435: callingName= Alex Anders, calledName= , redirectedTo =
*Jun  6 15:25:23.435: ephone-2[1][SEP000B5FF93258]:refreshDisplayLine for line 1
  DN 2 chan 1
*Jun  6 15:25:23.435: ephone-2[1]:OpenReceiveChannelAck:IP 10.1.1.102, port=30148,
  dn_index=2, dn=2, chan=1
*Jun  6 15:25:23.435: Calling DN 1 chan 1 from Called DN 2 chan 1 explicit
*Jun  6 15:25:23.435: ephone-1[2][SEP000DBDBEF372]:Calling ephone-1 is bound to
  Calling DN 1 chan 1
*Jun  6 15:25:23.435: ephone-2[1]:Incoming called DN 2 chan 1 Far-ephone-1 calling
  DN 1 chan 1
*Jun  6 15:25:23.435: SkinnyGetCallState for DN 2 chan 1 CONNECTED
*Jun  6 15:25:23.435: called DN -1 chan 1, calling DN 1 chan 1 phone 2 incoming
  s2s:1
*Jun  6 15:25:23.435: ephone-2[1][SEP000B5FF93258]:s2s=1 DN:2 chan 1
*Jun  6 15:25:23.435: SkinnyGetCallState for DN 1 chan 1 CONNECTED
*Jun  6 15:25:23.435: called DN 2 chan 1, calling DN -1 chan 1 phone 1 s2s:1
*Jun  6 15:25:23.435: ephone-1[2]:StartMedia 10.1.1.102 port=30148
*Jun  6 15:25:23.435: DN 1 chan 1 codec 4:G711Ulaw64k duration 20 ms bytes 160
*Jun  6 15:25:23.687: ephone-1[2]:OpenReceiveChannelAck:IP 10.1.1.101, port=29062,
  dn_index=1, dn=1, chan=1
*Jun  6 15:25:23.687: ephone-1[2]:Outgoing calling DN 1 chan 1 Far-ephone-2 called
  DN 2 chan 1
*Jun  6 15:25:23.687: SkinnyGetCallState for DN 1 chan 1 CONNECTED
*Jun  6 15:25:23.687: called DN 2 chan 1, calling DN -1 chan 1 phone 1 s2s:1
*Jun  6 15:25:23.687: ephone-1[2][SEP000DBDBEF372]:s2s=1 DN:1 chan 1
*Jun  6 15:25:23.687: SkinnyGetCallState for DN 2 chan 1 CONNECTED
*Jun  6 15:25:23.687: called DN -1 chan 1, calling DN 1 chan 1 phone 2 incoming
  s2s:1
*Jun  6 15:25:23.687: ephone-2[1]:StartMedia 10.1.1.101 port=29062
*Jun  6 15:25:23.687: DN 1 chan 1 codec 4:G711Ulaw64k duration 20 ms bytes 160
*Jun  6 15:25:23.939: ephone-1[2]:Refresh Display for line 1 chan 1
*Jun  6 15:25:23.939: SkinnyGetCallState for DN 1 chan 1 CONNECTED
*Jun  6 15:25:23.939: called DN 2 chan 1, calling DN -1 chan 1 phone 1 s2s:1
*Jun  6 15:25:23.939: ephone-1[2]:DisplayCallInfo outgoing call
*Jun  6 15:25:23.939: ephone-1[2]:SkinnyTryCall to 1002 instance 1 start at 0
  secondary 0
SkinnyTryCall to 1002 instance 1 match DN 2
*Jun  6 15:25:23.939: ephone-1[2]:Call Info DN 1 line 1 ref 3 called 1002 calling
```

Example 16-22   *Establishing Media (Continued)*

```
   1001 origcalled 1002 calltype 2
*Jun  6 15:25:23.939: ephone-1[2]:Call Info for chan 1
*Jun  6 15:25:23.939: ephone-1[2]:Original Called Name Bill Bryce
*Jun  6 15:25:23.939: ephone-1[2]: Alex Anders calling
*Jun  6 15:25:23.939: ephone-1[2]: Bill Bryce
*Jun  6 15:25:23.939: ephone-2[1]:Refresh Display for line 1 chan 1
*Jun  6 15:25:23.939: SkinnyGetCallState for DN 2 chan 1 CONNECTED
*Jun  6 15:25:23.939: called DN -1 chan 1, calling DN 1 chan 1 phone 2 incoming
  s2s:1
*Jun  6 15:25:23.939: ephone-2[1]:DisplayCallInfo incoming call
*Jun  6 15:25:23.939: ephone-2[1]:SkinnyTryCall to 1002 instance 1 start at 0
  secondary 0
SkinnyTryCall to 1002 instance 1 match DN 2
*Jun  6 15:25:23.939: ephone-2[1]:Call Info DN 2 line 1 ref 4 called 1002 calling
  1001 origcalled 1002 calltype 1
*Jun  6 15:25:23.939: ephone-2[1]:Call Info for chan 1
*Jun  6 15:25:23.939: ephone-2[1]:Original Called Name Bill Bryce
*Jun  6 15:25:23.939: ephone-2[1]: Alex Anders calling
*Jun  6 15:25:23.939: ephone-2[1]: Bill Bryce
```

Example 16-23 shows the call clearing. Phone 2 disconnects the call by going on-hook. Cisco CME sends the other phone a "Close Receive" message followed by a "Stop Media" message to both the phones. This tears down the media path between the two phones. Also, an on-hook message is sent to phone 1.

Example 16-23   *Call Clearing*

```
CME_HQ#debug ephone detail
*Jun  6 15:25:29.231: ephone-2[1]:ONHOOK (from phone msgID=7)
!output omitted for brevity
*Jun  6 15:25:29.231: called DN 2 chan 1, calling DN -1 chan 1 phone 1 s2s:1
*Jun  6 15:25:29.231: ephone-1[2]:CloseReceive
*Jun  6 15:25:29.231: ephone-1[2]:StopMedia
*Jun  6 15:25:29.231: ephone-2[1]:call clean up this DN 2 chan 1 was called by
  other DN 1 chan 1
*Jun  6 15:25:29.231: this ephone-2 other ephone-(1) other DN state CONNECTED
*Jun  6 15:25:29.231: ephone-2[1]:CloseReceive
*Jun  6 15:25:29.231: ephone-2[1]:StopMedia
*Jun  6 15:25:29.231: UpdateCallState DN 2 chan 1 state 0 phone-ref -1 calleddn
  -1 calleddn_chan 1
*Jun  6 15:25:29.231: DN 2 chan 1 End Voice_Mode
*Jun  6 15:25:29.231: Reset called DN binding for DN 1 (was 2)
*Jun  6 15:25:29.231: SetCallInfo calling dn -1 chan 1 dn 2 chan 1
calling [] called []
!output omitted for brevity
*Jun  6 15:25:29.231: ephone-2[1]:SelectPhoneSoftKeys set 0 mask FFBE for line 1
  ref 4
*Jun  6 15:25:29.231: SkinnyGetCallState for DN 2 chan 1 IDLE
*Jun  6 15:25:29.231: called DN -1 chan 1, calling DN -1 chan 1 phone -1 s2s:0
*Jun  6 15:25:29.231: ephone-2[1]:Clean Up Speakerphone state
*Jun  6 15:25:29.231: ephone-2[1]:SpeakerPhoneOnHook
```

continues

Example 16-23 *Call Clearing (Continued)*

```
*Jun  6 15:25:29.231: ephone-2[1]:Clean up activeline 1
*Jun  6 15:25:29.231: ephone-2[1]:is_auto_local 0 for DN -1
*Jun  6 15:25:29.231: ephone-2[1]:Tone Off ignored - already sent
*Jun  6 15:25:29.235: SkinnyGetCallState for DN 2 chan 1 IDLE
*Jun  6 15:25:29.235: called DN -1 chan 1, calling DN -1 chan 1 phone -1 s2s:0
*Jun  6 15:25:29.235: ephone-2[1]:SetLineLamp 1 to OFF
!output omitted for brevity
*Jun  6 15:25:29.235: ephone-1[2]:ClearCallPrompt line 1 ref 3
*Jun  6 15:25:29.235: ephone-1[2]:SelectPhoneSoftKeys set 0 mask FFBF for line 1
  ref 3
*Jun  6 15:25:29.235: SkinnyGetCallState for DN 1 chan 1 IDLE
*Jun  6 15:25:29.235: called DN -1 chan 1, calling DN -1 chan 1 phone -1 s2s:0
*Jun  6 15:25:29.235: ephone-1[2]:Clean Up Speakerphone state
*Jun  6 15:25:29.235: ephone-1[2]:SpeakerPhoneOnHook
*Jun  6 15:25:29.235: ephone-1[2]:Clean up activeline 1
*Jun  6 15:25:29.235: ephone-1[2]:is_auto_local 0 for DN -1
*Jun  6 15:25:29.235: ephone-1[2]:Tone Off ignored - already sent
*Jun  6 15:25:29.235: ephone-1[2]:Clean Up phone offhook state
*Jun  6 15:25:29.235: SkinnyGetCallState for DN 1 chan 1 IDLE
*Jun  6 15:25:29.235: called DN -1 chan 1, calling DN -1 chan 1 phone -1 s2s:0
*Jun  6 15:25:29.235: ephone-1[2]:SetLineLamp 1 to OFF
*Jun  6 15:25:29.235: UnBinding ephone-1 from DN 1 chan 1
*Jun  6 15:25:29.235: ephone-1[2]:SkinnyArmPhoneCallbacks scan 6 lines
*Jun  6 15:25:29.235: ephone-1[2]:SkinnyArmPhoneCallbacks for 1 targets
*Jun  6 15:25:29.235: ephone-1[2][SEP000DBDBEF372]:CallPrompt line 0 ref 0: Cisco
  CME Head Quarters
*Jun  6 15:25:29.235: ephone-1[2]:SkinnyCheckPendingCallBackPhone scan 6 lines
*Jun  6 15:25:29.235: ephone-2[1]:Far-end cleanup skiping ephone-1 DN 1 chan 1
  non-active line 0
*Jun  6 15:25:29.239: SkinnyGetCallState for DN 2 chan 1 IDLE
*Jun  6 15:25:29.239: called DN -1 chan 1, calling DN -1 chan 1 phone -1 s2s:0
*Jun  6 15:25:29.239: ephone-2[1]:SpeakerPhoneOnHook
*Jun  6 15:25:29.239: ephone-2[1]:ClearCallPrompt line 0 ref 0
*Jun  6 15:25:29.239: ephone-2[1]:SelectPhoneSoftKeys set 0 mask FFBE for line 0 ref 0
*Jun  6 15:25:29.239: ephone-2[1]:SkinnyArmPhoneCallbacks scan 2 lines
*Jun  6 15:25:29.239: ephone-2[1]:SkinnyArmPhoneCallbacks for 1 targets
*Jun  6 15:25:29.239: ephone-2[1][SEP000B5FF93258]:CallPrompt line 0 ref 0: Cisco
  CME Head Quarters
*Jun  6 15:25:29.239: ephone-2[1]:SkinnyCheckPendingCallBackPhone scan 2 lines
```

The highlighted output shown in Examples 16-20 to 16-23 points out the key messages to look for when troubleshooting call flow issues. For example, if the problem is no dial tone when the phone goes off-hook, you should look for the "StartTone" message (shown in Example 16-20) that the Cisco CME router sends to the phone. If the problem is that the call does not connect, you should look for the "OpenReceive" and "StartMedia" message exchanges (shown in Example 16-22) between the endpoints. The output of the debugs can be quite verbose. Looking for the key messages can help you identify the problem easier.

SCCP to H.323 Call

Figure 16-3 shows a sample exchange of messages between an H.323 endpoint and an SCCP endpoint during call setup and teardown. The exchange is very similar to the call setup discussed in the previous section except for the signaling messages specific to the H.323 protocol. You can view the call setup and teardown messages by turning on the **debug h225 asn1** and **debug h245 asn1** commands. The output of these debug commands shows the contents of the incoming and outgoing H.225 and H.245 messages.

Figure 16-3   *H.323 to SCCP Call Setup Messages*

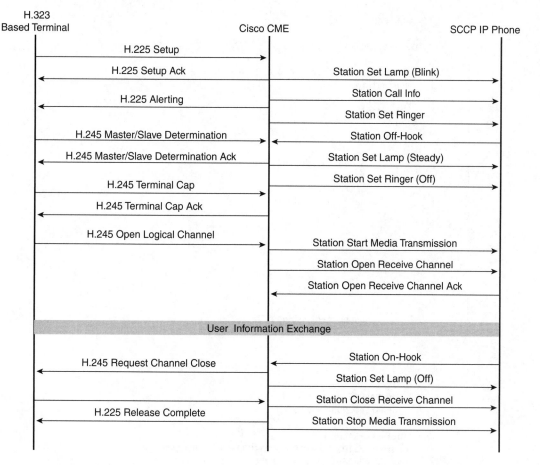

NOTE   The output of **debug** commands can be quite verbose and shouldn't be turned on in Cisco CME in a production environment with large call volumes. Doing so can degrade the router's performance considerably.

Examples 16-24 and 16-25 show sample output of these **debug** messages. Example 16-24 shows the incoming H.225 setup messages. Relevant portions of the messages are highlighted to help you understand how to read them. The first line of the debug shows that it is an incoming H.225 message. Also, you can see that it is a setup message, which contains various other parameters, such as IP address and port number. These values are represented in hexadecimal.

Example 16-24 *Debug Showing an H.225 Setup Message*

```
CME_HQ#debug h225 asn1
*Jul 27 15:20:06.099: H225.0 INCOMING PDU ::=
value H323_UserInformation ::=
    {
        h323-uu-pdu
        {
            h323-message-body setup :
            {
              protocolIdentifier { 0 0 8 2250 0 4 }
              sourceInfo
              {
                vendor
                {
                  vendor
                  {
                    t35CountryCode 181

                    t35Extension 0
                    manufacturerCode 18
                  }
                }
                gateway
                {
                  protocol
                  {
                    voice :
                    {
                      supportedPrefixes
                      {
                      }
                    }
                  }
                }
              }
              mc FALSE
              undefinedNode FALSE
            }
            activeMC FALSE
            conferenceID 'D07ADDD6569911D68053CA040EE6AAC4'H
            conferenceGoal create : NULL
            callType pointToPoint : NULL
            sourceCallSignalAddress ipAddress :
            {
              ip '0A010201'H
              port 11002
            }
            callIdentifier
```

Example 16-24 *Debug Showing an H.225 Setup Message (Continued)*

```
                         {
                            guid 'D07ADDD6569911D68055CA040EE6AAC4'H
                         }
                         fastStart
                         {
                            '0000000D4001800B050001000A0102014B2B80'H,
                            '400000060401004D40018012150001000A010201...'H
                         }
                         mediaWaitForConnect FALSE
                         canOverlapSend FALSE
                         multipleCalls TRUE
                         maintainConnection TRUE
                         symmetricOperationRequired NULL
                      }
                      h245Tunneling TRUE
                      nonStandardControl
                      {

                         {
                            nonStandardIdentifier h221NonStandard :
                            {
                               t35CountryCode 181
                               t35Extension 0
                               manufacturerCode 18
                            }
                            data 'E0011200011C3B1C399E0100036774640000002E...'H
                         }
                      }
                      tunnelledSignallingMessage
                      {
                         tunnelledProtocolID
                         {
                            id tunnelledProtocolAlternateID :
                            {
                               protocolType "gtd"
                            }
                         }
                         messageContent
                         {
                            '49414D2C0D0A4743492C64303761646464363536...'H
                         }
                      }
                   }
                }
             }

*Jul 27 15:20:06.107: H225 NONSTD INCOMING ENCODE BUFFER::=
   E0011200011C3B1C399E0100036774640000002E49414D2C0D0A4743492C
   643037616464643635363939313164363830353336361303430656536616333
   40D0A0D0A088006000400000003
*Jul 27 15:20:06.107:
*Jul 27 15:20:06.107: H225 NONSTD INCOMING PDU ::=
```

continues

Example 16-24 *Debug Showing an H.225 Setup Message (Continued)*

```
value H323_UU_NonStdInfo ::=
    {
        version 18
        protoParam qsigNonStdInfo :
        {
          iei 28
          rawMesg '1C399E01000036774640000002E49414D2C0D0A47...'H
        }
        progIndParam progIndIEinfo :
        {
          progIndIE '00000003'H
        }
    }
```

Example 16-25 shows an H.245 "OpenLogicalChannel message", which is an outgoing message. You can also see the parameters such as codec, IP address of the gateway, and port address. Some of these debugs are used in the following chapters to discuss various troubleshooting scenarios related to Cisco CME integration with H.323 endpoints and Cisco UE.

Example 16-25 *Debug Showing an H.245 OpenLogicalChannel Message*

```
CME_HQ#debug h245 asn1
*Jul 27 15:20:06.119: H245 FS OLC OUTGOING PDU ::=
value OpenLogicalChannel ::=
    {
        forwardLogicalChannelNumber 1
        forwardLogicalChannelParameters
        {
          dataType nullData : NULL
          multiplexParameters none : NULL
        }
        reverseLogicalChannelParameters
        {
          dataType audioData : g729 : 2
          multiplexParameters h2250LogicalChannelParameters :
          {
            sessionID 1
            mediaChannel unicastAddress : iPAddress :
            {
              network '0A010201'H
              tsapIdentifier 19242
            }
            mediaControlChannel unicastAddress : iPAddress :
            {
              network '0A010101'H
              tsapIdentifier 17373
            }
            silenceSuppression TRUE
          }
        }
    }
```

When using the debugs shown in Examples 16-24 and 16-25, you should look for possible errors during a call setup. For example, a codec mismatch or a wrong IP address can cause the call to fail. By looking at the debugs, you can verify that the values exchanged during the call setup are correct. For example, the codec highlighted in Example 16-25 is G.729. Verify that this is the correct codec. Similarly, you can verify the IP address highlighted in Example 16-25 (in hexadecimal).

NOTE   You can convert the IP address shown in hexadecimal in the debug output by converting every two hexadecimal digits into binary. For example, the IP address for the hexadecimal value of 0A010101 is 10.1.1.1.

Troubleshooting the Cisco IPC Express GUI

The GUI is a very useful tool for configuring and maintaining both Cisco CME and Cisco UE, especially for a system with a higher number of ephones and ephone-dns configured. The GUI is a shared interface for Cisco IPC Express and, therefore, contains elements for both Cisco CME and Cisco UE.

Common GUI Problems and Solutions

This section explains some of the basic problems that may come up while using GUI:

- The browser doesn't start
- Lack of IP connectivity
- Incorrect browser version and wrong browser settings
- The HTTP server isn't enabled on the router
- GUI files are unavailable in the router's flash

You also learn how to determine what the problem is.

The Browser Doesn't Start

When the browser doesn't start, take the following approach to narrow down the problem:

Step 1   Check IP connectivity between your PC and the Cisco CME router.

Step 2   Check the browser and revision. Only Internet Explorer (IE) 6.0 with JScript 5.6 or later is supported.

Step 3   Check the IOS configuration. You should see the **ip http server** and **ip http path flash:** statements in the router configuration.

Step 4 Ensure that all the required Cisco CME GUI files are present in the router's flash. Missing a crucial GUI file, or having the wrong version of the file, causes the browser not to launch properly.

Step 5 Determine if the problem is with the browser. Use the same browser to access Internet web pages to see if the problem persists.

Step 6 There may be conflicts with other Java installations running on the PC. Disable other Java applications to see if that improves the situation.

IP Connectivity

To check IP connectivity between your PC and the Cisco CME router, open a DOS command window on your PC and ping the IP address of the Cisco CME router. The PC should be able to ping the router with a 100% success rate.

The HTTP Server Isn't Enabled on the Router

The HTTP server on a router is disabled by default. For a PC to access the Cisco IPC Express GUI, you must enable the HTTP server on the router. You can do this using the following commands:

```
ip http server
ip http path flash:
```

Also, if the system is using secure HTTP (HTTPS), you cannot access the Cisco UE GUI from a PC. Cisco CME supports HTTPS.

GUI Files Are Unavailable in Flash

The GUI uses a number of files that must be present in the Cisco CME router's flash. You can download these files from the Cisco.com software center in .tar or .zip format. If you copy the files in .tar format to flash, extract these files using the **archive** command before accessing the GUI from a PC.

The list of files required to be present in the router's flash for the GUI to work correctly was given in Chapter 13, "Cisco IPC Express General Administration and Initial System Setup."

NOTE The GUI files change for every release of Cisco CME, so ensure that you have the correct GUI files in flash that match the release of Cisco CME installed on your router.

Cisco CME and Cisco UE GUI Pages

When the system is working correctly, it doesn't matter which of the integrated GUI pages are sourced by Cisco CME and which are sourced by Cisco UE. When troubleshooting GUI problems, however, you have to be aware that there are two different HTTP servers and that some pages come from one source (Cisco CME or the router) and others come from the HTTP server in Cisco UE. Cisco UE is an optional component of Cisco CME, so some of the basic pages for phones and extensions are sourced by Cisco CME. All automated attendant and voice mail-related pages are sourced by Cisco UE, so these GUI menus show up only if you have Cisco UE on your system.

The GUI pages sourced by Cisco CME are

- Configure > Extensions
- Configure > Phones
- Configure > System Parameters
- Reports > Call History

All other menu items are sourced by Cisco UE. If problems develop in the GUI, check to see whether the problems are seen in the four preceding pages or only on the Cisco UE sourced pages.

Additionally, you could try to access the Cisco CME GUI separately from the integrated Cisco CME and Cisco UE GUI. You access the Cisco CME GUI by pointing your browser to the URL http://*a.b.c.d*/ccme.html, where *a.b.c.d* is the Cisco CME router's IP address. The login used is the username defined by the **web admin** command under **telephony-service** on the Cisco CME router.

When Cisco UE is present on the system, you access the combined Cisco IPC Express GUI by pointing your browser to the URL http://*f.g.h.i*/, where *f.g.h.i* is the Cisco UE module's IP address. The login used here is any username defined on Cisco UE that is a member of the administrators group and, therefore, has administrative access to the system.

Troubleshooting the Cisco UE GUI Pages

If the problem lies in the Cisco UE portion of the GUI, you can use the Cisco UE **trace** command to help troubleshoot the problem.

Cisco UE WebInterface Trace Tool

The **trace** command in Cisco UE is a powerful tool to troubleshoot Cisco UE-related problems. To use the output of the **trace** command, you must activate the corresponding trace first. The options for the **trace** command are shown in Example 16-26.

Example 16-26 *Cisco UE* **trace** *Command Options*

```
CUE#trace ?
  BackupRestore  Module
  all            Every module, entity and activity
  ccn            Module
  config-ccn     Module
  voicemail      Module
  webInterface   Module
```

The webInterface option deals particularly with GUI. As soon as the area (in this case, the WebInterface area) is determined, go to the next level of the submenu to set up the required trace.

Before displaying the trace content, you should use the **clear trace** command to clear the trace buffer of any remaining output from previous tracing activity that may confuse the output gathered for this tracing session. To display the output captured by the **trace** command, enter the following to show the last portion of a running trace:

```
#show trace buffer tail
```

Use the following command to show the complete existing trace content in the buffer:

```
#show trace buffer long
```

User Logins and Access Privileges

You can log into the Cisco IPC Express system as an administrator or as a general user, with different privileges and therefore different menus. If you want to see the full menu with all the options, ensure that you are logging in with a user ID that is a member of the administrators group and therefore has administrative privileges on the system.

Multiple users can be logged in simultaneously, but only one administrator can log in at any given time. If a second administrator logs in, the system automatically logs out the first administrator.

The Apply Button

When you make configuration changes to the system, the changes are not committed (or saved) until you click the apply button that is present on many of the pages and screens. If you make changes and walk away from your PC, the login session may time out. If you close the Browser window without clicking apply, the changes are discarded. Although this may appear like the GUI is operating incorrectly, it really isn't. Ensure that you always click apply to save changes before closing the Browser pop-up window or logging out.

The Browser Starts with Blank or Error Pages

You may be able to start the browser and log in successfully, but when you click some of the menu options, a blank or error page is returned. If it is a Cisco UE GUI page, determine in which functional area the problem lies by using the **trace webInterface** command. The functional areas under **webInterface** are shown in Example 16-27.

Example 16-27 *Cisco UE WebInterface Trace Areas*

```
CUE#trace webInterface ?
  all            Every entity and activity
  autoAttendant  Entity
  backupRestore  Entity
  controller     Entity
  database       Entity
  group          Entity
  initwizard     Entity
  mailbox        Entity
  prompt         Entity
  proxyAgent     Entity
  session        Entity
  synchronize    Entity
  sysdb          Entity
  syslogdaemon   Entity
  trigger        Entity
  user           Entity
```

Activate and collect traces in the appropriate area. Use **all** if you are unsure which category to select. Most of the time, **trace webinterface** all is adequate because usually not much web traffic is going to Cisco UE. In some instances, it is also helpful to use the **debug ip http** [**all** | **transactions** | **error** | **...**] router debug command to capture additional information.

Summary

This chapter covered some of the initial system setup problems you may encounter, such as the registration of IP phones with Cisco CME and GUI connectivity operation.

You learned various ways of identifying phone registration problems and the configuration changes to solve them. The phone display is one of the key tools used to isolate problems with phone registration and operation. The areas of VLAN, DHCP, and TFTP configurations were examined. You saw how these settings may affect phone registration issues.

Basic call flow debugging was covered. You learned how to trace a call setup from off-hook to dialing, and media establishment to call disconnect. You can use this knowledge if you have to troubleshoot a call setup or establishment problem.

This chapter also discussed the basic techniques of troubleshooting GUI issues when administering Cisco IPC Express. It showed the steps required to narrow down the problem and then use the available commands on Cisco CME and Cisco UE, such as **debug** and **trace**, to obtain more detailed information to determine the problem. This chapter covered the basic setup options for ensuring that the GUI works properly and the browser settings are correct.

The following chapters look at more advanced troubleshooting topics for particular applications, call flow, and network connectivity aspects of Cisco IPC Express systems.

This chapter covers the following topics:

- Debugging and correcting dial plan patterns
- Fixing call transfer patterns
- Troubleshooting call conferencing
- Correcting music on hold (MOH) problems
- Troubleshooting directory services
- Working with the Class of Restriction (COR) feature

Troubleshooting Advanced Cisco CME Features

Chapter 16, "Troubleshooting Basic Cisco IPC Express Features," explained the basic operation of the Cisco CallManager Express (CME) system. It also looked at some of the problems you might encounter during the registration of IP phones, configuration of network technologies such as Dynamic Host Configuration Protocol (DHCP) and virtual LANs (VLANs), and basic considerations for the correct operation of the Cisco IPC Express GUI. At this point, your phones should be successfully registered to the Cisco CME system and operational.

The next step is to expand your basic two-phone system to a completely functional telephony system suited to your needs. The requirements can vary from system to system, so the potential problems also vary. This chapter explores the issues that may arise while adding configuration and features to a basic Cisco CME system.

Before learning about advanced Cisco CME troubleshooting, one of the most important concepts to understand is the difference between an ephone and an ephone-dn and how these fit into the Cisco IOS software voice architecture. Chapter 5, "Cisco CME Call Processing Features," covered the basic building blocks of a Cisco CME system; you should read it before this chapter. In review

- An ephone (Ethernet phone) is the configuration of the physical device.
- An ephone-dn is the configuration of the phone line or extension. Each ephone-dn has a virtual voice port and dial peer as its subcomponents.

The need to troubleshoot Cisco CME is most likely to arise out of features such as the following:

- The dialplan patterns and transfer patterns associated with the system configuration
- Call transfer and conference scenarios
- Advanced features such as music on hold (MOH), directory services, and Class of Restriction (COR)

This chapter discusses how to troubleshoot some of the problems you may encounter in these areas.

Dialplan Pattern Configuration Problems

A dialplan pattern is an essential element of the Cisco CME configuration to integrate the Cisco CME and PSTN dial plans. If the dialplan patterns are not properly configured, calls to or from the PSTN may not terminate correctly. This section describes some of the common pitfalls in configuring dialplan patterns and how to troubleshoot them.

Figure 17-1 shows the Cisco CME configuration for a company with two geographically separate headquarters and customer support center offices, with Cisco CME deployed at both sites. There are 20 employees in the headquarters office and five employees in the customer support center. Calls between the two sites are routed over the IP WAN using voice over IP (VoIP). This saves the company money and also provides the convenience of uniform four-digit dialing between the sites. Both offices have PSTN connectivity via a Primary Rate Interface (PRI) line.

Figure 17-1 *System Configuration*

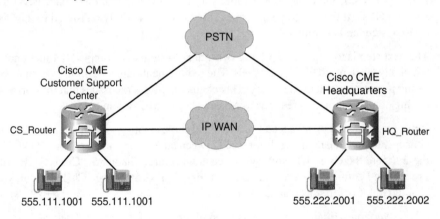

In Figure 17-1, the extension numbers for the support office start at 1001, with an E.164 prefix of 555111, making the PSTN Direct Inward Dial (DID) number for employees at the office start at 555.111.1001. The E.164 prefix for the headquarters site is 555222. Mapping the DID number to the extension number is achieved by using the **dialplan-pattern** command.

In this scenario, everything seems to be working fine for the company. Employees can call each other by dialing the appropriate four-digit extension number, and PSTN customers can call the support center by dialing the full PSTN DID number. Example 17-1 shows the relevant portions of the configuration of the headquarters Cisco CME router (HQ_router).

Example 17-1 *Headquarters Cisco CME Configuration*

```
HQ_Router#show running-config
dial-peer voice 1 voip
 destination-pattern 1...
 session target ipv4:10.10.10.1
```

Example 17-1 *Headquarters Cisco CME Configuration (Continued)*

```
 dtmf-relay h245-alphanumeric
 !
telephony-service
 load 7960-7940 P00303020214
 max-ephones 24
 max-dn 48
 ip source-address 10.10.10.2 port 2000
 create cnf-files version-stamp 7960 Jan 10 2004 14:22:22
 dialplan-pattern 1 55522220.. extension-length 4 extension-pattern 20..
 max-conferences 4
 transfer-pattern 1...
 !
ephone-dn  1
 number 2001
 !
ephone-dn  2
 number 2002
 !
ephone  1
 mac-address 0009.B7DA.0461
 button  1:1
```

Example 17-2 shows an extract from the customer support center Cisco CME router
(CS_router) configuration.

Example 17-2 *Customer Support Center Cisco CME Configuration*

```
CS_router#show running-config
!Output omitted for brevity
...
dial-peer voice 1 voip
 destination-pattern 2...
 session target ipv4:10.10.10.2
 dtmf-relay h245-alphanumeric
 !
dial-peer voice 2 voip
 destination-pattern 3...
 session target ipv4:10.10.10.3
 dtmf-relay h245-alphanumeric
 !
dial-peer voice 3 pots
 destination-pattern 9..........
 direct-inward-dial
 port 2/0:23
 forward-digits 11
telephony-service
 load 7960-7940 P00303020214
 max-ephones 24
 max-dn 48
 ip source-address 10.10.10.1 port 2000
 timeouts ringing 30
```

continues

Example 17-2 *Customer Support Center Cisco CME Configuration (Continued)*

```
 url authentication http://10.10.10.1/CCMCIP/authenticate.asp
 create cnf-files version-stamp 7960 Dec 05 2002 03:25:07
 dialplan-pattern 1 555111100. extension-length 4 extension-pattern 100.
 max-conferences 8
 transfer-pattern 2...
!
ephone-dn  1
 number 1001
 name CS Engineer1
!
ephone-dn  2
 number 1010
 name CS Engineer2

ephone  1
 mac-address 0007.EB46.299E
 type 7960
 button  1:1
```

A recent increase in sales for the company has led to an increased call volume to the support center. Therefore, the company has decided to hire five more people. Each new employee is provided with a new phone. John, the last person hired, is assigned extension number 1010. He is happy not to receive any customer calls on his first day, even though every one of his colleagues fields multiple customer calls. On the second day, John also receives no calls, and the next day and the day after. He can make calls from his phone to another extension and also can dial out via the PSTN. Colleagues from the headquarters office can call him, but no customer calls reach John directly. The next sections look at some of the **show** and **debug** commands that help identify and fix this problem.

Debugging Dialplan Patterns

One of the most useful debug commands for call processing issues involving Cisco CME phones is the **debug ephone detail** command. Because of the verbose nature of its output, use this command with caution in configurations that have a large number of phones and high call volumes. You can add a **mac-address** option to this command to show output for only a particular phone.

If you were to turn on **debug ephone detail mac-address 0003.E373.76FB** and make a call from the PSTN to John's number, 555.111.1010, you would see absolutely no debug output. This means that there is no incoming call to John's phone, which has a Media Access Control (MAC) address of 0003.E373.76FB. For a call to terminate on a particular extension, there must be a dial peer with a destination pattern matching that number. If you refer to the configuration of CS_router in Example 17-2, you see that the **destination pattern 555.111.1010** is not configured explicitly anywhere in the configuration. In fact, you have not configured the E.164

(PSTN DID) number for any of the phones. The Cisco CME **dialplan-pattern** command is taking care of this conversion from DID number to extension number.

For each ephone-dn that matches the wildcard characters (dots) in the **dialplan-pattern** command, an additional dial peer was automatically created with the destination pattern being the full E.164 number. The original dial peer has the actual destination pattern as the number configured with the **ephone-dn** command. For example, **ephone-dn 1** configured with the number 1001 has two dial peers with destination patterns of 1001 and 555.111.1001, respectively. These additional configurations are not seen as part of the router's running configuration, because they are Cisco CME-specific, internally generated configurations. You can see these configurations by issuing the **show telephony-service** command followed by the appropriate options. The output of the **show telephony-service dial-peer** command for the CS_router configuration is shown in Example 17-3.

NOTE   The dial peers for extension numbers 1003 to 1008 have been removed from the output to save space.

Example 17-3   show telephony-service dial-peer *Command Output*

```
CS_router#show telephony-service dial-peer
dial-peer voice 20001 pots
 destination-pattern 1001
 huntstop
 progress_ind setup enable 3
 port 50/0/1

dial-peer voice 20003 pots
 destination-pattern 1010
 huntstop
 progress_ind setup enable 3
 port 50/0/2

dial-peer voice 20016 pots
 destination-pattern 1009
 huntstop
 progress_ind setup enable 3
 port 50/0/9

dial-peer voice 20018 pots
 destination-pattern 1010
 huntstop
 progress_ind setup enable 3
 port 50/0/10

dial-peer voice 20029 pots
 destination-pattern 5551111001
 huntstop
```

continues

Example 17-3 **show telephony-service dial-peer** *Command Output (Continued)*

```
progress_ind setup enable 3
port 50/0/1

dial-peer voice 20036 pots
 destination-pattern 5551111009
 huntstop
 progress_ind setup enable 3
 port 50/0/9
```

As you can see from the output in Example 17-3, for each number configured under an ephone-dn, there are two dial peers with destination patterns—one with the extension number and another with the full E.164 version of the number.

Correcting the Dialplan Pattern

By now you realize that there is a missing dial peer for John's extension matching the E.164 version of his number (his PSTN DID number), 555.111.1010. You can also see that John's extension is the only number in the configuration with a missing dial peer for the E.164 extension.

Initially, when only five phones were connected to the system, the dialplan pattern configured was correct. The extension pattern of **100**. in the command **dialplan-pattern 1 555111100. extension-length 4 extension-pattern 100**. was valid for the extension numbers 1001 to 1005 that existed on the system at the time. With the addition of five more phone lines, the configuration became invalid for the most recent number: John's extension of 1010. This is the reason for the missing dial peer with the E.164 number as the destination pattern.

Changing the dialplan pattern from the existing configuration to the new configuration of **dialplan pattern 1 5551111... extension-length 4 extension-pattern 1...** solves the problem. With this change, you do not need to worry about adding extensions all the way to 1999, because they are all taken care of. However, you should certainly look at the configuration again after that.

Missing Transfer Patterns

Call transfer is one of most commonly used functions in Cisco CME. Transferring calls between multiple Cisco CME systems or to PSTN destinations requires the necessary configuration. This section describes some of the common mistakes made during system configuration (when integrating multiple sites) that prevent call transfer from working.

Call Transfer Doesn't Work

With further business growth, the company adds another office in a new location, and a third Cisco CME system is installed in this location. Figure 17-2 shows the new network configuration for the company with this additional office.

Figure 17-2   *System Configuration with the New Office*

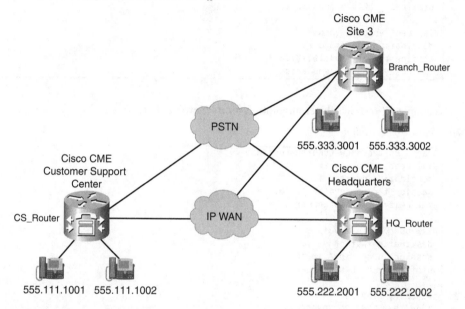

The configuration of the Cisco CME in the new location is not much different from the customer support site, except for the numbers assigned to the ephone-dns and the local PSTN DID number. Appropriate dial peers are added to the headquarters and customer support sites for full connectivity. The relevant dial peer configurations for all three Cisco CME routers are shown in the following examples. Example 17-4 shows the dial peer configuration for the headquarters site.

Example 17-4   *Headquarters Site Configuration*

```
HQ_Router#show running-config
dial-peer voice 1 voip
 destination-pattern 1...
 session target ipv4:10.10.10.1
 dtmf-relay h245-alphanumeric
!
dial-peer voice 2 voip
 destination-pattern 3...
 session target ipv4:10.10.10.2
 dtmf-relay h245-alphanumeric
```

Example 17-5 shows the configuration for the customer support center site.

Example 17-5 *Customer Support Center Configuration*

```
CS_router#show running-config
dial-peer voice 1 voip
 destination-pattern 2...
 session target ipv4:10.10.10.2
 dtmf-relay h245-alphanumeric
!
dial-peer voice 2 voip
 destination-pattern 3...
 session target ipv4:10.10.10.3
dtmf-relay h245-alphanumeric
```

Example 17-6 shows the configuration for the new site (site 3).

Example 17-6 *Site 3 Configuration*

```
Branch_Router#show running-config
dial-peer voice 1 voip
 destination-pattern 1...
 session target ipv4:10.10.10.1
dtmf-relay h245-alphanumeric
!
dial-peer voice 2 voip
 destination-pattern 2...
 session target ipv4:10.10.10.2
 dtmf-relay h245-alphanumeric
!
telephony-service
 load 7960-7940 P00303020214
 max-ephones 24
 max-dn 48
 ip source-address 10.10.10.3 port 2000
 create cnf-files version-stamp Jan 01 2002 00:00:00
 dialplan-pattern 1 5553333... extension-length 4 extension-pattern 3...
 max-conferences 4
 transfer-pattern 1...
 transfer-pattern 2...
```

Employees at each site now can call each other and receive calls from the PSTN. A new problem is reported, however. Employees at the headquarters and customer support sites cannot transfer calls to the new site 3 office even though they can make a direct call to the same destination extension. An incoming call from the new site 3 office can be transferred successfully to the headquarters or customer support sites.

To understand why the call transfer is failing, turn on the **debug ephone detail** command for the CS_router. Example 17-7 shows the relevant portions of the output of the **debug ephone detail** command for a call from an HQ_router phone to a CS_router phone.

Example 17-7 *Output of the* **debug ephone detail** *Command for the Incoming Call*

```
CS_router#debug ephone detail
!Output omitted for brevity
...
06:45:57: SetCallInfo DN 1 chan 1 is not skinny-to-skinny
06:45:57: SkinnyGetCallState for DN 1 chan 1 IDLE
06:45:57: called DN -1 chan 1, calling DN -1 chan 1 phone -1 incoming s2s:0
06:45:57: SkinnyUpdateDnState by EFXS_RING_GENERATE
  for DN 1 chan 1 to state RINGING
!Output omitted for brevity
...

06:45:57: ephone-1[1]:Call Info DN 1 line 1 ref 31 called 1001 calling 5552222001
  origcalled 1001 calltype 1
06:45:57: ephone-1[1]:Original Called Name CS Engineer1
06:45:57: ephone-1[1]: Janet Phillip calling
06:45:57: ephone-1[1]: CS Engineer1
06:45:57: ephone-1[1]:External RINGING
06:45:57: ephone-1[1]:Ringer Outside Ring On
06:45:57: SkinnyGetCallState for DN 1 chan 1 RINGING
06:45:57: called DN -1 chan 1, calling DN -1 chan 1 phone -1 incoming s2s:0
06:45:57: ephone-1[1]:SetLineLamp 1 to BLINK
06:45:57: Check AUTO phone -1
06:46:03: ephone-1[1]:OFFHOOK
06:46:03: ephone-1[1]:Disable Ringer line 1
06:46:03: ephone-1[1]:STOP RINGING
06:46:03: ephone-1[1]:Ringer Off
06:46:03: SkinnyGetCallState for DN 1 chan 1 RINGING
06:46:03: called DN -1 chan 1, calling DN -1 chan 1 phone -1 incoming s2s:0
06:46:03: ephone-1[1][SEP0007EB46299E]:Auto select answer line 1 dn -1 chan 1
06:46:03: ephone-1[1]:ANSWER call
...
06:46:03: defer_start for DN 1 chan 1 at CONNECTED
06:46:03: Skinny Call State change for DN 1 chan 1 CONNECTED from RINGING
06:46:03: ephone-(1) DN 1 chan 1 calledDn -1 chan 1 callingDn -1 chan 1 0.0.0.0
  port=0 incoming
!Output omitted for brevity
...
06:46:03: dn_support_g729 true DN 1 chan 1 ephone-1
06:46:03: dn_support_g723 false DN 1 chan 1 ephone-1
06:46:03: SetDnCodec clear_defer media start
06:46:03: SetDnCodec DN 1 chan 1 codec 11:G729  vad 250 size 20
06:46:03: Skinny clear media defer_start
06:46:03: DN 1 chan 1 Voice_Mode
06:46:03: SkinnyGetCallState for DN 1 chan 1 CONNECTED
...
06:46:03: SkinnyUpdateDnState by EFXS_OPEN_VOICE_PATH
  for DN 1 chan 1 to state CALL_START
```

continues

Example 17-7 *Output of the* **debug ephone detail** *Command for the Incoming Call (Continued)*

```
06:46:03: calling= 5552222001 called= 1001 origCalled=
06:46:03: callingName= Janet Phillip, calledName= , redirectedTo =
06:46:03: ephone-1[1][SEP0007EB46299E]:refreshDisplayLine for line 1 DN 1 chan 1
06:46:03: ephone-1[1]:OpenReceiveChannelAck:IP 10.10.10.141, port=27358,
  dn_index=1, dn=1, chan=1
06:46:03: ephone-1[1]:StartMedia 10.10.10.1 port=2000
06:46:03: DN 1 chan 1 codec 11:G729 duration 20 ms bytes 20
06:46:03: ephone-1[1]:Original Called Name CS Engineer1
06:46:03: ephone-1[1]: Janet Phillip calling
06:46:03: ephone-1[1]: CS Engineer1
```

A quick look at the debug shows that Janet Phillip (at headquarters number 555.222.2001) called CS Engineer1 at extension number 1001. The call was answered after it entered the ringing state, and the codec selected for the call is G.729 with 20 milliseconds (ms) sampling.

Example 17-8 shows the output of the **debug ephone detail** command during the call transfer to a phone at site 3.

Example 17-8 **debug ephone detail** *Command Output During Call Transfer*

```
CS_router#debug ephone detail
!Output omitted for brevity
...
07:12:21: ephone-1[1][SEP0007EB46299E]:SoftKeyEventMessage event 4 line 1
  callref 31
07:12:21: ephone-1[1]:SK TRANSFER line 1 ref 31
07:12:21: ephone-1[1]:TransferButtonPress
07:12:21: ephone-1 TRANSFER using transfer-system local DN 1 blind transfer
07:12:21: ephone-1[1]:HoldButtonPress (allow_toggle = 0)
07:12:21: SkinnyGetCallState for DN 1 chan 1 CONNECTED
07:12:21: called DN -1 chan 1, calling DN -1 chan 1 phone 1 incoming s2s:0
07:12:21: ephone-1[1]:HoldButtonPress HOLD activated for DN 1 chan 1
07:12:21: ephone-1[1]:HoldButtonPress DN 1 chan 1 other DN -1 chan 1 other
  ephone-(-1)
07:12:21: ephone-1[1]:UpdateCallState DN 1 chan 1 state 9 calleddn -1 chan 1
07:12:21: ephone-1[1]:Binding ephone-1 to DN 1 chan 1 s2s:0
07:12:21: Adding DN 1 chan 1 to MOH
07:12:21: Skinny Call State change for DN 1 chan 1 HOLD from CONNECTED
!Output omitted for brevity
...
07:12:21: SkinnyGetCallState for DN 1 chan 1 HOLD
07:12:21: called DN -1 chan 1, calling DN -1 chan 1 phone -1 incoming s2s:0
07:12:21: ephone-1[1]:SetLineLamp 1 to WINK
07:12:21: UnBinding ephone-1 from DN 1 chan 1
07:12:21: ephone-1[1]:CloseReceive
07:12:21: ephone-1[1]:StopMedia
07:12:21: ephone-1[1]:HoldButtonPress keep call plane for transfer
!Output omitted for brevity
...
07:12:21: Skinny StartTone 33 sent on  ephone socket [1] DtInsideDialTone
07:12:21: ephone-1[1][SEP0007EB46299E]:CallPrompt line 1 ref 31:
```

Example 17-8 **debug ephone detail** *Command Output During Call Transfer (Continued)*

```
07:12:21: ephone-1[1]:SelectPhoneSoftKeys set 2 mask FFFF for line 1 ref 31
07:12:22: ephone-1[1]:Update Stats Total for DN 1 chan 1
07:12:22: ephone-1[1]:KeypadButtonMessage 3
07:12:22: ephone-1[1]:is_auto_local 0 for DN -1
07:12:22: ephone-1[1]:StopTone sent to ephone
07:12:22: ephone-1[1][SEP0007EB46299E]:CallPrompt line 1 ref 31: Transfer 3
07:12:22: ephone-1[1][SEP0007EB46299E]:SkinnyTryCall to 3 instance 1 start at 0
07:12:22: ephone-1[1]:No Transfer DN match for 3
07:12:22: ephone-1[1]:No Transfer-Pattern match for 3
07:12:22: ephone-1[1]:is_auto_local 0 for DN -1
07:12:22: Skinny StartTone 37 sent on  ephone socket [1] DtReorderTone
07:12:23: ephone-1[1]:KeypadButtonMessage 0
07:12:23: ephone-1[1][SEP0007EB46299E]:CallPrompt line 1 ref 31: Transfer 0
07:12:23: ephone-1[1][SEP0007EB46299E]:SkinnyTryCall to 0 instance 1 start at 0
07:12:23: ephone-1[1]:No Transfer DN match for 0
07:12:23: ephone-1[1]:No Transfer-Pattern match for 0
07:12:23: ephone-1[1]:is_auto_local 0 for DN -1
07:12:23: Skinny StartTone 37 sent on  ephone socket [1] DtReorderTone
07:12:23: ephone-1[1]:KeypadButtonMessage 0
07:12:23: ephone-1[1][SEP0007EB46299E]:CallPrompt line 1 ref 31: Transfer 0
07:12:23: ephone-1[1][SEP0007EB46299E]:SkinnyTryCall to 0 instance 1 start at 0
07:12:23: ephone-1[1]:No Transfer DN match for 0
07:12:23: ephone-1[1]:No Transfer-Pattern match for 0
07:12:23: ephone-1[1]:is_auto_local 0 for DN -1
07:12:23: Skinny StartTone 37 sent on  ephone socket [1] DtReorderTone
07:12:23: ephone-1[1]:KeypadButtonMessage 1
07:12:23: ephone-1[1][SEP0007EB46299E]:CallPrompt line 1 ref 31: Transfer 1
07:12:23: ephone-1[1][SEP0007EB46299E]:SkinnyTryCall to 1 instance 1 start at 0
07:12:23: ephone-1[1]:No Transfer-Pattern match for 1
CS_router#
```

The debug output in Example 17-8 shows that Janet pressed the transfer softkey on her phone. This action automatically puts the original call on hold and starts playing dial tone. The phone then collects the digits (3001) of the destination where the call should be transferred. Each digit pressed generates a KeypadButtonMessage message, followed by the actual digit pressed.

A couple of lines below the KeypadButtonMessage 3 you can see the messages "No transfer DN match for 3" and "No transfer-pattern match for 3." This explains why the call wasn't transferred successfully. Even though necessary dial peers were added on both the headquarters and customer service Cisco CME routers, the transfer pattern necessary to enable transfer between these sites is still missing.

Fixing Transfer Patterns

The addition of the command **transfer-pattern 3...** on both the headquarters and customer service Cisco CME routers allows users to transfer a call to the phones connected to the site 3 Cisco CME. For each transfer destination, you should have a matching transfer pattern to enable a successful transfer to that extension. You can also use the **.T** dial peer terminology in the **transfer-pattern** command to match all possible numbering schemes.

Conference Failures

This section examines troubleshooting techniques for the conference feature, which is one of the most frequently used features in any typical office environment. Two common issues related to conference are discussed in this section:

- Conference failure because of unavailable lines
- Conference failure because of a codec mismatch

Conference Failure Because of Unavailable Lines

Example 17-9 shows the configuration of CS_router with the phones for the additional employees added to the system. With this configuration in place, when CS Engineer1 tries to initiate a conference with fellow support engineers, it fails. After making the first call when the conference softkey is pressed, CS Engineer1 gets a "No line available" message on the phone display.

Example 17-9   *Configuration of CS_router with Additional Phones*

```
CS_router#show running-config
!Output omitted for brevity
...
ephone-dn  1
 number 1001
 name CS Engineer1
 call-forward all 3001
!
ephone-dn  2
 number 1010
 name CS Engineer2
!
ephone-dn  3
 number 1003
 name CS Engineer3
!
ephone  1
 mac-address 0007.EB46.299E
 type 7960
 button  1:1
!
ephone  2
 mac-address 0003.E373.76FB
 type 7960
 button  1:2
!
ephone  3
```

Example 17-9   *Configuration of CS_router with Additional Phones (Continued)*

```
 mac-address 0030.94C2.9919
 button 1:3
!
ephone  4
 mac-address 000D.BDBE.F372
 button  1:4
```

The **debug ephone detail** output for the phone of CS Engineer1 is shown in Example 17-10.

Example 17-10   **debug ephone detail** *Output During a Conference Setup Failure*

```
CS_router#debug ephone detail
!Output omitted for brevity
...
3d01h: ephone-1[1][SEP0007EB46299E]:SoftKeyEventMessage event 13 line 1 callref 45
3d01h: ephone-1[1]:SK CONFERENCE line 1 ref 45
3d01h: SkinnyGetCallState for DN 1 chan 1 CONNECTED
3d01h: called DN 3 chan 1, calling DN -1 chan 1 phone 1 s2s:1
3d01h: SkinnyGetCallState for DN 1 chan 1 CONNECTED
3d01h: called DN 3 chan 1, calling DN -1 chan 1 phone 1 s2s:1
3d01h: SkinnyGetCallState for DN 1 chan 1 CONNECTED
3d01h: called DN 3 chan 1, calling DN -1 chan 1 phone 1 s2s:1
3d01h: ephone-1[1]:DisplayMessage: No Line Available
3d01h: ephone-1[1]:Conference with no idle line available: abort
```

The debug output shown in Example 17-10 displays a message similar to the one seen on the phone display. As indicated by the debug and the phone display messages, the phone is running out of ephone-dns to make the second call. When the conference softkey is pressed, the phone automatically puts the first line on hold and allocates the next available line to initiate the second call. You can solve this "No Line Available" problem by adding another line to the existing phone or by changing the existing line to a dual line.

You can modify the configuration example so that ephone-dn 1 is now a dual-line DN. You must delete the existing ephone-dn, and then add it again with the option **dual-line**. After you reconfigure the ephone-dn and restart the phone, you notice that the phone is registered without a number assigned to it. When you removed the existing ephone-dn, the software automatically also removed that extension (ephone-dn) from the configuration of ephone 1, because the extension does not exist anymore. If you look at the configuration, you can see that there is no longer a button 1:1 configuration under ephone 1. The button configuration is not added automatically when the ephone-dn is reconfigured as a dual-line DN. You should manually configure the buttons so that the phone gets registered with a number assigned to it.

Conference Failure Because of a Codec Mismatch

With the new configuration in place, CS Engineer1 now can make a conference call to all the employees in the customer service office. But the conference call still fails if one of the parties in the conference is located at the headquarters office. In this example, the conference originator can make the call to the destination party and gets connected but is unable to conference together all three parties. When the conference originator presses the conference button the second time to complete the conference, the phone displays the message "Cannot complete the conference." The output of the **debug ephone detail** command during the conference attempt is shown in Example 17-11.

Example 17-11 **debug ephone detail** *Output During a Conference with an Unsupported Codec*

```
CS_router#debug ephone detail
!Output omitted for brevity
...
C 3d03h: SkinnyGetCallState DN error -1
3d03h: SkinnyGetCallState for DN 4 chan 1 CONNECTED
3d03h: called DN -1 chan 1, calling DN 1 chan 1 phone 4 incoming s2s:1
3d03h: SkinnyGetCallState for DN 4 chan 1 CONNECTED
3d03h: called DN -1 chan 1, calling DN 1 chan 1 phone 4 incoming s2s:1
3d03h: ephone-4[3]:is_auto_local 1 for DN 4
3d03h: Skinny StartTone 53 sent on  ephone socket [3] DtHoldTone
3d03h: ephone-1[1][SEP0007EB46299E]:SoftKeyEventMessage event 13 line 1 callref 54
3d03h: ephone-1[1]:SK CONFERENCE line 1 ref 54
3d03h: SkinnyGetCallState for DN 1 chan 2 CONNECTED
3d03h: called DN -1 chan 1, calling DN -1 chan 1 phone 1 s2s:0
3d03h: ephone-1[1]:Conference attempt with unsupported codec
```

The last line of the debug explains the problem. Conference calling requires G.711 codecs unless digital signal processor (DSP) transcoding is provisioned (available only with Cisco CME 3.2 or later). To fix the problem, you should configure the G.711 codec on the dial peers or upgrade to Cisco CME 3.2 with the necessary transcoding hardware. Another important point is that even if the router uses DSP resources for transcoding, the media mixing for the conference is done in software by the router. The transcoder converts all G.729 packets to G.711 and sends them to the Cisco CME router. There the software mixes the media from the three parties involved in the conference and sends the mixed media back out to the three phones.

The three debug segments in the next several examples show the output of **show ephone** during various states of a conference call. The conference initiator is 1001, and the other parties involved in the call are 1003 and 1004.

Example 17-12 shows the output after the first call is made.

Example 17-12 **show ephone** *Output After the First Call*

```
CS_router#show ephone
ephone-1 Mac:0007.EB46.299E TCP socket:[1] activeLine:1 REGISTERED
mediaActive:1 offhook:1 ringing:0 reset:0 reset_sent:0 paging 0 debug:0
IP:10.10.10.141 49648 Telecaster 7960  keepalive 56 max_line 6
button 1: dn 1  number 1001 CH1   CONNECTED    CH2   IDLE
Active Call on DN 1 chan 1 :1001 10.10.10.141 24462 to 10.10.10.159 28488 via
   10.10.10.141
G711Ulaw64k  160 bytes no vad
Tx Pkts 451 bytes 77572 Rx Pkts 452 bytes 77744 Lost 0
```

Example 17-12   show ephone *Output After the First Call (Continued)*

```
Jitter 0 Latency 0 callingDn -1 calledDn 3 (media path callID 113 srcCallID 114)

ephone-3 Mac:0030.94C2.9919 TCP socket:[4] activeLine:1 REGISTERED
mediaActive:1 offhook:1 ringing:0 reset:0 reset_sent:0 paging 0 debug:0
IP:10.10.10.159 52063 Telecaster 7960  keepalive 339 max_line 6
button 1: dn 3  number 1003 CH1   CONNECTED
Active Call on DN 3 chan 1 :1003 10.10.10.159 28488 to 10.10.10.141 24462 via
   10.10.10.159
G711Ulaw64k  160 bytes no vad
Tx Pkts 452 bytes 77744 Rx Pkts 451 bytes 77572 Lost 0
Jitter 0 Latency 0 callingDn 1 calledDn -1
```

Example 17-13 shows the output after the second call is made.

Example 17-13   show ephone *Output After the Second Call*

```
CS_router#show ephone
ephone-1 Mac:0007.EB46.299E TCP socket:[1] activeLine:1 REGISTERED
mediaActive:1 offhook:1 ringing:0 reset:0 reset_sent:0 paging 0 debug:0
IP:10.10.10.141 49648 Telecaster 7960  keepalive 66 max_line 6
button 1: dn 1  number 1001 CH1   HOLD      CH2   CONNECTED
Active Call on DN 1 chan 2 :1001 10.10.10.141 20472 to 10.10.10.1 2000
via 10.10.10.141
G711Ulaw64k  160 bytes no vad
Tx Pkts 223 bytes 38356 Rx Pkts 224 bytes 38528 Lost 0
Jitter 0 Latency 0 callingDn -1 calledDn 4

ephone-3 Mac:0030.94C2.9919 TCP socket:[4] activeLine:1 REGISTERED
mediaActive:0 offhook:1 ringing:0 reset:0 reset_sent:0 paging 0 debug:0
IP:10.10.10.159 52063 Telecaster 7960  keepalive 348 max_line 6
button 1: dn 3  number 1003 CH1   CONNECTED
Active Call on DN 3 chan 1 :1003 10.10.10.159 28488 to 10.10.10.141 24462
via 10.10.10.159
G711Ulaw64k  160 bytes no vad
Tx Pkts 28296 bytes 4866912 Rx Pkts 28296 bytes 4866912 Lost 0
Jitter 0 Latency 0 callingDn 1 calledDn -1

ephone-4 Mac:000D.BDBE.F372 TCP socket:[3] activeLine:1 REGISTERED
mediaActive:1 offhook:1 ringing:0 reset:0 reset_sent:0 paging 0 debug:0
IP:10.10.10.158 50900 Telecaster 7960  keepalive 357 max_line 6
button 1: dn 4  number 1004 CH1   CONNECTED
Active Call on DN 4 chan 1 :1004 10.10.10.158 24508 to 10.10.10.1 2000
via 10.10.10.158
G711Ulaw64k  160 bytes no vad
Tx Pkts 476 bytes 81872 Rx Pkts 475 bytes 81700 Lost 0
Jitter 0 Latency 0 callingDn 1 calledDn -1
(media path callID 118 srcCallID 117)
```

Example 17-14 shows the output after all three parties are in the conference call.

Example 17-14 *Output After All Three Parties Are in the Conference*

```
CS_router#show ephone
ephone-1 Mac:0007.EB46.299E TCP socket:[1] activeLine:1 REGISTERED
mediaActive:1 offhook:1 ringing:0 reset:0 reset_sent:0 paging 0 debug:0
IP:10.10.10.141 49648 Telecaster 7960  keepalive 72 max_line 6
button 1: dn 1  number 1001 CH1   CONNECTED    CH2   CONNECTED
CH1 conferencedCH2 conferenced

Active Call on DN 1 chan 2 :1001 10.10.10.141 20472 to 10.10.10.1 2000
via 10.10.10.141
G711Ulaw64k  160 bytes no vad
Tx Pkts 8968 bytes 1542496 Rx Pkts 8968 bytes 1542496 Lost 0
Jitter 3 Latency 0 callingDn -1 calledDn 4

ephone-3 Mac:0030.94C2.9919 TCP socket:[4] activeLine:1 REGISTERED
mediaActive:1 offhook:1 ringing:0 reset:0 reset_sent:0 paging 0 debug:0
IP:10.10.10.159 52063 Telecaster 7960  keepalive 354 max_line 6
button 1: dn 3  number 1003 CH1   CONNECTED
Active Call on DN 3 chan 1 :1003 10.10.10.159 26034 to 10.10.10.1 2000
via 10.10.10.159
G711Ulaw64k  160 bytes no vad
Tx Pkts 14348 bytes 2467856 Rx Pkts 14349 bytes 2468028 Lost 0
Jitter 0 Latency 0 callingDn -1 calledDn -1 (media path callID 116
srcCallID 115)

ephone-4 Mac:000D.BDBE.F372 TCP socket:[3] activeLine:1 REGISTERED
mediaActive:1 offhook:1 ringing:0 reset:0 reset_sent:0 paging 0 debug:0
IP:10.10.10.158 50900 Telecaster 7960  keepalive 363 max_line 6
button 1: dn 4  number 1004 CH1   CONNECTED
Active Call on DN 4 chan 1 :1004 10.10.10.158 24508 to 10.10.10.1 2000
via 10.10.10.158
G711Ulaw64k  160 bytes no vad
Tx Pkts 9220 bytes 1585840 Rx Pkts 9220 bytes 1585840 Lost 0
Jitter 0 Latency 0 callingDn 1 calledDn -1
(media path callID 118 srcCallID 117)
```

Examples 17-12 and 17-13 show that the media is sent directly between the phones involved in the call. In Example 17-14, as soon as the conference is active, the destination's IP address changes to the Cisco CME router's IP address for all three phones. All the routers send the Real-Time Protocol (RTP) packets directly to the Cisco CME router, which mixes them and sends them back to the respective phones. This can take a considerable amount of CPU cycles and, hence, affects system performance. You can configure the maximum number of simultaneous conferences on a Cisco CME system with the command **max-conference**. The default value for this command varies, depending on the type of platform you are using.

Unable to Hear Music on Hold

The music on hold (MOH) feature provides a mechanism for the contents of a file stored on the router's Flash to be played to a remote phone when a call is put on hold. If a file does not exist, a short beep (tone on hold) is played to the held party. For IP phones local to the Cisco CME router, the phone itself generates the tone on hold. Hence, even if a music file is present on the router's Flash, a call directly between two IP phones local to the Cisco CME system when put on hold hears only short, intermittent beeps.

Debugging the MOH Problem

The company's system administrator wants to add the MOH feature to both the headquarters and customer support sites. This way, both customers and employees can hear music instead of tones when put on hold. A file, in .au format, is copied to the router's Flash, and the appropriate configurations are added. Example 17-15 shows the relevant Cisco CME configuration.

Example 17-15 show flash *Output and MOH Configuration for Cisco CME*

```
CS_router#show flash:
-#- --length-- ---------date/time--------- path
1       474338 Dec 5 2002 07:03:14 +00:00 minuet.au
CS_router#show running-configuration
!Output omitted for brevity
...
telephony-service
 load 7960-7940 P00303020214
 max-ephones 24
 max-dn 24
 ip source-address 10.10.10.1 port 2000
 timeouts ringing 30
 url authentication http://10.10.10.1/CCMCIP/authenticate.asp
 create cnf-files version-stamp 7960 Dec 05 2002 03:25:07
 dialplan-pattern 1 555111100. extension-length 4 extension-pattern 100.
 max-conferences 8
 moh minuet.au
```

With the configuration in place, customer calls arriving from the PSTN can hear the MOH. However, calls between the headquarters and customer service sites, when put on hold, still hear a beep tone instead of music.

To analyze this problem, a useful debug command is **debug ephone moh**. The output of this command on the CS_router is shown in Example 17-16 when a call from headquarters is put on hold.

Example 17-16 *Output of* **debug ephone moh**

```
CS_router#debug ephone moh
CS_router#
02:34:51: No MOH resources available for DN 1 chan 1 codec 11
CS_router#
```

continues

Example 17-16 *Output of* **debug ephone moh** *(Continued)*

```
CS_router#
02:35:38: Added DN 1 chan 1 to MOH in position 0 with 1 clients
02:35:38: Startup MOH/media streams MOH:1 Media:0
02:36:08: Removed DN 1 from MOH 0 clients at position 0
02:36:08: Shutdown MOH/media streams, no active clients
```

The debug output segment in Example 17-16 shows the output of the **debug ephone moh** command for a PSTN call put on hold and then retrieved from hold again after some time. From the debug, you can see the ephone-dn listed as one of the MOH stream recipients.

The output of the debug alone doesn't explain the problem sufficiently. The key point to note is that a live MOH feed is supported only for G.711 calls. However, the call between the headquarters and customer service sites is a G.729 call. Hence, the router is unable to provide MOH and provides the *tone on hold* feature instead. When you know this, the word "codec" in the debug makes more sense.

Fixing the MOH Problem

There are two ways you can fix the codec-mismatch problem so that calls between the headquarters and customer service sites can hear music when put on hold:

- Use the G.711 codec for calls between the sites.
- Use a live music feed via an ear and mouth (E&M) port on the router instead of an .au file in flash. (Configuring MOH is described in Chapter 14, "Configuring and Managing Cisco IPC Express Systems.")

Missing Directory Services Option

One of the features on a Cisco CME system is a real-time directory search function on the phone. The search pattern can be directly entered on the phone keypad, and matching results are displayed. Directory services can be accessed by pressing the directories button on the phone and selecting the appropriate options.

Consider, for example, that when the Directories button is pressed on one of the phones connected to the CS_router, you see the options for missed calls, received calls, and placed calls, but no options for directory services. This section describes how to pinpoint and fix this problem.

Chapter 16 covers downloading a file named SEP*xxxxyyyyzzzz*.cnf.xml to the phone. This file contains information needed for phone registration. The URL for directory access is one of the pieces of information contained in this file. This file is stored on the router system memory and can be viewed by issuing the command **show telephony-services tftp-bindings**. The output of this command for the CS_router is shown in Example 17-17.

Example 17-17 *Output of* **show telephony-service tftp-bindings**

```
CS_router#show telephony-service tftp-bindings
tftp-server system:/its/SEPDEFAULT.cnf
tftp-server system:/its/SEPDEFAULT.cnf alias SEPDefault.cnf
tftp-server system:/its/XMLDefault.cnf.xml alias XMLDefault.cnf.xml
tftp-server system:/its/ATADefault.cnf.xml
tftp-server system:/its/united_states/7960-tones.xml
 alias United_States/7960-tones.xml
tftp-server system:/its/united_states/7960-font.xml
alias English_United_States/7960-font.xml
tftp-server system:/its/united_states/7960-dictionary.xml alias
  English_United_States/7960-dictionary.xml
tftp-server system:/its/united_states/7960-kate.xml
alias English_United_States/7960-kate.xml
tftp-server system:/its/united_states/SCCP-dictionary.xml alias
  English_United_States/SCCP-dictionary.xml
tftp-server system:/its/XMLDefault7960.cnf.xml
alias SEP0007EB46299E.cnf.xml
tftp-server system:/its/XMLDefault7960.cnf.xml
alias SEP0003E37376FB.cnf.xml
```

In Example 17-17, you can see that a filename is associated with the MAC address of each phone on the system. The individual files are aliases of the original XMLDefault7960.cnf.xml file, which is the XML file created for the Cisco 7960 IP Phones. You can see this file's contents by issuing the command **more** followed by the filename with the path. In the example, the **more system:/its/XMLDefault7960.cnf.xml** command should return the file's contents. The output of this command for the SEP*xxxxyyyyzzzz*.cnf.xml file is shown in Example 17-18.

Example 17-18 *Contents of the XMLDefault7960.cnf.xml File*

```
CS_router#more system:/its/XMLDefault7960.cnf.xml
<device>
<devicePool>
<callManagerGroup>
<members>
<member  priority="0">
<callManager>
<ports>
<ethernetPhonePort>2000</ethernetPhonePort>
</ports>
<processNodeName>10.10.10.1</processNodeName>
</callManager>
</member>
</members>
</callManagerGroup>
</devicePool>
<versionStamp>{7960 Dec 05 2002 03:25:07}</versionStamp>
<loadInformation>P00303020214</loadInformation>
```

continues

Example 17-18 *Contents of the XMLDefault7960.cnf.xml File (Continued)*

```
<userLocale>
<name>English_United_States</name>
<langCode>en</langCode>
</userLocale>
<networkLocale>United_States</networkLocale>
<idleTimeout>0</idleTimeout>
<authenticationURL>http://10.10.10.1/CCMCIP/authenticate.asp</authenticationURL>
<directoryURL>http://10.10.10.1/localdirectory</directoryURL>
<idleURL></idleURL>
<informationURL></informationURL>
<messagesURL></messagesURL>
<proxyServerURL></proxyServerURL>
<servicesURL></servicesURL>
</device>
```

Example 17-18 shows that the file contains the directory URL information. You can visually verify that the phone has this information from the file by pressing the settings button and selecting Network Configuration. This displays a long list of network parameters for the phone. Using the rocker button on the phone, scroll down to an entry called directories URL. The entry on the phone matches the entry in the file.

The phone has all the necessary information required to query directory services, yet you cannot see the directory service option. The reason is that the URL for directory services is pointing to a file on the HTTP server of the Cisco CME router. The HTTP server function on Cisco routers is not enabled by default, so the phone cannot access the URL even though it is aware of it. Enable the HTTP server by entering the commands **ip http server** and **ip http path flash** on the Cisco CME router, and then press the directories key on the phone again. You can see a few more options than before, including the directory services entry.

Working with the Class of Restriction Feature

This section examines issues you may face while configuring the Class of Restriction (COR) feature for Cisco CME phones. COR is an existing Cisco IOS feature used to apply restrictions on originating and terminating calls from the router. COR is a feature applied to voice dial peers. Because dial peers are a subcomponent of the Cisco CME ephone-dn configuration, COR configurations can also be applied to ephone-dns.

First this section offers a brief discussion of COR's operating principles. Then you'll learn how to apply COR to a Cisco CME system and troubleshoot some of the possible errors that may come up. COR is like a lock-and-key mechanism. If the COR applied to an incoming dial peer for incoming calls is a superset of, or equal to, the COR applied to the outgoing dial peer for outgoing calls, the call is allowed to complete successfully.

Figure 17-3 shows a simple setup with two phones illustrating the relationship between the ephone-dn, dial peer, and voice port. Consider a call from Phone A to Phone B. From the perspective of the voice port associated with ephone-dn 1 attached to Phone A, this is an incoming call. Similarly, it is an outgoing call from the perspective of the voice port associated with ephone-dn 2 attached to Phone B.

Figure 17-3   *Call Setup from a Voice Port Perspective*

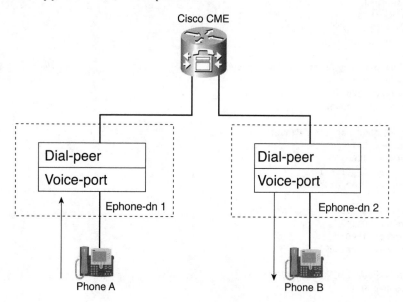

Even though the call is an incoming call for Phone B, it is going out of the voice port associated with ephone-dn 2. This concept is very important to understanding COR configurations. The dial peer associated with ephone-dn 1 is the incoming dial peer, and the dial peer associated with ephone-dn 2 is the outgoing dial peer. The key point here is the voice port: the configuration is done from a voice port perspective, not from a phone perspective.

The next thing to clarify is how COR configurations are applied to an incoming or outgoing call. Assume you need a configuration to restrict calls between Phone A and Phone B. To achieve this, two configurations are required:

- One to restrict calls from Phone A to Phone B
- One to restrict calls from Phone B to Phone A

Restrictions always apply in one way only. Hence, COR configurations are needed individually for both incoming and outgoing calls.

COR configuration involves creating a unique COR name and attaching it to various lists. The members of the list determine if the list is a subset or superset of another list. A sample configuration is shown in Example 17-19 with four names and seven COR lists.

Example 17-19 *Configuring COR*

```
router#show running-config
dial-peer cor custom
name 911
name 1800
name LocalCall
name LongDistance
!
dial-peer cor list RegularEmployee
member 911
member 1800
member LocalCall
!
dial-peer cor list Manager
member 911
member 1800
member LocalCall
member  LongDistance
!
dial-peer cor list Contractor
member 911
member 1800
member LocalCall
!
dial-peer cor list Call911
member 911
!
dial-peer cor list Call1800
member 1800
!
dial-peer cor list CallLocal
member LocalCall
!
dial-peer cor list CallLongDistance
member LongDistance
```

The unique names are configured under the **dial-peer cor custom** command. The COR lists are uniquely named lists configured from global configuration mode. The COR list named Manager is a superset of all other lists. The lists named RegularEmployee and Contractor are equal, and both are a subset of the list Manager. Note that the RegularEmployee and Contractor lists are not a subset or superset of the list named CallLongDistance.

The configuration is taken a step further by adding a few more dial peers to the existing set. Three dial peers are added with the destination patterns of 1800..., 1..., and 911, respectively.

Example 17-20 shows a simple configuration to prevent Phone A from making any calls out of dial peer 2.

Example 17-20   *COR Configuration to Prevent Phone A from Making Calls Out of Dial Peer 2*

```
router#show running-config
Dial-peer voice 1 voip
Destination-pattern 1800...
Session target:ipv4:10.10.10.2
dtmf-relay h245-alphanumeric

Dial-peer voice 2 voip
Destination-pattern 1...
Session target ipv4:10.10.10.2
dtmf-relay h245-alphanumeric
Cor outgoing LongDistance

Dial-peer voice 3 voip
Destination-pattern 911
Session target ipv4:10.10.10.2
dtmf-relay h245-alphanumeric

Ephone-dn 1
Number 1001
Cor incoming LocalCall
```

The COR list applied for incoming calls on ephone-dn 1 is not equal to or a superset of the COR list applied to outgoing calls on dial peer 2. Hence, a call originated from ephone-dn 1 cannot be terminated or connected via dial peer 2.

A more complex restriction is put in place by applying the COR list to the various dial peers and ephone-dns. Assume that Phone A is an employee's work phone and Phone B is a manager's phone. The employee is allowed to make only local calls, toll-free 1-800 calls, and emergency 911 calls. The manager is allowed to make calls without any restriction. The COR configurations are changed accordingly, and the new configuration is shown in Example 17-21.

Example 17-21   *COR Configuration with Multiple Levels of Restriction*

```
router#show running-config
Dial-peer voice 1 voip
Destination-pattern 1800...
Session target:ipv4:10.10.10.2
dtmf-relay h245-alphanumeric
Cor outgoing 1800

Dial-peer voice 2 voip
Destination-pattern 1...
Session target:ipv4:10.10.10.2
dtmf-relay h245-alphanumeric
Cor outgoing LongDistance

Dial-peer voice 3 voip
```

continues

Example 17-21 *COR Configuration with Multiple Levels of Restriction (Continued)*

```
Destination-pattern 911
Session target ipv4:10.10.10.2
dtmf-relay h245-alphanumeric
Cor outgoing 911

Ephone-dn 1
Number 1001

Ephone-dn 2
Number 1002
Cor incoming Manager
```

In this configuration, the COR list for incoming calls associated with ephone-dn 2 is a superset of the COR list for outgoing calls on all voice over IP (VoIP) dial peers. So a call originated from ephone-dn 2 can choose any one of the VoIP dial peers as the outgoing dial peer. On the other hand, no COR list is assigned for incoming calls on ephone-dn 1. Do not assume that because no COR list is assigned for incoming calls under ephone-dn 1 that it is a subset of all the VoIP dial peers. If you are familiar with the **deny any any** statement applied to an access list, the behavior is exactly the opposite for a COR list. If no COR list is applied to a dial peer, calls originating from that dial peer can be terminated on any dial peer irrespective of the COR configuration on the outgoing dial peers.

This means a call that originated from any of the dial peers can be terminated on this dial peer irrespective of the COR list configured for an incoming call on the originating dial peer. Example 17-22 illustrates the subset-superset problem. A summary of this behavior is explained in Table 17-1 .

Example 17-22 *COR Configuration to Illustrate the Subset-Superset Concept*

```
router#show running-config
Dial-peer cor custom
Name phone1
Name phone2
Name phone3
Name phone4

Dial-peer cor list phoneone
Member phone1
Dial-peer cor list phonetwo
Member phone2
Dial-peer cor list phonethree
Member phone3
Dial-peer cor list phonefour
Member phone4
Dial-peer cor list all
Member phone1
Member phone2
Member phone3
```

Example 17-22 *COR Configuration to Illustrate the Subset-Superset Concept (Continued)*

```
Ephone-dn 1
Number 1001
Cor outoing phoneone

Ephone-dn 2
Number 1002
Cor incoming phonetwo

Ephone-dn 3
Number 1003
Cor incoming all
Cor outoing phonethree

Ephone-dn 4
Number 1004
Cor incoming phonefour
```

Table 17-1 *Summary of COR Configuration Scenarios*

COR List on Incoming Dial Peer	COR List on Outgoing Dial Peer	Result	Reason/Example
No COR	No COR	The call succeeds.	COR is not applicable. Example: ephone-dn 1 calling ephone-dn 2
No COR	The COR list is applied for outgoing calls.	The call succeeds.	The incoming dial peer by default has the highest COR priority when no COR is applied. So if you apply no COR for an incoming call leg to a dial peer, this dial peer can make calls out of any other dial peer irrespective of the COR configuration on the outgoing dial peer. Example: ephone-dn 1 calling ephone-dn 3
The COR list is applied for incoming calls.	No COR	The call succeeds.	By default, the outgoing dial peer has the lowest priority. Because there are some COR configurations for incoming calls on the incoming/originating dial peer, it is a superset of the outgoing call COR configurations on the outgoing/terminating dial peer. Example: ephone-dn 2 calling ephone-dn 4

Table 17-1 *Summary of COR Configuration Scenarios (Continued)*

The COR list is applied for incoming calls. (A superset of the COR list is applied for outgoing calls on the outgoing dial peer.)	The COR list is applied for outgoing calls. (A subset of the COR list is applied for incoming calls on the incoming dial peer.)	The call succeeds.	The COR list for incoming calls on the incoming dial peer is a superset of the COR list for outgoing calls on the outgoing dial peer. Example: ephone-dn 3 calling ephone-dn 1
The COR list is applied for incoming calls. (A subset of the COR list is applied for outgoing calls on the outgoing dial peer.)	The COR list is applied for outgoing calls. (A superset of the COR list is applied for incoming calls on the incoming dial peer.)	The call fails.	The COR list for incoming calls on the incoming dial peer is *not* a superset of the COR list for outgoing calls on the outgoing dial peer. Example: ephone-dn 4 calling ephone-dn 1

To summarize, COR configurations are applied to the ephone-dns in Cisco CME. Also, when no COR configuration is applied to a dial peer or ephone-dn, it has the highest priority for an incoming call and the lowest priority for an outgoing call.

Summary

In this chapter you learned how to troubleshoot some of the more sophisticated features commonly used in Cisco CME, such as dialplan patterns, call transfer and conference, MOH, directory services, and COR. Some of the important debugs and **show** commands, such as **debug ephone detail**, **debug ephone moh**, and **show ephone**, were also discussed in detail. The output of these **debug** commands is a very useful tool for troubleshooting other Cisco CME features as well.

The next chapter focuses more on issues related to the integration of Cisco CME with Cisco Unity and H.323 gatekeepers.

This chapter covers the following topics:

- Integrating Cisco CallManager Express (CME) with Cisco Unity voice mail
- Using a centralized Cisco Unity system with a network of Cisco CMEs
- Troubleshooting call transfers and call forwards
- Troubleshooting transcoding
- Troubleshooting H.323 GK integration

## CHAPTER 18

Troubleshooting Cisco CME Network Integration

In the preceding chapters, you learned about the Cisco CallManager Express (CME) architecture, as well as how to implement and troubleshoot its different features.

This chapter discusses advanced troubleshooting topics in which Cisco CME is networked with other systems, such as other Cisco CMEs at multiple sites in your network and with a Cisco Unity system for voice mail. This chapter also discusses troubleshooting supplementary services, such as call transfer and call forward and integrating Cisco CME with an H.323 gatekeeper (GK).

Integrating Cisco CME with Cisco Unity Voice Mail

As discussed in Chapter 11, "Cisco CME External Voice Mail Options," Cisco Unity is a unified messaging application running on Windows 2000. It uses the Skinny Client Control Protocol (SCCP) to integrate with Cisco CME. This section discusses troubleshooting the integration of Cisco Unity with Cisco CME.

Configuring Cisco CME for Cisco Unity

Cisco Unity connects to Cisco CME as an SCCP device. You configure ephone-dns and ephones for Cisco Unity ports to register with Cisco CME. Cisco Unity uses its Windows Telephony Application Programming Interface (TAPI) to integrate with Cisco CME. A Telephony Service Provider (TSP) is implemented to interface with Cisco CME and provide call control services to the Cisco Unity application. Hence, the Cisco Unity TSP and Cisco CME configuration should match.

Example 18-1 shows a sample Cisco CME configuration for a five-port Cisco Unity system.

TIP
This configuration is used in the next troubleshooting sections, so you might want to bookmark this page until you finish this section on Cisco Unity integration.

Example 18-1 *CME Configuration for Cisco Unity to Integrate Using SCCP*

```
cme#show running-config
ephone-dn 8
 number 9050
 preference 0
 huntstop
 mwi on
!
ephone-dn 9
 number 9051
 preference 0 secondary 9 huntstop
 huntstop
 mwi off
!
ephone-dn 10 dual-line
! We need dual-line for Unity to execute consult transfers at its Auto Attendant number
8050
 name Voicemail 1
 preference 1 secondary 9
 no huntstop
!
ephone-dn 11 dual-line
 number 8050
 name Voicemail 2
 preference 2 secondary 9
 no huntstop
!
ephone-dn 12 dual-line
 number 8050
 name Voicemail 3
 preference 3 secondary 9
 no huntstop
!
ephone-dn 13 dual-line
 number 8050
 preference 4 secondary 9
 huntstop
!
ephone-dn 14
 number A8
 preference 0 secondary 9
 huntstop
!
ephone 3
```

Example 18-1   *CME Configuration for Cisco Unity to Integrate Using SCCP (Continued)*

```
  vm-device-id CiscoUM1-VI1
  button  1:10
 !
 ephone 4
  vm-device-id CiscoUM1-VI2
  button  1:11
 !
 ephone 5
  vm-device-id CiscoUM1-VI3
  button  1:12
 !
 ephone 6
  vm-device-id CiscoUM1-VI4
  button  1:13
 !
 ephone 7
  vm-device-id CiscoUM1-VI5
  button  1:14
```

Example 18-1 shows seven ephone-dns configured on Cisco CME even though the Cisco Unity system has only five ports. Two of these ephone-dns (8 and 9) are meant for the message waiting indicator (MWI), which is discussed in the "Troubleshooting MWI" section. The remaining five ephone-dns are meant for call completion to each of the Cisco Unity ports. The voice mail pilot number in this example is 8050.

Note that four of the ephone-dns have the same number (8050), forming a hunt group, and that the last one has a different number (preferably nondialable). The reason for this is that Cisco Unity uses an outdial mechanism to turn MWI on or off. Hence, it needs one or more ports to place the MWI calls to Cisco CME. There is a possibility that a port can be seized by Cisco CME and Cisco Unity at the same time, resulting in a glare condition. Therefore, it is good practice to dedicate one or more ports (depending on the number of subscribers in your system) to MWI calls. In Example 18-1, the last ephone-dn (ephone-dn 14, with number A8) is dedicated to MWI only: A8 cannot be dialed from a phone keypad.

Figure 18-1 shows the Cisco Unity port allocation configuration for taking calls and for MWI notification. This allocation is done depending on the number of subscribers in your system and the amount of outdialing, consisting of notifications, traps, and possibly networked calls for Audio Messaging Interchange Specification (AMIS).

Figure 18-1 *Cisco Unity Port Allocation*

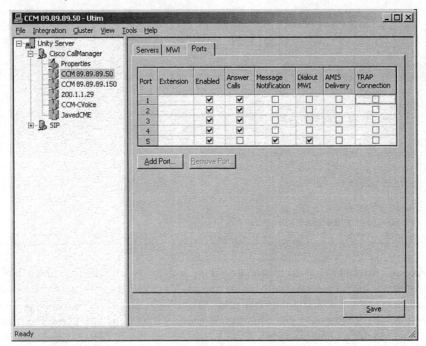

Note that the ephone-dns 10, 11, and 12 shown in Example 18-1 include a **no-huntstop** and **preference** configuration. This creates hunt group functionality for the Cisco Unity ports so that when a call is diverted to voice mail, it is connected using one of the available ports. In some instances (depending on your dialplan configuration), you might have to change the IOS dial peer **hunt** algorithm as shown in Example 18-2. For more information about dial peer hunt options, you can refer to Cisco IOS dial peer configuration guide at Cisco.com. Under normal circumstances, this configuration is not needed.

Example 18-2 *Dial Peer Hunt Configuration*

```
cme#show running-config

CME#configure terminal
CME(config)#dial-peer hunt 2
```

In addition to the ephone-dns, special ephone configurations are shown in Example 18-1. These ephones are needed for the Cisco Unity TSP to register with Cisco CME. Note that instead of the **mac-address** command under the ephone, this configuration uses the **vm-device-id** command, indicating that this ephone is meant for Cisco Unity ports rather than a Cisco IP phone.

The device identifiers used in the ephone configuration have to match the identifiers used by the Cisco Unity TSP configuration, as shown in Figure 18-2.

Figure 18-2 *Cisco Unity TSP Configuration*

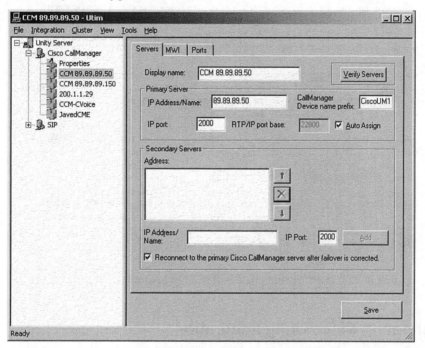

The next important item is the configuration of the MWI DNs. Cisco Unity uses an outdial mechanism to turn MWI on or off. In this mechanism, Cisco Unity goes off-hook (just like any other phone), but it uses a special off-hook SCCP message that lets Cisco Unity use a different calling number. When it wants to do an MWI operation, Cisco Unity initiates a call with the calling number equal to the extension for which MWI must be turned on or off. Then it dials a special number called an MWI directory number (DN). In Example 18-1, that special number is 9050 for ON and 9051 for OFF. The call processing mechanism for these special DNs in Cisco CME is that it turns the MWI on or off for the corresponding IP phone, depending on the called number. You'll take a closer look at these protocol messages in the troubleshooting sections.

The call processing mechanism for these speical DNs in Cisco CME is such that after you have configured both Cisco CME and Cisco Unity properly, you should see that Cisco Unity has registered its ports to Cisco CME, as shown in Example 18-3.

Example 18-3 *Cisco Unity Ports Registered to Cisco CME*

```
cme#show ephone registered
ephone-3 Device:CiscoUM1-VI1 TCP socket:[5] activeLine:0 REGISTERED
mediaActive:0 offhook:0 ringing:0 reset:0 reset_sent:0 paging 0 debug:0
```

continues

Example 18-3 *Cisco Unity Ports Registered to Cisco CME (Continued)*

```
IP:200.1.1.30 1510 Unity Voice Port  keepalive 425 max_line 1
button 1: dn 10 number 8050 CH1    IDLE


ephone-4 Device:CiscoUM1-VI2 TCP socket:[1] activeLine:0 REGISTERED
mediaActive:0 offhook:0 ringing:0 reset:0 reset_sent:0 paging 0 debug:0
IP:200.1.1.30 1497 Unity Voice Port  keepalive 425 max_line 1
button 1: dn 11 number 8050 CH1    IDLE


ephone-5 Device:CiscoUM1-VI3 TCP socket:[2] activeLine:0 REGISTERED
mediaActive:0 offhook:0 ringing:0 reset:0 reset_sent:0 paging 0 debug:0
IP:200.1.1.30 1505 Unity Voice Port  keepalive 425 max_line 1
button 1: dn 12 number 8050 CH1    IDLE


ephone-6 Device:CiscoUM1-VI4 TCP socket:[4] activeLine:0 REGISTERED
mediaActive:0 offhook:0 ringing:0 reset:0 reset_sent:0 paging 0 debug:0
IP:200.1.1.30 1509 Unity Voice Port  keepalive 425 max_line 1
button 1: dn 13 number 8050 CH1    IDLE


ephone-7 Device:CiscoUM1-VI5 TCP socket:[3] activeLine:0 REGISTERED
mediaActive:0 offhook:0 ringing:0 reset:0 reset_sent:0 paging 0 debug:0
IP:200.1.1.30 1508 Unity Voice Port  keepalive 425 max_line 1
button 1: dn 14 number A8 CH1    IDLE
```

The next section describes the process of troubleshooting the integration.

Troubleshooting Cisco Unity Integration

After you have correctly configured Cisco CME and Cisco Unity to interwork, as discussed in the preceding section, the system should work fine. However, in case you face any issues in this area, this section provides you with ways to identify and fix the problem.

Here are the most important aspects of integrating Cisco Unity with Cisco CME:

- Passing correct call information (calling number, called number, last redirecting/original called number, call type, and reason if the call is forwarded to Cisco Unity) to Cisco Unity so that it identifies the correct mailbox for leaving a message

- Passing correct dual-tone multifrequency (DTMF) information from different call legs

- Executing transfers to extensions from the Cisco Unity automated attendant (AA)

- Turning MWI on and off when appropriate

Verifying Call Information—Wrong Mailbox Selection

If your users complain of reaching the wrong mailbox or no mailbox after a call forward to Cisco Unity, the reason may be because the wrong call information is passed to Cisco Unity from Cisco CME. Turn on the **debug ephone state** on Cisco CME to verify that the original Called Number field is correct. Sample output from this command is shown in Example 18-4.

In the example, extension 9001 calls extension 9002, but 9002 does not answer. The call rolls over to the Cisco Unity system voice mail.

Example 18-4   debug ephone state *Command for Forwarded Calls*

```
cme#debug ephone state
*Oct 31 21:11:15.765: ephone-1[8]:OFFHOOK
*Oct 31 21:11:15.765: ephone-1[8]:SIEZE on activeLine 1 activeChan 1
*Oct 31 21:11:15.765: ephone-1[8]:SetCallState line 1 DN 1 chan 1 ref 198
  TsOffHook
*Oct 31 21:11:15.765: ephone-1[8]:SpeakerPhoneOffHook mute 0
*Oct 31 21:11:15.769: DN 1 chan 1 Voice_Mode
*Oct 31 21:11:15.769: dn_tone_control DN=1 chan 1 tonetype=33:DtInsideDialTone
  onoff=1 pid=158
*Oct 31 21:11:15.769: dn_tone_control DN=1 chan 1 tonetype=0:DtSilence onoff=0
  pid=158
*Oct 31 21:11:15.769: dn_tone_control DN=1 chan 1 tonetype=0:DtSilence onoff=0
  pid=158
*Oct 31 21:11:15.777: ephone-1[8]:SetCallState line 1 DN 1 chan 1 ref 198
  TsRingOut
*Oct 31 21:11:15.777: ephone-1[8]:Call Info DN 1 line 1 ref 198
  called 9002 calling 9001 origcalled 9002 calltype 2
*Oct 31 21:11:15.777: ephone-1[8]:Call Info for chan 1
*Oct 31 21:11:15.777: ephone-1[8]: name-9001 calling
*Oct 31 21:11:15.777: ephone-1[8]: No-Name
*Oct 31 21:11:15.781: ***Fixed called DN binding DN 1 chan 1 called 2
  chan 1 (was called -1 chan 1)
*Oct 31 21:11:15.781: ephone-2[7]:SetCallState line 1 DN 2 chan 1 ref
  199 TsRingIn
*Oct 31 21:11:15.781: ephone-2[7]:Call Info DN 2 line 1 ref 199
  called 9002 calling 9001 origcalled 9002 calltype 1
*Oct 31 21:11:15.781: ephone-2[7]:Call Info for chan 1
*Oct 31 21:11:15.781: ephone-2[7]: name-9001 calling
*Oct 31 21:11:15.781: ephone-2[7]: name-9002
*Oct 31 21:11:15.781: ephone-2[7]:Ringer Inside Ring On
*Oct 31 21:11:15.781: dn_tone_control DN=1 chan 1 tonetype=36:DtAlertingTone
  onoff=1 pid=158
*Oct 31 21:11:25.781: SkinnyUpdateRedirectNumber DN 1 chan 1 to 8050 reason 2
*Oct 31 21:11:25.781: ephone-2[7]:DN 2 disc reason 19 no answer state RINGING
*Oct 31 21:11:25.781: Reset called DN binding for DN 1 (was 2)
*Oct 31 21:11:25.781: ephone-2[7]:SetCallState line 1 DN 2 chan 1 ref 199 TsOnHook
*Oct 31 21:11:25.781: dn_tone_control DN=2 chan 1 tonetype=0:DtSilence onoff=0
  pid=158
*Oct 31 21:11:25.781: ephone-2[7]:SpeakerPhoneOnHook
*Oct 31 21:11:25.781: ephone-2[7]:Ringer Off
*Oct 31 21:11:25.785: ***Fixed called DN binding DN 1 chan 1 called 10 chan 1
  (was called -1 chan 1)
*Oct 31 21:11:25.785: ephone-3[5]:SetCallState line 1 DN 10 chan 1 ref 200
  TsRingIn
*Oct 31 21:11:25.789: ephone-3[5]:Call Info DN 10 line 1 ref 200 called 8050
  calling 9001 origcalled 9002 calltype 3
*Oct 31 21:11:25.789: ephone-3[5]:Call Info for chan 1
*Oct 31 21:11:25.789: ephone-3[5]: name-9001 calling
*Oct 31 21:11:25.789: ephone-3[5]: Voicemail 1
*Oct 31 21:11:25.789: ephone-3[5]:Ringer Inside Ring On
```

If you have access to the Cisco Unity graphical user interface (GUI), you can view the call information shown in Example 18-4 in a graphical manner using the Call Viewer application available on Cisco Unity server. Two of the fields shown in Example 18-4 might help you understand the call flow better—calltype and reason. The Calltype field refers to how the call was set up. The values are

- **1**—Inbound call
- **2**—Outbound call
- **3**—Forwarded call

Similarly, the Reason field signifies why the call was forwarded (such as no answer, busy, or unconditional).

If you are using the Cisco CME **dialplan-pattern** command, calls may come into Cisco CME using the complete E.164 number associated with the phones. Example 18-5 shows such an example. Here the call is placed by dialing 4085559002 instead of 9002, the number that would be used if the call came in from a Public Switched Telephone Network (PSTN) caller. Some of the output in the example is omitted for brevity. For Cisco Unity to understand this correctly, you must configure an alternate extension for these subscribers on Cisco Unity, as shown in Figure 18-3.

Example 18-5 *Call Dialed Using the E.164 Number of a Phone Forwarded to Voice Mail*

```
cme#debug ephone state
*Oct 31 21:11:15.765: ephone-1[8]:OFFHOOK
*Oct 31 21:11:15.765: ephone-1[8]:SIEZE on activeLine 1 activeChan 1
*Oct 31 21:11:15.765: ephone-1[8]:SetCallState line 1 DN 1 chan 1 ref 198
  TsOffHook
......
*Oct 31 21:11:15.777: ephone-1[8]:SetCallState line 1 DN 1 chan 1 ref 198
   TsRingOut
*Oct 31 21:11:15.777: ephone-1[8]:Call Info DN 1 line 1 ref 198
  called 4085559002 calling 9001 origcalled 4085559002 calltype 2
*Oct 31 21:11:15.777: ephone-1[8]:Call Info for chan 1
......
*Oct 31 21:11:25.781: SkinnyUpdateRedirectNumber DN 1 chan 1 to 8050 reason 2
*Oct 31 21:11:25.781: ephone-2[7]:DN 2 disc reason 19 no answer state RINGING
*Oct 31 21:11:25.781: Reset called DN binding for DN 1 (was 2)
*Oct 31 21:11:25.781: ephone-2[7]:SetCallState line 1 DN 2 chan 1 ref 199 TsOnHook
*Oct 31 21:11:25.781: dn_tone_control DN=2 chan 1 tonetype=0:DtSilence onoff=0
  pid=158
*Oct 31 21:11:25.781: ephone-2[7]:SpeakerPhoneOnHook
*Oct 31 21:11:25.781: ephone-2[7]:Ringer Off
*Oct 31 21:11:25.785: ***Fixed called DN binding DN 1 chan 1 called 10 chan 1
   (was called -1 chan 1)
*Oct 31 21:11:25.785: ephone-3[5]:SetCallState line 1 DN 10 chan 1 ref 200 TsRingIn
*Oct 31 21:11:25.789: ephone-3[5]:Call Info DN 10 line 1 ref 200 called 8050
  calling 9001 origcalled 4085559002 calltype 3
*Oct 31 21:11:25.789: ephone-3[5]:Call Info for chan 1
*Oct 31 21:11:25.789: ephone-3[5]: name-9001 calling
*Oct 31 21:11:25.789: ephone-3[5]: Voicemail 1
*Oct 31 21:11:25.789: ephone-3[5]:Ringer Inside Ring On
```

Figure 18-3 *Configuring Alternate Extensions on Cisco Unity*

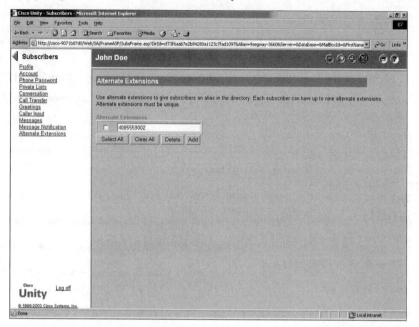

Troubleshooting DTMF—No Response to Digit Presses from Cisco Unity

When callers communicate with a voice mail system, the interface they use is called the Telephony User Interface (TUI). The user instructs the voice mail system what to do by pressing digits on the phone. Each digit usually maps to a specific action in the voice mail system.

If you are using Cisco Unity with Cisco CME, the calls can come to Cisco Unity from another Cisco CME or PSTN gateway using the H.323 protocol or from a PSTN interface on the local Cisco CME system. If the call arrives from H.323, the **h245-alphanumeric** DTMF relay option must be used between Cisco CME and the calling PSTN gateway. The other two DTMF options are not supported for IP phones later than H.323. For calls coming in from other interfaces, such as ISDN Basic Rate Interface/Primary Rate Interface (BRI/PRI) and analog PSTN lines, as well as from local IP phones, there is no need for a specific DTMF relay configuration. Cisco CME and Cisco IOS automatically handle relaying the digits to the Cisco Unity system.

Cisco CME then translates the incoming H.245 DTMF messages to SCCP KeypadButtonPress messages for Cisco Unity. Similarly, if the call is coming from a local PSTN trunk on your Cisco CME system, Cisco CME translates the incoming inband DTMF digits from the PSTN trunk to SCCP messages. If you are facing any issues in this area, turn on the following combination of debugs on Cisco CME to troubleshoot this situation:

- **debug ephone detail**—For calls originating from local IP phones

- **debug cch323 h245** and **debug ephone detail**—For calls originating from a far-end H.323 device

- **debug vtsp all** and **debug ephone detail**—For calls coming in from local PSTN interfaces

The highlighted lines in Example 18-6 show DTMF events coming from an H.323/H.245 leg relayed onto an SCCP leg to Cisco Unity.

Example 18-6 *DTMF Relay from an H.245 Call Leg to an SCCP Call Leg to Cisco Unity*

```
cme#debug cch323 h245
H245 State Machine tracing is enabled
cme#debug ephone detail
*Oct 31 21:25:15.445: //326/8E5B321F806C/H323/run_h245_iwf_sm: received
  IWF_EV_PROC_TUNNEL while at state IWF_ACTIVE
*Oct 31 21:25:15.449: //326/8E5B321F806C/H323/cch323_h245_user_input_ind:
  Received User Input Indication
*Oct 31 21:25:15.449: //326/8E5B321F806C/H323/cch323_h245_user_input_alpha:
  Processing alphanumeric ind (#)
*Oct 31 21:25:15.449: dn_tone_control DN=10 chan 1 tonetype=15:DtDtmfPound
  onoff=1 pid=158
.....
*Oct 31 21:25:15.449: called DN -1 chan 1, calling DN -1 chan 1 phone 3
  incoming s2s:0
*Oct 31 21:25:15.449: ephone-3[5]:is_auto_local 0 for DN 10
*Oct 31 21:25:15.449: Skinny StationKeypadButtonMessage 15 sent on socket [5]
  DtDtmfPound
*Oct 31 21:25:15.649: dn_tone_control DN=10 chan 1 tonetype=0:DtSilence onoff=0
  pid=158
*Oct 31 21:25:21.765: //326/8E5B321F806C/H323/run_h245_iwf_sm: received
  IWF_EV_PROC_TUNNEL while at state IWF_ACTIVE
*Oct 31 21:25:21.765: //326/8E5B321F806C/H323/cch323_h245_user_input_ind:
  Received User Input Indication
*Oct 31 21:25:21.765: //326/8E5B321F806C/H323/cch323_h245_user_input_alpha:
  Processing alphanumeric ind (3)
*Oct 31 21:25:21.765: dn_tone_control DN=10 chan 1 tonetype=3:DtDtmf3 onoff=1
  pid=158
...........
*Oct 31 21:25:21.765: called DN -1 chan 1, calling DN -1 chan 1 phone 3
  incoming s2s:0
*Oct 31 21:25:21.765: ephone-3[5]:is_auto_local 0 for DN 10
*Oct 31 21:25:21.765: Skinny StationKeypadButtonMessage 3 sent on
  socket [5] DtDtmf3
*Oct 31 21:25:21.965: dn_tone_control DN=10 chan 1 tonetype=0:DtSilence
  onoff=0 pid=158
*Oct 31 21:25:21.965: SkinnyGetCallState for DN 10 chan 1 CONNECTED
*Oct 31 21:25:21.965: called DN -1 chan 1, calling DN -1 chan 1 phone 3
  incoming s2s:0
*Oct 31 21:25:21.965: SkinnyGetCallState for DN 10 chan 1 CONNECTED
*Oct 31 21:25:21.965: called DN -1 chan 1, calling DN -1 chan 1 phone 3
  incoming s2s:0
*Oct 31 21:25:21.965: SkinnyGetCallState for DN 10 chan 1 CONNECTED
```

Example 18-6 *DTMF Relay from an H.245 Call Leg to an SCCP Call Leg to Cisco Unity (Continued)*

```
*Oct 31 21:25:21.965: called DN -1 chan 1, calling DN -1 chan 1 phone 3
  incoming s2s:0
*Oct 31 21:25:21.965: ephone-3[5]:is_auto_local 0 for DN 10
*Oct 31 21:25:21.965: ephone-3[5]:StopTone sent to ephone
*Oct 31 21:25:30.097: //326/8E5B321F806C/H323/run_h245_iwf_sm: received
  IWF_EV_PROC_TUNNEL while at state IWF_ACTIVE
*Oct 31 21:25:30.097: //326/8E5B321F806C/H323/cch323_h245_user_input_ind:
  Received User Input Indication
*Oct 31 21:25:30.097: //326/8E5B321F806C/H323/cch323_h245_user_input_alpha:
  Processing alphanumeric ind (1)
  ......
*Oct 31 21:25:30.101: SkinnyGetCallState for DN 10 chan 1 CONNECTED
*Oct 31 21:25:30.101: called DN -1 chan 1, calling DN -1 chan 1 phone 3
  incoming s2s:0
*Oct 31 21:25:30.101: ephone-3[5]:is_auto_local 0 for DN 10
*Oct 31 21:25:30.101: Skinny StationKeypadButtonMessage 1 sent
  on socket [5] DtDtmf1
*Oct 31 21:25:30.297: dn_tone_control DN=10 chan 1 tonetype=0:DtSilence
  onoff=0 pid=158
*Oct 31 21:25:30.297: SkinnyGetCallState for DN 10 chan 1 CONNECTED
```

If you are not seeing the digits in the H.323/H.245 debugs, make sure that the calling gateway has the correct configuration under the dial peer pointing to the Cisco CME hosting the Cisco Unity system. For the preceding Cisco Unity integration configuration, every far-end calling gateway should have a dial peer like the one shown in Example 18-7.

Example 18-7 *H.323 Dial Peer for Cisco Unity Ports Pointing to a CME Hosting Cisco Unity*

```
dial-peer voice 1 voip
  description "H.323 Dial peer pointing to CME hosting Cisco Unity"
  destination-pattern 8050
  session target ipv4:1.1.1.1
  dtmf-relay h245-alphanumeric
  codec G711ulaw
```

Troubleshooting Cisco Unity AA Integration

Callers may complain that when they dial an extension using the Cisco Unity AA, the call is not transferred to the correct user. This might be caused by an incorrect configuration on Cisco Unity or Cisco CME for AA integration.

Because Cisco Unity is an SCCP device like an IP phone, it uses the same methods to transfer a caller to the desired extension. Every extension that is a transfer target has to be present in the Cisco Unity database; otherwise, Cisco Unity cannot transfer the call. This avoids toll fraud by a caller who can call from the PSTN into the AA and then transfer to another PSTN number and end up charging the call to the business that owns the AA.

Cisco Unity can use a consult transfer (sometimes called a *supervised transfer*) or a blind transfer mechanism to transfer the call to the desired extension. A consult transfer allows the caller to recover and try again if the intended party is busy. Using this method requires a particular setting on Cisco Unity and configuring the **transfer-system full-consult** command on Cisco CME. Also, all the ephone-dns configured for Cisco Unity port registration must be set for dual line, as shown in Example 18-1. The Cisco Unity setting is shown in Figure 18-4. The important settings here are yes, ring subscriber's extension and supervise transfer for the user the caller is trying to reach. You select options on this page depending on the behavior you want for different subscribers.

Figure 18-4   *Configuring Call Transfer Settings*

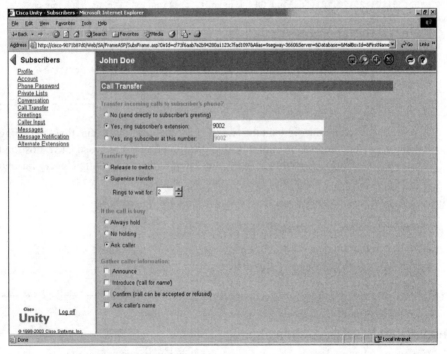

If you experience any issues with Cisco Unity AA transfers, verify the configuration needed for that particular scenario. This means checking the call transfer setting for the user involved in the call. If all the configurations on Cisco Unity are correct, troubleshoot the issue on Cisco CME.

Troubleshooting this issue on Cisco CME is no different from troubleshooting any other call-transfer issue on Cisco CME. Cisco Unity is just another SCCP device like any other IP phone and uses the same protocol mechanism that a real IP phone would use. The debugs of a sample consult call transfer initiated by the Cisco Unity AA are shown in Example 18-8. This example shows a caller placing a call to the Cisco Unity AA and dialing 9003. Cisco Unity establishes a consult call while putting the original call on hold. In this particular case, extension 9003 is busy and Cisco Unity AA retrieves the original call to give the caller an option to try other extensions or leave a message for 9003. If the option selected for this user is blind transfer, the call flow will be different. In this case, Cisco Unity releases the call and asks Cisco CME to set up a call to the specified extension. If the extension is busy, the caller hears busy tone or reaches the user's mailbox, depending on the configuration. You can use the same **debug** commands to troubleshoot blind transfers.

Example 18-8   *Cisco Unity AA Consult Transfer Call Flow*

```
CME#debug ephone detail
*Oct 31 21:51:57.561: ephone-3[5]:SetCallState line 1 DN 10 chan 1 ref 238 TsRingIn
*Oct 31 21:51:57.565: ephone-3[5]:Call Info DN 10 line 1 ref 238 called calling
  2903 origcalled 8050 calltype 1
*Oct 31 21:51:57.565: ephone-3[5]:Call Info for chan 1
*Oct 31 21:51:57.565: ephone-3[5]:Original Called Name Voicemail 1
*Oct 31 21:51:57.565: ephone-3[5]: No-Name calling
*Oct 31 21:51:57.565: ephone-3[5]: Voicemail 1
*Oct 31 21:51:57.565: ephone-3[5]:Ringer Outside Ring On
*Oct 31 21:51:57.797: ephone-3[5]:OFFHOOK
*Oct 31 21:51:57.797: ephone-3[5]:Ringer Off
*Oct 31 21:51:57.797: ephone-3[5]:ANSWER call
*Oct 31 21:51:57.797: ephone-3[5][CiscoUM1-VI1]:Answer Incoming call from
  ephone-(-1) DN -1 chan 1
*Oct 31 21:51:57.797: ephone-3[5]:Incoming Answer: can't find ephone
  calling DN 10 chan 1
*Oct 31 21:51:57.797: defer_start for DN 10 chan 1 at CONNECTED
*Oct 31 21:51:57.797: ephone-3[5]:SetCallState line 1 DN 10 chan 1 ref 238
  TsConnected
*Oct 31 21:51:57.801: DN 10 chan 1 Voice_Mode
*Oct 31 21:51:57.801: ephone-3[5]:OpenReceive DN 10 chan 1 codec 4:G711Ulaw64k
    duration 20 ms bytes 160
*Oct 31 21:51:57.801: ephone-3[5]:OpenReceiveChannelAck:IP 200.1.1.30,
port=22866, dn_index=10, dn=10, chan=1
*Oct 31 21:51:57.801: ephone-3[5]:StartMedia 200.1.1.29 port=2000
*Oct 31 21:51:57.801: DN 10 chan 1 codec 4:G711Ulaw64k duration 20 ms bytes 160
*Oct 31 21:51:58.813: ephone-3[5]:Call Info DN 10 line 1 ref 238 called
  calling 2903 origcalled 8050 calltype 1
*Oct 31 21:51:58.813: ephone-3[5]:Call Info for chan 1
*Oct 31 21:51:58.813: ephone-3[5]:Original Called Name Voicemail 1
*Oct 31 21:51:58.813: ephone-3[5]: No-Name calling
*Oct 31 21:51:58.813: ephone-3[5]: Voicemail 1
*Oct 31 21:52:02.953: dn_tone_control DN=10 chan 1 tonetype=9:DtDtmf9
  onoff=1 pid=158
*Oct 31 21:52:03.153: dn_tone_control DN=10 chan 1 tonetype=0:DtSilence
  onoff=0 pid=158
*Oct 31 21:52:03.253: dn_tone_control DN=10 chan 1 tonetype=10:DtDtmf0
  onoff=1 pid=158
*Oct 31 21:52:03.453: dn_tone_control DN=10 chan 1 tonetype=0:DtSilence onoff=0
  pid=158
*Oct 31 21:52:03.553: dn_tone_control DN=10 chan 1 tonetype=10:DtDtmf0
  onoff=1 pid=158
*Oct 31 21:52:03.753: dn_tone_control DN=10 chan 1 tonetype=0:DtSilence
  onoff=0 pid=158
```

continues

Example 18-8 *Cisco Unity AA Consult Transfer Call Flow (Continued)*

```
*Oct 31 21:52:03.853: dn_tone_control DN=10 chan 1 tonetype=3:DtDtmf3
  onoff=1 pid=158
*Oct 31 21:52:04.053: dn_tone_control DN=10 chan 1 tonetype=0:DtSilence
  onoff=0 pid=158
*Oct 31 21:52:07.385: ephone-3[5]:TransferButtonPress
*Oct 31 21:52:07.385: ephone-3 TRANSFER using transfer-system full
  DN 10 consult transfer
*Oct 31 21:52:07.385: ephone-3[5]:Transfer with consult line 1 DN 10
  chan 1 using second line 1 DN 10 chan 2
*Oct 31 21:52:07.385: ephone-3[5]:Consult for line 1 DN 10 chan 1 using line 1
  DN 10 chan 2
*Oct 31 21:52:07.385: ephone-3[5]:HoldButtonPress (allow_toggle = 0)
*Oct 31 21:52:07.385: ephone-3[5]:HoldButtonPress HOLD activated for DN 10
  chan 1
*Oct 31 21:52:07.385: ephone-3[5][CiscoUM1-VI1]:SetCallState line 1 ref 238
  state 10 TsCallTransfer ignored
*Oct 31 21:52:07.385: ephone-3[5]:CloseReceive
*Oct 31 21:52:07.385: ephone-3[5]:StopMedia
*Oct 31 21:52:08.397: PredictTarget match 9003 DN 3 not idle: SIEZE
*Oct 31 21:52:08.397: PredictTarget no idle match for 9003 after 1 attempts
*Oct 31 21:52:08.649: ephone-3[5]:ONHOOK (from phone msgID=7)
*Oct 31 21:52:08.649: ephone-3[5]:TRANSFER quit on line 1 DN 10
*Oct 31 21:52:08.649: ephone-3[5]:SetCallState line 1 DN 10 chan 1
  ref 238 TsHold
*Oct 31 21:52:10.581: dn_tone_control DN=3 chan 1 tonetype=37:DtReorderTone
  onoff=pid=158
*Oct 31 21:52:18.729: ephone-3[5]:SpeakerPhoneOffHook mute 0
*Oct 31 21:52:18.729: ephone-3[5]:OFFHOOK
*Oct 31 21:52:18.729: ephone-3[5]:RestoreHoldCall DN 10 chan 1
*Oct 31 21:52:18.729: ephone-3[5]:RestoreHoldCall using activeLine 1
  activeChan 1
*Oct 31 21:52:18.729: ephone-3[5]:SetCallState line 1 DN 10 chan 1
    ref 238 TsConnected
*Oct 31 21:52:18.729: ephone-3[5]:OpenReceive DN 10 chan 1 codec
  4:G711Ulaw64k  duration 20 ms bytes 160
*Oct 31 21:52:18.729: ephone-3[5]:SetCallState line 1 DN 10 chan 1
  ref 238 TsConnected
*Oct 31 21:52:18.733: ephone-3[5]:OpenReceiveChannelAck:IP 200.1.1.30,
  port=22866,  dn_index=10, dn=10, chan=1
*Oct 31 21:52:18.733: ephone-3[5]:StartMedia 200.1.1.29 port=2000
*Oct 31 21:52:18.733: DN 10 chan 1 codec 4:G711Ulaw64k duration 20 ms
  bytes 160
*Oct 31 21:52:33.769: dn_tone_control DN=10 chan 1 tonetype=3:DtDtmf3
  onoff=1 pid=158
```

Troubleshooting MWI

Cisco Unity uses a dialout mechanism for MWI. Cisco Unity places a call to a preconfigured number on Cisco CME by going off-hook using a special SCCP message. This special message lets Cisco Unity insert a different calling number than its own. Assume that there is a new voice message for extension 9002. Cisco Unity uses 9002 as the calling number in this special off-hook message and then places a call to one of the MWI DNs (9050 and 9051 in Example 18-1). The special processing of calls by these DNs turns on the MWI light on all the phones associated with extension 9002.

If extension 9002 is associated with button 1 of a phone, the MWI light turns on for that phone. If extension 9002 is associated with any button on the phone other than 1, you see a blinking envelope next to the line on the phone. Example 18-9 shows debug output for turning on MWI for extension 9002. This example uses **debug ephone detail**. Some of the insignificant debug output has been removed. Important things to note in this debug output are the off-hook message by a Cisco Unity port, dialing the MWI DN by Cisco Unity (KeypadButtonMessage), and the calling number. The call should be from the port assigned just to outdial to the MWI DNs. Also notice the "Set MWI" message for the ephone with extension 9002.

Example 18-9 *MWI Call Flow Debugs*

```
CME#debug ephone detail
*Oct 31 22:01:04.505: ephone-7[3]:OFFHOOK with calling party 9002
*Oct 31 22:01:04.505: SkinnyGetCallState for DN 14 chan 1 IDLE
*Oct 31 22:01:04.505: called DN -1 chan 1, calling DN -1 chan 1 phone -1 s2s:0
*Oct 31 22:01:04.505: ephone-7[3]:OFFHOOK
.........
*Oct 31 22:01:04.513: SkinnyGetCallState for DN 14 chan 1 SIEZE
*Oct 31 22:01:04.513: called DN -1 chan 1, calling DN -1 chan 1 phone 7 s2s:0
*Oct 31 22:01:04.513: ephone-7[3]:is_auto_local 0 for DN 14
*Oct 31 22:01:04.513: Skinny StartTone 33 sent on  ephone socket [3]
  DtInsideDialTone
*Oct 31 22:01:04.517: ephone-7[3]:KeypadButtonMessage 9
......
*Oct 31 22:01:04.517: ephone-7[3]:StopTone sent to ephone
......
*Oct 31 22:01:04.521: ephone-7[3]:KeypadButtonMessage 0
*Oct 31 22:01:04.521: SkinnyGetCallState for DN 14 chan 1 SIEZE
.........
*Oct 31 22:01:04.521: ephone-7[3]:Store ReDial digit: 90
*Oct 31 22:01:04.521: ephone-7[3]:SkinnyTryCall to 90 instance 1
  start at 0 secondary 0
*Oct 31 22:01:04.525: ephone-7[3]:KeypadButtonMessage 5
*Oct 31 22:01:04.525: SkinnyGetCallState for DN 14 chan 1 SIEZE
......
*Oct 31 22:01:04.525: ephone-7[3]:Store ReDial digit: 905
*Oct 31 22:01:04.525: ephone-7[3]:SkinnyTryCall to 905 instance 1
  start at 0 secondary 0
*Oct 31 22:01:04.525: ephone-7[3]:KeypadButtonMessage 0
*Oct 31 22:01:04.525: SkinnyGetCallState for DN 14 chan 1 SIEZE
*Oct 31 22:01:04.525: called DN -1 chan 1, calling DN -1 chan 1 phone 7 s2s:0
......
*Oct 31 22:01:04.525: ephone-7[3]:SkinnyTryCall to 9050 instance 2
  start at 9 secondary 0
*Oct 31 22:01:04.529: SkinnyUpdateDnState by EFXS_PROCEEDING
  for DN 14 chan 1 to state ALERTING
.........
```

continues

Example 18-9   *MWI Call Flow Debugs (Continued)*

```
*Oct 31 22:01:04.533: SkinnyGetCallState for DN 14 chan 1 ALERTING
*Oct 31 22:01:04.533: called DN -1 chan 1, calling DN -1 chan 1 phone 7 s2s:0
*Oct 31 22:01:04.533: ephone-7[3]:SetLineLamp 1 to ON
*Oct 31 22:01:04.533: SkinnyUpdateDnState set call info for DN 14 chan 1
*Oct 31 22:01:04.533: SetCallInfo calling dn 14 chan 1 dn 14 chan 1
calling [A8] called [9050] calling name
*Oct 31 22:01:04.533: SetCallInfo DN 14 chan 1 is not skinny-to-skinny
*Oct 31 22:01:04.533: SkinnyGetCallState for DN 14 chan 1 ALERTING
*Oct 31 22:01:04.533: called DN -1 chan 1, calling DN -1 chan 1 phone 7 s2s:0
*Oct 31 22:01:04.533: ephone-7[3]:DisplayCallInfo outgoing call
*Oct 31 22:01:04.533: ephone-7[3]:SkinnyTryCall to 9050 instance 1
   start at 0 secondary 0
SkinnyTryCall to 9050 instance 1 match DN 8
*Oct 31 22:01:04.533: ephone-7[3]:Call Info DN 14 line 1 ref 248 called
   calling A8 origcalled 9050 calltype 2
*Oct 31 22:01:04.533: ephone-7[3]:Call Info for chan 1
*Oct 31 22:01:04.533: ephone-7[3]: No-Name calling
*Oct 31 22:01:04.537: ephone-7[3]: No-Name
*Oct 31 22:01:04.537: Phone 1 DN 2 MWI on 0 messages
*Oct 31 22:01:04.537: ephone-2[7]:Set MWI line 1 to ON count 0
*Oct 31 22:01:04.537: ephone-2[7]:Set MWI line 0 to ON count 0
```

A Cisco Unity System with a Network of Cisco CMEs— Centralized Voice Mail Architecture

Cisco Unity can support thousands of subscribers, so when it is used with Cisco CME, it often makes sense to share a single Cisco Unity system among many Cisco CMEs in a network of Cisco CME nodes. The advantages of doing this instead of using a Cisco Unity Express (UE) system at each site are that voice mail administration can be done at a single central location, and a voice mail networking configuration is not needed to exchange messages between users located at different sites. However, you still need a Cisco CME collocated with Cisco Unity because Cisco Unity registers with only a single local Cisco CME system. This configuration was discussed in Chapter 11.

A centralized Cisco Unity system also means that all calls that access voice mail have to travel over the WAN. This requires a quality of service (QoS)-enabled WAN backbone as well as more bandwidth, especially if Cisco Unity is configured to use the G.711 codec. You can reduce bandwidth consumption in several ways:

- Configure Cisco Unity to use the G.729 codec. In this case, Cisco Unity can accept both G.729 and G.711 calls.

- Use a hardware transcoder in front of Cisco Unity to convert G.729 audio streams to G.711. Cisco CME 3.2 and greater supports a transcoding function.

One more thing to consider in centralized voice mail architecture is that all the IP phone extensions in the network must be unique. In other words, no two Cisco CMEs can share the same phone extension. Also, if you use central Cisco Unity as the AA for all the Cisco CME sites, you need to enable H.450 services in the network for call transfers to extensions appearing on different Cisco CMEs, and configure transfer patterns on the central Cisco CME. Figure 18-5 shows a sample topology of such a network.

Figure 18-5 *Centralized Cisco Unity with Distributed Cisco CME Sites*

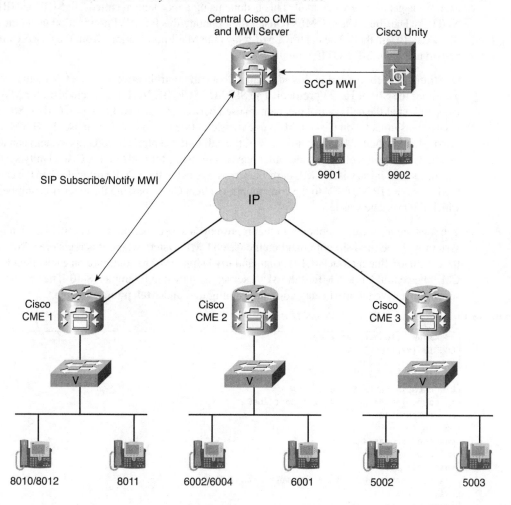

The preceding section covered how MWI integration works between Cisco CME and Cisco Unity. However, it assumed that all the phones subscribed to Cisco Unity are on the same Cisco CME where the Cisco Unity ports are registered. In the case of the centralized voice mail architecture discussed in this section, not all the phones are on the same Cisco CME. They are registered to different Cisco CMEs in the network. To propagate MWIs to the appropriate phone(s) in the network, the MWI indication has to be relayed from the central Cisco CME where Cisco Unity is registered to the remote Cisco CME where the appropriate phone is registered.

To achieve this, the Cisco CME hosting the Cisco Unity server acts as an *MWI server*, and the remote Cisco CMEs that share the central Cisco Unity server act as *MWI clients*. The client Cisco CMEs receive notifications from the central Cisco CME server when one of their extensions gets a new voice mail. This is done using a mechanism called SIP SUBSCRIBE/NOTIFY. The client Cisco CMEs register their ephone-dns for MWI notification using the SIP SUBSCRIBE method. The central CME relays the MWI notifications from the Cisco Unity system using the SIP NOTIFY method.

One thing to keep in mind in this scenario is that call control between Cisco CMEs may still use either the SIP or H.323 protocol. The SIP SUBSCRIBE/NOTIFY mechanism for MWI is independent of the call control mechanism used between the networked Cisco CMEs. So a call from extension 5002 on Cisco CME3 to extension 6002 Cisco CME2 can use the H.323 protocol, and when 6002 does not answer, the call to the central Cisco Unity system can also use the H.323 protocol. When the caller leaves a message for 6002 on the Cisco Unity system, it informs the central Cisco CME of the new message using the SCCP protocol. Then the central CME sends a SIP NOTIFY to the corresponding client CME, passing the extension number for which the message was left.

You must configure each ephone-dn that represents a subscriber on the central Cisco Unity system with the **mwi sip** command on the Cisco CME system where it is registered. You use the command-line interface (CLI) command **mwi sip-server** to configure on each client Cisco CME the central Cisco CME as the MWI server, as shown in Example 18-10. The Cisco CME server must have the **mwi relay** command configured under **telephony-service**.

Example 18-10 *Configuration for MWI Client Cisco CME*

```
cme#show telephony-service
CONFIG (Version=3.1)
=====================
Version 3.1
Cisco CallManager Express
ip source-address 17.17.17.1 port 2000
max-ephones 48
max-dn 15
max-conferences 4
max-redirect 5
voicemail 8050
mwi sip-server 200.1.1.29 transport tcp
mwi expires 86400
transfer-system full-blind
local directory service: enabled.

ephone-dn 1
number 2902
preference 0 secondary 9
huntstop
call-forward noan 8050 timeout 10
```

Example 18-10   *Configuration for MWI Client Cisco CME (Continued)*

```
mwi sip

ephone-dn 2
number 2903
preference 0 secondary 9
huntstop
mwi sip

ephone-dn 4
number 2904
preference 0 secondary 9
huntstop
mwi sip
```

Each ephone-dn that has **mwi sip** configured is subscribed to the central MWI server Cisco CME for MWI notifications. This is done using the SIP SUBSCRIBE method. You can see the subscriptions on the MWI server Cisco CME, as shown in Example 18-11.

Example 18-11   *List of Subscribed Clients for MWI Notifications*

```
cme#show mwi relay clients
Client        IPADDR            EXPIRES(sec)   MWI
============  ================  ============   ====
2902          49.23.48.2        61319          OFF
2903          49.23.48.2        86359          OFF
2904          49.23.48.2        86365          OFF
```

When the MWI server Cisco CME gets an MWI notification from the Cisco Unity server, it relays the notification by sending a SIP NOTIFY to the client Cisco CME, informing it that a particular extension has a new message. The client Cisco CME then turns on the MWI for the appropriate phone using the normal SCCP message.

Example 18-12 shows that ephone 7, which is the Cisco Unity port for MWI notifications, goes off-hook with calling number (subscriber extension number) 2902 and dials 9051, which is the MWI off DN. In the highlighted line, the called number is missing but the original Called Number field is set to 9051. It is confusing, but that is the way the fields appear in the debug output.

The MWI server in Cisco CME looks to see if 2902 is a local ephone-dn in its configuration. If it is not, the server looks for SIP subscriptions for MWI notifications. If it finds a subscription for extension 2902, it sends a SIP NOTIFY to the IP address received in the subscription, as shown in Example 18-12. The receiving (client) Cisco CME sends a "200 OK" SIP message acknowledging receipt of the MWI notification. This results in the client Cisco CME's turning on the MWI lamp for the phone using the usual SCCP.

Example 18-12   *SCCP and SIP Debugs for MWI Relay*

```
CME#debug ephone state
CME#debug ccsip messages
*Oct 31 22:29:22.433: ephone-7[3]:OFFHOOK with calling party 2902
*Oct 31 22:29:22.433: ephone-7[3]:OFFHOOK
*Oct 31 22:29:22.433: ephone-7[3]:SIEZE on activeLine 0 activeChan 1
*Oct 31 22:29:22.433: ephone-7[3]:SetCallState line 1 DN 14 chan 1
  ref 257 TsOffHook
*Oct 31 22:29:22.437: DN 14 chan 1 Voice_Mode
*Oct 31 22:29:22.437: dn_tone_control DN=14 chan 1 tonetype=33:DtInsideDialTone
   onoff=1 pid=158
*Oct 31 22:29:22.437: dn_tone_control DN=14 chan 1 tonetype=0:DtSilence
  onoff=0 pid=158
*Oct 31 22:29:22.441: dn_tone_control DN=14 chan 1 tonetype=0:DtSilence
  onoff=0 pid=158
*Oct 31 22:29:22.445: ephone-7[3]:SetCallState line 1 DN 14 chan 1
  ref 257 TsRingOut
*Oct 31 22:29:22.449: ephone-7[3]:Call Info DN 14 line 1 ref 257
  called  calling A8 origcalled 9051 calltype 2
*Oct 31 22:29:22.449: ephone-7[3]:Call Info for chan 1
*Oct 31 22:29:22.449: ephone-7[3]: No-Name calling
*Oct 31 22:29:22.449: ephone-7[3]: No-Name
*Oct 31 22:29:22.449: ephone-7[3]:SetCallState line 1 DN 14 chan 1
   ref 257 TsProceed
*Oct 31 22:29:22.449: UpdateCallState DN 9 chan 1 operating in mode 2
*Oct 31 22:29:22.449: UpdateCallState DN 9 chan 1 operating in mode 2
*Oct 31 22:29:22.453: dn_tone_control DN=14 chan 1 tonetype=36:DtAlertingTone
   onoff=1 pid=158
*Oct 31 22:29:22.497: //-1/xxxxxxxxxxxx/SIP/Msg/ccsipDisplayMsg:
Sent:
NOTIFY sip:2902@49.23.48.2:5060 SIP/2.0
Via: SIP/2.0/TCP  200.1.1.29;branch=z9hG4bKFC3
From: "2902"<sip:2902@200.1.1.29>
To: <sip:2902@49.23.48.2>;tag=99F03BFD-2307
Date: Thu, 31 Oct 2002 22:29:22 UTC
Call-ID: B77C4F4E-68B011D8-80B9958B-10B1AC79
User-Agent: Cisco-SIPGateway/IOS-12.x
Max-Forwards: 6
Timestamp: 1036103362
CSeq: 6 NOTIFY
Event: message-summary
Contact: <sip:2902@200.1.1.29:5060;transport=tcp>
Content-Length: 22
Content-Type: application/simple-message-summary

Messages-Waiting: no

*Oct 31 22:29:22.569: //-1/xxxxxxxxxxxx/SIP/Msg/ccsipDisplayMsg:
Received:
SIP/2.0 200 OK
```

Example 18-12   *SCCP and SIP Debugs for MWI Relay (Continued)*

```
Via: SIP/2.0/TCP  200.1.1.29;branch=z9hG4bKFC3
From: <sip:2902@200.1.1.29>
To: "2902" <sip:2902@49.23.48.2>;tag=99F03BFD-2307
Date: Fri, 27 Feb 2004 23:29:14 UTC
Call-ID: B77C4F4E-68B011D8-80B9958B-10B1AC79
CSeq: 6 NOTIFY
Timestamp: 1077924554
Event: message-summary
Content-Length: 0
```

Troubleshooting Call Transfers and Call Forwards

Chapter 7, "Connecting Multiple Cisco CMEs with VoIP," covered the call transfer and forward mechanisms and protocols used to implement network call transfers using H.323 and SIP. It is recommended that you review Chapter 7 to effectively troubleshoot any problems in this area. This section discusses how to troubleshoot issues with local and network call transfers and forwards and describes how to detect and fix common configuration issues.

Troubleshooting Call Transfers—Transfer Attempts Get Reorder Tone

Transfers to local extensions on a Cisco CME are enabled by default. For all the other transfers, including those to local PSTN numbers, you must configure transfer patterns. Sometimes transfer attempts may not work because either a transfer pattern is not configured or the transfer target's number may not match any transfer patterns configured on the system.

The easiest way to fix this situation is to use the **transfer-pattern .T** command, which allows transfers to all numbers. However, this solution might be undesirable if you are concerned about fraudulent use of call transfers. To see if a transfer pattern is matched, turn on the Cisco CME **debug ephone state** command to see which ones are not matching, and fix them with modifications to the transfer patterns for the desired transfer targets. This is shown in the debugs in Example 18-13. The user presses the transfer softkey when the call is in the connected state, gets dial tone, and starts dialing the transfer-to number. However, no transfer pattern matches this nonlocal number, so the caller hears reorder tone.

Example 18-13   *Missing Transfer Pattern*

```
CME#debug ephone state
SkinnyTryCall to 8010 instance 1 match DN 1
Feb 22 18:29:42: ephone-1[2]:Call Info DN 1 line 1 ref 244 called 8010 calling
   4085555002 origcalled 8010 calltype 1
Feb 22 18:29:42: ephone-1[2]:Call Info for chan 1
Feb 22 18:29:42: ephone-1[2]:Original Called Name Waugh
Feb 22 18:29:42: ephone-1[2]: lleyton hewitt calling
Feb 22 18:29:42: ephone-1[2]: Waugh
Feb 22 18:29:47: ephone-1[2][SEP003094C29D3C]:SoftKeyEventMessage event 4
   line 1 callref 244
```

continues

Example 18-13   *Missing Transfer Pattern (Continued)*

```
Feb 22 18:29:47: ephone-1[2]:SK TRANSFER line 1 ref 244
Feb 22 18:29:47: ephone-1[2]:TransferButtonPress
Feb 22 18:29:47: ephone-1 TRANSFER using transfer-system full DN 1
  consult transfer
Feb 22 18:29:47: SkinnyGetCallState for DN 1 chan 1 CONNECTED
Feb 22 18:29:47: called DN -1 chan 1, calling DN -1 chan 1 phone 1
  incoming s2s:0
Feb 22 18:29:47: SkinnyGetCallState for DN 1 chan 1 CONNECTED
Feb 22 18:29:47: called DN -1 chan 1, calling DN -1 chan 1 phone 1
  incoming s2s:0
Feb 22 18:29:47: SkinnyGetCallState for DN 3 chan 1 IDLE
Feb 22 18:29:47: called DN 2 chan 1, calling DN -1 chan 1 phone 1 s2s:0
Feb 22 18:29:47: ephone-1[2]:Transfer with consult line 1 DN 1 chan 1
  using second line 2 DN 1 chan 1
Feb 22 18:29:47: ephone-1[2]:Consult for line 1 DN 1 chan 1 using
  line 2 DN 3 chan 1
Feb 22 18:29:47: ephone-1[2]:HoldButtonPress (allow_toggle = 0)
Feb 22 18:29:47: SkinnyGetCallState for DN 1 chan 1 CONNECTED
Feb 22 18:29:47: called DN -1 chan 1, calling DN -1 chan 1 phone 1
  incoming s2s:0
Feb 22 18:29:47: ephone-1[2]:HoldButtonPress HOLD activated for DN 1 chan 1
Feb 22 18:29:47: ephone-1[2]:HoldButtonPress DN 1 chan 1 other DN -1 chan 1
    other ephone-(-1)
Feb 22 18:29:47: ephone-1[2]:Binding ephone-1 to DN 1 chan 1 s2s:0
Feb 22 18:29:47: Adding DN 1 chan 1 to MOH
.........
Feb 22 18:29:47: ephone-1[2]:CloseReceive
Feb 22 18:29:47: ephone-1[2]:StopMedia
Feb 22 18:29:47: ephone-1[2]:HoldButtonPress keep call plane for transfer
Feb 22 18:29:47: called DN -1 chan 1, calling DN -1 chan 1 phone -1
  incoming s2s:0
Feb 22 18:29:47: ephone-1[2]:is_auto_local 0 for DN -1
Feb 22 18:29:47: Skinny StartTone 33 sent on  ephone socket [2]
  DtInsideDialTone
Feb 22 18:29:47: ephone-1[2][SEP003094C29D3C]:CallPrompt line 1 ref 244:
Feb 22 18:29:47: ephone-1[2]:SelectPhoneSoftKeys set 2 mask FFFF for
  line 1 ref 244
Feb 22 18:29:47: ephone-1[2]:Update Stats Total for DN 1 chan 1
Feb 22 18:29:48: ephone-1[2]:KeypadButtonMessage 5
Feb 22 18:29:48: ephone-1[2]:is_auto_local 0 for DN -1
Feb 22 18:29:48: ephone-1[2]:StopTone sent to ephone
Feb 22 18:29:48: ephone-1[2][SEP003094C29D3C]:CallPrompt line 1
  ref 244: Transfer 5
Feb 22 18:29:48: ephone-1[2]:SkinnyTryCall to 5 instance 1 start at 0
  secondary 0
Feb 22 18:29:48: ephone-1[2]:No Transfer-Pattern match for 5
Feb 22 18:29:48: ephone-1[2]:KeypadButtonMessage 0
Feb 22 18:29:48: ephone-1[2][SEP003094C29D3C]:CallPrompt line 1
  ref 244: Transfer 50
Feb 22 18:29:48: ephone-1[2]:SkinnyTryCall to 50 instance 1 start at 0
  secondary 0
```

Example 18-13 *Missing Transfer Pattern (Continued)*

```
Feb 22 18:29:48: ephone-1[2]:No Transfer DN match for 50
Feb 22 18:29:48: ephone-1[2]:No Transfer-Pattern match for 50
Feb 22 18:29:48: ephone-1[2]:is_auto_local 0 for DN -1
Feb 22 18:29:48: Skinny StartTone 37 sent on  ephone socket [2] DtReorderTone
Feb 22 18:29:51: ephone-1[2]:ONHOOK (from phone msgID=7)
Feb 22 18:29:51: ephone-1[2]:TRANSFER quit on line 1 DN 1
Feb 22 18:29:51: ephone-1[2]:Clear DN 1 chan 1 transfer
Feb 22 18:29:51: UpdateCallState DN 1 chan 1 state 10 phone-ref -1 calleddn -1
  calleddn_chan 1
Feb 22 18:29:51: No active phone for DN 1 chan 1 instance 1 (mode 0)
Feb 22 18:29:51: DN 1 chan 1 End Voice_Mode
Feb 22 18:29:51: SetCallInfo calling dn -1 chan 1 dn 1 chan 1
calling [] called []
```

Troubleshooting Network Call Transfers—Attempts to Transfer H.323 Calls Fail

Troubleshooting network call transfers and forwards involves understanding the capabilities of all voice over IP (VoIP) devices in the network. This primarily involves identifying which devices support network call transfer protocols and which don't. The devices that support network call transfers are those that also support H.450.2, H.450.3, and H.450.12. The most important aspect of the configuration to verify is that all the devices involved in call transfers or forwards have appropriate call routing dial peers.

Cisco CME 3.1 and later can hairpin incoming H.323 calls to outgoing H.323 calls. Hairpinning calls can be the result of call transfers or forwards involving hybrid network devices or incorrect configuration. Hairpinned calls caused by hybrid network devices are acceptable, but those caused by incorrect configuration should be rectified to optimize call processing and resource consumption.

This section discusses how to troubleshoot such issues and gives possible solutions. Chapter 7 showed the protocol exchange sequence for a call transfer involving two or three devices. The first discussion in this section presents debug output for a successful network call transfer. This should help you understand the call transfer mechanism itself. The discussion following that covers a few scenarios in which call transfers fail or result in hairpinned calls.

Using Debugs to Understand Successful Network Call Transfers

Figure 18-6 shows the sample topology for the troubleshooting in this section. It consists of three sites where Cisco CME 3.2 is running for local call processing. The sites are connected with an IP WAN network engineered to carry H.323 calls between the sites.

Figure 18-6 *Topology for Troubleshooting Network Call Transfers*

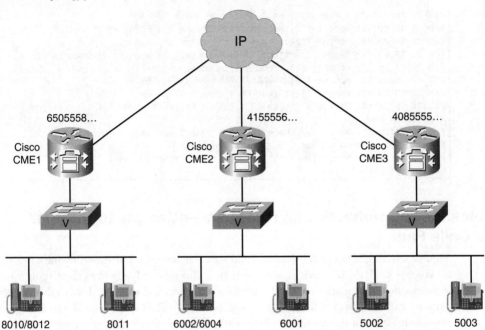

For this example, assume that **dialplan-pattern** commands are not configured under **telephony-service** and that all the call setups use extensions. The next section walks through the debug traces of a call transfer scenario involving the three sites. Extension 8010 at Cisco CME1 places a call to extension 6002 at Cisco CME2. This is shown in Example 18-14.

Example 18-14 *Transferee Calls the Transferor*

```
CME1#debug voip application supplementary-service
supplementary service debugging is on
CME1#debug ephone state
EPHONE state debugging is enabled
CME1#
Mar  9 14:24:37: ephone-1[2]:OFFHOOK
Mar  9 14:24:37: ephone-1[2]:SIEZE on activeLine 1 activeChan 1
Mar  9 14:24:37: ephone-1[2]:SetCallState line 1 DN 1 chan 1 ref 109 TsOffHook
Mar  9 14:24:37: ephone-1[2]:SpeakerPhoneOffHook mute 0
Mar  9 14:24:37: DN 1 chan 1 Voice_Mode
Mar  9 14:24:37: //-1//APPL:/SSProcessH450CommonInfoEvent:
CI_INFORM featureList=0xC0000000 featureValue[0][0] featureControl=0x0
Mar  9 14:24:37: dn_tone_control DN=1 chan 1 tonetype=36:DtAlertingTone onoff=1
   pid=159
Mar  9 14:24:43: //-1//APPL:/SSProcessH450CommonInfoEvent:
CI_INFORM featureList=0xC0000000 featureValue[0][0] featureControl=0x0
Mar  9 14:24:43: ephone-1[2]:SetCallState line 1 DN 1 chan 1 ref 109 TsConnected
Mar  9 14:24:43: ephone-1[2]:OpenReceiveChannelAck:IP 89.89.89.3,
```

Example 18-14 *Transferee Calls the Transferor (Continued)*

```
port=25124, dn_index=1, dn=1, chan=1
Mar  9 14:24:43: ephone-1[2]:StartMedia 89.89.89.1 port=2000
Mar  9 14:24:43: DN 1 chan 1 codec 4:G711Ulaw64k duration 20 ms bytes 160
Mar  9 14:24:43: ephone-1[2]:Call Info DN 1 line 1 ref 109 called 6002 calling
  8010 origcalled 6002 calltype 2
Mar  9 14:24:43: ephone-1[2]:Call Info for chan 1
......
```

The transferor at Cisco CME 2 receives the call and answers it. The call is now in a connected
state with media channels (Real-Time Transport Protocol [RTP]) set up. This is shown in
Example 18-15.

Example 18-15 *Transferor Receives the Call and Answers It*

```
CME2#debug voip application supplementary-service
CME2#debug ephone state
Mar  9 14:37:26: ephone-2[1]:Ringer Off
Mar  9 14:37:26: ephone-2[1]:ANSWER call
Mar  9 14:37:26: ephone-2[1][SEP0009B7F757AB]:Answer Incoming call from
  ephone-(-1) DN -1 chan 1
Mar  9 14:37:26: ephone-2[1]:OpenReceive DN 2 chan 1 codec 4:G711Ulaw64k duration
  20 ms bytes 160
Mar  9 14:37:26: //-1//APPL:/AppPrepareCommonInfoRequestReceived: Leg
  peer_tag=1000
Mar  9 14:37:26: //-1//APPL:/AppPrepareCommonInfo:
Global H450_2=1 H450_3=1 H450_12_ADV=1 H450_12_USAGE=0
Mar  9 14:37:26: //-1//APPL:/AppPrepareCommonInfoContent:
SS_CI ss_evt=18 featureList=0xC0000000 featureValues=[0][0][0][0]
  featureControl=0x0
Mar  9 14:37:27: ephone-2[1]:Call Info DN 2 line 1 ref 459 called 6002 calling
  8010 origcalled 6002 calltype 1
......
Mar  9 14:37:27: ephone-2[1]:OpenReceiveChannelAck:IP 28.28.28.3,
port=17856, dn_index=2, dn=2, chan=1
Mar  9 14:37:27: ephone-2[1]:StartMedia 28.28.28.1 port=2000
Mar  9 14:37:27: DN 2 chan 1 codec 4:G711Ulaw64k duration 20 ms bytes 160
```

The transferor at Cisco CME 2 decides to transfer this call to extension 5003 on Cisco CME 3.
As you see from the traces shown in Example 18-16, the original call is put on hold and the call
to 5003 (the transfer target) is set up using the second line (associated with DN 4 having
extension 6004) available on the transferor's phone.

Example 18-16 *Consult Call to Transfer Target Is Set Up*

```
CME2#debug voip application supplementary-service
CME2#debug ephone state
Mar  9 14:37:59: ephone-2[1]:TransferButtonPress
Mar  9 14:37:59: ephone-2 TRANSFER using transfer-system full DN 2 consult
  transfer
......
Mar  9 14:37:59: ephone-2[1]:HoldButtonPress (allow_toggle = 0)
```

continues

Example 18-16 *Consult Call to Transfer Target Is Set Up (Continued)*

```
Mar  9 14:37:59: ephone-2[1]:HoldButtonPress HOLD activated for DN 2 chan 1
Mar  9 14:37:59: ephone-2[1][SEP0009B7F757AB]:SetCallState line 1 ref 459 state
  10 TsCallTransfer ignored
Mar  9 14:37:59: ephone-2[1]:CloseReceive


Mar  9 14:37:59: ephone-2[1]:StopMedia
Mar  9 14:38:02: PredictTarget no idle match for 5003 after 0 attempts
Mar  9 14:38:02: ephone-2[1]:Consult for line 1 DN 2 chan 1 using line 2 DN 4
  chan 1 to 5003
Mar  9 14:38:02: ephone-2[1][SEP0009B7F757AB]:SkinnyPhoneDeselectLine 0 chan 1
  to 2
Mar  9 14:38:02: ephone-2[1]:OFFHOOK
Mar  9 14:38:02: ephone-2[1]:SIEZE on activeLine 2 activeChan 1
Mar  9 14:38:02: ephone-2[1]:SetCallState line 2 DN 4 chan 1 ref 460 TsOffHook
Mar  9 14:38:02: DN 4 chan 1 Voice_Mode
Mar  9 14:38:02: dn_tone_control DN=4 chan 1 tonetype=33:DtInsideDialTone onoff=1
  pid=154
Mar  9 14:38:02: //-1//APPL:/AppPrepareCommonInfo:
Global H450_2=1 H450_3=1 H450_12_ADV=1 H450_12_USAGE=0
Mar  9 14:38:02: //-1//APPL:/AppPrepareCommonInfoContent:
SS_CI ss_evt=18 featureList=0xC0000000 featureValues=[0][0][0][0]
  featureControl=0x0
Mar  9 14:38:02: ephone-2[1]:SkinnySelectPhoneSoftKeys DN 4 chan 1 change
  TsRingOut to TsCallTransfer
Mar  9 14:38:02: ephone-2[1]:Call Info DN 4 line 2 ref 460 called 5003
  calling 6004 origcalled 5003 calltype 2
.........
Mar  9 14:38:02: //-1//APPL:/AppPrepareCommonInfoRequestReceived: Leg
  peer_tag=20004
Mar  9 14:38:02: //-1//APPL:/AppPrepareCommonInfo: Not voip dialpeer, no common
  info sent.
Mar  9 14:38:02: dn_tone_control DN=4 chan 1 tonetype=36:DtAlertingTone onoff=1
  pid=154
Mar  9 14:38:06: //-1//APPL:/SSProcessH450CommonInfoEvent:
CI_INFORM featureList=0xC0000000 featureValue[0][0] featureControl=0x0
.........
Mar  9 14:38:06: ephone-2[1]:OpenReceiveChannelAck:IP 28.28.28.3,
port=21832, dn_index=4, dn=4, chan=1
Mar  9 14:38:06: ephone-2[1]:StartMedia 28.28.28.1 port=2000
Mar  9 14:38:06: DN 4 chan 1 codec 4:G711Ulaw64k duration 20 ms bytes 160
Mar  9 14:38:07: ephone-2[1]:Call Info DN 4 line 2 ref 460 called 5003
  calling 6004 origcalled 5003 calltype 2
```

The debug output for the transfer target (Cisco CME 3) is shown in Example 18-17.

Example 18-17 *Transfer Target Answers the Consult Call*

```
CME3#debug voip application supplementary-service
CME3#debug ephone state
*Mar  9 22:02:01.543: ephone-2[1]:OFFHOOK
```

Example 18-17   *Transfer Target Answers the Consult Call (Continued)*

```
*Mar  9 22:02:01.543: ephone-2[1]:Ringer Off
*Mar  9 22:02:01.543: ephone-2[1]:ANSWER call
......
*Mar  9 22:02:01.555: ephone-2[1]:OpenReceive DN 3 chan 1 codec 4:G711Ulaw64k
  duration 20 ms bytes 160
*Mar  9 22:02:01.559: //-1//APPL:/AppPrepareCommonInfoRequestReceived: Leg
  peer_tag=1000
*Mar  9 22:02:01.559: //-1//APPL:/AppPrepareCommonInfo: Global H450_2=1 H450_3=1
  H450_12_ADV=1 H450_12_USAGE=0
*Mar  9 22:02:01.559: //-1//APPL:/AppPrepareCommonInfoContent:
SS_CI ss_evt=18 featureList=0xC0000000 featureValues=[0][0][0][0]
  featureControl=0x0

*Mar  9 22:02:01.812: ephone-2[1]:Call Info DN 3 line 1 ref 186 called 5003
  calling 6004 origcalled  calltype 1
......
*Mar  9 22:02:01.816: ephone-2[1]:OpenReceiveChannelAck:IP 40.40.0.13,
  port=20502, dn_index=3, dn=3, chan=1
*Mar  9 22:02:01.816: ephone-2[1]:StartMedia 40.40.0.1 port=2000
*Mar  9 22:02:01.816: DN 3 chan 1 codec 4:G711Ulaw64k duration 20 ms bytes 160
```

At this point, the original call between extensions 8010 (Cisco CME 1) and 6002 (Cisco CME 2) is on hold while a call is active between 6004 (Cisco CME 2) and 5003 (Cisco CME 3). The call between 6004 and 5003 is the consultation call for the consult transfer. After the consultation, the transferor on Cisco CME 2 decides to commit the transfer so that extension 8010 (Cisco CME 1) and extension 5003 (Cisco CME 3) can talk. At this point, the H.450.2 call transfer protocol exchanges covered in Chapter 7 take place.

The transferor (Cisco CME 2) requests a consult ID from the transfer target (Cisco CME 3). When it is successful, the transferor gives the consult ID to the transferee (Cisco CME 1). The transferee then sets up a new call to the transfer target, replacing the consult call. In the debug shown in Example 18-18, note the consult ID request that is generated and exchanged and the consult ID of 13 that is returned.

Example 18-18   *Transferor Requests and Receives the Consult ID from the Transfer Target*

```
CME2#debug voip application supplementary-service
CME2#debug ephone state
Mar  9 14:38:33: ephone-2[1]:TransferButtonPress
Mar  9 14:38:33: ephone-2[1]:Commit Transfer with Consult for DN 2 chan 1 using
  consult DN 4 chan 1
......
Mar  9 14:38:33: ephone-2[1]:Request Consult ID for DN 2 chan 1 using consult DN 4
  chan 1
Mar  9 14:38:33: ephone-2[1]:SkinnyRequestConsultID for DN 4 chan 1
Mar  9 14:38:33: //3254//APPL:/SSMapEvent:
SS_IDENTIFY_REQUEST: rerouteNo[] invokeID[3256]
Mar  9 14:38:33: //3255//APPL:/AppConsultRequest:
Mar  9 14:38:33: AppLegH450TransferNotSupported: remote end is h450.2 capable
Mar  9 14:38:33: //3255//APPL:/AppIdentifyRequest:
```

continues

Example 18-18 *Transferor Requests and Receives the Consult ID from the Transfer Target (Continued)*

```
Mar  9 14:38:33: //3255//APPL:/SSMapEvent:
SS_IDENTIFY_RESP: identify[13] rerouteNo[5003] invokeID[1476]
Mar  9 14:38:33: //3254//APPL:/AppConsultResponseSuccess: consuldID[13]
Mar  9 14:38:33: //3254//APPL:/AppSSReturnResult:
Mar  9 14:38:33: ephone-2[1]:SkinnyConsultIDResponse DN 2 chan 1 explicit target
  5003 orig 5003 redirected= []
Mar  9 14:38:33: ephone-2[1]:SkinnyConsultIDResponse ActivateTransfer DN 2 chan 1
  to 5003 id [13]
......
Mar  9 14:38:33: DN 2 Call Transfer ID=[13] for callID 3253 to 5003 (expanded)
Mar  9 14:38:33: ephone-2[1]:Transfer Request OK for DN 2 chan 1
Mar  9 14:38:33: //3253//APPL:/SSMapEvent:
SS_INIT_IND: rerouteNo[5003] identify[13] invokeID[3257] transferringNo[6002]
  peer[0] xto_callID[0]
Mar  9 14:38:33: AppLegH450TransferNotSupported: remote end is h450.2 capable
Mar  9 14:38:33: //3252//APPL:/AppTransferInitiateRequest:  to [5003] with ID[13]
Mar  9 14:38:33: //3252//APPL:/AppTransferRequest:
Mar  9 14:38:33: AppLegH450TransferNotSupported: remote end is h450.2 capable
Mar  9 14:38:33: //3252//APPL:/AppTransferRequest: SS_INIT:rerouteNo[5003] ID[13]
Mar  9 14:38:33: //3252//APPL:/SSMapEvent:  SS_RETURN_RESULT
Mar  9 14:38:33: //3253//APPL:/AppSSReturnResult:
Mar  9 14:38:33: ephone-2[1]:DN 2 disc reason 16 normal state HOLD
```

The traces in Example 18-19 show the transfer target (Cisco CME 3) generating and issuing a consult ID to the transferor (Cisco CME 2). Later in this section you will see that after the transferred call is set up, the caller ID is updated on the transfer target, as shown.

Example 18-19 *Transfer Target Generates a Consult ID and Issues It to the Transferor*

```
CME3#debug voip application supplementary-service
CME3#debug ephone state
*Mar  9 22:02:28.624: //441//APPL:/SSMapEvent:
SS_IDENTIFY_REQUEST: rerouteNo[] invokeID[1476]
*Mar  9 22:02:28.624: //442//APPL:/AppConsultRequest:
*Mar  9 22:02:28.624: //442//APPL:/AppIdentifyRequest:
*Mar  9 22:02:28.624: //441//APPL:/AppSSGenerateConsultID:
*Mar  9 22:02:28.624: ID=13
*Mar  9 22:02:28.624: //441//APPL:/AppConsultResponseSuccess: consuldID[13]
```

After the transferor (Cisco CME 2) and the transfer target (Cisco CME 3) exchange the consult IDs, the transferor gives the consult ID to the transferee (Cisco CME 1) to use to set up a new call to replace the consult call on the transfer target.

In Example 18-20, the transferee (Cisco CME 1) receives the consult ID and asks to set up a new call to complete the transfer. In the end, all of the call information is updated to reflect the complete transfer.

Example 18-20 *Transferee Receives the Consult ID and Sets Up the Call*

```
CME1#debug voip application supplementary-service
CME1#debug ephone state
Mar  9 14:25:49: //239//APPL:/SSMapEvent:  SS_INIT_IND: rerouteNo[5003]
  identify[13] invokeID[1477] transferringNo[6002] peer[0] xto_callID[0]
Mar  9 14:25:49: //-1//APPL:/TRDTransferInitiate:
Mar  9 14:25:49: //238//APPL:/AppTransferRequest:
Mar  9 14:25:49: //-1//APPL:HN00000000:/TRD_transferSetup:
Mar  9 14:25:49: //-1//APPL:HN00000000:/TRDSetState:  -->
  [<TRD_await_destroy_done>]
Mar  9 14:25:49: //-1//APPL:HN00000000:/TRDHndHandler:
Mar  9 14:25:49: //-1//APPL:HN00000000:/TRDHndHandler:
Get event TRD_ev_destroyDone in state <TRD_await_destroy_done>
Mar  9 14:25:49: //-1//APPL:HN00000000:/TRD_destroyDone:
Mar  9 14:25:49: //-1//APPL:LG238:LG239:/AppHandOffLocalTRT:
Leg 238's protocol=1       Leg 239's protocol=2
Mar  9 14:25:49: //-1//APPL:/AppPrepareTransferSetup:  SS_SETUP:rerouteNo[5003]
  transferringNo[6002] ID[13] peer[0]
Mar  9 14:25:49: //-1//APPL:/AppPrepareCommonInfo:
ssInfo already set by opcode(10), skip common info.
Mar  9 14:25:49: //-1//APPL:HN00000000:/TRDSetState:  -->
  [<TRD_await_setup_resp>]
Mar  9 14:25:49: //-1//APPL:HN00000000:/TRDHndHandler:
Mar  9 14:25:49: //-1//APPL:HN00000000:/TRDHndHandler:
Get event TRD_ev_handlerDone in state <TRD_await_setup_resp>
Mar  9 14:25:49: //-1//APPL:HN00000000:/TRD_handlerDone:
Mar  9 14:25:49: //239//APPL:/AppSSReturnResult:
Mar  9 14:25:49: //-1//APPL:HN00000000:/TRDSetState:  -->[<TRD_idle>]
Mar  9 14:25:49: //-1//APPL:HN00000000:/TRD_returnIfDone:
Mar  9 14:25:49: //-1//APPL:HN00000000:/TRDSetState:  -->[<TRD_idle>]
Mar  9 14:25:49: //-1//APPL:HN00000000:/TRDHndCleanUp:
Mar  9 14:25:49: //-1//APPL:HN00000000:/TRDSetState:  -->[<TRD_clearing>]
Mar  9 14:25:49: //-1//APPL:HN00000000:/TRDHndFree:
Mar  9 14:25:50: ephone-1[2]:Call Info DN 1 line 1 ref 109 called 5003
  calling 8010 origcalled 5003 calltype 2
```

Example 18-21 shows the call information update on the transfer target (Cisco CME 3).

Example 18-21 *Caller ID Update on the Transfer Target*

```
CME3#debug voip application supplementary-service
CME3#debug ephone state
*Mar  9 22:02:28.624: //441//APPL:/AppSSReturnResult:
*Mar  9 22:02:28.664: //-1//APPL:/AppPrepareCommonInfoRequestReceived: Leg
  peer_tag=2000
*Mar  9 22:02:28.668: //-1//APPL:/AppPrepareCommonInfo:
Global H450_2=1 H450_3=1 H450_12_ADV=1 H450_12_USAGE=0
*Mar  9 22:02:28.668: //-1//APPL:/AppPrepareCommonInfoContent: SS_CI ss_evt=18
  featureList=0xC0000000 featureValues=[0][0][0][0] featureControl=0x0
......
*Mar  9 22:02:28.840: ephone-2[1]:Call Info DN 3 line 1 ref 186 called 5003
  calling 8010 origcalled  calltype 1
*Mar  9 22:02:28.840: ephone-2[1]:Call Info for chan 1
```

Troubleshooting Common Problems with Network Call Transfers

So far you have seen how a consult transfer in an H.323 network is implemented and how to interpret the debugs for such a scenario. In some cases, transfer attempts are unsuccessful or result in hairpinned calls. These situations are discussed next.

Assume that you want to use Cisco CME's **dialplan-pattern** command to implement the internal (extensions) and external (full E.164 numbers) phone number design discussed in Chapter 7. You also want to accept incoming calls dialed using the complete E.164 number of a phone number. The Cisco CME configuration for implementing these features looks in part like the one shown in Example 18-22.

Example 18-22   dialplan-pattern *Commands*

```
CME3#show telephony-service
CONFIG (Version=3.1)
=====================
Version 3.1
Cisco CallManager Express
ip source-address 40.40.0.1 port 2000
max-ephones 10
max-dn 20
max-conferences 3
max-redirect 5
dialplan-pattern 1 4085555... extension-length 4 extension-pattern 5...
dialplan-pattern 2 4155556... extension-length 4 extension-pattern 6...
dialplan-pattern 3 6505558... extension-length 4 extension-pattern 8...

CME2#show telephony-service
CONFIG (Version=3.1)
=====================
Version 3.1
Cisco CallManager Express
ip source-address 28.28.28.1 port 2000
max-ephones 100
max-dn 228
max-conferences 6
max-redirect 5
dialplan-pattern 1 4155556... extension-length 4 extension-pattern 6...
dialplan-pattern 2 4085555... extension-length 4 extension-pattern 5...
dialplan-pattern 3 6505558... extension-length 4 extension-pattern 8...
voicemail 3200

CME1#show telephony-service
CONFIG (Version=3.1)
=====================
Version 3.1
Cisco CallManager Express
ip source-address 89.89.89.1 port 2000
load 7960-7940 P00303010102
max-ephones 24
max-dn 120
max-conferences 8
```

Example 18-22   dialplan-pattern *Commands (Continued)*

```
max-redirect 5
dialplan-pattern 1 6505558... extension-length 4 extension-pattern 8...
dialplan-pattern 2 4155556... extension-length 4 extension-pattern 6...
dialplan-pattern 3 4085555... extension-length 4 extension-pattern 5...
voicemail 8900
```

The next discussion steps through the same call transfer scenario that was discussed in the preceding section. The call goes from extension 8010 on Cisco CME 1 to extension 6002 on Cisco CME 2. The person at extension 6002 wants to transfer to extension 5003 on Cisco CME 3. He presses the transfer key, gets dial tone, and dials 5003. He hears fast-busy tone instead of ringback. You will look at how this new configuration affects call forwarding in the section "Troubleshooting Common Problems with Network Call Forward."

Example 18-23 shows the **debug voip ccapi inout** and **debug ephone state** output of this call transfer attempt. As you can see in the debug output, the Cisco IOS call control application programming interface (API) processes a call for 408.555.5003 as the digits come in.

Example 18-23   *Call Transfer Attempt Fails Because of the Lack of an E.164 Dial Peer*

```
CME2#debug voip ccapin inout
CME2#debug ephone state
Mar  9 15:01:08: ephone-2[1]:TransferButtonPress
Mar  9 15:01:08: ephone-2 TRANSFER using transfer-system full DN 2 consult
  transfer
Mar  9 15:01:08: ephone-2[1]:Transfer with consult line 1 DN 2 chan 1 using second
  line 2 DN 2 chan 1
Mar  9 15:01:08: ephone-2[1]:Consult for line 1 DN 2 chan 1 using line 2 DN 4
  chan 1
Mar  9 15:01:08: ephone-2[1]:HoldButtonPress (allow_toggle = 0)
Mar  9 15:01:08: ephone-2[1]:HoldButtonPress HOLD activated for DN 2 chan 1
Mar  9 15:01:08: ephone-2[1][SEP0un al009B7F757AB]:
SetCallState line 1 ref 473 state 10 TsCallTransfer ignored
Mar  9 15:01:08: ephone-2[1]:CloseReceive
Mar  9 15:01:08: ephone-2[1]:StopMedia
Mar  9 15:01:10: PredictTarget no idle match for 5003 after 0 attempts
Mar  9 15:01:10: ephone-2[1]:Consult for line 1 DN 2 chan 1 using line 2 DN 4
  chan 1 to 5003
Mar  9 15:01:10: ephone-2[1]:SetCallState line 1 DN 2 chan 1 ref 473 TsHold
Mar  9 15:01:10: ephone-2[1][SEP0009B7F757AB]:
SkinnyPhoneDeselectLine 0 chan 1 to 2
Mar  9 15:01:10: ephone-2[1
c3725-NM#1]: Mar  9 15:01:10: ephone-2[1]:SIEZE on activeLine 2 activeChan 1
Mar  9 15:01:10: ephone-2[1]:SetCallState line 2 DN 4 chan 1 ref 474 TsOffHook
Mar  9 15:01:10: //-1/xxxxxxxxxxxx/CCAPI/ccTDConstructTDUsrContainer:
TD Container Constructed <<<<<< container-0x64F5D55C >>>>>>
Mar  9 15:01:10: //-1/xxxxxxxxxxxx/CCAPI/ccTDUtilAddDataToUsrContainer:
container=0x64F5D55C, tagID=6, dataSize=16, instID=-1,modifier=1
Mar  9 15:01:10: //-1/xxxxxxxxxxxx/CCAPI/ccTDConstructDataObject:
TD Data Object Cons
c3725-NM#
```

continues

Example 18-23 *Call Transfer Attempt Fails Because of the Lack of an E.164 Dial Peer (Continued)*

```
c3725-NM#tructed 0x63C227D8<<r-1,t-6,l-16,d-0x63C227F8,m-1,u-1202104,g-FACE0FFF>>
Mar  9 15:01:10: //-1/xxxxxxxxxxxx/CCAPI/ccTDConstructInstanceTDObject:
TD Queuable Instance Constructed 0x63C6317C[0x0,t-6,o-0x63C227D8<<r-1,t-6,l-16,
  d-0x63C227F8,m-1,u-1202104,g-FACE0FFF>>]
Mar  9 15:01:10: //-1/xxxxxxxxxxxx/CCAPI/ccTDPvtAddObjectToContainer:
Inserting Queuable TDObject into Container; [tagID-6, container-0x64F5D55C,
  Queuable-TDObject-0x63C6317C]
Mar  9 15:01:10: //-1/xxxxxxxxxxxx/CCAPI/cc_api_display_ie_subfields:
Mar  9 15:01:10: cc_api_call_setup_ind_common:
Mar  9 15:01:10:  cisco-username=
Mar  9 15:01:10: ----- ccCallInfo IE subfields -----
Mar  9 15:01:10:  cisco-ani=4155556004
Mar  9 15:01:10:  cisco-anitype=0
Mar  9 15:01:10:  cisco-aniplan=0
Mar  9 15:01:10:  cisco-anipi=0
Mar  9 15:01:10:  cisco-anisi=0
Mar  9 15:01:10:  dest=
Mar  9 15:01:10:  cisco-desttype=0
Mar  9 15:01:10:  cisco-destplan=0
Mar  9 15:01:10:  cisco-rdn=
Mar  9 15:01:10:  cisco-rdntype=0
Mar  9 15:01:10:  cisco-rdnplan=0
Mar  9 15:01:10:  cisco-rdnpi=0
Mar  9 15:01:10:  cisco-rdnsi=0
Mar  9 15:01:10:  cisco-redirectreason=0
Mar  9 15:01:10: //-1/xxxxxxxxxxxx/CCAPI/cc_api_call_setup_ind_common:
  (vdbPtr=0x643D9BE4, callInfo={called=,called_oct3=0x80,calling=4155556004,
calling_oct3=0x0, calling_oct3a=0x0,calling_xlated=false,
subscriber_type_str=RegularLine,fdest=0,peer_tag=20115, prog_ind=3,
callingIE_present 1, src_route_label=,
tgt_route_label= clid_transparent=0},callID=0x650EE1EC)
.........
Mar  9 15:01:10: //3288/xxxxxxxxxxxx/CCAPI/ccSetDigitTimeouts: initial=-1000,
  inter=-1000
Mar  9 15:01:10: //3288/xxxxxxxxxxxx/CCAPI/ccCallReportDigits: (callID=0xCD8,
  enable=0x1)
Mar  9 15:01:10: //3288/xxxxxxxxxxxx/CCAPI/cc_api_call_report_digits_done:
(vdbPtr=0x643D9BE4, callID=0xCD8, disp=0)
Mar  9 15:01:10: DN 4 chan 1 Voice_Mode
Mar  9 15:01:10: dn_tone_control DN=4 chan 1 tonetype=33:DtInsideDialTone onoff=1
  pid=154
Mar  9 15:01:10: dn_tone_control DN=4 chan 1 tonetype=0:DtSilence onoff=0 pid=154
Mar  9 15:01:10: //3288/xxxxxxxxxxxx/CCAPI/cc_api_call_digit_begin:
(dstVdbPtr=0x0, dstCallId=0xFFFFFFFF, srcCallId=0xCD8,
  digit=4, digit_begin_flags=0x0, rtp_timestamp=0x641130
  rtp_expiration=0x0, dest_mask=0x1)
Mar  9 15:01:10: dn_tone_control DN=4 chan 1 tonetype=0:DtSilence onoff=0 pid=154
Mar  9 15:01:10: //3288/xxxxxxxxxxxx/CCAPI/cc_api_call_digit_end:
(dstVdbPtr=0x0, dstCallId=0xFFFFFFFF, srcCallId=0xCD8,
  digit=4,duration=100,xruleCallingTag=0,xruleCalledTag=0, dest_mask=0x1),
  digit_tone_mode=0
```

Example 18-23   *Call Transfer Attempt Fails Because of the Lack of an E.164 Dial Peer (Continued)*

```
Mar  9 15:01:10: //3288/xxxxxxxxxxxx/CCAPI/cc_api_call_digit_begin:
(dstVdbPtr=0x0, dstCallId=0xFFFFFFFF, srcCallId=0xCD8,
    digit=0, digit_begin_flags=0x0, rtp_timestamp=0x648E30
    rtp_expiration=0x0, dest_mask=0x1)
Mar  9 15:01:10: //3288/xxxxxxxxxxxx/CCAPI/cc_api_call_digit_end: (dstVdbPtr=0x0,
  dstCallId=0xFFFFFFFF, srcCallId=0xCD8,
    digit=0,duration=100,xruleCallingTag=0,xruleCalledTag=0, dest_mask=0x1),
  digit_tone_mode=0
Mar  9 15:01:10: //3288/xxxxxxxxxxxx/CCAPI/cc_api_call_digit_begin: (dstVdbPtr=0x0,
    dstCallId=0xFFFFFFFF, srcCallId=0xCD8,
    digit=8, digit_begin_flags=0x0, rtp_timestamp=0x650B30
    rtp_expiration=0x0, dest_mask=0x1)
Mar  9 15:01:10: //3288/xxxxxxxxxxxx/CCAPI/cc_api_call_digit_end: (dstVdbPtr=0x0,
    dstCallId=0xFFFFFFFF, srcCallId=0xCD8,
    digit=8,duration=100,xruleCallingTag=0,xruleCalledTag=0, dest_mask=0x1),
    digit_tone_mode=0
Mar  9 15:01:10: //3288/xxxxxxxxxxxx/CCAPI/cc_api_call_digit_begin: (dstVdbPtr=0x0,
    dstCallId=0xFFFFFFFF, srcCallId=0xCD8,
    digit=5, digit_begin_flags=0x0, rtp_timestamp=0x658830
    rtp_expiration=0x0, dest_mask=0x1)
Mar  9 15:01:10: //3288/xxxxxxxxxxxx/CCAPI/cc_api_call_digit_end: (dstVdbPtr=0x0,
    dstCallId=0xFFFFFFFF, srcCallId=0xCD8,
    digit=5,duration=100,xruleCallingTag=0,xruleCalledTag=0, dest_mask=0x1),
    digit_tone_mode=0
Mar  9 15:01:10: //3288/xxxxxxxxxxxx/CCAPI/cc_api_call_digit_begin: (dstVdbPtr=0x0,
    dstCallId=0xFFFFFFFF, srcCallId=0xCD8,
    digit=5, digit_begin_flags=0x0, rtp_timestamp=0x660530
    rtp_expiration=0x0, dest_mask=0x1)
Mar  9 15:01:10: //3288/xxxxxxxxxxxx/CCAPI/cc_api_call_digit_end: (dstVdbPtr=0x0,
    dstCallId=0xFFFFFFFF, srcCallId=0xCD8,
    digit=5,duration=100,xruleCallingTag=0,xruleCalledTag=0, dest_mask=0x1),
    digit_tone_mode=0
Mar  9 15:01:10: //3288/xxxxxxxxxxxx/CCAPI/cc_api_call_digit_begin: (dstVdbPtr=0x0,
    dstCallId=0xFFFFFFFF, srcCallId=0xCD8,
    digit=5, digit_begin_flags=0x0, rtp_timestamp=0x668230
    rtp_expiration=0x0, dest_mask=0x1)
Mar  9 15:01:10: //3288/xxxxxxxxxxxx/CCAPI/cc_api_call_digit_end: (dstVdbPtr=0x0,
    dstCallId=0xFFFFFFFF, srcCallId=0xCD8,
    digit=5,duration=100,xruleCallingTag=0,xruleCalledTag=0, dest_mask=0x1),
    digit_tone_mode=0
Mar  9 15:01:10: //3288/xxxxxxxxxxxx/CCAPI/cc_api_call_digit_begin: (dstVdbPtr=0x0,
    dstCallId=0xFFFFFFFF, srcCallId=0xCD8,
    digit=5, digit_begin_flags=0x0, rtp_timestamp=0x66FF30
    rtp_expiration=0x0, dest_mask=0x1)
Mar  9 15:01:10: //3288/xxxxxxxxxxxx/CCAPI/cc_api_call_digit_end: (dstVdbPtr=0x0,
    dstCallId=0xFFFFFFFF, srcCallId=0xCD8,
    digit=5,duration=100,xruleCallingTag=0,xruleCalledTag=0, dest_mask=0x1),
    digit_tone_mode=0
Mar  9 15:01:10: //3288/xxxxxxxxxxxx/CCAPI/cc_api_call_digit_begin: (dstVdbPtr=0x0,
    dstCallId=0xFFFFFFFF, srcCallId=0xCD8,
    digit=0, digit_begin_flags=0x0, rtp_timestamp=0x677C30
```

continues

Example 18-23 *Call Transfer Attempt Fails Because of the Lack of an E.164 Dial Peer (Continued)*

```
      rtp_expiration=0x0, dest_mask=0x1)
Mar  9 15:01:10: //3288/xxxxxxxxxxxx/CCAPI/cc_api_call_digit_end:
Mar  9 15:01:10: //3288/xxxxxxxxxxxx/CCAPI/ccTDUtilGetDataByValue: CallID[3288],
  tagID[31], instID[-1]
Mar  9 15:01:10: dn_tone_control DN=4 chan 1 tonetype=37:DtReorderTone onoff=1
  pid=154
Mar  9 15:01:10: ephone-2[1]:DN 4 disc reason 28 invalid number state SIEZE
Mar  9 15:01:10: ephone-2[1]:SkinnySelectPhoneSoftKeys DN 4 chan 1 change
  TsRingOut to TsCallTransfer
Mar  9 15:01:10: //3288/xxxxxxxxxxxx/CCAPI/cc_api_call_disc_cause_update:
  (callID=0xCD8, cause=0x10)
Mar  9 15:01:10: //3288/7DB9A8D89271/CCAPI/cc_api_call_disc_cause_update:
  setting disc_cause to 0x10
```

The reason for this failed call transfer attempt is that Cisco CME takes the transfer target number (5003) and matches it with any **dialplan-pattern** commands configured. If there is a match, Cisco CME expands the transfer target extension (5003) to its complete E.164 number (408.555.5003) and uses that for call transfer instead of just the extension. The reason for this is that if the incoming call is from a PSTN gateway, it may not know about the extensions at all. All it might know is the phones' E.164 external numbers.

The attempt to set up a call to 408.555.5003 will fail, because Cisco CME 2 does not have a dial peer with destination pattern 408.555.5003 to route this call to Cisco CME 3.

To solve this problem, configure a dial peer on Cisco CME 2 with destination pattern 4085555... pointing to Cisco CME 3, as shown in Example 18-24. With this configuration, the transfer works fine. However, more adjustments may still be needed, as discussed next.

Example 18-24 *Dial Peer from Cisco CME 2 to Cisco CME 3*

```
CME2#show running-config
dial-peer voice 101 voip
  destination-pattern 4085555...
  session target ipv4:40.40.0.1
```

In Example 18-25, the transferor (Cisco CME 2) now can set up the consult call to the expanded E.164 number of extension 5003, which is 408.555.5003. However, when the transferor (Cisco CME 2) commits the transfer after the consultation call, an error occurs, even though the end-to-end consult call transfer worked. What happens is that the transferor (Cisco CME 2) asks the transferee (Cisco CME 1) to set up a call to the transfer target (Cisco CME 3), passing the complete E.164 number of the transfer target (408.555.5003). However, the transferee (Cisco CME 1) does not have a dial peer for that destination pattern, so it returns an error indicating that it cannot set up the transferred call.

After receiving the error from the transferee (Cisco CME 1), the transferor (Cisco CME 2) hairpins the transferee-transferor (Cisco CME 1–2) call leg to the transferor-transfer target (Cisco CME 2–3) call leg. Two call legs exist on the transferor (Cisco CME 2) even though the transferor phone is no longer part of the call. You can verify this situation by using the **show voip rtp connections** command on the transferor node, as shown in Example 18-25.

Example 18-25   *Hairpin Call Caused by the Lack of an E.164 Dial Peer on the Transferee*

```
CME2#debug voip ccapin inout
CME2#debug ephone state
Mar 10 14:51:38: ephone-2[1]:TransferButtonPress
Mar 10 14:51:38: ephone-2[1]:Commit Transfer with Consult for DN 2 chan 1 using
  consult DN 4 chan 1
Mar 10 14:51:38: ephone-2[1]:HoldButtonPress (allow_toggle = 0)
......
Mar 10 14:51:38: //3298//APPL:/AppConsultRequest:
Mar 10 14:51:38: AppLegH450TransferNotSupported: remote end is h450.2 capable
Mar 10 14:51:38: //3298//APPL:/AppIdentifyRequest:
Mar 10 14:51:38: //3298//APPL:/SSMapEvent:  SS_IDENTIFY_RESP: identify[17]
  rerouteNo[4085555003] invokeID[1508]
Mar 10 14:51:38: //3297//APPL:/AppConsultResponseSuccess: consuldID[17]
Mar 10 14:51:38: //3297//APPL:/AppSSReturnResult:
Mar 10 14:51:38: ephone-2[1]:SkinnyConsultIDResponse DN 2 chan 1 explicit target
  4085555003 orig 5003 redirected= []
Mar 10 14:51:38: ephone-2[1]:SkinnyConsultIDResponse ActivateTransfer DN 2 chan 1
  to 4085555003 id [17]
Mar 10 14:51:38: ephone-2[1]:Bator Call Transfer DN 2 chan 1 consult_dn 4 chan 1
  to 4085555003 id [17]
Mar 10 14:51:38: ephone-2[1]:SkinnyConsultIDResponse DN 2 chan 1  Fix Up eDSP
  state can't find local transferee DN (resetting)
Mar 10 14:51:38: DN 2 Call Transfer ID=[17] for callID 3296 to 4085555003
  (expanded)
Mar 10 14:51:38: ephone-2[1]:Transfer Request OK for DN 2 chan 1
Mar 10 14:51:38: //3296//APPL:/SSMapEvent:  SS_INIT_IND: rerouteNo[4085555003]
  identify[17] invokeID[3300] transferringNo[6002] peer[0] xto_callID[0]
Mar 10 14:51:38: AppLegH450TransferNotSupported: remote end is h450.2 capable
Mar 10 14:51:38: //3295//APPL:/AppTransferInitiateRequest:  to [4085555003] with
  ID[17]
Mar 10 14:51:38: //3295//APPL:/AppTransferRequest:
Mar 10 14:51:38: AppLegH450TransferNotSupported: remote end is h450.2 capable
Mar 10 14:51:38: //3295//APPL:/AppTransferRequest: SS_INIT:rerouteNo[4085555003]
  ID[17]
Mar 10 14:51:38: //3295//APPL:/SSMapEvent:  SS_RETURN_ERROR [10]
Mar 10 14:51:38: AppRedirectStatusUpdateAVlist:
Mar 10 14:51:38: //3295//APPL:/AppRedirectStatusUpdateAVlist: unable to get CallID
  to update AVlist
Mar 10 14:51:38: RD_Transferring_FAILED: ***** convert SSXFER 10 to RD status 14
  *********

Mar 10 14:51:38: //-1//APPL:LG3295:/AppHandOffLocalTRT: Leg 3295's protocol=2
  Leg -1's protocol=-1
Mar 10 14:51:38: //-1//APPL:HN4CC44348:LG3295:/AppHandOffLocalTRT:
ccSetupIndQueryRegistration
Mar 10 14:51:38: //3295//APPL:/AppHandOffLocalTRT:  handoff to local TRT, transfer
  is done

CME2#show voip rtp connections
```

continues

Example 18-25   *Hairpin Call Caused by the Lack of an E.164 Dial Peer on the Transferee (Continued)*

```
VoIP RTP active connections :
No. CallId  dstCallId  LocalRTP  RmtRTP  LocalIP     RemoteIP
1   3295    3298       18768     17956   1.3.28.28   1.3.6.26
2   3298    3295       18810     17720   1.3.28.28   1.3.6.33
Found 2 active RTP connections
```

NOTE   The transferor (Cisco CME 2) has two RTP streams: one to the transferee (Cisco CME 1) and one to the transfer target (Cisco CME 3). This is undesirable if all the devices involved in the call transfer can support the H.450.2 protocol, because this can consume more bandwidth on your WAN than it is engineered for. To fix this problem, configure a dial peer on the transferee (Cisco CME 1) with destination pattern 4085555... pointing to the transfer target (Cisco CME 2). This dial peer is exactly the same as the one you added on Cisco CME 2, as shown in Example 18-24.

Using Hairpinned Calls

The previous discussion covered how an erroneous configuration can lead to a transfer failure or an inefficient transfer. There are some scenarios where you may have to use hairpinned calls and plan for the additional bandwidth and resource use. An example of such a scenario is a PSTN gateway that is running an old version of Cisco IOS, such as 12.2.8T, or you have a non-Cisco H.323 device in the network. These devices don't support the H.450 protocol.

If any of the Cisco CME nodes receives a call from such a gateway and that call is transferred to another gateway, using hairpinned calls is the only option. However, you may notice in such cases that after you commit the transfer, it takes a few seconds for the transfer to complete. That is because the transferor is waiting for the transferee to acknowledge the successful call setup between transferee and transfer target. Because the transferee cannot use H.450, it cannot set up that call, and the transferor waits for a timeout period before it hairpins the transfer. To avoid this delay, configure H.450.12 on the transferor Cisco CME, as discussed in Chapter 7.

Troubleshooting Common Problems with Network Call Forward

In the preceding sections, you learned how some configuration items affect network call transfers. This section explores how configurations affect network call forwards.

Cisco CME supports three types of H.323 call forward implementations:

- A Cisco-proprietary method implemented before the industry-standard H.450 suite of protocols was supported by Cisco IOS

- An H.450-based call forward method

- A method called a *hairpinned call forward*, in which the forwarding gateway sets up a call leg to the forward-to target and then bridges it with the call leg that was supposed to be forwarded

The H.450 method is the recommended and most efficient call forwarding mechanism, provided that all the network devices in your network support it. For this method to be invoked by Cisco CME, a **call-forward pattern** configuration is required, as shown in Example 18-26. This configuration informs Cisco CME which calling numbers support the H450.3 method of call forwarding. If every network device in your network supports this method, using **call-forward pattern .T** is the easiest way to configure the feature globally to apply to all calls. If this configuration is missing in Cisco CME, call forwards may not work.

Example 18-26 *Configuring and Displaying the Call Forward Pattern*

```
CME3(config)#telephony-service
CME3(config-telephony)#call-forward pattern .T
......
CME#show telephony-service
CONFIG (Version=3.1)
======================
Version 3.1
Cisco CallManager Express
ip source-address 40.40.0.1 port 2000
max-ephones 10
max-dn 20
max-conferences 3
max-redirect 5
dialplan-pattern 1 4085555... extension-length 4 extension-pattern 5...
dialplan-pattern 2 6505558... extension-length 4 extension-pattern 8...
dialplan-pattern 3 4155556... extension-length 4 extension-pattern 6...
dialplan-pattern 4 5105559... extension-length 4 extension-pattern 9...
voicemail 7200
mwi relay
mwi expires 68000
time-format 12
date-format mm-dd-yy
call-forward pattern .T
```

There is another common scenario in which H.450.3 call forward fails. Assume that Cisco CME1 in Figure 18-6 has an analog PSTN line with a caller ID blocking configuration. A call from this line arrives at a far-end Cisco CME, such as Cisco CME2, with no calling number. For Cisco IOS to complete an incoming call, it must have an incoming dial peer to associate with the call so that it can negotiate call attributes. The problem being faced here is that the Cisco CME receiving this call (CME2) cannot identify an incoming dial peer to associate with the call, because it arrives with no calling number. So the attributes selected for this call are from default dial peer 0, where H.450 is disabled. You can see this problem in the debug shown in Example 18-27. Notice the empty calling number.

Example 18-27 *H450.3 Is Disabled When a Call Arrives with No Caller ID*

```
CME2#debug voip ccapin inout
CME2#debug voip ivr supplementary-service
Dec 13 20:29:00.860: //-1/529ACE8D8189/CCAPI/cc_api_display_ie_subfields:
   cc_api_call_setup_ind_common:
   cisco-username=1.4.14.28
   ----- ccCallInfo IE subfields -----
   cisco-ani=
   cisco-anitype=0
   cisco-aniplan=0
   cisco-anipi=0
   cisco-anisi=0
   dest=5002
   cisco-desttype=0
   cisco-destplan=0
   cisco-rdn=
   cisco-rdntype=-1
   cisco-rdnplan=-1
   cisco-rdnpi=-1
   cisco-rdnsi=-1
   cisco-redirectreason=-1
Dec 13 20:29:00.860: //-1/529ACE8D8189/CCAPI/cc_api_call_setup_ind_common:
   Interface=0x4481252C, Call Info(
   Calling Number=(TON=Unknown, NPI=Unknown, Screening=Not Screened,
   Presentation=Allowed),
   Called Number=5002(TON=Unknown, NPI=Unknown),
   Calling Translated=FALSE, Subsriber Type Str=Unknown,
   FinalDestinationFlag=TRUE,
   Incoming Dial-peer=0, Progress Indication=ORIGINATING SIDE IS NON ISDN(3),
   Calling IE Present=FALSE,
   Source Trkgrp Route Label=, Target Trkgrp Route Label=,
   CLID Transparent=FALSE), Call Id=14501
......
Dec 13 20:29:05.868: //-1/xxxxxxxxxxxx/CCAPI/ccUpdateRedirectNumber:
   Original Called Number=5002, Calling Number=, Calling DN=-1,
   Redirect Number=7200, Redirect Reason=2
Dec 13 20:29:05.868: ephone-1[3]:SetCallState line 2 DN 2 chan 1 ref 2620 TsOnHook
Dec 13 20:29:05.868: dn_tone_control DN=2 chan 1 tonetype=0:DtSilence onoff=0
   pid=160
Dec 13 20:29:05.868: //14502/529ACE8D8189/CCAPI/cc_api_call_disconnect_done:
   Disposition=0, Interface=0x44F05038, Tag=0x0, Call Id=14502,
   Call Entry(Disconnect Cause=19, Voice Class Cause Code=0, Retry Count=0)
Dec 13 20:29:05.868: //14502/529ACE8D8189/CCAPI/cc_api_call_disconnect_done:
   Call Disconnect Event Sent
Dec 13 20:29:05.868: ephone-1[3]:SpeakerPhoneOnHook
Dec 13 20:29:05.868: ephone-1[3]:Ringer Off
Dec 13 20:29:05.872: AppLegH450CallFwdNotSupported: h450.3 is being disabled on
   this voip dial-peer
Dec 13 20:29:05.872: //-1//APPL:/AppPrepareForwardSetup:
```

The first thing to do to fix this problem is to assign (on CME1) a caller ID on the incoming analog PSTN line using the **station-id number** and **station-id name** commands in Cisco IOS under the **voice-port** for corresponding analog voice ports on Cisco CME1, as shown in Example 18-28.

The next thing to do is to configure (on CME2) an explicit VoIP dial peer to match the caller ID that will be delivered by the analog trunks on CME1. Or, if all the devices in your network support H.450.3, and there is no specific pattern for calling numbers, the easiest way is to have a VoIP dial peer that matches all calling numbers. Explicit VoIP dial peers have H.450.3 enabled by default. The added dial peer should also have other parameters, such as codec and DTMF relay configurations, according to your needs. Example 18-28 shows a sample configuration.

Example 18-28   *Configuration to Match the Incoming Dial Peer for H.450*

```
!On Cisco CME1
CME1(config)#voice-port 2/1/0
CME1(config-voiceport)#station-id number 9
CME1(config-voiceport)#station-id name PSTN

!On Cisco CME2
CME2(config)#dial-peer voice 1 voip
CME2(config-dial-peer)#incoming called-number .
CME2(config-dial-peer)#dtmf-relay h245-alphanumeric
```

Troubleshooting Transcoding

Cisco CME 3.2 introduces support for transcoding services. You need transcoding services when you have devices and applications in the network that don't support lower-bandwidth codecs, and you don't have enough bandwidth available in your network. In such a case, the devices that don't support lower-bandwidth codecs are colocated with a transcoding device that converts media streams of different codecs. This section discusses the configuration and troubleshooting of such transcoding devices.

Configuring Transcoding Services

One key example of a transcoding scenario is when Cisco UE terminates AA or voice mail calls that must be G.711. If these calls originate from other sites across your WAN, they likely use G.729 to conserve bandwidth. For such calls to divert successfully into Cisco UE, transcoding services are needed. Also, if Cisco CME has to establish a three-party conference in which one of the endpoints is on a G.729 gateway, a transcoder is needed to complete and mix the conference. This section discusses the configuration of a transcoding device for Cisco CME and how to troubleshoot issues relating to transcoding services.

Assume in the topology given earlier in Figure 18-6 that Cisco CME 2 has a high-density voice network module (NM-HDV2) with digital signal processors (DSPs) that can be configured for transcoding services. Example 18-29 shows such a configuration with the NM-HDV2 present in slot 4 of the Cisco CME 2 router.

Example 18-29 *DSP Farm Configuration for Transcoding Services*

```
CME2#show running-config
voice-card 4
 dspfarm
 dsp services dspfarm
```

The DSP farm (for transcoding services) has to register with Cisco CME. The DSP farm does not need to be physically present in the Cisco CME router chassis with which it is registered. It may be present in a separate PSTN gateway router chassis at the same site. In this example, however, the DSP farm is hosted on the Cisco CME router itself, which is a common deployment.

Example 18-30 shows the configuration required to register the DSP farm to Cisco CME 2. You have to identify an interface whose IP address can be used in media setup for the services. In Example 18-30, FastEthernet interface 0/0 is used. The Cisco CME IP address that this transcoding device registers with is also configured (192.168.0.1 in Example 18-30). A transcoding profile is created in which you mention all the codecs that should be transcoded. Several commands start with **sccp**, because the transcoding device uses SCCP to register with Cisco CME, and it is controlled by using SCCP.

Example 18-30 *Configuration to Register the DSP Farm to a Cisco CME*

```
CME2#show running-config
sccp local FastEthernet0/0
sccp ccm 192.168.0.1 identifier 1
sccp ip precedence 3
sccp
!
sccp ccm group 1
 bind interface FastEthernet0/0
 associate ccm 1 priority 1
 associate profile 1 register mydsp1
!
dspfarm profile 1 transcode
 codec g711ulaw
 codec g711alaw
 codec g729ar8
 codec g729r8
 codec g729br8
 maximum sessions 4
 associate application SCCP
......
telephony-service
 max-ephones 100
 max-dn 288
 ip source-address 192.168.0.1 port 2000
 system message Sopranos
```

Example 18-30 *Configuration to Register the DSP Farm to a Cisco CME (Continued)*

```
sdspfarm units 1
sdspfarm transcode sessions 4
 create cnf-files version-stamp 7960 Apr 10 2004 15:27:09
 voicemail 6800
max-conferences 4
 web admin system name aesop password aesop
 transfer-system full-consult
 transfer-pattern 5...
 transfer-pattern 6...
```

After you enter this configuration, ensure that the transcoding device is registered with Cisco CME. Example 18-31 shows the output of the **show sccp all** command used to check the status of the transcoding device.

Example 18-31 *Checking the Status of a Transcoding Device*

```
CME2#show sccp all
SCCP Admin State: UP
Gateway IP Address: 192.168.0.1, Port Number: 0
IP Precedence: 3
User Masked Codec list: None
Call Manager: 192.168.0.1, Port Number: 2000
                  Priority: N/A, Version: 3.1, Identifier: 1

Transcoding Oper State: ACTIVE - Cause Code: NONE
Active Call Manager: 192.168.0.1, Port Number: 2000
TCP Link Status: CONNECTED, Profile Identifier: 1
Reported Max Streams: 8, Reported Max OOS Streams: 0
Supported Codec: g711ulaw, Maximum Packetization Period: 30
Supported Codec: g711alaw, Maximum Packetization Period: 30
Supported Codec: g729ar8, Maximum Packetization Period: 60
Supported Codec: g729r8, Maximum Packetization Period: 60
Supported Codec: g729br8, Maximum Packetization Period: 60
Supported Codec: rfc2833 dtmf, Maximum Packetization Period: 30

SCCP Application Service(s) Statistics:

Profile ID: 1, Service Type: Transcoding
TCP packets rx 114, tx 110
Unsupported pkts rx 1, Unrecognized pkts rx 0
Register tx 1, successful 1, rejected 0, failed 0
KeepAlive tx 103, successful 103, failed 0
OpenReceiveChannel rx 2, successful 2, failed 0
CloseReceiveChannel rx 2, successful 2, failed 0
StartMediaTransmission rx 2, successful 2, failed 0
StopMediaTransmission rx 2, successful 2, failed 0
Reset rx 0, successful 0, failed 0
MediaStreamingFailure rx 0
Switchover 0, Switchback 0

CCM Group Identifier: 1
```

continues

Example 18-31 *Checking the Status of a Transcoding Device (Continued)*

```
Description: None
Binded Interface: FastEthernet0/0, IP Address: 192.168.0.1
Associated CCM Id: 1, Priority in this CCM Group: 1
Associated Profile: 1, Registration Name: mydsp1
Registration Retries: 3, Registration Timeout: 10 sec
Keepalive Retries: 3, Keepalive Timeout: 30 sec
CCM Connect Retries: 3, CCM Connect Interval: 10 sec
Switchover Method: GRACEFUL, Switchback Method: GRACEFUL_GUARD
Switchback Interval: 10 sec, Switchback Timeout: 7200 sec
Signaling DSCP value: default, Audio DSCP value: default

Total number of active session(s) 0, and connection(s) 0
Total number of active session(s) 0, and connection(s) 0
Total number of active session(s) 0, connection(s) 0, and callegs 0

SCCP Application Service(s) Statistics Summary:
Total Conferencing Sessions: 0, Connections: 0
Total Transcoding Sessions: 0, Connections: 0
Total MTP Sessions: 0, Connections: 0
Total SCCP Sessions: 0, Connections: 0
```

Debugging Transcoded Calls

Now that the transcoding device is successfully registered with a Cisco CME, this section
covers how it is used in calls that require transcoding services. Assume that extension 6002 on
Cisco CME 2 receives a call from the PSTN. This call uses the G.711 codec, as shown in
Example 18-32.

Example 18-32 *Call Between the PSTN and Extension 6002*

```
CME2#show ephone offhook
ephone-90 Mac:0030.94C2.D2C6 TCP socket:[2] activeLine:1 REGISTERED
mediaActive:1 offhook:1 ringing:0 reset:0 reset_sent:0 paging 0 debug:0
IP:19.19.19.2 49500 Telecaster 7960  keepalive 5 max_line 6
button 1: dn 62 number 6002 CH1   CONNECTED
button 2: dn 64 number 6004 CH1   IDLE
Active Call on DN 62 chan 1 :6002 19.19.19.2 29146 to 1.4.13.29 2000 via
    19.19.19.2
G711Ulaw64k  160 bytes no vad
Tx Pkts 225 bytes 38700 Rx Pkts 227 bytes 39044 Lost 0
Jitter 0 Latency 0 callingDn -1 calledDn -1 (media path callID 12 srcCallID 11)
```

Assume further that extension 6002 wants to conference in extension 8010 on Cisco CME 1 and
that the configuration on Cisco CME 2 is such that calls to Cisco CME 1 use G.729. Setting up
this conference requires transcoding from G.729 to G.711. At this point, Cisco CME recognizes
that it must insert the transcoder in the media path for this call to succeed. Example 18-33 shows
that the consult call before the conference uses G.729 between extension 6002 and extension
8010.

Example 18-33 *Extension 6002 on Cisco CME 2 Calls 8010 on Cisco CME 1 for a Conference*

```
CME2#debug ephone state
CME2#debug ephone mtp
Apr 11 15:34:22: ephone-90[2]:HoldButtonPress (allow_toggle = 0)
Apr 11 15:34:22: ephone-90[2]:HoldButtonPress HOLD activated for DN 62 chan 1
Apr 11 15:34:22: ephone-90[2]:SetCallState line 1 DN 62 chan 1 ref 3 TsHold
Apr 11 15:34:22: ephone-90[2]:CloseReceive
Apr 11 15:34:22: ephone-90[2]:StopMedia
Apr 11 15:34:22: ephone-90[2]:SpeakerPhoneOffHook mute 0
Apr 11 15:34:22: ephone-90[2]:OFFHOOK
Apr 11 15:34:22: ephone-90[2]:SIEZE on activeLine 2 activeChan 1
Apr 11 15:34:22: ephone-90[2]:SetCallState line 2 DN 64 chan 1 ref 5 TsOffHook
Apr 11 15:34:22: ephone-90[2]:Check Plar Number
Apr 11 15:34:22: DN 64 chan 1 Voice_Mode
Apr 11 15:34:22: dn_tone_control DN=64 chan 1 tonetype=33:DtInsideDialTone
  onoff=1 pid=159
Apr 11 15:34:24: dn_tone_control DN=64 chan 1 tonetype=0:DtSilence onoff=0
  pid=159
Apr 11 15:34:24: dn_tone_control DN=64 chan 1 tonetype=0:DtSilence onoff=0
  pid=159
Apr 11 15:34:26:   20
Apr 11 15:34:26: ephone-90[2]:SetCallState line 2 DN 64 chan 1 ref 5 TsProceed
Apr 11 15:34:26: ephone-90[2]:SetCallState line 2 DN 64 chan 1 ref 5 TsRingOut
Apr 11 15:34:26: ephone-90[2]::callingNumber 6004
Apr 11 15:34:26: ephone-90[2]::callingParty 6004
Apr 11 15:34:26: ephone-90[2]:Call Info DN 64 line 2 ref 5 called 8010
  calling 6004 origcalled 8010 calltype 2
Apr 11 15:34:26: ephone-90[2]:Call Info for chan 1
Apr 11 15:34:26: ephone-90[2]: No-Name calling
Apr 11 15:34:26: ephone-90[2]: No-Name
Apr 11 15:34:26: dn_tone_control DN=64 chan 1 tonetype=36:DtAlertingTone onoff=1
  pid=159
Apr 11 15:34:30: dn_tone_control DN=64 chan 1 tonetype=0:DtSilence onoff=0
  pid=159
Apr 11 15:34:30: DN 64 chan 1 End Voice_Mode
Apr 11 15:34:30: DN 64 chan 1 Voice_Mode
Apr 11 15:34:30: SKINNY_CALL_RESTART for DN 64 ignored
Apr 11 15:34:30: ephone-90[2]:OpenReceive DN 64 chan 1 codec 11:G729  duration
  20 ms bytes 20
Apr 11 15:34:30: ephone-90[2]:SetCallState line 2 DN 64 chan 1 ref 5 TsConnected
Apr 11 15:34:30: ephone-90[2]:OpenReceiveChannelAck:IP 19.19.19.2, port=17770,
                 dn_index=64, dn=64, chan=1
Apr 11 15:34:30: ephone-90[2]:StartMedia 1.4.13.29 port=2000
Apr 11 15:34:30: DN 64 chan 1 codec 11:G729 duration 20 ms bytes 20
Apr 11 15:34:31: ephone-90[2]::callingNumber 6004
Apr 11 15:34:31: ephone-90[2]::callingParty 6004
Apr 11 15:34:31: ephone-90[2]:Call Info DN 64 line 2 ref 5 called 8010 calling
  6004 origcalled 8010 calltype 2
Apr 11 15:34:31: ephone-90[2]:Call Info for chan 1
Apr 11 15:34:31: ephone-90[2]: No-Name calling
Apr 11 15:34:31: ephone-90[2]: No-Name
```

After the consultation, extension 6002 decides to conference in all three parties. Cisco CME 2 now introduces the transcoding device. Example 18-34 shows that Cisco CME 2 instructs the transcoding device to open two RTP streams (using SCCP messages): one for G.729 and another for G.711. The messages that have MTP-1 in them go to the transcoding device. Note the IP addresses and RTP port numbers used in these messages. The IP addresses used for the transcoder are the same as that of the Cisco CME router, because the transcoding device is hosted in the Cisco CME router. You should see different IP addresses if the transcoder device is hosted in a separate router.

Example 18-34   *Cisco CME 2 Inserts a Transcoder for the Conference*

```
CME2#debug ephone state
CME2#debug ephone mtp
Apr 11 16:59:36: SkinnyXcodeGetStreamsForDn: dn=64, chan=1, codec=4, bytes=160
Apr 11 16:59:36: skinny_xcode_associate_stream: seize stream 3, confID=3, peer=4,
  far_end=0
Apr 11 16:59:36: skinny_xcode_associate_stream: seize stream 4, confID=3, peer=3,
  far_end=1
Apr 11 16:59:36: ***SkinnyResetDnCodec DN 64 chan 1 to skinny-codec 4 bytes 160
  was codec 11 ephone-(90)
Apr 11 16:59:36: ephone-90[2]:SkinnyResetDnCodec DN 64 chan 1 OpenReceiveAck
  already done
Apr 11 16:59:36: ephone-90[2][SEP003094C2D2C6]:SkinnyAssignConference line 2 conf
_dn 64 conf_chan 1
Apr 11 16:59:36: ephone-90[2]:SetCallState line 1 DN 62 chan 1 ref 1
  TsCallRemoteMultiline
Apr 11 16:59:36: ephone-90[2]:SkinnyAssignConference 0 OK with 1 active
Apr 11 16:59:36: ephone-90[2]:DN 62 chan 1 state changed to CONNECTED for
  conference with DN 64 chan 1 codec 4
Apr 11 16:59:36: ephone-90[2]:SetCallState line 2 DN 64 chan 1 ref 2 TsConnected
Apr 11 16:59:36: ephone-90[2]:SpeakerPhoneOffHook mute 0
Apr 11 16:59:36: skinny_xcode_open_receive_channel:        stream=4, confID=3,
  pTPartyId=4
Apr 11 16:59:36:        mtp=1, socket=1
Apr 11 16:59:36: MTP-1[1]:OpenReceive stream 4 codec 11:G729  duration 20 ms
  bytes 20
Apr 11 16:59:36: skinny_xcode_open_receive_channel:        stream=3, confID=3,
  pTPartyId=3
Apr 11 16:59:36:        mtp=1, socket=1
Apr 11 16:59:36: MTP-1[1]:OpenReceive stream 3 codec 4:G711Ulaw64k   duration 20 ms
  bytes 160
Apr 11 16:59:36: ephone-90[2]:CloseReceive
Apr 11 16:59:36: ephone-90[2]:StopMedia
Apr 11 16:59:36: ephone-90[2]:OpenReceive DN 64 chan 1 codec 4:G711Ulaw64k
  duration 20 ms bytes 160
Apr 11 16:59:36: MTP-1[1]: SkinnyXcodeOpenReceiveChannelAck:       stream=4,
  addr=1.4.13.29 port=18918 laddr=1.4.13.29 lport=2000
Apr 11 16:59:36: SkinnyXcodeStartMedia:          stream=4, confID=3, pTPartyId=4
Apr 11 16:59:36: MTP-1[1]:StartMedia 1.4.13.29 port=18918
Apr 11 16:59:36: stream 4 codec 11:G729 duration 20 ms bytes 20
Apr 11 16:59:36: MTP-1[1]: SkinnyXcodeOpenReceiveChannelAck:       stream=3,
  addr=1.4.13.29 port=17834 laddr=1.4.13.29 lport=2000
Apr 11 16:59:36: SkinnyXcodeStartMedia:          stream=3, confID=3, pTPartyId=3
```

Example 18-34   *Cisco CME 2 Inserts a Transcoder for the Conference (Continued)*

```
Apr 11 16:59:36: MTP-1[1]:StartMedia 1.4.13.29 port=17834
Apr 11 16:59:36: stream 3 codec 4:G711Ulaw64k duration 20 ms bytes 160
Apr 11 16:59:36: ephone-90[2]:OpenReceiveChannelAck:IP 19.19.19.2, port=21848,
               dn_index=64,dn=64, chan=1
Apr 11 16:59:36: ephone-90[2]:StartMedia 1.4.13.29 port=2000
Apr 11 16:59:36: DN 64 chan 1 codec 4:G711Ulaw64k duration 20 ms bytes 160
```

At this point, the transcoder is successfully inserted into the conference, and all three parties are in the conversation.

You can use the commands shown in Example 18-35 to view the current transcoding sessions and the endpoints involved.

Example 18-35   *Checking the Transcoding and RTP Sessions*

```
CME2#show voip rtp connections
VoIP RTP active connections :
No. CallId  dstCallId  LocalRTP RmtRTP LocalIP       RemoteIP
1   7       6          17652    18554  1.4.13.29     1.4.14.34
2   8       9          18918    2000   1.4.13.29     1.4.13.29
3   10      9          17834    2000   1.4.13.29     1.4.13.29
Found 3 active RTP connections

CME2#show sdspfarm sessions
Stream-ID:1 mtp:1 0.0.0.0  0  Local:0 IDLE
 usage: Ip-Ip (Res)
 codec:G711Ulaw64k  duration:20 vad:0 peer Stream-ID:2

Stream-ID:2 mtp:1 0.0.0.0  0  Local:0 IDLE
 usage: Ip-Ip (Res)
 codec:G711Ulaw64k  duration:20 vad:0 peer Stream-ID:1

Stream-ID:3 mtp:1 1.4.13.29  17834  Local:2000 START
 usage: Conf (DN=64 , CH=1) FE=FALSE
 codec:G711Ulaw64k  duration:20 vad:0 peer Stream-ID:4

Stream-ID:4 mtp:1 1.4.13.29  18918  Local:2000 START
 usage: Conf (DN=64 , CH=1) FE=TRUE
 codec:G729  duration:20 vad:0 peer Stream-ID:3

Stream-ID:5 mtp:1 1.4.13.29  16722  Local:2000 START
 usage: Ip-Ip
 codec:G711Ulaw64k  duration:20 vad:0 peer Stream-ID:6

Stream-ID:6 mtp:1 1.4.13.29  18550  Local:2000 START
 usage: Ip-Ip
 codec:G729AnnexA  duration:20 vad:0 peer Stream-ID:5

Stream-ID:7 mtp:1 0.0.0.0  0  Local:0 IDLE
 usage:
 codec:G711Ulaw64k  duration:20 vad:0 peer Stream-ID:0
```

continues

Example 18-35 *Checking the Transcoding and RTP Sessions (Continued)*

```
Stream-ID:8 mtp:1 0.0.0.0  0  Local:0 IDLE
  usage:
  codec:G711Ulaw64k  duration:20 vad:0 peer Stream-ID:0
```

The **show voip rtp connections** command shows the RTP streams established from the Cisco CME router to the other endpoints. This also includes the far-end Cisco CME router with an endpoint that is part of the conference. The **show sdspfarm session** command shows the RTP streams set up for transcoding purposes. This includes only the streams between the Cisco CME router and transcoding device.

Also note here the Usage field in the output of the **show sdspfarm session** command. In the first highlighted lines in Example 18-35, the Usage field says Conf, indicating that this transcoding is used for a conference session.

A few lines lower, you see a session where the Usage field is IP-IP. This means that this transcoding session is used for an IP-IP hairpinned call that Cisco CME has bridged and that the two call legs involved in the hairpin use different codecs. An example of such a scenario is a G.729 H.323 call coming from another PSTN gateway to Cisco UE. In this case, Cisco CME bridges the H.323 call from the PSTN gateway to the SIP call toward Cisco UE and introduces a transcoder. Another example is a call transfer from Cisco CME 2 to another PSTN gateway that does not support H450.2 and, hence, the call legs bridged by Cisco CME 2. The far-end PSTN gateway uses G.729 in this case—hence, the need for a transcoder.

Troubleshooting H.323 GK Integration

The section "Troubleshooting Common Problems with Network Call Transfers" covered common problems with call routing (dial peer) configurations. You can manage routing configuration between nodes in a network effectively if you have only a handful of Cisco CME sites in your network. As the number of Cisco CMEs and PSTN gateways increases, it becomes increasingly cumbersome to use manual dial peers pointing to each Cisco CME and PSTN gateway in the network at each of the sites. This is where a GK becomes a useful addition to the network. You can configure a Cisco IOS voice-enabled router as an H.323 GK by using the appropriate Cisco IOS image.

Figure 18-7 shows a sample topology with four Cisco CMEs in the network and using one of the Cisco CMEs as a GK. With this kind of network, all the call routing information can be centralized in the GK. All the extension-based and E.164 dial peers on the remote Cisco CME systems point to the GK. Only the GK has true knowledge of the dialing plan. This minimizes issues with call transfers and forwards caused by a lack of appropriate call routing dial peers on all Cisco CMEs.

Figure 18-7   *Topology for the GK in a Cisco CME Network*

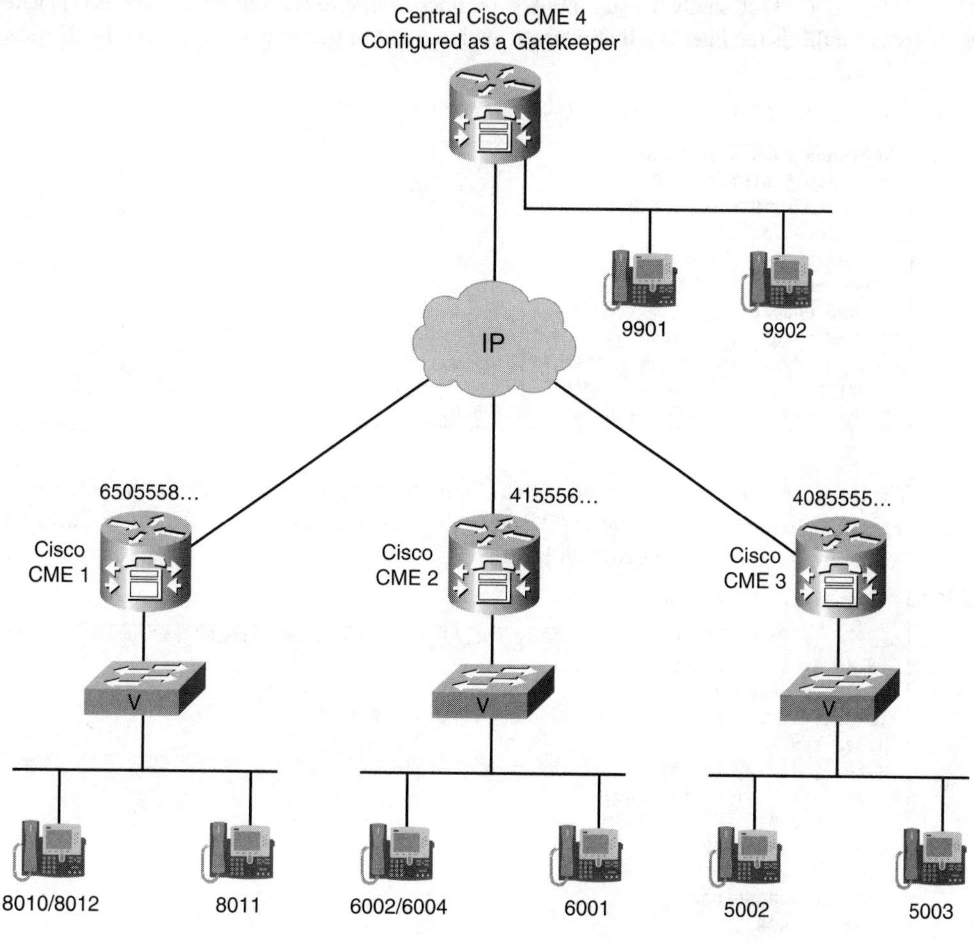

Example 18-36 shows the relevant part of the GK configuration. The name of the zone containing all the Cisco CMEs is gk.

Example 18-36   *GK Configuration*

```
CME4#show running-config
gatekeeper
 zone local gk cisco.com 192.168.0.1
 no shutdown
```

All the PSTN gateways and remote Cisco CME systems must be configured as shown in Example 18-37. Usually the serial WAN interface is used to configure H.323 on PSTN gateways because this is the interface that interacts with the rest of the network. Example 18-37 uses an Ethernet interface.

Example 18-37 *Gateway and Remote Cisco CME Configuration for the GK*

```
CME3#show running-config
interface FastEthernet0/0
 ip address 192.168.0.1 255.255.0.0
 load-interval 30
 duplex auto
 speed auto
 no cdp enable
 h323-gateway voip interface
 h323-gateway voip id gk ipaddr 192.168.0.1 1719
 h323-gateway voip h323-id cme6
 h323-gateway voip bind srcaddr 192.168.0.1
```

The most common problem faced with a GK in the network is that some of the gateways fail to register with the GK. Example 18-38 shows the message displayed to the Cisco CME/gateway console when it fails to register with the GK.

Example 18-38 *Gateway Fails to Register*

```
Dec  4 11:18:02.680: %CCH323-2-GTWY_REGSTR_FAILED: Gateway cme2 failed to register
  with GK gk even after 2 retries
CME3#show gateway
H.323 ITU-T Version: 4.0    H323 Stack Version: 0.1
 H.323 service is up
 Gateway  cme2  is not registered to any GK
Alias list (CLI configured)
 E164-ID 5001
 E164-ID 4085555001
 E164-ID 5002
 E164-ID 4085555002
 E164-ID 5003
 E164-ID 4085555003
 E164-ID 5004
 E164-ID 4085555004
 E164-ID 5005
 E164-ID 4085555005
 H323-ID cme2
Alias list (last RCF) is empty
```

The most common reason for this problem is that the gateway is using the same H.323 ID as an already registered gateway. Try changing the H.323 ID of this gateway to a different one using the **h323-gateway voip h323-id** command. If successful, you should see the output shown in Example 18-39 when you execute the **show gateway** command on the Cisco CME system.

Example 18-39 *Gateway Successfully Registers with the GK*

```
CME3#show gateway
H.323 ITU-T Version: 4.0   H323 Stack Version: 0.1
 H.323 service is up
 Gateway  cme7  is registered to GK gk
Alias list (CLI configured)
 E164-ID 5001
 E164-ID 4085555001
 E164-ID 5002
 E164-ID 4085555002
 E164-ID 5003
 E164-ID 4085555003
 E164-ID 5004
 E164-ID 4085555004
 E164-ID 5005
 E164-ID 4085555005
 H323-ID cme7
Alias list (last RCF)
 E164-ID 5001
 E164-ID 4085555001
 E164-ID 5002
 E164-ID 4085555002
 E164-ID 5003
 E164-ID 4085555003
 E164-ID 5004
 E164-ID 4085555004
 E164-ID 5005
 E164-ID 4085555005
 H323-ID cme7
```

Summary

This chapter covered advanced troubleshooting topics, including Cisco CME integration with
Cisco Unity for voice mail and AA and various call transfer scenarios across multiple Cisco
CME nodes in an H.323 network. H.450 operation and troubleshooting were discussed, as well
as scenarios that require transcoding of codecs to complete a call flow. This chapter also
covered network topologies with GK configurations.

This chapter covers the following topics:

- General Cisco Unity Express (UE) system troubleshooting techniques
- Troubleshooting problems that might occur during system installation
- Troubleshooting Cisco UE startup problems
- Troubleshooting the Cisco UE Initialization Wizard
- Troubleshooting the system backup and restore operations

## CHAPTER 19

Troubleshooting Cisco UE System Features

The previous chapters in Part IV, "Maintenance and Troubleshooting," took a closer look at Cisco CallManager Express (CME) troubleshooting of the call processing and phone components of your system, as well as some voice mail scenarios with external voice mail systems such as Cisco Unity. This chapter takes an in-depth view of troubleshooting Cisco CME's integrated voice mail application, Cisco Unity Express (UE).

Cisco UE's hardware and software architecture was discussed in Chapter 3, "Cisco IPC Express Architecture Overview." This fundamental architectural knowledge is required to understand the troubleshooting tools and techniques discussed in this chapter. In Chapter 3, you learned how a Cisco IOS router interfaces with the Cisco UE hardware module using the Router Blade Communication Protocol (RBCP), which is the fundamental mechanism used as the communication path between Cisco UE and the Cisco CME router and is integral to understanding later sections in this chapter.

This chapter covers troubleshooting the system-level aspects of Cisco UE, such as general problem isolation techniques, installation, startup, and backup and restore.

General Troubleshooting Techniques

Cisco UE offers several types of tools to help you isolate problems on the system:

- Viewing system information and status (using a variety of **show** commands)
- Event logging to log files including information, warning, error, and fatal messages
- A tracing facility showing detailed information on system events, information, and decisions (similar to Cisco IOS **debug** information)

Viewing Generic System Information

This book provides you with information about Cisco UE so that you can troubleshoot and fix most of the common problems you might encounter. In case you still have to contact the Cisco Technical Assistance Center (TAC) for additional support, however, it is helpful to provide the Cisco TAC with some basic information about your system. This basic information includes the software version, the software license, the current configuration of the Cisco CME and Cisco UE components, and some information about the current usage of the system. This section describes how to view that basic information.

Example 19-1 uses the **show version** command to provide information about the hardware form factor of the Cisco UE module, the model type of the router that is hosting the Cisco UE, the speed with which CPU is running, and additional hardware-specific information. One thing to note is that the AIM-CUE runs at 150 MHz if it is hosted on 2600XM or 2691 series access routers. In other routers, it runs at 300 MHz.

Example 19-1 *Displaying the System Version*

```
CUE#show version
CPU Model:                Celeron (Coppermine)
CPU Speed (MHz):          154.926
CPU Cache (KByte):        128
Chassis Type:             C2600
Chassis Serial:           FSJC0400673
Module Type:              AIM
Module Serial:            FHH07330001
```

Example 19-2 uses the **show software version** command to display the versions of the Cisco UE software components installed on the system. Identifying the installed software versions is important when troubleshooting interworking issues. For example, some Cisco UE features might be supported only with a certain version of Cisco CME or Cisco UE.

Example 19-2 *Displaying the Software Version*

```
CUE#show software version
Installed Packages:
 - Bootloader (Primary)  1.0.17
 - Global  2.0.0.12
 - Voice Mail  2.0.0.12
 - Bootloader (Secondary)  2.0.0
 - Core  2.0.0.12
 - Auto Attendant  2.0.0.12

Installed Languages:
 - US English  2.0.0.0
```

Example 19-3 shows the license installed on the system by using the **show software licenses** command.

Example 19-3 *Displaying Licenses*

```
CUE#show software licenses
Core:
 - application mode: CCME
 - total usable system ports: 4
Voicemail/Auto Attendant:
 - max system mailbox capacity time: 480
 - max general delivery mailboxes: 15
```

Example 19-3 *Displaying Licenses (Continued)*

```
 - max personal mailboxes: 50
Languages:
 - max installed languages: 1
 - max enabled languages: 1
```

Example 19-4 uses **show voicemail usage** to show the current usage of the different resources in the system, including the number of personal mailboxes, general delivery mailboxes (GDMs), and the voice mail capacity allocation.

Example 19-4 *Displaying the System's Current Usage*

```
CUE#show voicemail usage
personal mailboxes:                 50
general delivery mailboxes:         0
orphaned mailboxes:                 0
capacity of voicemail (minutes):    480
allocated capacity (minutes):       350.0
message time used (seconds):        15227
message count:                      856
average message length (seconds):   17.78855140186916
greeting time used (seconds):       0
greeting count:                     0
average greeting length (seconds):  0.0
total time used (seconds):          15227
total time used (minutes):          253.78334045410156
percentage used time (%):           53
```

The **show voicemail limits** command, shown in Example 19-5, shows the limits currently enforced on the voice mail system (based on the system's license). These limits include the default mailbox size, default recording limit for callers and subscribers, and message expiration duration.

Example 19-5 *Displaying System Voice Mail Limits*

```
CUE#show voicemail limits
Default Mailbox Size (seconds):         420
Default Caller Message Size (seconds):  60
Maximum Recording Size (seconds):       900
Default Message Age (days):             30
System Capacity (minutes):              480
Default Prompt Language:                en_US
Operator Telephone:                     0
```

Logging in Cisco UE

Cisco UE provides a full-fledged logging facility. Messages are logged to the console, to a Syslog server, or to the messages.log file on the disk or flash. Cisco UE has four levels of logging. Table 19-1 shows the Cisco UE logging levels mapped to Syslog logging levels.

Table 19-1 *Cisco UE Logging Levels*

Cisco UE Logging Level	Syslog Logging Level
INFO	Debug, Info, and Notice
WARNING	Warning
ERROR	Error
FATAL	Critical, Alert, and Emergency

If you are monitoring straightforward issues, such as whether the Cisco UE system reloaded, you might want to look at the Syslog messages before you start troubleshooting by turning on traces. These messages provide a brief problem description, a possible reason for the event, and other relevant information about a problem. These messages might be displayed on the console, written to a Syslog server, or stored in the Cisco UE messages.log file, depending on the system's configuration. Example 19-6 shows different ways of turning on logging in Cisco UE. Logging to the console displays the log messages on the console when they occur.

Example 19-6 *Logging Levels and Configuration*

```
cue(config)#log console ?
  errors      Error messages
  filter      Filter events from syslog
  info        Information messages
  warning     Warning messages
cue(config)#log console info

Logging to a server
cue(config)#log server 1.4.53.1
```

If you are using a Network Module Cisco UE (NM-CUE), the log messages are also written to a file called messages.log on the hard disk. If you want offline access to the file, you can use command-line interface (CLI) commands to copy the messages.log file to an FTP server. Example 19-7 shows the log files on the system.

Example 19-7 *Viewing Log Files on Cisco UE*

```
cue#show logs
linux_session.log
dmesg
syslog.log
shutdown.log
atrace.log
```

Example 19-7   *Viewing Log Files on Cisco UE (Continued)*

```
debug_server.log
memmon.log
klog.log
messages.log
```

The following steps show you how to copy the log file to an external server:

Step 1   Have an FTP server ready that the Cisco UE system can reach. Ensure that the FTP server is active.

Step 2   Set up a session to the Cisco UE CLI from the router using the **service-module service-engine** *<slot/port>* **session** command. Enter the **show logs** command, as shown in Example 19-7, to make sure that the desired log files are available.

Step 3   Enter the following command for each file you need to transfer:

```
CUE#copy log log_file url ftp://ftp_ip_address/
```

where *log_file* is the filename of the desired log file and *ftp_ip_address* is the IP address of the FTP server. An example of a command to copy messages.log to an FTP server is

```
cue#copy log messages.log url ftp://user:password@1.3.61.16/messages.log
```

Tracing Techniques

Cisco UE provides an extensive CLI-based tracing and debugging facility. It provides tracing commands for most of the system's important components, such as voice mail, the Customer Response Solutions (CRS) component, the web GUI interface, the Session Initiation Protocol (SIP) call processing component, and voice mail networking. Tracing uses the concepts of *module, entity,* and *activity.* For example, consider the following command:

```
cue#trace ccn managerappl dbug
```

In this example, **trace** is the command, **ccn** is the module that represents the CRS component, and **managerappl** (which stands for application manager) is the entity within the ccn module. The **dbug** parameter is the activity to be traced.

By default, trace output is stored in a memory buffer. You can use commands to view the trace buffer contents on the console. You also have the option of configuring the trace output to write to a file called atrace.log. If you are using an NM-CUE, writing trace output to the disk is enabled by default. On the Advanced Integration Module (AIM-CUE) hardware, tracing is disabled by default. You should enable it with care, because the AIM-CUE flash card has space limitations and a finite lifetime in terms of the number of write cycles before you must replace it. Doing indiscriminate tracing to your flash card shortens its life unnecessarily. Instead, if you are using an AIM-CUE, it is recommended that you use an external FTP server as the destination device for writing trace files.

trace Command Summary

Table 19-2 lists the most important **trace** commands. You can find the complete list of commands for tracing, modules, entities, and activities in the "Cisco UE System Administration and CLI Guides" available on Cisco.com.

Table 19-2   *Cisco UE **trace** Commands*

Command	Description
trace *module entity activity*	Turns on the trace for a desired module, entity, and activity.
show trace	Displays the current trace settings.
show trace buffer	Shows the current contents of the trace buffer. This output can be voluminous, depending on what traces were turned on, so use it carefully. This command displays the complete contents of the trace buffer from top to bottom.
show trace buffer containing *regexp pattern*	Displays the lines in the trace buffer that contain a particular pattern.
show trace buffer tail *N*	Shows the latest trace entries to the trace buffer in real time as and when they happen. If *N* is given, it shows the last *n* most recent trace entries and then continues displaying subsequent trace entries as and when they happen. If *N* is omitted, only new events are shown as they occur.
show trace buffer tail *N* **long**	Prints the traces in long format. The long format expands on the internal codes for different events and messages so that the trace output is more readable. For example, when you use **trace voicemail vxml all**, the output prints the text equivalent of the prompt file instead of just giving the prompt names.
clear trace	Clears the trace buffer. Usually used when troubleshooting problems in real time and when you don't need the previous contents of the trace buffer.

Turning on Traces

Depending on the problem area you are facing, you turn on traces for specific modules and entities. You might often have to turn on traces for several different modules and entities simultaneously to see how each module handles a particular data item or event. You might have to clear the trace buffer between different trace activities to make the troubleshooting output more readable and manageable, especially because the console connection speed is hard-coded to 9600 baud.

Each trace message in the output contains a time stamp of when the trace was generated. It also contains the module and entity that issued the trace output line so that when you read the trace, it is easy to understand which trace line was originated by which module. For example, in the following trace line, ACCN is the module (and stands for the CCN/CRS component), and VBRO is the entity (and stands for the voice browser).

```
2699 10/10 12:23:30.115 ACCN VBRO 0 Task:18000000079 Invoke:
http://localhost/voicemail/vxmlscripts/login.vxml
```

For most problems, turning on trace for a couple of modules and entities is sufficient, and the trace output is a manageable volume. More complex problems might require tracing to be turned on for many modules and entities, and the trace output can become cumbersome.

If a trace is turned on for only a couple of modules, it is easy to view the trace in real time. Thus, you turn on the trace, clear the trace buffer, issue the **show trace buffer tail** command, and make the call to trigger the system events you want to trace. As the call enters the Cisco UE application, you see trace output printed on the console. You can stop the trace output by pressing Ctrl-C, as shown in Example 19-8. The trace is cut off the moment you press Ctrl-C.

Example 19-8 *Viewing a Trace in Real Time*

```
cue#trace ccn VbrowserCore dbug
cue#clear trace
cue#show trace buffer tail
Press <CTRL-C> to exit...
DefaultCompilationConfig is now set to JVM en_US
2043 09/25 15:56:22.305 ACCN VBRW 0 Task:20000000089 enterLevel: SESSION_LEVEL
2043 09/25 15:56:22.306 ACCN VBRW 0 callContact.getSessionID() = 6000000059
2043 09/25 15:56:22.306 ACCN VBRW 0 Task:20000000089 VoiceBrowser sessionid:
  6000000059, taskid: 20000000089
2043 09/25 15:56:22.306 ACCN VBRW 0 callContact.getCallingNumber() = 5702
2043 09/25 15:56:22.306 ACCN VBRW 0 callContact.getCallingNumber() = 5702
2043 09/25 15:56:22.306 ACCN VBRW 0 callContact.getDNIS() = null
2043 09/25 15:56:22.306 ACCN VBRW 0 callContact.getCalledNumber() = 5800
2043 09/25 15:56:22.307 ACCN VBRW 0 callContact.getDNIS() = null
2043 09/25 15:56:22.307 ACCN VBRW 0 callContact.getCalledNumber() = 5800
2043 09/25 15:56:22.307 ACCN VBRW 0 callContact.getANIIIDigits() = null
2043 09/25 15:56:22.307 ACCN VBRW 0 callContact.getUserToUserInfo() = null
2043 09/25 15:56:22.307 ACCN VBRW 0 callContact.getRDNIS() = null
2043 09/25 15:56:22.307 ACCN VBRW 0 callContact.getLastRedirectedNumber() = null
2043 09/25 15:56:22.307 ACCN VBRW 0 callContact.getSessionID() = 6000000059
2043 09/25 15:56:22
cue#
```

If you run into a situation where you have to turn on tracing for many modules and entities, or even **trace all**, it is better not to attempt to watch the trace output in real time, because it becomes very difficult to follow. All the trace output is written to a file called atrace.log. On the NM-CUE, this file is written by default. On an AIM-CUE, use the **log trace local enable** command to allow the trace buffer to be written to flash. You can also use **log trace server** so that trace output is written to an FTP server instead of a flash on your Cisco UE, as shown in Example 19-9.

Example 19-9 *Writing Trace Output to a File*

```
cue(config)#log trace server url ftp://userid:password@192.168.0.1/trace
cue(config)#log trace server enable
```

After you make the preceding configuration, the trace file is created on the specified server.

Copying a Trace File to an FTP Server

After you make the test call to trigger the events you want to capture to a trace file, you must copy the atrace.log file to an FTP server, as shown in Example 19-10.

Example 19-10 *Displaying and Copying a Trace File*

```
cue#show logs
linux_session.log
dmesg
syslog.log
shutdown.log
atrace.log
debug_server.log
memmon.log
klog.log
messages.log
cue#copy log atrace.log url ftp://user:password@1.3.61.16/atrace.log
```

The atrace.log file is a binary file that you must decode to view in a text editor. You can get the utility to decode the trace file from the Cisco TAC. The utility consists of three files:

- atrace_decode (an executable)
- trace.tcmd
- trace.tmsg

Decode the atrace.log file as shown in Example 19-11. This creates an output file (dtmf_issue.log, in this example) that you can now view in a text editor. Currently, **atrace_decode** runs only on a Linux platform.

Example 19-11 *Decoding an atrace.log Trace File*

```
[test@CUE-core ftp]$ ./atrace_decode
Usage: ./atrace_decode <file_to_decode> <format> <out_file> <trace_command_file>
<trace_message_file>
format = 0 for short, 1 for long
[test@CUE-core ftp]$./atrace_decode atrace.log 1 dtmf_issue.log ./trace.tcmd
  ./trace.tmsg
```

Troubleshooting System Time Issues and NTP

Many of the Cisco UE features depend on a reliable clock. The voice message envelope information is one important example. As discussed in Chapter 13, "Cisco IPC Express General Administration and Initial System Setup," Cisco UE's clock is managed entirely by Network Time Protocol (NTP) and cannot be set manually.

Another Cisco UE feature that requires clock information is the trace and log messages that carry time stamps. If the clock on the Cisco UE system is not set correctly, troubleshooting might become very difficult, because log and trace messages cannot be correlated with real time.

You should configure an NTP source for Cisco UE that is the clock's source. An NTP source can be the host Cisco CME router (although this is not recommended because the low-end routers do not have a very reliable onboard clock source) or any other clock source in your network. Sometimes, for many reasons, the clock on Cisco UE might not be synchronized to its configured source. You can verify the status of NTP and the location of the clock's source with CLI commands. Example 19-12 shows these commands.

Example 19-12 *NTP-Related Commands*

```
NTP not working due to wrong configuration:
CUE#show ntp status
NTP reference server :        1.3.6.190
Status:                       reject
Time difference (secs):       0.0
Time jitter (secs):           4.0

NTP in Sync:
CUE#show ntp status
NTP reference server :        1.4.13.190
Status:                       sys.peer
Time difference (secs):       0.02110639284364879
Time jitter (secs):           0.019472182961180806

Trace commands available to debug NTP synchronization issues:
CUE#trace ntp ?
  all          Every entity and activity
  ntp          Entity
CUE#trace ntp ntp ?
  all          Every activity
  clkadj       Activity
  clkselect    Activity
  clkvalidity  Activity
  clockstats   Activity
  event        Activity
  loopfilter   Activity
  loopstats    Activity
  packets      Activity
  peerstats    Activity
```

Troubleshooting Installation Problems

When you install a Cisco UE module, problems might occur in downloading the software package. These problems might be caused by network connectivity or package issues. This section discusses some common problems that might occur during software installation of Cisco UE and ways to troubleshoot them.

Network Connectivity Issues

If the Cisco UE module is unable to establish contact with the FTP server where the software load resides, the error shown in Example 19-13 occurs when you attempt to install the software.

Example 19-13 *Installation Failed*

```
cueinstaller#>software install package url ftp://username:password@1.3.61.61/
  cue-vm.1.1.0.6.pkg
RAMDisk mounted
Connecting to host...
curl: (7) Connect failed
ERROR: Host did not respond.
Please check the host ip and try again.
RAMDisk unmounted
```

First ensure that the IP address of the FTP server is correct. Verify all the parameters given in the **install** command. If you are sure these are all correct, verify the IP connectivity from the Cisco UE module to the router. Reboot the Cisco UE module, as shown in Example 19-14, and press ******* at the first prompt. This action takes you to the bootloader prompt.

Example 19-14 *Checking IP Connectivity Between Cisco UE and the FTP Server*

```
cueinstaller#>reboot
WARNING: This will reboot the Service Engine!
Do you wish to continue (y,n) [n] y
```

The bootloader has a **ping** command, as shown in Example 19-15.

Example 19-15 *Checking IP Connectivity from the Bootloader*

```
ServicesEngine boot-loader> ping 1.3.61.61
Sending 5, 32 byte ICMP Echos to 1.3.61.61:
.....
Success rate is 0% (0/5)

ServicesEngine boot-loader> ping 1.3.61.16
Sending 5, 32 byte ICMP Echos to 1.3.61.16:
!!!!!
Success rate is 100% (5/5)
```

If the Cisco UE system cannot ping the FTP server, you might have the wrong configuration of IP parameters in the bootloader. Example 19-16 shows how to check the bootloader configuration. If you see anything wrong, you can use the bootloader **config** command to make modifications.

Example 19-16 *Checking the Bootloader Configuration*

```
ServicesEngine boot-loader>show config
IP addr:              1.4.13.90
Netmask:              255.255.0.0
TFTP server :         1.4.53.1
GW IP addr:           1.4.13.190
Default boot:         disk
Bootloader Version:   1.0.17
Default Helper-file:  cue-installer.1.1.1
Default BIOS:         primary
Default bootloader:   primary
Default cpu throttle: 50%
```

Another reason why the **ping** command might not be successful is the routing configuration on the Cisco IOS router. With an **ip unnumbered** configuration for the service-engine interface, you can verify the routing as follows:

- Ping the FTP host from the Cisco IOS router to ensure that the host can be reached. If this fails, examine the Cisco IOS routing configuration.

- If the FTP host can be reached from the router, verify the Cisco UE module's connectivity, as shown in Example 19-17.

Example 19-17 *Verifying Routing Table Information for Cisco UE Connectivity*

```
router#show ip route
Codes: C - connected, S - static, R - RIP, M - mobile, B - BGP
       D - EIGRP, EX - EIGRP external, O - OSPF, IA - OSPF inter area
       N1 - OSPF NSSA external type 1, N2 - OSPF NSSA external type 2
       E1 - OSPF external type 1, E2 - OSPF external type 2
       i - IS-IS, su - IS-IS summary, L1 - IS-IS level-1, L2 - IS-IS level-2
       ia - IS-IS inter area, * - candidate default, U - per-user static route
       o - ODR, P - periodic downloaded static route
Gateway of last resort is 1.3.0.1 to network 0.0.0.0
     1.0.0.0/8 is variably subnetted, 2 subnets, 2 masks
C       1.3.0.0/16 is directly connected, FastEthernet0/0
S       1.3.6.129/32 is directly connected, Service-Engine1/0
     20.0.0.0/24 is subnetted, 1 subnets
S       20.20.20.0 [1/0] via 1.3.6.26
     10.0.0.0/24 is subnetted, 1 subnets
C       10.10.10.0 is directly connected, FastEthernet0/1
     41.0.0.0/24 is subnetted, 1 subnets
S       41.41.41.0 [1/0] via 1.3.6.28
S*   0.0.0.0/0 [1/0] via 1.3.0.1
```

When the **show ip route** command is executed, a host route similar to the one highlighted in Example 19-17 should be displayed (where 1.3.6.129 is the IP address of your Cisco UE module and Service-Engine1/0 is the Cisco UE module seated in NM slot 1 of the router). If such a route does not show in your routing table, use the following command to add it:

```
router(config)#ip route 1.3.6.129 255.255.255.255 Service-Engine1/0
```

Software Package Issues

Sometimes a problem might occur in downloading the software, such as if binary mode was not used in the FTP command. This causes a problem when installing the software, such as the error shown in Example 19-18.

Example 19-18   *Failed Installation Caused by Corrupted Files*

```
cueinstaller#>software install package ftp://username:password@1.3.61.16/pkg/
cue-vm.1.1.0.6.pkg
RAMDisk mounted
Connecting to host...
  % Total    % Received % Xferd  Average Speed           Time           Curr.
                                 Dload  Upload Total   Current  Left    Speed
100 92785  100 92785    0      0   221k      0 0:00:00 0:00:00 0:00:00 2623k
RAMDisk unmounted
ERROR:: Security Header Validation Failed.
```

The error shown in Example 19-19 indicates that not all the files needed for installation are present on the FTP server.

Example 19-19   *Failed Installation Caused by a Missing File*

```
cueinstaller#>software install package ftp ://username :password@1.3.61.16/
cue-vm.1.1.1pkg
Created RAMDisk.
File System Type = reiser
RAMDisk mounted
Connecting to host...
  % Total    % Received % Xferd  Average Speed           Time           Curr.
                                 Dload  Upload Total   Current  Left    Speed
100 92811  100 92811    0      0   361k      0 0:00:00 0:00:00 0:00:00 8822k
Core File List is Signed
Retrieving cue-vm.1.1.1.manifest from 1.3.61.16
Retrieve manifest from server failed.
RAMDisk unmounted
Connecting to host...
curl: (19) cue-vm.1.1.1.manifest: No such file or directory
ERROR: The requested file does not exist on host.
Please check the package name and try again.
```

To recover from these software package installation errors, again download the software to the FTP server. Ensure that three types of files are present on the FTP server:

- .pkg

- .prt1

- .manifest (this file no longer exists separately in Cisco UE releases after 2.0)

Along with the available software image packages, a bootloader package is available. All Cisco UE software versions have a minimum bootloader version requirement. The manifest does not check that the minimum bootloader version is present in the system. Refer to the Cisco UE documentation to identify the bootloader version that is compatible with the Cisco UE software version you're trying to install. The exact files that comprise the installation might also vary from release to release. The examples in this section pertain to Cisco UE 1.1.1.

Troubleshooting Cisco UE Startup

You might experience situations in which the basic IP communication between the host router and the Cisco UE module fails even after proper configuration of the host router. You can identify such a problem by looking for *waiting* events such as those shown in an extract of the installation output in Example 19-20.

Example 19-20 *Installation Output Extract Showing Cisco UE Waiting for the Host Router*

```
==> only eth0 exists, we must be running on an AIM
==> only eth0 exists, we must be running on an AIM

Router communications servers initializing...complete.
Waiting for IOS to register IP address.
 - waited 10 seconds...
Waiting for IOS to register IP address.
 - waited 20 seconds...
```

Cisco UE is waiting for commands from the Cisco IOS router to configure Cisco UE with its IP address and default gateway parameters so that Cisco UE can communicate with the rest of the network. However, it is not receiving any response from the router. This process of configuring the Cisco UE module through the host Cisco IOS router uses the RBCP, as discussed in Chapter 3. There might be some situations in which you have to troubleshoot this protocol exchange between the host router and Cisco UE.

When Cisco UE successfully communicates with the router using RBCP and receives its IP parameters, you see the message shown in Example 19-21 on the Cisco UE console during application bootup.

Example 19-21 *Correct Response from the Host Router to Cisco UE*

```
==> only eth0 exists, we must be running on an AIM
==> only eth0 exists, we must be running on an AIM

Router communications servers initializing...complete.
IOS IP Address Registration complete.
```

The following few sections discuss troubleshooting problems during application bootup and communication issues between Cisco UE and the host router.

Checking Console Output on the Cisco UE Hardware

If you are having a problem opening a session to the Cisco UE module, or you don't see any output on the console, you can use the following command to check the console messages on the Cisco UE module without needing to open a session to the Cisco UE module:

```
router#test service-module service-engine slot/unit console
```

By default, this command displays the most recent 80 lines stored in the console buffer. However, it is possible to specify an offset of greater or less than 80, or to view all the messages stored in the console buffer.

Checking the RBCP Communication

To check the RBCP status on the Cisco UE module from the router, you can use the following test command:

```
router#test scp ping slot
```

This command sends a ping to the Cisco UE module as an RBCP message using operational code (opcode) 0x11. If the RBCP process on the Cisco UE module is up and running, the ping succeeds, and the output of the test command should look as shown in Example 19-22.

Example 19-22 *Testing Ping Output*

```
router#test scp ping 3
pinging addr 3(0x3)
assigned sap 0x4
addr 3(0x3) is alive
```

Debugging the RBCP Communication

There are situations in which you have to troubleshoot the RBCP messages between the Cisco UE module and the router. One situation is when the interface configuration has been verified but you still cannot ping the Cisco UE module.

First, check the interface's status and ensure that the interface and line protocol are up, as shown in Example 19-23.

Example 19-23 *Checking the Status of the Service-Engine Interface*

```
router#show interfaces service-engine 1/0
Service-Engine1/0 is up, line protocol is up
  Hardware is I82559FE, address is 0001.b912.f510 (bia 0001.b912.f510)
  Interface is unnumbered. Using address of FastEthernet0/0 (1.3.6.29)
```

Next, you should verify the RBCP state machine status on the router, as shown in Example 19-24. The Cisco UE module should be in steady state for proper operation. The example shows the status of service-engine 1/0.

Example 19-24   *Checking the Status of the RBCP State Machine*

```
ccme#service-module service-Engine 1/0 status
Service Module is Cisco Service-Engine1/0
Service Module supports session via TTY line 33
Service Module is in Steady state
cisco service engine 1.0
```

If you are still unable to ping the Cisco UE module IP address, troubleshoot the RBCP messages exchanged between the Cisco UE module and the host router. Table 19-3 describes the flags and how they are used for the scp-tx message. scp-tx stands for Switch Communication Protocol transmission, meaning that the router transmits this message to the Cisco UE module.

Table 19-3   *Flags for the scp-tx RBCP Message*

Opcode	Action	Action Description	Type	Interface Description
0054	01	Configure	01	Internal IP address
0054	00	Unconfigure	01	Internal IP address
0059	01	Configure	—	—
0059	00	Unconfigure	—	—

Table 19-4 describes the flags and how they are used for the scp-rx message, which is a "Switch Communication Protocol" message the router receives from the Cisco UE module.

Table 19-4   *Flags for the scp-rx RBCP Message*

Opcode	Type	Type Description
0054	01	Internal IP address rejected
0054	02	Internal IP address OK
0054	03	External IP address rejected (not used for NM-CUE)
0054	04	External IP address OK (not used for NM-CUE)
0059	00	Default IP gateway OK
0059	01	Default IP gateway rejected

The output of **debug scp all** is shown in Example 19-25. An IP address (192.168.0.2/ 255.255.0.0) is being configured on the Ethernet interface of the Cisco UE module.

Example 19-25   *IP Address RBCP Message Being Sent from the Router*

```
router#debug scp all
router(config-if)#service-module ip address 192.168.0.2 255.255.0.0
router(config-if)#
*Mar  2 18:07:24.673: scp-tx: SA:0F/01 DA:01/01 Op:0054 Sq:13C7 Ln:000A I:00
*Mar  2 18:07:24.673: 000: 01 01 C0 A8 00 02 FF FF 00 00    .....L....
*Mar  2 18:07:24.681: scp-rx: SA:0E/01 DA:0F/01 Op:0054 Sq:13C7 Ln:000A I:01
*Mar  2 18:07:24.681: 000: 02 00 00 00 00 00 00 00 00 00
```

The output shows that the scp-tx message transmitted has the Source Address (SA) field set to 0F/01, which indicates that the message originated from the router. The Destination Address (DA) field is set to 01/01, which indicates that the Cisco UE module is present in slot 1. The opcode of 0054 indicates that this is an IP address configuration. The sequence number (Sq) field is 0B26, and the length of the payload is 10 bytes.

The first parameter on the second line is the type, and the second parameter is the action. In the message, the type is 01 and the action is 01, indicating that the Cisco UE module interface is being configured. The next 8 bytes are the IP address and subnet mask.

In the output shown for the scp-rx message, the SA field is set to 0E/01, indicating that it originated from the Cisco UE module in slot 1. The DA field is set to 0F/01, indicating that the message is destined for the router. The Opcode and Sq fields are the same as in the scp-tx message. The Type field in the second line is set to 02, which means that the Cisco UE module IP address was set properly. The rest of the parameters have no significance.

Example 19-26 shows the Cisco UE module's **default-gateway** parameter being set.

Example 19-26   *Default Gateway Configuration RBCP Message*

```
router#debug scp all
router(config)#int content-engine 1/0
router(config-if)#service-module ip default-gateway 192.168.0.1
1d23h: scp-tx: SA:0F/01 DA:01/01 Op:0059 Sq:0B28 Ln:0005 I:00
1d23h: 000: 01 C0 A8 00 01                                  .....
1d23h: scp-rx: SA:01/01 DA:0F/01 Op:0059 Sq:0B28 Ln:0005 I:01
1d23h: 000: 00 FF FF FF E0
```

The debug output of the scp-tx message shows that the opcode is different. The value 0059 indicates that this message pertains to the IP **default-gateway** configuration parameter. The length of the payload is 5 bytes. The payload is shorter than the scp-tx message shown in Example 19-25 (it's 5 bytes in Example 19-26 and 10 bytes in Example 19-25), because no subnet mask is associated with the default gateway IP address. The action flag is set to 01, which indicates that the default gateway is being configured. In the output of scp-rx message, the action flag is set to 00, confirming that the configuration of the IP default gateway address was successful.

Table 19-5 summarizes some of the common problems encountered when installing and configuring a Cisco UE module, and possible solutions to those problems.

Table 19-5   *Common Installation Problems and Resolutions*

Problem	Possible Reason	Possible Solution
You can't open a session into the NM-CUE.	The TTY line associated with the NM-CUE is already occupied.	Use the **service-module service-engine** *slot/port* **session clear** command, or **clear line** *xx* to clear the TTY line.
The session, when invoked, results in a connection refused error message.	The TTY line associated with the NM-CUE is occupied.	Configure **no exec** under the TTY line associated with the NM-CUE. This prevents the line from being unavailable because of a rogue EXEC process.
Service module commands do not seem to take effect.	The service module status might not be in steady state. RBCP configuration messages go through only when the service module is in steady state.	It is possible that the service module is not responding. Try reloading the service module. If that doesn't work, use the **reset** command.
You can't ping the internal address when using the IP unnumbered scheme.	The IP route table is incorrect.	When using **ip unnumbered**, always remember to add a static route pointing toward the service-engine interface.
IOS doesn't let you change or remove the IP address of the CE NM interface.	The default gateway of the CE NM must be pointing to the same IP subnet as the interface being changed or removed.	First remove the IP default gateway from under the service-engine interface. Then change the interface's IP address and add back the IP default gateway.
You can set the speed of the terminal line from the router side, but you can't see any CLI for doing the same on the CE side.	There is no CLI to change the speed. The speed is hard-set to 9600, 8-N-1 on both the IOS and CE sides. Even though IOS allows you to change the speed settings, this doesn't take effect.	—

Troubleshooting the Initialization Wizard

The Cisco UE Initialization Wizard is a GUI tool provided to complete the installation of the system, as covered in Chapter 13. After new software is loaded on the system, you must run the Initialization Wizard. You invoke a browser on a PC with a URL pointing to Cisco UE. After logging in, you go through a number of steps, including

- Importing users from Cisco CME
- Defining the various pilot numbers

Here are a couple common issues encountered when running the Initialization Wizard:

- You are unable to log on to the Initialization Wizard
- After all the procedures are complete, the system returns with a failure

The next sections describe how to identify both issues.

Unable to Log into the Initialization Wizard

At the login window, you enter the administrator username and password assigned during the post-installation procedures. If you are unable to log in, the issue could be that the username and password were not entered properly or that uppercase or special characters have been used. To verify that the administrator username is legitimate, go to the CLI and check the Cisco UE configuration. The username entered should be one of the administrators defined on the system. You can verify that the username admin belongs to the Administrators group, as shown in Example 19-27.

Example 19-27 *Displaying Members of the Administrators Group*

```
cue#show group detail groupname Administrators
Full Name:          Administrators
Description:
Phone:
Phone(E.164):
Language:           systemDefault(ga_IE)
Owners:
Members:            admin
Privileges:         superuser ManagePrompts ManagePublicList ViewPrivateList
```

If you have verified that the username is an administrator but you still cannot log in, you can bypass this by assigning a new password for the login, as shown in Example 19-28.

Example 19-28 *Defining an Administrator*

```
CUE#username temp password temp
CUE#config terminal
CUE(config)#group Administrators member temp
```

temp is any name you choose for this purpose.

NOTE   Note that the group is Administrators; take care with both the case of the letters and the spelling. If you enter it wrong, it creates the wrong group and you still cannot access the system.

Initialization Wizard Reports Failures

During the process of running the Initialization Wizard, the most common problem experienced is that the Cisco UE GUI cannot log into Cisco CME to read the user and extension information.

This might be because the configuration on Cisco CME is missing some mandatory items. Cisco UE asks you to enter the username and password for Cisco CME, so ensure that you are using the correct Cisco CME username and password in these fields. Example 19-29 shows debugs on Cisco CME where a Cisco UE login fails because of wrong authentication information.

Example 19-29 *Failed Cisco CME Login by Cisco UE*

```
cme#debug ip http authentication
Dec 14 01:35:49.915: its_urlhook url: /telephony_service.html, method 1
Dec 14 01:35:49.915: Tue, 14 Dec 2004 01:35:49 GMT 1.4.13.153
/telephony_service.html auth_required  Protocol = HTTP/1.1 Method = GET
Dec 14 01:35:49.915:
Dec 14 01:35:49.923: its_urlhook url: /ITSMain, method 1
Dec 14 01:35:49.923: validate_username_password (asfd, sdf)validate_
admin_user (asfd: sdf)
validate_admin_user: validate admin [0] locally
validate_admin_user (asfd: sdf)
validate_username_password: check password for phone[-1]

Dec 14 01:35:49.923: HTTP: Authentication failed for realm its_access
Dec 14 01:35:49.923: HTTP: Authentication failed for level 15
Dec 14 01:35:51.923: Tue, 14 Dec 2004 01:35:51 GMT 1.4.13.153
/ITSMain auth_failed
        Protocol = HTTP/1.1 Method = GET
Dec 14 01:35:51.923:
Dec 14 01:35:51.927: its_urlhook url: /ipkeyswitch, method 1
Dec 14 01:35:51.927: lds_urlhook, url=/ipkeyswitch
```

You can see the current Cisco CME administration account details using the **show telephony-service** command on Cisco CME, as shown in Example 19-30.

Example 19-30 *Verifying Cisco CME Administrator Account Details*

```
CME#show telephony-service
CONFIG (Version=3.2)
======================
Version 3.2
Cisco CallManager Express
For on-line documentation please see:
www.cisco.com/univercd/cc/td/doc/product/access/ip_ph/ip_ks/index.htm
ip source-address 1.4.13.53 port 2000
max-ephones 48
max-dn 192
.........
web admin system name admin  password admin
web admin customer name Customer
edit DN through Web:  disabled.
edit TIME through web:  disabled.
```

The rest of the Initialization Wizard usually proceeds smoothly. If you encounter issues, turn on the traces shown in Example 19-31. The trace output is intuitive, so you should be able to identify any problems that might arise. Example 19-31 shows Cisco UE trace output when an administrator uses the wrong username and password for Cisco CME.

Example 19-31 *Cisco UE Trace Output When the Cisco CME Login Fails*

```
cue#trace webinterface all
cue#show trace buffer tail
Press <CTRL-C> to exit...
3662 12/15 15:06:10.904 webI init 5
3715 12/15 15:07:09.898 webI ctrl 0 Enter /Web/IW/InitWizard.do
3715 12/15 15:07:09.898 webI sydb 0 /sw/apps/monitor//ctrl/offline
3715 12/15 15:07:09.899 webI sydb 2 0
......
3715 12/15 15:07:09.903 webI ctrl 2 null
3715 12/15 15:07:09.903 webI ctrl 0 Center /Web/IW/InitWizard.do
3715 12/15 15:07:09.905 webI sydb 0 /sw/limits/global/applicationMode
3715 12/15 15:07:09.905 webI sydb 2 ITS
3715 12/15 15:07:09.905 webI sydb 0 /sw/limits/global/applicationMode
3715 12/15 15:07:09.906 webI sydb 2 ITS
3715 12/15 15:07:09.906 webI prxy 2 Call to connection.getInputStream()
3715 12/15 15:07:09.911 webI prxy 2 Response code 401. Receiving data from Router
3715 12/15 15:07:09.912 webI prxy 2 Receiving data from Router...done
3715 12/15 15:07:09.912 webI prxy 2 Detected Lambretta 1+ Image
3715 12/15 15:07:09.912 webI prxy 2 ITSL2Connection initiated
3715 12/15 15:07:09.912 webI prxy 2 Enter ITSL2 Login Center
3715 12/15 15:07:09.913 webI prxy 2 Call to connection.getInputStream()
3715 12/15 15:07:11.917 webI prxy 2 UNREACHABLE: Unable to contact Router
3715 12/15 15:07:11.917 webI prxy 2 Enter ITSL2 Login Center
3715 12/15 15:07:11.918 webI prxy 2 Call to connection.getInputStream()
3715 12/15 15:07:11.925 webI prxy 2 UNREACHABLE: Unable to contact Router
3715 12/15 15:07:11.925 webI init 5
3715 12/15 15:07:11.929 webI sydb 0 /sw/limits/global/applicationMode
3715 12/15 15:07:11.930 webI sydb 2 ITS
3715 12/15 15:07:11.932 webI sydb 0 /sw/limits/global/applicationMode
3715 12/15 15:07:11.933 webI sydb 2 ITS
3715 12/15 15:07:11.945 webI ctrl 0 Exit /Web/WEB-INF/screens/iw/InitWizard.jsp
```

Troubleshooting Backup and Restore

This section discusses problem scenarios you might encounter when performing a backup or restore operation of the Cisco UE configuration or voice message data, including the following:

- Cannot find or connect to the backup/restore server.
- Backup or restore cannot start.
- Backup or restore is incomplete.
- The restore operation cannot restore the correct configuration or data.

The next sections describe techniques for troubleshooting each of these issues.

Cannot Find or Connect to the Backup/Restore Server

To start a backup or restore operation, you must first configure the FTP server URL and corresponding directory. Backup and restore are done to the same server location. The CLI to configure the backup server is

```
cue(config)#backup server url ftp://server_ip_address/directory [username
    name password password]
```

Use the following processes to troubleshoot server connectivity problems:

- Check the Cisco UE configuration to ensure that all the backup and restore configuration parameters are correct. The critical parameters are the server's IP address and the appropriate directory path.

- Use the commands **show backup server** and **show backup history** to ensure that the configuration is set up properly.

- Ping the FTP server to ensure that it can be reached.

- The backup path specified in the Cisco UE configuration shows the default FTP path. Check the path set on the server to ensure that the proper directory has been selected.

Backup or Restore Cannot Start

The FTP server for backup and restore might require a user login and password (this is an optional but recommended configuration). Also, some FTP servers limit the transferable block of data to a certain size. If a login is configured on your FTP server, verify that you have permission to read and write on the FTP server.

If the backup server has been configured but cannot be reached when the backup process starts, the system shows an error message, as shown in Example 19-32.

Example 19-32 *Backup Restore Error Message*

```
cue#show backup server
Backup Restore: Unable to connect to backup server
```

The following Cisco UE **trace** command is useful in capturing the activities while a backup or restore is progressing:

```
cue#trace BackupRestore all
```

Example 19-33 shows traces indicating that the backup server has not been configured.

Example 19-33 *Backup Trace*

```
996 02/28 19:59:59.448 bare bare 0 BackupRestore: Backupsysdbnode get
996 02/28 19:59:59.448 bare bare 0 BackupRestore: done Backupsysdbnode get, val:
997 02/28 19:59:59.449 bare bare 0 BackupRestore: Backupsysdbnode get
997 02/28 19:59:59.449 bare bare 0 BackupRestore: done Backupsysdbnode get, val:
996 02/28 19:59:59.452 bare bare 0 in isServerConfigured
```

continues

Example 19-33 *Backup Trace (Continued)*

```
996 02/28 19:59:59.454 bare bare 0 in isServerConfigured,
  url:ftp://127.0.0.1/ftp user:backupadmin password:backupadminpassword
996 02/28 19:59:59.454 bare bare 129
996 02/28 19:59:59.454 bare bare 130
996 02/28 19:59:59.454 bare bare 0 out isServerConfigured, backup server not
  configured
996 02/28 19:59:59.454 bare bare 0 history sysdbprovider: backup server not
  configured
997 02/28 19:59:59.457 bare bare 0 BackupRestore: Backupsysdbnode get
997 02/28 19:59:59.457 bare bare -1 BackupRestore: done Backupsysdbnode get, val:
998 02/28 19:59:59.457 bare bare 0 BackupRestore: Backupsysdbnode get
998 02/28 19:59:59.457 bare bare 0 BackupRestore: done Backupsysdbnode get, val:
1082 02/28 19:59:59.458 bare bare 0 BackupRestore: Backupsysdbnode get
1082 02/28 19:59:59.458 bare bare 0 BackupRestore: done Backupsysdbnode get, val

On the other hand, if the FTP server is not present or reachable,
  the trace includes these outputs:
1186 03/01 01:40:56.823 bare bare 130
1186 03/01 01:40:56.825 bare bare 0 in isServerReachable, Unable to reach backup
  server
1186 03/01 01:40:56.825 bare bare 0 backup sysdbprovider: backup server
  unreachable
```

Backup or Restore Is Incomplete

When the backup or restore has been started but is aborted or incomplete, first check the integrity of the network between the Cisco UE system and the server. If available, use a sniffer to see if there are excessive packet drops. The other possibility is that the FTP server might not be configured properly to transfer large blocks of data. Some FTP servers might have the block size default set to smaller than 16 MB. Configure the FTP server to transfer and accept larger blocks of data. If the FTP server cannot be configured, use a different one. In addition, verify that the FTP server supports passive FTP.

Restore Doesn't Restore the Correct or Complete Configuration or Data

When the restore operation cannot restore the proper configuration or data, users notice wrong parameters and missing stored messages or greetings. Use the **trace** command shown in Example 19-34 to troubleshoot this situation.

Example 19-34 **trace backrestore** *Output*

```
cue#trace backrestore backrestore ?
  CONF        Activity
  HISTORY     Activity
  INIT        Activity
```

Example 19-34   **trace backrestore** *Output (Continued)*

```
OPERATION     Activity
SERVER        Activity
all           Every activity
```

Each of these traces records the detailed activities of the operation. Turn on the appropriate trace and repeat the failed activity. The activities are recorded accordingly and can then be examined for the cause of the failure.

Summary

This chapter provided an overview of the troubleshooting tools and techniques to be used with the Cisco UE system. You learned about potential problems with basic connectivity between the host router and the Cisco UE application, including tracing the RBCP messages. Isolating installation, startup, and other connectivity problems were covered next. This chapter also discussed backup and restore functions to show how to troubleshoot problems in this area.

The next chapters cover Cisco UE troubleshooting specific to the AA and voice mail applications.

This chapter covers the following topics:

- Troubleshooting problems that may occur with a customized automated attendant (AA)
- Tracing a call flow through AA from call arrival at the AA pilot number to the call's transfer to the destination extension

## CHAPTER 20

Troubleshooting Cisco UE Automated Attendant

This chapter discusses how to troubleshoot operational and runtime issues with developing and deploying the Cisco Unity Express (UE) customized automated attendant (AA) application.

Chapter 3, "Cisco IPC Express Architecture Overview," provides an overview of the Cisco UE AA and voice mail system components and architecture. As such, it is a good foundation for the topics discussed in this chapter. A key software component of Cisco UE is the Customer Response Solutions (CRS) software. CRS is the infrastructure leveraged by all other Cisco UE applications, including the AA. CRS is also the component used to implement the customized AA applications.

Troubleshooting a Customized AA

As discussed in Chapter 9, "Cisco IPC Express Automated Attendant Options," Cisco UE allows you to create up to five customized AA applications or top-level scripts for each Cisco UE system. Creating and deploying such applications involves the following steps:

Step 1   Establish clear requirements for your AA application, and draw a flow chart for the desired menu flow.

Step 2   Determine the wording of the prompts for the application.

Step 3   Record the prompts using the tool of your choice, such as a PC-based recorder or Cisco UE Administration Via Telephony (AVT) (called the Greeting Management System [GMS] before Cisco UE release 2.1). You also can outsource the creation of the prompts to a recording studio.

Step 4   Name the prompts (.wav files) appropriately.

Step 5   Convert the application flow chart you created in Step 1 into one or more scripts using the Cisco UE AA Script Editor. (Use appropriate variables, and make sure you use the right prompt names in the script.)

Step 6   Validate the scripts by selecting **Tools > Validate** in the Cisco UE AA Script Editor.

Step 7   Upload the scripts and prompts to the Cisco UE system using the GUI or (CLI).

Step 8   Create an AA application from the **Voice Mail > Auto Attendant** GUI menu. This allows you to associate the script with a dial-in phone number (the AA pilot number for this script) and prepares the application to take live calls.

Step 9   Ensure that the Cisco CME router has a Session Initiation Protocol (SIP) dial peer with the correct dual-tone multifrequency (DTMF) relay and codec options pointing to the new AA pilot number (called a trigger internally in the Cisco UE software) created in the preceding step.

Even though you have followed all the necessary precautions in creating the AA, some issues may still come up. When issues occur, you should use the troubleshooting techniques discussed in this chapter.

The following sections discuss possible problems you might encounter during the configuration of an AA application. These are not runtime issues. Instead, they are problems you may experience during the configuration or deployment of the system or a new AA menu.

Ensuring a Correct Configuration

An AA application may have multiple physical script files. In this case, a main .aef file calls other .aef files using the Call Subflow step. It is possible that you uploaded the main script but forgot to upload all the subflows needed by this script. Or you might have an undefined variable in the script if you forgot to validate the script in the AA script Editor before uploading.

You can find and fix many such issues when you configure the system instead of finding them during runtime when active user calls are placed to the application. You can find and eliminate most of these issues when creating the AA application using the Cisco UE administration GUI, as shown in Figure 20-1.

Figure 20-1   *Creating an AA Application*

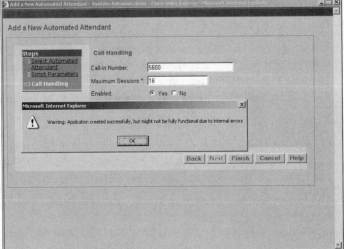

Although the GUI pop-up window shown in Figure 20-1 tells you an error has been detected, it does not tell you exactly what the error is. To understand what has gone wrong, turn on the **trace config-ccn** trace on Cisco UE. In the trace shown in Example 20-1, the problem is that a subflow called dialbyextension.aef has not been uploaded into Cisco UE.

Example 20-1 *Missing Subflow File During Application Configuration*

```
cue#trace config-ccn all
cue#show trace buffer tail
7634 12/14 02:37:39.916 ACCN STGN 0 Preprocessing GetListMember Step
748 12/14 02:39:36.252 WFSP APP 0 WFSysdbNdApp::check enter
747 12/14 02:39:36.388 WFSP APP 0 WFSysdbNdApp::isScriptExist name=main.aef
747 12/14 02:39:36.388 WFSP APP 0 WFSysdbNdApp::writeLDAPApplication saving app to
  ldap
747 12/14 02:39:36.735 WFSP APP 0 WFSysdbNdApp::writeLDAPApplication saving app to
  ldap done
747 12/14 02:39:36.735 WFSP APP 0 WFSysdbNdApp::setLDAPApplication exit
747 12/14 02:39:36.749 WFSP APP 0 WFSysdbNdApp::remoteAppReload rmi reload
  app=myaa
747 12/14 02:39:36.981 WFSP APP 0 com.cisco.app.InvalidApplicationException:
  failed to initialize configuration; nested exception is:
  com.cisco.app.InvalidApplicationException: failed to load script; nested
  exception is:
  com.cisco.wfapi.WFPreprocessException: Failed to preprocess the application:
  main.aef; nested exception is:
  com.cisco.wfapi.WFPreprocessException: Failed to load the sub-workflow:
  dialbyextension.aef; nested exception is:
  com.cisco.wfapi.WFException: Failed to load application from the repository:
  dialbyextension.aef; nested exception is:
  com.cisco.wfframework.repository.NoSuchObjectException: Can't find
  dialbyextension.aef
    at sun.rmi.transport.StreamRemoteCall.exceptionReceivedFromServer
(StreamRemoteCall.java:257)
    at sun.rmi.transport.StreamRemoteCall.executeCall(StreamRemoteCall.java:232)
    at sun.rmi.server.UnicastRef.invoke(UnicastRef.java:135)
    at com.cisco.app.remote.rmi.RMIApplicationManagerImpl_
Stub.reload(RMIApplication
  ManagerImpl_Stub.java:309)
    at com.cisco.wf.wfsysdb.WFSysdbNdApp.remoteAppReload(WFSysdbNdApp.java:172)
......
  com.cisco.wfapi.WFException: Failed to load application from the repository:
dialbyextension
747 12/14 02:39:36.984 WFSP APP 0 com.cisco.aesop.sysdb.xactSysdbException:
  Application created successfully, but might not be fully functional due to
  internal errors
    at com.cisco.wf.wfsysdb.WFSysdbNdApp.remoteAppReload(WFSysdbNdApp.java:180)
    at com.cisco.wf.wfsysdb.WFSysdbNdApp.commit(WFSysdbNdApp.java:804)
    at com.cisco.aesop.sysdb.nativeProvider.commit(nativeProvider.java:64)
    at com.cisco.aesop.sysdb.sysdbNative.node_handle_wait(Native Method)
    at com.cisco.aesop.sysdb.sysdbProducer$1.run(sysdbProducer.java:238)
    at java.lang.Thread.run(Thread.java:512)
```

The trace shown in Example 20-2 shows an undefined variable being used in a Menu step of the script. This might be caused by the script developer's having forgotten to run the Validation step on the AA Script Editor.

Example 20-2 *Missing Variable in the Menu Step*

```
cue#trace config-ccn application all
cue#show trace buffer tail
835 01/08 11:23:14.637 WFSP APP 0 WFSysdbNdApp::getLdapApplication access ldap
  start
835 01/08 11:23:14.932 WFSP APP 0 WFSysdbNdApp::getLdapApplication access ldap
  end
835 01/08 11:23:14.933 WFSP APP 0 WFSysdbNdApp::get value=main.aef
835 01/08 11:23:14.933 WFSP APP 0 WFSysdbNdApp::get exit
834 01/08 11:23:14.937 WFSP APP 0 WFSysdbNdCfgVars::get enter
834 01/08 11:23:14.937 WFSP APP 0 WFSysdbNdCfgVars::get attribute=operator done
835 01/08 11:23:25.687 WFSP APP 0 WFSysdbNdApp::setLDAPApplication exit
835 01/08 11:23:25.925 WFSP APP 0 WFSysdbNdApp::remoteAppReload rmi reload
  app=customaa
Jan  8 11:23:26 localhost java: WARNING ccn_config application debug com.cisco.
  app.InvalidApplicationException: failed to initialize configuration; nested
  exception is:
Jan  8 11:23:26 localhost java: com.cisco.app.InvalidApplicationException:
  failed to load script; nested exception is:
Jan  8 11:23:26 localhost java: com.cisco.wfapi.WFPreprocessException:
  Failed to preprocess the
Jan  8 11:23:26 localhost java: WARNING ccn_config application debug com.cisco.
  aesop.sysdb.xactSysdbException:
  Application created successfully, but might not be fully functional due to
  internal errors
835 01/08 11:23:26.308 WFSP APP 0 com.cisco.app.InvalidApplicationException:
  failed to initialize configuration; nested exception is:
  com.cisco.app.InvalidApplicationException: failed to load script; nested
  exception is:
  com.cisco.wfapi.WFPreprocessException: Failed to preprocess the application:
  main.aef; nested exception is:
  com.cisco.wfapi.WFPreprocessException: MenuStep: Variable 'menuprompt' not
  defined; nested exception is:
  com.cisco.wfapi.expression.WFSemanticException: Variable 'menuprompt' not
  defined
  at sun.rmi.transport.StreamRemoteCall.exceptionReceivedFromServer(StreamRemote
  Call.java:257)
  at sun.rmi.transport.StreamRemoteCall.executeCall(StreamRemoteCall.java:232)
  at sun.rmi.server.UnicastRef.invoke(UnicastRef.java:135)
```

The previous two examples show possible issues that can occur during the development and configuration of AA applications. These are by no means the only problems that might be encountered. If you are facing any issues during this stage of AA development, it is advisable to turn on one or more of the **trace config-ccn** traces shown in Example 20-3 to look for any exceptions reported by the system.

Example 20-3 *Sample config-ccn Traces*

```
cue#trace config-ccn ?
  all
  application
  group
  http-trigger
  jtapi-subsystem
  jtapi-trigger
  miscellaneous
  prompt
  script
  sip-subsystem
  sip-trigger
```

Now that you understand how to troubleshoot and correct script development and configuration issues, the next section covers runtime troubleshooting techniques.

Understanding SIP Call Flow to the AA

Troubleshooting AA applications requires an understanding of the SIP protocol and the architecture of the CRS software component of Cisco UE, as described in Chapter 3. There you learned about the different components of Cisco UE and how the CRS software is used inside Cisco UE.

Figure 20-2 shows a SIP call flow between Cisco CME and Cisco UE. It demonstrates how an incoming SIP call's signaling and media traverse the CRS component.

Figure 20-2 shows what happens when a SIP call is placed to Cisco UE from a Cisco CME phone or the Public Switched Telephone Network (PSTN). A SIP INVITE arrives at Cisco UE's SIP stack. This event is relayed to the application framework within the CRS component of Cisco UE. Upon receiving this call setup message, the application framework consults the configuration to determine which application is associated with the called number in the setup message. Depending on the system's configuration, the appropriate application is started—in this case, the Cisco UE AA script.

Any CRS application (for example, the AA) is a logical collection of steps programmed into a script. As soon as the application is started, control of the call is handed off to the application, which starts executing the steps in the script.

The first step in an application script is almost always the Accept step, which answers the call. Answering the call results in the appropriate SIP message (a 200 OK, in this case) being sent to the gateway, which in turn sends it to the PSTN. As a result of the exchange of the call setup and call answer messages between the PSTN gateway and Cisco UE, a Real-Time Transport Protocol (RTP) media channel is established between the two software components.

Figure 20-2 *SIP Call Flow to CRS*

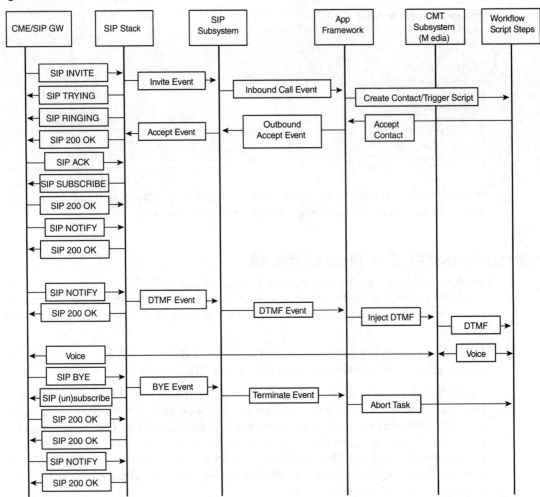

To open an RTP media channel, Cisco UE uses the services of the Cisco Media Termination (CMT) component. The application must be notified of the DTMF keypresses on the caller's phone to receive the correct events, so the application subscribes to the digit press notifications from Cisco CME or the PSTN gateway. After this protocol exchange, the application execution continues, depending on the application's events and programmed logic.

Verifying Why the AA Doesn't Answer Calls

Sometimes when calls are placed to the AA, either they don't ring or they ring but are not answered. There are many possible reasons for this behavior. One of the basic reasons is that Cisco CME or the PSTN gateway originating the call does not have a dial peer pointing to the AA pilot number (trigger). You can verify this configuration by doing a **show running-config** or **show dial-peer voice summary** command on Cisco CME or the PSTN gateway. Ensure that the dial peer has the correct configuration with respect to the SIP protocol and codec to be used (G.711 μ-law only), as shown in Example 20-4.

Example 20-4 *Correct SIP Dial Peer Configuration*

```
router#show running-config
dial-peer voice 6000 voip
 description AA
 destination-pattern 6...
 session protocol sipv2
 session target ipv4:10.19.153.37
 dtmf-relay sip-notify
 codec g711ulaw
 no vad
```

If the Cisco CME SIP dial peer configuration is correct, but the AA still doesn't answer calls, the next step is to turn on SIP debugs on Cisco CME, and check at what point in the call flow the call is failing. One of the reasons could be that the number dialed is not associated with the AA's pilot number. This is demonstrated by the SIP debug shown in Example 20-5.

Example 20-5 *Missing/Disabled Trigger or a Wrong Dialed Number*

```
cue#trace ccn stacksip dbug
cue#show trace buffer tail
2641 12/29 14:13:01.551 ACCN SIPL 0 -------
INVITE sip:6600@1.3.6.129:5060 SIP/2.0
Via: SIP/2.0/UDP  1.3.6.27:5060;branch=z9hG4bK2047
From: <sip:6019@1.3.6.27>;tag=66CAF308-EA1
To: <sip:6600@1.3.6.129>
Date: Mon, 29 Dec 2003 23:54:30 GMT
Call-ID: 2DA98768-399111D8-A2ADAECA-10549FA0@1.3.6.27
Supported: 100rel,timer
Min-SE: 1800
Cisco-Guid: 766004863-965808600-2729094858-273981344
User-Agent: Cisco-SIPGateway/IOS-12.x
Allow: INVITE, OPTIONS, BYE, CANCEL, ACK, PRACK, COMET, REFER, SUBSCRIBE, NOTIFY,
   INFO, UPDATE, REGISTER
CSeq: 101 INVITE
Max-Forwards: 6
Remote-Party-ID: <sip:6019@1.3.6.27>;party=calling;screen=no;privacy=off
Timestamp: 1072742070
Contact: <sip:6019@1.3.6.27:5060>
Call-Info: <sip:1.3.6.27:5060>;method="NOTIFY;Event=telephone-event;Duration=2000"
Expires: 180
Allow-Events: telephone-event
```

continues

Example 20-5 *Missing/Disabled Trigger or a Wrong Dialed Number (Continued)*

```
Content-Type: application/sdp
Content-Length: 179

v=0
o=CiscoSystemsSIP-GW-UserAgent 4326 3924 IN IP4 1.3.6.27
s=SIP Call
c=IN IP4 1.3.6.27
t=0 0
m=audio 19542 RTP/AVP 0
c=IN IP4 1.3.6.27
a=rtpmap:0 PCMU/8000
a=ptime:20

2643 12/29 14:13:01.551 ACCN SIPL 0 PROTOCOL_MSG:Protocol Stack Message:
  Stack Message=LocalLine to process DN 6600 in url sip:6600@1.3.6.129:5060 not
  found, try to process request on '*' line
2643 12/29 14:13:01.552 ACCN SIPL 0 PROTOCOL_MSG:Protocol Stack Message:
  Stack Message=Not found LocalLine for DN=6600, url=sip:6600@1.3.6.129:5060
2643 12/29 14:13:01.552 ACCN SIPL 0 PROTOCOL_MSG:Protocol Stack Message:
  Stack Message=Send Not found for request for INVITE sip:6600@1.3.6.129:5060
2643 12/29 14:13:01.553 ACCN SIPL 0 --- send message --- to 1.3.6.27:5060
SIP/2.0 404 Not Found
Via: SIP/2.0/UDP  1.3.6.27:5060;branch=z9hG4bK2047
From: <sip:6019@1.3.6.27>;tag=66CAF308-EA1
To: <sip:6600@1.3.6.129>;tag=9b277769-411
Call-ID: 2DA98768-399111D8-A2ADAECA-10549FA0@1.3.6.27
CSeq: 101 INVITE
Content-Length: 0
```

As shown in the trace, Cisco UE is sending a "404/Not Found" message in response to the SIP INVITE to number 6600. One of the reasons why the called number used in the INVITE is wrong may be because of an unintentional or incorrect number translation configuration in Cisco IOS, such as an incorrect **translation-rule** statement.

NOTE You might notice that when calling from some phones or PSTN interfaces, you don't see any SIP calls going to Cisco UE. That may be because of a Class of Restriction (COR) configuration in Cisco IOS.

Here are two other reasons why a "404/Not Found" may be sent from a Cisco UE:

- The SIP trigger (the pilot number configured for the AA) does not match the dialed number received from Cisco CME.
- The SIP trigger is disabled.

Example 20-6 shows a disabled trigger for the AA (the customaa application).

Example 20-6 *Disabled Trigger*

```
cue#show ccn trigger
Name:                             6800
Type:                             SIP
Application:                      voicemail
Locale:                           en_US
Idle Timeout:                     5000
Enabled:                          yes
Maximum number of sessions:       8

Name:                             6700
Type:                             SIP
Application:                      autoattendant
Locale:                           en_US
Idle Timeout:                     5000
Enabled:                          yes
Maximum number of sessions:       8

Name:                             6600
Type:                             SIP
Application:                      customaa
Locale:                           en_US
Idle Timeout:                     10000
Enabled:                          no
Maximum number of sessions:       8
```

Sometimes you might hear a prompt saying, "I am sorry. We are currently experiencing system problems." One of the reasons for this message is that the application may be disabled, but the trigger (pilot number) is not. Example 20-7 shows an example of where the AA application (customaa) is disabled.

Example 20-7 *Disabled AA Application*

```
cue#show ccn application
Name:                             ciscomwiapplication
Description:                      ciscomwiapplication
Script:                           setmwi.aef
ID number:                        0
Enabled:                          yes
Maximum number of sessions:       8
strMWI_OFF_DN:                    2221
strMWI_ON_DN:                     2222
CallControlGroupID:               0

Name:                             voicemail
Description:                      voicemail
Script:                           voicebrowser.aef
ID number:                        1
Enabled:                          yes
Maximum number of sessions:       8
```

continues

Example 20-7   *Disabled AA Application (Continued)*

logoutUri:
  mbxLogout.jsp
uri:
  login.vxml
	http://localhost/voicemail/vxmlscripts/
	
	http://localhost/voicemail/vxmlscripts/

Name:	customaa
Description:	customaa
Script:	main.aef
ID number:	4
Enabled:	no
Maximum number of sessions:	4
operator:	0

You can also turn on the Cisco UE command **trace ccn managerappl dbug**, as shown in Example 20-8, to see whether the application is enabled or disabled. This is handy in case the **show ccn application** command shows that the application is enabled, but it is, in fact, disabled internally because of a software error.

Example 20-8   *Trace Example for a Disabled Application*

```
cue#trace ccn managerappl dbug
cue#show trace buffer tail
3463 01/08 11:46:49.430 ACCN APMG 0 APP_RELOADED:Application reloaded:
  Application=customaa
Jan  8 11:47:21 localhost java:
  ERROR ccn ManagerAppl DBUG UNABLE_INVOKE_APP:Unable to invoke application:
  Application=customaa,Exception=com.cisco.app.ApplicationDisabledException:
  application 'customaa' is disabled
Jan  8 11:47:21 localhost java:   ERROR ccn ManagerAppl DBUG
  EXCEPTION:com.cisco.app.ApplicationDisabledException: application 'customaa'
  is disabled
Jan  8 11:47:21 localhost java:   ERROR ccn ManagerAppl DBUG EXCEPTION:
  at com.cisco.app.impl.ApplicationManagerImpl.invoke(ApplicationManagerImpl.java
  (Compiled Code))
Jan  8 11:47:21 localhost java:   ERROR ccn ManagerAppl DBUG EXCEPTION:
  at com.cisco.app.Application.invoke(Application.java(Inlined Compiled Code))
Jan  8 11:47:21 localhost java:   ERROR ccn ManagerAppl DBUG EXCEPTION:
  at com.cisco.app.Application.invoke(Application.java(Inlined Compiled Code))
Jan  8 11:47:21 localhost java:   ERROR ccn ManagerAppl DBUG EXCEPTION:
  at com.cisco.wf.subsystems.callcontrol.AppLineListener$1.run(AppLineListener.
  java(Compiled Code))
Jan  8 11:47:21 localhost java:   ERROR ccn ManagerAppl DBUG EXCEPTION:
  at EDU.oswego.cs.dl.util.concurrent.PooledExecutor$Worker.run(PooledExecutor.
  java(Compiled Code))
```

You can enable the application as shown in Example 20-9 or via the GUI.

Example 20-9 *CLI to Enable the AA Application*

```
cue(config)#ccn application customaa
Modifying existing application
cue(config-application)#enabled
```

If the application is not disabled and you still cannot place calls to it, the maximum number of allowed sessions for the trigger may have been exceeded. You can check this situation by tracing the SIP messages between Cisco CME and Cisco UE, as shown in Example 20-10. You see that Cisco UE returns the message "480 Temporarily Unavailable".

Example 20-10 *Trace Example for Maximum Calls to Trigger Active*

```
cue#trace ccn stacksip dbug
cue#show trace buffer tail
Press <CTRL-C> to exit...
3470 01/07 15:46:36.296 VMSS vxml 0x00000003b9ad1332 0 TIMEOUT
3544 01/07 15:46:53.251 ACCN SIPL 0 -------
INVITE sip:5800@1.3.6.127:5060 SIP/2.0
Via: SIP/2.0/UDP  1.3.6.27:5060;branch=z9hG4bKEF7
From: <sip:6019@1.3.6.27>;tag=951D3478-12C8
To: <sip:5800@1.3.6.127>
Date: Wed, 07 Jan 2004 23:46:53 GMT
Call-ID: 9ABD8318-40A211D8-8907AECA-10549FA0@1.3.6.27
Supported: 100rel,timer
Min-SE: 1800
Cisco-Guid: 2573390720-1084363224-2298785482-273981344
User-Agent: Cisco-SIPGateway/IOS-12.x
Allow: INVITE, OPTIONS, BYE, CANCEL, ACK, PRACK, COMET, REFER, SUBSCRIBE, NOTIFY,
    INFO, UPDATE, REGISTER
CSeq: 101 INVITE
Max-Forwards: 6
Remote-Party-ID: <sip:6019@1.3.6.27>;party=calling;screen=no;privacy=off
Timestamp: 1073519213
Contact: <sip:6019@1.3.6.27:5060>
Call-Info: <sip:1.3.6.27:5060>;method="NOTIFY;Event=telephone-event;Duration=2000"
Expires: 180
Allow-Events: telephone-event
Content-Type: application/sdp
Content-Length: 179

v=0
o=CiscoSystemsSIP-GW-UserAgent 5995 4148 IN IP4 1.3.6.27
s=SIP Call
c=IN IP4 1.3.6.27
t=0 0
m=audio 17524 RTP/AVP 0
c=IN IP4 1.3.6.27
a=rtpmap:0 PCMU/8000
a=ptime:20
```

continues

Example 20-10 *Trace Example for Maximum Calls to Trigger Active (Continued)*

```
3546 01/07 15:46:53.252 ACCN SIPL 0 Substring > telephone-event/8000< not found
3546 01/07 15:46:53.257 ACCN SIPL 0 --- send message --- to 1.3.6.27:5060
SIP/2.0 480 Temporarily Unavailable
Via: SIP/2.0/UDP  1.3.6.27:5060;branch=z9hG4bKEF7
From: <sip:6019@1.3.6.27>;tag=951D3478-12C8
To: <sip:5800@1.3.6.127>;tag=a3cfd31b-135700
Call-ID: 9ABD8318-40A211D8-8907AECA-10549FA0@1.3.6.27
CSeq: 101 INVITE
Content-Length: 0
```

Fixing Abnormal Exits and System Problems

It is always recommended that you try a newly developed AA in a test environment before deploying it for live calls, because runtime errors may affect your office's operations. This kind of testing eliminates possible runtime errors from the AA.

This section discusses how to identify and fix these potential issues. The most common error is a message from the system that says, "I am sorry. We are currently experiencing system problems. Please try again later." The system plays this prompt when it encounters an unexpected problem in the call processing, such as a missing prompt file or a missing subflow script (.aef) file.

The trace to turn on for such problems is the **trace ccn managerappl dbug** command, which you used earlier, in Example 20-8, and look for any exceptions that might point to any other misconfigurations, missing prompts, or files.

Missing Prompt File

If a prompt used in the script is not present on the system, an exception is generated when running the application, as shown in Example 20-11.

Example 20-11 *Missing Prompt File*

```
cue#trace ccn managerappl dbug
cue#show trace buffer tail
4131 01/08 11:38:07.969 ACCN APMG 0 APP_RELOADED:Application reloaded:
  Application=promptmgmt
Jan  8 11:40:13 localhost java:
  ERROR ccn ManagerAppl DBUG TASK_ABORTED:Application task aborted:
  Application=App[name=customaa,type=Cisco Script Application,id=4,desc=customaa,
  enabled=true,max=4,valid=true,
  optional=[cfgVars=[Lcom.cisco.wfapi.util.WFNameValuePair;@2a44c3c4,script=
  main.aef]],Application Trigger=Co
Jan  8 11:40:13 localhost java:
  ERROR ccn ManagerAppl DBUG EXCEPTION:com.cisco.prompt.UndefinedPromptException:
  user prompt '/usr/wfavvid/Prompts/user/ga_IE/menuprompt.wav'
```

There are two ways to configure system behavior when a prompt file is missing. If the system finds that a prompt referred to by a script is not present in the system, it can either ignore it and continue with the script execution, or stop the application execution and play an error prompt to the caller. You can configure this behavior in the Step Configuration window for each step using the continue on prompt errors option. Figure 20-3 shows this configuration for the Menu step.

Figure 20-3 *Customizing System Behavior on Prompt Errors*

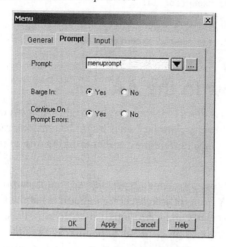

Missing Subflow Script File

The trace output shown in Example 20-12 shows a missing subflow .aef file.

Example 20-12 *Missing Subflow Error at Runtime*

```
cue#trace ccn managerappl dbug
cue#show trace buffer tail
Jan 11 01:30:45 localhost java:   ERROR ccn ManagerAppl DBUG UNABLE_INVOKE_APP:
  Unable to ......
Jan 11 01:30:45 localhost java:   ERROR ccn ManagerAppl DBUG EXCEPTION:
  at sun.rmi.server.UnicastServerRef.dispatch(UnicastServerRef.java
  (Compiled Code))
3604 01/11 01:30:45.785 ACCN APMG 0
  UNABLE_INVOKE_APP:Unable to invoke application: Application=App[name=customaa,
  type=Cisco Script Application,id=4,desc=customaa,enabled=true,max=4,
  valid=false,optional=[cfgVars=[Lcom.cisco.wfapi.util.WFNameValuePair;@731403c5,
  script=main.aef]],Exception=com.cisco.app.InvalidApplicationException:
  failed to load script; nested exception is:
  com.cisco.wfapi.WFPreprocessException: Failed to preprocess the application:
   main.aef; nested exception is:
  com.cisco.wfapi.WFPreprocessException: Failed to load the sub-workflow:
  dialbyextension.aef; nested exception is:
  com.cisco.wfapi.WFException: Failed to load application from the repository:
  dialbyextension.aef; nested exception is:
  com.cisco.wfframework.repository.NoSuchObjectException: Can't find
```

continues

Example 20-12 *Missing Subflow Error at Runtime (Continued)*

```
dialbyextension.aef
3604 01/11 01:30:45.786 ACCN APMG 0
   EXCEPTION:com.cisco.app.InvalidApplicationException: failed to load script;
   nested exception is:
3604 01/11 01:30:45.786 ACCN APMG 0 EXCEPTION:
   com.cisco.wfapi.WFPreprocessException: Failed to preprocess the application:
   main.aef; nested exception is:
3604 01/11 01:30:45.786 ACCN APMG 0 EXCEPTION:
   com.cisco.wfapi.WFPreprocessException: Failed to load the sub-workflow:
   dialbyextension.aef; nested exception is:
```

Tracing a Call Flow in the AA

The previous sections discussed some problems that may occur when deploying customized AA applications. However, similar issues might be encountered with other applications on Cisco UE because of misconfiguration or interworking difficulties with other applications in the network.

To effectively troubleshoot such unexpected issues, it is helpful to understand the complete operation of the AA from the point when a call arrives at the Cisco UE software to the point where the AA script starts and CRS steps are executed. The sample script that is used to demonstrate this section is available in Appendix B, "Sample Cisco UE AA Scripts." You can also download this script from the Cisco Press website at http://www.ciscopress.com/title/158705180X.

SIP Call Delivered to the AA Pilot Number

Figure 20-2 showed a SIP call flow for a call into Cisco UE. This section describes an incoming SIP call to a particular trigger (the AA pilot number) and the call being answered by the application. You also see how the media is set up using the RTP protocol and how the AA script steps are executed. The example used is a custom AA that does the following:

- Plays a menu to the caller for dial-by-extension and dial-by-name

- Transfers the call to the selected user

- Plays the spoken name if the user selected has recorded one

Example 20-13 shows the **trace** commands used to troubleshoot issues with SIP calls arriving at the AA. A SIP INVITE is the first message to arrive at the AA trigger.

Example 20-13 *Incoming INVITE to the AA*

```
cue#trace ccn stacksip dbug
cue#trace ccn managerappl dbug
cue#trace ccn libmedia dbug
cue#trace ccn subsystemcmt dbug
cue#show trace buffer tail
```

Example 20-13 *Incoming INVITE to the AA (Continued)*

```
3544 01/12 11:09:14.523 ACCN SIPL 0 ·······
INVITE sip:5600@1.3.6.127:5060 SIP/2.0
Via: SIP/2.0/UDP  1.3.6.27:5060;branch=z9hG4bKC96
From: <sip:6019@1.3.6.27>;tag=ADDECF6C-134D
To: <sip:5600@1.3.6.127>
Date: Mon, 12 Jan 2004 19:09:14 GMT
Call-ID: A56DFF23-446911D8-8934AECA-10549FA0@1.3.6.27
Supported: 100rel,timer
Min-SE: 1800
Cisco-Guid: 2755249499-1147736536-2301734602-273981344
User-Agent: Cisco-SIPGateway/IOS-12.x
Allow: INVITE, OPTIONS, BYE, CANCEL, ACK, PRACK, COMET, REFER, SUBSCRIBE,
   NOTIFY, INFO, UPDATE, REGISTER
CSeq: 101 INVITE
Max-Forwards: 6
Remote-Party-ID: <sip:6019@1.3.6.27>;party=calling;screen=no;privacy=off
Timestamp: 1073934554
Contact: <sip:6019@1.3.6.27:5060>
Call-Info: <sip:1.3.6.27:5060>;method="NOTIFY;Event=telephone-event;Duration=2000"
Expires: 180
Allow-Events: telephone-event
Content-Type: application/sdp
Content-Length: 179

v=0
o=CiscoSystemsSIP-GW-UserAgent 2947 2413 IN IP4 1.3.6.27
s=SIP Call
c=IN IP4 1.3.6.27
t=0 0
m=audio 18932 RTP/AVP 0
c=IN IP4 1.3.6.27
a=rtpmap:0 PCMU/8000
a=ptime:20
```

If the trigger number is correct and it can accept incoming calls, a 180 Ringing SIP message is
sent from Cisco UE to the calling party, as shown in Example 20-14. If the trigger number is
wrong or cannot accept calls, a 404 Not Found or 480 Temporarily Unavailable message is sent
from Cisco UE, as discussed earlier, in the section "Verifying Why the AA Doesn't Answer
Calls."

Example 20-14 *Outgoing 180 Ringing*

```
cue#show trace buffer tail
3546 01/12 11:09:14.530 ACCN SIPL 0 --- send message --- to 1.3.6.27:5060
SIP/2.0 180 Ringing
Via: SIP/2.0/UDP  1.3.6.27:5060;branch=z9hG4bKC96
From: <sip:6019@1.3.6.27>;tag=ADDECF6C-134D
To: <sip:5600@1.3.6.127>
Call-ID: A56DFF23-446911D8-8934AECA-10549FA0@1.3.6.27
CSeq: 101 INVITE
Content-Length: 0
```

Starting a New Call in the AA Script

Provided that the trigger number is correct and can accept incoming calls, the Cisco UE software starts a task to run the application, as shown in Example 20-15. It is important that the correct application be started with the correct script (main.aef in this case). Also note that the called and calling numbers are part of the trace. In most cases, the calling number is unimportant, but some scripts might behave differently depending on the calling numbers. In that case, this trace helps identify the calling number delivered to the application. (The sample script used here does not depend on the calling number.)

Example 20-15 *Cisco UE AA Script Starts*

```
cue#show trace buffer tail
3476 01/12 11:09:14.542 ACCN APMG 0 TASK_STARTING:Application task starting:
  Application=App[name=customaa,type=Cisco Script Application,id=4,desc=customaa,
  enabled=true,max=4,valid=true,
  optional=[cfgVars=[Lcom.cisco.wfapi.util.WFNameValuePair;@1bb03c4,
  script=main.aef]],Application Trigger=ContactApplicationTrigger
    [time=1073934554532,contact=SIPCallContact[id=46457,type=Cisco SIP Call,
    implId=A56DFF23-446911D8-8934AECA-10549FA0@1.3.6.27,active=true,
    state=CALL_RECEIVED,inbound=true,handled=false,locale=en_US,aborting=false,
    app=App[name=customaa,type=Cisco Script
  Application,id=4,desc=customaa,enabled=true,max=4,valid=true,
  optional=[cfgVars=[Lcom.cisco.wfapi.util.WFNameValuePair;@1bb03c4,
  script=main.aef]],task=16000029510,session=Session[id=0xb2d0d150,parent=null,
  active=true,state=SESSION_IN_USE,time=1073934554524],seqNum=0,
  time=1073934554524,cn=5600,dn=null,cgn=6019,ani=null,dnis=null,
  clid=sip:6019@1.3.6.27,atype=DIRECT,lrd=null,ocn=null,odn=null,uui=null,
  aniii=null,ced=null,route=TR[num=5600],port=
```

After the application starts, it answers the call. Then it starts executing the steps in the script, and the system takes action, depending on the logic prescribed by the script. The first step in any script is always the Start step, and the next step is almost always the Accept step. When the Accept step executes, the call is answered and goes to connect state. This is propagated to the SIP call leg using the "200 OK" SIP message. For reference, Figure 20-2 showed the SIP message flows. The trace is shown in Example 20-16.

Example 20-16 *Accept Step Executes, Resulting in a 200 OK SIP Message*

```
cue#show trace buffer tail
3476 01/12 11:09:14.543 ACCN APMG 0 EXECUTING_STEP:Executing a step:
  Application=App[name=customaa,type=Cisco Script Application,
    id=4,desc=customaa,enabled=true,max=4,valid=true,optional=
    [cfgVars=[Lcom.cisco.wfapi.util.WFNameValuePair;@1bb03c4,script=main.aef]],
    Task id=16,000,029,510,Step id=0,
    Step Class=com.cisco.wfframework.steps.core.StepStart,Step Description=Start
3476 01/12 11:09:14.544 ACCN APMG 0 EXECUTING_STEP:Executing a step:
  Application=App[name=customaa,type=Cisco Script Application,
    id=4,desc=customaa,enabled=true,max=4,valid=true,optional=
    [cfgVars=[Lcom.cisco.wfapi.util.WFNameValuePair;@1bb03c4,script=main.aef]],
    Task id=16,000,029,510,Step id=281,
    Step Class=com.cisco.wfframework.steps.core.StepComment,
```

Example 20-16 *Accept Step Executes, Resulting in a 200 OK SIP Message (Continued)*

```
          Step Description=/* New AA attendant */
3476 01/12 11:09:14.544 ACCN APMG 0 EXECUTING_STEP:Executing a step:
  Application=App[name=customaa,type=Cisco Script Application,
    id=4,desc=customaa,enabled=true,max=4,valid=true,optional=
    [cfgVars=[Lcom.cisco.wfapi.util.WFNameValuePair;@1bb03c4,script=main.aef]],
    Task id=16,000,029,510,Step id=1,Step Class=com.cisco.wf.steps.ivr.AcceptStep,
    Step Description=Accept (contact: --Triggering Contact--)
3476 01/12 11:09:14.547 ACCN SIPL 0 --- send message --- to 1.3.6.27:5060
SIP/2.0 200 OK
Via: SIP/2.0/UDP  1.3.6.27:5060;branch=z9hG4bKC96
From: <sip:6019@1.3.6.27>;tag=ADDECF6C-134D
To: <sip:5600@1.3.6.127>;tag=b46a7ccf-135780
Call-ID: A56DFF23-446911D8-8934AECA-10549FA0@1.3.6.27
CSeq: 101 INVITE
Server: Jasmin server / ver 1.1
Contact: sip:5600@1.3.6.127:5060
Content-Type: application/sdp
Content-Length: 216

v=0
o=CiscoSystemsSIP-Workflow-App-UserAgent 1458 1458 IN IP4 1.3.6.127
s=SIP Call
c=IN IP4 1.3.6.127
t=0 0
m=audio 16902 RTP/AVP 0 111
a=rtpmap:0 pcmu/8000
a=rtpmap:111 telephone-event/8000
a=fmtp:111 0-11
```

Script Interaction with a Connected Call

After the call is connected, the RTP media path must be established between Cisco UE and
Cisco CME or the calling PSTN gateway. The trace shown in Example 20-17 shows the IP
addresses and RTP port numbers used for the RTP channel. Two RTP channels are set up: one
for the outgoing audio and one for the incoming audio. The outgoing media stream is set to the
Cisco CME IP address (or the calling PSTN gateway), and the incoming media stream is set to
its own IP address. Note that the port numbers used are the ones previously exchanged in the
INVITE and 200 OK messages between the PSTN gateway and Cisco UE in the m=audio field.

Example 20-17 *RTP Channels Are Established*

```
cue#show trace buffer tail
3476 01/12 11:09:14.549 ACCN LMED 0
  RTP_PROPERTIES_REASSIGNED:RTP Properties Reassigned: Method Name=
  setTxDestination(),
  HOST NAME=1.3.6.27,PORT NUMBER=18,932,PACKET SIZE=20
3476 01/12 11:09:14.549 ACCN LMED 0 Enter RTPRecorder:setInputProperties
3476 01/12 11:09:14.549 ACCN LMED 0
  RTP_PROPERTIES_REASSIGNED:RTP Properties Reassigned:
  Method Name=setInputProperties(),HOST NAME=1.3.6.127,PORT NUMBER=16,902,PACKET
  SIZE=20
```

The call is now in a connected state and a two-way audio path is established between Cisco UE and the calling PSTN gateway. The AA script execution continues according to the program logic present in the script. The traces in Example 20-18 show the steps executing one by one.

The script checks for the day of the week and the time of day. Different behavior results depending on the current day and time on the system. In Example 20-18, the script takes the working hours path and presents a menu to the caller. The prompt for the menu is referenced by a variable called **menuprompt**.

Example 20-18 *Script Steps Executing*

```
cue#show trace buffer tail
3476 01/12 11:09:14.570 ACCN APMG 0 EXECUTING_STEP:Executing a step:
  Application=App[name=customaa,type=Cisco Script Application,
    id=4,desc=customaa,enabled=true,max=4,valid=true,optional=
    [cfgVars=[Lcom.cisco.wfapi.util.WFNameValuePair;@1bb03c4,script=main.aef]],
    Task id=16,000,029,510,Step id=351,
    Step Class=com.cisco.wf.steps.ivr.GetContactInfoStep,
    Step Description=Get Contact Info (contact: --Triggering Contact--)
3476 01/12 11:09:14.571 ACCN APMG 0 EXECUTING_STEP:Executing a step:
  Application=App[name=customaa,type=Cisco Script Application,
    id=4,desc=customaa,enabled=true,max=4,valid=true,optional=
    [cfgVars=[Lcom.cisco.wfapi.util.WFNameValuePair;@1bb03c4,script=main.aef]],
    Task id=16,000,029,510,Step id=469,
    Step Class=com.cisco.wf.steps.ivr.DayOfWeekStep,Step Description=Day of Week
3476 01/12 11:09:14.572 ACCN APMG 0 EXECUTING_STEP:Executing a step:
  Application=App[name=customaa,type=Cisco Script Application,
    id=4,desc=customaa,enabled=true,max=4,valid=true,optional=
    [cfgVars=[Lcom.cisco.wfapi.util.WFNameValuePair;@1bb03c4,script=main.aef]],
    Task id=16,000,029,510,Step id=480,
    Step Class=com.cisco.wf.steps.ivr.TimeStep,Step Description=Time of Day
3476 01/12 11:09:14.573 ACCN APMG 0 EXECUTING_STEP:Executing a step:
  Application=App[name=customaa,type=Cisco Script Application,
    id=4,desc=customaa,enabled=true,max=4,valid=true,optional=
    [cfgVars=[Lcom.cisco.wfapi.util.WFNameValuePair;@1bb03c4,script=main.aef]],
    Task id=16,000,029,510,Step id=481,
    Step Class=com.cisco.wfframework.steps.core.StepGoto,
  Step Description=Goto Weekdays
3476 01/12 11:09:14.574 ACCN APMG 0 EXECUTING_STEP:Executing a step:
  Application=App[name=customaa,type=Cisco Script Application,
    id=4,desc=customaa,enabled=true,max=4,valid=true,optional=
    [cfgVars=[Lcom.cisco.wfapi.util.WFNameValuePair;@1bb03c4,script=main.aef]],
    Task id=16,000,029,510,Step id=313,
    Step Class=com.cisco.wfframework.steps.core.StepLabel,
  Step Description=Weekdays:
3476 01/12 11:09:14.575 ACCN APMG 0 EXECUTING_STEP:Executing a step:
  Application=App[name=customaa,type=Cisco Script Application,
    id=4,desc=customaa,enabled=true,max=4,valid=true,optional=
    [cfgVars=[Lcom.cisco.wfapi.util.WFNameValuePair;@1bb03c4,script=main.aef]],
    Task id=16,000,029,510,Step id=444,
    Step Class=com.cisco.wf.steps.ivr.MenuStep,Step Description=Menu
    (contact: --Triggering Contact--, prompt: menuprompt)
```

Next, the prompt referenced by the variable **menuprompt** is played, as shown in Example 20-19.

Example 20-19 *Prompt Is Played*

```
cue#show trace buffer tail
3476 01/12 11:09:14.580 ACCN LMED 0 In PromptPlayer.playPromptQueue
3476 01/12 11:09:14.580 ACCN LMED 0 PromptPlayer.initializeDataSource()
3476 01/12 11:09:14.580 ACCN LMED 0 In play !!!!!
3476 01/12 11:09:14.580 ACCN LMED 0 play() promptQ.size=1
3476 01/12 11:09:14.583 ACCN LMED 0 Adding File: /usr/wfavvid/Prompts/user/
  en_US/menuprompt.wav
```

At this point the menu is played to the caller. In this sample script, the menu prompt is "Press 1 for dial-by-extension. Press 2 for dial-by-name." The caller presses 2 to select dial-by-name, as shown in Example 20-20. A SIP NOTIFY message comes from the PSTN gateway and is translated to the appropriate event to the AA application, and the application receives digit 2. For the menu in this script, digit 2 maps to the choice for dial-by-name. The way the script is designed, it calls a subflow named dialbyname.aef for dial-by-name. The traces show a Call Subflow step executing. More prompts are played according to the script logic, advising the caller to dial the last name and first name of the party he or she wants to talk to.

Example 20-20 *Script Continues Executing and More Prompts Are Played*

```
cue#show trace buffer tail
3544 01/12 11:09:24.095 ACCN SIPL 0 not found header for Event
3544 01/12 11:09:24.096 ACCN SIPL 0 -------
NOTIFY sip:5600@1.3.6.127:5060 SIP/2.0
Via: SIP/2.0/UDP  1.3.6.27:5060;branch=z9hG4bKDEE
From: <sip:6019@1.3.6.27>;tag=ADDECF98-1B3A
To: "Cisco SIP Channel3" <sip:5600@1.3.6.127>;tag=b46a7ccf-135780
Date: Mon, 12 Jan 2004 19:09:14 GMT
Call-ID: A56DFF23-446911D8-8934AECA-10549FA0@1.3.6.27
User-Agent: Cisco-SIPGateway/IOS-12.x
Max-Forwards: 6
Timestamp: 1073934564
CSeq: 102 NOTIFY
Event: telephone-event;rate=1000
Contact: <sip:6019@1.3.6.27:5060>
Content-Length: 10
Content-Type: audio/telephone-event
0x02800064
3546 01/12 11:09:24.097 ACCN SIPL 0 --- send message --- to 1.3.6.27:5060
SIP/2.0 200 OK
Via: SIP/2.0/UDP  1.3.6.27:5060;branch=z9hG4bKDEE
From: <sip:6019@1.3.6.27>;tag=ADDECF98-1B3A
To: "Cisco SIP Channel3" <sip:5600@1.3.6.127>;tag=b46a7ccf-135780
Call-ID: A56DFF23-446911D8-8934AECA-10549FA0@1.3.6.27
CSeq: 102 NOTIFY
Server: Jasmin server / ver 1.1
Contact: sip:5600@1.3.6.127:5060
Content-Length: 0
3546 01/12 11:09:24.099 ACCN LMED 0 stopPlay() called.
```

continues

Example 20-20 *Script Continues Executing and More Prompts Are Played (Continued)*

```
3546 01/12 11:09:24.099 ACCN LMED 0 PromptPlayer.destroy() called.
3519 01/12 11:09:24.137 ACCN LMED 0 fileSendDone(), finished=false
3476 01/12 11:09:24.137 ACCN LMED 0 In play(): After the wait()
3476 01/12 11:09:24.137 ACCN CMTS 0 process digit 2 tag=2
3476 01/12 11:09:24.138 ACCN APMG 0 POPING_ACTION:Poping action:
  Application=App[name=customaa,type=Cisco Script Application,
    id=4,desc=customaa,enabled=true,max=4,valid=true,optional=
    [cfgVars=[Lcom.cisco.wfapi.util.WFNameValuePair;@1bb03c4,script=main.aef]],
    Task id=16,000,029,510,Action=com.cisco.wf.cmt.dialogs.
    CMTSimpleRecognitionDialogImpl@5c6683c2,Type=Interruptible action
3476 01/12 11:09:24.139 ACCN CMTS 0
  MediaDialogChannel id=0,state=IN_USE MDC::clear com.cisco.wf.cmt.dialogs.
  CMTSimpleRecognitionDialogImpl@5c6683c2 abortWaiting=false
3476 01/12 11:09:24.140 ACCN APMG 0 EXECUTING_STEP:Executing a step:
  Application=App[name=customaa,type=Cisco Script Application,
    id=4,desc=customaa,enabled=true,max=4,valid=true,optional=
    [cfgVars=[Lcom.cisco.wfapi.util.WFNameValuePair;@1bb03c4,script=main.aef]],
    Task id=16,000,029,510,Step id=446,
    Step Class=com.cisco.wfframework.steps.core.StepCallSubflow,
    Step Description=Call Subflow -- dialbyname.aef
3476 01/12 11:09:24.141 ACCN APMG 0 PUSHING_ACTION:Pushing action:
  Application=App[name=customaa,type=Cisco Script Application,
    id=4,desc=customaa,enabled=true,max=4,valid=true,optional=
    [cfgVars=[Lcom.cisco.wfapi.util.WFNameValuePair;@1bb03c4,script=main.aef]],
    Task id=16,000,029,510,Action=dialbyname.aef,Type=Interruptible subflow
3476 01/12 11:09:24.142 ACCN APMG 0 EXECUTING_STEP:Executing a step:
  Application=App[name=customaa,type=Cisco Script Application,
    id=4,desc=customaa,enabled=true,max=4,valid=true,optional=
    [cfgVars=[Lcom.cisco.wfapi.util.WFNameValuePair;@1bb03c4,script=main.aef]],
    Task id=16,000,029,510,Step id=0,
    Step Class=com.cisco.wfframework.steps.core.StepStart,Step Description=Start
3476 01/12 11:09:24.143 ACCN APMG 0 EXECUTING_STEP:Executing a step:
  Application=App[name=customaa,type=Cisco Script Application,
    id=4,desc=customaa,enabled=true,max=4,valid=true,optional=
    [cfgVars=[Lcom.cisco.wfapi.util.WFNameValuePair;@1bb03c4,script=main.aef]],
    Task id=16,000,029,510,Step id=3,
    Step Class=com.cisco.wfframework.steps.core.StepComment,
    Step Description=/* Dial By Name */
3476 01/12 11:09:24.144 ACCN APMG 0 EXECUTING_STEP:Executing a step:
  Application=App[name=customaa,type=Cisco Script Application,
    id=4,desc=customaa,enabled=true,max=4,valid=true,optional=
    [cfgVars=[Lcom.cisco.wfapi.util.WFNameValuePair;@1bb03c4,script=main.aef]],
    Task id=16,000,029,510,Step id=154,
    Step Class=com.cisco.wfframework.steps.core.StepAssign,Step Description=Set
  again = 2
3476 01/12 11:09:24.145 ACCN APMG 0 EXECUTING_STEP:Executing a step:
  Application=App[name=customaa,type=Cisco Script Application,
    id=4,desc=customaa,enabled=true,max=4,valid=true,optional=
    [cfgVars=[Lcom.cisco.wfapi.util.WFNameValuePair;@1bb03c4,script=main.aef]],
    Task id=16,000,029,510,Step id=75,
    Step Class=com.cisco.wfframework.steps.core.StepLabel,
  Step Description=tryagain:
3476 01/12 11:09:24.146 ACCN APMG 0 EXECUTING_STEP:Executing a step:
```

Example 20-20 *Script Continues Executing and More Prompts Are Played (Continued)*

```
    Application=App[name=customaa,type=Cisco Script Application,
       id=4,desc=customaa,enabled=true,max=4,valid=true,optional=
       [cfgVars=[Lcom.cisco.wfapi.util.WFNameValuePair;@1bb03c4,script=main.aef]],
       Task id=16,000,029,510,Step id=129,
       Step Class=com.cisco.wf.steps.ivr.NameToAddressStep,
       Step Description=Name To User (contact: --Triggering Contact--,
       result user:dialname)
    3476 01/12 11:09:24.148 ACCN CMTS 0
       MediaDialogChannel id=0,state=IN_USE MDC::set: com.cisco.wf.cmt.dialogs.
       CMTUserDialogImpl@27b003c2 enter OK
    3476 01/12 11:09:24.149 ACCN APMG 0 PUSHING_ACTION:Pushing action:
       Application=App[name=customaa,type=Cisco Script Application,
          id=4,desc=customaa,enabled=true,max=4,valid=true,optional=
          [cfgVars=[Lcom.cisco.wfapi.util.WFNameValuePair;@1bb03c4,script=main.aef]],
          Task id=16,000,029,510,Action=com.cisco.wf.cmt.dialogs.
          CMTUserDialogImpl@27b003c2,Type=Interruptible action
    3476 01/12 11:09:24.150 ACCN CMTS 0 init:: flushDTMF=false DTMFBuffer.size=0
    3476 01/12 11:09:24.208 ACCN CMTS 0 In MediaManagerImpl.playPromptQueue:
       before check for p
    3476 01/12 11:09:24.209 ACCN CMTS 0 In MediaManagerImpl.playPromptQueue:
       before calling final playPromptQueue
    3476 01/12 11:09:24.209 ACCN LMED 0 In PromptPlayer.playPromptQueue
    3476 01/12 11:09:24.209 ACCN LMED 0 PromptPlayer.initializeDataSource()
    3476 01/12 11:09:24.209 ACCN LMED 0 In play !!!!!
    3476 01/12 11:09:24.209 ACCN LMED 0 play() promptQ.size=3
    3476 01/12 11:09:24.213 ACCN LMED 0 Adding File: /usr/wfavvid/Prompts/system/
    en_US/UserDialog/name_dial.wav
    3476 01/12 11:09:24.217 ACCN LMED 0 Adding File: /usr/wfavvid/Prompts/system/
    en_US/UserDialog/Cancel_Start.wav
    3476 01/12 11:09:24.221 ACCN LMED 0 Adding File: /usr/wfavvid/Prompts/system/
    en_US/gen/phone/star.wav
    3476 01/12 11:09:24.221 ACCN LMED 0 In play: before dataSource.start
    3476 01/12 11:09:24.221 ACCN LMED 0 In play: after dataSource.start
    3476 01/12 11:09:24.221 ACCN LMED 0 In play: before startOutput
```

Customizing the Menu Step

Before proceeding with AA application tracing, this is a good place to discuss some of the features of customizing prompt playing and the Menu step in a script.

In Figure 20-3, you saw in the Prompt tab for the Menu step the option to select the Barge In property. If you select yes for this property, the caller can press DTMF when the prompt is playing, and it takes effect immediately. If you select no for Barge In, the caller has to wait until the prompt is completed to make a selection, and the script ignores input from the caller during the prompt. So if your users are complaining that their DTMF presses are not taking effect, this is one place to look.

This operation is often confused with the interruptible option in the General tab, shown in Figure 20-4. The interruptible option controls whether the execution of this step can be interrupted by external events, such as a caller hanging up.

Figure 20-4 *Interruptible Option in the Menu Step*

Also, in the Properties window for the menu and other similar steps, you see a tab called Input, as shown in Figure 20-5. If you select yes for the flush input buffer option, the system flushes all the previously entered input before capturing caller input for this step. These are some of the options that can be used to get a desired behavior in your AA application.

Figure 20-5 *Flush Input Buffer Option in the Menu Step*

Processing Digit Input from the Caller

At this point in the script execution, the caller is pressing the digits to spell the subscriber's last and first names, and SIP NOTIFY messages are arriving at Cisco UE, as shown in Example 20-21. In these traces, the caller is trying to dial John Doe, so the digits 363 are pressed and transmitted to the AA application. Some of the unimportant trace output is omitted.

Example 20-21 *Caller Dials the Name of a Subscriber*

```
cue#show trace buffer tail
3544 01/12 11:09:34.680 ACCN SIPL 0 -------
NOTIFY sip:5600@1.3.6.127:5060 SIP/2.0
Via: SIP/2.0/UDP  1.3.6.27:5060;branch=z9hG4bK240B
From: <sip:6019@1.3.6.27>;tag=ADDECF98-1B3A
To: "Cisco SIP Channel3" <sip:5600@1.3.6.127>;tag=b46a7ccf-135780
Date: Mon, 12 Jan 2004 19:09:14 GMT
Call-ID: A56DFF23-446911D8-8934AECA-10549FA0@1.3.6.27
User-Agent: Cisco-SIPGateway/IOS-12.x
Max-Forwards: 6
Timestamp: 1073934574
CSeq: 103 NOTIFY
Event: telephone-event;rate=1000
Contact: <sip:6019@1.3.6.27:5060>
Content-Length: 10
Content-Type: audio/telephone-event
0x03800064
3546 01/12 11:09:34.681 ACCN SIPL 0 --- send message --- to 1.3.6.27:5060
SIP/2.0 200 OK
Via: SIP/2.0/UDP  1.3.6.27:5060;branch=z9hG4bK240B
From: <sip:6019@1.3.6.27>;tag=ADDECF98-1B3A
To: "Cisco SIP Channel3" <sip:5600@1.3.6.127>;tag=b46a7ccf-135780
Call-ID: A56DFF23-446911D8-8934AECA-10549FA0@1.3.6.27
CSeq: 103 NOTIFY
Server: Jasmin server / ver 1.1
Contact: sip:5600@1.3.6.127:5060
Content-Length: 0
!Output omitted for brevity
NOTIFY sip:5600@1.3.6.127:5060 SIP/2.0
Via: SIP/2.0/UDP  1.3.6.27:5060;branch=z9hG4bKFFC
From: <sip:6019@1.3.6.27>;tag=ADDECF98-1B3A
To: "Cisco SIP Channel3" <sip:5600@1.3.6.127>;tag=b46a7ccf-135780
Date: Mon, 12 Jan 2004 19:09:14 GMT
Call-ID: A56DFF23-446911D8-8934AECA-10549FA0@1.3.6.27
User-Agent: Cisco-SIPGateway/IOS-12.x
Max-Forwards: 6
Timestamp: 1073934575
CSeq: 104 NOTIFY
Event: telephone-event;rate=1000
Contact: <sip:6019@1.3.6.27:5060>
Content-Length: 10
Content-Type: audio/telephone-event
0x06800064
3546 01/12 11:09:35.689 ACCN SIPL 0 --- send message --- to 1.3.6.27:5060
SIP/2.0 200 OK
Via: SIP/2.0/UDP  1.3.6.27:5060;branch=z9hG4bKFFC
From: <sip:6019@1.3.6.27>;tag=ADDECF98-1B3A
To: "Cisco SIP Channel3" <sip:5600@1.3.6.127>;tag=b46a7ccf-135780
Call-ID: A56DFF23-446911D8-8934AECA-10549FA0@1.3.6.27
CSeq: 104 NOTIFY
Server: Jasmin server / ver 1.1
Contact: sip:5600@1.3.6.127:5060
```

continues

Example 20-21   *Caller Dials the Name of a Subscriber (Continued)*

```
Content-Length: 0
3476 01/12 11:09:35.691 ACCN CMTS 0 process digit 6
!Output omitted for brevity
NOTIFY sip:5600@1.3.6.127:5060 SIP/2.0
Via: SIP/2.0/UDP  1.3.6.27:5060;branch=z9hG4bK217B
From: <sip:6019@1.3.6.27>;tag=ADDECF98-1B3A
To: "Cisco SIP Channel3" <sip:5600@1.3.6.127>;tag=b46a7ccf-135780
Date: Mon, 12 Jan 2004 19:09:14 GMT
Call-ID: A56DFF23-446911D8-8934AECA-10549FA0@1.3.6.27
User-Agent: Cisco-SIPGateway/IOS-12.x
Max-Forwards: 6
Timestamp: 1073934576
CSeq: 105 NOTIFY
Event: telephone-event;rate=1000
Contact: <sip:6019@1.3.6.27:5060>
Content-Length: 10
Content-Type: audio/telephone-event
0x03800064
 !Output omitted for brevity
3546 01/12 11:09:36.192 ACCN SIPL 0 --- send message --- to 1.3.6.27:5060
SIP/2.0 200 OK
Via: SIP/2.0/UDP  1.3.6.27:5060;branch=z9hG4bK217B
From: <sip:6019@1.3.6.27>;tag=ADDECF98-1B3A
To: "Cisco SIP Channel3" <sip:5600@1.3.6.127>;tag=b46a7ccf-135780
Call-ID: A56DFF23-446911D8-8934AECA-10549FA0@1.3.6.27
CSeq: 105 NOTIFY
Server: Jasmin server / ver 1.1
Contact: sip:5600@1.3.6.127:5060
Content-Length: 0
3476 01/12 11:09:36.194 ACCN CMTS 0 process digit 3
!Output omitted for brevity
NOTIFY sip:5600@1.3.6.127:5060 SIP/2.0
Via: SIP/2.0/UDP  1.3.6.27:5060;branch=z9hG4bK2226
From: <sip:6019@1.3.6.27>;tag=ADDECF98-1B3A
To: "Cisco SIP Channel3" <sip:5600@1.3.6.127>;tag=b46a7ccf-135780
Date: Mon, 12 Jan 2004 19:09:14 GMT
Call-ID: A56DFF23-446911D8-8934AECA-10549FA0@1.3.6.27
User-Agent: Cisco-SIPGateway/IOS-12.x
Max-Forwards: 6
Timestamp: 1073934577
CSeq: 106 NOTIFY
Event: telephone-event;rate=1000
Contact: <sip:6019@1.3.6.27:5060>
Content-Length: 10
Content-Type: audio/telephone-event
0x0B800064
```

Upon receiving the digits, the Cisco UE AA has to search its Lightweight Directory Access Protocol (LDAP) database for a last name/first name combination that starts with the string of digits the caller pressed. Appendix B shows the dial-by-name part of the AA script.

In the traces shown in Example 20-22, the digit string 363 is matched to the single username John Doe, whose extension is 6001. The script checks to see if this user has a spoken name recorded. If he does, the script plays it so that the caller can recognize that this is the person she wants to talk to.

Example 20-22 *Script Resolves the Subscriber Name and Confirms the Spoken Name for the Caller*

```
cue#show trace buffer tail
3476 01/12 11:09:37.202 ACCN CMTS 0 UserDialog get getNumMatchesCached() for 363
3476 01/12 11:09:37.230 ACCN CMTS 0 UserDialog: getNumMatches(363) is 1
3476 01/12 11:09:37.231 ACCN CMTS 0 UserDialog get getUserIdMatches() for 363
3476 01/12 11:09:37.405 ACCN CMTS 0 Create user UserDialogResult:
  name=<John Doe>, firstN=John, lastN=Doe, ext=6001, e-mail=null, id=a1, type=
3476 01/12 11:09:37.406 ACCN APMG 0 POPING_ACTION:Poping action:
  Application=App[name=customaa,type=Cisco Script Application,
    id=4,desc=customaa,enabled=true,max=4,valid=true,optional=
    [cfgVars=[Lcom.cisco.wfapi.util.WFNameValuePair;@1bb03c4,script=main.aef]],
    Task id=16,000,029,510,Action=com.cisco.wf.cmt.dialogs.
    CMTUserDialogImpl@27b003c2,Type=Interruptible action
3476 01/12 11:09:37.407 ACCN CMTS 0
  MediaDialogChannel id=0,state=IN_USE MDC::clear com.cisco.wf.cmt.dialogs.
  CMTUserDialogImpl@27b003c2 abortWaiting=false
3476 01/12 11:09:37.415 ACCN APMG 0 EXECUTING_STEP:Executing a step:
  Application=App[name=customaa,type=Cisco Script Application,
    id=4,desc=customaa,enabled=true,max=4,valid=true,optional=
    [cfgVars=[Lcom.cisco.wfapi.util.WFNameValuePair;@1bb03c4,script=main.aef]],
    Task id=16,000,029,510,Step id=130,
    Step Class=com.cisco.wf.steps.ivr.GetUserInfoStep,
    Step Description=Get User Info (user: dialname)
3476 01/12 11:09:38.318 ACCN APMG 0 EXECUTING_STEP:Executing a step:
  Application=App[name=customaa,type=Cisco Script Application,
    id=4,desc=customaa,enabled=true,max=4,valid=true,optional=
    [cfgVars=[Lcom.cisco.wfapi.util.WFNameValuePair;@1bb03c4,script=main.aef]],
    Task id=16,000,029,510,Step id=131,
    Step Class=com.cisco.wfframework.steps.core.StepIf,
    Step Description=If ( spokenname == null ) Then
3476 01/12 11:09:38.320 ACCN APMG 0 EXECUTING_STEP:Executing a step:
  Application=App[name=customaa,type=Cisco Script Application,
    id=4,desc=customaa,enabled=true,max=4,valid=true,optional=
    [cfgVars=[Lcom.cisco.wfapi.util.WFNameValuePair;@1bb03c4,script=main.aef]],
    Task id=16,000,029,510,Step id=133,
    Step Class=com.cisco.prompt.steps.CreateContainerPromptStep,
    Step Description=Create Container Prompt (output prompt: spelledname)
3476 01/12 11:09:38.322 ACCN APMG 0 EXECUTING_STEP:Executing a step:
  Application=App[name=customaa,type=Cisco Script Application,
    id=4,desc=customaa,enabled=true,max=4,valid=true,optional=
    [cfgVars=[Lcom.cisco.wfapi.util.WFNameValuePair;@1bb03c4,script=main.aef]],
    Task id=16,000,029,510,Step id=134,
    Step Class=com.cisco.wf.steps.ivr.ImplicitConfirmStep,
    Step Description=Implicit Confirmation (contact: --Triggering Contact--)
3476 01/12 11:09:38.363 ACCN CMTS 0
  MediaDialogChannel id=0,state=IN_USE MDC::set: com.cisco.wf.cmt.dialogs.
  CMTImplicitConfirmDialogImpl@52f103c5 enter OK
3476 01/12 11:09:38.364 ACCN APMG 0 PUSHING_ACTION:Pushing action:
```

continues

Example 20-22 *Script Resolves the Subscriber Name and Confirms the Spoken Name for the Caller (Continued)*

```
      Application=App[name=customaa,type=Cisco Script Application,
        id=4,desc=customaa,enabled=true,max=4,valid=true,optional=
        [cfgVars=[Lcom.cisco.wfapi.util.WFNameValuePair;@1bb03c4,script=main.aef]],
        Task id=16,000,029,510,Action=com.cisco.wf.cmt.dialogs.
        CMTImplicitConfirmDialogImpl@52f103c5,Type=Interruptible action
3476 01/12 11:09:38.365 ACCN CMTS 0 init:: flushDTMF=false DTMFBuffer.size=0
3476 01/12 11:09:38.378 ACCN CMTS 0
 In MediaManagerImpl.playPromptQueue: before check for p
3476 01/12 11:09:38.378 ACCN CMTS 0
 In MediaManagerImpl.playPromptQueue: before calling final playPromptQueue
3476 01/12 11:09:38.378 ACCN LMED 0 In PromptPlayer.playPromptQueue
3476 01/12 11:09:38.378 ACCN LMED 0 PromptPlayer.initializeDataSource()
3476 01/12 11:09:38.378 ACCN LMED 0 In play !!!!!
3476 01/12 11:09:38.378 ACCN LMED 0 play() promptQ.size=2
3476 01/12 11:09:38.394 ACCN LMED 0 Adding File: /usr/wfavvid/Prompts/system/
  en_US/AA/AACalling.wav
3476 01/12 11:09:38.395 ACCN LMED 0 In play: before dataSource.start
3476 01/12 11:09:38.395 ACCN LMED 0 In play: after dataSource.start
```

If you encounter any difficulty with matching digit strings to subscriber names, the problem can be because either the caller made a mistake when dialing the user's name or the user's name is misspelled in the Cisco UE system configuration. One way to verify the keypad mapping of a user's last and first names to the system configuration is to check the database (the sysdb component) setting for the user, as shown in Example 20-23.

Example 20-23 *Checking a Subscriber's Name-to-Digit Mapping*

```
cue#show sysdb sw/local/users/autosub1
Name/commonName                      John Doe
Name/givenName                       John
Name/surname                         Doe
Name/displayName                     John Doe
TelephoneNumbers/primaryE164Number   4085556001
TelephoneNumbers/primaryExtension    6001
Password/userPassword
Password/userPin
Password/userPasswordInitial
Password/userPinInitial
Password/userPasswordGen             0
Password/userPinGen                  0
SpokenName/FormatType
SpokenName/SpokenNameURL
Language/preferredLanguage           en_US
AutoAttendantProfile/keyPadMapping   3635646
```

AA Call Transfer to the Selected Destination

When the script has identified the subscriber the caller wants to reach, it transfers the call to that subscriber's extension (6001, in this case) using the Call Redirect step. The execution of the Redirect step results in a blind transfer of the call using the SIP BYE/Also mechanism. This step is shown in Example 20-24.

Example 20-24   *Script Executes the Redirect Step*

```
cue#show trace buffer tail
3476 01/12 11:09:43.902 ACCN APMG 0 POPING_ACTION:Poping action:
  Application=App[name=customaa,type=Cisco Script Application,
    id=4,desc=customaa,enabled=true,max=4,valid=true,optional=
    [cfgVars=[Lcom.cisco.wfapi.util.WFNameValuePair;@1bb03c4,script=main.aef]],
    Task id=16,000,029,510,Action=com.cisco.wf.cmt.dialogs.
    CMTImplicitConfirmDialogImpl@52f103c5,Type=Interruptible action
3476 01/12 11:09:43.903 ACCN CMTS 0
  MediaDialogChannel id=0,state=IN_USE MDC::clear com.cisco.wf.cmt.dialogs.
  CMTImplicitConfirmDialogImpl@52f103c5 abortWaiting=false
3476 01/12 11:09:43.905 ACCN APMG 0 EXECUTING_STEP:Executing a step:
  Application=App[name=customaa,type=Cisco Script Application,
    id=4,desc=customaa,enabled=true,max=4,valid=true,optional=
    [cfgVars=[Lcom.cisco.wfapi.util.WFNameValuePair;@1bb03c4,script=main.aef]],
    Task id=16,000,029,510,Step id=136,
    Step Class=com.cisco.wf.steps.ivr.RedirectStep,
    Step Description=Call Redirect (contact: --Triggering Contact--,
    extension: extension)
3476 01/12 11:09:43.908 ACCN SIPL 0 --- send message --- to 1.3.6.27:5060
SUBSCRIBE sip:6019@1.3.6.27 SIP/2.0
Via: SIP/2.0/UDP 1.3.6.127:5060
From: "Cisco SIP Channel3" <sip:5600@1.3.6.127>;tag=b46a7ccf-135780
To: <sip:6019@1.3.6.27>;tag=ADDECF98-1B3A
Call-ID: A56DFF23-446911D8-8934AECA-10549FA0@1.3.6.27
CSeq: 52 SUBSCRIBE
Max-Forwards: 50
Contact: <sip:5600@1.3.6.127:5060>
Event: telephone-event;duration=2000
Expires: 0
Content-Length: 0
3476 01/12 11:09:43.910 ACCN SIPL 0 --- send message --- to 1.3.6.27:5060
BYE sip:6019@1.3.6.27:5060 SIP/2.0
Via: SIP/2.0/UDP 1.3.6.127:5060
From: <sip:5600@1.3.6.127>;tag=b46a7ccf-135780
To: <sip:6019@1.3.6.27>;tag=ADDECF6C-134D
Call-ID: A56DFF23-446911D8-8934AECA-10549FA0@1.3.6.27
CSeq: 53 BYE
User-Agent: Jasmin UA / ver 1.1
Max-Forwards: 50
Content-Length: 0
Also: <sip:6001@1.3.6.27;user=phone>
```

Summary

In this chapter, you learned how to troubleshoot call execution by the AA scripts in your system. This chapter covered the call flows for the calls coming into the AA and how to troubleshoot common problems at runtime. This chapter also presented the traces of a typical AA call to help you understand how the steps execute and what information to look for in the various traces. At this point, you should be able to troubleshoot most of the problems you might encounter when deploying a Cisco UE AA.

This chapter covers the following topics:

- Common voice mail show commands
- Troubleshooting mailbox graphical user interface (GUI) configuration problems
- Troubleshooting Cisco Unity Express (UE) and Cisco CallManager Express (CME) integration
- Troubleshooting the Telephony User Interface (TUI) and VXML browser
- Troubleshooting the database, Lightweight Directory Access Protocol (LDAP), and mailbox activities
- Troubleshooting the message waiting indicator (MWI)
- Troubleshooting voice mail Voice Profile for Internet Mail (VPIM) networking

## CHAPTER 21

Troubleshooting Cisco UE Integrated Voice Mail Features

This chapter discusses the debugging and tracing aspects of the Cisco Unity Express (UE) voice mail application for Cisco IP Communications (IPC) Express. The discussion starts by looking at configuration problems that show up in the graphical user interface (GUI) and how to address them. Another area of possible problems is the interface between Cisco UE and Cisco CallManager Express (CME), which you also will learn how to troubleshoot. The Voice Browser step of the Cisco Customer Response Software (CRS) is used to implement the Telephony User Interface (TUI), and in this chapter you learn how to interpret voice browser traces and TUI sessions.

Voice mail interacts with back-end data stores such as the Lightweight Directory Access Protocol (LDAP) directory and the Structured Query Language (SQL) database to retrieve user and mailbox information. This chapter covers the troubleshooting of issues that might require you to look at the LDAP and SQL aspects of the voice mail application.

A common problem with voice mail systems includes incorrect operation of the message waiting indicator (MWI), so you also learn about this area of problem isolation. The last area of voice mail troubleshooting covered in this chapter is when multiple Cisco UE systems are networked via Voice Profile for Internet Mail (VPIM).

Chapter 3, "Cisco IPC Express Architecture Overview," gave an overview of the voice mail system components and architecture and provide a good foundation for the topics discussed in this chapter.

Common Voice Mail show Commands

Although tracing is one of the key troubleshooting tools in Cisco UE, it is not always necessary. Many of the **show** commands are sufficient to identify certain problems. The following sections discuss the most common **show** commands you can use to pinpoint trouble spots.

Listing Mailboxes with Usage Statistics

The **show voicemail mailboxes** command gives a very helpful summary of each mailbox. Although you can display the same data for each mailbox in the GUI, no GUI screen provides the same comprehensive system summary that is given by the output of this command-line interface (CLI) command. The **show voicemail mailboxes** command lists mailbox statistics in table format and contains the following fields:

- Total number of messages
- Number of new and saved messages
- Total time used for the mailbox
- Total mailbox size and the percentage of the mailbox used

Example 21-1 shows sample output of the **show voicemail mailboxes** command. In this output, Jane Smith's mailbox does not contain any messages, but still the message time (MSGTIME) associated with the mailbox is given as 9 seconds. That is because Jane Smith has recorded one or more greetings, and the time for the greetings is counted as part of the total mailbox message time. However, spoken names are not considered part of the mailbox time, because they are stored in LDAP rather than the SQL database.

Example 21-1 *Displaying Mailbox Statistics*

```
cue#show voicemail mailboxes
OWNER              MSGS NEW  SAVED  MSGTIME  MBXSIZE   USED
"johnsmith"          4    2    2      60      3000     2 %
"janesmith"          0    0    0       9      3000     1 %
"group1"             0    0    0       0      3000     0 %
"group2"             0    0    0       0      3000     0 %
"group3"             0    0    0       0      3000     0 %
"group4"             0    0    0       0      3000     0 %
"group5"             0    0    0       0      3000     0 %
"johndoe"            0    0    0       0      3000     0 %
"janedoe"            0    0    0      14      3000     1 %
```

Displaying Mailbox Details

To display the details of a particular mailbox, use the **show voicemail detail mailbox** *userid* command. As shown in Example 21-2, it displays a mailbox's characteristics, including the message counts, date of creation, and last-modified time stamp.

Example 21-2 *Displaying Single Mailbox Details*

```
cue#show voicemail detail mailbox johndoe
Owner:                       /sw/local/users/johndoe
Type:                        Personal
Description:                 johndoe mailbox
Busy state:                  idle
Enabled:                     disabled
Mailbox Size (seconds):      3000
Message Size (seconds):      60
Play Tutorial:               false
Space Used (seconds):        0
Total Message Count:         0
New Message Count:           0
Saved Message Count:         0
```

Example 21-2   *Displaying Single Mailbox Details (Continued)*

```
Expiration (days):             30
Greeting:                      standard
Created/Last Accessed:         Oct 10 2003 05:17:04 PDT
```

Displaying Voice Mail Usage Details

To get a summary of the entire voice mail system, including the number of mailboxes and summary usage statistics, use the **show voicemail usage** command. Sample output of this command is shown in Example 21-3.

Example 21-3   *Displaying System Voice Mail Usage Details*

```
cue#show voicemail usage
personal mailboxes:                 67
general delivery mailboxes:         9
orphaned mailboxes:                 0
capacity of voicemail (minutes):    6000
allocated capacity (minutes):       3800.0
message time used (seconds):        31
message count:                      2
average message length (seconds):   15.5
greeting time used (seconds):       115
greeting count:                     11
average greeting length (seconds):  10.454545454545455
total time used (seconds):          146
total time used (minutes):          2.433333396911621
percentage used time (%):           1
```

Displaying System Licenses

If you are experiencing problems creating new users, groups, or mailboxes, check the license installed on the Cisco UE system, and make sure that the system limits are not exceeded.

Sample output for the **show software licenses** command is shown in Example 21-4. If you have exceeded the number of mailboxes allowed by the license, you cannot create more until the license is upgraded. The number of users allowed on a Cisco UE system is typically double the number of mailboxes specified by the license.

The maximum amount of voice mail that you can store on the system is a licensed feature. On an NM-CUE system, it is 100 hours, and on the AIM-CUE it is 14 hours for the 1-GB flash card. You can allocate this total number of voice mail hours among your mailboxes in any manner suitable to your needs. Although this is the default system operation, there is no requirement to divide the amount of time equally among all mailboxes. As soon as the total of all the allocated voice mailboxes' storage equals the maximum allowed system storage, you cannot create any more mailboxes, even though you may not yet have reached the mailbox limit.

Example 21-4 *Verifying System License Limits*

```
cue#show software licenses
Core:
 - application mode: CME
 - total usable system ports: 4
Voicemail/Auto Attendant:
 - max system mailbox capacity time: 480
 - max general delivery mailboxes: 15
 - max personal mailboxes: 50
Languages:
 - max installed languages: unlimited
 - max enabled languages: 1
```

Displaying Default Voice Mailbox System Settings

The **show voicemail limits** command shows the default system settings for different voice mail parameters. These settings are applied to every new mailbox created. Although the administrator can override these settings on a per-mailbox basis, these system settings are the defaults applied. Sample output of this command is shown in Example 21-5.

Example 21-5 *Verifying Voice Mail Default Limits*

```
cue#show voicemail limits
Default Mailbox Size (seconds):         420
Default Caller Message Size (seconds):  60
Maximum Recording Size (seconds):       900
Default Message Age (days):             30
System Capacity (minutes):              480
Default Prompt Language:                en_US
Operator Telephone:                     5700
```

Troubleshooting Mailbox GUI Configuration Problems

You can select to create mailboxes manually when users or groups are added, or you can add mailboxes in bulk fashion during the Cisco UE Initialization Wizard when user definitions are imported from Cisco CME. The following issues may occur in the GUI:

- Mailbox configuration problems
- Orphaned mailboxes
- User and group configuration problems
- General delivery mailbox problems

Mailbox Configuration

To troubleshoot mailbox configuration problems in the GUI, the mailbox **trace** command **trace webInterface mailbox all** is useful.

Example 21-6 shows sample output of this command where the user attempts to access a mailbox that does not exist. The administrator creates a new mailbox, deletes another mailbox, and then verifies that the new mailbox has been created successfully by checking the mailbox GUI page. Other mailboxes are also shown on the GUI page. The PERSONAL_000000000000000000000009 text shown in the trace is an internal unique identifier for each mailbox. You can use this identifier to isolate operations and events that pertain to a particular mailbox in the system.

Example 21-6 *Mailbox Trace*

```
cue#trace webInterface mailbox all
cue#show trace buffer tail

2607 02/28 19:39:30.308 webI mail 1 Attempt to read mailbox
  PERSONAL_000000000000000000000006
2178 02/28 19:40:23.483 webI mail 1 Error while reading Mailbox by owner. no such
  attribute
2178 02/28 19:40:23.563 webI mail 2 Created mailbox:
  PERSONAL_000000000000000000000009
2178 02/28 19:40:23.564 webI mail 2 Proceeding to Populate other values for new
  mailbox
2178 02/28 19:40:23.564 webI mail 2 Saving Mailbox
2178 02/28 19:40:23.625 webI mail 2 Finished populating other values for new
  mailbox
2667 02/28 19:40:23.893 webI mail 1 Filter for mailboxes : (&(ownerDn=*))
2667 02/28 19:40:23.899 webI mail 1 Attempt to read mailbox
  PERSONAL_000000000000000000000004
2667 02/28 19:40:23.902 webI mail 1 Attempt to read mailbox
  GENERAL_000000000000000000000000
2667 02/28 19:40:23.904 webI mail 1 Attempt to read mailbox
  PERSONAL_000000000000000000000008
2667 02/28 19:40:23.906 webI mail 1 Attempt to read mailbox
  PERSONAL_000000000000000000000002
2667 02/28 19:40:23.909 webI mail 1 Attempt to read mailbox
  PERSONAL_000000000000000000000009
2667 02/28 19:40:23.918 webI mail 1 Attempt to read mailbox
  PERSONAL_000000000000000000000005
2667 02/28 19:40:23.919 webI mail 1 Attempt to read mailbox
  PERSONAL_000000000000000000000006
2672 02/28 19:40:39.660 webI mail 3 Going to sysdb to delete Mailbox for :
  /sw/local/users/test
2672 02/28 19:40:39.699 webI mail 3 Deleted mailbox: /sw/local/users/test Mailbox
  deleted
2672 02/28 19:40:39.699 webI mail 3 Returned from sysdb. Mailbox delete for :
  /sw/local/users/test
2672 02/28 19:40:39.700 webI mail 1 Filter for mailboxes : (&(ownerDn=*))
2672 02/28 19:40:39.700 webI mail 1 Attempt to read mailbox
  PERSONAL_000000000000000000000004
```

continues

Example 21-6 *Mailbox Trace (Continued)*

```
2672 02/28 19:40:39.703 webI mail 1 Attempt to read mailbox
   GENERAL_00000000000000000000000000
2672 02/28 19:40:39.705 webI mail 1 Attempt to read mailbox
   PERSONAL_00000000000000000000000008
2672 02/28 19:40:39.708 webI mail 1 Attempt to read mailbox
   PERSONAL_00000000000000000000000002
2672 02/28 19:40:39.711 webI mail 1 Attempt to read mailbox
   PERSONAL_00000000000000000000000005
2672 02/28 19:40:39.712 webI mail 1 Attempt to read mailbox
   PERSONAL_00000000000000000000000006
```

Orphaned Mailboxes

An *orphaned* mailbox is a mailbox without an owner. This can occur when the owner (the user profile) is deleted but the mailbox remains in the system, now unassociated with a valid user. When a user is deleted using the Cisco UE GUI, the attached mailbox is automatically deleted as well, so the orphaned mailbox condition does not occur if you do system administration via the GUI. The CLI does not operate this way, however. When the user is deleted via the Cisco UE CLI, the mailbox remains in the system (unless explicitly deleted with a separate command), and it appears as an orphaned mailbox.

To check the status of all mailboxes in the system, use the **show voicemail usage** command. Example 21-7 shows sample output for this command.

Example 21-7 *Checking Mailbox Status*

```
cue#show voicemail usage
personal mailboxes:                    100
general delivery mailboxes:            9
orphaned mailboxes:                    1
capacity of voicemail (minutes):       6000
allocated capacity (minutes):          5450.0
message time used (seconds):           1183
message count:                         38
average message length (seconds):      31.13157894736842
greeting time used (seconds):          63
greeting count:                        8
average greeting length (seconds):     7.875
total time used (seconds):             1246
total time used (minutes):             20.766666412353516
percentage used time (%):              0
```

Example 21-7 shows that one orphaned mailbox exists in this system. To find out the details of the orphaned mailbox, use the command **show voicemail mailbox orphaned** (see Example 21-8).

Example 21-8 *Showing an Orphaned Mailbox*

```
cue#show voicemail mailbox orphaned
OWNER              TYPE           ORPHANED TIME
"Bill"             Personal       Jul 28 2004 18:18:06 PST
```

In the GUI, orphaned mailboxes are shown in the **Voice Mail > Mailboxes** screen. The mailbox is marked as orphaned. An orphaned mailbox does not affect the overall Cisco UE operation, but it does count as one of the licensed mailboxes. An orphaned mailbox indicates that a mailbox defined in the system cannot be used by any of the subscribers, so it is desirable to reassociate orphaned mailboxes with a valid user or remove them. To delete an orphaned mailbox in the GUI, go to the **Voice Mail > Mailboxes** screen, and select the orphaned mailboxes to delete. Or create a user with the same user ID as the one the orphaned mailbox belongs to. The system prompts you to reassociate the mailbox with this user.

User and Group Configurations

Users and groups are the owners of personal and general delivery mailboxes, respectively. The following are some problems you might encounter with users and groups:

- A deleted user still appears in the GUI
- A user is not associated with a voice mailbox
- A user is not associated with a group

Use the command **trace webinterface user all** or **trace webinterface group all** to troubleshoot these problems.

Deleted User Appears in the GUI

To troubleshoot a deleted user who still appears in the GUI, in the CLI first enter **trace webinterface user all** to turn on the traces to be monitored. In the GUI, click the deleted user to prompt more detailed information. A new window should appear. A normal **webinterface** trace for a valid user is given in Example 21-9.

Example 21-9 *Normal User Trace*

```
cue#trace webinterface user all
cue#show trace buffer
2604 03/01 01:03:21.383 webI user 1 Resetting UserForm
2604 03/01 01:03:21.750 webI user 1 Start reading user Bill
2604 03/01 01:03:21.753 webI user 1 End reading user Bill
```

Because the user has been deleted, it is likely that no user window pops up and no trace is collected. This indicates that the user is no longer a valid user in the system and that the database does not have any record of that person. Use the CLI command **show voicemail users** to verify whether the user is in the user list. Enter the command **user** *name* **delete** to delete the unwanted user.

User Is Not Associated with a Voice Mailbox in the GUI

It is possible that you have configured a user with a voice mailbox but the voice mailbox does not show up in the GUI. Verify with the command **show voicemail users** that the user appears in the system. If the voice mail user is in the system but the mailbox does not show up in the GUI, the problem is likely a GUI issue.

To troubleshoot this problem, enable **trace webinterface user all** and clear the trace buffer. In the GUI, select **Configure > Users** and then select the user whose mailbox does not show up. A User Profile window opens. Click the **Mailboxes** tab. The mailbox information should appear in the same window, as shown in Figure 21-1.

Figure 21-1 *User Mailbox*

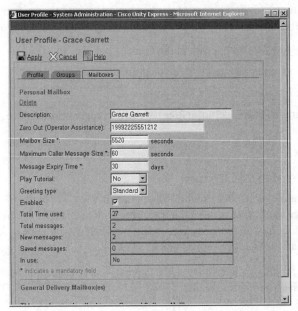

If no mailbox information appears, go to the CLI and examine the trace buffer. Example 21-10 shows a normal trace showing a user with a legitimate mailbox.

Example 21-10 *Normal Mailbox Trace*

```
cue#trace webinterface user all
cue#show trace buffer
3125 03/01 04:57:48.737 webI user 1 Start reading user Bill
3125 03/01 04:57:48.740 webI user 1 End reading user Bill
3125 03/01 04:57:48.943 webI user 1 1 entries read for authorized mailboxes
```

If no such trace is collected, delete and re-add the user. Also add the voice mailbox, and verify that the problem has been resolved.

User Is Not Associated with a Group in the GUI

For a user who has been configured as a member of a group but the group association does not show up in the GUI, the first step is to determine whether this is a system issue or a GUI issue. The useful CLI commands are

- **show users**—Lists all the users in the system

- **show groups**—Lists all the groups in the system

- **show group detail groupname group_name**—Lists all the members of the particular group

Execute all these commands on your system and note the output. If the voice mail user shows up in the group but in the GUI the user is not associated with the group, check the GUI interface.

To troubleshoot, enable the **trace webinterface group all** command and clear the trace buffer. In the GUI, select **Configure > Users**, and then click the user under investigation. The User Profile window opens. In this window, click the **Groups** tab, as shown in Figure 21-2, and then go to the CLI to examine the trace buffer.

Figure 21-2   *User's Group Membership*

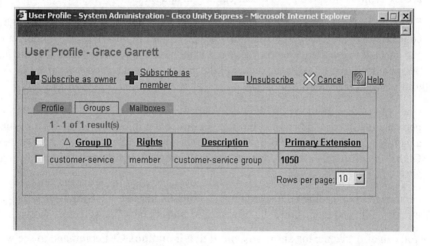

Example 21-11 shows a normal trace showing a user belonging to a legitimate group.

Example 21-11   *Normal Group Trace*

```
cue#trace webinterface group all
cue#show trace buffer
3237 03/01 13:01:15.520 webI grup 1 Start reading group Sales
3237 03/01 13:01:15.521 webI grup 1 End reading group Sales
3237 03/01 13:01:15.521 webI grup 1 Reading owners for Sales
3237 03/01 13:01:15.522 webI grup 1 Reading members for Sales
3237 03/01 13:01:15.522 webI grup 1 Bill
```

If no such trace is collected, delete and readd the user. Assign the user to a group, and verify that the problem has been resolved.

General Delivery Mailboxes

General delivery mailboxes (GDMs) are similar to personal mailboxes. However, they are associated with groups (as opposed to individual users), and more than one user (member) can access them, although only one user can log in at a time.

Problems with GDMs can be configuration-related. When a GDM gets a message, it is not copied to every member's personal mailbox; it resides in the GDM. Any member of the group can check to see if there are new messages in a GDM by pressing 9 after logging into his or her personal mailbox. Note that an owner of the group does not have access to the GDM unless that user is also a member of the group.

One of the most common problems users experience with GDMs is that when they log into their personal mailboxes, they do not have the option to log into the GDMs they are supposed to be a member of. This might be because the user is not a member of the group associated with the GDM. To ensure that a user is part of the group in question, follow the steps described next with either the GUI or the CLI.

Go to the Group Profile GUI screen by selecting **Configure > Groups**, click the group you are interested in, and then choose the **Owners/Members** tab. This screen is shown in Figure 21-3.

You can also execute the **show voicemail detail mailbox** CLI command to see which GDM a particular user is a member of. This command is executed for user johndoe in Example 21-12. The output shows that he is part of the sales GDM.

Note that the first part of the mailbox information in Example 21-12 describes johndoe's personal mailbox (of which he is the owner). The following section of the output describes his associations with GDMs. The example shows that he is associated with the sales GDM, which is owned by a group called sales.

Figure 21-3 *Group Profile*

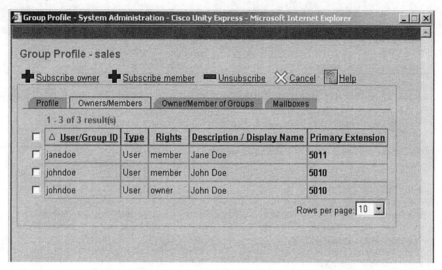

Example 21-12 *Verifying a User's GDM Membership*

```
cue#show voicemail detail mailbox johndoe
Owner:                              /sw/local/users/johndoe
Type:                               Personal
Description:                        johndoe mailbox
Busy state:                         idle
Enabled:                            true
Mailbox Size (seconds):             420
Message Size (seconds):             60
Play Tutorial:                      true
Space Used (seconds):               0
Total Message Count:                0
New Message Count:                  0
Saved Message Count:                0
Expiration (days):                  30
Greeting:                           standard
Created/Last Accessed:              Dec 04 2003 04:09:25 EET

Owner:                              /sw/local/groups/sales
Type:                               General Delivery
Description:                        sales mailbox
Busy state:                         idle
Enabled:                            true
Mailbox Size (seconds):             420
Message Size (seconds):             60
Play Tutorial:                      true
Space Used (seconds):               0
Total Message Count:                0
```

continues

Example 21-12 *Verifying a User's GDM Membership (Continued)*

```
New Message Count:                      0
Saved Message Count:                    0
Expiration (days):                      30
Greeting:                               standard
Created/Last Accessed:                  Dec 04 2003 04:08:11 EET
```

The **show voicemail detail mailbox** command can also be used to show the details of the sales GDM, as shown in Example 21-13.

Example 21-13 *Details of the GDM*

```
cue#show voicemail detail mailbox sales
Owner:                                  /sw/local/groups/sales
Type:                                   General Delivery
Description:                            sales mailbox
Busy state:                             idle
Enabled:                                true
Mailbox Size (seconds):                 420
Message Size (seconds):                 60
Play Tutorial:                          true
Space Used (seconds):                   0
Total Message Count:                    0
New Message Count:                      0
Saved Message Count:                    0
Expiration (days):                      30
Greeting:                               standard
Created/Last Accessed:                  Dec 04 2003 04:08:11 EET
```

You can check this same information in the GUI by selecting **Configure > Groups**, clicking the group of interest (sales, in this example), and then selecting the Mailboxes tab. This screen is shown in Figure 21-4. By clicking the **Owner/Member** tab on this screen, you can list the users who currently have access to this GDM.

Figure 21-4 *General Delivery Mailbox*

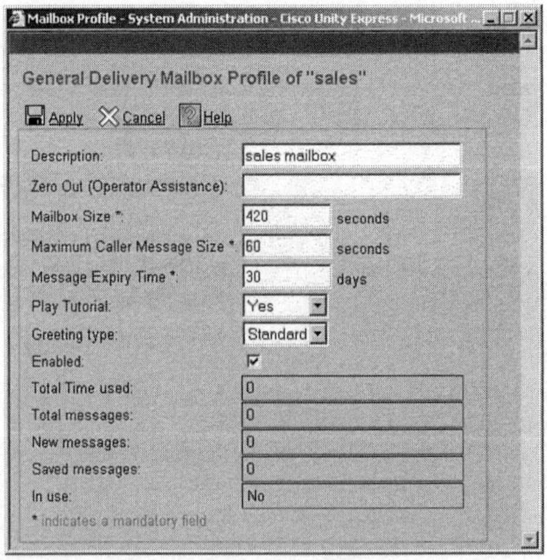

Apart from the **show** commands described in this section, you can also use all mailbox- and message-related trace commands to troubleshoot GDMs. The CLI command **show group detail groupname** *name* also has very helpful output.

Troubleshooting Cisco CME and Cisco UE Integration

Cisco CME is the system's call control engine. All calls coming into voice mail to leave or retrieve messages involve an interaction (via SIP) between Cisco CME and Cisco UE. Cisco CME integration with Cisco UE voice mail includes the following activities:

- Forwarding of a call to Cisco UE on busy or ring-no-answer
- Dual-tone multifrequency (DTMF) relay to interact with the voice mail system
- A call transfer from the automated attendant (AA) that forwards into voice mail
- Turning the MWI on or off

Call forwarding into voice mail requires passing the right original called number to the voice mail system so that the correct user's mailbox is selected to play the greeting and leave a message. DTMF relay encompasses the conversion of IP phone keypad digit presses sent via Skinny Client Control Protocol (SCCP) messages from the phone to Cisco CME call control, and from there to Cisco UE via SIP NOTIFY messages. Call transfer from the AA is implemented as a blind transfer using the SIP BYE/Also message sequence.

The most common problems encountered with calls into voice mail are caused by incorrect or incomplete configuration:

- The wrong mailbox selection or no mailbox selection on call forward to voice mail (which might also result in the wrong greeting being played to the caller)
- Digit presses from the phone do not get the required response (in other words, DTMF messages do not reach the application)
- Call transfers from the AA do not work
- Fast-busy tone is heard for calls going to voice mail
- MWI does not operate properly

Correcting each of these problems is discussed in the following sections.

Wrong Mailbox Selection or Unexpected Greeting

Calls to a Cisco CME IP phone can arrive from two different sources:

- A call received from an internal extension, where the dialed number is the phone's extension
- A call received from the PSTN or from another site (routed via H.323 or SIP), where the called number may be the phone's E.164 number

Therefore, depending on what number was dialed, the original called number (also called the *last redirecting number* in the case of multiple forwards) sent from Cisco CME to Cisco UE is either the internal extension of the called IP phone or the complete E.164 number dialed to reach the IP phone. Cisco UE voice mail must be able to recognize both types of numbers.

Furthermore, when a subscriber calls Cisco UE voice mail directly (for example, to check voice mail), the *calling number* is used to identify the appropriate mailbox. This calling number may also be an internal extension or a fully qualified E.164 phone number (if the **dialplan-pattern** command is configured on Cisco CME). Therefore, it is important that the calling number be delivered correctly to Cisco UE for these calls. Various PSTN and Cisco CME configurations may transform (via digit manipulation) the calling number, which may cause the voice mail system to play the wrong prompt. The following sections demonstrate how to identify and rectify these problems.

Call from an Internal Extension to Voice Mail

Example 21-14 shows the output of the **debug ccsip messages** command on Cisco CME when a call to extension 5010 arrives from internal extension 7010. A SIP INVITE message is sent from Cisco CME to Cisco UE. 7010 is the calling number, used to recognize whether the caller is a subscriber on the system. Subsequently, when the called person listens to the message left in voice mail, this Calling Number field determines which prompts are played. If the calling number of the original call (extension 7010) matches a valid subscriber with a mailbox on Cisco UE, the voice mail system plays "Extension 7010 sent message 1...." If the caller has a spoken name recorded in the system, the system plays "*Spoken name sent message 1....*" On the other hand, if the calling number does *not* match any user in the system, the voice mail plays "An unknown caller sent message 1..." or "7010 sent message 1..." if the **voicemail callerid** configuration on Cisco UE is enabled.

Example 21-14 *SIP Debugs for a Call Forwarded to Cisco UE*

```
ccme#debug ccsip messages
INVITE sip:6800@192.168.0.2:5060 SIP/2.0
Via: SIP/2.0/UDP  192.168.0.1:5060
From: "7010" <sip:7010@192.168.0.1>;tag=691AE6E4-223C
To: <sip:6800@192.168.0.2>
Call-ID: E5D39E6A-8FC011D7-9025DAEC-459632B0@192.168.0.1
CSeq: 101 INVITE
Max-Forwards: 6
Remote-Party-ID: <sip:7010@192.168.0.1>;party=calling;screen=no;privacy=off
Timestamp: 1054070868
Contact: <sip:7010@192.168.0.1:5060>
Diversion: <sip:5010@192.168.0.1>;reason=no-answer;counter=1
```

The voice mail pilot number (extension 6800 in Example 21-14) is shown in the To: field of the SIP INVITE message. The most important part of this trace is the Diversion field. It contains the number (extension 5010) that the caller originally called (extension 7010, which shows up in the From: field) before the call was forwarded to voice mail. The value in the Diversion header (5010) is the mailbox number for which the message will be left. Also, the SIP message has a Reason field, which indicates whether the called party did not answer the call or was busy on the phone. Some voice mail systems play different greetings depending on these reason codes, but Cisco UE voice mail currently plays the same prompt for both situations.

There is a case in which a call is forwarded more than once before it reaches voice mail. For example, if extension 5010 forwards its calls to 5012 on busy or ring-no-answer and then 5012 forwards all calls to voice mail, the Diversion header contains 5012 instead of 5010. This can create confusion, because the caller thinks he called 5010 and wants to leave a message for 5010, but instead he gets the voice mail greeting for the person at extension 5012. Cisco CME uses the last redirecting number rather than the original called number for mailbox selection.

Call Using an E.164 Number to Voice Mail

Example 21-15 shows a slightly different variation of a call-forward-to-voice-mail situation. The call comes from the PSTN and goes to an IP phone in E.164 number format (444.555.5010). The original Called Number field in the Diversion header is populated with this E.164 number. If the E.164 field is not configured for this subscriber within the Cisco UE voice mail application, this call does not reach a mailbox, and the caller does not hear the right greeting.

NOTE   In the following debugs, some output has been removed to show only the most important parts of the trace.

Example 21-15   *Call Forward When the Called Number Is in E.164 Format*

```
ccme#debug ephone state
ccme#debug ccsip messages
*Mar  4 00:19:34.566: ephone-2[2]:SetCallState line 1 DN 1 chan 1 ref 7 TsRingIn
*Mar  4 00:19:34.566: ephone-2[2]:Call Info DN 1 line 1 ref 7 called 4445555010
  calling 5702 origcalled 4085255010 calltype 1
*Mar  4 00:19:34.566: ephone-2[2]: No-Name calling
*Mar  4 00:19:34.566: ephone-2[2]: 5010
*Mar  4 00:19:34.566: ephone-2[2]:Ringer Outside Ring On
*Mar  4 00:19:44.566: ephone-2[2]:SetCallState line 1 DN 1 chan 1 ref 7 TsOnHook
*Mar  4 00:19:44.566: dn_tone_control DN=1 chan 1 tonetype=0:DtSilence onoff=0
  pid=137
*Mar  4 00:19:44.566: ephone-2[2]:SpeakerPhoneOnHook
*Mar  4 00:19:44.566: ephone-2[2]:Ringer Off
*Mar  4 00:19:44.570: Sent:
INVITE sip:5800@1.3.6.129:5060 SIP/2.0
Via: SIP/2.0/UDP  1.3.6.29:5060
From: "5702" <sip:5702@1.3.6.29>;tag=F85274C-2696
To: <sip:5800@1.3.6.129>
Date: Thu, 04 Mar 1993 00:19:44 GMT
```

continues

Example 21-15 *Call Forward When the Called Number Is in E.164 Format (Continued)*

```
Remote-Party-ID: <sip:5702@1.3.6.29>;party=calling;screen=no;privacy=off
Timestamp: 731204384
Contact: <sip:5702@1.3.6.29:5060>
Call-Info: <sip:1.3.6.29:5060>;method="NOTIFY;Event=telephone-event;Duration=2000"
Diversion: <sip:4445555010@1.3.6.29>;reason=no-answer;counter=1
Expires: 180
```

If a call fails to get a greeting from the right mailbox, make sure that the recipient subscriber has the E.164 number field configured, as shown in Example 21-16. This also can be done through the GUI's user profile page.

Example 21-16 *Checking for an E.164 Number for a Subscriber*

```
cue#show user detail username johndoe
Full Name:        John Doe
First Name:       John
Last Name:        Doe
Nickname:         John Doe
Phone:            5010
Phone(E.164):     4445555010
Language:         en_US
```

If this field is not yet configured, populate it as follows:

```
cue(config)#username johndoe phonenumberE164 4445555010
```

Sometimes, when a subscriber directly calls Cisco UE to check voice mail, the person hears the "Enter your ID" prompt instead of the "Enter your password" prompt. The reason could be that the calling number is not delivered properly to the Cisco UE application or the application doesn't recognize the number because of configuration mismatches.

Digit Manipulation

Often Cisco UE voice mail doesn't recognize a calling number because of digit manipulation done by the PSTN voice gateway router or the Cisco CME call control software.

One of the digit manipulation features is the Cisco CME **dialplan-pattern** command. If configured, Cisco CME call control promotes the extension of an IP phone to the fully qualified E.164 number by inserting the appropriate digits. For instance, extension 5010 is promoted to 444.555.5010.

In this case, the From field in the SIP INVITE from Cisco CME call control to Cisco UE is populated with the E.164 number. For this to work properly, you have to configure the E.164 field for the Cisco UE subscribers, as shown in Example 21-16. To check whether Cisco CME has dial plan patterns configured, use the **show telephony-service** command, as shown in Example 21-17.

Example 21-17 *Verifying the Cisco CME Dial Plan Pattern Configuration*

```
ccme#show telephony-service
CONFIG (Version=3.0)
=====================
Version 3.0ip source-address 10.10.10.1 port 2000
max-ephones 12
max-dn 48
max-conferences 8
huntstop
dialplan-pattern 1 4445555... extension-length 4
time-format 12
date-format mm-dd-yy
```

The debug traces shown in Example 21-18 demonstrate the calling number being populated with the E.164 number when the call is sent to the Cisco UE voice mail application.

Example 21-18 *Calling Number Delivered in E.164 Format*

```
ccme#debug ccsip messages
SIP Call messages tracing is enabled
c2600-ITS-NM#
Jun  9 08:55:04.214: Sent:
INVITE sip:5800@1.3.6.130:5060 SIP/2.0
Via: SIP/2.0/UDP  1.3.6.30:5060;branch=z9hG4bK373
From: <sip:4445555010@1.3.6.30>;tag=1F5DE9-996
To: <sip:5800@1.3.6.130>
Date: Sun, 09 Jun 2002 08:55:04 GMT
Call-ID: 6C827377-7ABD11D6-800FA41E-A3784778@1.3.6.30
Supported: timer,100rel
Min-SE:  1800
Cisco-Guid: 1767160890-2059211222-2148312094-2742568824
User-Agent: Cisco-SIPGateway/IOS-12.x
Allow: INVITE, OPTIONS, BYE, CANCEL, ACK, PRACK, COMET, REFER, SUBSCRIBE, NOTIFY,
   INFO, UPDATE, REGISTER
CSeq: 101 INVITE
Max-Forwards: 6
```

Another digit manipulation feature that may convert the calling number is the Cisco IOS translation rule feature. Translation rules might be configured for the calling ephone-dn or for the dial peers governing the incoming PSTN or VoIP calls. Or a global translation rule might be translating calling numbers for every incoming VoIP call using the Cisco IOS **voip-incoming** CLI. This translation rule might convert the calling number to a different digit string that Cisco UE does not recognize. In this case, correct the Cisco IOS configuration such that the translated calling number matches either the extension or the E.164 field value in the Cisco UE user configuration for the subscriber.

Troubleshooting DTMF—No Response for Digit Presses from Cisco UE

During calls to either voice mail or the AA, the system might not respond to the caller's digit presses. This may be caused by an incorrect configuration on the SIP dial peer directing calls to Cisco UE. It also might be caused by a failed SIP SUBSCRIBE/NOTIFY transaction.

Example 21-19 shows a working DTMF configuration for the SIP dial peer on the Cisco CME router to direct calls to Cisco UE applications. Note the DTMF relay specified as sip-notify. Currently, this is the only DTMF relay option supported by Cisco UE applications. Also note that voice activity detection (VAD) is turned off. The CRS component does not detect DTMF correctly if VAD is enabled for calls.

Example 21-19 *SIP Dial Peer on Cisco CME for Cisco UE*

```
ccme#show running-config
dial-peer voice 6800 voip
 destination-pattern 5...
 session protocol sipv2
 session target ipv4:1.3.6.127
 dtmf-relay sip-notify
 codec g711ulaw
 no vad
```

In the SIP-NOTIFY DTMF relay mechanism, the Cisco UE application *subscribes* internally to Cisco CME call control for telephony events (in this case, the event is the pressing of a digit) as soon as the call is established. Cisco CME accepts this subscription and sends a NOTIFY to Cisco UE whenever a digit is pressed on the phone.

If the DTMF digits for a call to Cisco UE do not take effect, the configuration of the SIP dial peer is the first place to inspect. There may be other causes of DTMF recognition problems, but the incorrect configuration of the dial peer is by far the most common mistake.

The trace shown in Example 21-20 demonstrates how a digit press on an IP phone is translated to a SIP-NOTIFY DTMF relay event to the application. For every KeypadButtonMessage from the phone, you can see a SIP-NOTIFY message going toward Cisco UE. If these messages do not match, this indicates a failure in the Cisco CME code to translate digit presses to the application, effectively breaking DTMF relay.

Example 21-20 *Debug Traces Showing DTMF Relay*

```
ccme#debug ephone detail
EPHONE detail debugging is enabled
ccme#debug ccsip messages
SIP Call messages tracing is enabled
ccme#
*Mar  4 00:34:55.649: ephone-2[2]:Call Info DN 1 line 1 ref 11 called 5700 calling
  5010 origcalled 5700 calltype 2
*Mar  4 00:34:55.649: ephone-2[2]: 5010 calling
*Mar  4 00:34:55.649: ephone-2[2]: No-Name
*Mar  4 00:35:01.949: ephone-2[2]:KeypadButtonMessage 1
*Mar  4 00:35:01.949: SkinnyGetCallState for DN 1 chan 1 CONNECTED
```

Example 21-20 *Debug Traces Showing DTMF Relay (Continued)*

```
*Mar  4 00:35:01.949: called DN -1 chan 1, calling DN -1 chan 1 phone 2 s2s:0
*Mar  4 00:35:01.949: Sent:
NOTIFY sip:5700@1.3.6.129:5060 SIP/2.0
Via: SIP/2.0/UDP  1.3.6.29:5060
From: <sip:4085255010@1.3.6.29>;tag=F930B80-674
To: "Cisco SIP Channel3" <sip:5700@1.3.6.129>;tag=c2e25d00-284
CSeq: 102 NOTIFY
Event: telephone-event;rate=1000
Contact: <sip:4085255010@1.3.6.29:5060>
Content-Length: 10
Content-Type: audio/telephone-event

0x01800064
*Mar  4 00:35:01.949: Received:
SIP/2.0 200 OK
Via: SIP/2.0/UDP  1.3.6.29:5060
From: <sip:4085255010@1.3.6.29>;tag=F930B80-674
CSeq: 102 NOTIFY

*Mar  4 00:35:05.225: ephone-2[2]:KeypadButtonMessage 5
*Mar  4 00:35:05.225: SkinnyGetCallState for DN 1 chan 1 CONNECTED

NOTIFY sip:5700@1.3.6.129:5060 SIP/2.0
Via: SIP/2.0/UDP  1.3.6.29:5060
From: <sip:4085255010@1.3.6.29>;tag=F930B80-674
To: "Cisco SIP Channel3" <sip:5700@1.3.6.129>;tag=c2e25d00-284
CSeq: 103 NOTIFY
Contact: <sip:4085255010@1.3.6.29:5060>
Content-Type: audio/telephone-event

0x05800064
```

The highlighted hexadecimal number represents the digits pressed for the SIP protocol
NOTIFY message. Table 21-1 shows the mapping of hex values to digit buttons on a phone. The
important thing is the first byte in the hex value. The remaining bytes can vary depending on
the configuration on the calling gateway.

Table 21-1 *Digit-to-SIP Protocol Value Mapping*

Digit	SIP Protocol Value
0	0x00800064
1	0x02800064
2	0x02800064
3	0x03800064
4	0x04800064
5	0x05800064

continues

Table 21-1 *Digit-to-SIP Protocol Value Mapping (Continued)*

Digit	SIP Protocol Value
6	0x06800064
7	0x07800064
8	0x08800064
9	0x09800064
*	0x0A800064
#	0x0B800064

The trace segment shown in Example 21-20 ensures that Cisco CME is correctly translating and sending the digits to the Cisco UE application. This does not necessarily mean that digits are reaching the correct component within Cisco UE to which the call is established. Other components of the Cisco UE software must work properly for the digits to take effect. For example, the CRS SIP stack must handle the incoming SIP-NOTIFY event properly, and send the digit to the CRS application software. If this application software is using the voice browser component, the digits have to reach the voice browser properly. As you saw in Chapter 20, "Troubleshooting Cisco UE Automated Attendant," many CRS step customizations change the behavior of DTMF handling in applications. Be sure to verify those customizations if the application script was not supplied as part of the Cisco UE software.

Troubleshooting Automated Attendant Transfers

It may happen that a caller interacting with the Cisco UE AA presses the extension of the user he wants to speak to, but then the call to the extension is unsuccessful, and the caller hears overflow tone instead of a ringing phone. When a caller chooses an extension in the AA, the Cisco UE AA application does a blind transfer operation. This operation might fail for various reasons.

The simplest reason is that the extension chosen does not exist on the Cisco CME router. Other reasons could be a mistake in either the Cisco IOS, Cisco UE software, or Class of Restriction (COR) configuration. For more information on COR and troubleshooting, refer to Chapter 17, "Troubleshooting Advanced Cisco CME Features."

For example, suppose a call goes from the PSTN to the AA, and the caller presses the extension of a phone in the break room. A COR may be configured for the ephone-dn associated with the break room phone such that it may receive calls only from internal phones and not from the PSTN. Check for this kind of configuration before looking more deeply into troubleshooting AA call transfer failures.

Cisco UE uses the SIP BYE/Also message to instruct Cisco CME call control software to execute a call transfer to a requested extension. The SIP BYE/Also mechanism triggers a blind transfer. This means that there are no intermediate steps between initiating the transfer, making sure the destination phone rings, and completing the transfer. A blind transfer is a one-step mechanism in which control of the call is relinquished at the same time that the call is redirected to the new extension, so the Cisco UE application has no further control over the call after the transfer has been executed. So if the caller dials a nonexistent extension or an extension where the phone isn't registered, the caller hears fast-busy (also called overflow) tone.

In the trace shown earlier in Example 21-20, assume that the call was to the Cisco UE AA (instead of voice mail) and that the caller selected dial-by-extension and then pressed the extension of the destination user to talk to.

The trace shown in Example 21-21 shows how Cisco UE executes the transfer using the BYE/ Also mechanism. The BYE message is the SIP message to disconnect the original call. The BYE message additionally includes a header called Also, which further tells the Cisco CME call control software to set up a new call to the number specified in the message. This sequence effectively transfers the call.

Example 21-21   *SIP Blind Transfer Using BYE/Also by Cisco UE*

```
ccme#debug ccsip messages
*Mar  4 00:35:13.769: Received:
BYE sip:4085255010@1.3.6.29:5060 SIP/2.0
Via: SIP/2.0/UDP 1.3.6.129:5060
From: <sip:5700@1.3.6.129>;tag=c2e25d00-284
To: "5010" <sip:4085255010@1.3.6.29>;tag=F930B44-165C
Call-ID: E7B1CE85-174E11CC-802B8935-B1821821@1.3.6.29
CSeq: 53 BYE
User-Agent: Jasmin UA / ver 1.1
Max-Forwards: 50
Content-Length: 0
Also: <sip:5012@0.0.0.0;user=phone>
```

The Cisco UE AA before release 2.1 allowed transfers to any digit string. It did not mandate that the destination telephone number must be available or configured in the Cisco UE system's LDAP database.

Using the mechanism just described, a local PSTN caller can potentially call the Cisco CME AA and dial a long-distance or even an international destination telephone number, and the call will be transferred to that number. This effectively executes a hairpinned call (in from the PSTN and back out to the PSTN on the same router) and charges the call to the business hosting Cisco UE. This process can result in toll fraud. If you are using Cisco UE release 2.0 or earlier, you can avoid this by configuring the COR feature on the dial peers pointing to long-distance PSTN numbers so that only select phones may call these numbers. In such cases, it is especially important to consider COR configurations while troubleshooting AA call transfer failures.

The COR configuration introduces some complexity into Cisco CME operation. The other option is to use Cisco UE release 2.1 or higher, which has a configurable parameter in the AA for allowing (or disallowing) external transfers. The GUI screen where you can configure this parameter is shown in Figure 21-5.

Figure 21-5 *Allowing or Blocking AA Transfers to External Numbers*

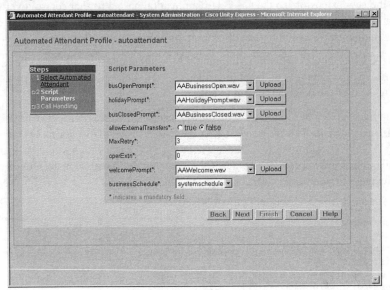

If you are writing your own customized AA scripts, you can use the *Extension To User* step provided in the release 2.1 Cisco UE Script Editor to block transfers to external numbers.

Calls to Cisco UE Get Fast-Busy

Sometimes when a call is placed to Cisco UE (to either the AA or voice mail applications), you may hear fast-busy tone unexpectedly. That may be because the call setup from the originating system (such as a Cisco CME or PSTN voice gateway at another site) may not be using the right codec.

Cisco UE supports only the G.711 μ-law codec with 20-ms packetization. It is important that all the dial peers pointing to Cisco UE on Cisco CME, or from any other PSTN voice gateway, are configured with this codec type. If calls with other types of codecs must be supported, a transcoder must be used to change the call to G.711 before it enters the Cisco UE application. Transcoding with Cisco CME is supported as of release 3.2.

You can check that the codec in the Cisco CME configuration is correct as shown in Example 21-22.

Example 21-22 *Dial Peer Configuration for a Codec*

```
ccme#show running-config
dial-peer voice 6800 voip
 destination-pattern 5...
 session protocol sipv2
 session target ipv4:1.3.6.127
 dtmf-relay sip-notify
 codec g711ulaw
 no vad
```

If Cisco UE is getting calls from other PSTN gateways in the network apart from the Cisco CME host router, another way to verify the codec type used for the calls to Cisco UE is to enable SIP debugging on Cisco UE. In the **trace ccn stacksip dbug** output shown in Example 21-23, you see that the codec used is pcmu (which is G.711 μ-law).

Example 21-23 *SIP Traces on Cisco UE to Identify a Codec*

```
cue#trace ccn stacksip dbug
cue#show trace buffer tail
Press <CTRL-C> to exit...
2407 07/26 19:34:50.582 ACCN SIPL 0 -------
INVITE sip:5800@1.4.14.134:5060 SIP/2.0
Via: SIP/2.0/UDP  1.4.14.34:5060;branch=z9hG4bK165B
From: <sip:5010@1.4.14.34>;tag=372DC22C-19CA
To: <sip:5800@1.4.14.134>
Date: Mon, 26 Jul 2004 12:27:48 GMT
Call-ID: A3342E0-DE3611D8-80A2AFCE-EEF507D3@1.4.14.34
Supported: 100rel,timer
Min-SE: 1800
Cisco-Guid: 155931842-3728085464-2157948878-4009035731
User-Agent: Cisco-SIPGateway/IOS-12.x
Allow: INVITE, OPTIONS, BYE, CANCEL, ACK, PRACK, COMET, REFER, SUBSCRIBE, NOTIFY,
   INFO, UPDATE, REGISTER
CSeq: 101 INVITE
Max-Forwards: 70
Remote-Party-ID: <sip:5010@1.4.14.34>;party=calling;screen=no;privacy=off
Timestamp: 1090844868
Contact: <sip:5010@1.4.14.34:5060>
Call-Info: <sip:1.4.14.34:5060>;method="NOTIFY;Event=telephone-event;
   Duration=2000"
Expires: 180
Allow-Events: telephone-event
Content-Type: application/sdp
Content-Length: 182

v=0
o=CiscoSystemsSIP-GW-UserAgent 2366 3655 IN IP4 1.4.14.34
s=SIP Call
c=IN IP4 1.4.14.34
t=0 0
m=audio 16506 RTP/AVP 0
c=IN IP4 1.4.14.34
a=rtpmap:0 PCMU/8000
a=ptime:20
Content-Length: 0
```

In countries where G.711 a-law is used, the conversion from G.711 a-law to G.711 μ-law is done automatically by the Cisco IOS voice infrastructure software and is not a cause for concern for calls to Cisco UE. No additional configuration is needed.

Troubleshooting the TUI and VXML Browser

The main interface used to interact with a voice mail system such as Cisco UE is the Telephony User Interface (TUI). When a call arrives at a voice mail system, the system starts playing specific prompts depending on the call type (for example, an external caller, a subscriber, or a call forwarded into voice mail). To interact with the system, the user presses DTMF digits on his phone's keypad, and the voice mail system responds by playing more prompts until the end of the session. This is implemented using a Voice Extensible Markup Language (VXML) browser, also called a voice browser. Think of the voice browser as a web browser that fetches VXML scripts instead of HTML pages over HTTP. VXML is mainly used for voice-based interactive systems such as interactive voice response (IVR) and voice mail. In Cisco UE, the voice browser fetches VXML scripts over HTTP from an internal web server and interprets them to implement the TUI. The Tomcat web server uses Java Server Pages (JSP) to query the voice mail back-end databases to build VXML scripts, depending on the call information and subscriber's mailbox properties.

Sometimes it may be necessary to troubleshoot this aspect of the caller voice mail system interaction, because the caller might hear unexpected prompts or no prompts at all after pressing a digit. When this situation occurs, it is quite possible that the digit pressed on the phone (and translated to a SIP NOTIFY message) did not reach the CRS application or the voice browser software components of the Cisco UE voice mail application.

To understand what is happening if this situation arises, it is useful to troubleshoot the voice browser's operation. It is very difficult to be specific about common problems encountered in this area, so instead this section uses an example of an active TUI session to Cisco UE and discusses the salient aspects of the trace output. Showing how the TUI session should work helps you understand how to troubleshoot any problem that might arise in this area.

You can use the same tracing techniques to troubleshoot any issues with response time for DTMF from the voice mail system. For example, if you feel that the voice mail system's response to DTMF digits pressed on a phone is too slow, you can view the response time in these traces. Look at the time stamp at which the digit arrives at the voice mail application and the time stamp at which the next prompt is played. A large delay between the two time stamps might point to a performance issue on the Cisco UE system.

Example 21-24 shows a voice browser trace for a call forwarded to Cisco UE voice mail. You can use task ID (Task:18000000082, in this case) to differentiate between multiple simultaneous calls. This task ID is generated from the CRS Workflow infrastructure. As discussed in the preceding section, the calling, called, and original called numbers are important for the proper functioning of voice mail. Because voice mail is implemented using a VXML voice browser software component, these Call Information fields have to be passed to the voice browser. As you can see in the voice browser trace in Example 21-24, the voice browser receives all these Call Information fields.

Example 21-24   *Start of Voice Browser Traces*

```
cue#trace ccn vbroswercore dbug
cue#show trace buffer tail
2702 10/10 12:31:10.338 ACCN VBRW 0 Task:18000000082 Here is the
  DefaultCompilationConfig set in the JVM en_US
2702 10/10 12:31:10.338 ACCN VBRW 0 Task:18000000082 DefaultCompilationConfig will
  be set to en_US
2702 10/10 12:31:10.338 ACCN VBRW 0 Task:18000000082 DefaultCompilationConfig is
  now set to JVM en_US
2702 10/10 12:31:10.341 ACCN VBRW 0 Task:18000000082 enterLevel: SESSION_LEVEL
2702 10/10 12:31:10.341 ACCN VBRW 0 callContact.getSessionID() = 5000000007
2702 10/10 12:31:10.341 ACCN VBRW 0 Task:18000000082 VoiceBrowser sessionid:
  5000000007, taskid: 18000000082
2702 10/10 12:31:10.341 ACCN VBRW 0 callContact.getCallingNumber() = 6003
2702 10/10 12:31:10.341 ACCN VBRW 0 callContact.getDNIS() = null
2702 10/10 12:31:10.341 ACCN VBRW 0 callContact.getDNIS() = null
2702 10/10 12:31:10.341 ACCN VBRW 0 callContact.getCalledNumber() = 5800
2702 10/10 12:31:10.342 ACCN VBRW 0 callContact.getANIIIDigits() = null
2702 10/10 12:31:10.342 ACCN VBRW 0 callContact.getUserToUserInfo() = null
2702 10/10 12:31:10.342 ACCN VBRW 0 callContact.getRDNIS() = null
```

The first trace line shown in Example 21-25 is important, especially when calls are forwarded into voice mail. The LastRedirectingNumber field comes into play when a call to an extension on Cisco CME is forwarded on busy or no-answer to voice mail. This identifies the original extension dialed and, hence, is the extension associated with the mailbox for which this message must be left.

If a value for the callContact.getLastRedirectedNumber() field is present in the trace, you can safely assume that this was a forwarded call and not a direct call to voice mail. This is shown in Example 21-25.

Example 21-25   *Voice Browser Trace Showing the Last Redirected Number*

```
cue#show trace buffer tail
2702 10/10 12:31:10.342 ACCN VBRW 0 callContact.getLastRedirectedNumber() = 5010
2702 10/10 12:31:10.342 ACCN VBRW 0 callContact.getRDNIS() = null
2702 10/10 12:31:10.342 ACCN VBRW 0 callContact.getLastRedirectedNumber() = 5010
2702 10/10 12:31:10.342 ACCN VBRW 0 callContact.getSessionID() = 5000000007
2702 10/10 12:31:10.348 ACCN VBRW 0 Task:18000000082 VBContext::pushLang language
  = en_US
2702 10/10 12:31:10.348 ACCN VBRW 0 Task:18000000082 VBContext::pushLang Adding
  new language : en_US
2702 10/10 12:31:10.348 ACCN VBRW 0 Task:18000000082
```

After processing the call information, the voice browser starts the first VXML script, login.vxml, which is the top-level login script for the voice mail system. Depending on the type of call, either the external caller login script (if it is a forwarded call, the script to leave a message is executed) or the subscriber login script (if it is a direct call, the user is asked to identify himself) is executed next, as shown in Example 21-26.

Example 21-26 *Voice Browser Executing a Login Script*

```
cue#show trace buffer tail
2702 10/10 12:31:10.349 ACCN VBRW 0 Task:18000000082
  VoiceBrowser.invokeApplication(level:0): [URI=http://localhost/voicemail/
  vxmlscripts/login.vxml fragment=null]
2702 10/10 12:31:10.349 ACCN VBRW 0 Task:18000000082 enterScope: application
2702 10/10 12:31:10.349 ACCN VBRW 0 Task:18000000082 enterLevel: APPLICATION_LEVEL
2702 10/10 12:31:10.349 ACCN VBRW 0 Task:18000000082 Got document:
  http://localhost/voicemail/vxmlscripts/login.vxml from cache.
..........
2702 10/10 12:31:10.349 ACCN VBRW 0 Task:18000000082 enterLevel: APPLICATION_LEVEL
2702 10/10 12:31:10.349 ACCN VBRW 0 Task:18000000082
  VoiceBrowser.invokeRootDocument: [URI=http://localhost/voicemail/vxmlscripts/
  systemLangID.jsp fragment=null]
2702 10/10 12:31:10.357 ACCN VBRW 0 Task:18000000082 Fetch: HTTP 200 OK
2702 10/10 12:31:10.357 ACCN VBRW 0 Task:18000000082 Fetch: HTTP Response is not
  from Cache
2702 10/10 12:31:10.358 ACCN VBRW 0 Task:18000000082 Browser:
  com.cisco.voicebrowser.browser.CookieSet@3df95571: 1 cookies:
  JSESSIONID=mqh3bxs2a1;Path=/voicemail;Domain=localhost
2702 10/10 12:31:10.358 ACCN VBRW 0 Task:18000000082 Successfully fetched bytes:
  239, duration(s): 0.0090, URI: http://localhost/voicemail/vxmlscripts/
  systemLangID.jsp
```

This call is a forwarded call, so the caller login script to leave a message in a mailbox is executed. This interchange is shown in Example 21-27.

Example 21-27 *Caller Login Script Is Executed for a Forwarded Call*

```
cue#show trace buffer tail
2702 10/10 12:31:10.389 ACCN VBRW 0 Task:18000000082 VoiceDomTraverser:
  handleElementBlock(): is called
2702 10/10 12:31:10.390 ACCN VBRW 0 Task:18000000082 <goto> destination:
  [URI=http://localhost/voicemail/vxmlscripts/caller_login.vxml fragment=null]
2702 10/10 12:31:10.391 ACCN VBRW 0 Task:18000000082 Got document:
  http://localhost/voicemail/vxmlscripts/caller_login.vxml from cache.
2702 10/10 12:31:10.391 ACCN VBRW 0 Task:18000000082 exitScope: anonymous
2702 10/10 12:31:10.391 ACCN VBRW 0 Task:18000000082 exitLevel: FIELD_LEVEL
2702 10/10 12:31:10.391 ACCN VBRW 0 Task:18000000082 exitLevel: DIALOG_LEVEL
2702 10/10 12:31:10.391 ACCN VBRW 0 Task:18000000082 Form context:
  check_pin_status=not defined
  _block1001="_defined"
  validate_id=not defined
  _block1000="_defined"
```

Because this is a forwarded call originally directed to extension 5010, the voice mail application must ensure that extension 5010 has a mailbox in this system. It verifies this by executing extValidation.jsp, as shown in Example 21-28.

Example 21-28 *Voice Browser Executes JSP to Validate the Extension*

```
cue#show trace buffer tail
2702 10/10 12:31:10.401 ACCN VBRW 0 Task:18000000082 Invoke subdialog[mbox_check]
  [URI=http://localhost/voicemail/vxmlscripts/extValidation.jsp fragment=null]
  Params: null
2702 10/10 12:31:10.401 ACCN VBRW 0 Task:18000000082 VBContext.pushContext level:1
2702 10/10 12:31:10.401 ACCN VBRW 0 Task:18000000082
  VoiceBrowser.invokeApplication(level:1):
  [URI=http://localhost/voicemail/vxmlscripts/extValidation.jsp fragment=null]
2702 10/10 12:31:10.402 ACCN VBRW 0 Task:18000000082 enterScope: application
2702 10/10 12:31:10.402 ACCN VBRW 0 Task:18000000082 enterLevel: APPLICATION_LEVEL
2702 10/10 12:31:10.420 ACCN VBRW 0 Task:18000000082 Fetch: HTTP 200 OK
2702 10/10 12:31:10.421 ACCN VBRW 0 Task:18000000082 Successfully fetched bytes:
  815, duration(s): 0.019, URI: http://localhost/voicemail/vxmlscripts/
  extValidation.jsp
2702 10/10 12:31:10.423 ACCN VBRW 0 Task:18000000082 exitLevel: APPLICATION_LEVEL
2702 10/10 12:31:10.424 ACCN VBRW 0 Task:18000000082 exitScope: application
2702 10/10 12:31:10.424 ACCN VBRW 0 Task:18000000082 enterScope: application
2702 10/10 12:31:10.424 ACCN VBRW 0 Task:18000000082 enterLevel: APPLICATION_LEVEL
2702 10/10 12:31:10.424 ACCN VBRW 0 Task:18000000082 enterScope: document
2702 10/10 12:31:10.425 ACCN VBRW 0 Task:18000000082 enterLevel: DOCUMENT_LEVEL
2702 10/10 12:31:10.425 ACCN VBRW 0 Task:18000000082 traverseDocument:
  http://localhost/voicemail/vxmlscripts/extValidation.jsp
  base=http://localhost/voicemail/vxmlscripts/extValidation.jsp
2702 10/10 12:31:10.425 ACCN VBRW 0 Task:18000000082
  VoiceDomParser:handleMetaElement(): - NodeName=meta:NodeValue=null:LocalName=
```

As you can see from this trace, the voice mail system continues to execute the appropriate JSP, which, in turn, access data from the LDAP and SQL databases to build dynamic VXML scripts and deliver these to the voice browser to execute.

The previous set of trace examples demonstrate the voice browser's operation. Sometimes it is necessary to troubleshoot TUI sessions for some calls. An example is when a caller hears unexpected prompts. You may need to see the DTMF digits the user is pressing and the prompts the voice mail system plays in response.

The following trace examples demonstrate TUI troubleshooting. In the voicemail vxml trace output, you can see a hexadecimal number (0x0000000430e2344f in the trace output). This is the unique call identification (or call ID) from the voice mail system's point of view. It is used to differentiate between multiple simultaneous calls.

This section discusses TUI operation with a sample TUI session where a subscriber logs in and addresses a message to another subscriber. As soon as you understand this example, it is very easy to troubleshoot any other TUI-related situations that might crop up. Use the following commands to troubleshoot these types of issues:

- **trace ccn vbrowseroutput dbug**
- **trace voicemail vxml all**
- **show trace buffer tail**

One tip for using these commands is to clear the trace buffer before troubleshooting (**clear trace**) and turn off all other traces (**no trace all**). Then turn on the **trace ccn vbrowseroutput dbug** and **trace voicemail vxml all** commands and make the test call. Use the show trace buffer long command to see the trace buffer contents, because this command shows detailed messages about prompts, including the text that is the content of the voice mail prompt. The long format of traces helps you understand the TUI interaction much better. One thing to note while looking at these traces is that **voicemail vxml** trace output is coming from the voicemail back end running as part of the Tomcat web server, and the trace lines containing VBRO are from the voice browser (client).

When the voice mail system answers a direct (not forwarded) incoming call, the voice browser takes the following actions:

- It starts accessing VXML scripts.
- It checks the default system language (which is only English until Cisco UE release 2.0).
- It validates the extension.
- It asks the user to enter a PIN.

The trace in Example 21-29 shows the output from the voice browser and voice mail VXML scripts. Note that traces come from modules ACCN and voicemail and entities VBRO and VXML, respectively.

Example 21-29 *Voice Browser Logs in a Subscriber*

```
cue#show trace buffer tail
2699 10/10 12:23:30.115 ACCN VBRO 0 Task:18000000079 Invoke:
  http://localhost/voicemail/vxmlscripts/login.vxml
2699 10/10 12:23:30.118 ACCN VBRO 0 Task:18000000079 Fetch:
  http://localhost/voicemail/vxmlscripts/systemLangID.jsp
2699 10/10 12:23:30.141 ACCN VBRO 0 Task:18000000079 Fetch:
  http://localhost/voicemail/vxmlscripts/extValidation.jsp
2699 10/10 12:23:30.165 ACCN VBRO 0 Task:18000000079 Fetch:
  http://localhost/voicemail/vxmlscripts/checkPinStatus.jsp
```

At this point, the voice mail application requests that the prompt AvSubSignInENU002.wav (which contains the phrase "Please enter your password") be played. This is shown in the **voicemail vxml** trace in Example 21-30.

Example 21-30 *VXML Script Requesting That a Prompt Be Played*

```
cue#show trace buffer tail
2699 10/10 12:23:30.234 voicemail vxml "Please enter your password.<1.5 sec
  silence>" 0x0000000430e2344f AvSubSignInENU002.wav
2699 10/10 12:23:30.235 ACCN VBRO 0 Task:18000000079 Play:
  ../prompts/ENU/AvSubSignIn/AvSubSignInENU002.wav
```

The DTMF digits pressed by the user are received by the voice browser, as shown in Example 21-31. These digits are delivered by the SIP stack (as discussed earlier, in the section "Troubleshooting DTMF—No Response for Digit Presses from Cisco UE") and CRS infrastructure components to the voice browser. This is another place where you should look for correct processing of digits in a case where voice mail is not responding as expected to digits pressed by a caller. This is to ensure that the digits are indeed reaching the voice browser application component.

Example 21-31 *Digits Pressed by the User Are Received by the Voice Browser*

```
cue#show trace buffer tail
2699 10/10 12:23:30.238 ACCN VBRO 0 Task:18000000079 Listen:
2699 10/10 12:23:34.332 ACCN VBRO 0 Task:18000000079 Heard:    'dtmf-2 dtmf-2
  dtmf-2 dtmf-#'
```

At this point, the voice mail system must execute a JSP to validate the caller's password. The interaction between the user and voice mail system continues in this manner until the end of the TUI session. If you are facing any issues with the voice mail TUI (including TUI performance), the traces discussed in this section are the best way to understand which component is not working as expected and why.

Example 21-32 shows the continuation of the direct call. This example shows that the voice mail system has successfully logged in the subscriber.

Example 21-32 *Voice Mail System Logs in the User*

```
cue#show trace buffer tail
2699 10/10 12:23:34.337 ACCN VBRO 0 Task:18000000079 Fetch:
  http://localhost/voicemail/vxmlscripts/validate_password.jsp
2699 10/10 12:23:34.416 ACCN VBRO 0 Task:18000000079 Fetch:
  http://localhost/voicemail/vxmlscripts/setSubSession.jsp
2699 10/10 12:23:34.430 ACCN VBRO 0 Task:18000000079 Fetch:
  http://localhost/voicemail/vxmlscripts/playSpokenName.jsp
2699 10/10 12:23:34.453 ACCN VBRO 0 Task:18000000079 Fetch:
  http://localhost/voicemail/vxmlscripts/root.jsp
2699 10/10 12:23:34.617 voicemail vxml "hello." 0x0000000430e2344f
  AvSubMsgCountENU128.wav
2699 10/10 12:23:34.618 ACCN VBRO 0 Task:18000000079 Play:
  ../prompts/ENU/AvSubMsgCount/AvSubMsgCountENU128.wav
2699 10/10 12:23:35.023 voicemail vxml "You have no new messages."
  0x0000000430e2344f AvSubMsgCountENU001.wav
2699 10/10 12:23:35.023 ACCN VBRO 0 Task:18000000079 Play:
  ../prompts/ENU/AvSubMsgCount/AvSubMsgCountENU001.wav
```

At this point, the user presses 2 to choose to send a message, as shown in Example 21-33.

Example 21-33 *User Chooses to Send a Message*

```
cue#show trace buffer tail
2699 10/10 12:23:35.029 ACCN VBRO 0 Task:18000000079 Play:
  ../prompts/ENU/AvSubMenu/AvSubMenuENU006.wav
```

continues

Example 21-33 *User Chooses to Send a Message (Continued)*

```
2699 10/10 12:23:35.030 ACCN VBRO 0 Task:18000000079 Listen:
2699 10/10 12:23:42.340 ACCN VBRO 0 Task:18000000079 Heard:    'dtmf-2'
2699 10/10 12:23:42.353 voicemail vxml "Spell the name of the person or group."
  0x0000000430e2344f AvAesopCustomENU002.wav
2699 10/10 12:23:42.354 ACCN VBRO 0 Task:18000000079 Play:
  ../prompts/ENU/AvAesopCustom/AvAesopCustomENU002.wav
2699 10/10 12:23:42.354 voicemail vxml "Spell the last and first name"
  0x0000000430e2344f AvAddrSearchENU005.wav
2699 10/10 12:23:42.355 ACCN VBRO 0 Task:18000000079 Play:
  ../prompts/ENU/AvAddrSearch/AvAddrSearchENU005.wav
2699 10/10 12:23:42.355 voicemail vxml "For Q, press 7. For Z, press 9."
  0x0000000430e2344f AvAddrSearchENU030.wav
2699 10/10 12:23:42.356 ACCN VBRO 0 Task:18000000079 Play:
  ../prompts/ENU/AvAddrSearch/AvAddrSearchENU030.wav
2699 10/10 12:23:42.357 voicemail vxml "To switch between spelling and number
  entry, press ##." 0x0000000430e2344f AvAddrSearchENU075.wav
2699 10/10 12:23:42.357 ACCN VBRO 0 Task:18000000079 Play:
  ../prompts/ENU/AvAddrSearch/AvAddrSearchENU075.wav
```

The user presses ## to select addressing by extension number, as shown in Example 21-34.

Example 21-34 *User Chooses to Dial-by-Extension*

```
cue#show trace buffer tail
2699 10/10 12:23:42.358 ACCN VBRO 0 Task:18000000079 Listen:
2699 10/10 12:23:45.990 ACCN VBRO 0 Task:18000000079 Heard:    'dtmf-#'
2699 10/10 12:23:45.994 ACCN VBRO 0 Task:18000000079 Listen:
2699 10/10 12:23:46.251 ACCN VBRO 0 Task:18000000079 Heard:    'dtmf-#'
2699 10/10 12:23:46.292 ACCN VBRO 0 Task:18000000079 Fetch:
  http://localhost/voicemail/vxmlscripts/setAddressingMode.jsp
2699 10/10 12:23:46.305 voicemail vxml "Enter the extension." 0x0000000430e2344f
  AvAddrSearchENU037.wav
2699 10/10 12:23:46.305 ACCN VBRO 0 Task:18000000079 Play:
  ../prompts/ENU/AvAddrSearch/AvAddrSearchENU037.wav
2699 10/10 12:23:46.306 voicemail vxml "To switch between spelling and number
  entry, press ##." 0x0000000430e2344f AvAddrSearchENU075.wav
2699 10/10 12:23:46.306 ACCN VBRO 0 Task:18000000079 Play:
  ../prompts/ENU/AvAddrSearch/AvAddrSearchENU075.wav
2699 10/10 12:23:46.307 ACCN VBRO 0 Task:18000000079 Listen:
```

The user enters the extension of the recipient mailbox, as shown in Example 21-35.

Example 21-35 *User Addresses the Message to an Extension*

```
cue#show trace buffer tail
2699 10/10 12:23:52.081 ACCN VBRO 0 Task:18000000079 Heard:    'dtmf-6 dtmf-0
  dtmf-0 dtmf-1 dtmf-#'
2699 10/10 12:23:52.111 ACCN VBRO 0 Task:18000000079 Fetch:
  http://localhost/voicemail/vxmlscripts/extValidation.jsp
2699 10/10 12:23:52.136 ACCN VBRO 0 Task:18000000079 Fetch:
  http://localhost/voicemail/vxmlscripts/getAddrParts.jsp
```

The user's interaction with the voice mail system continues like this until the end of the call.

Troubleshooting the Database, LDAP, and Mailbox Activities

This section discusses troubleshooting the Cisco UE voice mail system's interaction with its back-end databases. Here you learn how to interpret SQL database traces, voice mail's interaction with the LDAP database for user information, and message and mailbox activities. These topics are discussed by looking at an example of a subscriber addressing a voice message to another subscriber and sending it. The **trace** commands needed for this section include

- **trace voicemail database all**
- **trace voicemail ldap all**
- **trace voicemail message all**
- **trace voicemail mailbox all**
- **show trace buffer tail**

In the trace segment shown in Example 21-36, a call arrives at the voice mail system with a calling number of 6001. As you can see from the traces, voice mail accesses the LDAP database to resolve the calling number to a user configured on the system to check whether the caller is a valid subscriber on the system or an outside (PSTN) caller calling into the voice mail system. Depending on the outcome of this query, the voice mail system plays different prompts.

In this example, the calling number 6001 is resolved to the user johndoe. Following that action, the system retrieves the user's preferred language (English only in the system used to generate these traces) to select the appropriate prompts to play.

Example 21-36 *System Retrieves User Information Based on Calling Extension*

```
cue#show trace buffer tail
6082 09/30 18:39:48.614 voicemail ldap "getUserByPhoneNo" 6001
6082 09/30 18:39:48.617 voicemail ldap "getUserByPhoneNo: userDn." /sw/local/
  users/johndoe
6082 09/30 18:39:48.617 voicemail ldap 0 getAttributeValue:
  /sw/local/users/johndoe/Language/preferredLanguage
6082 09/30 18:39:48.618 voicemail ldap 0 getAttributeValue:
  /sw/local/users/johndoe/TelephoneNumbers/primaryExtension
6082 09/30 18:39:48.618 voicemail database 0 Got connection: 2, inUse: 3, active:
  2
```

After the calling user has been identified, the voice mail system verifies that the user has a mailbox, because it is not necessary for every user defined in the system to have an associated voice mailbox.

The SQL statement shown in Example 21-37 is executed and returns the mailbox ID of the given user (for example, the mailbox ID returned here is PERSONAL_00000000000000000000022).

Example 21-37   *Retrieving Mailbox Information Based on User Information*

```
cue#show trace buffer tail
6082 09/30 18:39:48.619 voicemail database "SQL: " select mailboxid from
  vm_mbxusers where owner=true and userdn='/sw/local/users/johndoe';
6082 09/30 18:39:48.621 voicemail database "Database query results"
  PERSONAL_00000000000000000000022
6082 09/30 18:39:48.621 voicemail database 0 Freed connection: 2, inUse: 3,
  active: 2
```

Next, the voice mail system retrieves the details of the mailbox for johndoe by executing the SQL statement shown in the trace output in Example 21-38. The database returns a row of data. To interpret this data, you need the database schema. The SQL database schema for Cisco UE is given in Appendix C, "Cisco Unity Express Database Schema." The schema-related trace output is shown in Example 21-38.

Example 21-38   *Sample Schema and Trace Output for Table vm_mailbox*

```
create table vm_mailbox
(
    MailboxId            varchar(64)          not null,
    MailboxType          integer              not null default 0,
    Description          varchar(64)          ,
    MailboxSize          integer              ,
    MessageSize          integer              ,
    Tutorial             boolean              not null default true,
    TotalMessageTime     integer              ,
    MessageExpiryTime    integer              ,
    Enabled              boolean              not null default true,
    GreetingType         integer              not null default 10,
    OrphanedTime         bigint               not null default 0,
    primary key          (MailboxId)
);

cue#show trace buffer tail
6082 09/30 18:39:53.085 voicemail database "SQL: " select * from vm_mailbox where
  mailboxid='PERSONAL_00000000000000000000022';
6082 09/30 18:39:53.090 voicemail database "Database query results"
  PERSONAL_00000000000000000000022,0,johndoe mailbox, 3000, 60, f,0,30, t,10,0,
  1064946956019
```

From the trace output and schema definition, the following are the characteristics of johndoe's mailbox:

- **Mailbox ID**—PERSONAL_00000000000000000000022

- **MailboxType**—0, personal mailbox

- **Description**—johndoe mailbox
- **Mailboxsize**—3000 seconds
- **MessageSize**—60 seconds
- **Tutorial**—0, tutorial flag is OFF
- **TotalMessageTime**—0, meaning that the mailbox is empty
- **MessageExpiryTime**—30, messages expire after 30 days
- **Enabled**—t, True, the mailbox is enabled
- **GreetingType**—10, the standard greeting is active
- **OrphanedTime**—0, not an orphaned mailbox

The data returned from the back-end SQL database affects the prompts played to the caller via VXML. The JSP create dynamic VXML scripts for the TUI depending on the values returned from the back-end databases. For example, if the tutorial flag is set for the mailbox, the prompts played to the user start with the tutorial prompt "Welcome to Cisco Unity Express messaging system. To get the most from the system...."

After checking that the mailbox is enabled, the voice mail system lets the user log into the mailbox. At the same time, the voice mail system retrieves the user's spoken name from the LDAP database to play it after the login. The traces in Example 21-39 show this exchange.

Example 21-39 *Voice Mail System Plays the User's Spoken Name After Login*

```
cue#show trace buffer tail
6082 09/30 18:39:53.104 voicemail mailbox "User login" /sw/local/users/johndoe
6082 09/30 18:39:53.104 voicemail database 0 Got connection: 3, inUse: 3,
  active: 2
6082 09/30 18:39:53.106 voicemail database "SQL: " update vm_mailbox set
  lastaccessed=1064947193104 where mailboxid='PERSONAL_00000000000000000000022';
6082 09/30 18:39:53.111 voicemail database "Commiting transaction"
6082 09/30 18:39:53.114 voicemail database 0 Freed connection: 3, inUse: 3,
  active: 2
6082 09/30 18:39:53.160 voicemail ldap "getSpokenNameByName: userDn."
  /sw/local/users/johndoe
6082 09/30 18:39:53.160 voicemail ldap "normalizeDN" /sw/local/users/johndoe
6082 09/30 18:39:53.160 voicemail ldap "getSpokenName: dn."
  uid=johndoe,ou=users,ou=branch123,o=cisco.com
```

After having logged into the mailbox, user johndoe chooses to send a voice message to another subscriber at extension 6003. At this time, the voice mail system resolves extension 6003 to a subscriber called janedoe. janedoe's spoken name is retrieved, if recorded, from LDAP and is played as a confirmation to johndoe. Finally, the voice mail system finds janedoe's mailbox ID (PERSONAL_00000000000000000000023), as shown in Example 21-40.

Example 21-40 *User Addresses a Message to Another Extension*

```
cue#show trace buffer tail
6081 09/30 18:40:07.825 voicemail ldap "getUserByPhoneNo" 6003
6081 09/30 18:40:07.828 voicemail ldap "getUserByPhoneNo: userDn." /sw/local/
  users/janedoe
6081 09/30 18:40:07.828 voicemail ldap 0 getAttributeValue:
  /sw/local/users/janedoe/Language/preferredLanguage
6081 09/30 18:40:07.829 voicemail ldap 0 getAttributeValue:
  /sw/local/users/janedoe/TelephoneNumbers/primaryExtension
6081 09/30 18:40:07.829 voicemail database 0 Got connection: 3, inUse: 3, active:
  2
6081 09/30 18:40:07.830 voicemail database "SQL: " select mailboxid from
  vm_mbxusers where owner=true and userdn='/sw/local/users/janedoe';
6081 09/30 18:40:07.832 voicemail database "Database query results"
  PERSONAL_00000000000000000000023
```

janedoe's spoken name, if recorded, is retrieved from LDAP and is played so that the sender can recognize the extension by spoken-name confirmation, as shown in Example 21-41.

Example 21-41 *Message Recipient's Spoken Name Is Played if Recorded*

```
cue#show trace buffer tail
6082 09/30 18:40:07.846 voicemail ldap "getSpokenNameByName: userDn." /sw/local/
  users/janedoe
6082 09/30 18:40:07.846 voicemail ldap "normalizeDN" /sw/local/users/janedoe
6082 09/30 18:40:07.847 voicemail ldap "getSpokenName: dn." uid=janedoe,ou=users,
  ou=branch123,o=cisco.com
```

As soon as the recipient of the voice message is identified, the caller records a message. The voice mail system creates a message, assigns it a message ID, and sets the message's size. As shown in the trace output in Example 21-42, a message with ID 1064947237095_0, 43258 bytes long, is created. This message is 5.2 seconds long (5281 ms).

Example 21-42 *Message Is Created*

```
cue#show trace buffer tail
6082 09/30 18:40:37.096 voicemail message "Creating Message" 1064947237095_0
6082 09/30 18:40:37.096 voicemail message "Message Length" 5281, Message Size:
  43258
```

The next few lines of trace output (as given in Example 21-43) show that a message is sent from user johndoe to extension 6003 and that a message with ID 1064947237095_0 is received for mailbox ID PERSONAL_00000000000000000000023. The total usage time for the destination mailbox is updated in the database. After sending the message, the user logs out of the mailbox.

Example 21-43 *Message Is Sent and Database Tables Are Updated*

```
cue#show trace buffer tail
6082 09/30 18:40:37.096 voicemail mailbox "Sending message(s) from"
  0x000000037e11d61a /sw/local/users/johndoe
```

Example 21-43 *Message Is Sent and Database Tables Are Updated (Continued)*

```
6082 09/30 18:40:37.096 voicemail mailbox "Sending message to" 0x000000037e11d61a
  6003
.......
6082 09/30 18:40:37.096 voicemail database 0 Got connection: 2, inUse: 3,
  active: 2
6082 09/30 18:40:37.097 voicemail mailbox "Message received"
  0x0000000000000000 PERSONAL_00000000000000000000023,1064947237095_0
............
6082 09/30 18:40:37.099 voicemail database "SQL: " update vm_message
  set messageid='1064947237095_0',messagetype=1,sender='/sw/local/users/johndoe',
  urgent=false,private=false,attachedmsgid=null where messageId='OID_16693';
6082 09/30 18:40:37.104 voicemail database "SQL: " insert into vm_usermsg
  values('PERSONAL_00000000000000000000023','1064947237095_0',1,1064947237095);
6082 09/30 18:40:37.108 voicemail database "SQL: " select totalmessagetime from vm
  _mailbox where mailboxid='PERSONAL_00000000000000000000023' for update;
6082 09/30 18:40:37.111 voicemail database "Database query results" 2409
6082 09/30 18:40:37.111 voicemail database "SQL: " update vm_mailbox set
  totalmessagetime=7690 where mailboxid='PERSONAL_00000000000000000000023';
6082 09/30 18:40:37.115 voicemail database "Commiting transaction"
6082 09/30 18:40:37.118 voicemail ldap 0 getAttributeValue:
  /sw/local/users/janedoe/TelephoneNumbers/primaryExtension
6082 09/30 18:40:37.131 voicemail database 0 Freed connection: 2, inUse: 3,
  active: 2
6081 09/30 18:40:43.994 voicemail mailbox "User logout" 0x000000037e11d61a
  /sw/local/users/johndoe
```

Example 21-44 explores what happens when Jane Doe logs into her mailbox and listens to the
message just sent by John Doe. First, the calling number (6003) is resolved to a subscriber on
the system, and the subscriber's details are retrieved. The calling subscriber's mailbox ID is
checked, and the details of that mailbox are retrieved from the vm_mailbox table. Then the
voice mailbox entity logs the subscriber into the mailbox, updates the last access time for the
mailbox, and retrieves the user's spoken name.

Example 21-44 *Message Recipient Logs in to Check the Message*

```
cue#show trace buffer tail
6082 09/30 18:40:48.912 voicemail ldap "getUserByPhoneNo" 6003
6082 09/30 18:40:48.915 voicemail ldap "getUserByPhoneNo: userDn."
  /sw/local/users/janedoe
6082 09/30 18:40:48.916 voicemail ldap 0 getAttributeValue:
  /sw/local/users/janedoe/Language/preferredLanguage
6082 09/30 18:40:48.916 voicemail ldap 0 getAttributeValue:
  /sw/local/users/janedoe/TelephoneNumbers/primaryExtension
6082 09/30 18:40:48.917 voicemail database 0 Got connection: 3, inUse: 3,
  active: 2
.......
6082 09/30 18:40:48.918 voicemail database "SQL: " select mailboxid from vm
  _mbxusers where owner=true and userdn='/sw/local/users/janedoe';
6082 09/30 18:40:48.920 voicemail database "Database query results"
  PERSONAL_00000000000000000000023
```

continues

Example 21-44 *Message Recipient Logs in to Check the Message (Continued)*

```
6082 09/30 18:40:48.921 voicemail database 0 Freed connection: 3, inUse: 3,
  active: 2
6081 09/30 18:40:57.002 voicemail database 0 Got connection: 2, inUse: 3,
  active: 2
6081 09/30 18:40:57.003 voicemail database "SQL: " select * from vm_mailbox where
  mailboxid='PERSONAL_000000000000000000000023';
6081 09/30 18:40:57.009 voicemail database "Database query results"
  PERSONAL_000000000000000000000023,0,janedoe
  mailbox,3000,60,f,7690,30,t,10,0,1064947025206
6081 09/30 18:40:57.009 voicemail database "SQL: " select userdn from vm_mbxusers
  where owner=true and mailboxid='PERSONAL_000000000000000000000023';
6081 09/30 18:40:57.012 voicemail database 0 Freed connection: 2, inUse: 3,
  active: 2
6081 09/30 18:40:57.013 voicemail database 0 Got connection: 3, inUse: 3,
  active: 2
6081 09/30 18:40:57.013 voicemail database "SQL: " 0x000000037e11d61c select
  mailboxid from vm_mbxusers where owner=true and userdn='/sw/local/users/
  janedoe';
6081 09/30 18:40:57.016 voicemail database "Database query results"
  0x000000037e11d61c PERSONAL_000000000000000000000023
6081 09/30 18:40:57.017 voicemail database "SQL: " 0x000000037e11d61c select
  distinct vm_mbxusers.mailboxid, orphanedtime from vm_mbxusers, vm_mailbox where
  vm_mailbox.mailboxid=vm_mbxusers.mailboxid and (userdn='/sw/local/users/
  janedoe') and orphanedtime=0 and owner=false;
6081 09/30 18:40:57.022 voicemail database 0 0x000000037e11d61c Freed connection:
  3, inUse: 3, active: 2
6081 09/30 18:40:57.022 voicemail mailbox "User login" /sw/local/users/janedoe
6081 09/30 18:40:57.023 voicemail database 0 Got connection: 2, inUse: 3,
  active: 2
6081 09/30 18:40:57.024 voicemail database "SQL: " update vm_mailbox set
  lastaccessed=1064947257023 where mailboxid='PERSONAL_000000000000000000000023';
6081 09/30 18:40:57.028 voicemail database "Commiting transaction"
6081 09/30 18:40:57.030 voicemail database 0 Freed connection: 2, inUse: 3,
  active: 2
6081 09/30 18:40:57.165 voicemail ldap "getSpokenNameByName: userDn."
  /sw/local/users/janedoe
6081 09/30 18:40:57.165 voicemail ldap "normalizeDN" /sw/local/users/janedoe
6081 09/30 18:40:57.165 voicemail ldap "getSpokenName: dn."
  uid=janedoe,ou=users,ou=branch123,o=cisco.com
```

The voice mail system now gets details about the messages for this particular mailbox from the vm_usermsg and vm_message tables in the SQL database, as shown in Example 21-45. You can see as part of this SQL transaction that all the message attributes are returned, including

- The message's sender (/sw/local/users/johndoe)
- The message's length (5281 seconds)
- The message's size (43258 bytes)
- When the message was left (30-Sep-03 18:40:25 UTC)

Also note the value 16693, which is the object ID of the message stored as an object in the SQL database. References to this appear in the later traces also. Right now the messages in the mailbox are ordered according to urgency and secondarily by the time when they were left. Urgent messages are played out first, and then the remaining messages are played in the order in which they were received.

Example 21-45 *Information About the Message Is Retrieved*

```
cue#show trace buffer tail
5047 09/30 18:40:57.207 voicemail database 0 Got connection: 3, inUse: 3,
  active: 2
5047 09/30 18:40:57.208 voicemail database "SQL: " 0x000000037e11d61c select *
  from vm_usermsg,vm_message where mailboxid='PERSONAL_00000000000000000000023'
  and vm_usermsg.messageid=vm_message.messageid;
5047 09/30 18:40:57.225 voicemail database "Database query results"
  0x000000037e11d61c PERSONAL_00000000000000000000023,1064947237095_0,1,
  1064947237095,1064947237095_0,1,1,/sw/local/users/johndoe,f,f,5281,43258,
  1064947225155,null,16693,30-Sep-03 18:40:25 UTC
5047 09/30 18:40:57.225 voicemail database 0 0x000000037e11d61c Freed connection:
  3, inUse: 3, active: 2
6081 09/30 18:41:01.912 voicemail database 0 Got connection: 2, inUse: 3, active:
  2
6081 09/30 18:41:01.913 voicemail database "SQL: " 0x000000037e11d61c select
  mailboxid, vm_usermsg.messageid, urgent, messagetime from vm_usermsg, vm_message
  where vm_usermsg.messageid=vm_message.messageid and state=1 and mailboxid=
  'PERSONAL_00000000000000000000023' and messagetype<10 order by urgent desc,
  messagetime asc;
6081 09/30 18:41:01.918 voicemail database "Database query results"
  0x000000037e11d61c PERSONAL_00000000000000000000023,1064947237095_0,f,
  1064947225155
```

Note that the message ID was received in the last SQL transaction. In the traces shown in Example 21-46, the voice mail system creates a message to be played using that message ID.

Example 21-46 *Voice Mail System Readies the Message to Be Played*

```
cue#show trace buffer tail
6081 09/30 18:41:01.919 voicemail database 0 0x000000037e11d61c Freed connection:
  2, inUse: 3, active: 2
6081 09/30 18:41:01.919 voicemail database 0 Got connection: 3, inUse: 3, active:
  2
6081 09/30 18:41:01.920 voicemail message 0 1064947237095_0
6081 09/30 18:41:01.924 voicemail message "Creating Message" 1064947237095_0
6081 09/30 18:41:01.925 voicemail database "Database query results"
  0x000000037e11d61c 1064947237095_0,1,/sw/local/users/johndoe,f,f,5281,43258,
  1064947225155,null,16693,30-Sep-03 18:40:25 UTCh
6081 09/30 18:41:01.925 voicemail database 0 0x000000037e11d61c Freed connection:
  3, inUse: 3, active: 2
```

Because John Doe is the sender of the message, the voice mail system now has to retrieve details such as his spoken name and extension to play as part of the message's envelope information, as shown in Example 21-47.

Example 21-47 *System Retrieves and Plays the Sender's Information as Part of the Envelope*

```
cue#show trace buffer tail
6081 09/30 18:41:01.926 voicemail ldap 0 getAttributeValue:
  /sw/local/users/johndoe/TelephoneNumbers/primaryExtension
6081 09/30 18:41:01.926 voicemail ldap "getUserByPhoneNo" 6001
6081 09/30 18:41:01.929 voicemail ldap "getUserByPhoneNo: userDn."
  /sw/local/users/johndoe
6081 09/30 18:41:01.929 voicemail ldap 0 getAttributeValue:
  /sw/local/users/johndoe/Language/preferredLanguage
6081 09/30 18:41:01.929 voicemail ldap 0 getAttributeValue:
  /sw/local/users/johndoe/TelephoneNumbers/primaryExtension
6081 09/30 18:41:01.930 voicemail database 0 Got connection: 2, inUse: 3,
  active: 2
6081 09/30 18:41:01.931 voicemail database "SQL: " select mailboxid from vm
  _mbxusers where owner=true and userdn='/sw/local/users/johndoe';
6081 09/30 18:41:01.934 voicemail database "Database query results"
  PERSONAL_000000000000000000000022
6081 09/30 18:41:01.934 voicemail database 0 Freed connection: 2, inUse: 3,
  active: 2
6081 09/30 18:41:01.934 voicemail ldap "getUserByDn" /sw/local/users/johndoe
6081 09/30 18:41:01.934 voicemail ldap "normalizeDN" /sw/local/users/johndoe
6081 09/30 18:41:01.934 voicemail ldap 0 getAttributeValue:
  /sw/local/users/johndoe/TelephoneNumbers/primaryExtension
6081 09/30 18:41:01.935 voicemail ldap 0 getAttributeValue:
  /sw/local/users/johndoe/Language/preferredLanguage
6081 09/30 18:41:01.935 voicemail database 0 Got connection: 3, inUse: 3,
  active: 2
6081 09/30 18:41:01.936 voicemail database "SQL: " select mailboxid from vm
  _mbxusers where owner=true and userdn='/sw/local/users/johndoe';
6081 09/30 18:41:01.938 voicemail database "Database query results"
  PERSONAL_000000000000000000000022
6081 09/30 18:41:01.938 voicemail database 0 Freed connection: 3, inUse: 3,
  active: 2
6081 09/30 18:41:01.938 voicemail ldap "getSpokenNameByName: userDn."
  /sw/local/users/johndoe
6081 09/30 18:41:01.939 voicemail ldap "normalizeDN" /sw/local/users/johndoe
6081 09/30 18:41:01.939 voicemail ldap "getSpokenName: dn."
  uid=johndoe,ou=users,ou=branch123,o=cisco.com
5047 09/30 18:41:12.757 voicemail database 0 Got connection: 2, inUse: 3,
  active: 2
```

In the trace shown in Example 21-48 you can see the message entity of the voice mail system retrieving message object 16693 from the database. After Jane Doe listens to the message, she opts to delete it. In the traces shown in Example 21-48, you see that the message and large object are deleted, and the mailbox properties (for example, mailbox time remaining) are updated in the database. Then the user logs out of the mailbox.

Example 21-48   *User Listens to and Deletes the Message and Logs Out*

```
cue#show trace buffer tail
5047 09/30 18:41:12.757 voicemail message 16693 get
5047 09/30 18:41:12.757 voicemail database "Large object open" 16693 0
  0x000000037e11d61c
5047 09/30 18:41:12.758 voicemail database "Large object close" 0x000000037e11d61c
5047 09/30 18:41:12.758 voicemail database 0 0x000000037e11d61c Freed connection:
  2, inUse: 3, active: 2
6081 09/30 18:41:14.970 voicemail mailbox "Message deleted" 0x000000037e11d61c
  PERSONAL_00000000000000000000023,1064947237095_0
6081 09/30 18:41:14.970 voicemail database 0 Got connection: 3, inUse: 3,
  active: 2
6081 09/30 18:41:14.971 voicemail database "SQL: " 0x000000037e11d61c delete from
  vm_usermsg where messageid='1064947237095_0' and
  mailboxid='PERSONAL_00000000000000000000023';
6081 09/30 18:41:14.974 voicemail database "SQL: " 0x000000037e11d61c select
  usecount,messagelength,attachedmsgid, messageoid from vm_message where
  messageId='1064947237095_0' for update;
6081 09/30 18:41:14.977 voicemail database "Database query results"
  0x000000037e11d61c 1,5281,null,16693
6081 09/30 18:41:14.978 voicemail message "Deleting Message" 1064947237095_0
6081 09/30 18:41:14.978 voicemail database "SQL: " 0x000000037e11d61c delete from
  vm_message where messageid='1064947237095_0';
6081 09/30 18:41:14.982 voicemail database 16693 0x000000037e11d61c Deleted large
  object id:
6081 09/30 18:41:14.982 voicemail database "Commiting transaction"
  0x000000037e11d61c
6081 09/30 18:41:14.985 voicemail database 0 0x000000037e11d61c Freed connection:
  3, inUse: 3, active: 2
6081 09/30 18:41:14.985 voicemail database 0 Got connection: 2, inUse: 3,
  active: 2
6081 09/30 18:41:14.986 voicemail database "SQL: " 0x000000037e11d61c select
  totalmessagetime from vm_mailbox where mailboxid='PERSONAL
  _00000000000000000000023' for update;
6081 09/30 18:41:14.989 voicemail database "Database query results"
  0x000000037e11d61c 7690
6081 09/30 18:41:14.989 voicemail database "SQL: " 0x000000037e11d61c update vm
  _mailbox set totalmessagetime=2409 where mailboxid='PERSONAL
  _00000000000000000000023';
6081 09/30 18:41:14.993 voicemail database "Commiting transaction"
  0x000000037e11d61c
6081 09/30 18:41:14.995 voicemail database 0 Got connection: 3, inUse: 4,
  active: 2
6081 09/30 18:41:14.996 voicemail database "SQL: " 0x000000037e11d61c select
  count(*) from vm_usermsg where state=1 and mailboxid='PERSONAL
  _00000000000000000000023';
6081 09/30 18:41:14.999 voicemail database "Database query results"
  0x000000037e11d61c 0
6081 09/30 18:41:15.000 voicemail database 0 0x000000037e11d61c Freed connection:
  3, inUse: 4, active: 2
```

continues

Example 21-48 *User Listens to and Deletes the Message and Logs Out (Continued)*

```
6081 09/30 18:41:15.000 voicemail ldap 0 getAttributeValue:
  /sw/local/users/janedoe/TelephoneNumbers/primaryExtension
6081 09/30 18:41:15.031 voicemail database 0 0x000000037e11d61c Freed connection:
  2, inUse: 3, active: 2
6082 09/30 18:41:15.108 voicemail ldap "getUserByPhoneNo" 80016003
6082 09/30 18:41:15.112 voicemail ldap "getUserByPhoneNo: No entry found."
6082 09/30 18:41:15.200 voicemail database 0 Got connection: 3, inUse: 3,
  active: 2
6082 09/30 18:41:15.201 voicemail database "SQL: " 0x000000037e11d61c select *
  from vm_usermsg,vm_message where mailboxid='PERSONAL_00000000000000000000023'
  and vm_usermsg.messageid=vm_message.messageid;
6082 09/30 18:41:15.206 voicemail database 0 0x000000037e11d61c Freed connection:
  3, inUse: 3, active: 2
6082 09/30 18:41:20.357 voicemail mailbox "User logout" 0x000000037e11d61c
  /sw/local/users/janedoe
```

In a similar way, you can isolate any other voice mail back-end-related issues using the preceding **trace** commands and referring to the database schema. The Cisco UE Database Schema changes from one release to another as more features are added, but the basic nature of the schema and troubleshooting using the schema remain the same. The key to effective troubleshooting in this area is understanding what data is stored in which database.

Troubleshooting the Message Waiting Indicator

The message waiting indicator (MWI) is one of the most important and basic features of any voice mail system. Sometimes, because of many factors, the subscriber does not see the correct MWI changes on the phone. This could be because somehow Cisco CME and Cisco UE got out of sync with each other concerning the MWI status for subscribers. (For example, perhaps Cisco CME was reloaded and it does not keep track of MWI state across reloads.) This section discusses MWI configuration and troubleshooting MWI-related issues.

MWI Operation

With Cisco CME deployments, Cisco UE uses what is called a *callout* mechanism to change MWI status on the phone. In this mechanism, Cisco CME defines two special extensions: the MWI ON and MWI OFF DNs. These extension definitions have a very specific number format.

For example, the pattern can be 2222.... for the MWI ON DN and 2221.... for the MWI OFF DN, where 2222 and 2221 are prefixes, and the number of dots is equal to the length of the extensions in your Cisco CME dial plan. If Cisco UE must turn on MWI for extension 6001, it places an outgoing call to number 22226001. Cisco CME terminates the call on the MWI ON DN (because the called number matches the dial peer for the MWI ON DN). Cisco CME processes the called number of the call and extracts extension 6001 from it, which is matched by the four dots defined on the MWI ON DN. It then finds all the phones with appearances of extension 6001 on them (there can be several if 6001 is a shared line), and then sends an SCCP MWI ON message to each of the phones. A similar sequence of steps is followed to turn off an MWI lamp by Cisco UE outcalling to the MWI OFF DN. For example, 22216001 is used to turn off MWI for extension 6001.

You can test the operation of your MWI DNs on Cisco CME by dialing the MWI DN prefix followed by the extension from any phone. For example, if you dial 22226001 from any phone, you should see the MWI light activated on phones with extension 6001. This verifies that your MWI DNs are correctly configured and operational.

When you choose the patterns for MWI DNs, keep in mind that such a pattern must not overlap with any other extension or dial peer patterns configured on Cisco CME. Those configurations can interfere with the MWI calls that come from Cisco UE, effectively breaking MWI operation. Also look for any Cisco IOS translation rules that might translate the called numbers for the MWI DN call. This also breaks the MWI operation.

Now that you understand the mechanism between Cisco CME and Cisco UE for turning MWI on or off, the next step is to investigate what happens inside the Cisco UE software components to affect MWI when a voice message is left in or deleted from a mailbox.

When a new message is left in a mailbox, or a subscriber deletes the last new message in the mailbox, the voice mail system has to change the MWI state on the subscriber's phone. However, the voice mail back-end component does not have access to any call control mechanism to place the outcall to Cisco CME. Instead, it depends on the CRS component, which contains a SIP stack for call control. However, there is no direct interface between the voice mail back end and the CRS component.

The CRS component, as discussed in Chapter 3, can start applications on three kinds of triggers:

- E-mail
- HTTP
- Call

To affect MWI changes, the voice mail system (internally) sends an HTTP trigger to the CRS software. A system-level CRS application called ciscomwiapplication, with an associated script called setMWI.aef, exists and is configured to respond to this HTTP request.

When voice mail sends an HTTP request specifying the extension for MWI operation and the state to be set (ON or OFF), this CRS application starts up and places a call to the appropriate Cisco CME MWI ON or OFF DN using the parameters passed.

Verifying MWI Configuration

For MWI to work correctly, it is important that the configurations on Cisco CME and Cisco UE are correct and match. To verify the configuration, use the commands shown in Example 21-49.

Example 21-49 *MWI DN Configuration*

```
ccme#show telephony-service ephone-dn
ephone-dn 20
number 7701
preference 0 secondary 9
huntstop
call-forward busy 5800
call-forward noan 5800 timeout 10
hold-alert 30 originator

ephone-dn 21
number 7010
preference 0 secondary 9
huntstop

ephone-dn 22
number 7011
preference 0 secondary 9
huntstop
call-forward busy 5800
call-forward noan 5800 timeout 10

ephone-dn 23
number 7012
preference 0 secondary 9
huntstop

ephone-dn 50
number 2222....
preference 0 secondary 9
huntstop
mwi on

ephone-dn 51
number 2221....
preference 0 secondary 9
huntstop
mwi off

ephone-dn 61
number 6001
preference 0 secondary 9
huntstop
call-forward all 5800
call-forward busy 5800
call-forward noan 5800 timeout 10
```

On Cisco UE, ensure that the ciscomwiapplication CRS application is created and configured properly, as shown in Example 21-50.

Example 21-50 *MWI Application Configuration on Cisco UE*

```
cue#show ccn application
Name:                                    ciscomwiapplication
Description:                             ciscomwiapplication
Script:                                  setmwi.aef
ID number:                               0
Enabled:                                 yes
Maximum number of sessions:              1
strMWI_OFF_DN:                           2221
strMWI_ON_DN:                            2222
CallControlGroupID:                      0

Name:                                    voicemail
Description:                             voicemail
Script:                                  voicebrowser.aef
ID number:                               1
Enabled:                                 yes
Maximum number of sessions:              1
logoutUri:                               http://localhost/voicemail/vxmlscripts/m
bxLogout.jsp
uri:                                     http://localhost/voicemail/vxmlscripts/l
ogin.vxml

Name:                                    autoattendant
Description:                             autoattendant
Script:                                  aa.aef
ID number:                               2
Enabled:                                 yes
Maximum number of sessions:              1
MaxRetry:                                3
operExtn:                                7701
welcomePrompt:                           AAWelcome.wav

Name:                                    promptmgmt
Description:                             promptmgmt
Script:                                  promptmgmt.aef
ID number:                               3
Enabled:                                 yes
Maximum number of sessions:              1
```

You can also verify the current MWI DN settings in the Cisco UE sysDB settings, as shown in Example 21-51. Note that in the output of both the Cisco UE **show ccn application** (Example 21-50) and **show sysdb** (Example 21-51) commands, MWI DNs appear without the dots. This does not mean that they are without dots on Cisco CME. (See the output of the **show telephony-service ephone-dn** command shown earlier in Example 21-49.)

Example 21-51   *Verifying MWI DN Configuration on Cisco UE in sysDB*

```
cue#show sysdb /sw/apps/ccn/wf/applications/craAesop/applications/
  ciscomwiapplication
app/applicationId             0
app/applicationType           Cisco Script Application
app/description               ciscomwiapplication
app/enabled                   1
app/maxSessions               8
app/script                    setmwi.aef
app/aeAccess                  0
app/aeEnd                     1
cfgVars/strMWI_OFF_DN         2221
cfgVars/strMWI_ON_DN          2222
cfgVars/CallControlGroupID    0
cfgVarsType/strMWI_OFF_DN     java.lang.String
cfgVarsType/strMWI_ON_DN      java.lang.String
cfgVarsType/CallControlGroupID java.lang.Integer
```

There can be some inconsistency between the Cisco CME and Cisco UE MWI DN configurations if the Cisco CME configuration is changed directly through the Cisco CME GUI or via Cisco IOS CLI. If you see that an inconsistency exists, synchronize both configurations. You can achieve this by navigating to the **Administration > Synchronize Information** screen in the GUI, as shown in Figure 21-6.

If there are any inconsistencies between the Cisco CME and Cisco UE configurations with respect to MWI DNs or other fields, these are listed on the **Administration > Synchronize Information** page. You must synchronize the information on this screen for the MWI mechanism to work correctly. After you synchronize the information, the MWIs are not automatically refreshed at that time.

You can refresh the MWI states on subscribers' phones in two ways:

- You can refresh a particular subscriber's MWI using the **mwi refresh telephonenumber** *number* command in the Cisco UE CLI.

- You can refresh MWI for all the subscribers in your Cisco CME system using the **mwi refresh all** command.

You can perform both operations via the GUI by navigating to the **Voice Mail > Message Waiting Indicators > Refresh** screen.

NOTE   Cisco UE sends an MWI update every time there is a new message in a subscriber's mailbox, not just when there is a state change in a mailbox. Also, Cisco UE does not have the capability to synchronize MWI states automatically at a configured time (or midnight routines), so manual synchronization is a must in case the states get out of synchronization.

Figure 21-6 *Synchronizing MWI Information*

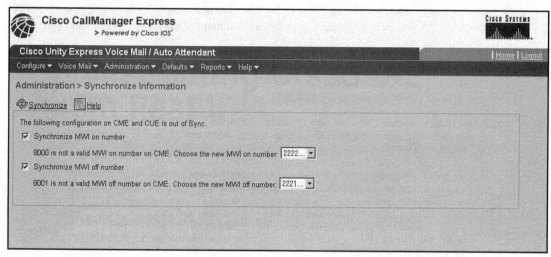

One other configuration that can affect MWI operation is the SIP gateway address configuration in Cisco UE. This should point to the Cisco CME with which Cisco UE is integrated. You can verify this setting by using the **show ccn subsystem sip** Cisco UE CLI command.

Tracing MWI

This section investigates which traces to turn on to troubleshoot MWI-related problems, as well as how to interpret the traces to verify that all the subsystems involved in MWI operation are working correctly. The following **trace** commands are used to troubleshoot problems in this area:

- **trace ccn stacksip dbug**
- **trace voicemail mwi all**
- **trace ccn managerappl dbug**
- **show trace buffer tail**

In the traces shown in Example 21-52, extension 5010 has received a new voice message, so the voice mail system sets the MWI state for this extension to true (the ON state). This action by the voice mail system results in an HTTP trigger being sent to the CRS software component, as discussed in the previous sections. In the third line in Example 21-52, you can see the HTTP message going to port 8080, passing the extension number (5010 in this example) and the desired state of the MWI (1 for ON).

Example 21-52   *Voice Mail Back End Sends an HTTP Trigger to Turn on MWI*

```
cue#show trace buffer tail
2487 10/01 14:26:54.309 voicemail mwi "setMessageWaiting" 0x0000000000000000 5010,
  true
2487 10/01 14:26:54.309 voicemail mwi " job state" adding job
1792 10/01 14:26:54.309 voicemail mwi "job state" http://localhost: 8080/
  mwiapp?extn=5010&state=1

2317 10/01 14:26:54.316 ACCN APMG 0 TASK_CREATED:Application task created:
  Application=App[name=ciscomwiapplication,type=Cisco Script Application,id=0,
  desc=ciscomwiapplication,enabled=true,max=8,valid=true,optional=[cfgVars=
  [Lcom.cisco.wfapi.util.WFNameValuePair;@6786a090,script=setmwi.aef]],Application
  Trigger=ContactApplicationTrigger[time=1065018436314,contact=HttpContact[id=54,
  type=Cisco Http Contact,implId=null,active=true,state=CONTACT_RECEIVED,
  inbound=true,handled=false,
  locale=en_US,aborting=false,app=App[name=ciscomwiapplication,type=Cisco Script
  Application,id=0,desc=ciscomwiapplication,enabled=true,max=8,valid=true,
  optional=[cfgVars=[Lcom.cisco.wfapi.util.WFNameValuePair;@6786a090,script=
  setmwi.aef]],task=null,session=null,seqNum=-1,time=1065018436314,req=org.apache.
  tomcat.facade.HttpServletRequestFacade@7ce36091]],Task id=16,000,000,031,Task
  Class=com.cisco.wfframework.engine.core.WFEngineWorkflowDebugTask,New Task
  Class=com.cisco.app.impl.WFWorkflowAppDebugTaskWrapper
2317 10/01 14:26:54.317 ACCN APMG 0 APP_SESSION_ACTIVE:Active application session:
  Application=App[name=ciscomwiapplication,type=Cisco Script Application,id=0,
  desc=ciscomwiapplication,enabled=true,max=8,valid=true,optional=[cfgVars=
  [Lcom.cisco.wfapi.util.WFNameValuePair;@6786a090,script=setmwi.aef]],Application
  Trigger=ContactApplicationTrigger[time=1065018436314,contact=HttpContact[id=54,
  type=Cisco Http
```

As shown in the preceding trace, CRS starts its outcalling application in response to the HTTP trigger received from the voice mail component. Example 21-53 is the step-by-step trace of the CRS application executing this operation.

Example 21-53   *MWI Application Starts Executing as a Result of the HTTP Trigger*

```
cue#show trace buffer tail
2317 10/01 14:26:54.318 ACCN APMG 0 EXECUTING_STEP:Executing a step:
  Application=App[name=ciscomwiapplication,type=Cisco Script Application,id=0,
  desc=ciscomwiapplication,enabled=true,max=8,valid=true,optional=[cfgVars=
  [Lcom.cisco.wfapi.util.WFNameValuePair;@6786a090,script=setmwi.aef]],Task
  id=16,000,000,031,Step id=0,Step Class=com.cisco.wfframework.steps.core.
  StepStart,Step Description=Start
2317 10/01 14:26:54.319 ACCN APMG 0 EXECUTING_STEP:Executing a step:
  Application=App[name=ciscomwiapplication,type=Cisco Script Application,id=0,
  desc=ciscomwiapplication,enabled=true,max=8,valid=true,optional=[cfgVars=
  [Lcom.cisco.wfapi.util.WFNameValuePair;@6786a090,script=setmwi.aef]],Task
```

Example 21-53 *MWI Application Starts Executing as a Result of the HTTP Trigger (Continued)*

```
    id=16,000,000,031,Step id=1,Step Class=com.cisco.wf.steps.ivr.AcceptStep,Step
    Description=Accept (contact: --Triggering Contact--)
2317 10/01 14:26:54.319 ACCN APMG 0 EXECUTING_STEP:Executing a step:
    Application=App[name=ciscomwiapplication,type=Cisco Script Application,id=0,
    desc=ciscomwiapplication,enabled=true,max=8,valid=true,optional=[cfgVars=
    [Lcom.cisco.wfapi.util.WFNameValuePair;@6786a090,script=setmwi.aef]],Task
    id=16,000,000,031,Step id=111,Step Class=com.cisco.wf.steps.http.
    GetHttpHeaderStep,Step Description=Get Http Contact Info (contact: --Triggering
    Contact--)
2317 10/01 14:26:54.320 ACCN APMG 0 EXECUTING_STEP:Executing a step:
    Application=App[name=ciscomwiapplication,type=Cisco Script Application,id=0,
    desc=ciscomwiapplication,enabled=true,max=8,valid=true,optional=[cfgVars=
    [Lcom.cisco.wfapi.util.WFNameValuePair;@6786a090,script=setmwi.aef]],Task
    id=16,000,000,031,Step id=142,Step Class=com.cisco.wfframework.steps.core.
    StepIf,Step Description=If ( mwistatus != "0" ) Then
2317 10/01 14:26:54.320 ACCN APMG 0 EXECUTING_STEP:Executing a step:
    Application=App[name=ciscomwiapplication,type=Cisco Script Application,id=0,
    desc=ciscomwiapplication,enabled=true,max=8,valid=true,optional=[cfgVars=
    [Lcom.cisco.wfapi.util.WFNameValuePair;@6786a090,script=setmwi.aef]],Task
    id=16,000,000,031,Step id=143,Step Class=com.cisco.wfframework.steps.core.
    StepAssign,Step Description=Set strMWI_DN = strMWI_ON_DN
2317 10/01 14:26:54.321 ACCN APMG 0 EXECUTING_STEP:Executing a step:
    Application=App[name=ciscomwiapplication,type=Cisco Script Application,id=0,
    desc=ciscomwiapplication,enabled=true,max=8,valid=true,optional=[cfgVars=
    [Lcom.cisco.wfapi.util.WFNameValuePair;@6786a090,script=setmwi.aef]],Task
    id=16,000,000,031,Step id=144,Step Class=com.cisco.wfframework.steps.core.
    StepAssign,Step Description=Set mwiOn = true
2317 10/01 14:26:54.321 ACCN APMG 0 EXECUTING_STEP:Executing a step:
    Application=App[name=ciscomwiapplication,type=Cisco Script Application,id=0,
    desc=ciscomwiapplication,enabled=true,max=8,valid=true,optional=[cfgVars=
    [Lcom.cisco.wfapi.util.WFNameValuePair;@6786a090,script=setmwi.aef]],Task
    id=16,000,000,031,Step id=78,Step Class=com.cisco.wfframework.steps.core.StepIf,
    Step Description=If ( mwistatus != "" ) Then
2317 10/01 14:26:54.322 ACCN APMG 0 EXECUTING_STEP:Executing a step:
    Application=App[name=ciscomwiapplication,type=Cisco Script Application,id=0,
    desc=ciscomwiapplication,enabled=true,max=8,valid=true,optional=[cfgVars=
    [Lcom.cisco.wfapi.util.WFNameValuePair;@6786a090,script=setmwi.aef]],Task
    id=16,000,000,031,Step id=83,Step Class=com.cisco.wfframework.steps.core.StepIf,
    Step Description=If ( strDeviceNum != "" ) Then
2317 10/01 14:26:54.322 ACCN APMG 0 EXECUTING_STEP:Executing a step:
    Application=App[name=ciscomwiapplication,type=Cisco Script Application,id=0,
    desc=ciscomwiapplication,enabled=true,max=8,valid=true,optional=[cfgVars=
    [Lcom.cisco.wfapi.util.WFNameValuePair;@6786a090,script=setmwi.aef]],Task
    id=16,000,000,031,Step id=84,Step Class=com.cisco.wfframework.steps.core.
    StepAssign,Step Description=Set strMWI_CompleteNum = strMWI_DN + strDeviceNum
2317 10/01 14:26:54.322 ACCN APMG 0 EXECUTING_STEP:Executing a step:
    Application=App[name=ciscomwiapplication,type=Cisco Script Application,id=0,
    desc=ciscomwiapplication,enabled=true,max=8,valid=true,optional=[cfgVars=
    [Lcom.cisco.wfapi.util.WFNameValuePair;@6786a090,script=setmwi.aef]],Task
    id=16,000,000,031,Step id=189,Step Class=com.cisco.wf.steps.ivr.MWIStep,Step
    Description=Set Message Waiting Indicator (DN: strDeviceNum)
```

continues

Example 21-53 *MWI Application Starts Executing as a Result of the HTTP Trigger (Continued)*

```
2317 10/01 14:26:54.323 ACCN APMG 0 EXECUTING_STEP:Executing a step:
  Application=App[name=ciscomwiapplication,type=Cisco Script Application,id=0,
  desc=ciscomwiapplication,enabled=true,max=8,valid=true,optional=[cfgVars=
  [Lcom.cisco.wfapi.util.WFNameValuePair;@6786a090,script=setmwi.aef]],Task
  id=16,000,000,031,Step id=193,Step Class=com.cisco.wfframework.steps.core.
  StepComment,Step Description=/* Don't return fail since ... */
2317 10/01 14:26:54.323 ACCN APMG 0 EXECUTING_STEP:Executing a step:
  Application=App[name=ciscomwiapplication,type=Cisco Script Application,id=0,
  desc=ciscomwiapplication,enabled=true,max=8,valid=true,optional=[cfgVars=
  [Lcom.cisco.wfapi.util.WFNameValuePair;@6786a090,script=setmwi.aef]],Task
  id=16,000,000,031,Step id=175,Step Class=com.cisco.wf.steps.ivr.CreateCallStep,
  Step Description=Place Call (to strMWI_CompleteNum )
2317 10/01 14:26:54.329 ACCN SIPL 0 --- send message --- to 1.3.6.29:5060
```

As a result of the last step, which sets up a call to the value contained in strMWI_CompleteNum, you can see in the traces shown in Example 21-54 that a SIP INVITE message is sent from Cisco UE to Cisco CME to change the state of the MWI lamp.

Example 21-54 *Application Execution Results in a SIP Outcall to Cisco CME*

```
cue#trace ccn stacksip dbug
cue#show trace buffer tail
INVITE sip:22225010@1.3.6.29;user=phone SIP/2.0
Via: SIP/2.0/UDP 1.3.6.129:5060
From: "Cisco SIP Channel5" <sip:outbound-0@1.3.6.29>;tag=5bed1e99-272
To: <sip:22225010@1.3.6.29;user=phone>
Call-ID: c91b8616-270@1.3.6.129:5060
CSeq: 51 INVITE
Contact: sip:outbound-0@1.3.6.129:5060
User-Agent: Jasmin UA / ver 1.1
Accept: application/sdp
Content-Type: application/sdp
Content-Length: 216

v=0
o=CiscoSystemsSIP-Workflow-App-UserAgent 2792 2792 IN IP4 1.3.6.129
s=SIP Call
c=IN IP4 1.3.6.129
t=0 0
m=audio 16906 RTP/AVP 0 111
a=rtpmap:0 pcmu/8000
a=rtpmap:111 telephone-event/8000
a=fmtp:111 0-11

2272 10/01 14:26:54.335 ACCN SIPL 0 receive 357 from 1.3.6.29:5060
2273 10/01 14:26:54.336 ACCN SIPL 0 not found header for Date
2273 10/01 14:26:54.336 ACCN SIPL 0 not found header for Allow-Events
2273 10/01 14:26:54.336 ACCN SIPL 0 -------
SIP/2.0 100 Trying
Via: SIP/2.0/UDP 1.3.6.129:5060
From: "Cisco SIP Channel5" <sip:outbound-0@1.3.6.29>;tag=5bed1e99-272
```

Example 21-54 *Application Execution Results in a SIP Outcall to Cisco CME (Continued)*

```
To: <sip:22225010@1.3.6.29;user=phone>;tag=EFCE8-E51
Date: Fri, 01 Mar 2002 00:16:22 GMT
Call-ID: c91b8616-270@1.3.6.129:5060
Server: Cisco-SIPGateway/IOS-12.x
CSeq: 51 INVITE
Allow-Events: telephone-event
Content-Length: 0
```

In the traces shown in Example 21-55, Cisco CME sends a 1 "80 Ringing" message to Cisco UE, indicating that the call terminated on a valid MWI DN and that the MWI request is being processed.

Example 21-55 *MWI Call Goes to Alerting State and Disconnects*

```
cue#trace ccn stacksip dbug
cue#show trace buffer tail
SIP/2.0 180 Ringing
Via: SIP/2.0/UDP 1.3.6.129:5060
From: "Cisco SIP Channel5" <sip:outbound-0@1.3.6.29>;tag=5bed1e99-272
To: <sip:22225010@1.3.6.29;user=phone>;tag=EFCE8-E51
Date: Fri, 01 Mar 2002 00:16:22 GMT
Call-ID: c91b8616-270@1.3.6.129:5060
Server: Cisco-SIPGateway/IOS-12.x
CSeq: 51 INVITE
Allow: UPDATE
Allow-Events: telephone-event
Contact: <sip:22225010@1.3.6.29:5060>
Content-Length: 0

.........
CANCEL sip:22225010@1.3.6.29;user=phone SIP/2.0
Via: SIP/2.0/UDP 1.3.6.129:5060
From: "Cisco SIP Channel5" <sip:outbound-0@1.3.6.29>;tag=5bed1e99-272
To: <sip:22225010@1.3.6.29;user=phone>
Call-ID: c91b8616-270@1.3.6.129:5060
CSeq: 51 CANCEL
Max-Forwards: 50
Content-Length: 0
```

At this point, Cisco UE has finished notifying Cisco CME about a change in MWI status. It is now the responsibility of the Cisco CME call control software to complete the MWI notification to the IP phone to turn the lamp on or off. To troubleshoot this portion of the transaction, turn on the **debug ephone mwi** or **debug ephone detail** traces in Cisco IOS software. The traces in Example 21-56 show the SCCP messages sent by Cisco CME to the phone(s) for turning MWI on and off.

Example 21-56 *SIP Outcall from Cisco UE Results in an SCCP MWI Message to the IP Phone*

```
ccme#debug ephone state
ccme#debug ephone mwi
...........
Jun 11 05:51:57.663: calling [private] called [22225010]
Jun 11 05:51:57.663: SkinnyTryCall to 5010 instance 1 start at 0SkinnyTryCall to
  5010 instance 1 match DN 1
Jun 11 05:51:57.663: Phone 0 DN 1 MWI on 0 messages
Jun 11 05:51:57.667: ephone-1[1]:Set MWI line 1 to ON count 0
Jun 11 05:51:57.667: ephone-1[1]:Set MWI line 0 to ON count 0
Jun 11 05:51:57.667: UpdateCallState DN 10 chan 1 operating in mode 1
Jun 11 05:52:01.874: ephone-1[1]:ONHOOK (internal)
Jun 11 05:52:01.874: ephone-1[1]:call clean up this DN 1 chan 1 was calling other
  DN -1 chan 1
Jun 11 05:52:01.874: this ephone-1 other ephone-(-1) other DN state UNKNOWN
Jun 11 05:52:01.878: ephone-1[1]:CloseReceive
Jun 11 05:52:01.878: ephone-1[1]:StopMedia
Jun 11 05:52:01.878: DN 1 chan 1 End Voice_Mode
Jun 11 05:52:01.878: ephone-1[1]:SetCallState line 1 DN 1 chan 1 ref 13 TsOnHook
Jun 11 05:52:01.882: ephone-1[1]:SpeakerPhoneOnHook
Jun 11 05:52:01.886: ephone-1[1]:SpeakerPhoneOnHook
```

Troubleshooting Voice Mail VPIM Networking

Chapter 10, "Cisco IPC Express Integrated Voice Mail," explained Cisco UE support for voice mail networking using Voice Profile for Internet Mail (VPIM). It interworks with other Cisco UE systems and Cisco Unity systems in a network. This section discusses some common problems faced in deploying this feature and how to troubleshoot and fix them.

Cannot Send and Receive Network Messages from a Location

If you notice that you cannot send or receive any messages from a particular location, a probable cause is that the local location ID is not configured in the system. Until you configure this on a Cisco UE system, voice mail networking is not enabled. If you are trying to send a network message from a system where a local location ID is not configured, the system plays the prompt "Sorry. The extension you requested is not available." You can verify whether you have configured a local location by using the Cisco UE CLI shown in Example 21-57.

Example 21-57 *Displaying Network Locations*

```
cue#show network locations
ID          NAME                        ABBREV  DOMAIN
303         'Boston'                    BOS     cueunity.cisco.com
401         'Bangalore'                 BAN     bang.cue.cisco.com
201         'Los Angeles'               LAX     lax.cue.cisco.com

Local location id:
```

In Example 21-57, the local location ID is empty, which indicates that voice mail networking is disabled. You can configure this parameter using the following CLI to set the local location ID to 401:

```
cue(config)#network local location id 401
```

Cannot Send Messages to Cisco Unity

Assume that you have a network with a centralized Cisco Unity at the main campus site, smaller offices with Cisco UEs, and voice mail networking configured between all the sites. You may be able to send messages between the Cisco UE sites and send a message from Cisco Unity to Cisco UE, but you are unable to send a message from Cisco UE to Cisco Unity.

The reason for this problem may be that the sending Cisco UE site is configured in the same domain as that of the Cisco Unity system. The Microsoft Exchange server used by Cisco Unity does not allow other VPIM locations to be in the same domain as itself. For example, the network location configuration shown in Example 21-58 does not work if iptel.cisco.com points to a Cisco Unity server.

Example 21-58   *Erroneous DNS Configuration for Cisco Unity*

```
cue#show network locations
ID       NAME                         ABBREV  DOMAIN
303      'Boston'                     BOS     iptel.cisco.com
401      'Bangalore'                  BAN     bang.iptel.cisco.com
201      'Los Angeles'                LAX     lax.iptel.cisco.com
```

Separating the domains for the Cisco UE and Cisco Unity systems fixes the problem, as shown in Example 21-59.

Example 21-59   *Correct DNS Configuration for Cisco Unity*

```
cue#show network locations
ID       NAME                         ABBREV  DOMAIN
303      'Boston'                     BOS     bos.iptel.cisco.com
401      'Bangalore'                  BAN     bang.cue.cisco.com
201      'Los Angeles'                LAX     lax.cue.cisco.com
```

When deploying Cisco UE and Cisco Unity voice mail networking, remember that DNS is mandatory in such a network. Cisco Unity is not supported in a network where DNS service is unavailable. It is important that all the network locations on Cisco UE and Cisco Unity be configured using host names and domain names, not explicit IP addresses. If you have a network of Cisco UEs only, you can use explicit IP addresses or DNS host names in network location configurations. This alternative configuration eliminates the dependency on DNS service or DNS cache consistency for voice mail networking.

Unable to Address Messages to Network Locations

There may be occasions when users are unable to address messages to network locations. The Cisco UE system plays a message informing the user that the extension he or she dialed is unavailable. The probable reason for this issue is a misconfiguration in the network location setting with respect to extension lengths. For example, if you have accidentally configured an extension length of 3 for a location where the actual extension length is 4, the system responds with this message when a user addresses a message with a four digit extension. You can verify the configuration as shown in Example 21-60.

Example 21-60 *Displaying Location Details*

```
BANG#show network detail location id 201
Name:                          Los Angeles
Abbreviation:                  LAX
Email domain:                  lax.cue.cisco.com
Minimum extension length:      4
Maximum extension length:      4
Phone prefix:
VPIM encoding:                 G711ulaw
Send spoken name:              enabled
Sent msg count:                1
Received msg count:            0
```

Troubleshooting Nondelivery Receipts

When you send voice mail messages to different networked locations, you might receive nondelivery receipts (NDRs) for many reasons. When you listen to the NDR, it describes why that particular message could not be delivered.

The following sections discuss the most common reasons why a message cannot be delivered. It also covers how to identify the underlying problem and correct it.

Invalid Extension at the Receiving System

The invalid extension error at the receiving system occurs when a message is sent to an extension that does not exist on the destination system's configuration. You can verify whether the extension the message is addressed to is available on the destination system by checking the extension in the mailbox page of the Cisco UE GUI.

Another reason you might run into this situation is that in your network location configuration for the recipient location, you might have configured **voicemail extension-length min** and **voicemail extension-length max**. If this is the configuration, and the user dials the wrong length for a location and extension when addressing the message, Cisco UE cannot detect that until the message reaches the destination system. So the message is sent anyway, resulting in an invalid extension NDR from the destination system. For example, assume that you have a location called Boston where all the extensions are four digits in length. At another location in the network, such as Los Angeles, you have a configuration for the Boston location, as shown in Example 21-61.

Example 21-61 *Extension Length Configuration for Boston Location*

```
cue#show running-config
network location id 303
 abbreviation "BOS"
 email domain cueunity.cisco.com
 name "Boston"
 voicemail extension-length min 3 max 10
 end location
```

This configuration allows users to address a network message to location 303 (Boston) with any strings of digits between three and ten digits in length, even though all the extensions in Boston are four digits long. So if a user makes a mistake in addressing the message, the sending system cannot detect it. You should use the minimum and maximum extension length configuration if you have mixed-length extensions. Otherwise, it is recommended that you use a fixed-extension-length value to minimize addressing errors.

Remote Location Is Unavailable

The destination location may be unavailable for a few reasons, including the following:

- The Cisco UE system is offline for an extended period of time.
- The network link serving the location may be down.

A simple IP **ping** test can confirm the network status.

DNS Service Is Unavailable and Local DNS Cache Is Inconsistent

If you are using host and domain names in your network location configurations, the availability of DNS service is compulsory to send messages across the network. Cisco UE has a DNS cache, so even if the DNS server on the network is unavailable for a brief period, Cisco UE should still be able to send messages to remote locations as long as the cache is consistent and has entries for the location the message is addressed to.

You can verify the availability of a DNS server using IP **ping**. Cisco UE checks the Mail Exchange (MX) DNS record for a remote location, so it is important that an MX record and a normal DNS record are available for the remote location. You can check Cisco UE's DNS cache by using the **show ip dns** cache command, shown in Example 21-62, to check the consistency of the entries.

Example 21-62 *Displaying DNS Cache*

```
BANG#show ip dns cache
BANG.localdomain.       2147483647 IN A         1.4.13.90
1.0.0.127.in-addr.arpa. 2147483647 IN PTR          localhost.
localhost.       2147483647 IN A          127.0.0.1
90.13.4.1.in-addr.arpa. 2147483647 IN PTR          BANG.localdomain.
lax.cue.cisco.com.       3600 IN MX          10 lax.cue.cisco.com.
lax.cue.cisco.com.       3600 IN A          1.4.14.134
```

If the IP address of the remote Cisco UE has changed since this cache was last updated, voice mail messages cannot be sent to this location. As soon as the DNS server is again available, you can use the **clear ip dns cache** command to clear the cache, and build a new one with updated values.

Recipient Mailbox at the Remote Location Is Full or Disabled

If the recipient's mailbox is full or disabled, an NDR is generated by the destination Cisco UE system. You can check mailbox usage by using the CLI discussed in the section "Common Voice Mail **show** Commands."

Recipient Location Has No Configuration for the Sending Location

For successful operation of Cisco UE voice mail networking, it is important that each location know about every other location in the network. For security reasons, Cisco UE does not accept any incoming messages from an IP address or host name that is not present in its network location configuration. You can verify the location configuration by using the **show network locations** command.

Tracing Voice Mail Networking

The preceding sections discussed common problems and their solutions. This section demonstrates how to debug voice mail networking with tracing. Voice mail networking is implemented using VPIM, which in turn uses Simple Mail Transfer Protocol (SMTP) for message transfer.

When you troubleshoot, a basic understanding of SMTP is helpful. Example 21-63 shows the output of a networking trace in which a message was sent to a nonexistent mailbox and an NDR was received by the sending system. The first half of the trace shows a voice mail message being sent from extension 5501 at the sending location to extension 9008 at the receiving side. The second half of the trace shows an NDR coming back from the remote location to 5501 with a **mailbox full** reason. The important information to look for while troubleshooting is as follows (also highlighted in the trace output):

- The EHLO SMTP message sent and received by the systems.
- The MAIL FROM and RCPT TO headers, which identify the sender and recipient's information.
- The From and To VPIM headers.
- The VPIM message ID. This is a globally unique message ID that can be useful in troubleshooting on the receiving side.
- The vCard information sent and received. This is useful in Cisco UE release 2.1 and later when the vCard information is cached on the receiving system to identify remote users.

- The encoding format for the audio message. This can be G.711 or G.726 (32-KB Adaptive Differential Pulse Code Modulation [ADPCM]).

- In the NDR message delivery, the NDR status that gives the reason why the message could not be delivered.

Example 21-63   *Tracing Voice Mail Networking*

```
cue#trace networking smtp all
cue#trace networking vpim send
cue#trace networking vpim receive
cue#show trace buffer tail
Press <CTRL-C> to exit...
6018 12/26 22:56:50.091 netw smtp 3 192.168.0.200
6018 12/26 22:56:50.106 netw smtp 4
6018 12/26 22:56:50.129 netw smtp 6 220 192.168.0.200 Simple Mail Transfer Service
  Ready
6018 12/26 22:56:50.129 netw smtp 5 EHLO
6018 12/26 22:56:50.137 netw smtp 6 250-192.168.0.200 (Cisco Unity Express)
6018 12/26 22:56:50.137 netw smtp 6 250-X-VPIM-Wave
6018 12/26 22:56:50.139 netw smtp 6 250-DSN NOTIFY
6018 12/26 22:56:50.141 netw smtp 6 250 SIZE
6018 12/26 22:56:50.714 netw smtp 5 MAIL FROM 5501@192.168.0.100
6018 12/26 22:56:50.729 netw smtp 6 250 ok
6018 12/26 22:56:50.730 netw smtp 5 RCPT TO 9008@192.168.0.200
6018 12/26 22:56:50.736 netw smtp 6 250 ok
6018 12/26 22:56:50.737 netw smtp 5 DATA
6018 12/26 22:56:50.743 netw smtp 6 354 Start mail input; end with <CRLF>.<CRLF>
6018 12/26 22:56:50.750 netw vpim 3 VPIM
6018 12/26 22:56:50.793 netw vpim 3 VPIM: To: <9008@192.168.0.200>
6018 12/26 22:56:50.811 netw vpim 3 VPIM: From: Auto SubOne<5501@192.168.0.100>
6018 12/26 22:56:50.867 netw vpim 3 VPIM: Date: Sun, 26 Dec 2004 22:56:49 -0800
  (PST)
6018 12/26 22:56:50.867 netw vpim 3 VPIM: MIME-Version: 1.0 (Voice 2.0)
6018 12/26 22:56:50.867 netw vpim 3 VPIM: Content-Type: Multipart/Voice-Message;
  Version=2.0;
6018 12/26 22:56:50.867 netw vpim 3 VPIM:       Boundary="==VpimMsg==1104130610745"
6018 12/26 22:56:50.868 netw vpim 3 VPIM: Content-Transfer-Encoding: 7bit
6018 12/26 22:56:50.868 netw vpim 3 VPIM: Message-ID:
  <JAB054980L7-NM-JAD06390I66-1104130214514>
6018 12/26 22:56:50.869 netw vpim 3 VPIM:
6018 12/26 22:56:50.872 netw vpim 3 VPIM: --==VpimMsg==1104130610745
6018 12/26 22:56:50.872 netw vpim 3 VPIM: Content-Type: text/directory;
  charset=us-ascii; profile=vCard
6018 12/26 22:56:50.872 netw vpim 3 VPIM: Content-Transfer-Encoding: 7bit
6018 12/26 22:56:50.873 netw vpim 3 VPIM: Content-Disposition: attachment;
  filename="Auto SubOne.vcf"
6018 12/26 22:56:50.873 netw vpim 3 VPIM:
6018 12/26 22:56:50.873 netw vpim 3 VPIM: BEGIN:vCard
6018 12/26 22:56:50.873 netw vpim 3 VPIM: FN:Auto SubOne
6018 12/26 22:56:50.874 netw vpim 3 VPIM: EMAIL;TYPE=INTERNET;
  TYPE=VPIM:5501@192.168.0.100
6018 12/26 22:56:50.874 netw vpim 3 VPIM: TEL:5501
6018 12/26 22:56:50.874 netw vpim 3 VPIM: VERSION: 3.0
```

continues

Example 21-63 *Tracing Voice Mail Networking (Continued)*

```
6018 12/26 22:56:50.874 netw vpim 3 VPIM: END:vCard
6018 12/26 22:56:50.874 netw vpim 3 VPIM:
6018 12/26 22:56:50.909 netw vpim 3 VPIM: --==VpimMsg==1104130610745
6018 12/26 22:56:50.909 netw vpim 3 VPIM: Content-Type: Audio/x-wav
6018 12/26 22:56:50.909 netw vpim 3 VPIM: Content-Transfer-Encoding: Base64
6018 12/26 22:56:50.910 netw vpim 3 VPIM: Content-Description: VPIM Message
6018 12/26 22:56:50.910 netw vpim 3 VPIM: Content-Disposition: inline;
  voice=Voice-Message
6018 12/26 22:56:50.910 netw vpim 3 VPIM: Content-ID:
  JAB054980L7-NM-JAD06390I66-1104130214514
6018 12/26 22:56:50.910 netw vpim 3 VPIM:
6018 12/26 22:56:51.124 netw vpim 3 VPIM:
6018 12/26 22:56:51.125 netw vpim 3 VPIM: --==VpimMsg==1104130610745--
6018 12/26 22:56:51.143 netw smtp 5 End of DATA
6018 12/26 22:56:54.230 netw smtp 6 250 2.6.0 Message queued for delivery
5762 12/26 22:56:55.242 netw smtp 2
5762 12/26 22:56:55.247 netw smtp 3 socket hostName: 192.168.0.200,
  hostAddress: 192.168.0.200
5762 12/26 22:56:55.248 netw smtp 3 hostname: 192.168.0.200 found in good address
  cache
5762 12/26 22:56:55.255 netw smtp 1
6023 12/26 22:56:55.257 netw smtp 5 Initial connection message
6023 12/26 22:56:55.269 netw smtp 6 UNKNOWN: EHLO 192.168.0.200
6023 12/26 22:56:55.269 netw smtp 5 250-192.168.0.100
6023 12/26 22:56:55.774 netw smtp 6 EHLO : MAIL FROM: <9008@192.168.0.200>
6023 12/26 22:56:55.777 netw smtp 5 250 ok
6023 12/26 22:56:55.791 netw smtp 6 MAIL FROM:: RCPT TO: <5501@192.168.0.100>
6023 12/26 22:56:55.792 netw smtp 5 250 ok
6023 12/26 22:56:55.797 netw smtp 6 RCPT TO:: DATA
6023 12/26 22:56:55.797 netw smtp 5 354 Start data
6023 12/26 22:56:55.895 netw vpim 4 VPIM: To: <5501@192.168.0.100>
6023 12/26 22:56:55.896 netw vpim 4 VPIM: From: <9008@192.168.0.200>
6023 12/26 22:56:55.897 netw vpim 4 VPIM: Date: Sun, 26 Dec 2004 22:56:49 -0800 (PST)
6023 12/26 22:56:55.900 netw vpim 4 VPIM: MIME-Version: 1.0 (Voice 2.0)
6023 12/26 22:56:55.902 netw vpim 4 VPIM: Content-Type: Multipart/report;
  report-type=delivery-status;Boundary="==VpimNdrMsg==1104187978982"
6023 12/26 22:56:55.906 netw vpim 4 VPIM: Message-ID:
  <JAB054980L7-NM-JAD06390I66-1104130214514@192.168.0.200>
6023 12/26 22:56:55.907 netw vpim 4 VPIM:
6023 12/26 22:56:55.910 netw vpim 4 VPIM: --==VpimNdrMsg==1104187978982
6023 12/26 22:56:55.919 netw vpim 4 NDR: Content-Type: text/plain
6023 12/26 22:56:55.920 netw vpim 4 NDR:
6023 12/26 22:56:55.921 netw vpim 4 NDR: Your message could not be delivered
6023 12/26 22:56:55.922 netw vpim 4 NDR:
6023 12/26 22:56:55.924 netw vpim 4 NDR: --==VpimNdrMsg==1104187978982
6023 12/26 22:56:55.925 netw vpim 4 NDR: Content-Type: message/delivery-status
6023 12/26 22:56:56.029 netw vpim 4 NDR:
6023 12/26 22:56:56.031 netw vpim 4 NDR: Reporting-MTA: dns; CUE
6023 12/26 22:56:56.033 netw vpim 4 NDR: Original-Recipient: rfc822; 9008@192.168.0.200
6023 12/26 22:56:56.034 netw vpim 4 NDR: Final-Recipient: rfc822; 9008@192.168.0.200
6023 12/26 22:56:56.036 netw vpim 4 NDR: Action: failed
```

Example 21-63 *Tracing Voice Mail Networking (Continued)*

```
6023 12/26 22:56:56.038 netw vpim 4 NDR: Status: 5.1.1 (Mailbox does not exist)
6023 12/26 22:56:56.043 netw vpim 4 NDR: Last-Attempt-Date: Sun, 26 Dec 2004
  22:56:49 -0800 (PST)
6023 12/26 22:56:56.044 netw vpim 4 NDR:
6023 12/26 22:56:56.046 netw vpim 4 NDR: --==VpimNdrMsg==1104187978982
6023 12/26 22:56:56.047 netw vpim 4 NDR: Content-type: Message/RFC822
6023 12/26 22:56:56.048 netw vpim 4 VPIM: Content-Transfer-Encoding: 7bit
6023 12/26 22:56:56.050 netw vpim 4 VPIM:
6023 12/26 22:56:56.051 netw vpim 4 VPIM: To: <9008@192.168.0.200>
6023 12/26 22:56:56.053 netw vpim 4 VPIM: From: <5501@192.168.0.100>
6023 12/26 22:56:56.054 netw vpim 4 VPIM: Date: Sun, 26 Dec 2004 22:56:49 -0800
  (PST)
6023 12/26 22:56:56.058 netw vpim 4 VPIM: MIME-Version: 1.0 (Voice 2.0)
6023 12/26 22:56:56.059 netw vpim 4 VPIM: Content-Type: Multipart/Voice-Message;
  Version=2.0;Boundary="==VpimMsg==1104187979064"
6023 12/26 22:56:56.061 netw vpim 4 VPIM: Content-Transfer-Encoding: 7bit
6023 12/26 22:56:56.063 netw vpim 4 VPIM: Message-ID:
  <JAB054980L7-NM-JAD06390I66-1104130214514>
6023 12/26 22:56:56.064 netw vpim 4 VPIM:
6023 12/26 22:56:56.066 netw vpim 4 VPIM: --==VpimMsg==1104187979064
6023 12/26 22:56:56.070 netw vpim 4 VPIM: Content-Type: Audio/32KADPCM
6023 12/26 22:56:56.071 netw vpim 4 VPIM: Content-Transfer-Encoding: Base64
6023 12/26 22:56:56.073 netw vpim 4 VPIM: Content-Description: VPIM Message
6023 12/26 22:56:56.084 netw vpim 4 VPIM: Content-Disposition: inline;
  voice=Voice-Message
6023 12/26 22:56:56.085 netw vpim 4 VPIM: Content-ID:
  JAB054980L7-NM-JAD06390I66-1104130214514
6023 12/26 22:56:56.144 netw vpim 5 83787
6023 12/26 22:56:56.144 netw vpim 8
6023 12/26 22:56:56.496 netw vpim 6 16074
6023 12/26 22:56:57.228 netw vpim 6 15446
6023 12/26 22:56:57.457 netw vpim 10
6023 12/26 22:56:57.602 netw vpim 4 VPIM: --==VpimMsg==1104187979064--
6023 12/26 22:56:57.603 netw vpim 4 VPIM: --==VpimNdrMsg==1104187978982--
6023 12/26 22:56:57.621 netw vpim 4 NDR: .
6023 12/26 22:56:58.000 netw smtp 5 260 Message queued
6023 12/26 22:56:58.016 netw smtp 6 DATA: RSET
6023 12/26 22:56:58.017 netw smtp 6 RSET: QUIT
6023 12/26 22:56:58.017 netw smtp 5 221 closing channel
```

Summary

This chapter covered voice mail problems. Cisco UE commands to verify the system's voice mail configuration were given, and various GUI-related issues were discussed. The call handoff interface between Cisco CME and the Cisco UE application was covered to illustrate how potential problems in this area may be investigated. The operation of the voice browser, interpreting traces of TUI sessions, and MWI issues were discussed. Numerous examples showed which traces to turn on and how to interpret the fields in the output.

Cisco IPC Express Features, Releases, and Ordering Information

The first part of this appendix lists the more common features available in Cisco CallManager Express (CME) 3.2.2 and Cisco Unity Express (UE) 2.1. The second part is a quick guide to ordering a Cisco IPC Express system.

Cisco IPC Express Features and Releases

Highlights of the Cisco CME and UE features are described in this section. For more explanation of the features and how they function, refer to the system administrator guides at Cisco.com:

- **Cisco CME**—http://www.cisco.com/go/ccme
- **Cisco UE**—http://www.cisco.com/go/cue

Cisco CME Feature Overview

The Cisco IOS releases corresponding to the more recent versions of Cisco CME are

- 3.0—12.3(4)T
- 3.1—12.3(7)T
- 3.2—12.3.11T
- 3.2.1—12.3.11XL
- 3.2.2—12.3.11XL1

The Cisco CME features are divided into the categories of system, call processing and phone, attendant phone, administrative, call coverage, network, and Public Switched Telephone Network (PSTN) trunking. These categories are described in the following sections.

System Features

Cisco CME system features include

- Account codes and call detail record (CDR) field entry
- Station message detail recording (SMDR)/CDR support

Call Processing and Phone Features

Cisco CME call processing and phone features are as follows:

- Cisco CME supports the following Cisco IP phone types:
  - Single-line phones—7902G, 7905G, 7910G, 7912G
  - Wireless 802.11b phone—7920
  - Conference phones—7935G, 7936G
  - Multi-button phones—7940G, 7960G, 7970G
  - Cisco IP Communicator softphone
- Secondary dial tone
- Last number redial
- Caller ID display (on display phones)
- Caller ID blocking
- Call hold
- Call waiting (with beep suppression)
- Call transfer (consultative and blind)
- Call forward on busy, no-answer, unconditional (all)
- Call forward all digit restriction
- Call park
- Call pickup of ringing and on-hold extensions
- Call pickup local group
- Call pickup explicit group
- Call back busy subscriber/camp-on
- Time of day, day of week, call blocking
- Do not disturb
- Do not disturb, divert call to voice mail
- Auto line selection on multi-button phones
- Three-party ad hoc conferencing (requires additional transcoding digital signal processor [DSP] for conferencing compressed voice over IP [VoIP] G.729 calls)
- Convert conference to call transfer
- Shared lines
- Silent and feature ring options
- Intercom
- Paging

- Call back busy subscriber
- System and station speed dial
- Fast dial
- Directory services (display phone)
- Directory of missed, received, and dialed calls
- Local directory lookup
- On-hook dialing
- XML phone application support
- Message waiting indication (MWI)
- Music on hold (internal or external)
- Transcoding of G.729 streams to G.711
- International language support (on the display phones):
  - Danish
  - Dutch
  - English
  - French
  - German
  - Italian
  - Japanese
  - Norwegian
  - Portuguese
  - Russian
  - Spanish
  - Swedish
- Private branch exchange (PBX) and Key System operation modes
- Direct PSTN line selection (private line)

Attendant Phone Features

Cisco CME attendant phone features include

- Busy lamp field (monitor line)
- Direct station select
- Night service bell
- Cisco 7914 14-button expansion module (up to two per phone)

Administrative Features

Cisco CME administrative features include

- After-hours call blocking and override
- Call forwarding restriction control
- Trunk-to-trunk call transfer control
- Called number restrictions
- Web browser graphical user interface (GUI)
- Automatic enrollment of new IP phones (optional)
- Three-level GUI access, including a customizable end-user administration level
- Telephony service setup wizard
- Softkey customization

Call Coverage Features

Cisco CME call coverage features include

- Hunt groups (sequential, parallel, and longest idle)
- Caller ID for hunt groups
- Shared lines
- Overlay lines (with called-name display)
- Basic (three queues) automatic call distribution (ACD)
- Dialed number identification service (DNIS) called-name display

Network Features

Cisco CME network features include

- H.323 networking
- End-to-end call transfer (H.450.2) and forwarding (H.450.3) using H.450 across H.323 networks
- H.450.2 and H.450.3 proxy function
- H.450.12 capabilities exchange
- Selective H.323 gatekeeper registration
- Session Initiation Protocol (SIP) trunking
- Cisco CallManager H.323 interoperability

- Skinny Call Control Protocol (SCCP) to RFC 2833 dual-tone multifrequency (DTMF) support
- SIP refer and redirect support for transfer and forwarding within a SIP network
- Message waiting indication relay
- Remote Authentication Dial-In User Service (RADIUS) integration

PSTN Trunking Features

Cisco CME PSTN trunking features include

- Caller ID, automatic number identification (ANI), and calling name
- Direct inward dial and direct outward dial
- Analog interfaces:
    — Foreign Exchange Office (FXO), Foreign Exchange Station (FXS), ear and mouth (E&M), and direct inward dial (DID)
    — FXO interface supports on-hook caller ID receipt and hookflash generation
    — FXS interface supports on-hook caller ID transmission
- Digital interfaces:
    — T1, E1
    — Many ISDN (such as Basic Rate Interface [BRI] and Primary Rate Interface [PRI]) and non-ISDN signaling variants
- Hookflash on analog trunks
- Direct FXO line select

Automated Attendant Options

Cisco CME automated attendant (AA) options include

- Cisco UE AA
- Toolkit Command Language (TCL)-based AA

Voice Mail Options

Cisco CME voice mail options include

- Cisco UE voice mail
- Cisco Unity server-based unified messages or voice mail (PC-based)
- Non-Cisco voice mail integration using H.323, SIP, or DTMF
- MWI

Application Integration

- Microsoft customer relationship management (CRM) integration
- Idle URL, periodically push messages to XML screen
- Computer telephony integration (CTI) using Telephony Application Programming Interface (TAPI)

Cisco UE Feature Overview

The Cisco UE features are divided into several categories, including AA, voice mail, system management, and networking. They are described in the following sections.

Automated Attendant Features

Cisco UE AA features include

- Up to five AAs per system
- A basic, default system AA with a canned menu and customizable welcome greeting
- A fully customizable, script-driven menu structure for building custom AAs
- Cisco UE Editor for AA script creation and modification
- A greeting management system (GMS) to listen to and record greetings (prompts) used in the AA menus
- Emergency alternate greeting (EAG)
- Transfer to operator
- Dial-by-name
- Dial-by-extension
- Standard AA scripts with business hours and holidays

Voice Mail Features

Cisco UE voice mail features include

- G.711 μ-law call termination and message storage
- Subscriber mailboxes
- Personal mailboxes
- General delivery mailboxes (GDMs)
- Message expiry

- Local broadcast messaging
- Simple voice mail networking via Voice Profile for Internet Mail (VPIM)
- Subscriber features:
  — Envelope information
  — Spoken name recording
  — Standard and alternate greeting
  — Set/reset password
  — Playback message controls—replay, skip, save, delete, pause, fast-forward, rewind
  — Undeletion of messages during the same session
  — Local name confirmation on message send
  — Nondelivery receipt (NDR) on send to local recipient
  — Message tagging—private and urgent
  — MWI for new messages
  — Mailbox full notification
  — Password and personal identification number (PIN)
- Caller features:
  — Programmable zero-out extension
  — Message editing—rerecord, listen
  — Message tagging—urgent
  — Nondelivery notification
  — Mailbox full notification
- Broadcast messaging
- Private and public distribution lists

System Management Features

Cisco UE system-level management features include

- User ID and password or PIN authentication for all system access
- Web GUI provisioning integrated with Cisco CME
- Command-line interface (CLI) for easy scripting, bulk provisioning, and troubleshooting
- Telephony User Interface (TUI) for caller and subscriber feature access

- GUI for system administrators:
  - User profiles—name, extension, set/reset passwords
  - Define personal mailboxes and general delivery mailboxes
  - Mailbox parameters—maximum recording time, maximum length per message, reset MWI, message expiry time
  - System statistics on storage space use
  - Setting system defaults (storage space, maximum message size)
- Administrator allocation of message storage on a per-mailbox basis
- Backup and restore
- Remote management:
  - HTTP for GUI
  - Console connection for CLI access via the Cisco IOS router **session** command
- Language localization (one language per Cisco UE system)
- Configuration synchronization with Cisco CME and host router
- Incremental upgrades
- Onboard installer
- Background downloads for software upgrades

Networking Features

Cisco UE networking features include

- Voice mail networking to other Cisco UE and Cisco Unity systems, including using Voice Profile for Internet Mail version 2 (VPIMv2)
- Blind addressing to all sites
- Spoken-name confirmation of names available in the directory or cache
- VCard exchange
- Nondelivery receipt (NDR)
- Delayed Delivery Receipt (DDR)
- Network broadcast messaging

Cisco IPC Express Ordering Information

There are two ways to order Cisco IP Communications (IPC) Express. You can choose one of the bundles, or you can choose a la carte, where you order each item separately:

- **Bundles**—Bundles offer the most popular hardware and software combinations. If you are deploying a new system, several discounted bundles that include both the hardware and software components of Cisco IPC Express are available to make the ordering process easier.

- **A la carte**—If you have a unique configuration, ordering a la carte gives you more flexibility in your choices. It is also the appropriate choice if you already have a Cisco access router for your data infrastructure. To deploy a Cisco IPC Express system, you have to upgrade your Cisco IOS software to a voice-capable image, check that your dynamic random-access memory (DRAM) and Flash capacity on the router are sufficient to support a voice image, purchase a Cisco CME feature license for the desired number of IP phones, and purchase an IP phone seat license for each phone. Cisco UE mailbox licenses can optionally be ordered if you plan on deploying voice mail and an AA application.

Ordering a Cisco IPC Express System a La Carte

Ordering the components of a Cisco IPC Express solution involves several steps:

Step 1 Select a Cisco IPC platform. Select an appropriate Cisco IPC Express platform for your office. Which one you choose depends on the number of users in your office, the number of IP phones you plan to support, future growth plans, and your budget. The range of available platforms is described in Chapter 1, "Introducing Cisco IPC Express."

Step 2 Verify memory requirements. Ensure that the platform you select has enough memory to support the solution. Check the memory requirements for the Cisco IOS release you intend to use on Cisco.com.

Step 3 Select the appropriate Cisco IOS software feature set and release. The following feature sets supported with Cisco IOS Release 12.3(4)T and later are required to deploy Cisco IPC Express: IP Voice, SP (Service Provider) Services, Advanced IP Services, Enterprise Services, and Advanced Enterprise Services. If you want to deploy voice and security features, the minimum feature set required is the Advanced IP Services image.

Next, find the version or release of Cisco CME and Cisco UE (if desired) from Table A-1.

You can also use the Cisco Feature Navigator, a web-based tool, to determine which features are supported in a specific Cisco IOS image. You need a Cisco.com account to access the Feature Navigator at http://www.cisco.com/go/fn.

Table V-1   *IOS Software Feature Sets and Releases for CME*

Minimum Cisco IOS Feature Set	Cisco IOS Software Version	Cisco CME	Cisco UE Hardware
IP Voice	12.3(4)T	Release 3.0	NM-CUE
IP Voice	12.3(7)T	Release 3.1	NM-CUE AIM-CUE
IP Voice	12.3(11)T	Release 3.2	NM-CUE AIM-CUE

Step 4   Choose a Cisco CME feature license. Choose the appropriate Cisco CME feature license from Table A-2, based on the number of phones you plan to deploy. The feature licenses can be combined to support more phones per router. For example, the FL-CCME-SMALL can be combined with the FL-CCME-72 to support a total of 96 phones.

A minimum of 12.3.11T is required to support more than 120 IP phones with Cisco IPC Express. Note that the Cisco CME licenses can be converted without additional cost to Survivable Remote Site Telephony (SRST) licenses later if you migrate to a Cisco CallManager network.

Table V-2   *Cisco CME Feature Licenses and Maximum Phones Supported*

Cisco CME Feature License	Number of Phones Supported
FL-CCME-SMALL	24 phones
FL-CCME-36	36 phones
FL-CCME-MEDIUM	48 phones
FL-CCME-72	72 phones
FL-CCME-96	96 phones
FL-CCME-120	120 phones
FL-CCME-144	144 phones
FL-CCME-168	168 phones
FL-CCME-192	192 phones
FL-CCME-240	240 phones

Step 5   Choose a Cisco IP phone license. Choose the appropriate Cisco phone license
if you are ordering new IP phones for your Cisco IPC Express solution (see
Table A-3). Replacement phones are exempt from this requirement. Note that
if you choose to migrate from Cisco CME to Cisco CallManager at some
point, these phone licenses can be migrated to Cisco CallManager without
additional cost.

Table V-3   *Cisco IP Phone Licenses for CallManager Express*

Phone Type	Cisco CME IP Phone License
CP-7970	SW-CCME-UL-7970(=)
CP-7960	SW-CCME-UL-7960(=)
CP-7940	SW-CCME-UL-7940(=)
CP-7935	SW-CCME-UL-7935(=)
CP-7920	SW-CCME-UL-7920(=)
CP-7912	SW-CCME-UL-7912(=)
CP-7905	SW-CCME-UL-7905(=)
CP-7902	SW-CCME-UL-7902(=)
ATA-186	SW-CCME-UL-ANA(=)

If you are a reseller, you must purchase a combined Cisco CME and phone
license, as shown in Table A-4.

Table V-4   *Combined Cisco CME and Phone Licenses for Resellers*

Phone and License SKU	Description
CP-7960G-CCME	Cisco 7960 IP Phone with one Cisco CME phone license
CP-7940G-CCME	Cisco 7940 IP Phone with one Cisco CME phone license
CP-7935-CCME	Cisco 7935 IP Phone with one Cisco CME phone license
CP-7920-CCME-K9	Cisco 7920 IP Phone assembly with one Cisco CME phone license
CP-7912G-CCME	Cisco 7912G IP Phone with one Cisco CME phone license
CP-7905G-CCME	Cisco 7905G IP Phone with one Cisco CME phone license
CP-7902G-CCME	Cisco 7902G IP Phone with one Cisco CME phone license

Step 6   Select the PSTN connectivity. Choose the appropriate voice interface cards required for the PSTN trunk connectivity required. The interface cards supported on the Cisco IPC Express platforms are described in Chapter 6, "Cisco CME PSTN Connectivity Options."

Step 7   Choose additional applications. Order additional applications, such as Cisco UE, as required. See the section "Ordering Cisco UE" for details.

Ordering Cisco IPC Express Bundles

A wide range of bundles is available, as shown in Table A-5. The bundles include the Cisco IPC Express platform, an appropriate Cisco IOS image, the recommended amount of memory, DSPs for PSTN connectivity, and the Cisco feature license supporting a specific number of IP phones.

Table V-5   *Cisco IPC Express Bundles*

Bundle	Platform	IOS Feature Set	Memory (Flash/ DRAM)	DSPs/ Voice Module	CME Feature License Support
CISCO1760-V-CCME	Cisco 1760	IP Plus	32/128 MB	PVDM-256K-4	24 phones
CISCO2611XM-V-CCME	Cisco 2611XM	SP Services	32/128 MB	NM-HD-2V (DSPs for eight voice calls)	36 phones
CISCO2651XM-V-CCME	Cisco 2651XM	SP Services	32/128 MB	AIM-ATM-VOICE-30 (DSPs for 30 voice calls)	48 phones
CISCO2801-V-CCME	Cisco 2801	SP Services	64/256 MB	PVDM2-8	24 phones
CISCO2811-V-CCME	Cisco 2811	SP Services	64/256 MB	PVDM2-16	36 phones
CISCO2821-V-CCME	Cisco 2821	SP Services	64/256 MB	PVDM2-32	48 phones
CISCO2851-V-CCME	Cisco 2851	SP Services	64/256 MB	PVDM2-48	96 phones
CISCO3725-V-CCME-A	Cisco 3725	SP Services	64/128 MB	NM-HD-2V (DSPs for eight voice calls)	48 phones
CISCO3725-V-CCME	Cisco 3725	SP Services	64/128 MB	AIM-ATM-VOICE-30 (DSPs for 30 voice calls)	48 phones
CISCO3745-V-CCME-A	Cisco 3745	SP Services	64/128 MB	NM-HD-2V	120 phones
CISCO3745-V-CCME	Cisco 3745	SP Services	64/128 MB	AIM-ATM-VOICE-30 (DSPs for 30 voice calls)	120 phones

Table V-5 *Cisco IPC Express Bundles (Continued)*

Bundle	Platform	IOS Feature Set	Memory (Flash/ DRAM)	DSPs/ Voice Module	CME Feature License Support
CISCO3825-V-CCME	Cisco 3825	SP Services	64/256 MB	PVDM2-64	168 phones
CISCO3845-V-CCME	Cisco 3845	SP Services	64/256 MB	PVDM2-64	240 phones

Ordering Cisco UE

Cisco UE is an optional voice mail and AA application to be added on to your Cisco IPC Express solution. Cisco UE integrates into your Cisco CME router platform. Because of this, the Cisco IOS software feature set and release requirements for the Cisco IPC Express platforms, and the feature license requirements for Cisco CME described earlier, also apply to Cisco UE. The following are the steps to add the Cisco UE application to your order:

Step 1 Select the Cisco UE hardware. Select either a network module (NM) or asynchronous interface module (AIM) form factor. Note that the minimum IOS software release required to support the NM-CUE is 12.3(4)T and 12.3(7)T for the AIM-CUE.

Step 2 Select the software release. Select the appropriate Cisco UE release you want to deploy. The following releases are available:

— SCUE-2.0

— SCUE-2.1

Step 3 Select the license level. Select the Cisco UE license level based on the number of mailboxes you require:

— SCUE-LIC-100CME—100 mailboxes

— SCUE-LIC-50CME—50 mailboxes

— SCUE-LIC-25CME—25 mailboxes

— SCUE-LIC-12CME—12 mailboxes

Step 4 Select the languages. If a language other than the default of U.S. English is required, select the desired language for the system:

— CUE-LANG-FRA

— CUE-LANG-ESP

— CUE-LANG-DEU

Sample Cisco UE AA Scripts

This appendix lists an example of a typical Cisco Unity Express (UE) automated attendant (AA) script. The high-level flow of logic in the script is as follows:

```
If (business hours) then
  Play <menuprompt>
    To enter the phone number of the person you are trying to reach, press 1
    To enter the name of the person you are trying to reach, press 2
  To transfer to the operator, press 0
else
  Play <weekend prompt>
```

The main script is implemented as main.aef, and the dial-by-extension logic (press 1) and dial-by-name logic (press 2) are implemented as the subflows—dialbyextension.aef and dialbyname.aef, respectively. Each of these three scripts is discussed in this appendix.

You can download the binary files (.aef files) for the scripts from the Cisco Press website (http://www.ciscopress.com/title/158705180x). You can view them with the Cisco UE AA Editor, which is a PC application you can download from Cisco.com. Follow these steps:

Step 1 Go to Cisco.com.

Step 2 Search for Software Center.

Step 3 Choose Voice Software.

Step 4 Page down to Cisco Unity Express Software.

Step 5 Choose a software release.

The Cisco UE AA Editor is listed among the files given for a particular release at the Cisco.com Software Center. For example, in the Cisco UE 1.1.2 release listing, the file called CUEEditor1.1.2.exe is the editor. A version of the editor is posted with each release of Cisco UE. Accessing this site requires a Cisco.com login ID. Along with the editor, several more sample AA scripts are posted at this site that you can use to build or customize your own Cisco UE AA.

The Cisco UE AA Editor is discussed in Chapter 9, "Cisco IPC Express Automated Attendant Options." As shown in several of the figures later in this appendix, the script content (steps) is shown in the top-right pane, the tool palette of steps to choose from is in the top-left pane, and the script variables are in the bottom-left pane. Any error or informational messages are in the bottom-right pane.

You construct a script by dragging the steps from the tool palette into the script content pane and filling out the properties for each step. This might include first creating variables and populating their values. To run this script sample on your Cisco UE system, you must record audio .wav files for all the prompts referenced and then upload all the script and prompt files to Cisco UE as described in Chapter 9. It is also important that all variables have values assigned.

The main.aef Script

The main.aef script does the following:

- Answers the incoming call (the accept step in the script shown in the next section)
- Checks for business hours and business days (the day of week and time of day steps in the script)
- Provides the normal welcome greeting if it is during business hours (the menu step following the weekdays label)
- Branches to a subflow (a separate script file called dialbyextension.aef) if the caller selects 1 for dial-by-extension (the call subflow to dialbyextension.aef step)
- Branches to a subflow (a separate script file called dialbyname.aef) if the caller selects 2 for dial-by-name (the call subflow to dialbyname.aef step)
- Transfers the caller to the operator (which is a variable) if he or she selects 0 (the Call Redirect step)
- Handles various error conditions

Figure B-1 shows a graphical user interface (GUI) view of the first page of the script, which maps to approximately the top 30 lines of the text representation of the script. Figure B-2 shows the second page, which maps to approximately the last 30 lines of the text representation of the script. The full text and variable definitions of the main.aef script are given in the next section.

Figure B-1   *First Page of the main.aef Script*

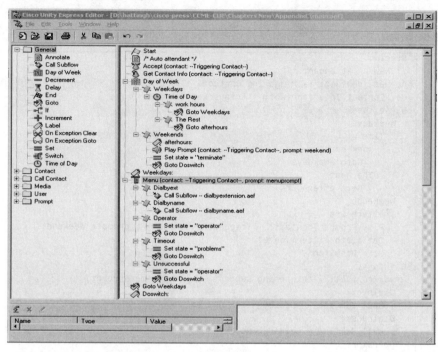

Figure B-2   *Second Page of the main.aef Script*

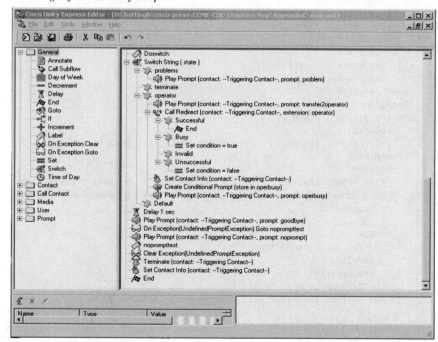

Script Content

Example B-1 is a text representation of the main.aef script contents.

Example B-64 *main.aef Script*

```
Start
/* New AA attendant */
Accept (contact: --Triggering Contact--)
Get Contact Info (contact: --Triggering Contact--)
Day of Week
  Weekdays
    Time of Day
      work hours
        Goto Weekdays
      The Rest
        Goto afterhours
  Weekends
    afterhours:
    Play Prompt (contact: --Triggering Contact--, prompt: weekend)
    Set state = "terminate"
    Goto Doswitch
Weekdays:
Menu (contact: --Triggering Contact--, prompt: menuprompt)
  Dialbyext
    Call Subflow -- dialbyextension.aef
  Dialbyname
    Call Subflow -- dialbyname.aef
  Operator
    Set state = "operator"
    Goto Doswitch
  Timeout
    Set state = "problems"
    Goto Doswitch
  Unsuccessful
    Set state = "operator"
    Goto Doswitch
Goto Weekdays
Doswitch:
Switch String ( state )
  problems
    Play Prompt (contact: --Triggering Contact--, prompt: problem)
  terminate
  operator
    Play Prompt (contact: --Triggering Contact--, prompt: transfer2oper)
    Call Redirect (contact: --Triggering Contact--, extension: operator
      Successful
        End
      Busy
        Set condition = true
      Invalid
      Unsuccessful
        Set condition = false
    Set Contact Info (contact: --Triggering Contact--)
```

Example B-64 *main.aef Script (Continued)*

```
        Create Conditional Prompt (store in operbusy)
        Play Prompt (contact: --Triggering Contact--, prompt: operbusy)
     Default
  Delay 1 sec
  Play Prompt (contact: --Triggering Contact--, prompt: goodbye)
  On Exception(UndefinedPromptException) Goto noprompttest
  Play Prompt (contact: --Triggering Contact--, prompt: noprompt)
  noprompttest:
  Clear Exception(UndefinedPromptException)
  Terminate (contact: --Triggering Contact--)
  Set Contact Info (contact: --Triggering Contact--)
  End
```

Variables

The variables defined in the main.aef script are shown in Figure B-3.

Figure B-3 *Variables of the main.aef Script*

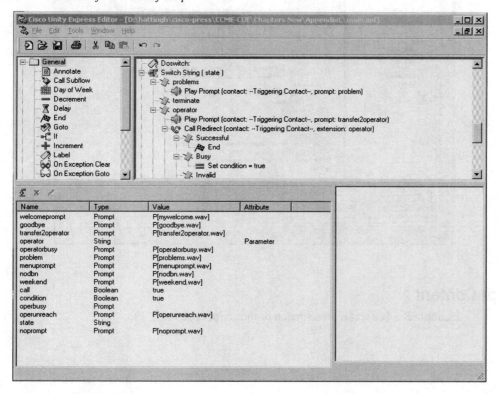

The dialbyname.aef Script

The dialbyname.aef script allows a caller to spell an employee's name (the name to user step in the script shown in the next section). When a match is found (the get user info step in the script), the caller is transferred (the call redirect step in the script) to that employee's extension.

The full text and variable definitions for the dialbyname.aef script are given in the next section. Figure B-4 shows a GUI view of the main portion of the script.

Figure B-4 *The dialbyname.aef Script*

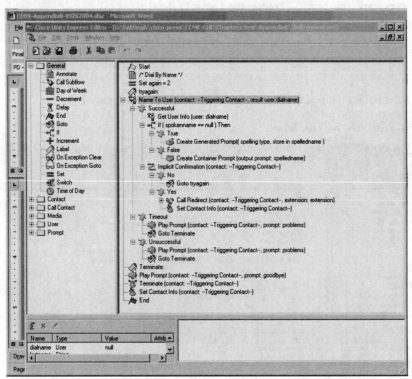

Script Content

Example B-2 is a text representation of the script contents.

Example B-65 *The dialbyname.aef Script*

```
Start
/* Dial By Name */
Set again = 2
tryagain:
Name To User (contact: --Triggering Contact--, result user:dialname)
  Successful
    Get User Info (user: dialname)
    If ( spokenname == null ) Then
      True
        Create Generated Prompt( spelling type, store in spelledname)
      False
        Create Container Prompt (output prompt: spelledname)
    Implicit Confirmation (contact: --Triggering Contact--)
      No
        Goto tryagain
      Yes
        Call Redirect (contact: --Triggering Contact--, extension: extension)
          Successful
            End
          Busy
            Play Prompt (contact: --Triggering Contact--, prompt: userbusy)
            Goto Terminate
          Invalid
            Play Prompt (contact: --Triggering Contact--, prompt: invaliduser)
            Decrement again
            If ( again == 0 ) Then
              True
                Play Prompt (contact: --Triggering Contact--, problems)
                Goto Terminate
              False
                Goto tryagain
          Unsuccessful
            Play Prompt (contact: --Triggering Contact--, prompt: invaliduser)
            Goto Terminate
          Set Contact Info (contact: --Triggering Contact--)
  Timeout
    Play Prompt (contact: --Triggering Contact--, prompt: problems)
    Goto Terminate
  Unsuccessful
    Play Prompt (contact: --Triggering Contact--, prompt: problems)
    Goto Terminate
Terminate:
Play Prompt (contact: --Triggering Contact--, prompt: goodbye)
Terminate (contact: --Triggering Contact--)
Set Contact Info (contact: --Triggering Contact--)
End
```

Variables

The variables defined in the dialbyname.aef script are shown in Figure B-5.

Figure B-5 *Variables of the dialbyname.aef Script*

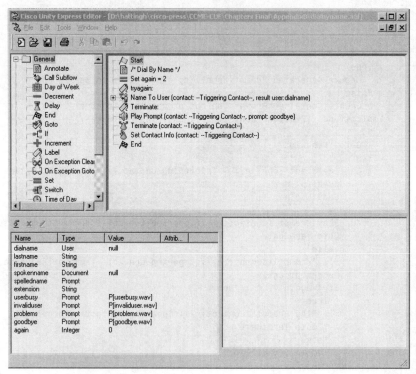

The dialbyextension.aef Script

The dialbyextension.aef script allows a caller to

- Dial the extension (the get digit string step in the script shown in the next section) of the employee he or she wants to contact

- Transfer the call to the selected extension (the call redirect step in the script)

Figure B-6 shows a GUI view of the main portion of the script. The full text and variable definitions for the dialbyextension.aef script are given in the next section.

Figure B-6   *The dialbyextension.aef Script*

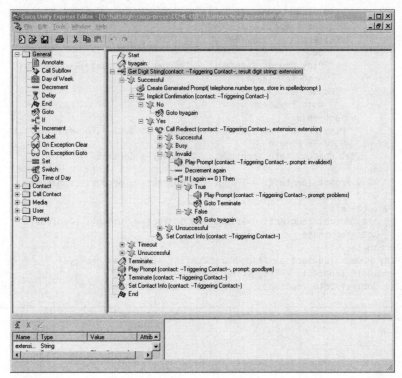

Script Content

Example B-3 is a text representation of the script contents.

Example B-66 *The dialbyextension.aef Script*

```
Start
tryagain:
Get Digit String(contact: --Triggering Contact--, result digit string: extension)
  Successful
  Create Generated Prompt(telephone.number type, store in spelledprompt)
  Implicit Confirmation (contact: --Triggering Contact--)
    No
      Goto tryagain
    Yes
      Call Redirect (contact: --Triggering Contact--, extension: extension)
        Successful
          End
        Busy
          Play Prompt (contact: --Triggering Contact--, prompt: extbusy)
          Goto Terminate
        Invalid
```

continues

Example B-66 *The dialbyextension.aef Script (Continued)*

```
                    Play Prompt (contact: --Triggering Contact--, prompt: invalidext)
                    Decrement again
                    If ( again == 0 ) Then
                      True
                        Play Prompt (contact: --Triggering Contact--, problems)
                        Goto Terminate
                      False
                        Goto tryagain
                  Unsuccessful
                    Play Prompt (contact: --Triggering Contact--, prompt: invalidext)
                    Goto Terminate
                  Set Contact Info (contact: --Triggering Contact--)
            Timeout
              Play Prompt (contact: --Triggering Contact--, prompt: problems)
              Goto Terminate
            Unsuccessful
              Play Prompt (contact: --Triggering Contact--, prompt: problems)
              Goto Terminate
      Terminate:
      Play Prompt (contact: --Triggering Contact--, prompt: goodbye)
      Terminate (contact: --Triggering Contact--)
      Set Contact Info (contact: --Triggering Contact--)
      End
```

Variables

The variables defined in the dialbyextension.aef script are shown in Figure B-7.

Figure B-7   *Variables of the dialbyextension.aef Script*

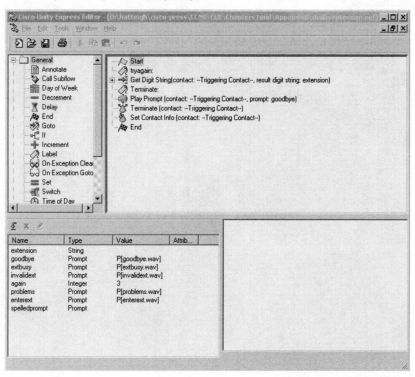

Cisco Unity Express
Database Schema

This appendix contains the SQL database schema for Cisco Unity Express (UE). The information in this appendix is relevant to interpreting traces from the voice mail component. It gives the layout of the different tables in the database schema.

Table vm_bcst_heard

```
create table vm_bcst_heard
(
    MessageId            varchar(128)    not null,
    MailboxId            varchar(64)     not null,

    foreign key (MessageId) references vm_message on delete cascade on update
    cascade,
    foreign key (MailboxId) references vm_mailbox on delete cascade on update
    cascade,
    primary key (MessageId, MailboxId)
);
```

Table vm_config

```
create table vm_config
(
    Parameter            varchar(32)     not null,
    Value                varchar(256)    not null,

    primary key (Parameter)
);
```

Table vm_dbversion

```
create table vm_dbversion
(
    dbversion            integer         not null,
    timestamp            date            not null,
    createtime           time            not null,

    primary key (dbversion)
);
```

Table vm_greeting

```
create table vm_greeting
(
    GreetingId          varchar(64)         not null,
    GreetingType        integer             not null,
    MessageLength       integer                     ,
    MessageSize         integer                     ,
    GreetingOid         OID                         ,
    MailboxId           varchar(64)         not null,

    foreign key (MailboxId) references vm_mailbox on delete cascade on update
    cascade,
    primary key (GreetingId)
);
```

Table vm_job

```
create table vm_job
(
    JobId               serial              not null,
    MessageId           varchar(128)        not null,
    Recipients          bytea               not null,
    LocalDomain         varchar(64)                 ,
    LocalPhonePrefix    varchar(20)                 ,
    HasSpokenName       boolean             not null default false,
    TaskId              bigint              not null default 0,

    primary key (JobId)
);
```

Table vm_mailbox

```
create table vm_mailbox
(
    MailboxId           varchar(64)         not null,
    MailboxType         integer             not null default 0,
    Description         varchar(64)                 ,
    MailboxSize         integer                     ,
    MessageSize         integer                     ,
    Tutorial            boolean             not null default true,
    TotalMessageTime    integer                     ,
    MessageExpiryTime   integer                     ,
    Enabled             boolean             not null default true,
    GreetingType        integer             not null default 10,
    OrphanedTime        bigint              not null default 0,
    LastAccessed        bigint                      ,
    ZeroOutNumber       varchar(32)                 ,

    primary key (MailboxId)
);
```

Table vm_mbxusers

```
create table vm_mbxusers
(
    MailboxId       varchar(64)         not null,
    UserDN          varchar(256)        not null,
    Owner           boolean             not null default false,

    foreign key (MailboxId) references vm_mailbox on delete cascade on update
    cascade,
    primary key (MailboxId, UserDN, Owner)
);
```

Table vm_message

```
create table vm_message
(
    MessageId           varchar(128)        not null,
    MessageType         integer             not null default 1,
    UseCount            integer             not null default 1,
    Sender              varchar(256)        not null,
    Urgent              boolean             not null default false,
    Private             boolean             not null default false,
    MessageLength       integer                 ,
    MessageSize         integer                 ,
    MessageTime         bigint                  ,
    AttachedMsgId       varchar(128)            ,
    MessageOid          OID                     ,
    UTCTime             varchar(32)             ,
    EndTime             bigint              not null default 9223372036854775807,
    ReceiveTime         bigint              not null default 0,
    NdrReason           integer                 ,
    StartTime           bigint              default 0,
    MWIOn               boolean             not null default false,
    TotalMessageLength  integer             not null default 0,

    foreign key (AttachedMsgId) references vm_message on delete cascade on update
    cascade,
    primary key (MessageId)
);
```

Table vm_usermsg

```
create table vm_usermsg
(
    MailboxId       varchar(64)         not null,
    MessageId       varchar(128)        not null,
    State           integer             not null default 1,
    StoreTime       bigint              not null,

    foreign key (MailboxId) references vm_mailbox on delete cascade on update
    cascade,
    foreign key (MessageId) references vm_message on delete cascade on update
    cascade,
    primary key (MailboxId, MessageId)
);
```

AA (automated attendant). A voice processing system that provides callers with a recorded message and directs them to specific extensions based on their responses to various prompts.

AAA/RADIUS (authentication, authorization, and accounting/Remote Authentication Dial-In User Service) server. Authentication and authorization for users and tracking of connection time provides the framework for access control using database information provided by a RADIUS server.

access control list. *See* ACL.

ACL (access control list). A list of devices such as routers, gateways, and servers that are allowed access to certain types of resources in a network.

ANI (Automatic Number Identification). Provides the calling phone number of an incoming call. In general usage, ANI is the same as CLID.

Asynchronous Transfer Mode. *See* ATM.

ATM (Asynchronous Transfer Mode). The standard for which multiple service types (such as voice, video, and data) are organized in fixed-length (53-byte) cells and transmitted over a physical medium such as E3, T3, or SONET. Because ATM cells are easily processed in hardware, faster processing and switching speeds ranging from 155.52 Mbps to 10 Gbps are possible.

authentication, authorization, and accounting/Remote Authentication Dial-In User Service. *See* AAA/RADIUS.

automated attendant. *See* AA.

Automatic Number Identification. *See* ANI.

blind transfer and consultation transfer. A blind transfer occurs when the called party transfers the call to a third party without first talking to the third party. With a consultation transfer, the transferring party speaks with the third party before connecting the original caller to the third party.

caller ID. A telephony feature that displays the name and number of the calling party. In general usage, the same as ANI and CLID.

Calling Line Identification. *See* CLID.

CAS (Channel Associated Signaling). In-band signaling when the call control signaling for a phone call is sent on the same channel as the media or speech path.

CCS (Common Channel Signaling). Out-of-band signaling when the call control signaling for a phone call is sent on the same channel as the medium or speech path. BRI (Basic Rate Interface) and PRI (Primary Rate Interface) use CCS because it has a separate D channel to transmit signaling information.

central office. *See* CO.

centralized and distributed network deployments. Network deployment alternatives in which the call routing intelligence is concentrated in a single, central location in the network, with client/server protocols between the central site (server) and the outlying devices (clients). Alternatively, each site can have its own configuration and intelligence with peer-to-peer protocols between the sites (distributed).

centrex service. A managed service offered by a central office that delivers telephony services for small-to-medium businesses that do not want to maintain their own private branch exchange (PBX) system.

Channel Associated Signaling. *See* CAS.

CLID (Calling Line Identification). The ISDN number of the calling party. The telephone company provides this in the call setup message.

CO (central office). A telephone company's local switching system that connects residential and other end users' (such as businesses) telephone equipment. This is the entry point into the Public Switched Telephone Network (PSTN) for most end users.

codec (coder-decoder). An integrated circuit device that typically uses pulse code modulation (PCM) to transform analog signals into a digital bit stream and digital signals back into analog signals. Also in VoIP, a digital signal processor (DSP) software algorithm used to compress or decompress speech or audio signals.

coder-decoder. *See* codec.

Common Channel Signaling. *See* CCS.

consultation transfer. *See* blind transfer and consultation transfer.

DHCP (Dynamic Host Configuration Protocol). A protocol that is used to dynamically allocate and assign IP addresses to devices such as computers or IP phones. This enables easy administration of a large IP network.

dial peer. A configuration structure that defines the mapping of a telephone number to a voice port or IP address

dial tone. The tone heard when a phone handset (receiver) is lifted, indicating that the switching equipment is ready to accept a number, or a line is available for use.

Dialed Number Identification Service. *See* DNIS.

DID (Direct Inward Dial). Allows an external caller to dial a business's internal extension number without needing to go through an operator or automated attendant. The dialed digits are passed to the business's telephone switching system, which then completes the call.

Digital Signal Processor. *See* DSP.

Digital Subscriber Line. *See* DSL.

Direct Inward Dial. *See* DID.

DNIS (Dialed Number Identification Service). A service that provides the number that the caller dialed. This allows the receiving switching system to automatically switch the call without operator assistance. *See also* DID.

DSL (Digital Subscriber Line). A public network technology that delivers high-bandwidth data, voice, and video over conventional copper telephone wiring at limited distances. The four types of DSL are ADSL, HDSL, SDSL, and VDSL. They differ according to their bandwidth upload and download speeds. For example, ADSL (asymmetric DSL) download speeds are 1.544 Mbps, and upload speeds are 128 kbps. SDSL (symmetric DSL) features similar download and upload speeds of 384 kbps.

DSP (Digital Signal Processor). This technology processes a voice signal, samples it into segments, and packs it into frames for transmission over a packet network.

DTMF (dual-tone multifrequency). The paired high- and low-frequency tones that make up touch-tone dialing.

DTMF relay (dual-tone multifrequency relay). Occurs when DTMF digits are detected before they enter a packet network, are packetized in message format, and are regenerated on the terminating side of the network.

dual-tone multifrequency. *See* DTMF.

dual-tone multifrequency relay. *See* DTMF relay.

Dynamic Host Configuration Protocol. *See* DHCP.

E1. A digital transmission scheme with a clock rate of 2.048 MHz used everywhere except in North America and Japan. It offers 31 simultaneous channels of 64 kbps each that can be used individually for voice or data traffic. It also has a 32nd 64-kbps channel used for control information.

Ethernet. The IEEE standard used to network computers on a LAN over twisted-pair cables or optical fiber. Data rates range from 10 Mbps (10Base-T Ethernet) to 100 Mbps (Fast Ethernet) to 1000 Mbps (Gigabit Ethernet).

File Transfer Protocol/Trivial File Transfer Protocol. *See* FTP/TFTP.

firewall. A hardware or software system that shields a business's internal network from external attacks, such as through the Internet. This is accomplished by allowing only certain types of traffic to enter the internal network.

foreign exchange office. *See* FXO.

foreign exchange station. *See* FXS.

Frame Relay. A high-speed packet-switched data communications protocol, similar to but more efficient than X.25, used to connect WANs. Frame Relay technology uses High-level Data Link Control (HDLC) encapsulation between devices. Frame Relay packets are carried over T1 and T3 lines, ranging from speeds of 56 kbps to 45 Mbps.

FTP/TFTP (File Transfer Protocol/Trivial File Transfer Protocol). Protocols used to transfer files from one computer to another over a network.

FXO (foreign exchange office). An FXO interface uses an RJ-11 connector to connect to the PSTN or an interface on a PBX.

FXS (foreign exchange station). An FXS interface uses a standard RJ-11 connector to connect directly to analog devices such as telephones, fax machines, and PBXs. An FXS interface supplies ring voltage and dial tone.

gatekeeper. An H.323 device that provides bandwidth management and address translation and that controls access for H.323 devices. H.323 devices register with a centralized gatekeeper, easing the provisioning, installation, and management of a large H.323 service provider or enterprise networks.

gatekeeper direct endpoint signaling. Multiple types of gatekeeper call signaling methods exist. Within direct endpoint signaling, the call setup messages are sent directly to the terminating devices. *See also* gatekeeper routed signaling.

gatekeeper routed signaling. Multiple types of gatekeeper call signaling methods exist. With gatekeeper routed call signaling, the call setup messages are sent via the gatekeeper. *See also* gatekeeper direct endpoint signaling.

glare. A situation that results when two switches with a connection between them decide to seize the same trunk at the same time to set up a new call. One of the two switches must back off to allow the call in the other direction to proceed and then select another trunk for the failed call setup attempt.

H.323. An ITU standard for multimedia communications over IP networks that addresses call control, multimedia management, and bandwidth management.

H.323 Fast Start. The H.323 standard provides two versions of a protocol exchange for call setup. The original standard specified a verbose message exchange that over time became known as H.323 Slow Start. To cut down on post-dial delays, the number of messages exchanged to set up a call was optimized in a later version of the H.323 standard. This version is known as Fast Start.

hairpinning. Redirecting voice traffic out the same interface where it was received, such as when an incoming PSTN call is looped back out onto the PSTN because it cannot be delivered via the VoIP network.

hookflash. The hookswitch on the telephone device is briefly depressed (going on-hook and off-hook within a certain short period of time), such as for call waiting or call transfer.

HTTP (Hypertext Transfer Protocol). The protocol used by web browsers and web servers to transfer files, such as text and graphics files.

Hypertext Transfer Protocol. *See* HTTP.

ICT (intercluster trunk). Used to connect Cisco CallManager clusters across an IP network.

IE (information element). A flexible method of encoding protocol messages such that the receiving system can parse different pieces of information from the message in any order. An IE typically consists of a unique ID, a length field, and a content-specific payload. ISDN is an IE-encoded protocol.

information element. *See* IE.

Integrated Voice Response system. *See* IVR system.

intercluster trunk. *See* ICT.

ISDN (2B+D, 23B+D, 30B+D). 2B+D is the BRI in ISDN. 23B+D is the PRI in the U.S. and Japan. 30B+D is the PRI service in ISDN in Europe and elsewhere.

ISDN BRI (Integrated Services Digital Network Basic Rate Interface). An ITU (International Telecommunication Union) standard communications protocol that permits telephone networks to carry data, voice, and other traffic. BRI is a basic service consisting of two 64-Kbps bearer (B) channels and one 16-kbps signaling (D) channel.

ISDN PRI (Integrated Services Digital Network Primary Rate Interface). An ITU standard communications protocol that permits telephone networks to carry data, voice, and other traffic. PRI is intended for greater-capacity users based on T1/E1 ports. In the U.S. and Japan, a PRI consists of 23 64-kbps bearer (B) channels and a signaling (D) channel. In Europe and elsewhere, a PRI consists of 30 B channels and a D channel.

IVR (Integrated Voice Response) system. A programmable voice processing system that accepts telephony/speech input and touch-tone keypad or voice recognition selection. It responds with information from a database or by directing calls to certain destinations.

key system. A small telephone system that features multiple lines and basic call features for small businesses.

line. A communication connection between a switching system and an end-user telephone device. *See also* trunk.

managed services. In a managed-services environment, enterprise branch offices or small and medium businesses outsource their network installation and management to a service provider (SP). This SP typically provides the customer premises equipment (CPE), the network backbone, and the network management expertise. This is ideal for businesses that do not have an in-house networking staff or that have only a small staff for their networking needs.

Media Termination Point. *See* MTP.

Message Waiting Indicator. *See* MWI.

MTP (Media Termination Point). Provides a termination and reorigination anchor point in the middle of the media path of a telephone call. This is often used to change IP addresses for security reasons on different segments of the call.

MWI (Message Waiting Indicator). A method of alerting a user when a voice mail message is waiting. Typical MWI alerts include a light, a phone display icon, and stutter dial tone.

NAT (Network Address Translation). A method of converting a local/private IP address to a global/public IP address or vice versa. This delivers security for businesses because private IP addresses are not visible to the outside world. NAT also lets a business use a single global IP address for its communication, conserving the number of global IP addresses that are needed.

Network Address Translation. *See* NAT.

off-hook. The lifting of the telephone receiver. *See also* on-hook.

on-hook. The receiver is resting or is not being used. *See also* off-hook.

PBX (private branch exchange). A privately owned telephone switching system used by businesses to connect desktop extensions and trunks to the PSTN.

Plain Old Telephone Service. *See* POTS.

POTS (Plain Old Telephone Service). An alternative term for PSTN.

private branch exchange. *See* PBX.

proxy/redirect server. A device in a Session Initialization Procol (SIP) network that terminates a connection, accepts requests from a user, potentially authenticates a user, and then either passes on the requests or processes them.

PSTN (Public Switched Telephone Network). International public telephone service.

Public Switched Telephone Network. *See* PSTN.

Real-Time Transport Protocol. *See* RTP.

Resource Reservation Protocol. *See* RSVP.

RFC 2833. An in-band DTMF relay method used predominantly in SIP networks.

RSVP (Resource Reservation Protocol). An Internet Engineering Task Force (IETF) specification that allows applications to request dedicated bandwidth before packets are transferred to ensure availability.

RTCP (RTP Control Protocol). The transport of an RTP session is augmented by a control protocol (RTCP) to allow monitoring of the delivery in a manner scalable to large multicast networks and to provide minimal control and identification functionality. Refer to IETF RFCs 1889 and 3550.

RTP (Real-Time Transport Protocol). Commonly used with IP networks, RTP is designed to provide end-to-end network transport functions for applications transmitting real-time data, such as audio and video. RTP provides such services as payload type identification, sequence numbering, time-stamping, and delivery monitoring to real-time applications. Refer to IETF RFCs 1889 and 3550.

RTP Control Protocol. *See* RTCP.

SCCP (Skinny Client Control Protocol). A VoIP signaling protocol used by Cisco CallManager and Cisco CallManager Express (the call agents) to send messages between the call agent and an IP phone to control phone and call state.

Session Initialization Protocol. *See* SIP.

SIP (Session Initialization Protocol). A protocol developed by an IETF Working Group as an alternative to H.323. Offers many of the same architectural features as H.323, including addressing voice and multimedia calls over IP networks. SIP's advantages are its simplicity, its flexibility, its ability to work alongside a host of other different protocols, and the ease with which it can be embedded in end-user devices and Internet technologies.

SIP UA (user agent). A device that transmits SIP packets over IP.

SIP user agent. *See* SIP UA.

Skinny Client Control Protocol. *See* SCCP.

T1. A North American transmission standard. T1 transmits DS-1 formatted data at 1.544 Mbps through a network, using alternate mark inversion (AMI) or B8ZS coding. It offers 24 simultaneous channels of 64 kbps each that can be used individually for voice or data traffic.

TCL (Tool Command Language). An IVR scripting environment that lets businesses create customized call control scripts for their needs.

Tool Command Language. *See* TCL.

transcoding. The ability to modify the codec of a VoIP phone call midstream between devices that support different codecs.

transferee. When transferring a call from party A to party B, the transferee (A) is the party being transferred to the new destination. *See also* transferor.

transferor. When transferring a call from party A to party B, the transferring party (B) is known as the transferor. *See also* transferee.

trunk. A communication connection between two switching systems. *See also* line.

virtual LAN. *See* VLAN.

virtual private network. *See* VPN.

VLAN (virtual LAN). A group of devices configured using software so that they appear as if they are physically located on the same wire, even though they are located on different LAN segments. This is useful to group users without redesigning the network.

VoATM (voice over ATM). The transport of voice traffic over an ATM network. The voice traffic can be encapsulated using a special AAL5 encapsulation for multiplexed voice or AAL2.

VoFR (voice over Frame Relay). The transport of voice traffic over a Frame Relay network.

Voice Extensible Markup Language. *See* VXML.

voice over ATM. *See* VoATM.

voice over Frame Relay. *See* VoFR.

voice over IP. *See* VoIP.

voice port. A voice interface on a networking device, such as a PBX or a router.

Voice Profile for Internet Mail. *See* VPIM.

VoIP (voice over IP). The technology to carry a normal telephony voice call over an IP-based packet network.

VoIP carrier services. Service providers that offer end-user and business "PSTN" services but use a packet-based network for these services instead of traditional PSTN equipment.

VPIM (Voice Profile for Internet Mail). An interoperability standard for sending voice mail between voice messaging systems.

VPN (virtual private network). Allows IP traffic to travel securely over a public TCP/IP network such as the Internet by encrypting all traffic from one network to another. A VPN uses "tunneling" to encrypt all information at the IP level.

VXML (Voice Extensible Markup Language). Allows businesses to create audio dialogs that interact with Internet XML servers through voice recognition technology such as synthesized speech, digitized audio, recognition of spoken and DTMF key input, and recording of spoken input.

WAN (wide-area network). A communications network or several LANs that connect computers and sites across a wide geographic area.

wide-area network. *See* WAN.

wireless LAN. *See* WLAN.

WLAN (wireless LAN). Ethernet LAN access with wireless technology using the 802.11 standard.

INDEX

H

I

K – L

M

U

V

W–Z

Cisco Press

Learning is serious business.

Invest wisely.

SEARCH THOUSANDS OF BOOKS FROM LEADING PUBLISHERS

Safari® Bookshelf is a searchable electronic reference library for IT professionals that features more than 2,000 titles from technical publishers, including Cisco Press.

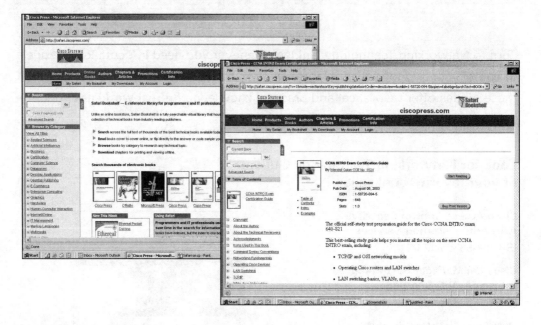

With Safari Bookshelf you can

- **Search** the full text of thousands of technical books, including more than 70 Cisco Press titles from authors such as Wendell Odom, Jeff Doyle, Bill Parkhurst, Sam Halabi, and Karl Solie.

- **Read** the books on My Bookshelf from cover to cover, or just flip to the information you need.

- **Browse** books by category to research any technical topic.

- **Download** chapters for printing and viewing offline.

With a customized library, you'll have access to your books when and where you need them—and all you need is a user name and password.

TRY SAFARI BOOKSHELF FREE FOR 14 DAYS!

You can sign up to get a 10-slot Bookshelf free for the first 14 days. Visit **http://safari.ciscopress.com** to register.

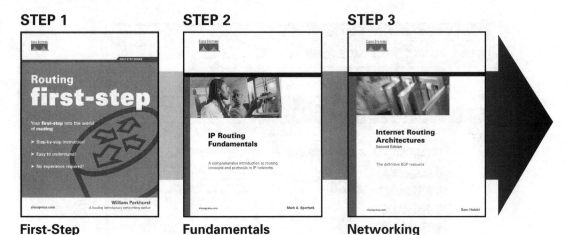

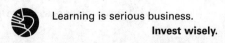